ARCHIBALD COX

Courtesy of the Cox Family

ARCHIBALD COX

CONSCIENCE OF A NATION

KEN GORMLEY

Foreword by Elliot Richardson

ADDISON-WESLEY

Reading, Massachusetts

Many of the designations used by manufacturers and sellers
to distinguish their products are claimed as trademarks. Where those
designations appear in this book and Addison-Wesley was aware of
a trademark claim, the designations have been printed in initial
capital letters (e.g., Frisbee).

Library of Congress Cataloging-in-Publication Data

Gormley, Ken.
    Archibald Cox : conscience of a nation / Ken Gormley ; foreword by
Elliot L. Richardson.
       p.   cm.
    Includes bibliographical references and index.
    ISBN 0-201-40713-2
    1. Cox, Archibald, 1912–   . 2. Special prosecutors—United
States—Biography. 3. Law teachers—Massachusetts—Cambridge—
Biography. 4. Watergate Affair, 1972–1974. I. Title.
KF373.C673G67   1997
345.73'01—dc21
[B]   97-27499
                                                 CIP

Addison-Wesley is an imprint of Addison Wesley Longman, Inc.

Jacket design by Suzanne Heiser
Jacket photograph courtesy of the Library of Congress
Text design by Ruth Kolbert
Set in 11-point Caledonia by Pagesetters

1 2 3 4 5 6 7 8 9-MA-0100999897
First printing, August 1997

Addison-Wesley books are available at special discounts for bulk purchases.
For more information about how to make such purchases in the U.S.,
please contact the Corporate, Government, and Special Sales Department
at Addison-Wesley, One Jacob Way, Reading, MA 01867, or call (800) 238-9682.

Find us on the World Wide Web at http://www.aw.com/gb/

To my wife Laura,
and my children, Carolyn, Luke, and Rebecca,
who have taught me that the most significant acts of public service
are performed without fanfare or promise of fame,
within the home

CONTENTS

PART THREE

WATERGATE AND BEYOND

EPILOGUE

HOME TO NEW ENGLAND

425

Foreword

by Elliot Richardson

This book opens with a dramatic scene: The House of Representatives has voted to impeach President Andrew Johnson; the Senate is trying the charges against him. Yet that scene occurred in 1868. The issues were unique to their time and context. Archibald Cox was not born until more than half a century later. Why, then, is this extraordinary episode an appropriate start for Cox's biography? The answer rests in the figure who rose to defend President Johnson: William Maxwell Evarts, a leading lawyer of his generation. Evarts was Cox's great-grandfather—but that alone does not explain the linkage. Like all of us, Cox had four great-grandfathers; he never knew Evarts. True, both Evarts and Cox played crucial roles in struggles over the ouster of a president—the only two such contests in this nation's history. But Evarts saved a president; Cox doomed one. The importance of this scene in Cox's life lies not just in common blood, but in the qualities Evarts embodied.

We soon discover how large the legacy of great-grandfather Evarts loomed in Archibald Cox's early years. Indeed, it may have been why the boy's family called him "Billy." As we go more deeply into the book, we continue to hear echoes of William Maxwell Evarts's voice. Born in 1818, he was a man of rigorous intellectual honesty and strong moral principles. He grew up, moreover, when the ideas and ideals that inspired this nation's government were still fresh, and his public career bears witness to the strength of their hold on him. In addition to defending Andrew Johnson, he served the United States as attorney general, secretary of state, and senator from New York.

Although the Evarts heritage undoubtedly influenced Cox's character and outlook, other familial influences were not dissimilar. All of his forebears (including Roger Sherman, signer of the Declaration of Independence and the U.S. Constitution) had roots deeply planted in American soil. Many achieved professional distinction. Most had first-class educations. Cox's father, an independent-minded lawyer, was a leader of the New York patent and trademark bar. Young Archie himself went to St. Paul's School, Harvard College, and the Harvard Law School.

A conspicuous merit of this biography is that the more we learn about Archibald Cox, the more clearly we see how the influences that formed his character also shaped his career. They surely played a part, for example, when he twice seized the opportunity to serve in the office of the solicitor general of the United States—first as a staff lawyer, later in the top job during the Kennedy administration. That office, after all, not only represents the national government before the Supreme Court but determines when the executive branch seeks review of a lower court's ruling. The solicitor general also takes part as a friend of the court in other cases of national significance. He and his colleagues thus have crucial roles in most of the cases that test our constitutional system. For a lawyer of Cox's lineage, the opportunity to debate such issues must have seemed irresistible. By the time he stepped down as solicitor general in 1965, he had argued and won more Supreme Court cases than any other lawyer of his era.

While the process that turned Cox into an authority on labor law is less obvious, a close look reveals the same influences. He got his first exposure to labor negotiations through representing management at a leading Boston law firm. Even then, Cox's deep-rooted commitment to the equal rights of every individual inclined him to want to make sure that the employees' side got a fair shake. He had barely returned to the same firm after World War II when the Harvard Law School invited him to teach labor law. In accepting this invitation he passed up a partnership partly because, as he later said, he "sympathized more with the labor people." To those of us in Cox's first labor law class, however, it was plain that he would never let sympathy override his sense of fairness. For him, respect for the merits of a case, wherever they might lie, would inevitably make mediation more congenial than advocacy. He had, in fact, the makings of a great judge. Were it not for John F. Kennedy's untimely death, Cox would all but certainly have been appointed to the Supreme Court.

A person of Archibald Cox's character and ability had little need, of course, to depend on luck to turn up rewarding opportunities in such well-established occupations as appellate advocacy, labor relations, and teaching. He never lost sight, however, of the ways in which chance can alter the course of one's life. And so it did in the two extraordinary situations that were to put his powers to their highest and best use.

First came the unprecedented mixture of cultural ferment, social unrest, and antiwar sentiment that swept the nation in the late 1960s. At Columbia University and then at Harvard, Archibald Cox was called upon to soothe outbreaks of disorder. He ended up representing the Harvard administration in its responses to student protesters and threats of violence. Throughout this ordeal he steadfastly maintained a level of objectivity and fair-mindedness that neither exhaustion nor abuse could lessen. His actions in this period are little known outside those campuses, but they demonstrated his strength of character.

Chance called upon Archibald Cox's character a second time through the implausible set of circumstances that eventually led Richard Nixon to resign the presidency. In this case, I was chance's improbable instrument. As the newly designated attorney general, I decided that I should delegate responsibility to investigating Watergate to an independent counsel and that this person should have substantial prosecutorial experience. Cox had no such experience. But then how could I have guessed that the seven former prosecutors I approached would all turn me down? When I dropped the prosecutorial prerequisite, that made eligible the man who should have been my choice in the first place.

Had Richard Nixon known Archie Cox as well as the readers of this biography will know him, Nixon would have realized that his only hope of salvation lay in full disclosure. Instead, he repeatedly let himself be victimized by his own cynicism. Cox was a Kennedy man, and to Nixon that meant that Cox was "out to get him." Try as I might, I could not convince Nixon or his staff that Archie would rather cut off his right arm than take any action not fully supported by the law and the facts. Had Nixon known how stubbornly Cox dealt with the Kennedys when he disagreed with their judgment in the sit-in and reapportionment cases, Nixon would have understood what I meant.

Nixon was equally mistaken in thinking that Cox might be induced to go along with a deal that limited his capacity to pursue any and all material evidence merely for the sake of retaining his highly visible position. Indeed, Nixon and his lawyers seemed to discount the risk of pushing Cox too far.

In the end, Nixon's most damaging misjudgment was his underestimation of Cox's ability to communicate the strength of his integrity. Nixon himself, like everyone else who watched Cox's press conference on the afternoon of October 20, 1973, must have felt that force. Indeed, in all the annals of public service there have been few finer examples of grace under pressure.

That demonstration of the linkage between Archibald Cox's background and behavior suggests one additional observation. The stereotypical features of his culture are old-line, cultivated, well-to-do, and WASPy. Those who share this background belong to one of the smaller minority groups making up our multicultural society, occasionally even seen as relics. At their best, however, they are prime transmitters of the distinctively American attributes that transcend other cultural lines. And though it is by and large good that the emergence of multiculturalism has alerted us to the limitations of the melting pot, it would be too bad if minority groups ceased to think of themselves as Americans. All of us have a stake in the cultural tradition to which Archibald Cox and his great-grandfather Evarts belong, because it is a tradition that bases its affirmation of diversity on a profound belief in the dignity and worth of every individual. In so doing, it helps to create unity even as it celebrates diversity.

Someday, perhaps, our society will be mature enough to create a pantheon of heroes who fought for this nation's indigenous values while also representing the distinctive attributes of their personal heritage. The man whose qualities and contributions are remembered in these pages surely deserves an honored place in that assemblage.

THE
IMPEACHMENT
TRIAL

William M. Evarts (1818–1901)

Library of Congress

W hen William M. Evarts rose to begin his closing argument on
behalf of the president, he appeared oddly like a specter of
Cicero with his aquiline nose and flowing hair. The semicircular rows
of senators sat entranced; the gallery remained stock-still. The sound
of a stray pocket watch could be heard ticking, accentuating the
perfect silence. The six managers from the House sat across the room
at the long table for the prosecution, fidgeting—John A. Bingham of
Ohio, George S. Boutwell and Benjamin F. Butler of Massachusetts,
James F. Wilson of Iowa, John A. Logan of Illinois, and Thomas F.
Williams and Thaddeus Stevens, both from Pennsylvania.[1] It was the
28th day of April, 1868.

Ladies in stiff white crinolines and men in waistcoats hung from the
galleries. Chief Justice Salmon P. Chase struck his gavel to a wooden
block, motioning for Evarts to begin. Attorney General Henry Stanberry had resigned his cabinet office in order to act as lead counsel for
the president,[2] but the crush of eleven articles of impeachment and
the circuslike atmosphere of the proceedings had caused Stanberry to
become ill from exhaustion and drop out as Andrew Johnson's principal hope against conviction.

The burden now fell on this erect, gaunt, intensely alert man—
William Maxwell Evarts—attorney from New York.[3] When he rose
from the defense table and addressed the clutch of fifty-four senators
who sat in judgment of the indicted president, it was with a strange
sort of conviction. Particularly strange, some whispered, because several months earlier he had delivered a passionate speech at the Cooper Union in New York, lashing out at President Johnson's uninspired,

lax policy toward Reconstruction in the South and calling Johnson the "President without a party."[4] Hardly the words, spectators whispered, of a man who should now be seated at lead counsel table, holding the fate of Andrew Johnson in a loose collection of notes in his leather satchel.

But William M. Evarts occupied a tall seat in the senate hall. In 1861, Evarts himself had been nominated to serve as U.S. senator from New York when William H. Seward resigned the senate to become Lincoln's secretary of state. Evarts (almost irrationally, some shook their heads) had thrown his votes to Judge Ira Harris and given away the nomination. Evarts had feared that if he stayed in the race, Horace Greeley, the irascible editor of the *New York Tribune,* might pull an upset victory and divide the Republican party.[5]

It was in the courtroom, not in politics, that Evarts's name sparkled with a dazzling string of achievements. He had argued the famous *Lemmon Slave Case* in 1860 for the state of New York, one of the first major pro-abolitionist cases that had attempted to choke off the shipment of slaves through the North by freeing blacks who entered the port of New York.[6] He had won the *Prize Cases* in 1863, on behalf of the U.S. government, successfully arguing that President Lincoln's blockade of Southern ports and his seizure of Confederate vessels at the outbreak of the Civil War was constitutional.[7]

So widespread was his reputation for excellence that the New York Court of Appeals had signed a unanimous petition to President Lincoln in October 1864, urging Evarts's appointment to the U.S. Supreme Court when Chief Justice Roger Taney died suddenly.[8] Evarts had refused to promote himself for this or any other office, however, and he was passed over for Salmon P. Chase, who now presided over this galling impeachment trial.

Evarts's trademark at the bar was his fierce independence—an independence now in full view as he sat stoically at counsel table for a Democratic president, a president who had actively resisted—fought against—his representation.

The radical Republican newspaper *Independent* called Evarts a "hireling counsel" who had "pawned his honor for a lawyer's fee."[9] Still, Evarts believed with every ounce of his reasoning that the grounds that his radical Republican colleagues had manufactured to launch this impeachment trial were pure political poppycock. The president stood accused of violating the Tenure of Office Act, which had been pushed through by the radical Republicans the previous year, making it a "high misdemeanor" for the president to remove any cabinet officer without the Senate's consent. The president's crime, according to the impeachment articles, was that he had fired Edwin M. Stanton, his own secretary of war, with "the deliberate purpose and intent to set himself above the Constitution and beyond the law."[10]

But Evarts knew, as every other lawyer who had ever studied Article 2 of the Constitution knew, that the Tenure of Office Act was most likely unconstitutional. He knew, as every other Washington insider knew, that the law had been enacted and Stanton's firing had been orchestrated by the radical Republicans to set the president up for this impeachment charade.[11]

Evarts would not sit quietly along the sidelines and allow the presidency to be destroyed, not even when the advantage went to his own political party. Extreme partisan mischief of this sort threatened the delicate balance between two coordinate branches of government in violation of the words and soul of the Constitution, to which he had pledged adherence.

Evarts surveyed the overflowing Senate chambers. His eyes were sharp, his nose steep. He was a "strikingly handsome" man, with a "markedly intellectual face."[12] But the face now showed strains of doubt. The president's case, so far, verged upon hopelessness. The rules of evidence had been skewed at every turn by the prosecution. Chief Justice Chase had become virtually powerless to control the proceedings. Spies had broken into Evarts's room at the Willard Hotel just days earlier and had rifled through his trash basket looking for scraps of strategy and notes.

Evarts came from a Puritan stock that thrived on challenges. His grandfather, Roger Sherman, had been a noted statesman of the American Revolution, architect of the Connecticut Compromise, one of the few Founders who had signed all three historic documents when the nation was formed: the Declaration of Independence, the Articles of Confederation, and the U.S. Constitution.[13] An interest in political affairs and public matters was viewed as a "hereditary instinct" in the family.[14] Evarts checked his pocket watch; it was time to begin.

The words flowing from Evarts's mouth, without note or prepared script, would eventually consume four days and fourteen hours.[15]

After challenging the senators to abide by their oaths of office, "for the Lord will not hold him guiltless that taketh his name in vain,"[16] Evarts pounced on the indictment leveled at the president and pulled it to shreds with methodical logic. The crowd in the Senate gallery consumed every word. Could one seriously question that the president had a right to test the constitutionality of the Tenure of Office Act? It was a shameless, unprecedented effort by Congress to encroach upon the powers reserved to the executive branch. The president owed no apology to Congress for challenging such a transparent piece of legislation. Indeed, it was the President's *duty* to disobey a law that he believed offended the higher frame of government and to leave it to the Supreme Court to tell him if he was right or wrong.[17]

This was not merely the trial of a chief executive, said Evarts, pounding his fist, "it is indeed the trial of the Constitution."[18] The future of all three branches of government was at stake in the room, he warned. "The House of Representatives is here as accuser; the president of the United States is here as the accused; and the Senate of the United States is here as the court to try him, presided over by the Chief Justice. . . ."

Evarts emphasized the absolute necessity, the urgency, of preserving a balance of power if the American system of government was to survive: "These powers of our government are here, this our Government is here, not for a pageant or a ceremony. . . ." The speaker shifted his left hand into the back pocket of his frock coat, an old habit. Rather, they were gathered here to determine "whether one of them shall be made to bow by virtue of constitutional authority confided to the others. . . ."[19]

One writer observed that the "gravity and deliberation of his [Evarts's] manner, emphasized by the sustained shaking of his forefinger above his head as he approached a climax, carried conviction."[20] Tall, pale, and lanky, Evarts strode back and forth in the Senate chambers like a gangling caricature of his own intellectualism. His suit was impeccable. The high collar was stiff and starched. The unruly hair sometimes slipped downward across his face. There was no smile at moments like this. "But occasionally he signalized the approach of something good by a queer relaxation of the lines about his mouth."[21]

Seizing upon Manager Boutwell's extravagant suggestion that there was a "hole in the sky" near the Southern Cross where president Johnson should be thrown into exile, Evarts straightened his collar and proceeded to describe the imaginary hole in the sky into which Manager Boutwell would attempt to launch the president. From the wings of Lady Liberty on the dome of the Capitol, Boutwell would shout, *"Sic itur ad astra!"* only to be hurled into orbit himself, making it difficult to determine "which is the sun and which is the moon?"[22] The spectators howled with approval; a faint smile crept across the lips of the orator.

Henry Cabot Lodge would later say that Evarts possessed a "phosphorescent" wit that flashed constantly. He now mixed wit with deadly accuracy. The utter folly of this proceeding was that President Johnson was accused—at bottom—of violating an *un*constitutional law. "Why, nobody ever violates an unconstitutional law," Evarts jabbed, "because there never is any such obstacle to a man's action . . . as an *un*constitutional law."[23]

By day number four, Evarts's oration had reached a crescendo. He was masterful, sentimental. Nearly overcome by emotion as he kept the blurry sea of senatorial faces riveted to his exhausted frame, Evarts addressed the crowd:

> And oh, if you could only carry yourselves back to the spirit and the purpose and the wisdom and the courage of the framers of the Government, how safe it would be in your hands! How safe is it now in your hands, for you who have entered into their labors will see to it that the structure of your work comports in durability and excellency with theirs.[24]

By the end of Evarts's performance, the tables of the prosecution had been turned. One historian wrote that Evarts's unparalleled appeal to honesty and duty had "lifted the whole proceedings, from the murky atmosphere in which it had its origin, to a region of lofty and patriotic wisdom."[25] The diary of a firsthand observer recorded: "There is an impression that the Radical cause is growing weaker, and indications that the radical leaders have apprehensions."[26]

On May 16, 1868, thousands of spectators spilled onto the terraces and streets outside the U.S. Capitol, fighting for tickets. At exactly noon, Chief Justice Salmon P. Chase shuffled forward into the same ornate Senate chamber where the prosecution had begun. The sergeant at arms bellowed his proclamation. Counsel for the defense, followed by the prosecuting managers, took their seats at the divided tables. Reporters hurriedly scribbled notes.[27] A congressman from Indiana recalled the tension gripping the Capitol at this uncertain moment in history. It was like a long, long jump into deep water: "The galleries were packed, and an indescribable anxiety was written on every face. Some of the members of the house near me grew sick under the burden of suspense. Such stillness prevailed that the breathing in the galleries could be heard at the announcement of each Senator's voice."[28]

The jury was heavily lopsided against the Democratic president. Only twelve "jurors" were Democrats; forty-two were Republicans, many of them radicals who had helped to orchestrate the prosecution in the first place.[29] Every spectator knew that the fate of the president hinged on the votes of a few wavering Republicans, several vacillating senators who were still debating as late as that morning whether to break ranks with their party.

The wait, the roll call, the maddening ticking of the Senate clock, were all interminable. When the final votes were tallied on Article 11 of the impeachment bill—the one most likely to succeed—President Andrew Johnson was acquitted by the margin of thirty-five for, nineteen against, just one short of the two-thirds majority necessary for conviction.[30]

The "reign of passion" that had threatened to destroy the tenuous equilibrium of power in American government had been held in check.[31] According to a noted nineteenth-century observer, A. Oakey Hall, "the logical strength of the Evarts argument . . . unquestionably decided wavering senators, and gave his client a majority of one for acquittal."[32] Charles Francis Adams, the American ambassador to England, wrote Evarts upon his return from London: "You are entitled to every credit in having done such good work in checking [the tempest's] fury." He added, "I hope it may prove a beacon to warn off all incompetent or intoxicated seamen from a perilous passage."[33]

Evarts served a brief eight-month stint as attorney general under President Johnson.[34] He returned home to cofound the Bar Association of the City of New York in 1869, helping to dismantle the corrupt Tweed Ring that had brought a tainted name to his legal profession.[35] He was prominently mentioned for a seat on the Supreme Court when

Salmon P. Chase died of a stroke in 1873. But Evarts, the victim of fate's final zigzag in his seemingly uncapped career, was passed over (once again) for Morrison Waite.[36]

Although he never occupied a seat on the Supreme Court—one of the few government positions that truly appealed to him—Evarts accepted each call to public service willingly. He served as a distinguished secretary of state under President Rutherford B. Hayes.[37] In his old age, Evarts was elected to the U.S. Senate by the legislature of New York. He served out an honorable six-year stint from 1885 to 1891,[38] a final journey into public service that ended with his vanishing eyesight.

Evarts lived out the last years of his life in relative obscurity at his summer estate Runnemede (named after the sacred ground where King John had signed the Magna Carta in 1215) in the remote town of Windsor, Vermont. It was one place on earth where politics and lost opportunities could be blotted out by the pine-covered ascent that led to Mount Ascutney, the soft rushing waters of the Connecticut River, and the wildflower-dotted woods known as "Paradise," where he and his wife had courted a half-century earlier.[39] Here in a whitewashed clapboard house in the center of a tiny New England town, he found all that he needed: several thousand citizens, three churches, some milking cows, a sawmill, a gristmill, and one seminary.[40]

William M. Evarts was a great man who never quite became great in the eyes of modern American history books. Although he argued and won more constitutional cases than any other person alive during his era, with the possible exception of Daniel Webster,[41] he never found time to lobby for his own appointment to the nation's highest Court. The very essence of his personality, which allowed him to achieve great deeds, prevented him from following a preordained script to the top. He was "not a politician in the usual sense," as one biographer noted. His fatal flaw, if it could be called a flaw, was that he was "too independent to please the political bosses."[42]

In old age, when presented with a beautifully bound, blank book for writing his own memoirs, Evarts "opened it and remarked what a spotless record it was and how wise to leave it thus."[43]

"It is difficult to understand," Evarts eulogized in 1891 when the cornerstone was laid on the tomb of President Ulysses S. Grant in New York, "until the work is completed, how the fabric of great men's lives is woven, for much of the playing of the loom is unnoticed until the conciliated colors are united and presented as the complete fabric of their lives."[44]

Evarts's principal biographer, Chester L. Barrows, would later sum up the completed fabric of this man's life by observing that Evarts "did not seek office, but let it seek him."[45] He was a rare public servant who did not mind being obscured by more aggressive office seekers, who valued integrity over the right to take a shot at the glittering prizes at the top of the nineteenth-century American pecking order. He was content to remain on the second rung of fame's precarious ladder, until history gave him the opportunity to protect the teetering balance of power between Congress and the president. Having risen to the task, on that one brilliant occasion, he indelibly shaped the future of American history.

It was not until one hundred years later, with the election of Richard M. Nixon as president, that the three branches of the American government would position themselves for another titanic clash of the magnitude that Evarts had witnessed.

But Evarts would never hear the word Watergate. Nor would his children or most of their children. Evarts would return to the solitude of his summer estate in Windsor until his eighty-third year. In early 1901 he died in New York and returned a final time; his remains were transported to Vermont, where he was buried underneath a simple gravestone in Ascutney Cemetery, at the base of a towering granite marker, down the road from his cherished Runnemede estate and the flower-swept woods of Paradise. A tiny cross of marble invited the arrival of future family members with the Biblical welcome: "My sheep hear my voice and I know them and they follow me."

A fellow nineteenth-century lawyer wrote an obituary for Evarts in a New York newspaper: "In his death a great light has been extinguished,—no, not altogether extinguished. It will long continue to shine in his many noble utterances which history and literature all preserve; in the memory of the patriotic services which he rendered to his country; in the affectionate regard of a thousand friends, and in the bright example he set as a citizen, statesman and man."[46]

As flowers grew over Evarts's grave in Windsor, Vermont, and a new century took root full of promise and change, a young, gangling boy walked the same paths of Windsor, across the same tract called Runnemede. Tramping through the woods of Paradise, he dreamed of the day that he would become a lawyer and perhaps have the opportunity to dabble in public service.

His name was Archibald Cox.

THE
MAKING
OF A
LAWYER

Archie Cox, Harvard Squash Team (1934)

Harvard University Archives

1

"BILLY" COX

The old Evarts estate in Windsor, with its sprawling collection of homes and wooded acres nestled under Mount Ascutney, left a brilliant impression on Archibald Cox, Jr., from the earliest days.

"The earliest days" for Archie began as soon as his mother could wrap him in a blanket and drive him from their home in Plainfield, New Jersey, to the mountains of Vermont. A worn, brown leather guest book that his grandmother Perkins kept for Runnemede Lodge beginning in 1907 recorded that Frances Perkins Cox and Archibald Cox, Jr. (Archie and his mother), arrived in Windsor from Plainfield on June 12, 1912, less than a month after young Archie was born on May 17. His name was inscribed in the guest book carefully, as if by a first-time mother hoping that someone would one day open the brown book searching for this special name, the ambitious dreams of a mother envisioning boundless success for her first-born child. (The leather book would of course be opened for just that purpose, eighty years later, but it was through no help of the boy himself.)

Archie's mother was the granddaughter of William Maxwell Evarts, once-famous statesman from New York who had defended President Andrew Johnson in his infamous impeachment trial. By 1912, not all Americans appreciated the full importance of the name Evarts; in Windsor, however, the Evarts family name was as good as the golden history of Vermont itself.

Frances Cox (her friends called her "Fanny") was a striking woman—five foot, eight—with a straight nose and chiseled chin that would be inherited by her oldest son and the six other children who

3

followed. She enjoyed playing bridge, reading, drinking tea, and reciting poetry with older ladies who came to spend the afternoon. Even after motherhood arrived, she still found time for card games, picnics, hikes up Mount Ascutney, and family swims announced at the drop of a hat—she simply carried the new baby in tow.[1]

The guest book recorded that Archibald Cox, Sr. (the father), arrived at Windsor on July 12, 1912, from New York. He visited his wife and baby for a long weekend and then vanished, traveling back in the Pullman car of the *White Mountain Express,* a common compromise for a busy lawyer from the city. He was the son of Rowland Cox, a Philadelphia Quaker who had served in the cavalry in Pennsylvania and was transferred to Illinois during the Civil War, but somehow wound up in Manhattan as a prominent nineteenth-century lawyer. He authored *Cox's Manual of Trade Marks* and gained prominence by defending the copyright of the Oxford Bible against a New York publishing company.[2] When he died suddenly in 1900, his son took over his father's law practice fresh out of Harvard Law School, quickly becoming an expert in copyrights, trademarks, and patents.

It was a settled part of family lore that neither Archibald, Sr., nor his father would consider having a partner in law practice, a symptom of the unabashed "streak of independence in the family."[3] Nevertheless, Archibald, Sr., managed "to hold the practice" with enough flair and verve to become one of the more well-established members of the community in Plainfield, New Jersey. That affluence only burst into greater prominence when he established Johnson & Johnson's right to use the "red cross" symbol as its trademark.

The Coxes and Perkinses (not coincidentally, when it came to Archie's parents pairing up) were both prominent families in Plainfield, a town of thirty or forty thousand on the New Jersey Central and B & O railroads, halfway between New York and Princeton.[4] According to family lore, Archibald, Sr., had spotted Frances Perkins walking down the steps of his parents' home in Plainfield when she was only seven years old. He announced, "There's the girl I'm going to marry."[5] Although he had to wait a decade (he was eighteen years older), the two ended up sweethearts and made up for lost time with seven children.

The senior Archibald grew into a tall, attractive man with silvery hair and a pipe in his teeth, who favored bow ties in the casual months of the summer. He was president of the Board of Education in Plainfield. The consummate host, he invited a swarm of Plainfield neighbors to visit his home for a gala gathering each Christmas, complete with blazing candles that dripped wax on a giant spruce tree, and his own fireman standing by "just in case."[6] He was a gregarious, outgoing, charming man, who was frequently asked to run for mayor.[7] But his busy law practice prevented extended forays into local government or politics. In 1911 Archibald Cox, Sr., wrote in his class report to old Harvard College friends: "There is nothing really to write. I have done nothing but practise law, and it is hardly worth while to write the things which I have not done."[8] Except for his natural charm and his ability to gulp down two eggs in a single breath before rushing off to catch the 7:55 train to New York,[9] even his seven children would learn regretfully little about him by the end of their time together.

One mystery that family members never unraveled was why young Archie was bestowed with the nickname "Billy" as soon as he was born. His father was certainly proud to have a boy; Frances Cox recorded that her husband walked up and down the hallway singing, "There'll be a Hot Time in the Old Town Tonight!" when his first son was born. But he made no secret that he disliked the idea of providing the world with an "Archibald, Jr."; he began calling his first son "Bill" the moment his wife introduced the baby.[10] The rest of the Coxes never figured out whether "Bill" was derived from the revered family name of William M. Evarts,[11] or whether it was a random selection that meant "anything is better than another Archibald." No matter how the nickname came about, as soon as Archie, Jr., became old enough to express an opinion, he made clear that he would just as soon use his *own* name. But the request was never quite honored by his family, who continued to call him "Bill"—out of force of habit—for the rest of their lives.[12]

By the time 1914 arrived and Archie was two, the boy was able to scribble a "B" next to his name in his grandmother's guest book in Windsor, presumably for "Billy." And by the time he reached the age of nine, in 1921, Archie's signature would appear in the same guest book with a clear, strong hand as "Archibald Cox, Jr."[13]

The trips from New Jersey to Vermont were recorded each summer like the steady ticking of a clock. Runnemede Lodge was a red brick house with white pillars, built in 1825, that Grandmother Perkins had inherited as one of the twelve children of William M. Evarts. It was the second of six houses (two were later torn down) tucked behind a long, white picket fence surrounded by wide lawns and sweeping ferns that the statesman had purchased along Main Street to allow his children the privilege of living this idyllic lifestyle in perpetuity. They were six magnificent storybook houses, fanned out like a lost millionaire's row in this private, withdrawn, unpretentious New England town. Here the Cox family grew its own network of Yankee roots.

As Archibald Cox, Jr., grew up tall and lanky, with blond hair and a sculpted chin of determination, summers remained synonymous with Windsor: swimming in "*the* Pond" out back, canoeing up to the sluice gates, riding Morgan horses down old carriage roads laden with pine needles, visiting his Evarts cousins at their forty-room farmhouse-mansion (with thirteen baths) on Juniper Hill, hitting baseballs, and exploring Paradise. The hike over to Paradise was less than twenty minutes at a brisk pace. Across the dike, a hiker followed a path overgrown with wild honeysuckle bushes. Turtles and unseen pond creatures plopped into the water with each footstep. Cool winds and trails wound through the Evarts property, past lily pads and trickling water, into woods that gobbled up summertime like an enchanted forest. From the high woods of Paradise, one could see the very top of Mount Ascutney. It almost touched the sky, towering over the rest of the granite hills (if one squinted) like the head of a proud father, arms outstretched, watching over this special domain. It was an ideal hiding place in the 1920s, where boys and girls could think high thoughts, try out phrases, experiment with daring ideas. Here, the Cox children could appreciate the family's glimmering past in one eyeful. And create their own visions of the future.

In this isolated New England setting, Archie grew up steeped in the family history of William M. Evarts: the lineal relationship to American statesman Roger Sherman; the famous speeches bound in leather on the bookcase; the town hall and church and public library that his great-grandfather had helped found in the 1800s. These not only shaped Archie's interest in history from the earliest days, but gave him "a strong sense of continuity."[14]

Windsor was an idyllic setting for a boy to spend summers. It was made even more special by the weather-worn covered bridge that led from Windsor to Cornish, New Hampshire, just across the Connecticut River. Here in Cornish an enchanted community burst to life each summer, drawing within its folds some of the greatest literary-artistic figures of the late 1800s and early 1900s: the sculptor Augustus

Saint-Gaudens, who had once been commissioned by William M. Evarts to make a bust of Chief Justice Waite for the Supreme Court in Washington; the artist and illustrator Maxfield Parrish, who used Mount Ascutney as a background in choice paintings; the American novelist Winston Churchill, who set several books in the quiet New Hampshire town; and the famous New York judge Learned Hand, who was already becoming a legend by the 1920s. Archie's uncle, Maxwell Evarts Perkins, noted editor at Scribner's in New York who was discoverer, silent collaborator, and father figure to some of the greatest literary talent of the 1920s and 1930s—F. Scott Fitzgerald, Ernest Hemingway, and Thomas Wolfe[15]—also settled into one of the six houses on the old Evarts estate each summer with his family, adding another spark to the tiny New England community. It was a world of creative thinkers and public success stories that left a permanent imprint in the minds of the Cox children.

When he wasn't hiking mountain trails and soaking up the outdoors in Windsor, Archie plunged into reading of all kinds—literature, history, poetry, light stories. Sunday nights (the maids' night off) were special occasions. The Cox children would gather together in the living room after supper, where they would select a favorite poem to recite under the flicker of a glass kerosene lamp. They sat beneath a portrait of Grandfather Perkins hung over the fireplace; he had been a promising art critic who helped found the Boston Museum of Fine Arts, but he was tragically killed in 1886 when his horses got spooked in a thunderstorm and crashed into a stone wall near Paradise.[16]

Under Grandfather Perkins's stern gaze, Archie had started off as a "frail and nervous" child, according to his sister Betty.[17] But with age he grew in confidence; his voice soon became "extremely loud" and certain. Archie's favorite poem came from the *Home Book of Verse*. He could deliver it with great style again and again by heart, even into old age:

> *Whar have you been for the last three year*
> *That you haven't heard folks tell*
> *How Jim Bludso passed in his checks*
> *The night of the* Prairie Belle?

It was a poem about the wreck of the *Prairie Belle* steamship on the Mississippi River, written by John Hay, Abraham Lincoln's private secretary and later secretary of state under Presidents William

McKinley and Theodore Roosevelt. The hero of the poem had two principles that guided him as a riverboat captain on the Mississippi. First, he would never let another steamboat pass him, because he wanted to be the best at what he did. Second, if the *Prairie Belle* ever took fire, he swore a thousand times that he would deliver each passenger safely to the shore, no matter what the costs. For a young Archie Cox, these two oaths of the rough-hewn riverboat engineer revealed a dogged virtue:

> *Through the hot, black breath of the burnin' boat*
> *Jim Bludso's voice was heard*
> *And they all had trust in his cussedness,*
> *And knowed he would keep his word.*
> *And sure's you're born, they all got off*
> *Afore the smoke-stacks fell—*
> *And Bludso's ghost went up alone*
> *In the smoke of the* Prairie Belle.[18]

One cousin described Archie as a "loner."[19] But this was not exactly the word. The lineup of the Cox children spanned sixteen years, making them actually two separate "generations": Archie (born in 1912); Betty (born 1913); Mary, called "Molly" (1916); followed by Rob (1919); Max (1922); Louis (1925); and Rowland (1928).[20] The next oldest boy in the family, Rob, was seven years younger. With such an age gap, Archie frequently found himself climbing, hiking, and reading away the time by himself. His sisters, Betty and Molly, were his friends, but they did things that girls did in the 1920s—cutting out dolls, playing pencil-and-paper games.[21] Archie's parents had bought him a collie back in Plainfield, but he was "the opposite of a boy devoted to his dog."[22] Trips across the river to Cornish, where he could play tennis with boys his own age, were more his style. Sunday baseball games in Paradise with pickup teams of summer transplants were a favorite pastime. Girls were welcome; the shortage of short-stops made it pointless to discriminate.

Archie was "comfortable with people. And they were comfortable with him."[23] He rarely got ruffled, even when intentionally pro-voked. His sisters were haunted by the fact that their father's name was Archibald, and flashed their tempers when friends recited the name with a stray inflection or a smirk. The only one in the family

who "didn't seem to mind" was Archibald, Jr.[24] He liked his name;
he didn't worry about meaningless jokes.

From his father, Archie would inherit an old-fashioned work ethic;
a tiny spark of wit (and an even deeper admiration of it in others); a
gracious, polite demeanor; and a general love for newspaper headlines, action, and public events. From his mother, he would inherit
less tangible qualities: an abundant willingness to accept; an interest in
the creative side of life rather than the commercial world; an optimist's view of humanity, assuming the best of all who entered his
doorway; a love for the outdoors; and a quiet Yankee reserve that in
later years would be mistaken by those who did not know him for
arrogance (when it came much closer to shyness).

From both parents, Archie would inherit an unusual merging of
New England and New Jersey dialects. "We all have a queer accent,"
sister Molly would smile.[25] It was precise and methodical. Lips were
pursed. The tones were high-sounding, mellifluous, as if the speaker
was reading from a book of old English verse while holding back any
trace of sentiment or emotion. In the Cox family, emotions and
exuberance and effusiveness were not paraded through the house.
These were best left for private settings, places like the woods or the
mountains.

For "Billy" Cox, a feel for history and an instinct toward pursuing
worthwhile opportunities in life did not end when his family packed
up their belongings each August and drove home from Vermont to
New Jersey.

The house on 1010 Rahway Road in Plainfield where Archie spent
much of his childhood was a long, low, white building with green
shutters, a Dutch colonial custom-designed by the architectural firm
of White and White. His father had it built in the early 1920s on a
nine-acre plot with a hillside that had been used to grow potatoes
during World War I. The house represented increasing profits from
the senior Cox's law firm and corresponded with the arrival of a fifth
child, Max, the only Cox child born in a hospital, because the house
was unfinished.[26]

Years later, Archie would preserve a vivid memory of this home, its
seven bedrooms, oil furnace, claw-foot bathtubs, fireplaces, maids'
quarters, tennis court (his father liked to beat him and proclaim,
"Brother, your tail hangs behind!"), and chauffeur's apartment over

the garage, all symbols of Roaring-Twenties wealth. Archie also remembered the presidential election of 1928, when his father brought home their first console radio (Archie himself had a tiny crystal set) to listen to the speeches of Al Smith, the Democratic presidential candidate running against Herbert Hoover. "He bought a big, heavy console," Cox remembered. "And I have a very vivid picture . . . of my father and mother, myself and my sister Betty . . . sitting in the living room, listening to the broadcasts of Al Smith's and maybe Hoover's speeches. And on the dining room chairs, shrouded in the dark would be sitting the maids. . . . I don't think they resented this. I think that the relations between my family and the 'retainers' were very good. At least that's my picture. But the symbols of status were probably much more important than any ideas of status themselves."[27]

Maids and nurses and chauffeurs were paid "New York wages" of $425 per month for the five of them, a tidy sum.[28] But young Archie discovered that he was one of the only boys in their affluent section of Plainfield whose father was supporting a progressive Democrat (a Catholic, no less) for president, a fact that summed up his early political consciousness much more than the swelling ledger in the family bank book.

Life in Plainfield during the nonsummer months was a solid, regular existence. All children under nine ate "supper" (hot cereal with prunes or applesauce) at 5:30 and then went to bed. The older children were expected to sit down to dinner as soon as Archibald, Sr., walked in the door from the train station. Boys wore coats and ties; girls wore dresses (or, if they had already worn a dress earlier in the day, a "new dress").[29] The parents had one cocktail of vermouth and fruit juice, never more, never less. Then the maids served dinner. A typical meal consisted of soup; roast beef, chops, or lamb; two vegetables; and a pudding.[30] After dinner the older children were allowed to read before going to bed, as long as they pulled up the covers and extinguished the lights by 8:00 sharp.

Archie found that he liked the sound of words, the flow and resonance of phrases carefully forged and sharpened by the writer. He liked to speak words almost as much as he liked to read them. But this posed certain hazards.

His first public speaking contest was at the Wardlaw School in Plainfield, a small private grade school that Archie rode to on a bicycle. The poem he had selected was "Farragut," about wooden Union warships going into Mobile Bay during the Civil War. Archie

o

would never forget clenching his fists at the Wardlaw School, planting his feet, and reciting:

> *Farragut, Farragut,*
> *Old Heart of Oak,*
> *Daring Dave Farragut*
> *Thunderbolt stroke . . .*

Then he stopped. "And I couldn't remember another word. I broke down completely as a tearful little boy."[31]

By his teens, however, Archie had become more polished, more confident of his talents. His father was "terribly excited that I wouldn't be admitted to St. Paul's [prep school], because he had read an English composition of mine and found it filled with mistakes of spelling."[32] Archibald, Sr., told his wife, "Well, the boy's a moron."[33] But Archie wasn't worried. He "regarded it, and always regarded it, as an unnecessary flap."[34] Still, it was enough of a flap, old letters reveal, that his father wrote directly to an administrator at St. Paul's School in April 1926. Reporting that young Archie was taking the entrance exams, his father conspicuously threw in some choice information: "I am told that, other things being equal, relationship to Alumni may count something in favor of a boy on the waiting list. If so, my boy can claim, in addition to his father and four uncles, a grandfather and five or six grand-uncles, and a Trustee in the generation before that."[35] A representative of St. Paul's quickly wrote back reassuringly: "You are right in understanding that relationship to Alumni counts in a boy's favor when he is trying for admission to the School. Your boy should score heavily in this regard when the time comes."[36]

Archie was safely admitted to St. Paul's in 1926. By this time, he had shaken much of the self-doubt that had plagued him as a boy. He could easily recite the saga of Admiral Farragut by heart.[37]

Archie entered St. Paul's at age fourteen, receiving a thick dose of New England culture that he enjoyed immensely. St. Paul's was a private Episcopal boys' school outside of Concord, New Hampshire, sixty miles from Windsor, in the middle of a wooded, secluded, bucolic nowhere. There were English Tudor buildings, tennis courts, ponds with footbridges, geese, swans, and absolute solitude.

Archie's great-grandfather Perkins had helped found St. Paul's, and his grandfather had been one of the first students in the 1870s, so the Cox, Evarts, and Perkins names all carried a special ring amid the chiming bells of the Episcopal prep school grounds. So nicely did Archie adapt that his younger brother Rob was planning to follow in his footsteps, a fact that pleased Archie and gave his own enrollment a delightful aura of pathfinding and experimentation.

Archie enjoyed rubbing elbows with a swarm of teenage boys of his own vintage, many of whom were sons of alumni. Along with the other third formers in the fall of 1926, Archie lived in an alcove in the "Old School" building. In this spartan setting, each boy had nothing but a bed and a bureau, some clothes on the floor until a master came along, and a ready comb.[38] "It was perfectly pleasant," recalled Archie's classmate and lifelong friend, Dr. Thomas W. Clark. "Sleeping and getting up in the morning is what you did."

As soon as the morning bells went off at an ungodly hour, the boys raced down, took showers, ate breakfast, went to chapel, and got ready for classes.[39] In the New England winters, it was still dark as they dashed across the dimly lit brick paths for lessons in Greek and trigonometry. Part of the unspoken challenge was to learn to face adversity head-on. "We took cold showers in the basement," Clark remembered. "You were sissy to [do otherwise] . . . even in the middle of winter," he explained. "There was plenty of hot water—we just didn't use it."[40]

Boys wore a coat and tie to classes and donned a stiff collar every night for dinner.[41] They attended chapel once a day, twice on Sundays. Immediately after students communed with God, infractions were read out loud at the "Big Study." Violations such as "up after lights," "swimming at night," and "out after check-in" were announced sternly by the rector, Dr. Samuel S. Drury, who was considered God's direct spokesman, and demerits were levied.[42]

For a boy who was used to going to bed at eight o'clock back in Plainfield, the hours at St. Paul's seemed long and difficult. Archie wrote home: "Tell Betty it's no fun sitting up so late, until 9:00."[43] Archie's classmate, William G. Foulke, remembered that hardships nevertheless created a bond: "It was a rigorous life—getting up when the sun was just coming up; it was cold; we were living in very little quarters. Circumstances like these bring people together."

The boys attending St. Paul's were hardly children of the struggling lower classes. The school was a WASPy affair, for the most part. Two Vanderbilts enrolled during Archie's entering year.[44] Parents assumed that they were sending their children to the "best school in the English-speaking world."[45] By and large, they were offspring of the rich and powerful in the great Northeast, who recognized that if their children were going to letter in college sports, make Phi Beta Kappa at Ivy League schools, run banks, head corporations, lead great law firms, become great diplomats, and make names for themselves in government and national politics, they had better learn rigorous habits in the earliest years.

Despite all these high-minded parental goals, a group of 428 boys had a way of softening the structure. Some boys tinkered with radios. Some wrote for the school magazine. Club football, hockey, baseball, and crew were institutions. "Teas" were a regular event at the homes of masters. Canoeing on the lakes and streams on campus was a popular pastime. By December, the ice was thick enough to skate on Mill Pond, "Big Turkey," and "the Everglades." There were other diversions. "We would go swimming in the quarry," recalled Tom Clark, "which was totally illegal. We would have to entice a janitor who had a car to take us there. It was no better than swimming in the lakes that the school owned. But it was illegal, so we did it."[46]

St. Paul's sponsored one dance a year. Boys would invite girls from home, usually Long Island or New Jersey, to dance fox-trots and waltzes.[47] Archie's only recollection of a date was Elizabeth "Zibby" Fiske from Plainfield, who was more comfortable sitting on the porch on Rahway Road with his sisters, but reluctantly made the trip to New Hampshire to see how prep school boys danced.[48]

Archie was viewed as "a bit more intellectually inclined" than many of his classmates. His sandy, almost blond hair was always cut short. At six feet tall, he was skinny, even "gangly." He was known neither for his athletic prowess nor his "sartorial" stylishness.[49] He was neverthe-less listed as a backup left tackle on his intramural Isthmian football team.[50] And he was a passable enough baseball player that he pitched an occasional intramural game.[51]

Still, athletics were not what had attracted Archie to St. Paul's. Nor did they keep him there. During fourth form (tenth grade), while Archie's roommate Edgar Rulon-Miller was busy perfecting the art of smoking cigarettes up the chimney to avoid the well-trained noses of the masters, Archie began developing his own interests. A young mas-ter named John Mayher frequently invited a group of boys to carry books to his room in New Upper "after lights," so they could read aloud. Here Archie and his roommates began expanding their curiosity and tastes in literature. They read H. H. Munro's work written under the pseudonym Saki, mostly light prose and irreverent political satire. They consumed the offbeat 1920s newspaper column *archy and mehitabel* featuring an alley cat, Mehitabel, and a cockroach named Archy (much to Archie Cox's delight), who climbed onto a typewriter at night and punched out dialogue in lowercase letters because he was too small to engineer the shift button. Typical of Archy-the-cockroach's astute observations on life was the following rumination, in lower case:

> *if you get gloomy just*
> *take an hour off and sit*
> *and think how*
> *much better this world*
> *is than hell*
> *of course it wont cheer*
> *you up if*
> *you expect to go there*[52]

Archie soon thrived at St. Paul's. He joined the "Greek Gang," a group of students who studied classical Greek and played intramural sports together. He teetered "on the edge of trouble," ducking into the dining hall for formal meals just before the heavy Gothic doors swung closed. He was regularly chastised for sporting a short, almost stubbly hairstyle that Dr. Drury viewed as much too short.[53]

Archie was never one of the top boys in the third or fourth forms, a fact published conspicuously in "half term rankings" in the school magazine. But he won the Keep Prize in English History for an essay that he signed under the nom de plume "William M. Evarts." By the end of fourth form, in 1928, he had joined the Propylean Literary Society, where he was judged best speaker in two separate debates. In one winning argument, Cox supported the affirmative on the issue "Resolved: That the war debt of the Allies to the United States ought to be cancelled by the United States."[54] In the second, he argued the negative on the proposition "Resolved: That the United States should enter the League of Nations."[55]

In the spring of 1928, Frances Cox wrote to Dr. Drury: "It is lovely to have Archie at home again and to see him so well, and so happy. We feel you are doing so much for him at St. Paul's, and that he is learning a great deal besides lessons in books."[56]

By sixth form (senior year), Archie was beginning to achieve a new level of confidence—just as it was time to leave. He was listed as one of the select members of the sixth form who "read the lessons at Sunday Evening" chapel.[57] With his large, strong hands he excelled at racket sports and was appointed to the Squash and Tennis Committees. He argued against Groton School in a major interschool debate, taking the negative on the question of whether the U.S.S.R. should be recognized by the United States, and "swinging the tide" in favor of a St. Paul's victory.[58] By this time, he was given the nickname "Solicitor" by his classmates, an undeniable tribute.[59] "The Six Rankings" listed him, academically, as one of the "leaders of the entire school."[60]

More important than this scholastic achievement, a reputation was starting to follow Archie Cox. "He was an independent," said his friend Charlie Kirkland. "Like all boys' schools, there were lots of cliques. He was on the edge of them. It was a hard role to play. Most kids had a herd instinct. But he didn't need it."[61]

This emerging perception of Archie as someone who "forged his own course" led the rector to appoint Archie and Joseph "Indian Joe" Barker to the Student Council, a distinct honor at St. Paul's.[62] Some skeptical friends saw an unflattering angle to Cox's appointment. It was widely known in the dormitories and locker rooms that there was "a good deal of illegal goings-on" in Twenty House. "Constantly," said Charlie Kirkland, who balked at describing the activity in any further detail. "Certainly he [Archie] and everyone else knew." The illegal activity that everyone knew about, including the administration, was smoking and gambling, a "moving crap game." Much of it involved friends of Archie. As Kirkland and other residents of Twenty House saw Dr. Drury's careful selection of Cox, "Drury put him on the council because he thought he could get information."

Whether or not that was the plan (Archie himself would never attribute this unseemly motive to the administration), his friends remained impressed that Cox could toe the line. He never condoned the improper activity, yet he never blew the whistle. "He somehow managed to walk that tight-rope of not being a part of it and not giving it away," Kirkland said. "He was on the side of authority but he didn't give in to it."[63]

Whenever he was preoccupied or troubled, Archie would walk around the Lower Pond below the red brick chapel, where mosquitoes and black flies swarmed in noisy hordes. On the narrow trail that circled behind the pond, Archie had a favorite path that took him a quarter of a mile around the perimeter. There was a stone marker built along the trail in the shape of a cross. He would pick his way to this end point, stop, read the one-sentence inscription on the marker, then turn around.

It was a familiar verse from the King James Version of the Bible, Ecclesiastes, chapter 12. It somehow made him feel good to read it: "REMEMBER NOW THE CREATOR IN THE DAYS OF THY YOUTH."

Archie captured the Hugh Camp Memorial Cup for public speaking at the end of sixth form, with a free-spirited address delivered in the Big Study entitled "The Age of Revolt." As part of the honor Archie was invited to publish his essay in the June 4, 1930, issue of *Horae Scholasticae,* the final edition of the school magazine. There, the eighteen-year-old Archie Cox wrote with confident style: "Two characteristics of man have hitherto impeded him: fear and authority. He is afraid to venture far from the established course. He dares not think too clearly about himself and his institutions, for he fears the result."[64]

Graduation was held on June 5, 1930, after a sentimental last night that included a quiet singing of "Salve Mater" under the faintly illuminated trees outside the Old Study. The crowd was so large that Archie's parents could not book a hotel; they stayed at a nearby farmhouse, where Archibald, Sr., coughed all night with a nagging cold. "I should have never made you come," Frances Cox told her husband. But, as Frances later recorded, Archie's father smiled back and replied, "Maybe it was the most important thing in the whole world."[65]

With his parents watching proudly, Archie delivered a speech entitled "Today" at the final Concordian-Cadmean dinner and received a silver medal in debating.[66] A letter of recommendation had already been written by Dr. Drury and mailed to Harvard: "Archibald Cox is one of our leading boys in the Sixth Form. . . . He comes of a good Harvard family, many of whom have been connected with Harvard. He is a fine public speaker, having led our recent debating team against Groton. We expect great things of Cox and believe that he will be a true contributor to the life of Harvard. He is a communicant of the Episcopal Church."[67]

St. Paul's was a narrow world, consisting of boys imported almost exclusively from the upper social stratum of New York, Philadelphia, and New England families. Despite the cloistered environment, however, something very positive had happened to Archie in the Tudor buildings, endless ballyards, and pristine woods of the New Hampshire prep school. Something so positive that he would feel compelled to "quietly revisit" St. Paul's throughout his life, particularly when he was faced with a career change or a difficult life-decision.[68]

Archie and his old classmates would be unable, years later, to dissect the precise causes, the exact sources of positive influence, when asked to explain how St. Paul's had profoundly touched their lives. Part of it was undoubtedly the positive example set by St. Paul's alumni, some of whom had become prominent figures of the time: men like John Winant, governor of New Hampshire, and Archibald Alexander, distinguished New York City lawyer and two-time candidate for the U.S. Senate from New Jersey. Part of the positive influence, too, certainly came from the rector, Dr. Drury. As one former student would recount during a debriefing after being shot down in a fighter plane during World War II, "Just about this point, I saw a big golden glow and the pearly gates. And I saw Dr. Drury's face looking over the top."[69]

Another positive factor was surely linked to the long, spiny chapel, with its sparkling panes of glass and gothic tower ringing chimes on the hour, that served as the physical and symbolic center of the campus. Archie and his old classmates agreed that religion—including daily trips to chapel (twice on Sunday), where Archie "passed the plate"—played a critical role in the moral shaping that took place at St. Paul's. This was true, even though, ironically, Archie and many of his cohorts never became "good churchmen."[70] Traditional wisdom at St. Paul's held that although a certain number of teenagers were destined to become heathens and agnostics no matter what training was drilled into their heads, at least at St. Paul's they "lost their faith under the best possible circumstances."[71]

Whatever the precise origin of its impact, St. Paul's would exert a strong influence on Archibald Cox for the rest of his life.[72] He would never find satisfactory words to sum up the importance of his education at that New England prep school. But his mother would do it for him, long after he reached mature years. "Billy," Frances Cox would say after she passed her eightieth birthday, "you certainly haven't done very well in your duty toward God but you have done, I'll have to confess, pretty well in your duty towards your neighbor."[73]

2

HARVARD

Years of new friends and the taste of new experiences at St. Paul's had silently turned into years of preparation for college. Few forces can match the fire that burns in adolescents as they begin to visualize the abundance of careers, the boundless opportunities that await them after graduation. As Archie Cox's life began to refocus with a new lens, the image in his mind's eye became unshakable and brilliant. There was, he remembered, "never a day when I wasn't going to be a lawyer."[1]

Archie read and reread Francis Wellman's *Art of Cross-Examination,* which included humorous and suspenseful passages of lawyers grilling witnesses with searing, sometimes provocative questions that "sort of made your jaw drop."[2] He also read Beveridge's *Life of John Marshall,*[3] a set of thick, red books that he would keep on his shelf for the rest of his life. The Marshall biography included an account of the trial of Aaron Burr in 1807, which raised fascinating issues of executive privilege. Archie jotted notes in the margin—always in pencil—and read for pleasure. The image of the legal profession taking shape in his mind, not only as a result of summers in Windsor but also from his studies at St. Paul's, was one of "great cases and great lawyers in great circumstances."[4]

And so, when Archie left the physical, social, and educational seclusion of St. Paul's and arrived that fall of 1930 at the bustling Harvard campus in Cambridge, he was quite sure he wanted to study courses that would one day make him a lawyer.

As an adult, Archie would preserve no recollection of the individuals who wrote letters of reference for his admission to Harvard

College; a seventeen-year-old boy views filling out such papers as far less important than do his parents. But the tiny packet of materials in Cox's permanent record at Harvard would reveal that one of those references was Judge Learned Hand. Although Archie had met Judge Hand only once or twice by 1930, seeing him occasionally on Main Street in Windsor picking up his mail in the summer, Learned Hand's name was a charmed one in the Cox family. Archie's father had practiced law in front of Judge Hand for years; both men had occupied offices in the Woolworth Building in New York City when Hand was a district judge, and they had become friends.[5] At the end of World War I, there was talk of Judge Hand joining President Wilson's entourage for the peace conference in Europe, and talk of Archie's father going with him. The Cox family considered it an exciting prospect, but the call from the president never materialized. On the day that the American commission sailed from New York, Archibald Cox, Sr., happened to be trying a case in Judge Hand's courtroom. "Mr. Cox," the judge said as he halted the proceeding and peered down from the bench, "would you like to adjourn court for a few minutes so that everybody can look out the window as they sail off without us?"[6]

By 1930, Judge Hand had been promoted to the U.S. Court of Appeals in New York. He was developing a national reputation as one of the most brilliant, original, and eloquent federal judges in American history. He was a close enough friend of Archie's father by this time that he agreed to help Cox's eldest son make good. "I know his father very well indeed," Learned Hand wrote in longhand on March 31, 1930, to Henry Pennypacker, the chairman of the admissions committee at Harvard, "and I am absolutely sure that any son of that man must have good stuff in him. He [the father] is one of the best patent lawyers in America, a man of character, energy, sagacity and wisdom. Tested by his blood, the boy must be good." Although the judge did not know Archie, Jr., personally, he added as an aside, "On his mother's side the boy is descended from William M. Evarts, another warrant for his capacity."[7]

On August 12, 1930, Archibald Cox, Sr., wrote an appreciative note in his elaborate script to A. C. Hanford, dean at Harvard. He indicated his great pleasure that his oldest son had now been admitted to the college. The senior Cox described Archie as "a sound, average boy, not without considerable promise in some directions," and expressed his confidence that he would meet passable standards: "Thus far he has gone his own way, with fair performance. . . ."[8]

Before he left for college, Archie's mother decided that it was time that his father give him some frank advice, now that his son was eighteen. "You've just got to talk to that boy about the facts of life before he goes off," she told her husband. She left them in the room together; in two minutes, they rejoined her. Frances Cox glared at her husband. "What did you say to him, anyhow?" she asked. "You certainly didn't spend much time talking." Archibald Sr. answered, "I told him if he'd keep away from drink, he'd be all right."[9]

Archie immediately plunged into Harvard life and became part of a loosely identified group of students known as the St. Grottlesex boys, a hodgepodge of young men who shared a common background from particularly WASPy New England prep schools: St. Paul's, Groton, and Middlesex.[10] It was vaguely understood by these young men, but perfectly understood by their parents, that if one was born into a traditional WASP family; attended a good prep school like Groton or St. Paul's; gained admission to Harvard, Yale, or Princeton; married the right kind of girl (one from the same background); and kept one's nose relatively clean, one was destined to become a "big success" in life. That is, unless one happened to become a drunk or an actor in the process. It was like escalator steps that moved a young man along effortlessly, higher and higher; extra steps were purely optional. It was the achiever lane, a well-defined path for certain children of success in early twentieth-century America. And Archie Cox had been born into it.

He quickly teamed up with old St. Paul's classmates Tom Clark and Charlie Kirkland, and moved into a small dorm room in Russell Hall, an old building slated to be torn down but spared the wrecking ball to accommodate the overflow of freshmen.[11] His feet were positioned on the correct tread. It was a comfortable, nontaxing existence.

One pleasant diversion came in the form of Archie's membership in the Delphic Club, one of the Harvard Finals Clubs, affectionately known among its spirited members as the Gas House.[12] In a museum-like building on Linden Street just off Harvard Square, filled with shadows, smoke, dark wood, and pictures of old members in suits, Archie took three meals a day and played bridge. Here he learned to drink homemade beer brewed by the steward (with an assistant named Archie), experimented with New Jersey apple jack, smoked Camel-brand cigarettes without filters, and otherwise became acquainted with college life during the raging years of Prohibition.[13]

Life was exactly what it was supposed to be at the Delphic Club—a "gas." There were "many, many parties" upstairs in the cavernous room decorated with moose heads and other symbols of college exuberance.[14] When a party was not in progress, "the guys would collect, buy a couple of drinks," settle in for dinner, then roll dice in cups to see who had to pay for each other's checks. Some Gas House members were willing to go "all the way to twelve or fourteen [dinners]," rolling dice recklessly until they were holding a wad of unpaid dinner checks, having lost the dangerous quest to escape from the Gas House free of charge.[15] Archie tended to be more conservative; a few meals totaling ten or twenty dollars was his limit. But he enjoyed throwing off the structured lifestyle of St. Paul's and replacing authority with a bit of self-indulgence.

The fact of life that Archie's father had really passed along in the room that day had been: "You go to college for growing up."[16] Archie embraced this philosophy with open arms, living "the life of those who were getting gentlemanly C's experimenting with drinks, social life, going to debutante parties, going out with debutantes or other girls."[17] A Gas House photo of this era showed Archie with a furrowed brow and an oversized suit jacket hanging off his thin shoulders. He was still more shy and serious than most of his peers. He was not much of a "ladies' man." He and Charlie Kirkland vied briefly over the same girl, Jean Read, but Kirkland won easily.[18] At the same time, Archie was undergoing his own transformation. Although far from distinguishing himself on the map of Harvard—other than as a respectable card player—he was achieving the ultimate success of a college student. He was finding a comfortable rut.

To his own surprise, with all the other demands on his time piling up (not to mention squash and tennis), his grades were usually ending up slightly better than "gentlemanly C's." Archie found that he liked classes. He developed colorful idols in the classroom such as Roger "Frisky" Merriman, a big, bald man who taught history from the fall of the Roman Empire,[19] and Frederick Merk, the famous American historian known for his frontier theories, who was "dry as dust" but "somehow again had a way of capturing the imagination."[20]

His lifelong friend from the Gas House, Teddy Chase, would describe the "bristly headed" Archie Cox as they settled into freshman life: "He was tall and thin. Wore a bow tie. Had a wonderful style. Rather clipped in his speech. He was bright. But his brightness was not really apparent until Law School."[21]

During the fall of 1930, an intermittent distraction plagued Archie, in the form of sporadic letters from home reporting that his father was suffering from lung trouble. As far back as Archie could remember, Archibald, Sr., had always had a handsome pipe clamped in his teeth and carried a sparkling silver pouch for his aromatic tobacco. The younger children's eyes grew large when the pouch was produced. They made a game of it, attempting to capture the silver prize, holding it for ransom until their father was ready to tamp down a new bowl of tobacco.[22]

But by early 1930, the silver pouch had caused the senior Archibald to spend a good part of the summer at St. Huberts resort in the Adirondack Mountains of New York—recognized therapy for lung conditions at the time. He said to his wife, "It's the queerest thing about this cough. I just feel as if it [doesn't] belong to me at all."[23] There were repeated trips to the hospital in New York. Time off from work. Positive reports from the doctors. He seemed to be improving greatly. So much so that he was allowed to return home from the hospital in early autumn and finish his recovery in Plainfield.[24] Archie would recall, "I expected all through the spring and summer of 1930 that he was going to get *better*."[25]

But things did not improve as Archie expected. By February 1931, Archibald Cox, Sr., was being lowered into a grave in Windsor under the towering winter pines, a casualty of the little-understood disease of lung cancer at the age of fifty-six. A service was held at the Grace Church in Plainfield, and a second at the redbrick church in Windsor, both brief Episcopal affairs.[26] Mount Ascutney loomed cold and forbidding this time of year. The Cox clan filed rigidly into the cemetery; the mountain peak cast its outstretched arms in long, craggy shadows over the procession. Archibald, Sr., now lay with departed members of his wife's family, across the cemetery road from William M. Evarts. His headstone reduced a promising life to a brief span: "Archibald Cox Sr. Born in Smyrna, Del. Nov. 26, 1874. Died in Plainfield, N.J. Feb. 28, 1931."

His children felt that the world had come to an end. Frances Cox tried to hold herself together. But those close to her knew that "it just crushed her."[27]

Not only was the elder Archibald's death a complete emotional shock, but it meant a radical change in life for Archie's mother if she was going to keep seven children clothed and educated. For a woman who "didn't even know how to empty the carpet sweeper,"[28] she suddenly had to dismiss all the maids, shift from a sprawling house of servants and amenities to an austere household of chores and cost cutting, and slash back the family's lifestyle.

The Depression had set in. The prosperity of the 1920s, which allowed a family with an income of twenty-five thousand dollars to buy a house outside New York City, a country home, a car, and a private school education for the children, all came to a crashing halt.[29] Fanny Cox would eventually take in boarders, most of them young school-teachers, to help pay for the upkeep.[30] More was expected of Archie. There was a new sense that "You're the oldest. You're the head of the family now, and you have responsibilities to go with it."[31] As his sister Molly would say of the new relationship between Archie and his mother, "She depended on [Bill] a great deal. It made him dependent on her."[32]

In a shaky hand, the widowed Frances Cox wrote to Dr. Drury at St. Paul's in response to his letter of condolence ten days after the funeral: "Archie has been such a help and comfort to me, and I hate to let him go back to college Saturday night. He is so self-reliant and so ready to face responsibility."[33] The most painful thought, she con-fided, was that she had been so anxious—so ready—to send her next eldest son, Rob, to St. Paul's. But her husband's death cast grave doubts on this prospect. Frances Cox ended the letter with a question that did not come easily for someone of her background: Was there any way that Dr. Drury could consider a scholarship for Rob? "He is a bright, promising boy. Like Archie in some ways, with a good mind and a gift for making friends."[34] He would not be able to follow in the family tradition without some form of help.

Archie was forced to move out of a relatively expensive room in Eliot House and relocate to cheaper quarters. His grades suffered a jolt at the end of freshman year. He received a D in English 28, the first bad grade ever. A note was scribbled on his permanent record: "Father of boy died recently. Boy has good enough mind so that he would be better off if he were doing good work, [and] had more contact with able men in faculty [if he] expects to go to law school."[35]

His father's death also meant that Archie would have to find a summer job. Before this, the only "work" assigned to Archie was drawing the chalk lines on the family tennis court in Plainfield. Now, in the summer of 1931, he took a position as a "tutor-companion" for the Stillman family in Connecticut. They were good friends of his parents; Dr. Stillman had cared for Archie's father during his last illness. Since the Cox family could no longer afford to keep a horse in

Windsor, their mare Sally was sold to the Stillmans and transported to Middlebury, where Archie took the boys, Rufus and Buddy, on slow rides through the trails.[36] He had to skip visiting the old Evarts's homestead during the summer of 1931, one of his first missed summers since he was born. The next time Archie visited his grandmother Perkins, just a year after the funeral, he signed the guest book at Runnemede Lodge with the self-conscious "Archibald Cox (Billy)." The "Jr." that had always followed his name was omitted. He had lost the right to use that now.

After a relatively subdued sophomore year, new setbacks awaited Archie. By his junior year, in the fall of 1932, Archie had developed a fairly serious relationship with a girlfriend, Connie Holmes, who came from a solid family in Stonington, Connecticut. She was a friend of Charlie Kirkland's girlfriend, a convenient link.

Connie Holmes had attended the finest girls' schools in the East. She was admitted to Radcliffe College at age sixteen, but had deferred enrollment for two years while traveling in Switzerland and pursuing unspecified studies. A note from the headmistress at Concord Academy to the Radcliffe admissions committee summed up this applicant: "She is by no means the average person, her school record indicates. She is from a gifted family, with defects and qualities of something akin to genius. Her work is sometimes spectacularly good, sometimes inexplicably poor."[37]

Connie Holmes and Archie grew close after she enrolled and got a dorm at Radcliffe during his junior year. Archie knew that Connie had some ill-defined problems; she was "very high strung" and suffered from seizures akin to epilepsy. "Going through sunlight, bright to shade, had some effect on her."[38] Yet they made a nice couple. Connie was short, dark, a "very attractive young woman." The Cox family loved her like one of their own. They were concerned when she suffered a setback later that autumn and was checked into the McLean, a private psychiatric hospital in Belmont, outside of Cambridge. But Archie accepted the medical problem as something that would work itself out.

Connie Holmes was discharged from the McLean and traveled to France with her mother during the winter of 1932–33. She seemed to be on the upswing. One night at the end of junior year, Archie's phone rang. He received the news in shock: Connie Holmes had committed suicide in France. Sleeping pills.[39]

Charlie Kirkland, who was close to Cox throughout this time, termed Connie's death a "disaster" for Archie. "We shared our confidences," said Kirkland. "He was set back for quite a while." "They were very deeply in love," explained his sister Betty. "It was very tragic."

Archie himself would speak in quiet tones when discussing Connie, even years later. "I was very fond of her," was all he would say. She had been an outgoing, warm, spirited young woman, his first real love. There had been vague references to marriage. Friends and family knew that they were "getting very serious." After six decades, Archie would still treat the subject haltingly. "We got on very well together," Cox would say softly.[40]

After Connie Holmes's suicide, there was a new period of confusion. Archie submerged himself deeply in his schoolwork.

When senior year arrived, Archie found himself a candidate for honors in American history. He scribbled notes to himself and began to think concretely about options. The thesis topic he decided to tackle was "The Senatorial Saucer," borrowed from the metaphor that George Washington had once used to explain the role of the Senate in American government. "Even as you pour tea into your saucer to cool it, so do we pour legislation into the senatorial saucer to cool it."[41] Archie's senior tutor, Paul Buck, who later became a Pulitzer Prize–winning historian, dismissed the project as too ambitious. He warned Archie, "You haven't got brains enough to do that."[42] But in the spring of 1934, Archie turned in a 125-page thesis entitled "Senatorial Saucer," earning himself honors in history and unearthing a new talent.

In this heavily researched, carefully typed and footnoted paper, Archie seemed to have found a rhythm, a style. Not only could he synthesize large chunks of complex material and work them together patiently into a single fabric like a colorful rug, but he enjoyed doing it.

He dug into the "great problems" and crises faced by the U.S. Senate between 1789 and the Civil War, and attempted to weave them together with careful threads of logic. He wrote about the clash between the Federalists, who represented businessmen, and the Republicans, who championed farmers and pioneers. He wrote about Jay's Treaty. He discussed the rifts created by the growing issue of slavery in the North and South. He explained how the adoption of the Missouri Compromise and the Kansas-Nebraska Act revealed the

Senate as it "sank under southern domination and at its lowest ebb," giving slaveholders "the whip hand."[43]

One of the most intriguing stories for Archie, as he developed a snapshot of the Senate's role in America during those tumultuous years, was the failed attempt by the Democratic-Republican Party in Congress to impeach Supreme Court Justice Samuel Chase in 1803, in order to create political chaos for the Federalists.[44] This piece of history had much in common with the impeachment trial of Andrew Johnson, something Archie had read about since he was a boy.

Fortunately, Archie typed away, six Democratic senators had been disciplined enough in their beliefs, true enough to their consciences, that they could see beyond party politics. They voted against impeachment despite the obvious hazards to their own careers. Chase was acquitted. And, Cox concluded, "one of the great crises in American history was safely passed. The inherent caution of the Senate had proved greater than the party whip."[45]

The spring of 1934 brought with it salve to help heal the lingering wounds that remained from the death of a girlfriend. It also brought warm weather, a lush green carpet of grass in the Yard, and the arrival of a letter of acceptance from Harvard Law School. Fifty years later, Cox would remember his move to the ivy-covered buildings of the Law School as vividly as if he had just taken a seat in one of its classrooms.

Archie was well aware, even before he applied, that his admission to Harvard Law School was almost a foregone conclusion. His father had graduated in the Class of 1899, but nepotism aside, during the 1930s almost any student with a bachelor's degree and the ability to scrape up enough tuition money (four hundred dollars per semester) could be admitted to the famous Harvard Law School. Dean Roscoe Pound believed that there was no way of telling who would do well in legal studies until they were thrown into the swamp and allowed to sink, swim, or vanish.[46] So although Archie's college grades "certainly wouldn't have gotten me into the Harvard Law School at any time from about 1950 forward,"[47] fate ushered him in the door in 1934.

In fact, fate did even better. Archie Cox soon became the "freak that bothered all the statisticians,"[48] achieving the highest grade average of any first-year student in his class. He was the number-one student out of a throng of 593, a ranking that surprised Archie more than anyone else.[49] Dean Pound, a world-famous legal educator who wore a green eyeshade in the classroom, originally because of eye trouble but later as his trademark, became Archie's early inspiration. "He was capable of splitting a hair into many more parts than anyone else."[50] Pound was both a lawyer and a botanist; he could "classify and organize" complicated legal decisions as easily as he could flowers or goldenrods, a talent that greatly impressed a young Cox.[51]

If Roscoe Pound provided the intellectual excitement, Edward H. "Bull" Warren, Property professor and disciplinarian, provided the raw thrill. He regaled his class with *in terrorem* tactics unlike anything Archie had seen in college. Students who failed to enter the door by exactly seven minutes past the hour (class time) faced the full force of Bull Warren's wrath, a distinction that Archie worked hard to avoid. After the door slammed shut and silence descended on the classroom, students stranded in the hallway "would try to open the door quietly and crawl in on their hands and knees."[52]

Archie enjoyed the challenge, the tension, the regular, hard hours of work. Steady routines and tedious attention to detail were the hallmarks of a solid, old-fashioned New England lifestyle. Archie's uncle Max Perkins, the editor, had once written to Charles Scribner as a young man applying for his first job in the publishing business: "I am anxious to make this change because of my desire for a regular life; and I have the strongest reasons a young man can have for desiring such a life, and for liking it once I have it."[53] This aptly summed up the family creed. After four years of experimentation in college, one aspired to hard work. Archie was ready to move into adulthood.

Dressed in jacket and necktie (he never attended class without a proper coat), Archie soon found himself excelling in the classroom and on exams. He was astounded when he received a personal letter from Dean Pound at the end of first year, informing him that his exam in Criminal Law was "one of the five or six very best books I have had the pleasure of reading in thirty-six years of law teaching."[54] The talent that Archie had unearthed in college—the ability to tackle mounds of complex material and neatly organize them like a puzzle—was now paying dividends. Law school was where, as one friend put it, Archie took off.[55]

Archie found an apartment at 20A Prescott Street and roomed with three other first-year students who had been fellow Gas House members.[56] Roommates brought with them welcome diversions. Archie had tried to block out the death of Connie Holmes, withdrawing from social activity and concentrating on academics. But by the middle of first year, Archie slowly developed an interest in another young woman, Priscilla Prince, a classmate of Teddy Chase's girlfriend. Priscilla's family owned a cabin in Dublin, New Hampshire, where the group would occasionally travel on weekends to chop wood, opening up a view of Windmill Hill.[57] Co-ed trips in the 1930s were very different from those of the latter twentieth century; males and females slept separately, and they really did chop wood. These excursions provided a chance for Archie to spend time with members of the opposite sex and to reenter the world of dating without committing himself emotionally.

Another benefit of these trips to New Hampshire was that the car often stopped at Teddy Chase's home on the return leg, where Teddy's father, a retired Massachusetts Superior Court judge, gave the boys a pep talk about the virtues of public service.[58] Archie was already thinking about the opportunities—and duties—of becoming a lawyer.

During his first year, Archie blocked off time from studying Torts, Contracts, and Property to do his part in the Massachusetts election of 1934. James Michael Curley, the notoriously corrupt mayor of Boston, was running against Gaspar Bacon for governor of Massachusetts. Archie enlisted the help of a young Gas House friend, Floyd Haskell—who later became U.S. senator from Colorado—to help campaign door-to-door for the Republican candidate, Bacon. The two of them marched through the affluent sections of Boston, down Commonwealth Avenue, rapping on giant metal door knockers. Archie would stand erect and ask the well-groomed residents, "Have you decided whom you will be voting for?"

"Yes, oh yes, we're voting for our friend Mr. Bacon. We're registered," was the inevitable response. This bucked Archie up, moving him along the tree-lined avenues, doing his civic duty.

But when he visited the rear of one massive home, the servants' quarters, Archie received his first blunt lesson in politics. A beautiful Irish girl with blue-black hair and sparkling blue eyes answered the door. Archie stood up straight with his crew cut and asked, "Miss, are you registered to vote?"

"Shure'n, I am," the young woman answered, with an Irish brogue.

"Whom, may I ask, are you voting for?"

"Shure'n, I'll vote for Mayor Curley."

Archie seemed knocked off guard. "Do you think Mayor Curley's exactly honest?" His voice squeaked.

The young woman rolled her blue eyes at this naive law student. "Shure'n, what of that?" She closed the door in his face. As Haskell would later translate her response: "Who gives a goddam? He's one of us."[59]

"It was quite a kick," Haskell remembered.

Mayor Curley won the election by 109,000 votes. Archie returned to studying Torts, Contracts, and Property. Still, he was proud to be joining one of the oldest and most honorable professions. There were certain privileges and duties that came with it, even if, as he was beginning to learn, the world wasn't always pure or perfect.

Even at the age of twenty-three, Archie still felt the summer allure of visiting Windsor and spending time at the old Evarts estate. While some classmates headed for summer jobs in New York or Boston or other bustling cities, Archie signed up to work at his Uncle Louis's law office on Main Street, a stone's throw away from the dirt driveway that led up to his grandmother Perkins's brick house.

In Uncle Louis's tiny office lined with *Vermont Reports,* Archie worked alongside Jeremiah Evarts (a grandson of William M. Evarts), handled title searches, and tracked down witnesses for court. He went to interview an unwed mother in a bastardy case in Brattleboro because Uncle Louis was "too embarrassed to do it" himself. When Archie arrived at the door with his yellow legal pad, the mother blurted out that her lawyer had instructed her not to talk to anyone, and closed the door in his face. Archie went home relieved.[60]

Working in a small Vermont law office was slow and uncomplex; it also allowed for some free time. Archie spent it hiking the White and Green Mountains, especially the Long Trail that ran between Massachusetts and Vermont.[61] He walked, planned, worked, and plotted out ideas about a career in law. As life worked out, he found something else instead.

As Cox would later sum it up, second year was unforgettable "because I had made the *Law Review* and also notable because early that fall at a cocktail party I met Phyllis Ames. . . ."[62]

Working on the *Harvard Law Review* was a top scholastic honor. It was a chance to edit articles by the nation's great legal scholars and work on shorter student pieces that were published together in a heavy bound volume. The *Law Review* represented the crème de la crème of legal scholarship. Archie earned the right to serve as an editor based upon his number-one performance on first year exams. He relished the work.

His mother's increasingly tight financial straits had once again forced Archie to move out of his apartment. At the beginning of second year, he accepted a position as a proctor at Wigglesworth House in Harvard Yard to earn free room and board. Archie spent spare minutes in his dorm writing letters on Gas House letterhead, arranging for his brother Rob's courses at St. Paul's, just as his father had done for him.[63] As Teddy Chase observed it, Archie was "literally the head of the family" now. When the two Harvard boys visited Plainfield on the weekends, with Fanny Cox running around, hair "flying wild," taking care of boarders and children,[64] it was Archie who sat across from his mother at the head of the table and "went up to the sideboard and carved the roast."[65]

Even after he moved out, however, the old first year apartment at 20A Prescott Street remained a welcome gathering spot. It was a good place for the old roommates to meet after Harvard football games. It was here, after a football game in the fall of second year, that Phyllis Ames would first lay eyes on Archie Cox. "He was tall and very thin," she said, squeezing her eyes and remembering that late fall afternoon. "Wearing a tweed coat and flannel trousers. To be honest, he looked a little shabby. Clothes didn't mean that much to him."[66]

One young man had already asked Phyllis out on a date that afternoon. She had turned him down. After the party broke up, she walked down the steps to the sidewalk. "I heard footsteps behind me. It was Archie." The serious-looking law student also wanted to take her out. "I said I promised my mother in Wayland that I was coming home to have dinner with her."[67] Before there was time for further negotiations, Phyllis found herself driving back to Wayland in her mother's blue Ford with a rumble seat, the "shabby" Archie Cox sitting beside her. "It just seemed it was meant to be somehow," she would later say. "He certainly had other women. I had other young men. I had to sign off with several in the next few evenings."[68]

Phyllis herself was tall, five feet, nine and a half inches, with blond-ish brown hair that she kept short. She was thin but sturdy, with broad shoulders and a "strong face."[69] For all of her energy and durability, she was extremely feminine, old-fashioned. "A little like Mrs. Cox [Archie's mother]," Teddy Chase would remember.[70] This young woman—who attracted Archie so strongly from the first moment—liked to ride horses, play bridge, hit tennis balls, tramp through the woods, and labor on the farm. "She always had a twinkle in her eye," said Anna Ela, who had known Phyllis Ames since they were young girls. "She was always up to something."[71]

Phyllis Ames was up to many things. She played field hockey on her college team at Smith, and forward on the all-women's basketball team. She had a lively, sophisticated wit and a boundless sense of humor, but she kept these hidden under a quiet poker face except among friends. "She was a person who made friends easily," said Anna Ela, who never attended college but remained one of Phyllis's best friends for life. "She was always very faithful to them."[72]

Phyllis's brother, James Barr Ames, a third year student at Harvard Law School, noticed signs of something unusual as his sister drove this Archie Cox fellow back to campus that night. "I think there was never any question of anyone else after that."[73]

The Ames family had roots that were generations long, linked to Harvard Law School and legal education. Phyllis's grandfather, James Barr Ames I, had been the dean of the Law School in the 1890s. Her own father, Richard Ames, had served as administrative secretary at the law school for a seeming eternity, sixteen years. Phyllis's maternal grandfather, Nathan Abbott, had been born in Maine but eventually migrated to California, where he founded Stanford Law School, serving as its first dean.[74] Years after Phyllis and Archie were married, they would attend a dinner at the home of Supreme Court Justice Harlan Stone, who would point to two pictures hanging over the desk in his study. One was a photo of Phyllis's grandfather Ames. The other was a picture of her grandfather Abbott.[75] Legal talent ran deep in the bloodline.[76]

But there was a dangerous twist in this seemingly fated romance. By the fall of 1935, Phyllis's parents were separated, soon to be divorced. It was a small family, just Phyllis and her brother. Her only cousins, Richard and Henry Ames from Wayland, with whom she had been very close, were drowned that summer in a trans-Atlantic yacht race, trying to save their father after he was swept overboard six hundred miles east of Newfoundland.[77]

Phyllis needed time to breathe. She had to move cautiously. She had already promised her mother that she would stay home for a year; her mother was "alone and quite sad" after the disintegration of her marriage.[78] Phyllis would shelve her plans to get a master's degree in education at the University of Vermont the next fall. She had spent her junior year in France and intended to teach French—but those plans could be put on hold. She would at least wait and see what happened with this Archie Cox fellow. But not too fast, she warned herself.[79]

Despite Phyllis's pledge to move cautiously, Archie's first overture toward marriage came swiftly. Directly. "We were stopped at a stoplight on the Main Street of Waltham, Massachusetts," Phyllis recalled. "We had been together only three or four times. He asked me to marry him." Inwardly, Phyllis was overjoyed. Outwardly, she was unsure. She had no desire to leap too fast and end up with children saddled with the same sort of devastating parental relationship that she had endured. "I didn't want to inflict that kind of problem on any child we had."[80]

Phyllis refused to give Archie an answer at the stoplight. She brushed him off.

There was, however, another unusual Harvard connection that seemed to charm their relationship. It came in the unlikely form of Professor Austin Wakeman Scott, an elderly, distinguished member of the Harvard Law faculty who had stood as best man at Phyllis's parents' wedding. Even after her parents' separation, "Mr. Scott" faithfully visited the Ames household in Wayland for Sunday luncheon, a loyal friend to both sides of the broken marriage. Archie soon began running into him at the Sunday luncheon table.

As far as Archie was concerned, Mr. Scott was a first-rate Trusts instructor. He was popular with the students. The opportunity to see one of his professors in the flesh, as part of a potential "extended family," made the visits even more exciting for Archie. But it also presented drawbacks for a young man attempting to get to know a young woman. "I have a vivid recollection of sitting in Mr. Scott's Trusts class on Monday morning," Cox would chuckle, "Mr. Scott having been out at Wayland for a Sunday lunch the day before, and he would invariably call on me. . . . I don't believe it ever entered his head that perhaps I had been spending the previous day at other things than preparing for Trusts class."[81]

Phyllis visited the Cox home in Plainfield, at the invitation of Archie's mother, when she and Archie drove down for the Harvard-Princeton game in November. Archie's sister Betty remembered that everyone "was greatly taken with her." Brother Max did not see how it could be otherwise: "She was just Phyllis."

Phyllis had been forceful enough to brush Archie off the first time he proposed. But the young man with a crew cut persisted; he seemed to know exactly what he wanted. For such a serious-looking fellow, he seemed almost impetuous; Phyllis liked this unlikely touch of free-spiritedness in an otherwise earnest law student. They rendezvoused several more times at the Scotts' house in Cambridge, where Phyllis stayed overnight to visit with Archie on weekends. Although the Scotts acted as proper New England chaperones and made their presence known, they regularly disappeared long enough to read the paper or clean dishes in the kitchen, giving Archie and Phyllis time to be alone. It was during one of these lulls that Archie popped the question a second time, in the middle of his Trusts professor's living room. With nothing but instinct to guide her, Phyllis Ames quietly said yes.[82]

To the tune of Cole Porter's "Night and Day" on the radio, Archie and Phyllis made plans to spend their lives together.[83]

Archie gave Phyllis an engagement ring in March 1936, purchased with the fruits of his "intellectual exploits" as winner of the Sears Prize as top student in the first year class.[84] A note from Felix Frankfurter, then a professor at the Law School, congratulated the betrothed couple: "My God, what a powerful legal combination!"[85] What Felix Frankfurter and other casual observers of the Cox-Ames engagement did not know, and what most observers would never know, was that this couple shared much more than their obvious legal bond.

For Phyllis, although her heritage in the law was part of her family history, it had brought problems to the family along with successes. In Phyllis's mind, the law was something to be tolerated, at best. More important than the "powerful legal combination" that the Cox and Ames names presented in the *Boston Herald* and the *New York Times*[86] engagement announcements in the spring of 1936 was a simple hard-working New England ethic, a shared love for the mountains and outdoors, a private vision of how life should be lived.

Archie would struggle to explain his own curious hybrid background by quoting his cousin Harrison Tweed, a well-known New York lawyer, who once pronounced drolly, "All Evartses are peasants at heart." To Archie, this spoke volumes. Intellectual exploits and public service notwithstanding, "an extraordinarily high proportion of us has liked to work the soil with our own hands. To grow things, to muck out our own horses and cows even though we didn't have to."[87]

Such a life precisely matched the dreams of Phyllis Ames, who had spent childhood summers on her grandfather's farm beside the ocean in Maine, riding horses and doing the work of a farmhand in the country. Money and success were necessary up to a point. But simpler pleasures, dirt on the hands and twigs in the hair after a solid day's work, were far more significant achievements. The greatest common bond shared by Archibald Cox and Phyllis Ames for the next sixty years—although only their closest friends and family would ever observe it—would be their mutual desire to preserve this simple, uncluttered, unelaborate, intensely private New England life.

Even after Archie had become, to his own surprise, a very public figure.

3

LEARNED HAND

O ne of the magical strokes of good fortune that touched Archie
Cox's life during Law School, besides meeting Phyllis Ames,
was his exposure to Professor Felix Frankfurter during third year.
Archie enrolled in Frankfurter's course on Public Utilities Law,
because Frankfurter was "*the* faculty member who was alert to, concerned with, and indeed an active part of what was going on in the
outside world."[1] What was going on was the New Deal, Franklin D.
Roosevelt's program for dragging the country out of the Great
Depression through "buoyant and dynamic" leadership.[2] A cavalcade
of new government agencies was sprouting up in Washington. Courts
were creating bold new legal principles by the dozens to accommodate the changes.

For eager young law students, the New Deal represented vigorous
government at its best. It meant an exciting new commitment to
public service. Freshly minted professionals, especially lawyers,
flocked to Washington. There were jobs, opportunities, and worthwhile glimmering causes.[3]

Felix Frankfurter added to this excitement by fostering a renewed
sense of purpose in the classroom, creating heroes and role models by
the dozens. "Felix had a wonderful way of making great figures in the
law come alive," Cox recalled. "The great Supreme Court lawyers, the
past solicitors general. People like Elihu Root [and] Henry L.
Stimson."[4]

Frankfurter himself exuded competence with a capital "C," based
upon a wealth of experience, mostly in government, that students like
Archie admired as a refreshing twist in the classroom. "Frankfurter

once said to me," Cox remembered, "that the great thing about Oliver Wendell Holmes, Jr., was that although his personal experience was very narrow, his reading was enormously wide and his imagination was very fertile and the result was he could live and feel the lives of the people he was called upon to judge."[5] Frankfurter possessed much of this same quality, opening students' minds to the fresh world of law and government that was emerging under President Roosevelt in Washington.

Archie's best friend Teddy Chase enrolled in Frankfurter's Federal Jurisdiction seminar during third year. He and fellow students were awestruck; Frankfurter seemed to be in the newspapers constantly, visiting the White House regularly "to tell Roosevelt what to do." When news hit the papers about FDR's notorious "court packing plan," by which the president would cram more justices onto the court to overpower the mutinous justices who were striking down his New Deal legislation, a pack of law students waited anxiously for Professor Frankfurter to walk through the door. They wanted to see "what Frankfurter the [presidential] adviser would say." Frankfurter strolled into class. He put one leg on a chair, wiped his spectacles with a handkerchief, and placed one hand on his knee. "Gentlemen," he began, "I have no doubt what you're thinking." There was a dramatic pause. "But as students of the law, we are to be concerned only with accomplished fact." Frankfurter then launched into the day's cases and never once mentioned the court packing plan.[6] It was this aura of power, mystery, knowledge, and utter mental discipline that made Felix Frankfurter a sparkling light on the Harvard Law School faculty, as far as students like Archie were concerned.

Working on the *Review* was an equally powerful and transfiguring experience for a graduate of the narrow world of St. Paul's. It meant exposure to classmates like John Sapienza, whom Archie had previously known only as a person who bused tables in the Harvard dining hall and whose father was a construction worker. It also meant trading barbs with Noel Hemindinger, who openly espoused communist views, the sort of discourse that had escaped Cox in the cocoon of his college and prep school life.

Archie's first assignment for the *Review* was to edit a piece that Hemindinger had written on communism. Hemindinger seemed flabbergasted when Cox's notes came back in bold red pen, pushing Hemindinger's somewhat left-wing ideas more clearly and further than the author had done. "Well, I conceived that to be my job as an editor," Cox explained, "to express what the piece tried to express, more clearly," even though he himself did not agree with the article in substance or philosophy.[7]

So it was a shock and disappointment when Archie developed serious eye problems, as a result of working eighty- to ninety-hour weeks in Langdell Library, and was forced to resign from the *Review*.[8] When he went to see an ophthalmologist, the doctor administered a test on depth perception. "Is the bird in the cage or is it out of the cage?" the doctor asked. Archie replied, "It's jumping in and out of the cage."[9] Keeping up with classes was difficult and exhausting. Phyllis would read to him at night, mangling legal pronunciations such as "curtorari" (certiorari), as they cut through the blur of pages.

Archie's physical problems only got worse before they got better. During the winter of his third year, he was unexpectedly laid up with a blood disease that set him even further back in his studies. The only positive aspect of this freak illness was that he was taken into the Ames house for over a month, "as an invalid, really."[10] Lying in bed, Archie spent long days and evenings recuperating with his fiancée at his side. It was a frustrating loss of time. But Archie and Phyllis used the long hours to grow acquainted in the way that young couples need to grow acquainted: planning, talking about the names and numbers of children they might have, considering the type of house they might one day own.[11]

When it came to career plans, Archie adopted the motto of friends who advised him, "First choose where you want to live; then make your decision about what kind of practice."[12] Phyllis felt most comfortable staying in Boston. Archie himself had grown fond of the city with its sparkling skyline, footbridges over the Charles River, and unique history linked with America's founding.

So as soon as Archie emerged from the sickbed in the winter of 1936–37, he took the rattling subway into Boston, a rickety, red train that reminded him of "the Toonerville Trolley" cartoon.[13] He decided to follow Teddy Chase's lead and accept a position at Palmer and Dodge, a well-established Boston firm that specialized in general litigation and insurance defense work. It would be a good place for Archie to begin his legal career after graduation that spring and shake off the curse of his third year health problems. It would also be a good way to begin his life with Phyllis.

Archie was now on the path to becoming a solid corporate lawyer. He was prepared to work long hours and cultivate important clients.

He was ready to buy a nice home in Boston for his future wife and future children, a home that would easily be financed by his large-firm salary. But all of this changed dramatically in December 1936, the day that Felix Frankfurter summoned Archie into his office.

The call to Frankfurter's office was not an ordinary event. Although he was taking Professor Frankfurter's class in Public Utilities Law, he had never been one of the students known as "hot dogs" around the Law School, who visited Frankfurter's home on Sunday for tea and otherwise formed a fan club at his heels.[14] What could the professor want? The office was on the second floor of Langdell Hall, in the west wing. It was cool and dark and smelled of old books. Frankfurter adjusted his spectacles and looked very serious. He was a short, vivid man with "lots of nervous energy."[15] Frankfurter tapped his pen. How would Cox like to clerk for Judge Learned Hand on the U.S. Court of Appeals in New York for a year, instead of entering private practice right away?

That simple question would change Archie's life forever.

Learned Hand was already a legend in the legal profession. He was the author of many of the most famous opinions printed in the Harvard casebooks. His name was quoted in Supreme Court opinions and scholarly publications more often than any other lower court judge in the history of the United States. His name was discussed in the same breath as were Oliver Wendell Holmes, Jr., Louis Brandeis, and Benjamin Cardozo. Hand was at the top of most lists of likely appointees to the U.S. Supreme Court, whenever there was a vacancy. It would later be written that Learned Hand was "universally acknowledged as the greatest living judge in the English-speaking world."[16]

There was also the intriguing personal connection. Although Archie had forgotten or never digested the fact that Learned Hand had written his letter of reference for Harvard College, he did know that his father had been a friend of the judge and had practiced law before him in New York. Archie had picked up snippets of conversations to the effect that his father, of Quaker background, and Judge Hand enjoyed rousing religious discussions of an iconoclastic brand, because they were both avowed religious skeptics.[17] As an overawed young boy, Archie remembered being ushered into the famous Judge Hand's chambers in New York City—a rare trip with his father downtown—where he quietly inspected the books on the shelf, the fountain pen on the desk, and the paper embossed with the seal of the United States as the two men talked in animated, adult tones about life, law, and religion.

It is unlikely that Hand selected Archie because of his old ties with his father. Hand had not followed Archie's career; he knew neither where the "Cox boy" was attending law school nor when he was graduating. Almost certainly, this was Felix Frankfurter's selection. For years, Frankfurter had recruited clerks for an elite group of judges, including Hand. Archie had been first in his class and won the Sears Prize; this was the sort of talent that Frankfurter sought out. Yet Judge Hand must have been surprised and pleased when he heard Frankfurter propose the name "Archibald Cox." Hand must have said something like "I know that boy's family; he comes from good stock. I suppose he's not exactly a boy anymore." No matter what form the discussion took, it produced a fortunate result for the law student sitting in front of Felix Frankfurter's desk that day.

For Archie, the prospect of working for Judge Hand presented "an honor and an opportunity that is hard to imagine anyone turning away from."[18] Although clerkships were still relatively uncommon in the 1930s—many judges had no clerk at all—a chance to work for Learned Hand was like a chance to study under Holmes or Brandeis. Archie left Felix Frankfurter's office feeling almost dizzy. He discussed the matter briefly with Phyllis. They agreed he should take it; they would worry about lost opportunities later. Archie immediately met with the hiring partner at Palmer and Dodge, asking for a one year deferment. Sitting down and shaking his head gravely, the partner strongly advised Archie not to accept the clerkship. "He told me yes, they would release me from any commitment but not to think that I had a job there when I got through with Learned Hand."[19]

Two details needed to be ironed out before the deal could be consummated, in fairness to Judge Hand. First, would Hand accept Archie Cox with his history of eye problems? Second, would Judge Hand tolerate a married clerk? Felix Frankfurter was especially concerned about the second issue. Learned Hand's cousin Augustus Hand, also a federal appeals judge, was known to drag his clerks along to the family stomping grounds in Elizabethtown, New York, whenever the spirit moved him. The question had arisen with one married clerk: Where would they put his wife?

Word soon flashed back that Learned Hand trusted that Archie's eye problems were behind him. He also had no problem accepting a clerk who had committed himself to the holy bond of matrimony, "particularly one who had married an Ames."[20] Hand had studied at Harvard Law in the 1890s under Phyllis's grandfather; Dean Ames had helped him out with advice as a young lawyer beginning his own career.[21] Archie and Phyllis would be acceptable as a package deal.

Archie quickly mailed a handwritten letter to Judge Hand from Rahway Road in Plainfield, during his trip home for Christmas. "I was much surprised to have Mr. Frankfurter recommend me," he wrote in a clear hand on December 31, 1936, "and am doubly pleased now it is settled."[22]

Archie finished his last Law School examination, a Tax exam given by Professor Erwin Griswold, on June 9, 1937. Three days later, he married Phyllis Ames. According to New England tradition, once a young man had nailed down a job suitable to provide for a family, marriage was the permissible prize. Archie wasted no time. The ink on his diploma was barely dry when he stood under the tall, white steeple of the Unitarian church in Wayland. The ceremony was being performed by the local Unitarian minister, the Reverend Mr. Foglesong, along with an Episcopal priest, the Reverend Mr. Davidson, a former master at St. Paul's whom the boys knew as the "Jolly Friar."[23] This dual ceremony was necessary, Phyllis smiled, because "otherwise Archie's mother wouldn't have considered us married."[24]

Frances Cox had arrived from Windsor with the younger boys and a pile of wedding gifts in the car.[25] The sun was bright, the day perfect. Guests streamed into the second floor of the church. Bells pealed noisily. Even Phyllis's father came to the wedding. Mr. Ames had moved to Castine, Maine, after the divorce and did not feel particularly comfortable returning to his wife's domain in Wayland. Still, he stayed long enough for the nuptial itself, smiling at his daughter from a front pew. As a wedding gift, he had already arranged for the newlyweds to spend a summer-long honeymoon in Europe, bicycling in the Cotswolds, punting on the Thames, returning on a turbine steamer from Rotterdam in early September.

Archie's niece walked down the aisle as flower girl. Phyllis's brother, James Barr Ames III, gave his sister away at the altar. The best man was Teddy Chase; Archie's brother Rob served as an usher. Phyllis chose to have no attendants. She wore a white chiffon gown and a veil made of lace from her grandmother's wedding dress, held in place by a wreath of orange blossoms. In her hands, she carried a fragrant bouquet of calla lilies. Archie wore a black cutaway with striped formal pants.[26]

Phyllis was happy but nervous. She began the vows: "I, Archibald, take you . . ." Laughter spread through the pews; luckily, she was able to recover smoothly and restate the vow using her own name.[27]

A reception of champagne and tea sandwiches followed the ceremony at Phyllis's mother's home on Glezen Lane. The air was crisp, and the smell of June flowers swept across the fresh-cut lawn. Archie would never suspect, walking across the grass and shaking hands on that sunny day, that he and Phyllis would live in this same clapboard house as husband and wife for nearly half a century.

On this bright day in Wayland, as he watched his new wife smiling at friends in front of her childhood home, Archie knew only that this picture suited him well.

The chambers of Judge Learned Hand occupied the twenty-fourth floor of the U.S. Courthouse Building in New York City at Foley Square, overlooking the Lower Hudson River. After a magical summer abroad in England, Archie and Phyllis drove from Boston to New York and established their first residence together, a walkup apartment on East 74th Street in a building that had been reclaimed and renovated in an "otherwise dingy neighborhood."[28] New York City would have been an unthinkable home to Phyllis Ames without a husband. But as Phyllis Cox, she went along with the move happily.

"To see what kind of a day it is," Phyllis liked to joke, "I had to stick my head outside the window and turn upside down."[29] Instead of riding horses, canning vegetables, and driving a hay rack, Phyllis now devoted her attention to "trying to learn to cook."[30] As Phyllis recalled, "We were newlyweds. He was starting a new career. Everything was wondrous."[31] For Archie, who was working six days a week—the norm for a young lawyer in New York City—his new job was as wondrous as the marriage.

The job description of "law clerk" to Judge Learned Hand was dramatically different from that of a modern law clerk preparing for a six-figure salary in a glittering Wall Street firm. Archie was paid a wage of $2,300, hardly a staggering sum even in 1937.[32] The judge and his clerk sat in a single room, surrounded by law books, a colorful Oriental rug on the floor. "He sat with his back toward the long wall that had the windows in it," Cox remembered, "and I sat with my back toward a short wall with the door into the lavatory so that I would be facing him."[33] Modern law clerks spend much of their time ghostwriting decisions. Judge Hand allowed none of that. He took enormous pride in drafting his own opinions, opinions known for their clear, brilliant, philosophical, near-poetic quality. Hand composed on a writing board, often with his feet propped up on the desk. He patiently filled his ink pen with an eyedropper and used his clerk almost entirely as a "sounding board."[34]

Although Judge Hand was a perfectionist who took his work with perfect seriousness, he was an incurable artiste who enjoyed amusing himself by writing in verse. Over fifty years later, Archie would be able to recite one memorable bench memo exchanged with other circuit judges, which his boss took great delight in authoring in an admiralty case. It began

Mable *had a rotten line*
Its hemp not worth a damn
But everywhere that Mable *went*
Her line would let her slam[35]

Judge Hand also amused himself by tweaking his law clerks. He called the clerks "Sonny," in the tradition of Oliver Wendell Holmes, and enjoyed springing unexpected questions on them. Early on in Archie's clerkship, Judge Hand hit him with a query. "Sonny," said the judge, staring at him, "what do you think about such and such a case?"

Archie opened his mouth and began to put together a string of words to formulate an answer. "Don't bother to go on," Judge Hand interrupted him. "I've not been listening." As Cox summed up his thoughts: "This was my new job? Much to look forward to! What was I going to do with this ogre?" Later that day, Judge Hand presented his clerk with a copy of the memo that he had been drafting when the fateful question was asked. Learned Hand's logic, Archie now saw on the paper in front of him, followed the precise train of thought that he had begun to articulate. The "ogre" had cut him off because he knew, in one sentence, that both of them agreed. Archie felt better about his new job.[36]

Such was the life of a clerk for a circuit judge in the U.S. Court of Appeals. Judge Hand would write three or four drafts of each opinion on long legal pads with his fountain pen twitching. He would agonize, rewriting draft after draft. Only then would he give the sheets of marked-up legal paper to his clerk for a final edit. If Archie proposed no changes, it usually elicited the stoic comment, "No pay today, Sonny."

At the end of most days, whenever Judge Hand decided that enough work had been accomplished, Archie and his mentor would travel together on the Lexington Avenue subway and get off at the 68th Street stop, where Judge Hand would continue by foot to his brownstone at 142 East 65th Street. Before entering the subway, the judge would insist on spending the nickel to buy Archie's evening paper,[37] one of the "privileges of age," Hand would say.

Many who observed Hand from afar took him for a surly, irascible man. As a questioner in the courtroom, Learned Hand could be "gruff," "overbearing," and "very abrupt" with lawyers.[38] Hand's biographer, Gerald Gunther (another former clerk), would acknowledge that "Hand could be downright sarcastic when dealing with incompetent lawyers and lower federal judges." If there was a bad argument in progress, Judge Hand would "simply turn his seat 180 degrees to express his contempt."[39] Much of this brusque demeanor, as Cox observed it, stemmed from the image Hand preserved of himself as a child. "He had been a very shy boy and young man socially. My authority for that is Learned Hand. Not only directly but various things he would tell me."[40] The result could be, depending on Hand's mood, an intimidating, offensive manner on the bench. Stripped of his robe, however, Hand could transform himself into one of the most charming, sought-after dinner companions in New York City.[41] As Cox explained, it was this inscrutable man "who had enormous influence on me, whom I loved as well as admired."[42]

One episode summed up the complex nature of Judge Hand for his young clerk. It was a Saturday, shortly after Archie had been hired. The clerk of courts ushered a woman into chambers who was attempting to file papers to stay the foreclosure on her husband's farm in upstate New York. It was at the tail end of the Depression; the courts were routinely open for emergencies on Saturdays, but the woman's lawyer had not deemed it important enough, or had not been paid enough, to travel to New York City. Judge Hand was noticeably irritated at being interrupted with such a stray administrative matter. Saturday was his day to get seven or eight hours of quiet, uninterrupted work done, wasn't it? Cox watched in horror as the judge tore into the woman's papers, grumbling, "Why does your petition say this? Why doesn't it say this? Blah, blah, blah."[43] The woman sank deeper into the chair, deeper into distress. Cox watched the scene dumbfounded: "I'm sitting there—here's my hero turning into this bully of a poor woman who's about to lose her home and after ten minutes of this, maybe, he tore the sheets off his pad and 'Here, take this down to the clerk.' He showed her out the door."[44]

When Judge Hand closed the door he muttered, "I hate to be appreciated," and went gruffly back to work. Cox later learned that at the same time the "bully" had been berating the woman and blustering, he had been scribbling out proper pleadings "and a letter-perfect order" that allowed her to stay foreclosure on the farm.[45]

This was the same Judge Hand who enjoyed dancing around the office after struggling over a particularly difficult opinion, singing, "The law is the true embodiment, of everything that's excellent!" from the Gilbert and Sullivan operetta *Iolanthe*.[46] He liked to refer to himself and his colleagues as "Circus Judges," and often provided the atmospherics himself.[47]

It was the same Judge Hand who stood up from his desk and scratched his head the day the famous ocean liner *Leviathan* was being pulled out of the Hudson River by tugs, to be sold to Japan for junk. For many years, the *Leviathan* was the biggest ship on the Atlantic; it had been seized from the Germans during World War I. "We may as well stop pretending that we're working," Judge Hand announced flatly to his young clerk as he turned to the windows. "Neither of us really is. We'll just stand and watch the *Leviathan*."[48] They watched the vessel move out slowly, just as Hand and Archie's father had once watched a different ship depart from New York harbor, two decades earlier.

Many would view it as a tragedy that this original-issue judge never earned a seat on the U.S. Supreme Court, despite universal recognition as one of the finest jurists in America. "Always the bridesmaid, never the bride," was a phrase Hand used in describing his own career.[49] As Cox observed it, there was certainly "some unhappiness" on Learned Hand's part that he repeatedly missed appointment to the highest Court.[50] At the same time, Cox would never accept the premise that Learned Hand fell short of true greatness simply because he was not rewarded with the title "Justice."

The Supreme Court would have been a different place in the 1920s and 1930s with Learned Hand on the bench. Almost surely, in Cox's view, there would have been "one less conservative vote and one more Holmes-Brandeis-Stone vote. So that the decisions of the early New Deal days would have been quite different."[51] But would Hand have earned a more illustrious spot in American history? Would he have contributed more to the development of American law, if there had been different, more brightly colored labels of success pinned on him?

Perhaps not, Cox felt. Hand's strong suit was dealing with obscure points that drove others mad with tedium: state tort law, contracts, tax law, and property. He could take a mass of cases—unorganized splinters and shards of ideas—and painstakingly fit them into a glittering stained glass window that illuminated an entire field for the rest of the legal world. Although there were occasional cases, such as the *Masses* decision dealing with the First Amendment, that brought him notoriety in the constitutional realm, his strength, his unusual artistry, related to much more mundane topics. Basic common law principles. Statutes. Subjects that were not the stuff of usual Supreme Court cases. Concluded Cox, "Cardozo, surely among lawyers, won much higher regard as Chief Judge of the New York Court of Appeals and made more of a mark generally, in that role, than he did as a Justice of the Supreme Court of the United States. Maybe it would have been the same with Learned Hand."[52]

When it was not raining, snowing, or hailing in the mornings, Archie and his boss would often meet and walk together from 65th Street to Foley Square, a four-mile trek that Judge Hand would make religiously until he was seventy-five. It was on one of these walks that Learned Hand, who never discussed legal cases on a good stroll, raised the topic: "Sonny, you know who I'd like to be if I could live my life over again?"

Of course, young Cox had no answer. "I'd be your cousin Harry Tweed," the judge quickly answered his own question.[53] Harrison Tweed was one of the many grandchildren of William Maxwell Evarts and a successful lawyer in the prestigious New York firm of Millbank Tweed. He was a high-profile attorney known for his frequent detours into public service. From bits and pieces of conversations, Archie soon figured out why Learned Hand wanted to be his cousin Harry Tweed. Tweed was "the polo player, the handsome young man at whose feet every young woman fell in New York City and on Long Island, the prominent figure in the Porcellian Club [at Harvard]."[54] As Cox summed up his mentor whom he so deeply loved and admired, "He was awfully complex."[55]

Hand's influence on American law was based in large part on the addresses and opinions that flowed from his fountain pen. But it was based as well upon the silent array of clerks that he molded during his gruff, playful, moody years as a federal judge. This unusual collection of young lawyers would go on to shape the American legal system for most of the twentieth century. They included Charles Wyzanski, New Dealer and later federal judge; Elliot Richardson, cabinet member and adviser to numerous presidents; Gerald Gunther, leading constitutional expert and Hand biographer; and, perhaps somewhat to Hand's own surprise, his law clerk from the year 1937–38, Archibald Cox.[56]

As Cox would later put it with some feeling, borrowing Holmes's phrase, Learned Hand taught "not by precept, but by example."[57]

Archie would remember one day toward the twilight of his clerkship, when the judge and his clerk sat together in the room overlooking the Hudson River. Suddenly Judge Hand looked up from his desk and asked urgently, "Sonny, to whom am I responsible?" Judge Hand looked around. "Everybody ought to be responsible to somebody. To whom am I responsible? Nobody can fire me. Nobody can cut my pay. Nobody can make me decide, tell me what to decide. Not even those nine bozos in Washington who sometimes reverse me. To whom am I responsible?"

After a long pause, Judge Hand pointed to the shelves of law books surrounding him. "To those books about us. That's to whom I am responsible."[58] And then he went back to work.

The one-year clerkship vanished in a blink. It presented Archie's first career dilemma. Should he go to Palmer and Dodge as originally planned? Despite their initial warnings and disclaimers, the members of that firm were anxious to have Archie come back; they offered a flattering salary. Or should he join Ropes and Gray in Boston? Phyllis's older brother, James, practiced there, as did a bright star in the Boston trial bar named Charlie Rugg.[59] Archie talked frequently and seriously to the judge, who raised his great eyebrows as they spoke. Should he lean toward the older Mr. Dodge as a potential mentor? Or toward the younger Charlie Rugg? Was his life's calling in insurance defense work? Or were there other possibilities if he hooked his future to a rising star like Rugg? Of course, there were no answers from Judge Hand. Just more questions.

Archie knew that he had to make a decision himself. He drafted four different letters. One was an acceptance letter to Palmer and Dodge, one a rejection letter. One was an acceptance to Ropes and Gray, another a rejection. The next morning he gripped them in his large right hand and began the trek to work. "I will walk downtown to the Federal Building," he told himself, "and when I get there, I'll post two letters, hopefully consistent, and that will be that."[60]

So Archie walked down the streets of New York City. He entered the Federal Building in Foley Square, placed a stamp on one acceptance letter, placed a stamp on one rejection letter, and took the elevator to work. He never thought about the decision again.[61] He would be working at Ropes and Gray.

Learned Hand commented more than once in the following years, as his relationship with Archie Cox aged into friendship, "The way you went back and forth and couldn't make up your mind and then when you posted these letters that was the end of it and [you] never worried about it again."[62] But for Cox, Learned Hand himself had set somewhat of an example over this. The judge always agonized before making decisions, but he never looked back once a case was marked "Affirmed" or "Reversed."[63]

As Phyllis would later describe her husband's decision-making powers, "When a choice has to be made, although he sometimes thinks days and nights about it, whatever he picks will turn out to be right. He got that from [his mother]."[64]

For Archibald Cox, the decision to go to Ropes and Gray was much simpler than that. It was, for a New Englander who viewed life with a steady ray of optimism, a recurring example of "how one's life is affected by luck, and mine," he said, knocking on a wooden desk, "always for the better."[65]

4

PIONEER
IN LABOR LAW

Cox's clerkship with Learned Hand had surpassed his abundant expectations, introducing him to the world of intellectual giants, prestige, and high-profile public service. In their cramped New York City walk-up, however, Archie and Phyllis were like a pair of New England squash in the wrong soil. They decided it was better to return to Phyllis's stomping grounds. They would rent a little cottage in Weston, near Wayland, and reacquaint themselves with a simpler Yankee lifestyle.[1] Now that they had been married for a year, it was time to set down some roots of their own.

Archie had passed the Massachusetts bar exam in November of 1937. He had an office at the prestigious firm of Ropes and Gray located in the center of the banking and professional district of Boston. What more could a young lawyer want?

He also found a mentor in the person of Charlie Rugg.[2] Archie had barely unpacked his law books before Rugg had asked him to work on Supreme Court briefs for H. P. Hood and Sons, the biggest milk company in Boston. It was a test case challenging the constitutionality of the Agricultural Marketing Agreement Act, a controversial piece of New Deal legislation. Archie thrashed out draft briefs in an absolute fog. Whenever he appeared at Rugg's door, Rugg would motion him to come in. "And from my point of view," Cox would recall warmly, "he would rewrite it with me sitting across the desk learning why he was rewriting it."[3]

Rugg soon gave Archie the chance to travel to Fall River, Massachusetts, a textile hub near Cape Cod, where a mysterious strike had erupted overnight at the American Thread Company. The lanky, unpolished new attorney found himself representing management at a secret meeting with organizers for the United Textile Workers (part of the Congress of Industrial Organizations, or CIO), holed up in a remote hotel room. Archie watched the union leaders put on a tough face, but he nudged them toward a plan that would allow the union to organize the mill without posing a threat to the company. In the end, both sides walked away beaming. Years later, when Archie would return to Fall River in the 1940s and 1950s as a well-established labor lawyer, he would hear the good-natured banter, "Oh, here comes the man who brought the CIO in."[4]

Another young partner, Charlie Wyzanski, soon took an interest in Archie's work. A brilliant graduate of Harvard Law School who had clerked for Learned Hand six years earlier than Archie, Wyzanski was a hotshot New Dealer who had recently served as solicitor of labor under President Roosevelt, then jumped to the solicitor general's office. By 1937, Wyzanski had a reputation as one of the top labor lawyers in the country. The story was widespread that Wyzanski had gotten the better of John W. Davis, famous Supreme Court advocate and former presidential candidate, in the *Associated Press v. Labor Board* case, which sustained the constitutionality of a major piece of New Deal legislation and helped persuade FDR to abandon his infamous court-packing plan.[5] The white-haired Davis had commented after one Supreme Court battle with his young opponent, "In my palmiest days I could not have touched that argument."[6]

"The young fry, including myself, all wanted to work for Charlie Wyzanski," Cox remembered, "and I was particularly lucky in hitting it off with him. I think it was because, for one reason or another, I was acute enough to realize that if he asked you to do something, you had to stay up all night and get it done by noon the next day or he'd have it done himself."[7]

Charlie Wyzanski was "young, short, Jewish, very bright."[8] He had been the first Jewish partner, and remained the only one, at the Yankee firm, blazing a path through sheer intellect that did not wait for laggards.[9] He was a portly man in his thirties who was just as "quick and impatient" as Charlie Rugg was mellow. Wyzanski had been an "early New Dealer," which meant that he could reminisce about visiting the White House at age twenty-six with "Miss Perkins" (Secretary of Labor Frances Perkins, the first female cabinet member) to strategize with President Roosevelt and his entire cabinet during the early FDR administration.[10]

Cox enjoyed practice immensely. Stress and work became two mainstays of his life. He regularly puffed Camel nonfilter cigarettes, a habit that he had picked up while playing bridge and drinking beer during Gas House days. He kept smoking until one Saturday when he woke up, drank his first cup of coffee, and coughed. His throat felt so raw that he had to crawl back into bed and miss a Saturday of writing memos at Ropes and Gray. An occasional vice was acceptable for Cox, but missed days of work were not. He never smoked again.[11]

It was a special time for a young lawyer cutting his teeth on labor law. It was also a special time for Archie and Phyllis as a family. Their first child, Sarah ("Sally"), was born in 1939,[12] followed by a second ("Archie, Jr.") the following year. The Coxes were enjoying a period of contentment and stability.

But in the spring of 1941, with the rumblings of World War II growing louder, Charlie Wyzanski abruptly left Ropes and Gray and returned to Washington as vice chairman of the National Defense Mediation Board. His appointment came directly from the president. The board was an emergency body that would mediate disputes in industries related to national defense. With Hitler's Germany on the march, strikes and lockouts at home might damage the war effort. All of this was a tremendous honor and opportunity for Charlie Wyzanski. It also turned into an opportunity for Cox: in June, Wyzanski asked him to serve as one of four assistants to the board. Cox later mused, "If there hadn't been a war, I'd have simply stayed on at Ropes and Gray all my life."[13]

Archie embraced the call to Washington as quickly as he had accepted the clerkship with Learned Hand. With the war coming, it seemed natural that he should go. He moved Phyllis and the children to a little house off Connecticut Avenue and took over a modest desk in the Social Security Building. It was understood at Ropes and Gray that this was a temporary commitment, for the good of Wyzanski's board and the war effort. Cox would be back as soon as the war was over.

Wyzanski's board immediately waded into a dispute involving the "captive" coal mines—those coal mines that directly supplied the steel industry. John L. Lewis, fiery leader of the United Mine Workers, was pressing hard for a union shop. If he did not get what he wanted, Lewis pledged to call a strike that would shut down steel production, World War II or not.[14] Wyzanski's board fumbled with various attempts to resolve the strike as President Roosevelt pushed and pushed, but the dispute ran in circles. On November 10, 1941, the board issued a wishy-washy opinion denying the union shop to the UMW. In a bitter display of protest, the labor members of the board resigned en masse.[15] The president's machinery for resolving emergency disputes was paralyzed. Only five months after Archie had arrived in Washington to serve his country, the National Defense Mediation Board had disintegrated.

In the chaotic period that followed, Charlie Wyzanski was appointed by President Roosevelt to the federal bench in Massachusetts. Although Archie was unaware of it, Wyzanski and Judge Hand quietly intervened on his behalf.[16] He landed on his feet in November 1941 with a surprising, almost incredible, offer to remain in Washington. He would be working as a young lawyer in the solicitor general's office at the U.S. Justice Department.

For Archie, the chance to join the solicitor general's office resuscitated a lifelong dream of public service. The office consisted of only seven or eight attorneys, an elite corps. Professor Frankfurter, feet propped up in the classroom, had often referred to it as the office of the "celestial general."[17] The picture painted in Archie's mind was one of great opportunities for a lawyer in government service, the chance to represent the United States in the nation's highest Court.

Almost immediately, Cox was assigned his first appellate argument in the Supreme Court. Solicitor General Charles Fahy, a gentle man with a hawklike nose, directed Archie to "confess error" in a California case called *Weber v. United States*. The U.S. government had denied citizenship to six resident aliens because they had become naturalized to take advantage of old-age pensions recently made available to U.S. citizens under California law.[18] The government had won in a lower court, but was now voluntarily waving the white flag. Confessing error was the Justice Department's way of admitting that it had made a mistake; it was willing to have the Supreme Court overturn its own victory. Cases like this were considered a sure win for the solicitor general's office.

Still, Archie prepared for his first Supreme Court argument as if it were the case of the century. He wrote and rewrote his short presentation, memorizing it like a cooking recipe. "I was practically programmed so that I couldn't think or say anything else," he confessed.[19]

The nervous new government lawyer stepped up to the lectern in the ornate Supreme Court chambers at the appointed hour on March 9, 1942. Phyllis watched anxiously from the front row of spectator seats. With her two children at home with scarlet fever, she hoped the argument would not last long. Archie organized his script. Eight justices (one was absent) peered down at him from their lofty perch on the bench, thumbing through stacks of briefs. Cox waited for the nod from the chief justice. Then he mustered all the strength and volume at his command. "And I had no sooner opened my mouth," Cox relived that unforgettable moment, "than eight justices jumped down my throat. . . . I was just totally taken aback. It must have verged on being a very pathetic scene if you were at all sympathetic to the young man."[20]

With lightning speed, the Supreme Court affirmed the denial of citizenship to Louis Weber and his fellow appellants. It upheld the government's original victory, even though the government had "confessed" that it should have been overturned. Solicitor General Charles Fahy received the "bad news" of his victory in good humor. He gently explained that even the Supreme Court occasionally made mistakes. Then he gave Archie another case.

Archie enjoyed the high level of practice. But his sense of satisfaction diminished as the war escalated in Europe, Africa, and the Pacific.

Archie's younger brother Rob, with whom he had been close since childhood, had already left Harvard College to join the British army in North Africa. Rob was one of a flock of young, enthusiastic Ivy Leaguers who saw the need for the United States to enter the war long before America had committed itself. There would not be much to American life, a host of young men like Rob believed, if Great Britain and France disappeared as the only buffer between Germany and the Atlantic Ocean.

Archie's mother was "scared" by Rob's decision. In the autumn of 1938 she had listened to Adolf Hitler on their old console radio in Plainfield and had felt frightened by "the power of that man." That same fall a great hurricane had swept into Windsor and uprooted many ancient trees on Main Street, knocking over virgin pines in Paradise "as if giants had been playing jackstraws."[21] It was an ominous sign, she felt, of the years to come. Yet Frances Cox understood the youthful wisdom behind Rob's decision. As a citizen rather than as a mother, she knew that "it was the right thing."[22]

For long hours, Archie talked over the decision with his younger brother before the commitment to go overseas was made. As Rob would later write in a letter to his mother, his oldest brother, "Billy," had identified four reasons for him to go: "Nothing better to do; adventure; curiosity; and belief." As Rob explained in a letter he wrote home in the summer of 1943, "I came for all four [reasons]. But mostly for shame. I was ashamed of America. I love America, and I could not sit mediocre while America was being attacked. For America is not just a place between two oceans. America is faith and because it is a faith must be dynamic or perish."[23]

With these noble thoughts, Rob had left the security of New England for the British service. He had been a popular student at St. Paul's, much more so than Archie. He had played on the Harvard hockey team, a distinction that attracted the attention of plenty of young women.[24] Rob shared the blond hair and sculpted features of his older brother, but unlike Archie, he wanted nothing to do with the family's stodgy legal profession. Rob was a free spirit; his ultimate dream lay in the field of writing. Uncle Max Perkins, the editor, had seen talent in Rob's work. Rob's secret ambition was to write a novel about Windsor: "Not the usual Jalna or . . . Forsyte thing," he wrote back to his mother from the war zone, "in which the Evarts and Perkins and people of the past and present are intertwined." Rather, he envisioned a book in which "the hero would be the place itself."[25]

By the summer of 1942, the Cox family was receiving photos of Rob in flashy British military attire, riding a camel in North Africa, as the Sphinx and pyramid shimmered in the background.[26] Archie now toyed with the idea of joining the marines in "intelligence"; he had heard that they were taking young lawyers. Archie had a family to worry about, but did that minimize his obligations to his country? Months passed filled with legal work. Archie called his mother regularly to hear the latest news from Europe. The family was excited when it learned that Rob's division of the British Rifle Corps had been part of the sweep in the Battle of El Alamein, Egypt. It had been a turning point in the war, the first time a major Nazi army had retreated and could not stop its retreat. At the end of one conversation, Archie blurted out, "Tell Robbie he's my inspiration."[27]

Solicitor General Fahy was well aware that Archie was "torn and uneasy." It was obvious that his young assistant wanted to get closer to the war effort.[28] In the spring of 1943, Archie got his wish. Through Fahy's help, Archie was given an "honorable discharge" from the "celestial" general's quarters that he loved so much, and was offered a post in the State Department as an assistant to Thomas K. Finletter, head of the Coordinating Committee North Africa. Finletter was responsible for overseeing the administration of U.S. and British affairs in North Africa, which included smuggling industrial diamonds from Switzerland into the United States. It was not frontline duty, but it was a small version of service.

Phyllis would recall these years as an utterly "discombobulating time." By now, the newlyweds were not so newly wed. They had two small children. Archie's bouncing from job to job in Washington did nothing to soften the sense of disorientation for any of them. But this was what Archie, and his family, had to do.[29]

Cables flowed from North Africa, Europe, and across the globe. Cox enjoyed the feeling of contributing to the war effort. In Rob's last letter home, he had been enthusiastic that his brother "Bill" might be sent to North Africa via his new job, and the two brothers could "meet up." "I suppose the chances would be about one in a hundred," Rob had scribbled, "but it's not impossible because one can do a certain amount of aerial hitch-hiking."[30] For Archie, there was a certain excitement about his vicarious participation in events overseas.

That is, until he received a phone call in Tom Finletter's office one afternoon in May, which rendered his own trifling contributions meaningless. In the mountains of Tunisia, Rob had suffered a wound that severed an artery. Because of inadequate medical staff on the front lines, the wound had been hastily wrapped in field dressing and had turned fatal from heavy bleeding. His British division had held firm and ultimately forced the Germans to surrender. But Archie's brother Rob was dead.[31]

A letter from Lieutenant G. A. Lyon, Rob's closest friend in the Second Battalion of the King's Royal Rifle Corps, described the final hours in serene detail: Rob had volunteered to join another officer in searching out an enemy seventy-five-millimeter German gun that was firing at close range, too close to his battalion. They had proceeded about seven hundred yards when Rob was suddenly hit by machine-gun fire from a German sniper hidden behind a haystack. The sniper had sprayed him in the arm and upper shoulder. Rob had died "a soldier's death" of internal bleeding, never complaining, just feeling "quite comfortable and very sleepy" until "he did go to sleep, never to wake up again."[32]

As Archie would later reconstruct the news, "It was an enormous shock. I don't know how to reduce it to words. An enormous shock."[33] Feelings of grief, shock, shame at his own failure to join the war, reflections about childhood, all crowded Archie's mind. His younger brother had led such an extraordinary, promising life. "To be cut off very young particularly when [a person is] not engaged in self-seeking . . . ," Archie would reflect, "is always sad even if it isn't your brother. It's a great deal sadder if it is your brother."[34]

Robert Hill Cox II was buried in a war cemetery in grave number 29, row F, plot A, near a tiny village, Sbikha, along the road to Kairouan in Tunisia. Only a makeshift wooden cross would mark his grave:[35] "Liet. R. H. Cox, 2/K.R.R.C."[36]

A memorial service was held in Windsor, under the somber shadows of Mount Ascutney. The Coxes gathered at the old Evarts house, which had been passed down to Archie's mother after Grandmother Perkins died in 1940. Black curtains were pulled across windows on Main Street. Frances Cox had sold the house in Plainfield in 1939 out of financial necessity and rented an apartment in New York City; a second service was scheduled there.

Condolences arrived from Rob's commanding officer in North Africa. A telegram of sympathy came from Buckingham Palace on May 19, 1943, signed by King George VI.[37] All of these tributes and accolades provided mild comfort to Archie's mother.[38] She was devastated. Archie's brother Louis summarized his mother's loss: "She was fond of all of her children. But none more so than my brother Rob."[39]

Along with Rob's personal possessions, Frances Cox received a letter that her son had written in advance, just in case he never returned. Now the words seemed almost haunting:

> Dearest M. . . .
>
> I think you would like a last word if anything did happen, a letter to tell you what I hope you already know—how glad a time you have given me—and to try to say what I think about life. . . .
> Possibly it was all too pleasant so that the trees we climbed and the paths we prowled in "the jungle," the brook we dammed and the secret places we found in Paradise made us soft dreamers. I do not think so. I think it near miraculous to have had such a childhood.

Rob ended the letter with words of poetic optimism: " 'Bless the friends I love so well,' " he wrote, "but above all you, M. 'Life is good, brother, there's a wind on the heath.' "[40]

Frances Cox wrote back in response to a letter of sympathy from Judge Learned Hand: "I know, hard as it is, that Robbie's going, and his living and dying as he did for his own and our integrity, made his life more complete than anything else could have done—though I must confess that that age-old cry 'my son—my son' is always in my heart." She confided in Judge Hand: "So Bob was worthy of his Father, and I just can't say anything better than that."[41]

Max Perkins, the uncle whom Rob had dreamed of emulating, composed a short tribute that was hung in St. Paul's Episcopal Church in Windsor, where it remains today. Amid prayer books and wooden pews and tiny white gates reserving seats for the members of the Evarts and Perkins, and now Cox, families, the simple tribute read: "Lieutenant in the King's Royal Rifle Corps, killed in the Battle of Tunisia April 19, 1943, who, at the age of twenty-two, convinced that his own country should share in the great war for human freedom, joined the British Army in July, 1941, and so gave to that cause all of America he could command."

It was a time of repeated upheavals for Archie, at home and at work. Jurisdictional disputes kept cropping up between Tom Finletter's office and other governmental agencies.[42] Finally, the flow of cables in Finletter's office ceased entirely. It was the State Department's way of isolating those "at odds with those who were in control."[43]

One day at the end of 1943, the phone in Archie's office rang. It was Miss Perkins, still a member of the president's cabinet. Was Archie interested in serving as associate solicitor in the Labor Department? On several other occasions Miss Perkins had called his office, but Archie had always assumed that her secretary "had made a mistake and gotten me on the phone instead of Oscar Cox [a prominent New Dealer]."[44] This time, there was no question that the call was for Archibald—not Oscar—Cox. The offer came as an enormous relief; it gave Archie a chance to salvage some meaningful occupation in Washington. Archie now moved to his fourth new job in less than two years.

The position as associate solicitor of labor, orchestrated almost certainly, once again, by Charlie Wyzanski and Judge Hand, was a "considerable step up in the Washington world." As Cox would describe this promotion, "I moved into an office . . . with a rug on the floor, a sofa, and a conference table. All the marks of importance."[45]

Most of the work was civil litigation, much of it enforcing the Fair Labor Standards Act. There were opportunities to argue appeals, plus a chance to sop up real-life experience. One case in Kentucky involved the failure to pay minimum wages and overtime to miners hired to open up outcroppings in abandoned, worked-out coal mines. Cox visited the mine and left with an image burned into his head of the tipple operator who got paid a set amount per ton, and "the blind man who drove the mule that would pull the coal over the track . . . the man got paid something like ten cents a ton for what his mule pulled."[46]

Archie enjoyed his new job and its fresh challenges. But he particularly enjoyed his unusual mode of transportation to and from work. Archie and Phyllis had rented a small home in rural Maryland, where Phyllis renewed ties with an old classmate from Smith College, Jane Ickes. Jane's husband (forty years older than his wife) was none other than Harold Ickes, the longest-serving secretary of the interior in U.S. history and a prominent fixture in the Roosevelt administration. Ickes was known for his dour personality and gruff demeanor; he was a hard-boiled individualist who had earned himself the nickname "Old Curmudgeon" in Washington and beyond. Moving to the country had meant that Archie had to deal with gas rationing imposed during the war, but Harold Ickes had a cabinet car with enough gasoline to drive to and from the capital each day. Phyllis and Jane had quietly discussed this fact, as they pondered how to bring their families closer together despite the Curmudgeon's harsh exterior.

"So, the wives engaged in a very delicate negotiation as to whether Harold would be willing to give me a ride into town and a ride out of town in the afternoon, at least when he could," Archie chuckled. "The 'treaty' was that if I would be standing . . . on the side of the road that ran off from [his] road at, I don't know, 7:10 or whatever it was in the morning, the car would stop and I could open a door and get in. But I was not allowed to speak to him."[47]

First Cox and Ickes exchanged "good mornings," but nothing more. Cox buttoned his lips and stared out the car window. Soon the Old Curmudgeon loosened up and began chatting about work, government, whatever was on his mind. Sunday nights turned into a standing invitation for the Coxes to have supper with Harold and Jane Ickes. On the morning car trips, Harold Ickes began thinking aloud freely, giving Archie a bird's-eye view of the world ticking inside Washington.

During the 1944 presidential campaign, as Governor Thomas Dewey of New York mounted an attack against FDR, Ickes tried out a new concept on his young traveling companion. He was working on a speech: it would be a spoof on Dewey (known for his fastidious dress and manners), poking fun at the candidate's campaign appearance in Philadelphia, where he had sported an overly fancy blue serge suit.

Ickes would deliver the speech to a convention of international union members in Grand Rapids, Michigan, the perfect crowd.[48] Archie and Ickes kicked around words and phrases; speechwriting seemed like great fun.

The next time Archie heard the speech, it was being broadcast over car radios and living room consoles across the nation. "The Man in the Blue Serge Suit," as the speech was dubbed, became one of the most memorable addresses of the 1944 campaign. What intrigued Archie most was that an avowed intellectual like Harold Ickes could merge his cerebral talents with the dog-eat-dog world of politics and somehow make them jibe. It was an unusual mixture of skills, Archie thought. One that he might like to try out, someday.

The death of FDR, the replacement of Miss Perkins as secretary of labor in July of 1945, and President Truman's decision to drop the atomic bomb on Hiroshima all hastened Archie's return to Boston and private practice. The war in Europe had come to an end. The conflict in the Pacific was winding down. The Coxes had always assumed, from both a family point of view and a professional one, that they would be moving back to Wayland once the war ended. "Change was in the wind," Archie felt.[49]

In one of their last drives in the government car, the Old Curmudgeon had offered Archie advice about his future in government. "You've reached the ceiling," said Ickes, peering through his spectacles. "The trouble with you is you don't *come* from anywhere."[50] In Washington, if one wanted to move beyond a dead-end position as a career bureaucrat, one had to have a solid political network and constituency from one's own state. Cox had none of this.

But in Cox's own mind, the equation was even simpler: "It was getting time to go home."[51] Archie had promised the lawyers at Ropes and Gray that he would return. He had promised Phyllis that Massachusetts would be their home.[52] As celebrations swept the country, as the triumphant nation wrapped itself in banners of red, white, and blue, Archie and his family left Washington. Presumably for good.

Every return includes change. Phyllis's father had died alone in the early 1940s, in a tragic fire in Maine. Phyllis's mother had moved to Palo Alto, California, marrying Rufus Kimball, a lawyer and an old beau.[53] The red clapboard house in Wayland with barn and fence, where Phyllis had grown up, was now offered to Archie and Phyllis as their own. It would be the perfect place to raise their family.

A new baby arrived in early November to help fill the sizable home. Archie himself picked the name "Phyllis" in honor of the baby's mother, as well as an aunt who had been very close. "It wasn't very original," Phyllis the mother laughed. "But that's how it came to be."[54]

So Phyllis and Archie and young Phyllis, Archie, Jr., and Sally settled into the family homestead in Wayland, content to submerge themselves in the country air, the sounds of chickens, the smells of horses and cats in the barn, and the pleasant chores that went along with country life on Glezen Lane.

In downtown Boston, the atmosphere was equally agreeable. As associate solicitor of labor, Archie had worked his way up to a civil service rating of P-6 with a salary of $5,600, next to the top-ranking brass. When he moved back to Ropes and Gray in the summer of 1945, he was offered $10,000 to start, nearly six times what he had earned there as a starting lawyer.

"I went back to Ropes and Gray thinking it was for life," Cox said. "Life turned out to be four or five weeks."[55]

Professor Austin Scott and his wife visited the house in Wayland one early fall afternoon for Sunday lunch, just as they had arrived countless Sundays when Phyllis's parents were still together. At some point after the lunch dishes were cleared, Mr. Scott turned unexpectedly to Archie. "Have you ever thought about teaching?" he asked.

There was silence. "Well, no, not really," came the answer.

Mr. Scott dabbed his mouth with a napkin. "Well, you'd better start thinking quick," he said. "Jim Landis is going to call you up tomorrow and invite you to join us."[56]

The call came, as predicted. Archie traveled out to Harvard Law School for an informal chat (he thought) with Dean Landis. He returned with a formal offer to join the Harvard Law School faculty, teaching Labor Law and first-year Torts. Archie told Landis that *if* he accepted the job—he was not accepting yet, but *if* he did— he would be willing to try his hand at anything other than Corporations, because he did not know anything about that subject, and Property, "because it was dull."[57] This stipulation was acceptable to Landis. In fact, the dean's only expectation was that Archie should become the top labor law expert in the country; not a particularly daunting requirement, as far as Archie saw it, since Harvard Law School professors were *supposed* to be "the best people in their fields."[58]

The offer was an intriguing one, but it produced a gnawing uncertainty as Archie began to debate it back and forth in his mind. Why should he give up something that he *knew* he could do reasonably well, practicing law at a top firm, for something unknown?[59] He didn't have a "calling," in the old-fashioned sense, to become a teacher. At the same time, there was no greater compliment a lawyer could receive, was there, than being asked to join the Harvard Law School faculty? Not to mention the fact that Phyllis had family roots dating back for generations at Harvard . . .

As he sifted through the positives and negatives, the most important drawing card, Cox concluded, was the independence that came with being a law professor. "What you said, what you wrote, the opinions you expressed, they'd be your own."[60] Archie never wanted to find himself beholden to a client's retainer check in hashing out his own ideas. There had always been an independent streak in the Cox family. His father, a confirmed solo practitioner, had always warned young lawyers who were approaching the age and stature of prospective partners, "Go somewhere else for your own good. You'll never be my partner."[61] Maybe Archie had inherited some of that same obstinance.

Archie met with Charlie Rugg, still his good friend and mentor at Ropes and Gray. What should he do? Rugg emphasized two things. "As soon as we open the firm up," he assured Archie, "you will be made a partner." And second, "You'll make a lot of money if you stay here. You won't get to keep much of it with the income taxes, but it's fun to see it flow through your bank account."[62]

Money had never been a dominant concern for Archie or Phyllis, in any job decision. They would be able to remain in the family home in Wayland, thanks in part to a trust established by Phyllis's father at the time of his divorce. A law professor's salary was plenty sufficient to live in the country, pay taxes, educate one's children, and "not worry that you were leaving your wife in poverty if something happened to you."[63]

There was another issue that nagged at Archie, not the sort of thing that he could discuss with Charlie Rugg, so he confided in his brother Max. Archie explained to his younger brother that he enjoyed representing management in labor disputes just fine; it was solid work. When it came right down to it, though, he "sympathized more with the labor people." If he practiced law at a big firm, there was a lingering concern that he would "always want to be on the other side."[64]

After thrashing the question around in his head a final time, Archie picked up the phone and accepted the job at Harvard Law School. He did not suspect that, aside from his marriage to Phyllis, this phone call would commence the longest-running chapter of his life.

Cox took a pay cut of nearly one-third, down to seven thousand dollars, and accepted the ambiguous title of Lecturer on Law, meaning the first year would be a trial period. Although his status was far from secure, there were still intangible payoffs.[65] The chance to teach Labor Law at Harvard was the chance to get in on the ground floor of a blossoming new field. He had already been asked by Foundation Press to rewrite Dean Landis's casebook—it would be the first modern Labor Law text in print. Authors like Clinton S. Golden from Pittsburgh (a senior staffer at the Steelworkers' union), whose work Archie had read carefully, had written that the key to a successful labor movement was to get the workers themselves involved in governing the workplace, through collective bargaining and union activity. This was an appealing concept to Cox. Independent lawyers, arbitrators, and professors would be in the best position to nudge American labor and management in the right direction. Perhaps Archie could do some of that nudging.[66]

Word came back that even Learned Hand approved of Archie's decision. Judge Hand thought that his old clerk was perfectly suited for teaching. The judge felt that Archie "was such a gentle soul," that he "wasn't sure I could stand the rigors of practice."[67]

Gentle soul or not, Archie first had to worry about becoming a competent, rigorous teacher. It had been years since he had sat in a classroom, and then only as a student. The prevailing teaching approach at Harvard, as in most American law schools, was the casebook method, developed by Christopher Columbus Langdell in the 1870s. Students read leading decisions from courts across the country, picked them apart, analyzed them as precedent, thus bringing to life Hand's homespun parable, "Sonny, to whom am I responsible? To these books about us." It was now Archie's turn to take a classroom full of students and guide them through the maze of "books about them."

Archie was apprehensive. He stopped by to see Warren Seavey, his old Torts professor. Seavey's office in Langdell North was in a quiet corner with a view of Holmes Field and a gentle easterly breeze wafting through the windows, partially cranked open. It would later become Cox's own office for three decades.

Archie began, "Mr. Seavey, as you know, I've not been in a law school class since 1937. That's eight or nine years now, and I'm not sure how well I remember how one does conduct a class. May I sit in the back of the room?" Seavey spun around in his chair. He stared at the tall oak tree in Holmes Field. "Don't sit in the back of the room," he insisted. "Come sit up on the platform and get a feeling for what it's like."[68]

The following day Archibald Cox appeared as a new faculty member on the riser with Professor Seavey, in front of the sprawling Langdell classroom. He watched Mr. Seavey pose "hypotheticals" dealing with the law of false imprisonment. "What if a plaintiff was *unconscious* when he or she had been locked into a room, could he or she have an action for false imprisonment?" It was standard drill for first year classes; Archie had gone through it many times as a student. His mind wandered.

Suddenly, Archie heard a single sentence clap him on the back like a thunderbolt. "Cox, what do *you* think?"

Young Professor Cox straightened himself up like an ironing board. The eyes of the entire class bore in on him. Archie organized some thought in his mind, stammered out some reply. It was all a blur. "My memory stops with the shock of, 'What do you think?' "[69]

The next day, Professor Seavey did not appear at class. The young Professor Cox was forced to stand up, clutch onto the lectern with both large hands, and begin teaching Torts at the famous Harvard Law School.

5

A CALL
FROM THE
WHITE HOUSE

The end of World War II brought GIs flooding back to law school, anxious to complete legal studies in order to cement their futures. Enrollment at Harvard Law School swelled. So did opportunities for young professors developing new classes, churning out record numbers of ambitious lawyers grateful to have a stake in the American dream. Cox was awarded tenure in 1946, just one year after joining the faculty, making him at age thirty-four one of the youngest men at Harvard Law School to hold that rank. Inside the walls of Langdell Hall, these were busy and productive years to be a labor expert.

Outside, life was not so calm. America was exploding into strikes, seizures, and fierce tangles between President Harry S. Truman and organized labor. The formal wage and price controls imposed during the war were slowly removed because of public skepticism, but the government's effort to segue into a nicely oiled economy was a mess.[1] There were steel strikes, coal strikes, railroad strikes, strikes among meat packers, strikes at General Motors and General Electric.[2]

By the summer of 1950, the United States had become mired in the Korean War. The need for uninterrupted production clearly required fresh action to keep the economy from spiraling out of control. Dozens of new federal agencies, patterned after the makeshift wage and price boards of the World War II era, were set up by the White House to stabilize key industries.

John Dunlop, a friend of Archie's and economics professor at Harvard, was named a "public member" of the new Wage Stabilization Board.[3] It was a tripartite board—one of those creatures unique to wartime America—that put labor, management, and a few neutral referees together in a single pot, in an effort to thrash out labor disputes. These three-sided boards were designed to control wages and prevent prices from skyrocketing in key industries. Dunlop now asked Archie to lend a hand on an offshoot of the board called the Construction Industry Stabilization Commission. This commission was created to iron out disputes in the volatile construction and building trades.[4] The job was not glamorous, but it seemed to fit Cox.

By 1952, Archie could rightfully be listed as one of the leading scholars in American labor law. His revision of *Cases on Labor Law* had been published by Foundation Press in 1948. He had pumped out a steady stream of law review articles on labor issues, using an arsenal of number-two pencils, art gum erasers, and notepads to bring order to a sprawling new body of case law. Fulfilling his promise to Dean Landis, he was slowly becoming to Labor Law what Austin Scott was to Trusts or Samuel Williston was to Contracts: the nation's leading expert.

Although Archie handled some labor arbitration work, he was much more identified with writing law review articles than slugging it out in the trenches. Robben Fleming, a fellow labor expert, explained the perception of Cox in 1952: "He was not the hands-on, jump-into-the-fracas type. . . . When you thought of the leading arbitrators or mediators, he was not on that list." Rather, Fleming recalled, Cox was "much more reserved. You would see him more often on a platform where he was delivering a paper on labor law."[5]

Professor Dunlop, in contrast, was a big name in the rough-and-tumble world of Washington labor battles. For Cox, the chance to work alongside Dunlop and be exposed to the inner workings of such a practical-minded board counted as valuable experience. With the Korean War escalating at the 38th parallel, the contribution seemed doubly important.[6] Archie quickly found himself spending back-to-back nights on the *Federal Express*, the overnight train between Boston and Washington, hashing out wage negotiations and getting his hands dirty in messy construction disputes.

Archie planned to write a book with John Dunlop on the Wage Stabilization Board experience. He would continue to develop an expertise in the construction field. It seemed to be a perfect blend of academics and hands-on labor work.

Those plans never materialized, however. In the spring of 1952, a major dispute over wages in the steel industry erupted as the Korean

War ground forward. President Truman, frustrated with the ineffectiveness of the Wage Stabilization Board and confronted with an imminent nationwide strike announced by the powerful steelworkers union, directed the secretary of commerce to seize the steel mills and keep them running.[7] As Truman would respond to his critics later, "Tell 'em to read the Constitution. . . . The President has the power to keep the country from going to Hell."[8]

Within two months, the U.S. Supreme Court would find President Truman's actions unconstitutional in the historic *Steel Seizure* case, holding that the president had usurped Congress's power and exceeded his prerogatives under Article 2.[9] The White House was beaten back, and licked its wounds. The steelworkers and management settled under terms almost identical to the ones the government had proposed months earlier. The Wage Stabilization Board, because of its ineffective decision-making, was dramatically overhauled by Congress and its powers scaled back.[10]

From the rubble of this botched exercise in labor negotiations came Archibald Cox's first major call to public service.

Hundreds of miles away from the political standoffs in Washington, the spring of 1952 was shaping up nicely for the Coxes. Archie and Phyllis had recently purchased their first pickup truck, a black and white two-tone Chevrolet. Archie drove the truck to work at the Law School all winter, a sight that aroused great curiosity among the law students who milled around the Langdell parking lot.[11] Now the Coxes were preparing the truck, the horse trailer, and the three children for their annual trek to the summer farm in Maine. The farm was part of a large tract of land originally purchased by the Ames family in the 1800s, now passed down to Archie and Phyllis to continue the summer tradition.

In May 1952, Archie celebrated his fortieth birthday with a modest gathering of extended family (including animals) in Wayland. His blond crew cut was turning darker now, but at least there were only stray gray hairs to mark the occasion. Archie's mother reported to Judge Learned Hand, who had just celebrated his own eightieth birthday and retired from "regular active service" on the court, that she was traveling to Wayland with a special birthday gift for Archie. She had bought her son a hardback edition of *Spirit of Liberty*, a collection of the judge's addresses and essays just published by

Alfred A. Knopf in New York, but was "keeping a copy for myself too."[12]

With three children and an assembly of dogs, cats, horses, chickens, and other assorted farm animals, Archie's fortieth birthday party proved to be a big success by Wayland standards. He received his *Spirit of Liberty* and promised his mother that he would read it in his spare time that summer.

O̲nly a man who was looking for challenges with small chance of reward," *Business Week* magazine would later observe, "would [take] the Chairmanship of the Wage Stabilization Board."[13] Having just turned forty, Archibald Cox was in the mood for challenges. In hindsight, however, he might have preferred to miss this one.

By the midsummer of 1952, it was becoming clear that the president had to patch back together the crippled Wage Stabilization Board if wage and price controls were going to keep the country from slipping into economic chaos. The Korean War dragged on. President Truman had committed himself to stabilizing the economy; he had few other options. Cox was at his Harvard office doing research when he received a telephone call from the East Wing of the White House. It was Dr. John R. Steelman, *the* assistant to the president, who advised Truman on a wide spectrum of policy matters, including labor.[14] Steelman knew Cox from labor circles and respected his work. Would Cox consider serving as chairman of the reconstituted Wage Stabilization Board? If he was willing to take the job, Steelman said that he and Roger Putnam (former mayor of Springfield, Massachusetts, and now administrator of the Economic Stabilization Agency) would pass along the nomination to the president's desk. Cox clutched the phone. Yes, he said. He would do his best.

President Truman was occupying his Missouri headquarters on the eleventh floor of the red brick Hotel Muehlenbach in downtown Kansas City when he signed the order. From this Midwest office, on July 30, 1952, the president announced the creation of a new tripartite Wage Stabilization Board, with Archibald Cox of Wayland, Massachusetts, to serve as its chairman.[15] It would consist of an equal number of labor, industry, and public members. The board started at eighteen appointees but soon dropped to fifteen. Although it would be charged with the duty of stabilizing wages, it would have no power to settle disputes on its own.[16] Cox would report to Putnam, who would answer directly to the president. Only Putnam and the president could reverse a decision of the board, a sufficient guarantee of autonomy, as far as Cox was concerned. With an enormous framed certificate personally signed by Harry S. Truman, Archie Cox took his first official leave from Harvard and moved back to Washington for a stay of uncertain length.[17]

Phyllis and the three children were firmly entrenched at the summer farmhouse along the ocean in South Brooksville, Maine. Horses, lupines, hiking, and sailing were too important for the children to give up, even in the name of President Truman. As Phyllis described the yearly migration to Maine that fit the mold for many Yankee families, "It's been that way for generations. The mother and children . . . go to a cooler clime, leaving the husband behind." Yankee tradition aside, Phyllis and Archie had decided, "One can disrupt children only so many times. They need a sense of continuity."[18]

The oldest Cox child, Sally, was now thirteen years old. A newspaper photographer captured her teaching her little sister, seven-year-old Phyllis, how to play scales on the piano as her father watched approvingly. There were reporters at the door, a bit of commotion. To the children, however, their father's departure for Washington seemed unremarkable. "It was just something that Dad did," recalled Sally.[19]

Archie's lone relocation to Washington, to an office on a side street near the Capitol off Pennsylvania Avenue, with a backlog of twelve thousand cases on his desk, was not the sort of storybook presidential appointment that he might have envisioned. The new board was like a "duckbilled platypus," an amalgam of right feet and left wings. It was burdened with an unusual mission: "We were holding a highly flexible, highly dangerous line," said one member. "We were dealing with the most powerful forces in America—big labor and big business. Neither of which wanted stabilization."[20] The board's job was to contain these opposing forces and at the same time avoid blowing itself to pieces.

An immediate problem slammed Cox's board broadside: The CIO and North American Aviation, one of the largest manufacturers of military airplanes in the country, had agreed to a ten-cent-per-hour wage increase in order to avert a strike.[21] This clearly exceeded the old Wage Stabilization Board guidelines established to keep wages and prices from mushrooming.[22] Cox's board was presented with a Hobson's choice. Should it approve this compromise, in the name of getting aviation workers back on the job, and forget about old guide-lines? Or should the board stick to its guns and tell the president that this wage increase was too high, even if it risked fouling up the settlement?

After a string of tense meetings, Cox decided that the board should approve the new wage hike. The old board had broken the guidelines so many times that it was silly to cling to them. "It was time to draw the generalization that there was a *new* ceiling," Cox argued.[23]

The industry members of the board were furious with this per-ceived act of pusillanimity. Cox would remember the scene with discomfort: he was stretched out on the sofa in his office, "utterly exhausted," praying for a few moments' sleep, when the industry members marched into the room to announce that they were resign-ing en masse. Archie knew what this meant. The board would be destroyed, reduced to rubble again, just as it had been after the *Steel Seizure* case. "And I remember lying there utterly exhausted and quite openly tearfully pleading with them to give me a chance, saying it was their duty to stay on, and that while this might look like having no guts to control wages, I did have a rationale and they should give it a chance."[24]

Cox reasoned that he was entitled to one shot. If he failed, he would pack up and go home. The old board had effectively established a new cap on wages, higher than its official cap but solid nonetheless. The new board could in good conscience honor it. Cox's group would establish its own limits and make clear that they were unbending. The industry members fussed and grumbled. But they gave in to Cox's logic. For now.[25]

Harold Enarson, one of the neutral board members (later president of Ohio State University), had mixed impressions of Cox's perfor-mance in his new role. He was intrigued by the persona Cox had cultivated: the Harvard tweeds, the sharp New England profile, the brisk walk on tall legs, the sentences that could be diagrammed with precision. "Obviously, there was a great intellect at work. But I couldn't see where the intellect connected with the sweaty substance of labor politics," Enarson said.[26] For Enarson, who had worked in factories as a young man and understood labor from an "emotional perspective," Cox seemed to be lacking in this department. "He had a kind of aloofness that I found . . . it was just Archie," said Enarson.[27]

Aloof or not, Cox was soon dumped into the dirty puddle of labor work, head first. In the fall of 1952, the board found itself in a mammoth fight with a particularly formidable opponent, John L. Lewis, head of the United Mine Workers. Lewis was by now an institution in American labor. His leonine head, white hair accentuated with bushy black eyebrows (that rivalled those of Learned Hand), and Elizabethan oratorical style were only a small part of what made Lewis a fearsome opponent for any gaggle of lawyers the president could drum up. His most potent weapon was his nerve, his power, his ability to control the army of workers at his fingertips. "He had an acute sense of power and how to push people around," admitted one White House observer.[28] While millions of Americans detested the hulking, portly, obstreperous, cigar-smoking Lewis, legions of coal-smeared mine workers revered him.

Of humble Midwest origin, Lewis had witnessed mine explosions. He had buried the dead after mine disasters and had passed through company towns where miner families lived like subterranean rats without proper medical care. Lewis had seen men with broken backs from cave-ins; he had heard the cough that meant black lung. He had watched his own father die too young from the rigors of the miner's life.[29]

John L. Lewis and Harry S. Truman had gone head-to-head many times. Of Lewis, Harry Truman had once written: "He is, as bullies are, as yellow as a hound dog pup."[30] Cox's Wage Stabilization Board now found itself in the middle of a bitter rivalry between these two powerful men.

The bituminous coal industry had negotiated a deal with Lewis and his mine workers for a wage increase of $1.90 per day, which broke even the board's new ceiling.[31] The *United Mine Workers Journal* called it "A Triumph of Collective Bargaining."[32] Over 375,000 soft coal miners threatened a silent strike—with a nationwide outbreak of an inexplicable "flu"—if the Wage Stabilization Board refused to approve the wage hikes in time for their next pay envelopes.[33] Chairman Archibald Cox promised to exercise "calm judgment" and render a decision on the proposed deal with "all deliberate haste."[34] Still, unannounced walkouts began in the Peabody Coal Mine in Harrisburg, Illinois, and swept like brushfire to other regions of the country.[35]

Despite the emotional appeals about the plight of the coal miners, Cox had reached the tough conclusion, "You couldn't decently pretend you were continuing a wage stabilization program and approve this increase."[36] Behind closed doors, the other public board members all agreed with Cox, with varying degrees of reluctance.[37] On October 18, the board announced that it would approve a pay raise of up to $1.50 per day. But no more. The additional 40 cents could *not* be placed in pay envelopes by coal companies, without violating federal law.[38] All four labor members of the board angrily dissented.[39] In a statement prepared for the media, Chairman Archibald Cox cautioned the mine workers against naked defiance of the law:

> The foundation of a free society is voluntary acceptance of the decisions reached under the processes of democratic government. A Congress elected by the people made wage stabilization the law of the land. . . . Both the miners and their leaders must know that freedom—their freedom—cannot long survive when the supremacy of law is challenged by naked power.[40]

Within a day of Cox's announcement, 300,000 of the nation's 375,000 soft coal miners were reported idle in an "unauthorized" walkout.[41] But Roger Putnam, head of the Economic Stabilization Agency, went on record declaring that Cox's board had exhibited "real courage" in rendering its decision.[42] The *New York Times* ran an editorial entitled "Statesmanship in the W.S.B.," for the first time drawing national attention to Cox. "Not only the public but the miners themselves must be impressed with the courage and the statesmanship that the Board brought to this situation. . . . Every American, we think, must have felt a little prouder to be one as he read [the] words of Archibald Cox, Chairman of the Board. . . ."[43]

The coal miners, however, hardly flushed pride at Cox's words. Cartoons appeared in newspapers across the country, depicting Cox as an ogre stealing milk from the bottles of coal miners' babies.[44] Lewis called the board's decision "attempted thievery."[45] He threatened a long, formal strike, which would have nasty repercussions on America's military operations overseas if the full increase was not approved. Lewis wrote a letter to Harry M. Moses, president of the Bituminous Coal Operators' Association, that was brutally poignant: "We have a contract. It is with your Association. It is complete. It speaks for itself. You signed it. It was negotiated in the American way—through collective bargaining. It is as pure as a sheep's heart."

Lewis went on to attack Cox directly, as a cowardly Harvard professor who, aided by his "timid trio of dilettante associates," would take nourishment from the mouths of infants: "Naturally miners resent such attempted thievery. Miners are people, Mr. Moses. They have children. Children need milk. The forty cents would buy milk each day. You of all men should know that the mineworkers will fight to protect the milk supply of their families."[46]

Moses quickly caved in. He joined his adversary Lewis in filing a petition directly to Roger Putnam, seeking reversal of the board's decision.[47] For Cox, none of this jockeying came as a great surprise. He understood that Lewis was "very much of the old school. When he had muscle, he believed in using it."[48]

Correspondence poured into the White House from across the country, recording irate positions on both sides. R. L. Darby of the Darby Coal Yards in Van Wert, Ohio, scribbled a note to President Truman: "Who is the biggest, who has the most power, John L. Lewis or the President of the United States?"[49] Mrs. Hazel Sholenberger of New Hampshire wrote a letter chiding the president. "You called off Steel Strike, R.R. strike and now are you going to let this Lewis call another coal strike?" she admonished. "He should be put in jail."[50]

From Ludlow, Kentucky, John J. Holloran wired this message: "BEFORE YOUR TERM ENDS RELIEVE SOME OF THE BOYS IN THE MINE FIELDS. . . ."[51] John DeVito, recording secretary of Local 45 UAW-CIO in Cleveland, cabled: "LOCAL 45 UAW-CIO VIGOROUSLY PROTESTS THE ACTION OF THE [Wage Stabilization Board]. . . . STATISTICS OF CASUALTIES AMONG MINE WORKERS INDICATE THAT THE $1.90 JOHN L. LEWIS AND THE MINERS DEMAND IS REASONABLE AND JUSTIFIABLE."[52]

During these stressful weeks as Lewis's appeal was placed in front of Putnam at the president's side, Cox took a series of walks with labor arbitrator David Cole. With Cole attempting to settle the coal strike on behalf of the Federal Mediation and Conciliation Service, the two men had similar goals in many ways. But Cole was a shirtsleeves arbitrator who "never saw a labor dispute that he didn't think he could settle."[53] Archie's strict adherence to wage-price controls was, frankly, a bother.

Cox and Cole took several long hikes in Rock Creek Park outside of Washington. As they kicked up decaying leaves under the umbrella of trees blown thin with the approach of winter, Cox stressed the importance of not giving in to the strike, not allowing the labor leaders to muscle their way to preferential treatment. Cole shot back, "A democracy must never reveal its weakness," citing Winston Churchill. He argued that a person in Cox's position had no choice but to allow labor and management to reach their own agreement if they could, even if it technically violated the "integrity" of Cox's board. Otherwise, Cole argued, Cox would expose the government's ultimate lack of power to enforce its own commands. Cole reminded Archie of the adage during World War II, "You can't mine coal with bayonets."[54] The stark reality was this: The president and his boards occasionally might have to sacrifice principle to expediency. It was important that the miners pick up their shovels and go back into the dark holes to do what America needed them to do most: dig coal.

But Cox remained unconvinced. His mind whirled with the thought, "Somehow we must muddle through without giving in; otherwise the program is bound to collapse." Thinking back on these nagging concerns, Cox would later latch onto a line from Robert Bolt's play *A Man for All Seasons,* based on the life of St. Thomas More: "And when the last law was down, and the Devil turned round on you—where would you hide . . . the laws all being flat?"[55]

Cox attended a round of meetings with Putnam and also met with top White House adviser John Steelman requesting a private audience with President Truman.[56] He was allocated exactly fifteen minutes in which to convince the president.

Cox and Putnam, who seemed to be paralyzed when it came to making a decision on the appeal, met with the president on Wednesday, November 12, 1952, at 12:45 P.M.[57] The five foot, nine inch president from Independence, Missouri, shook hands with the six foot, two and a half inch professor from New England. Cox recalled being "a bit overwhelmed and tongue-tied" at the thought of standing in the presence of the president of the United States.[58] "Having shaken hands," Cox recalled of this high-level conference, "President Truman began talking about the weather, the furniture, and every irrelevancy for thirteen minutes and then, 'Sorry, I have no more time.' " He excused himself for a two-hour lunch.[59] That was the one and only conference between Cox, head of the Wage Stabilization Board, and the president who had appointed him.[60]

In late October, Putnam took the United Mine Workers' appeal home with him to New York. As one board member described him, Putnam resembled a "well-meaning Rotarian from down the street," a friendly and rotund fellow without any "great intellectual or moral force in him."[61] Although he had blurted out earlier that the board had shown "real courage" in rejecting the increase, Putnam now backpedaled, telling the press that he refused to "act in a hurry" in deciding the mine workers' appeal.[62] The leisurely review dragged on, toward the November presidential election, into December. John L. Lewis badgered, "How long, O Lord, do we have to wait for this decision?"[63]

One morning during the interminable period of waiting, Cox walked into Charles Killingsworth's office. He told his vice chairman, "I just spent an hour sitting at the foot of the Lincoln Memorial down on the Potomac."

"Really," Killingsworth looked up at him. "What did Lincoln tell you?"

Cox opened and closed his large right hand, a habit that he had developed when he was under stress. "He said, stick in there."[64]

Shortly after this conversation with Mr. Lincoln came an abrupt invitation to join Putnam at his apartment for drinks and dinner. Cox remembered sensing that the cocktail hour had gone on too long. At one point Putnam went out of the room to get more liquor. "I remember Charlie saying in a low voice so that Roger couldn't hear, 'This makes it perfectly clear that he's getting up the courage to give us bad news.' " Which turned out to be the case.[65]

As President Truman prepared to leave on a last-minute whistle-stop campaign swing on behalf of Democratic presidential candidate Adlai Stevenson, he granted John L. Lewis a private audience at the White House. Lewis walked out of this closed-door White House session upbeat; he ordered his mine workers back to work, before leaving for an extended vacation in South America. An understanding had been reached.[66]

On December 3, 1952, Harry S. Truman, a lame duck president soon to be succeeded by Dwight D. Eisenhower, ordered approval of the full increase requested by the coal miners' union and industry bosses.[67] Cox's board had been overruled.[68]

Seated in his office with couch and fancy desk, Cox accepted the news in silent shock. He told friends and colleagues that he intended to resign "forthwith."

John Dunlop, the fellow professor from Harvard who had gotten Archie mixed up in this wage stabilization business in the first place, strongly pushed his colleague to change his mind.[69] "The president had a right to do it," Dunlop lectured Archie. "He probably shouldn't have done it, from an equity point of view. But he did it." Dunlop's advice was this: Archie should suck in his stomach, put the ordeal behind him, and stay.[70] Cox listened respectfully. He then repeated that he was resigning.

Harold Enarson saw too much "grandstanding" in Cox's approach. Archie's decision to resign "created some tensions with me," Enarson admitted. It was "a disservice to the president and the country to resign." The issue of whether wage controls would continue "was a decision for the new president to make. It wasn't a decision for us to make." Enarson concluded, "I never thought the moral issue was as crystal clear as Archie seemed to think."[71]

But the decision was made. The machinery of government in stress began to whirl. Charlie Killingsworth said to Cox, "Well, if you hadn't resigned, I'd have resigned but since you've gone, I have to stay."[72] It was a rationale that Cox understood and believed in: allow the top echelon to resign out of principle, but ensure that someone else stay to keep the board functioning.

Cox certainly could not condemn President Truman for his decision. At the same time, he felt that he could not be part of it. As Cox understood it, President Truman's logic had revolved around two important facts. First, the ever-vacillating Putnam had promised Lewis that if he did not declare a formal strike, his appeal would be considered "*very* carefully."[73] The president felt that Putnam had stepped over the line and committed the president to overturning Cox's board.[74] "Roger Putnam hung us" is what Cox learned from the White House.[75]

Second, Eisenhower had won the election. The Democrats had been thumped solidly. Wage-price controls were going to be extinct in a few months, no matter what Truman said or did. Ike had promised as much during the campaign. "We were custodians of a dying enterprise," explained Enarson.[76] So the coal dispute was not particularly important, as Truman sized it up. It made good political sense to bury it.[77]

Cox's answer to all of this was, "Well, but it goes to the integrity of the tripartite process and while you may not want to continue these controls now, there's a *future* to think of."[78] The future was in preserving a board, one that would stand as a model for many other such dispute resolution bodies; one that would stand for the notion that labor and management could be brought to the table and forced to act civilly toward one another when the country most demanded it. The future was in preserving a *process,* to which the president and his appointees had committed themselves.

For Cox's former colleagues, there was a fine line between his adherence to principle and plain stubbornness.[79] At the same time,

Enarson understood that there was an element of "New England fortitude and integrity" at work in Cox's decision-making. "The question of whether to quit or not to quit is still an intensely personal matter," conceded Enarson. "It goes to the heart and soul of the individual."[80] To that extent, Cox could not be second-guessed.

Cox contacted the president's White House counsel, Charlie Murphy, to tell him that he was drafting a letter to the president, explaining in detail his reasons for resigning. Cox would release the letter to the press as soon as he vacated his office.

Murphy was "very anxious that I just quietly resign and not give any reason,"[81] Cox remembered. When Cox rejected this suggestion, Murphy pushed him to keep it as quiet as possible. There was a transition to worry about. President Truman had other things on his mind; his wife's mother was dying upstairs in the White House and he had a farewell dinner for members of the cabinet and their wives the next night.[82] Why should Cox make a big fuss over such a minor event? Why not leave quietly, and pick up the battle in some new administration?

But this approach was unacceptable to Cox. The whole point of his quitting was not to display anger or disrespect for the president; it was to illuminate the matter for the public, bring it into sharp focus for debate, so that such errors of government did not repeat themselves. This was an important goal even if President Truman was vacating the White House. As Cox would later put it, "I don't think anybody's that important that *he* [or she] stay in office. I think it's more important to have the issues flushed out."[83]

The press observed Cox leaving his office on December 4 with "eyes misted," as "scores of fellow workers gathered around to say farewell."[84] Murphy made a last-ditch effort to reach Cox by telephone at 5:45 in the afternoon. He still hoped to convince the former chairman to disappear quietly, in the genteel Washington way. But the phone call never reached its recipient. Archie was already heading up the highway pointed toward Massachusetts.[85] The letter had gone out.

It was not the sort of letter that would be reprinted in gossip columns nationwide. But it was classic, unadulterated, unadorned, Archie. Cox courteously began the correspondence to President Truman by stating that he understood that the president's decision was made "after sincere and careful deliberation." Yet he went on to stand his ground:

It is my considered judgment that the decision to allow the negotiated increases in the coal industry, while retaining general wage
controls, will lead to one of two consequences. Either most em-
ployers and employees will be held to established wage stabilization
policies while a powerful few receive larger increases, or else wage
stabilization policies will be relaxed to the extent necessary to allow
increases as large as those approved for the coal miners. The former
alternative violates the democratic ideal of equality and puts a premium on the use of economic power to compel a change of government policies. The latter alternative would preserve the forms of
stabilization without the substance.

Archie concluded firmly:

Believing that one or the other of these consequences must follow,
and that both are fundamentally wrong, I cannot, either usefully or
conscientiously, continue in the administration of the stabilization
program.[86]

That same day, December 4, President Truman accepted Cox's
resignation in a brief, perfunctory letter on White House stationery.[87]
In less than five months, Cox's second tenure in Washington had come
to a jarring conclusion.

Little appeared in the next day's morning papers concerning Cox's
great expression of moral principle. A terse news account appeared in
the *New York Times,* accompanied by a picture of Cox wearing a
polka-dot bow tie.[88] Cox's letter of resignation was printed beside the
president's reply, on an inside page. That was the extent of the
national coverage.

Cox had faced down a president and stuck to his guns. In many
ways, however, it seemed foolhardy, pointless, the exhaltation of substance over form. He had left no perceptible mark on the small piece
of government machinery that he had set out to protect. He had
jeopardized, in the meantime, any future chance of working in Washington, in the tight labor circles that would view him as an academic
stickler lacking sufficiently thick political skin.

Nevertheless, Archie felt oddly comfortable with his decision.
Fame and notoriety in government, as he was beginning to see, were
more a product of luck and chance than something one could control
through premeditation. Whether the tumblers of chance spun into a
configuration yielding accolades and attention, or whether one walked

away in silence, was ultimately irrelevant. The important thing was that he, Cox, had established his own intellectual and moral compass. He had tried to stick to its needle.

The professor returned to the classroom at Harvard. He was convinced that he had agonized through "the most important and difficult decision" that he would ever make. In fact, Cox was quite certain, at the age of forty, that his excursions into public service were now over. Looking back at the Wage Stabilization Board crisis of 1952, he said, "I expected it all to be the biggest event in my life."[89]

A letter arrived at Cox's Harvard Law School office the following week from Edward H. Collins, a member of the editorial staff of the *New York Times*. In his hastily scribbled note, Collins told Cox that an editorial had been written about his resignation, one day after Cox had delivered his letter to the president. Unfortunately, the piece had "died" on the galley room floor because of the "rapidly changing nature of his situation" and the mad rush to get out a daily newspaper. But Collins thought Cox might like to see it.

The editorial had been captioned "A Resignation with Honor." The unpublished piece concluded: "Mr. Cox's letter of resignation was marked neither by bitterness nor by criticism of the motives of the President. But reading this compact and dignified statement of the issues, one finds himself wondering if an indictment could be drawn up that would be any more damaging and more unanswerable. . . ."[90]

Cox folded the letter and put it away. His high-minded moral stand had already blown away in the trash with one unprinted editorial in a single edition of the *New York Times*.

In the offices of the Wage Stabilization Board in Washington, a poem entitled "Coronach" (a Scottish lament for the dead, played on bagpipes) was stuffed inside a file belonging to one board member. It would remain there for over forty years:

> *Cox has gone, cox has gone,*
> *take the harvard banners down.*
>
> *quietly,*
> *without a blast.*
>
> *stack the cases*
> *at half mast.*

coal dust
settled from the fray
we've lost another boss today.

take the loss philosophically,
coal has finished more than he.[91]

6

A YANKEE
PROFESSOR

Coming home always represented the high point of any excursion for Cox, for reasons invisible to the casual observer.

Few people at Harvard, over the course of six decades, ever caught more than a fleeting glimpse of the private side of Archibald Cox. Few fellow professors pulled up in the driveway on a Sunday or laid eyes on the farm in Wayland. The Coxes, for their part, rarely showed up in Cambridge or attended Saturday night cocktail parties. This was not, as Archie's children would explain, out of any disaffection or disrespect for his colleagues. For a New England Yankee, some pleasures were not meant to be mixed. One sphere of Archie's life occupied the busy days. Another filled the nights and weekends. Professional and family activities were both anchors of his existence. Yet there was no reason to allow these two worlds to intersect.

As a tenured professor with a growing national reputation in the labor field, Cox had acquired new flexibility, something that had attracted him to the teaching profession in the first place. He had a strict rule against missing classes for "extracurricular" legal projects. Cox discovered, however, that if he scheduled classes for the beginning of the week, he could still block off a day or two for more worldly adventures at the end. This allowed him to follow the example of teachers like Felix Frankfurter, who believed in studying the law but meshing textbooks with the real-world tumble of events.

Cox was named to the American Arbitration Association, serving as a neutral umpire when union and management failed to reach agreement in the collective bargaining process, which was often.[1] He traveled to Philadelphia to hear Bell Telephone arbitrations. He handled a string of cases for the seafood industry in Gloucester, which took him up and down the New England seacoast. There were school-teacher disputes, battles involving the Upholsterers International Union, airlines arbitrations, and railroad work.[2]

Several cases even captured national attention, like the battle involving the Brotherhood of Locomotive Engineers in 1954. Cox and fellow arbitrator Dick Lester, an old friend and economics professor at Princeton, found themselves riding on a Milwaukee Railroad diesel engine from Milwaukee to Chicago, trying to get a feel for their subject. But they riled the eighty-thousand-member brotherhood by awarding a modest five-cent pay raise, denying the fatter "skill increases" that the railroaders had demanded.[3] On the same page of the *New York Times* that pictured President and Mrs. Dwight D. Eisenhower serenely eating ice cream at a White House lawn party, "Grand Chief" Guy L. Brown charged that Cox's panel "had killed the future usefulness of arbitration in railroad disputes." The railroad union leader fulminated, "This is the weak decision of weak men who refused to assume responsibility."[4]

At the same time, when Cox and Lester found themselves on an arbitration panel for the same Brotherhood of Locomotive Engineers in the spring of 1960, awarding a hefty 4 percent wage increase to the union, Brown now told the *New York Times* that the entire brotherhood was "very happy" with the arbitrators' work.[5]

Arbitration was a satisfying vocation; it was far more civilized than the blood and gore of traditional litigation work. Yesterday's losers were often tomorrow's victors; few parties stayed angry forever. An arbitrator could sit as Solomon and hand-fashion justice to fit the particular case, which was gratifying. Cox enjoyed the fact that arbitrations in the 1950s were still informal affairs with relaxed ground rules. "An old-time court reporter was present," Archie said with a smile, "who did it all with a pen. When we all began to talk at once, she would throw up her pen in the air, throw up her hands, and we would have to stop."[6]

Cox's reputation in labor circles had spread nationwide. He was elected secretary of the Labor Section of the American Bar Association. He worked with Governor Robert Bradford and Senator Christopher H. Phillips of Massachusetts, both Republicans, to draw up legislation dealing with "emergency labor disputes." Dubbed the "Cox-Phillips" bill, it was enacted into law by the Massachusetts legislature in 1950.[7]

Labor work was not always glamorous. But trying to make the process work, Cox believed, was a basic form of justice.

Going back to his earliest days as a professor, Cox also enjoyed handling a few pro bono criminal appeals in the U.S. Supreme Court. Most likely at the suggestion of Felix Frankfurter or some other member of the Court who remembered him from his wartime Washington days, Cox was appointed in the late 1940s to represent two indigent convicts, Francis Gryger and Frank Townsend, both serving long jail sentences in Philadelphia.

In *Gryger,* Cox felt a certain amount of sympathy for the defendant; he was a petty criminal who had been in and out of trouble most of his life. Judge Harry S. McDevitt had allowed Gryger to plead guilty to assault and battery, even though he had no lawyer, then hammered him with a sentence of life in prison under a special "habitual offender" law. Cox felt strongly that this violated his client's due process rights; he had been lulled into accepting an unduly harsh penalty. But the Supreme Court disagreed. It upheld Gryger's conviction.[8] *Townsend* was a different matter. The defendant had been sentenced to ten to twenty years for armed robbery and burglary, a punishment that Cox thought was well deserved. His client was "clearly guilty." But the same judge, Harry S. McDevitt, had acted like a "bully" at sentencing. Among other things, he had made a crack about Townsend playing his stolen saxophone "in the prison band." It turned out that Townsend's *brother* had stolen the saxophone. Although Judge McDevitt himself had caught the slip-up and corrected it on the next page of the printed record, Archie walked a tightrope on behalf of his "guilty" client and argued that the judge had been too "facetious" during sentencing. Although Archie's heart was not in this one, the Supreme Court bought the argument. Townsend's sentence was overturned.[9]

Justice was not pure, Cox learned. But he received a curious sense of satisfaction from these pro bono cases.[10] Even at the top of the pyramid of American law, he understood, there was an unavoidable margin of error. One accepted this as a part of the imperfect human condition and worked to surmount it on the next case, or the case after that.

Archie soon found himself deluged with letters from the Eastern State Penitentiary in Pennsylvania as convicts of all stripes got word that a Harvard professor might handle their cases, free of charge.[11]

Cox could not do anything about most letters. An occasional envelope caught his eye, however, or an occasional note troubled him, causing him to drum his hands against the steering wheel of his pickup truck as he drove home at night to Wayland.

One letter came from a convict named Rudolph Sheeler, who claimed to have been "railroaded" into confessing to the murder of a Philadelphia policeman. Cox read and reread the letter, bothered by the words.

"There was something about the letter that touched me," Cox remembered. "It made me think there was something unusual about this. I guess it was that he mentioned that while he had been in prison he had been very closely related with some Quaker organization, which would fit . . . in eastern Pennsylvania. And I did go to the trouble to get in touch with the Quaker organization, and they spoke very highly of this person. But his complaint was still that he had been railroaded, that the facts were falsified and the testimony was perjured and it all happened in Philadelphia."[12]

Cox carried the letter around in his briefcase. He dropped a note to Louis Schwartz, a fellow Justice Department lawyer from the World War II days, who taught Criminal Law at the University of Pennsylvania: Would Schwartz take a look at Sheeler's allegations? Perhaps from his strategic spot in Philadelphia, he could see if there was any truth to them.

"Well, damned if Lou didn't blow the lid off the Philadelphia Police Department," said Cox, shaking his head.[13] The truth came out that Sheeler had been beaten by the Philadelphia homicide squad during interrogation, then promised clemency if he confessed to the murder, a promise that the police never kept. Rudolph Sheeler had spent twelve years in jail for a crime he never committed. A chance note from Cambridge to Philadelphia had kept him from spending the rest of his life there.[14]

These pro bono cases taught Archie that "instinct" could be just as valuable as intellect. There was more to justice than the simple labels of "guilty" or "not guilty" slapped on individuals in the rush of business. Some "innocents" were guilty, some "guilty's" were innocent, and many souls lay somewhere in between. What made the system work was the presence of individual lawyers who threw themselves into the task with enough vigor that they would dig beyond the surface facts. But occasional triumphs of justice, like the one in *Sheeler,* only increased the pain for Cox as he continued to get letters from inmates for the rest of his career. For "most of them, there [is] almost surely no merit," Cox would conclude pensively, "but then there's always that doubt. . . ."[15]

Although extracurricular interests continued to pile up, Archie never forgot that "professoring" was his full-time occupation. In academics, publishing was the currency of the system. A top priority for Cox was keeping up with his writing. Austin Wakeman Scott, now one of the eldest members of the faculty and Archie's vigilant mentor, had dropped the hint early on: "Well, it always seemed to me that we always should sort of look forward to writing at least one law review article a year," Scott told him. At first, Cox struggled to meet Scott's benchmark. Then he exceeded it.[16] One afternoon, Scott wandered by Archie's office with a second piece of advice: it was not a bad idea to hire a full-time secretary, even though the law school would pay only a small percentage of the salary. "I've always had a full-time secretary," said Scott, scratching his large eyebrows, "and so I had to pay most of the salary myself, and it's rather a good thing to do because you have got to keep her busy and that means that you have to write something." So Cox hired himself a full-time secretary. He wrote incessantly, and got his money's worth.[17]

Cox wrote articles about labor unions and the Taft-Hartley Act. He composed commentary that flowed from his arbitration work.[18] He wrote articles for the *Harvard Law Review* and the *Rocky Mountain Law Review*.[19] In a special issue of the *Harvard Law Review* dedicated to Judge Learned Hand, Cox wrote a tribute to his old boss.[20] He traded barbs with Jimmy Hoffa, pugnacious leader of the teamsters' union, who blasted Cox for a statement made in the *Michigan Law Review* suggesting that a handful of labor unions had engaged in "outright thievery." Cox wrote a polite letter in reply, apologizing for Hoffa's upset feelings, but adding, "I know no better words for describing some of the instances than 'outright thievery.' "[21]

Through the 1950s, Cox averaged three major law review articles a year, while most law professors struggled to produce one in double that time.[22] W. Willard Wirtz, a major figure in national labor circles, wrote to Harvard from Northwestern University Law School in 1955: "The name of Cox comes up so often in the Labor Law course here that I sometimes feel almost apologetic about it."[23] When Dean Erwin Griswold, Cox's old Tax professor, was asked by younger faculty members who was producing enough scholarship to satisfy him, the notoriously demanding Griswold had a stock answer: "Well, Archie Cox."[24]

Professoring was Cox's lifeblood. Like countless educators who poured heart and soul into their work, however, Archie met with mixed reviews when it came to those unpredictable reviewers, his students.

Milton Kayle, a Labor Law student in the late 1940s, described Professor Cox in words that would be echoed by many fellow students. "He was kind of patrician," said Kayle, who later worked in the White House under President Truman. "He was not a warm . . . it was hard to pierce the shield of the professor."[25] Harry Wellington, later dean of the law schools at Yale and New York Law School, was a student of Cox's in the early 1950s. He remembered Cox as a "good and clear" instructor and a "popular teacher in those days." But Professor Cox earned his marks for clarity and intellect, rather than for warm, personal charms. "He was sort of a Boston Brahmin, a stiff fellow," Wellington remembered.[26]

Cox enjoyed the give-and-take of the classroom. Although he thrived on discussion and open debate, he required students to meet him on his own turf. Like most of his colleagues of the era, Cox believed in treating the students without leniency or coddling. Students were referred to as "Mr. Smith" and "Mr. Jones," never by first names. Cox's classroom philosophy was serious and without frills.[27]

Some students were turned off by Cox's seeming snobbishness, by his use of examples in the classroom that bore no relation to the average person's life. He discussed contracts by spinning off hypothetical examples that began, "I have a gold pocketwatch in my vest" or "on my farm I keep some quarter horses," examples that smacked of blue blood. Some called him "brilliant"; his name was cited in Supreme Court opinions as a leading labor expert.[28] Others called him "arrogant" or "insufferable."

First-year students in particular found Cox imposing as he strode back and forth in the front of the classroom. One referred to him as a "typical WASP, a stuffed shirt." Another described him in cartoonlike images: "There was a birdlike look to him. He was very thin with a bow tie and a crew cut. An angular guy. There were not many round parts to Archie. He was very erect and square-shouldered. Almost exaggeratedly so."

Several former first-year students told of the infamous day in 1959 that Cox arrived late for an Agency class in Austin Hall and found students already pushing their way out the door. Whether it was because he did not particularly enjoy teaching Agency, as some claimed, or because he was under stress from long train trips to Washington to consult on labor legislation, which had become frequent by this time, or because he was offended that students would consider walking out of his classroom for any reason, Archie lost his composure. "He was really angry," said one student describing Cox's uncharacteristic reaction. "He grabbed his roster. . . . It slid out from under him. His elbows were on the table. He was almost screaming. Nobody wanted to make eye contact. So we just continued to leave."[29]

But these were rare stories in the student grist mill.[30] For the most part, the Archibald Cox of the 1940s and 1950s got strong marks for his powerful grasp of legal material, lukewarm reviews for his ability to endear himself to students, but universal acclaim as a steady and unflappable teacher.

Daniel Mayers and Philip Heymann, both of whom went on to establish prominent legal careers of their own (Heymann later taught alongside Cox on the Harvard Law School faculty), enjoyed the dubious distinction of being "kicked out of class" by Professor Cox in 1959. "We just got the giggles one day. We were much too old for it," Mayers gave the account. "He just asked us very nicely, 'Please leave.' There was a New England calm to his demeanor."[31]

The supreme challenge to Cox's New England calm came in 1950, when a third-year student stumbled into Administrative Law class late. It was Archie's brother Maxwell Cox. Max had anguished over whether to take his older brother's course. Finally he asked "Bill" directly. "I discussed it, and he thought I ought to take a course in Administrative Law," explained the younger Cox. "He thought his was as good as any. He may have even put it higher. Being a dutiful brother, I took it."

Archie referred to his brother as "Mr. Cox" in the classroom. Max, in turn, treated his brother like any other professor. When he arrived late for class one day after missing the midnight bus home from Vassar, where he was courting a young woman who would later become his wife, Max "knocked over five chairs in Langdell," tripping over feet as he made his way to his seat. Professor Cox lost his train of thought. He "sort of stopped halfway." The entire classroom turned red, holding back laughter. Archie stood up straight.

"Gentlemen, we will forgive the disturbance." Professor Cox

looked around the room. He finally allowed himself to crack a smile. "Max has always been this way."[32]

Professor Cox's strong suit was not in the field of entertainment. He excelled at aspects of teaching that were far less visible. He helped students rework their law review notes, remembering how important this project had been in his own law school years. He faithfully judged moot court exercises for the Board of Student Advisers when other professors were scarce.[33] He met with small groups of students and tiny law clubs for lunches and dinners on his own time. He served as faculty adviser to the Learned Hand Club, in which students informally argued cases in order to develop oral advocacy skills.[34] He jotted notes of praise to students who had written particularly good pieces in the *Review*. He gave career advice to students, seated in his cramped office in the middle of the Langdell Library stacks.[35] These quiet acts of kindness and encouragement were very much a part of Cox's essence as an educator. Yet they were not widely broadcast among the masses of students, leaving the image of Professor Archibald Cox as a stiff and emotionless character.

One former student who would later credit Professor Cox with playing a "decisive role" in shaping his career was a member of the class of 1947 named Elliot Richardson. Richardson had taken Cox's Labor Law course after returning from active duty in the army during World War II. He followed in Cox's footsteps, clerking for Judge Learned Hand. He then accepted a clerkship with Felix Frankfurter at the Supreme Court. In late 1949, Richardson was offered a job in the State Department by the secretary of state, Dean Acheson. "The idea of being in the State Department was exciting," Elliot Richardson explained his predicament. "On the other hand, I always had in the back of my mind going into politics. If I stayed in Washington, I might end up . . . a government hack."

While Richardson was wrestling with the decision, he visited his old alma mater. Just as he was walking out the heavy front doors of Langdell Hall, Professor Archibald Cox came walking in. Both men stopped. Richardson remembered that his old teacher had worked in the secretary of labor's office in Washington; he also knew that he had spent time in the solicitor general's office. "He was the type of guy I naturally trusted," Richardson said. "Trusted his judgment. I asked him what he thought of my dilemma."

Cox cocked his head. He looked down at his former student "like a great blue heron."

"Well, Elliot," Cox told Richardson, remembering the advice that Harold Ickes had once given him. "When I was in Washington, I always thought it important to come *from* somewhere."[36]

Richardson took the advice. "I turned down the Acheson job," Richardson said slowly, savoring the memory. He returned to his home state of Massachusetts and entered private practice at Ropes and Gray, working closely with Charlie Rugg, Cox's first mentor. Later Richardson served as U.S. attorney in Boston, was elected lieutenant governor of Massachusetts, and eventually made his way back to Washington as, among other things, attorney general of the United States under President Richard M. Nixon.

Elliot Richardson would later muse, "I can't imagine what a different life I would have had, if I had stayed in Washington."[37]

As Archie's career grew and his side interests multiplied, so did his family, fifteen country miles away in Wayland. The old Ames place on Glezen Lane was technically a farm. To most eyes, however, it appeared as a sprawling country estate. The house was barn-red, typical for New England circa 1900. Long and thin and sheathed in clapboard, it sat on sixteen acres. There was a coal stove in the kitchen, three chimneys and four fireplaces (one usually burning wood after September), and ample trees outside for chopping. There was an old barn for horses, with a riding ring in a separate field. A little coop housed chickens. Somewhere on the grounds, one could always find a dog and a cat. The first cat was "Puff," followed by "Jimmy Skunk," or "Three Diamond Brand" (named for a brand of tuna fish).

On the first-floor landing was a tall grandfather's clock, "Grandpa," that had been a wedding gift to Phyllis's parents and remained on the landing as a sentimental link with the past. Otherwise, there were few dazzling showpieces or antiques inside. Most of the silverware had been moved to trunks in the basement; this made space for toys and a wide array of horse accoutrements that consumed the children's rooms.

Sally kicked off the family's love affair with animals when she received her own pony named Princess. Young Phyllis continued the tradition when she became the owner of a second, particularly limber pony named Mrs. Gregor, that hopped easily into the back of a station wagon. Archie, Jr., enjoyed bicycles and other wheeled transportation more than hoofed varieties, because they did not bite back.

The house on Glezen Lane was kept neat, but Phyllis tolerated the merging of outdoors and indoors that came with any farm. When she got a new vacuum cleaner, "which wasn't often," Phyllis kept the old one inside for housework and proudly hauled the new one outside "to clean the horses."[38] It was a working farm, to the extent that the Coxes drank the cows' milk, ate eggs from the chickens, and harvested vegetables from the sizable garden out back. They grew squash, potatoes, cauliflower, broccoli, carrots, beans, peas, corn, spinach, and Swiss chard. One of the principal allures of the Cox place for local children was that Phyllis, occasionally assisted by Archie, would chop the heads off chickens and dip the still-wriggling bodies into scalding water to get them ready for eating. "All of the neighbor kids came to watch," said young Phyllis. "Not all parents did that in Wayland."

The Coxes' division of labor was typical for an American family of the 1940s and 1950s. Phyllis did most of the cooking, cleaning, errands, banking, paying bills, taking the truck in for repairs, working on homework with the children, washing, mending, and scrubbing dishes after dinner. "If there was a flat tire," young Phyllis remembered, "my mother changed it." Archie's jobs were to earn a living by day, mow the yard with a push mower on weekends, and dry dishes after dinner.

Archie always made it a point to be home for supper. "Dinner hour was one of the most pleasant times," Sally remembered. "We ate in the dining room. It was family time." The family talked about the day's events, as well as current events and geography. "The only time you could be excused from the dinner table," said Sally, "was to look up something in an atlas or a dictionary."[39]

Phyllis tried never to buy a vegetable from the grocery store unless she was exiled in Washington or some other "unnatural" place. Even in the winter, the family ate fruits and legumes from the garden that were stewed and stored in the freezer or canned and lined along shelves in the cellar. Cooked cereal bubbled on the stove at night for the next morning's breakfast. Plates were cleared, and the cycle repeated itself. The children's most vivid memory of their parents would be as two silhouettes standing side by side at the sink, as Phyllis washed and Archie dried the china dishes. They were both tall, thin, and athletic. In many ways they resembled each other, except that Archie's hair stood up in a bristly crew cut, "which occasionally the barber cut too short," although not from his own perspective.[40]

After dishes were washed, the children finished homework, then brushed their teeth and went to bed early. There was no television, even after that form of entertainment had become popular in the 1950s. Phyllis handled most of the reading (the children enjoyed Thornton Burgess's books about animals) and put the children to bed, until Archie mastered his Law School courses sufficiently to help more regularly. To the older children, when he had the chance, Archie liked to read "good literature": Robert Louis Stevenson's *Treasure Island* and *Kidnapped* or Mark Twain's adventures. For young Phyllis, he picked poems out of the same large two-volume set of the *Home Book of Verse* that he had recited as a boy, including " 'Will you walk into my parlor?' said the spider to the fly? ' 'Tis the prettiest little parlor, that ever you did spy.' " He also read "The Walrus and the Carpenter" from Lewis Carroll's adventures of Alice in *Through the Looking-Glass*, one of her favorites.[41]

Archie's principal hobby on weekends was his work. The Coxes were never formal churchgoers; Archie had inherited a good deal of religious skepticism from his father. He had trouble believing in all the church dogma, all the colorful religious stories and parables, "since science proved they were all wrong." Like his own father, though, he tried to maintain a "simple faith."[42]

Archie regularly went to the Law School on Saturdays, sometimes Sundays. In the warmer months, he dug in the garden or chopped firewood. He was chairman of the Wayland United Nations Association that succeeded in bringing an occasional lecturer on world affairs to the small New England town.[43] In the winter months, Archie read in front of the fireplace—history, biographies, mysteries—while "Grandpa" the clock ticked regularly.

Phyllis's hobbies were more varied. Every morning she was up at dawn, riding and "driving" horses in preparation for weekend shows.[44] During the fall of 1946 she helped establish the first 4-H Club for horses in America. Phyllis threw her heart, soul, and two girls into 4-H activities.[45] She often took weekend trips for Morgan horse shows in other New England towns, or as far off as New York.[46]

At night, Phyllis knitted and collected stamps. She met with the Shakespeare Club, a group that her mother had once belonged to, gathering in members' homes to read parts in Shakespeare plays. She also kept up her college sports, at least through the late 1940s, playing forward on a Wayland pickup basketball team called "the Tired Mothers." They competed against local high school teams, the telephone company, and workers from the General Motors plant in

Framingham.[47] The team soon expanded into "the Tired Mothers and Others" when several women were allowed to join before their offspring arrived.

By the 1950s, Archie was traveling more regularly out of town for labor arbitrations, giving speeches to the American Bar Association, and working on weekends preparing speeches that he would give the following week. As far as the three Cox children were concerned, this was nothing unusual. "Going and coming" was what he did.[48] In the blur of his busy schedule, however, Archie became painfully aware, as all parents do eventually, that his children were growing up. In the summer of 1949, from his quiet desk in the stacks of Langdell Hall, where he was working on yet another law review article, Archie wrote to his son in Maine:

> Dear Archie—
>
> I miss all of you very much but I am especially sorry not to be home at your birthday. Nine is pretty old and you are an unusually big and grown up boy even for nine. I hope that you will have a happy birthday.
>
> I am sending you ten dollars in this letter as a birthday present. It would be nicer to get you something myself, but I didn't know what you wanted most. Probably you won't want to spend all the money in Maine because you can't buy many things there. So you could save some until you get home where there are more stores in the fall. But you do whatever you want with it.
>
> I got your letter and I hope that you will write again. Have a good time. Lots of love,
>
> Daddy[49]

The Coxes had a settled routine of spending summers in Maine. This meant that Phyllis and the children drove the truck to Maine, while Archie stayed behind to work. Each June the "Brookway Farm" truck was loaded up—"Brook" stood for Brooksville, "way" stood for Wayland. The pony, Mrs. Gregor, rode in the truck bed. A trailer was hitched to the rear to haul the Morgan horses.[50] The truck pulled out, and Archie was left to man the house in Wayland. He neatly printed one pre-trip note for Phyllis: "Will [you] please *write* a list of instructions for using the washing machine? Do you put soap in?"[51]

The small farmhouse in Maine overlooked a field of purple lupines that sloped down to the rocky shoreline of the Atlantic. Sailboats blew across the water, owned by families who "summered" in Brooksville. There were occasional boat rides and Ping-Pong games at the South Brooksville "Yacht Club." But for the most part, the children worked. Phyllis drove the tractor while Archie, Jr., raked hay and unloaded it in the barn. The pig, horses, and chickens all had to be fed; the cow, milked and fed. Mrs. Gregor had to be shooed out of the house; she was allowed in the kitchen if her hooves were clean, but occasionally she tried to extend her liberties by clomping into the dining room or bedrooms.

On weekends, Archie appeared from Boston to dig asparagus trenches or chop wood for chilly evenings. (He purposely avoided learning how to milk the cow.) After law school work was under control, he spent three weeks in South Brooksville with his family, as a vacation. Then it was late August, and another school year appeared as quickly as summer had vanished.[52]

Although summer months were consumed by the rituals of Maine, and the chores that came with owning a farm, Windsor was still a special place for the Cox family. Its allure had simply moved to a different season.

By the 1950s, Frances "Fanny" Cox had ripened into the unmistakable matriarch of the Cox family. She lived full time at the old Evarts homestead on Main Street. Her snow-white hair was tucked in a bun; her eyes radiated love for grandchildren. Grandma Cox had sledded in long skirts while her own children were growing up; in old age, she continued to act decades younger than the lines on her face showed. She would occasionally interrupt, "C'mon now. Enough homework. Let's play cards."[53] She had a "wonderful, gravelly voice" with a strong New England accent, remembered Adelia Moore, Fanny Cox's goddaughter. (Moore's father, Episcopal Bishop Paul Moore of New York, had attended school with Rob Cox.) Fanny Cox's face was accentuated with "great, deep-set, pale blue eyes" that listened intently with an almost spiritual expression.[54] Her firm chin bespoke a strong will to stay active reading, thinking, playing games, going on hikes, drinking tea on the sofa in front of the fireplace, and visiting with the stream of guests, old and young, who stopped by the rambling house to visit its celebrated occupant.

During the quiet months of spring and fall, Fanny Cox befriended local characters such as J. D. Salinger, the reclusive author of *Catcher in the Rye,* who lived a hermit's existence in Cornish, across the bridge—he had the mailbox next to hers at the post office. She also entertained an elderly Learned Hand and his wife in the sunroom whenever they swung through Windsor to do their marketing. "She loved everybody, so it was quite easy [to love her]," said one friend describing Fanny's charms.[55] Fanny Cox was an adventurer. In the early 1950s—already age sixty—she had taken a trip to Alaska to visit her son Rowland, an Episcopal clergyman assigned to a mission in the tiny Eskimo village of Point Hope. She traveled part of the way on a mail plane and the last leg on a dogsled.[56] She was also an avowed romantic. Fanny Cox donated regularly to a book fund at St. Paul's in memory of her son Rob, since he never had had the chance to become a writer and books were the closest thing to preserving his memory.[57] For the most part, however, the Cox matriarch did not live amid dreams and memories of the past. She was grounded in the present. The present was her children and grandchildren. This meant that the most important time of the year came in December.

New Englanders thrive on routines. For the Cox family, rearranged as it was by marriages and grandchildren and careers and distant addresses, the special routine began on December 24. Each Christmas Eve, the entire Cox family made its way to the old Evarts estate. Archie and Phyllis drove their three children in a car, not a truck. The animals were left behind with neighbors for once.

After a crèche was set up, holly was strung over pictures, tea was poured, and it was time for the "Christmas Service." As the oldest, Archie did the readings each year. First came the story from the Bible about the birth of the Christ child: "And it came to pass in those days . . ." Next came the singing of Christmas carols, which ended faithfully with "O Little Town of Bethlehem," Fanny Cox's favorite. Last came Archie's recitation of " 'Twas the Night before Christmas," out of a red book that Grandma Cox kept ready on the shelf all year.[58]

Santa's "supper" was carefully arranged by the fireplace in the "Blue Room": a tangerine, saltines, beer, or milk. Weary travelers excused themselves and went to bed.

On Christmas day, the children rushed down the stairs to see if Santa had arrived. (He had.) After they opened stockings and presents, the adults prepared Christmas dinner. Uncle Louis drew the curtains, blocking out light except for the flicker of red candles arranged on the table. "It was just beautifully dark," Phyllis remembered the scene. Grandma Cox supervised the serving of the meal, which featured turkey or goose. But the main attraction was not the food; it was the little square of paper sitting at each place around the table (sometimes as many as thirty-six places were set), containing a poem written about each member of the family.[59]

The tradition of the poems had begun in 1936 after the death of Archibald, Sr., when Fanny Cox had decided that it might bring joy back to the table to review the good points of the year in verse. Rob, the budding author, initially accepted much of the poem-writing duty. But after he left for the war, the job was shared. Each year, the yellowing scraps of paper were collected and placed in a special album, which was dragged out the next December for a new generation of entries, for children, in-laws, and grandchildren.

One handwritten poem in 1949 told the story of a new professor, "Billy" Cox, who was the envy of the faculty with a new vehicle:

> *When it comes to mounting up mileage*
> *Or to pacing with pocketed hands*
> *Or to rock back and forth in a lecture on torts,*
> *Why I do it to beat all the bands!*
> *Seavey, the dean, and Browker,*
> *Fuller and Leach and Scott,*
> *Own professorial autos,*
> *Dignified cars they've all got;*
> *Yet wait for a couple of fortnights*
> *And then they'll all think they are stuck,*
> *As with envious eyes, they stare in surprise*
> *At my truck that don't look like a truck!*[60]

A poem for "Aunt Phyllis" in 1955 told the story of her quite different occupation:

> *She's off to Middlebury in the morning*
> *She takes in Harrisburg by afternoon*
> *If she hears there's a horse*
> *A Morgan horse, of course—*
> *She can't get in her car too soon.*[61]

After poems, the rum pudding arrived, burning a "lovely blue flame" as Grandma Cox and Aunt Molly carried it from the kitchen to the dining room, along with a "great many pies." Archie would be excused from the table so that he could sneak into the "Strawberry Room," where he lit the candles on the Christmas tree, just as his father had done each year in Plainfield. Bathed in the scent of pine and melted wax, the adults would hand out a new round of gifts.[62] The sequence of events each Christmas was regular, predictable. Steady in its course.

Each year Archie bought Phyllis a piece of jewelry. He gave each child a book with an inscription. When the girls matured into teenagers in the 1950s, they were old enough to earn one item of jewelry. Archie, Jr., received a pair of cuff links or a tie clasp. "Dad has a good sense of proportion," said Sally. "He had good taste in jewelry. He still does."[63]

The old Evarts homestead in Windsor represented the enduring epicenter of the changing Cox family, a constant reference point for old and new. Fanny Cox would write on the first page of her Christmas album: "One thing is certain—through all the years to come, something of the past will linger in the present, blend with the future and be yours for always."[64]

It was appropriate that at Windsor, in the same "Blue Room" crowded with pictures of generations of Coxes and Evartses and Perkinses, surrounded by the smell of Vermont pine needles and the sight of poems strewn on the table, Archie would receive one of the most important phone calls of his life.

It came during the family Christmas celebration of 1960. It was from a young senator from Massachusetts, who had just won an election.

PART TWO

THE
KENNEDY
YEARS

Archibald Cox, Solicitor General (1961–1965)

7

YOUNG
SENATOR KENNEDY

Archibald Cox's aborted service in the Truman administration had been, as far as he was concerned, the pinnacle of his short-lived career in government.[1] He considered the return to the Harvard Law School faculty a "permanent decision."[2]

But Archie did not abandon his interest in public affairs; he viewed it more as a responsibility than as a job with a paycheck. He continued to take an active role in town government in Wayland, just as Phyllis's father had done. In New England, local government and small town halls held a special importance to the inhabitants, dating back to Colonial days. Archie was elected assessor in Wayland in the early 1950s, valuing real estate and assessing taxes. He also became chairman of a new Personnel Board, drawing up the personnel plan and salary scale and handling employment matters for the little town.

In March 1956 Cox ran for selectman, the equivalent of a town councilman, against John McEnroy, a salesman from the Cochituate end of Wayland, and lost by thirty-two votes.[3] In the fall of 1958 Archie would run again, this time with the valuable support of Tom Linnehan, the local coal and oil dealer. Of course, it did not hurt that by that date, Senator John F. Kennedy would walk into a small reception in Wayland and greet Archibald Cox as a close friend and adviser.

Kennedy had been in the Harvard College class of 1940, one year behind Archie's younger brother Rob. Rob had moved in "overlapping circles" with JFK. They had both served in the war, Rob dying and JFK nearly so. These facts stuck in the back of Archie's mind, making him particularly predisposed to help when the young senator wrote in 1953.[4]

In March of that year, just two months after JFK had moved from the House to the U.S. Senate, he wrote to Professor Cox, feeling him out as a potential labor adviser. Labor had been one of the first subjects that Kennedy had attempted to master to give himself credibility as a young man in his twenties aspiring toward politics.[5] He now used it as a building block in Congress. At Kennedy's request, Cox testified before a Senate Labor Committee on April 30. He discussed possible overhauls of the Taft-Hartley law, enacted in 1947 to equalize power between union and management, and suggested changes dealing with state-federal jurisdiction and secondary boycotts. The two men had lunch together at one o'clock that afternoon.[6] Kennedy's longtime secretary, Evelyn Lincoln, would describe the young senator during this period, "He looked like an elevator operator or a young boy. He didn't know how to fix his tie and the long end was generally way down below his waist."[7]

On June 1 of 1953, Senator Kennedy wrote to Professor Cox once more, requesting that he review a draft bill that would amend the Taft-Hartley law as it related to unions. The senator asked that Cox comment on key issues, including "the most feasible legislation dealing with communism in the labor movement."[8] Kennedy also wrote: "I would appreciate your guidance in transmitting these proposals into specific legislation," a request that Cox agreed to accommodate as soon as he could dig his way out from under "a mountain of examination papers."[9]

Whether Cox did anything further to fulfill these requests remains unclear. The correspondence between the two men, at least letters that have survived, dropped off until 1957. By this time, when it came to labor reform, the nation's eyes had focused on the Select Committee on Improper Activities in the Labor or Management Field, otherwise known as the McClellan Committee. Headed by Senator John L. McClellan, a Democrat from Arkansas, the so-called Rackets Committee was a high-profile group investigating scores of reported abuses within the trade union movement.[10] Senator Kennedy's younger brother Robert served as the aggressive chief counsel to the committee. He guided the inquisition through sensational televised sessions, exposing shocking stories of fraud and corruption in the labor world to the American public, including racketeering, kickbacks, violence, spying on nonunion members, and strong-arm tactics.

The Rackets Committee's public hearings began in early 1957. They lasted nearly two years, and filled fifty-eight volumes of published reports.[11] The bulk of the attention focused on Jimmy Hoffa, the colorful, belligerent president of the International Brotherhood of Teamsters, who "barked" his way through weeks of questioning and tangled with Robert Kennedy as a recurring witness.[12] With documented accounts of union corruption and fraudulent labor election procedures mounting, it was clear that some kind of reform legislation had to follow—some tough measures to curb these well-publicized abuses by labor bosses.

By 1957, a somewhat seasoned Senator Kennedy was a member of the Senate Committee on Labor and Public Welfare and chairman of the pivotal Subcommittee on Labor. Kennedy again contacted Cox, this time asking whether the professor would consider putting together an informal group of academic experts to make recommendations on specific labor reforms. As Cox remembered the offer, "He really gave no instructions or imposed no limits with respect to the substance. It was just the wonderful kind of invitation that a professor likes to get if the professor has any interest in ongoing public affairs, policy." In fact, the only condition that Senator Kennedy attached was that Cox should not invite anyone west of Chicago, since that might make it "too hard for us to get together."[13]

With this flexible invitation in his pocket, Cox put together a well-pedigreed group of academicians and friends.[14] This informal advisory group met over a period of five months in the late fall and early winter of 1957–58, assembling recommendations for the senator in a new, politically treacherous area of labor law.

A steady stream of letters flowed between Cox and Ralph Dungan, Kennedy's chief legislative assistant on labor issues. Cox's informal committee first drafted a report making recommendations to Kennedy in three principal areas of alleged abuses by unions: union elections, expulsions, and misuse of trusteeships and receiverships. At this point the senator asked Cox, "Well, how about putting this all in the form of legislation?"[15] He wanted a draft bill. When it came to reducing words onto paper, Cox preferred to work by himself. He decided to slug through this part of the assignment personally. After months of writing and three different redrafts sandwiched between teaching and labor arbitrations, Cox produced a proposed bill that he assured Kennedy would be palatable to labor union leaders—to the extent that anything could ever be palatable to labor union leaders.[16]

The young senator announced his plan to unveil the bill to a group of prominent union bosses by himself and get their reaction. Archie winced. He tried to steer JFK in a different direction. Nothing good could come out of this meeting. Cox had dealt with the most obstreperous union leaders up close; he had sat through negotiations in which labor bosses had raged on interminably. If Kennedy insisted on doing it, he should at least take Cox and some other reserve forces with him.

But JFK seemed hell-bent on assembling this group of unionists and testing out his new labor bill, and hell-bent on hosting the gathering alone. He would use his brother Bobby's place on Hickory Hill in McLean, Virginia, which was much bigger than his own row house in Georgetown. The guest list would include a powerful collection of "labor skates," or union bosses, including cigar-chomping George Meany of the AFL-CIO and A. J. Hayes of the Machinists Union, hardened figures from the top of the American labor pyramid.[17] In spite of Archie's concerns, the senator left with the labor bill tucked neatly in his leather briefcase.

When he returned, Senator Kennedy was ashen. "He came back exceedingly shaken," Cox recalled. JFK verged upon being accusatory. He suggested that Archie "had led him down a false trail by indicating this wasn't an extreme measure at all." Archie concluded that Kennedy's guests "gave him the conventional labor leaders' treatment of anybody with whom they're going to negotiate. They raved and blustered and screamed, and I, in due course, tried to explain that to him."[18]

In March 1958, the McClellan Committee had issued its first preliminary report, calling for tough new labor reforms.[19] A swarm of senators and congressmen gathered with proposed bills in hand. Despite the rocky reception that labor unionists had given his initial draft, JFK upstaged his rivals by pulling off the politically savvy feat of recruiting Senator Irving Ives, a Republican from New York who was well respected in labor circles, to cosponsor his bill.[20]

JFK had few friends in the Senate. It was obvious that his ultimate aspirations lay in higher stratospheres; this kind of youthful ambition was not rewarded in the jealous cloakrooms of the Senate.[21] He was able to pull off this coup on the labor bill, according to aides, only through skillful finagling. One afternoon JFK casually asked Senator Ives, who occupied the larger office next door, whether he would consider cosponsoring a labor bill. Ives offhandedly answered, "Okay, Jack . . ." At this point Kennedy immediately called in his secretary for dictation and "got a press release out before anybody had a chance to change his mind."

"So Jack Kennedy kind of flimflammed him on it," remembered Ralph Dungan. "When you get into that kind of situation, boy, he was damned aggressive."[22]

The Kennedy-Ives bill, as it was dubbed, seemed appealing on its face. It was tough on labor bosses, but not *too* tough. As Cox himself described the bill in a press release issued by Kennedy's office, the proposed legislation represented a balanced effort to end abuses in unions without unduly disadvantaging labor or management.[23]

So JFK was stunned when he discovered that both labor and management found reasons to hate it.[24] During hearings in the Subcommittee on Labor, chaired by Kennedy, the senator found himself clashing regularly with George Meany, president of the AFL-CIO. Kennedy defended his bill; it could not *possibly* be "antilabor." After all, he reminded Meany, the advisory group that had drafted the legislation was headed by Archie Cox of Harvard, and "made up of experts friendly to labor."

Meany glowered. "My only comment is," he spat back, in a much-quoted retort, " 'God save us from our friends.' "[25]

But most union leaders realized that they had to walk the gangplank gingerly. Shooting down a Democratic bill might lead to Republican legislation, at the start of the next Congress, which might be even more unpalatable.

On June 10, 1958, Senator John F. Kennedy reported the Kennedy-Ives bill out of committee for consideration by the full Senate, the first major piece of proposed legislation of his congressional career.[26] The bill was complex and expansive, covering thirty major items dealing with trade union reform.[27] As Ralph Dungan wrote in a buoyant letter to Cox, the Kennedy-Ives bill "follows very closely" many of the points initially recommended by the Cox advisory group.[28] Senator Kennedy expressed his gratitude to Cox, enclosing a check for $312.43 to cover the committee's expenses.[29]

Cox's early impressions of Senator Kennedy, for whom he was willing to put in such double time, were all positive. His "instincts were right," as Cox saw it. "He was highly intelligent and he was an important political figure who was really interested, I think, in substantive questions of policy quite apart from or in addition to their political impact."[30] Kennedy had a "sticky mind," as Cox would characterize it, and took the intellectual side of his job seriously. Cox would remember the time he flew back to Boston after a long week in Washington, seated next to Kennedy on the plane. Each of them pulled out a book. "The politician was reading Proust," Cox recalled with a smile, "and the professor was reading Perry Mason."[31]

Archie's Washington trips soon became longer and more frequent. Meetings were typically held in room 362 of the Senate Office Building, Kennedy's cramped office within a stone's throw of the Capitol. There was one room crammed with desks for all his aides, Ted Sorensen, Ted Reardon, Myer "Mike" Feldman, and Ralph Dungan; another room for his secretary, Evelyn Lincoln; and a larger office for the senator himself. Kennedy "could never sit still for five minutes," said one assistant describing the work atmosphere. "He was shuffling papers around or yelling for Evelyn Lincoln. . . . Every second was counting in his mind."[32] JFK's office contained a fireplace, a bookshelf, the ambassadorial desk that had belonged to his father, a rocking chair that the senator's father had bought as therapy for his son's bad back, and a sofa from Merchandise Mart in Chicago (owned by the senator's uncle). Here JFK could sleep away a few hours in the afternoon since Senate Majority Leader Lyndon Johnson had begun scheduling night sessions. Evelyn Lincoln kept pillows and sheets in the bookcase, waking JFK for roll calls.

Kennedy always found a few minutes to brush his hair, brown but tinted red from the sun, with a wooden brush kept handy in a desk drawer. "Of course, that hair was his trademark and he worked very hard to keep it," Evelyn Lincoln mused. "He brushed it, brushed it, and brushed it. I used to have to brush it, too."[33]

In this office Archie found himself meeting more frequently with JFK, at times crossing paths with Arthur Goldberg, principal lawyer for the AFL-CIO, and other labor guests. There was no compensation but lunch. This usually consisted of chicken, mashed potatoes, a vegetable, custard, rolls, and coffee, all prepared at JFK's home in Georgetown and set up on card tables as the men talked. "It was very simple," Evelyn Lincoln remembered. "They had to eat what he ate. That's what he liked."[34]

Evelyn Lincoln remembered Cox as "tall, good looking," with brownish hair that was starting to sprout gray. He typically wore a red bow tie with a dark suit. He was "very serious, very academic," she recalled. "The Professor" was cordial, not snobby, but extremely focused on "his subject or his work."[35]

Labor issues were complex and full of nasty little details, especially when it came to the labyrinth of the Taft-Hartley Act. Ralph Dungan remembered JFK listening to discussions in his blue pin-striped shirtsleeves, "kind of bored, really, with the legislative process of trying to design laws and amend and modify others."[36] In fact, Kennedy was so restless that he frequently missed committee and subcommittee meetings on the labor legislation, traveling steadily, dumping much of the work on Senator Wayne Morse, and then appearing at critical moments to deal with big votes and important policy questions.[37] In that sense, as Dungan admitted, "Jack Kennedy was not a very good senator, a very good legislator. . . ." He was, when it came down to these tedious details, "intolerant of a process."[38] The net result was that JFK "was bored and I was bored and almost everybody else was bored with the business of screwing around with that very intricate set of statutes known as our labor law." For this reason, Dungan would conclude, "Archie Cox with all of his pristine, puritanical, academic ways was just a wonderful help."[39]

JFK could digest massive bodies of complex information, after they had been sorted out in the minds of people like Cox, and transfer them into his own mental storehouse. He was able to listen, absorb, and apply bundles of freshly minted knowledge to broader policy questions that made for a politician's smorgasbord. "I would say that nearly all of this came through his ears rather than from reading," Cox observed.[40]

When it came to the labor issue, JFK had strong personal feelings. "He was genuinely outraged by the stuff that was coming out of the McClellan Committee," Dungan explained. In particular, Kennedy was disgusted with labor leaders who seemed unwilling to address themselves to their own obvious problems.[41] According to Dungan, JFK viewed George Meany as an "honest but dumb mick." Kennedy saw Walter Reuther as "being a little bit arrogant and not very helpful in this enterprise."[42] He viewed many of the labor bosses as "fakes" and "usurpers of power."[43] A person like Archie Cox represented an ace in the hole for the Kennedy operation. "He was a straight, pure academic—who didn't understand or give a hoot about political considerations," said Dungan. "Rather, 'What was right, what was good?' "[44]

As Kennedy's labor legislation moved forward in the Senate, with debate and dickering on the floor, JFK displayed Cox prominently. "The appearance he wanted to give," Dungan explained, "was serious and careful use of expertise."[45] JFK wanted to be seen as operating from a position of strength. By 1958 Cox was recognized, not only in academic circles, but around Washington, as one of the top labor experts in the country. That year, the law school named him "Royall Professor"—it was the oldest endowed chair, established in 1815, a mark of rising esteem among his colleagues.[46] Kennedy's staff took advantage of this rising stock, conspicuously referring to Cox as "the Professor" whenever other senators and staffers were within earshot.[47]

Archie did not resent being used as the conduit of tedious details and prepackaged information. The legislative process benefited. Senator Kennedy benefited. And Cox could remain relatively neutral in developing his ideas. In his judgment, JFK was putting the product of his work to good use. "I've always thought that, with a little bit of knowledge, . . ." Cox would say, "if John F. Kennedy hadn't been an elected office holder, he would have been a professor. Probably in the field of history or government at a very good liberal arts college."[48] This, of course, was the ultimate compliment coming from Cox. Particularly directed toward a politician.

As the Kennedy-Ives bill chugged through the Senate, the highly visible Professor Cox was treated as a senior member of Kennedy's staff. He engaged in dickering on the Senate floor. He lobbied hard in favor of the legislation and was frequently invited into the Senate cloakroom for informal banter and debate.[49]

The Kennedy-Ives labor reform bill was passed in the Senate by an overwhelming vote of eighty-eight to one, on June 17, 1958. The *Christian Science Monitor* commented: "It is a good bill and, for the purposes its sponsors set for it, a strong bill."[50]

On June 6 Senator Kennedy wrote to Erwin N. Griswold, dean of Harvard Law School, expressing his gratitude "for your kindness in freeing Professor Cox from his academic duties in order to assist the Senate Labor Committee in its work on the current labor legislation."[51] On June 12, Dean Griswold shot back a response: "Lest there be any misunderstanding, I think I should make it plain that Professor Cox was not freed from any academic duties here. . . . It is only because of his great ability and energy that he was able to carry on both duties at the same time."[52]

Just as quickly as the Kennedy-Ives bill coasted to near-unanimous passage in the Senate, it was killed in the House. The Eisenhower administration viewed the bill as not tough enough on labor. White House operatives managed to tie up the bill in Congress for months through a complex alliance of Democrats and Republicans, and allowed time to run out. Just before the Eighty-fifth Congress wound to a close, the bill gasped its last breath before it reached the House floor.[53] The Kennedy-Ives bill was successfully suffocated.

Archie went off to teach for the summer at Stanford, expressing "great disappointment" about events in the House of Representatives. He submitted an expense report for $132.74 to the senator's office. "I would gladly have expended this for the satisfaction of the experience," Cox wrote, "but the Cox family exchequer being what it is, it seems advisable to send you this statement."[54] Kennedy vowed, in a press release, that new labor reform would be "brought forward again next year."[55]

A Gallup poll conducted in November 1958 found that voters believed Congress's first order of business should be to resolve the messy school desegregation crisis that lingered after *Brown v. Board of Education,* but a close second was the need to "clean up corruption and racketeering in unions."[56]

In January 1959, JFK received approval from the Senate to establish a blue-ribbon advisory panel to study pro-union changes in the Taft-Hartley laws. Panels like this were a "well-worn technique" in the Kennedy office. They represented a way to ensure a high-quality output while creating a sparkling clean image for the public.[57] Archibald Cox was named chairman of the panel.[58] Other members included Arthur Goldberg, David Cole, Guy Farmer, and W. Willard Wirtz, all of them towering names in the labor field.[59]

In a quick follow-up move Kennedy introduced the Kennedy-Ervin bill, a slightly souped-up version of his original antiracketeering legislation. Irving Ives had retired, but Kennedy's new cosponsor was an equally shrewd choice, the influential Senator Sam Ervin from North Carolina. He too had said yes to Kennedy in a "weak moment."[60] A press release from Senator Kennedy's office described the bill in tough terms, calling it a "potent weapon" for driving out the "venal, selfish and criminal elements" in both labor and management.[61] Among other things, it required summary dismissal of all ex-convicts from union posts (aimed at the likes of Jimmy Hoffa), provided stiff jail terms for stealing or destroying union records, and gave the U.S. government power to investigate "crooked union elections."[62] As the *Nashville Tennessean* lauded, "The beauty about this new legislation is that it not only would virtually put Mr. Hoffa and his associates out of business . . . but would do the same to any others who trod the same path."[63]

The steelworkers, coal miners, and railway labor unions all bitterly opposed the legislation. Labor bosses were riding "high, wide, and handsome" on decisive victories in the 1958 congressional elections. They flatly rejected the notion that they should settle for any labor reform that did not include prolabor "sweeteners." If organized labor was going to swallow a bitter anti-union pill, it wanted some quid pro quo built into the legislation now.[64] Otherwise, no deal.

C. F. Early from Saratoga, California, wrote a sharp note to Senator Kennedy in Washington: "I would like to comment that I have read your book, *Profiles in Courage,* and believe that the bill which you are sponsoring will never win you any awards for courage.

"I know that you have stated that you would propose a second bill to correct labor abuses, however, I think that the both of us know that you haven't got a Chinaman's chance to get a second bill through Congress.

"If you are expecting to run for president, you are running in the wrong direction. . . ."[65]

Not only were pro-union forces angry, but management smelled blood. President Eisenhower delivered a special message to Congress, calling for stiffer Taft-Hartley amendments and tougher crackdowns on unions, a message enthusiastically cheered by Republicans.[66] Senator Kennedy was losing ground on both fronts.

Kennedy asked Professor Cox to spend more time in Washington. It was time for Archie to see Dean Erwin Griswold at the Law School. Whenever he was about to take on a large outside project during the teaching year, Archie felt bound to clear it with his old tax professor the dean. Griswold's standard approach was to "try to poke holes in any proposal." It was a "typical lawyer's approach," as Archie had long understood.[67] So Cox concluded that the best strategy was to enter Griswold's office suggesting exactly the opposite: "Senator Kennedy has proposed that I set up a group to get up . . . legislation for him reforming the National Labor Relations Act. I suppose I can't do it. It would take an awful lot of time in Washington."

The inevitable answer came back from Griswold: "What do you mean you *can't* do it?"[68]

As far as Dean Griswold was concerned, Cox's activities in Washington only enhanced his abilities as a teacher. Griswold was proud of his own commitment to public service; he stood behind Archie's. So Cox stepped up his work for the Massachusetts senator, entering a bloody battle that was no longer the neutral academic think tank that he had initially enjoyed.

The path of Kennedy's labor legislation was littered with explosives. Senator Kennedy caved in to labor leaders and agreed to inject prolabor sweeteners directly into the guts of the bill, even though he and Cox knew that by all rights, these provisions belonged in a separate piece of legislation.[69] Outraged, Senator Ervin disavowed his own bill. Senator McClellan pushed through an amendment called the "Bill of Rights" that despite its seductive name would stick a knife into the pro-union provisions and strongly favor management.[70] The *New York Times* called it a "grave defeat" for Kennedy.[71]

JFK and Archie scrambled. Kennedy lacked the votes necessary to tear the "Bill of Rights" out of the bill entirely. Under parliamentary rule, he had less than two days to substitute a new "Bill of Rights" for McClellan's proposal and attempt to salvage the new Kennedy legislation and the support of organized labor. After a day and a half of round-the-clock revisions, ripping the McClellan amendment apart and softening its bite with subtle linguistic massagings, Senator Kennedy asked Cox to meet with the McClellan Committee's counsel, his younger brother Bobby, to review the draft. "We were miles apart," Cox recalled.[72] Robert Kennedy's stance "lacked not only sympathy but understanding of organized labor."[73] After this meeting, Cox concluded bluntly, "I didn't form a very high opinion of Bobby."[74] But JFK and his staff did not worry much about Bobby's fickle responses: "We could always write him off as an uncontrollable, brash young man, which he was."[75]

The amendments sufficiently appeased senators, or sufficiently confused them. Propelled by the new hodgepodge of pro- and anti-union provisions, Senate bill 1555 (the revamped Kennedy bill) rocketed through the Senate on April 25 by a margin of ninety to one.[76] Senator Paul H. Douglas from Illinois remembered Kennedy's speech on the Senate floor in defense of his patched-together labor bill as an "amazing performance," "a combination of political and Ph.D."[77]

Not all reactions were so positive. Dick Lynch from Local 410 of the International Union of Electrical, Radio and Machine Workers, AFL-CIO, wrote Senator Kennedy: "Please stop calling your bill the 'Kennedy *Reform* Bill.' . . . The correct title should be: 'The Kennedy McClelland [*sic*] *Anti Labor* Bill.'" He added: "And that brother of yours—he is too much of a smart aleck."[78]

It was far too early to claim victory. President Eisenhower was determined to get a tougher labor reform bill. His hopes reposed in the House, in the form of Congressmen Philip Landrum, a Democrat from Georgia, and Robert Griffin, a junior Republican from Michigan. They patched together a new piece of legislation that rivaled the Senate version and was much less friendly to labor.[79] The Landrum-Griffin proposal, as it came to be known, galloped through the House by a wide margin of 303 to 125, knocking out several other contenders.[80]

The House and Senate Conference Committee met on August 18, 1959, in the Foreign Relations Room of the Capitol. JFK realized that he had "the crisis of his political life on his hands."[81] The path was narrow but treacherous: the two chambers of Congress had to sit down and thrash out a compromise or face consequences that might be worse. Seated at JFK's side was Professor Archibald Cox, who served as an "assistant." Congressman Graham Barden of North Carolina, the ranking House member, deferred to rank, allowing Senator Kennedy to act as chairman of the committee.[82]

The biggest stumbling block lay in Title VII, the section that would incorporate the controversial Taft-Hartley amendments. Here, the House and Senate versions were miles apart. The warring delegations of senators and representatives could not agree on pivotal issues such as secondary boycotts, picketing, and federal-state jurisdiction. Nerves were worn to a thread.[83] During one heated session in the old Supreme Court chamber, a long room "dense with tobacco smoke," Congressman Barden suddenly turned on Cox, seated in the chair beside Kennedy, and lashed out that he was tired of "these intellectual outsiders nitpicking and scratching for little holes." A grim-faced Kennedy shot back, "And I'm sick and tired of sitting here and having to defend my aide time and time again from your attacks." The conferees sat back in stunned silence.[84]

During another session of the House-Senate conference, Cox took his seat at Kennedy's side and joined in the debate. Soon a shouting match broke out. Congressman Landrum was pointing his finger at the "Harvard Professor" and accusing him of being a "Communist."[85] Senator Kennedy pummeled Landrum with a stinging defense of Cox, one of the few times Cox ever saw JFK's Irish temper take over. Senator Wayne Morse moved to adjourn the meeting until the following morning so that both sides could calm down. The *New York Times* reported that "tempers got out of hand today."[86] Senator Barry Goldwater later told Philip Landrum, Jr., of his father's performance that day: "Your daddy was my kind of man," he recounted. "Mr. Cox had a tendency to smirk. He told Cox if he didn't stop smirking, he'd knock it off."[87]

Cox had never seen this raw end of politics up close before. He did not like it.[88] Years later, after John F. Kennedy had moved into the White House, Congressman Phil Landrum would step up to Cox at a social event and insist that he should not take the episode of 1959 personally. "When you're in a fight," Landrum told him, "you can throw anything you get a hold of."[89] This logic was, perhaps, basic for a politician. For Cox, however, the incident left him nonplussed.

The House-Senate conference sessions dragged on. On many days, Cox woke up and wished he were back in Cambridge. Many events caused Cox professional and personal discomfort. During one key vote on the labor bill, Senator Lyndon Johnson reported to Kennedy that he had taken a nose count and that Kennedy was going to lose. He should withdraw his proposal. "Kennedy took his own nose count and found it wasn't true at all."[90] As Cox would conclude more and more frequently, the powerful Johnson "didn't play quite fair."[91]

There was no direct mention of JFK's likely candidacy for president when the labor bill was being pushed through Congress. Certainly the senator never suggested that Cox should modify his own judgment for purposes of advancing Kennedy's career ambitions. "No, categorically," Cox would say on this score.[92] At the same time, "no one had any doubt that he would be a major contender in 1960."[93]

Kennedy had run a strong Senate re-election campaign in 1958, building an overwhelming majority in Massachusetts to demonstrate his ability to amass votes.[94] Many prominent figures in the House and Senate were now gunning for the Massachusetts Democrat, viewing his labor bill as the potential springboard to a presidential nomination. Lyndon Johnson in particular—in the eyes of many political observers—was intentionally attempting to sabotage the bill in the Senate, in order to beef up his own chances for the White House.[95] Ralph Dungan would put it even more strongly: "He would schedule important votes deliberately on Friday afternoon, when JFK was not there. There was absolutely no doubt that LBJ snookered [him] at every chance he got, along with a friendly 'ha ha' and a big arm around his shoulder. . . . LBJ did it in spades, because he was a hater."[96]

All of this was a sobering eye-opener for Cox. Politics in its hardboiled form was not his calling, not at all. He nevertheless found himself surprisingly comfortable trading debate points with senators and representatives in the conference room or discussing details of the proposed labor legislation in the corridors of the narrow cloakroom. Even his most vociferous rival, Congressman Phil Landrum, would acknowledge that when it came to sorting out the sticky Taft-Hartley amendments, Cox was "the most dominant personality."[97]

Despite the many ugly days, Archie found himself intrigued by the world of Washington. As a younger lawyer, he had met important figures like Learned Hand, Harold Ickes, and Felix Frankfurter. Now, he was witnessing the center of the political cauldron in the Capitol, which rumbled with activity and turned into front page news on a daily basis. During the labor bill jockeying, he even had a chance to meet Vice President Richard M. Nixon, who occupied an office directly across from Kennedy in the old Senate Office Building. Nixon would occasionally poke his head into JFK's office and chuckle, "Don't work so late."[98] Once, Archie happened to run into the vice president, face-to-face. They stopped in the hall briefly. "We chatted for maybe five minutes. That was all there was to it. He was perfectly pleasant. I hope I was perfectly pleasant."[99] It was the first, but not the last, encounter between the California politician and the Harvard professor.

For two and a half weeks during the hottest part of the summer, the conference committee labored over the irreconcilable bills. Hordes of union members arrived on buses in Washington, attempting to influence congressmen.[100] After a long Sunday meeting between labor skates, lawyers, and Senate staffers (including Cox), at which each side grabbed concessions, the logjam finally broke.[101] The House and Senate hurriedly approved a single piece of legislation on September 3 and 4.[102]

The final compromise bill contained at least eleven changes to the Taft-Hartley Act. It included tough measures that required disclosure of labor union financial records, prohibited certain types of picketing, banned "hot cargo" contracts that prevented transportation of non-union goods, toughened restrictions on secondary boycotts, and incorporated other major overhauls.[103] At the same time, the legislation contained a hodgepodge of pro-union compromises, some of which reeked of political deal-making.[104] When it came to the boycott and picketing provisions, the final version was much closer to the Republican Landrum-Griffin bill than Kennedy's Democratic version. Yet most of the internal union reform provisions, representing a critical contribution to American labor law, had come from the Kennedy camp.[105]

"Compromises are never happy experiences," John F. Kennedy commented to the press after the odd, patchwork bipartisan piece of legislation won approval. "I think it's the best bill we can get—and get a bill."[106]

Archie's old boss, Judge Learned Hand, who had reached the "decrepit" age of eighty-seven (in his own words), wrote to his former clerk at the end of this intense blitz: "I have watched your progress with interest and great satisfaction. I know of nothing more critical in our social structure just at the moment than the relations between management and labor unions."[107]

Some union leaders condemned the final compromise. Others applauded it. President Eisenhower quickly signed the bill into law, believing that it was the best that he was going to get. Despite hooting and hollering from various labor camps, labor unions were "damned happy" to get some of the legitimate sweeteners that JFK had injected into the legislation.[108]

After nearly two years, Kennedy's germ of a labor bill, or at least part of it, had become law.[109] The long haul designed to correct "fraud, cruelty, exploitation and gangsterism" in labor union leadership, set into motion by the McClellan Rackets Committee hearings, was brought to a close.[110] The *Albuquerque Tribune* called it "one of the most useful and effective investigations Capitol Hill has seen."[111] An obviously pleased Senator Kennedy was asked by a reporter what the new piece of labor legislation should be named. He paused, then replied carefully, "The Labor-Management Reporting Act of 1959."[112]

"I haven't any doubt," Cox later observed, "that he had presidential politics in mind when he said it."[113] Kennedy could have easily dubbed the law the Kennedy-Ervin Act, based on rank, giving himself an extra trophy for his senatorial showcase.

But the Democratic convention of 1960, just a year away, was now taking center space in JFK's thoughts. Would the legislation be "good or bad politically"? It was best to accept credit for the leadership and workmanship, but not associate himself *too* closely with the final law, or indicate 100 percent approval. JFK's principal goal, to demonstrate that he was mature enough and savvy enough to forge a major bill and steer it through Congress, had now been achieved.

As Cox would explain the significance of that achievement, it was crucial for Kennedy to have at least one substantial piece of legislation under his belt before launching a presidential campaign. "I think this was really Senator John F. Kennedy's principal, if not only, major legislative accomplishment."[114] Ralph Dungan, who helped steer the legislation to its conclusion, put it more succinctly: "It was all he really took into the campaign, other than his charm and vision."[115]

8

THE
CANDIDATE'S
ACADEMIC ADVISER

rchie once met a lawyer in Portland, Oregon, a high-ranking officer in the American Bar Association, who proudly explained that ever since college "he had every detail of his life laid out. And had been lucky enough, pretty much, to follow it." Cox recalled that he had walked away from the fellow, puzzled. "I remember thinking, well, I never could have lived that way. I never did live that way. How extraordinary. With respect to public service, I guess if anybody had asked me—nobody did—my feelings would have been that, well, one expects to engage in what was called public service when the opportunities arise. It's a privilege as well as a responsibility. . . . But as to how often those opportunities will arise, what those opportunities will be, who knows?"[1]

In late 1959, after the triumph of the Landrum-Griffin Act, John F. Kennedy took Archie aside and told him directly that he was running for president. Of course, that news had been "in the wind" since 1956, when Kennedy had narrowly missed the vice presidential nomination.[2] But JFK had always kept his aspirations politely unspoken in dealings with Cox.

Archie himself had struggled to stay as apolitical as possible, while elbows were jabbed in the struggle over the labor bill. His only true political activity remained his involvement in Wayland town government. In the same 1958 issue of the local *Town Crier* that featured two Wayland girls twirling their hula hoops for a record twenty-five thousand spins, Archie was pictured standing in front of a microphone announcing his candidacy for a selectman post for the second time. His political speech-making was hardly flowery or memorable: "The fiasco in the handling of fire and police communications last summer," Cox declared in unveiling his candidacy, ". . . illustrates the unhealthy condition which has been developing for the past three years. I am convinced that a change is needed if we are to solve the serious problems which face Wayland during the coming years." The official response of Archie's opponent, incumbent John McEnroy, was no more stirring: "I have no comment to make at the moment."[3]

It was this same fall that John F. Kennedy ran his powerhouse campaign for re-election in the Senate. He had scheduled an appearance on October 19 at a town meeting at the Sandy Burr Golf Club in Wayland. Town officials were inexperienced in the art of political protocol; nobody knew exactly how to prepare for the arrival of a U.S. senator and his wife. Cox remembered the scene at Wayland's golf course with great amusement.

The senator arrived five or ten minutes late and walked in through the door. He looked around. There was no one to *greet* him. None of the town officials had prepared for this task; none of the party officials was on hand. After a few moments of uncomfortable silence and foot-shuffling, Archie stepped forward. "His face falls on me and we meet as old friends in the middle of the room and then matters go forward."

A day or two later in Washington, resuming their work on the labor legislation, Senator Kennedy asked Cox, "Archie, who was that dizzy blond who got hold of my hand and wouldn't let go in the receiving line? . . . She was complaining something about you were running against her husband and why was I giving you all this prominence?" Cox would later acknowledge, "It didn't hurt any, I am sure."[4]

This time Archie captured his unpaid seat as selectman in Wayland by a vote of 1,594 to 586.[5] JFK now asked a favor in return. Would Archie be involved with his campaign for the presidency? Kennedy needed key contacts in the academic world to serve as close advisers.

As early as 1957, Kennedy's aides had been fumbling to put together some ragtag version of an academic advisory group. The initial assemblage was headed by Professor Earl Latham of Amherst College, who had done polling work for Kennedy during his 1956 vice presidential bid. At least on paper, this first incarnation of the advisory group included a long list of prominent names, including Henry

Kissinger, Arthur Sutherland, and other well-known figures from the Harvard and Massachusetts Institute of Technology community.[6] The work of the group, however, was spotty and ill defined. Earl Latham, according to one member, "was not a great success in organizing these things."[7] He had moved to Brown University and was no longer accessible.

With the 1960 Democratic Convention just around the corner, Kennedy needed to formalize his academic contacts, in part to woo the intellectual crowd that had previously aligned itself with Adlai Stevenson, in part to begin generating position papers for a presidential campaign. The *Boston Sunday Globe* of December 13, 1959, reported that one of Kennedy's principal challenges as a newly ordained presidential candidate was to "corner an intellectual heavyweight of national stature to head his speechwriting group in the campaign setup."[8]

As the convention drew nearer, JFK told Dave Powers, his affable, jug-eared campaign manager who had been with him since Kennedy's first run for Congress in 1946, "I'm going to need the greatest brains in the country to win." Powers knew that the young senator was absolutely right. "It had to be a perfect campaign."[9]

JFK's group of academic advisers in late 1959 was an uncontained herd rather than a trained stable. Dozens of big names had been floated around as members of this elite coterie after Ted Sorensen presided over an exploratory meeting at the Cambridge Sheraton Commander Hotel in 1958.[10] But the group's membership remained vague. The *Boston Globe* drolly observed that the group was "so loosely drawn that a few of them also do chores for Adlai Stevenson, Nelson Rockefeller and Senator Hubert Humphrey . . . between giving Kennedy assists."[11]

Arthur Schlesinger, Jr., of Harvard, a veteran of the Adlai Stevenson campaign, explained during the early months of the primary campaign, "I guess I'm nostalgically for Stevenson, ideologically for Humphrey, and realistically for Kennedy." According to the *New York Times*, Schlesinger said that like many other intellectuals along the Charles River, he would "gladly work for any two-legged liberal mammal who might beat Nixon."[12]

Kennedy was a wild card for this liberal Ivy League bloc. When it came to economic issues, he was passable. When it came to other tests of political mettle, like speaking up against the shenanigans of Senator Joseph R. McCarthy, with whom father Joseph Kennedy appeared too closely aligned and for whom brother Bobby had worked briefly, JFK seemed to be somewhere else "physically or spiritually."[13] So the liberal academics cautiously gathered around the Kennedy bandwagon, ready to bolt at a moment's notice.

The story of how Archibald Cox became head of JFK's Academic Advisory Group is one that now can be pieced together from documents in the Kennedy Library archives. Although Cox himself never knew many of the forces that converged to make 1960 such an unusual year, the forces did converge and somehow thrust him into the forefront of a national presidential campaign.

At the start of 1960, Richard Goodwin, one of Senator Kennedy's chief aides, met with Professor Mark DeWolfe Howe of the Harvard Law School faculty. Howe had been one of Kennedy's informal advisers on civil rights for years. Would Professor Howe head up the new academic group that Senator Kennedy was contemplating, Goodwin asked? Correspondence in early January reveals Goodwin's pushing hard for an answer and expressing open regret when Howe turned him down.[14] Professor Howe explained that if the academicians were going to be made useful to the senator, "they must be put under the wing of an eagle, not of a sparrow." Howe went on: "The only man in this corner of the academic world who seems to me to have not only the essential sort of association with the Senator but to have the intellectual force and standing that would make him an effective leader of an organized group of scholars is Archie Cox."[15]

Several days later, a letter arrived at Cox's office from John F. Kennedy, dated January 18, 1960:

Dear Archie:

While I am reluctant to impose on you any further, I have come to the conclusion that you would be the ideal man to head up my efforts this year to tap intellectual talent in the Cambridge area. . . .

I hope you will be willing to take this on. I realize that riding herd on twenty or thirty college professors may, at times, be a demanding job. But I consider this group one of the most important elements in my campaign. Your services in leading it would be an invaluable contribution.

Jack[16]

Several days later, Archie wrote back:

> Dear Senator Kennedy:
>
> As I told you on the telephone, I am happy to head up the academic group—or for that matter do anything else I can in your campaign. Please regard it as my pleasure rather than an imposition.[17]

Cox would remember having "no conscious plan or thoughts" of a place in the Kennedy administration, if there ever was one. In fact, he had no intention of leaving Harvard. He was following the example of his father and countless other Coxes and Perkinses and Evartses, who believed that occasional excursions into public affairs were part of the privilege and duty of the legal profession. "I thought very well of him and his candidacy," he said of JFK. "I thought it would be interesting, fun."[18]

The new Academic Advisory Group took off with a burst of determination, as the battle for the Democratic presidential nomination between Kennedy, Adlai Stevenson, Lyndon Johnson, Hubert Humphrey, Stewart Symington of Missouri, and a handful of other favorite-son candidates began.[19] Cox and JFK met at Kennedy's apartment in Boston to discuss Archie's new role.[20] A reception and dinner for potential supporters were scheduled at the Harvard Club in Boston on Sunday afternoon, January 24, at 3:30 P.M. sharp.[21] At the appointed day and hour, approximately nineteen academicians and a handful of political types filed into the meeting room in the posh downtown club on Commonwealth Avenue. Guests included professors from MIT, Harvard Law School, and Brandeis University.[22]

The group sat around a long wooden semicircular table in a room with high ceilings. A stream of light shone through the windows.[23] Senator Kennedy sat at one end of the table and introduced Cox as the person who would be acting as his representative in the intellectual community.[24] Kennedy spoke without notes, emphasizing the importance of the academics' work in the campaign.

The professors at the Harvard Club would remain forever struck by minute signals, encouraging signals, that were emitted by the candidate. Walter Rosenblith was surprised, for one, that Kennedy was virtually "on time." This was not common for politicians.[25] Walt Rostow, an economist associated with the Center for International

Studies at MIT, remembered being captivated by Kennedy's opening remarks. "As you've gathered," Kennedy said calmly to them, "I shall be a candidate for the nomination. . . ." The young senator paused. "If I win, I believe that I can beat Mr. Nixon. Therefore, I ask . . . that you give the same [to me] as you would give to your president." It was a fair, honest, confident request.[26]

Economist Paul Samuelson came to the meeting leery of the prospect that a member of the Catholic Church could, or should, occupy the White House in 1961. "There was some concern because the church had its own agenda and was not regarded as being tolerant of deviations from it," he explained. Samuelson was also disturbed that Joseph Kennedy, JFK's father, had reputedly made his fortune in bootlegging and assorted other illicit businesses. The young senator who sat in front of them, however, seemed to absorb Samuelson's comments like a "sponge"; he gave the impression that he wanted plain, honest advice. "I decided that whatever Joe Kennedy was," Samuelson said, remembering his revised assessment, "and whatever JFK's inner beliefs were, his colors were nailed to the liberal side of the centrist spectrum." Samuelson now reached the conclusion that Kennedy was "more promising material for the White House than Stevenson."[27]

Kennedy rattled off the precise number of days left until the election. "This is not enough time for me to deeply study the issues," he told the academic attendees. "I need people who know about issues, who will be honest and will criticize things truthfully."[28]

Spontaneously, the group began to discuss policy questions that the presidential contenders, including JFK, might face. One academician happened to mutter, "politically [this] might not work." Kennedy abruptly halted the discussion. "I don't want any of you to worry about the politics of the situation. You don't have that skill. Forget it. I'll do that." The professors sat back in their chairs. "You just worry about the substance."

Lucian Pye, a political economist, remembered his reaction. "This was kind of a shocker to me. It violated my classical notion of politics."[29] Kennedy's admonition struck a perfect chord with these professors. He wanted them to help work out policy formulation, but to stay out of the messy business of politics.

Walter Rosenblith, a biophysicist, had come to the meeting feeling awkward, since there were "twice as many Harvard people as MIT." But he soon found himself absorbed by the young politician. Rosenblith raised his hand. "Senator," he asked in his strong European accent, "have you ever thought of the fact that if you are elected, the role of science is going to be more important than it ever has been before?"

Kennedy mulled over the question; he had apparently already considered the idea of an expanded interplay between science and government. The senator replied that issues such as the threat of nuclear war with Russia, and putting men in outer space, were going to be on the front burner of his campaign. This reaction was an eye-opener for Rosenblith and other academicians seated around the table. The notion of "culture" and "intellectualism" in America had been traditionally confined to the humanities. Science had always been a disfavored stepchild. Presidential candidates tended to surround themselves with lawyers and government types who lacked the background even to speak intelligently about such topics. This candidate, seated at the long table at the Harvard Club, sounded different. He seemed anxious to return to the philosophy of Jefferson and Franklin, "who blended these things into culture."

For Rosenblith, who had grown up in France where a broad intellectualism was more common than in America, the message of the Harvard Club meeting was exceedingly positive. "Even Jimmy Carter," Rosenblith later reflected, "who viewed himself as an atomic scientist, didn't have that [breadth]."[30]

By the end of JFK's extemporaneous discussion, there was a room full of converts. Ted Sorensen, who watched the performance from a chair at the semicircular table, saw the transformation vividly. "People were feeling very good," he smiled. Samuelson, once skeptical, completely revised his assessment of JFK: "He passed the test in my eyes as to whether this was an operation that I would participate in."[31]

JFK concluded by explaining that Archie would serve as the group's new coordinator. His immediate job was to act as "nudger" of material from a diverse team of academic advisers and recruit new volunteers from across the intellectual spectrum. He would synthesize detailed memos relating to science, macroeconomics, nuclear disarmament, labor law, the entire gamut of policy issues, and turn them into position papers that could be used by the candidate. Those in the room saw Cox as a good choice. "To essentially run a group of thirty or more intellectuals is not an easy thing," Rosenblith explained with good humor. "They all think that they have the truth, or something close to the truth."[32]

Archie's first task, as compiler of "the truth" from so many different sets of brain waves, was to gather up ideas and edit papers before passing them along to Sorensen, Goodwin, or Kennedy directly.[33] Archie's contact was Deirdre Henderson, a capable, young research assistant who worked out of the senator's Boston office in the Federal Building.[34] Henderson would travel to Cambridge and "pick people's brains," gather up materials from Cox and other scholars, then prepare summaries and reports for the senator.[35]

Henderson recalled that from the start, Senator Kennedy displayed a high level of trust in Cox, which lent impact to her own work. JFK's trust in Cox flowed, as Henderson observed the relationship, from his view of the Harvard professor as someone who did not want "something for himself."[36] In politics, this attribute was both scarce and invaluable.

Much of the attraction, for Kennedy, in tapping into the mine of intellectual talent at Harvard and MIT was pure image. He wanted to make the liberal elite of the country, who exerted great influence in newspapers, magazines, and television, feel as if they had access to the candidate. As the wife of one academic adviser put it, "The best way to get an intellectual on your side is to ask his opinion."[37] Creating the sense of access and allowing the ideas of scholars to "fall into [JFK's] mind along with all the rest" was more valuable than a million campaign buttons.[38]

Part of the attraction, however, was more than pure image. People like Ted Sorensen were talented wordsmiths who could manipulate language and make it dance and sing. Nevertheless, JFK knew that his campaign hinged equally on fresh ideas. The "egghead" group led by Professor Cox would be the vehicle that provided a stream of fresh concepts sufficient to last until Election Day.[39]

Ted Sorensen was quick to downplay the group, telling the *New York Times* in February 1960 that the advisory committee was "much more talked about than fact."[40] Cox, on the other hand, now forty-seven years old, with his salt-and-pepper hair still in a crew cut, and with a string of career successes behind him, took on the assignment with utter New England resolve. His job at the Law School was secure. His children were growing up. Sally was away at Smith College studying American history and reading the English classics. Archie, Jr.—a six-foot, seven-inch student at Harvard—was playing varsity basketball, intramural football, soccer, baseball, tennis, hockey, and track. At the age of ten young Archie had announced that he wanted to become either a fireman or a millionaire; he had since decided against being a fireman, because it required getting up in the middle of the night.[41] As a student of business and economics, he was moving nicely toward the other goal. Young Phyllis was enrolled at the Winsor School in Boston, a private girls' academy where she kept busy riding horses and winning 4-H Club ribbons as her mother watched as a faithful "railbird."[42] It was a sensible time in life for Archie to experiment with larger commitments outside the university, even in the otherwise doubtful world of presidential politics.

Cox was more comfortable than he expected as the pied piper of academics for a presidential contender. He felt an intellectual ease with Kennedy. "I think he had a deep, underlying philosophy," Cox would put it. "Something which, to draw a contrast, Jimmy Carter never seemed to have. I'm not sure that Richard Nixon, for all his intellectual power, had one."[43]

Because of his past work with Kennedy, Cox enjoyed a special status in the fledgling campaign structure. Dave Powers never forgot how instrumental Cox had been in the early stages of the campaign. Powers remembered flying with JFK into Atlantic City in October 1959, for the United Auto Workers Convention. It was a major political event because three potential presidential nominees, Kennedy, Humphrey, and Symington, were all going to speak. As soon as they had arrived, Kennedy phoned Archie Cox. It was nearly midnight. Deirdre Henderson stood next to the phone with a stenographer's pad, as JFK and Powers paced the floor asking Archie questions, calling out sentences and ideas about the Landrum-Griffin Act and Jimmy Hoffa, dictating labor thoughts long into the night.

"The next day Kennedy spoke and stole the show," Powers laughed. "Walter Reuther was so impressed, he started to lean towards our candidacy. The next year, he endorsed Kennedy."[44] Memories like this gave Cox a special niche in the Kennedy operation.

In June, just a month before the Democratic National Convention was set to select its candidate, Deirdre Henderson hosted a cocktail party at her apartment on Beacon Hill. The affair was swarming with academic contributors and Kennedy staffers. The presidential candidate himself drank ginger ale, but the room pulsed with a fast-paced buzz. Professor Walt Rostow, who had just returned from a tour across the country, suggested to Kennedy an opening line for his acceptance speech: "This country is ready to start moving again and I am prepared to lead it." Kennedy seemed to like the phrase. It was eventually spun into a principal theme in the campaign.[45]

The following night, at a state Democratic rally at the Sheraton Hotel in Boston, JFK assembled a table of "academic eggheads." He prominently displayed them near the head platform. The candidate observed with a characteristic wry smile "how out of place the academics looked [in relation to] the Boston pols." Everyone laughed and nodded their heads. It seemed "quite true."[46]

In one sense, Kennedy "didn't like intellectuals," or at least a "particular kind of pedantic fellow" who was constantly spinning off self-important comments, "well, suppose he does this," "suppose he does that," and so on. These people "irritated" him terribly, admitted one aide.[47] At the initial Harvard Club meeting, JFK had leaned over during dinner and whispered impatiently to Cox, "Get that bore off my back," shooting a glance at one prominent scholar who was pestering him with more academic drivel.[48]

With people like Cox and Henderson acting as a buffer zone, however, the union between politicians and "eggheads" worked well. JFK began openly experimenting with material from his new academic advisers. In Denver, the candidate delivered a speech dealing with urban renewal, based on a paper by Professor Robert C. Wood of MIT. "In those days," Wood recalled, "just to have a politician *talk* about urban problems was very rare."[49] As the abbreviated primary election season wrapped up with Kennedy victories in Wisconsin and West Virginia, the Kennedy bandwagon seemed to be picking up support.

It was another major boost for JFK, newspapers reported, when longtime Stevenson supporters and political ghostwriters Arthur Schlesinger, Jr., and John Kenneth Galbraith formally shifted to the Kennedy camp before the convention.[50] Galbraith had known Jack Kennedy since the late 1930s, when Galbraith was a young instructor at Harvard's Winthrop House and JFK was a student. Schlesinger had been a Harvard classmate of Joe Kennedy, Jr., who had been killed in the war. They increasingly engaged in a direct but discreet dialogue with the candidate, often with Jacqueline Kennedy or occasionally Cox acting as a silent intermediary.[51]

These were not "furtive" meetings, as the two men saw it.[52] But Schlesinger had a clear sense that he and Galbraith were meant to stay in the background, at least for now. The convention was just around the bend. Kennedy seemed concerned that the presence of intellectual heavyweights who also wrote speeches might ruffle the feathers of Ted Sorensen and Dick Goodwin, two young, talented, and ambitious speechwriters who were anxious to guard their own turf.[53] It turned out that Schlesinger and Galbraith were not the only "eggheads" who would feel the heat from these points of friction.

The Democratic Convention in Los Angeles in July 1960 delivered the nomination to a young, still unpolished John F. Kennedy, amid balloons, long-eared donkeys, and ticker-taped hoopla. Once the convention lights blinked off, Cox discovered that his role as "captain" of the Cambridge intellectuals had expanded by geometric proportions. Volunteers were cropping up across the entire country; anxious politicians were recommending "friends" in every city. The job of "academic adviser" was no longer a part-time avocation.

Shortly after the convention, Archie met with Kennedy at his home in Georgetown. The row house at 3307 N Street was a modest brick building, big enough for a wife and new baby. The two men had met there several times during their labor legislation work. This time they talked in the garden, behind the house. It was decorated with simple wicker chairs and garden furniture. Cox recalled, "And he asked me if I would be willing to take on the role—I can't quote how he described it—sort of full time in Washington, doing the sort of thing I had been doing at Harvard but much expanded."[54] The idea was that Archie would move to Washington, set up an office, hire full-time speechwriters, and coordinate the academic talent streaming in from across the country.

Cox said he would take the job, do his best.

The next question out of the lips of Senator Kennedy was, "Do you think you can get on with Ted Sorensen?" After a pause JFK continued, "Ted is very jealous of anyone who seems to have contact with me or a relationship with me threatening his."

Cox's response was simple: "Senator, I can think of only one person that I couldn't get on with in my life. There was one boy at St. Paul's School, and we were also at Harvard College together, whom I couldn't stand. But I've always been able to get on with anybody else. So, sure."[55]

JFK's words would soon prove to be prophetic.

9

TENSIONS
IN THE
1960 CAMPAIGN

When the Democratic and Republican nominees for president officially broke from the starting gate in August 1960, there were two different campaigns going on simultaneously. One was the political battle covered in the newspapers and on television, a battle of quotable lines and photogenic faces: Richard M. Nixon of California versus John F. Kennedy of Massachusetts. The other was a silent campaign that did not earn notoriety or glittering exposure in the press. It was the campaign of ideas, fought by an army of anonymous academicians who scurried below the line of camera fire, content with the prospect of an intangible victory (if there was a victory at all) on election day. If their candidate prevailed in November, they would shape the amorphous American engine called "policy." And for this ill-defined prospect, they were willing to work relentlessly.

The New Yorker ran a cartoon portraying a national campaign headquarters, with a worker holding up the telephone and mouthing the words, "It's Harvard, Professor. They want to know when you're going to grade last June's exams."[1] The joke around Cambridge was that Cox and his counterpart on the Nixon campaign, Lon Fuller (another Harvard law professor who had once taught Nixon at Duke University), were so influential that, "here at Harvard, the contest is not between Kennedy and Nixon. The question is whether you want to vote for Cox or Fuller."[2]

Immediately after the convention, Senator Kennedy asked Cox to gather a group of top scholars to "brief him" on economic issues.[3] They would meet on August 3 on the Kennedy boat in Hyannis Port.

It was a beautiful, cloudless day on Cape Cod. Photographers and reporters swarmed around the candidate's compound. Roads were blocked off. Crowds were held back by temporary police.[4] While the candidate completed a meeting with Walter Reuther, head of the United Auto Workers, Cox and his group waited, hands folded.

Cox had assembled an impressive lineup, most of whom required no introduction to the candidate: John Kenneth Galbraith and Seymour Harris of Harvard, Richard Lester of Princeton, and Paul Samuelson of MIT. Reuther concluded his meeting and lingered long enough to "lecture" Cox and his colleagues about labor economics. Jacqueline Kennedy, the candidate's wife, appeared in a yellow bathing suit and introduced herself to Galbraith. She had just finished reading his new book, *The Liberal Hour,* which contained a chapter on economics and art, which she had enjoyed immensely. Senator Kennedy, wearing duck trousers for sailing, ushered his guests to the boat and instructed them to "ignore everything you heard" from Reuther. "Start from scratch," he told them, climbing out onto the long yacht. "Tell me the best thing to do. I'll worry about any conflicts with Walter Reuther."[5]

"We went out on the senator's boat," Cox remembered, "and cruised around talking a great deal about the international economic situation, which was all an eye-opener to him." Senator Kennedy broke the ice by reminding the academicians that he had taken "Economics A" at Harvard with Professor Russ Nixon, and had received a passable C. The professors all smiled; Russ Nixon was known to be very close to the Communist party. "But apparently he hadn't had very much influence on the Senator," Seymour Harris chuckled.[6]

The men spent several hours aboard the *Marlin,* soaking in the sun and enjoying the intellectual repartee. Samuelson whispered to Harris that he was talking too fast in the candidate's face. He should slow down, especially in discussing the critical issues of "protecting the dollar and preventing inflation." These twin themes, both related to spurring the economy, would become major themes of the Kennedy campaign. "After I did slow up some," Harris remembered, "I was really quite surprised at how much the Senator picked up inside of one hour on this really crucial, very highly technical problem."[7]

At the conclusion of the briefing, the candidate offered his guests lunch aboard the yacht. "I was looking forward to a gourmet lunch," recalled Samuelson. "The chef took out frankfurters and beans. That wasn't my idea of a gourmet outing on Nantucket Sound."[8] The meeting proved successful, anyway, despite its gastronomical shortcomings.

When the others left, Cox stayed a few extra minutes. Senator Kennedy said he had been particularly impressed by Paul Samuelson, who had spoken forcefully about the problem of the international balance of payments. He would like to get him more closely involved as an adviser. Within a year, Samuelson would become a key consultant to the Council of Economic Advisors under a new Kennedy administration.[9]

For now, however, a Kennedy administration was still worlds away in the minds of the professors who drove home from Cape Cod that August day. First, there was a campaign to worry about.

As an adviser to a presidential contender, Archie did not always carry out high-powered political assignments. That same cloudless week in August, Archie was asked to attend a luncheon at Hyannis Port where, among other guests, Governor Averell Harriman was present. Harriman had started out as a strong contender for the Democratic nomination but quickly fizzled out. Senator Kennedy took Cox aside. "Be sure to take care of Averell," he instructed. "His nose is getting slightly out of joint here. Nobody's paying attention to him." Cox's assignment for the rest of the lunch was "to make sure that Averell's nose didn't get any further out of joint from neglect."[10]

Once he moved to Washington and set up the formal speechwriting and research group, Archie's tasks ricocheted from the mundane to the near impossible. It was no comfort that Phyllis and the family were waiting behind in Massachusetts, anticipating a longer period of separation. When Archie set up his desk in an empty office on L Street that was to be his home until the end of the campaign, he felt more uneasy than he had with other moves.

On August 8, after taking up temporary residence at the University Club in Washington, Archie mailed a private letter to Phyllis in South Brooksville, Maine. He wrote in neat lines of ink:

> My thoughts often strayed in your direction with a little worry while you were presumably en route. . . . I hope you will get some rest and relaxation. You looked so young and attractive at the airport as to disguise how much too hard you've had to work this summer.

In this letter, Archie worried openly about his new job, especially his powers of decision-making in hiring staff:

> Sorensen has made it plain that he doubts whether anyone that I have chosen is any good. I dread the consequences for the Senator's campaign if he turns out to be right.

Archie ended the three-page letter with a confession to his wife:

> It's hardly necessary to say how good it was to see you. I cure my homesickness [by] promising that after November 15th I shall shuck off everything except teaching, relax and then concentrate entirely on what I do best—writing upon legal subjects. I can dream, can't I? Or is the trouble that my real dreams flow too fast in another direction?
> Anyway I love you more each day.[11]

Not only did his new living space at the Washington University Club appear foreign, but Archie's paycheck looked different, too. For the first time, Cox was taking an actual salary from the senator. In seven years of traveling to Washington to advise JFK, Cox had never accepted any payment other than out-of-pocket expenses. He did keep an umbrella, cuff links, and a watch from Tiffany's in New York that the senator had sent him at Christmas and other holidays. These were "personal" gifts of the sort that "friends might exchange."[12] Archie's New England upbringing had allowed him to accept tokens of that sort, but money was something different. Now that he was on formal leave from Harvard, a salary was essential to keep his family afloat. His paycheck totaled two thousand dollars a month, a little less than his monthly Harvard salary, but sufficient. As he wrote to JFK's brother-in-law in Washington, Steven Smith, who was in charge of disbursements for the Democratic National Committee, the amount "will carry me."[13]

The press began paying attention to Cox as early as April 1960, describing him as "tall, lean and boyish looking," noting that he drove a pickup truck to work, that he was "terrifically shy," and that he wore an outdated crew cut hairstyle.[14] "The view which I hold with the greatest conviction," he told the *New York Times*, "is that Ezra Thayer was right in observing the central tragedy of life is that there are only twenty-four hours in the day."[15] Parallels were becoming frequent, such as that drawn in the *Montana Standard*, between Cox's academic group and the original "Brain Trust" that assisted in the election of

Franklin D. Roosevelt in 1932.[16] Archie's profile would make its way into *Vogue* magazine. He was featured in the monthly Italian magazine *Il Globo,* under the caption "Il Capo É Un Giurista."[17] The *St. Louis Post-Dispatch* described Cox as "Chief Brain Picker" for JFK, a man who "habitually wears a smile," a person who "likes to compare himself with the 'central' in a rural telephone exchange, feeding information to the Kennedy organization."[18]

Yet it was not clear if Archie would be a central player or a two-bit rural operator mechanically switching telephone plugs. Ted Sorensen, Kennedy's chief aide, remained publicly "unimpressed" by the new academic group, "even though he helped form it."[19] Archie himself did not know how his untitled position would shake out. As he unpacked boxes in a vacant office at 1737 L Street, just off Connecticut Avenue, and set up an operation that the press would soon dub the "Brain Trust," he had some misgivings of his own.

Archie was invited to tag along to some of the earliest strategy sessions of the campaign, usually meeting over breakfast at the Mayflower Hotel. The group was led by thirty-four-year-old campaign manager Bobby Kennedy.[20] It included Clark Clifford, J. William Fulbright, and Richard Bolling, all pivotal members of the candidate's election squad.[21] Although Archie was not much of an asset when it came to political masterminding, he sat politely at these powwows, eating his favorite breakfast (eggs over easy and bacon, no toast, coffee, orange juice, and milk) and finding it "good fun."[22]

The organizational chart of Cox's group was as fuzzy as that of Kennedy's amorphous campaign machinery. Archie was in charge of recruiting speechwriters, drafting major papers and speeches, and gathering material from academics across the country. Myer "Mike" Feldman, a longtime Kennedy assistant, headed up a research arm in the same building, collecting facts and quotes, including a body of information about Vice President Richard Nixon called the "Nixopedia." Bobby Kennedy was in charge of the "political" limb of the operation, managing the day-to-day presidential campaign and traveling from state to state to woo support and solidify existing Democratic contacts. Ted Sorensen and Dick Goodwin were on the road with the candidate as his principal speechwriters, taking material from the Cox and Feldman groups and melding these into final text as Kennedy swept across the countryside of America.[23]

On the advice of Sorensen and Bobby Kennedy, Cox recruited a handful of speechwriters with proven experience. These included Joe Kraft, a writer who had worked for the *New York Times* and *Washington Post;* James Sundquist, a political analyst who had written speeches for Harry Truman and advised Senator Joseph Clark of Pennsylvania; William Attwood, an editor from *Look Magazine* and former Stevenson speechwriter; and Robert Yoakum, a newspaper columnist.

Joe Kraft would remember the first and only meeting between the presidential candidate and this new team of speechwriters. Besides the lack of formal organization, Kraft was surprised by two things about JFK: "One was how very good looking he was. And the other was the superb tan that he had."[24] That was about all the speechwriters would have time to observe, as the campaign took to the road.

Archie and other key advisers prepared confidential memos for Senator Kennedy, spelling out their individual strategies for the candidate's speechwriting operation. John Kenneth Galbraith, who had worked on two of Adlai Stevenson's campaigns, stressed that "a narrower range of subjects, with more repetition and emphasis" would place "less strain" on the candidate. "Stevenson," he wrote, "covered so many subjects, he probably left the public less clear where he stood on any one."[25] John Bartlow Martin, who had also worked on the front lines for Stevenson and later became his biographer, warned JFK that "no matter how carefully you prepare in advance, a campaign is a fast-developing constantly changing affair." Most speeches had to be written "almost immediately before delivery." Martin admonished JFK to avoid the urge for too much preplanning. "A certain amount of helter-skelter confusion is inevitable," he wrote.[26]

Cox opposed such haphazard political adventures. Neat, rigid organization was the key. In his own confidential memo dated June 17, Cox urged Kennedy to "promptly select someone to act as executive officer for the policy-formulation and speech-writing side of the campaign, to organize the work of all academic advisors and speechwriters." Whether Cox viewed himself as the proper choice for this job he never stated, but he did underscore one fact: "The person selected should therefore be a regular part of your closest circle of advisors, dealing directly with you."[27]

Sorensen took sharp issue with Cox's approach. His memo, apparently written after Cox's, stressed the importance of his own "7½ years

of speech-writing and speech-coordinating in this office." In Sorensen's view, the most critical job in this (or any) campaign was to take a
pile of position papers and imperfect drafts from the desks of the
research people in Washington and "get an acceptable text, with fresh
ideas," done "sufficiently in advance of delivery for the candidate's
study and distribution to the press." The pivotal task fell upon the
writers traveling with the candidate on the road. Sorensen believed
that the Washington operation should generate raw materials. Period.
"Group authorship can never replace one man with a pen or typewriter," Sorensen wrote tersely.[28]

With these conflicting memoranda in front of him for John F.
Kennedy to review, the presidential campaign of 1960 took off at full
tilt.

Despite Ken Galbraith's admonition that "less was better," Archie
immediately set out to produce position papers and speeches on every
topic imaginable, any subject that would conceivably be thrown at the
candidate. In a July 29 memo to Mike Feldman, Cox directed the
creation of a central file containing papers on over a hundred topics.
These ranged from the Taiwan Straits to "Atoms for Peace" to debt
limits to grazing lands to school integration.[29] Research on all papers
was to be completed by September 1, which would create a stockpile
of major addresses ready to be unloaded for the heaviest campaign
push in the fall.

Speech texts slowly trickled out of Cox's office as the candidate hit
the campaign trail in late August. These drafts were handed off to
JFK's speechwriters on airport tarmacs and hotel verandas. But problems quickly surfaced.

For one, there seemed to be a hard-to-explain mismatch between
what Cox's group *thought* it was doing in its speechwriting and what
the candidate actually uttered. Cox and his staff in Washington
thought their job was to concentrate on "ideas, substance, policy
positions."[30] The words coming out of the candidate's mouth, however, seemed to be geared much more toward pleasing the media,
producing the "blip for the evening news."[31] In Cox's mind, JFK
needed more of that "dry, deadly, academic stuff" that Sorensen and
Goodwin shunned in order to cater to the new whims of television and
the press.[32]

In preparing speech material for stops in each state, Cox would carefully review speeches that FDR had delivered in the same city or town. Archie was struck by stark differences, differences that made him wince. "The contrast between the amount of substance in those speeches—the full speeches—and what I thought appropriate for Kennedy was enormous."[33] He wrote to Sorensen in alarm in early September, advising that the candidate should give at least two or three meatier speeches per week, to satisfy the more discerning voters. "Talking longer and quieter would be no harder on his voice," Archie lobbied.[34]

But the problems only seemed to intensify. One early warning sign came with a major address that Archie had personally written at considerable effort for a Labor Day audience on September 5 in Detroit. Kennedy stood under a broiling sun in Cadillac Square before an estimated crowd of sixty thousand. He "hacked" his way through the speech and suddenly chucked Cox's text in middelivery, ad-libbing the remainder. The *Detroit News* called it a "diffuse" address "booby-trapped with clumsy figures of speech." Word swiftly got back to Washington that the Detroit speech was not regarded as a "very happy" one; it was burdened with too many facts and figures and percentages and "average annual rates of interest," which did nothing to inspire the crowd. Senator Kennedy publicly complained to the *New York Times* that his speechwriters were not "producing materials that satisfied him," a direct slap in the face for Archie's group.[35]

There were also disagreements on policy. They were not unusual disagreements or insurmountable disagreements. But they contributed to a creeping sense of alienation within Cox's operation. Archie and Congressman Chester Bowles, who was heavily involved in the campaign from the Washington angle, both felt strongly that the Cuba issue should be handled gingerly. Like much of the intellectual community of America, Bowles and Cox felt that Castro's rise to power was understandable in view of the nature of the previous regime. U.S. policy toward Castro, they believed, should begin with the postulate "that he could be won over as a friend."[36] Ted Sorensen's view, on the other hand, "was that Kennedy must be tougher than Nixon" on Cuba. Sorensen's view prevailed; end of discussion.[37]

But the most serious problem of morale in Cox's office did not flow from policy differences. These could be endured. The bigger problem flowed from a lack of basic self-esteem. Few, if any, of the speeches being sent to the candidate seemed to translate into even a morsel of text when the final speech appeared on the evening news or in the morning newspapers. A number of writers and staffers recruited by Cox were "feeling cut off."[38] So much so that Cox met with Senator Kennedy at his home in Georgetown for breakfast, during a lull in the campaign, and "pleaded with him to lay down some clearer lines of responsibility."[39]

The clearer lines never materialized.[40] By late summer, there was no hiding the frayed connection between the Sorensen-Goodwin team on the road and the Cox operation in Washington. In one letter home to Phyllis, Archie called Sorensen "haughty."[41] Archie and his staff referred to Goodwin as the "junior Sorensen." He "tended to throw his weight around a little too aggressively," as far as Cox was concerned.[42] "Personal frictions" were producing an unpleasant sense of discordance, like two repelling magnets. "I'm not the one who can judge who was right and who was wrong," Cox would later say. "It's interesting that the senator in the very beginning had foreseen them."[43]

From Sorensen's perspective, the problems went deeper than mere personality clashes. Some of the friction was fueled by Kennedy himself, who was not always satisfied with the work product of the academic contingency. There were times, Sorensen remembered, "when JFK felt the material from Cox's group in Washington was not responsive to what he wanted." When this happened, "I took the brunt." On one unforgettable occasion, Sorensen recalled, Kennedy completely lost his composure and gave him "heat" for the unacceptable quality of papers coming out of Washington. "Heat" from JFK, especially when he was operating without sleep on the road, was not a pleasant natural element. This "no doubt created some resentment," Sorensen admitted.

The center of the campaign was shifting further and further away from Washington, further away from Cox's "speech factory" on L Street. The speechwriters Cox had recruited to work beside him were now plucked out of Washington and dispersed onto the road to act as "advance men," mimicking the system developed by Stevenson in 1956. They fanned out across the country to every city where Kennedy was to give a speech, interviewing local citizens and politicians, learning the right names to drop in speeches, developing openers and closers, sopping up local color, making it a point to "stand in the same spot the candidate was going to stand, to get a feel for the atmosphere."[44] After joining the candidate and his entourage on Kennedy's private plane, the *Caroline*, long enough to prep him for the speech and see their own drafts chewed up by Sorensen and Goodwin, the advance men would leapfrog across the country repeating the process in another venue.[45] This system, however haphazard, seemed to work well for Kennedy. JFK was "just very, very good at taking a fast briefing, just very, very good at switching gears and picking up something."[46]

Despite the growing tensions in August and September, Cox took a few campaign swings with the candidate, at JFK's own request, to offer quick advice, usually on labor matters. On September 14, Archie attended the Liberal Party dinner at the Commodore Hotel in New York City to hear JFK deliver a speech on liberalism and national citizenship. Two thousand cheering guests handed Kennedy the Liberal Party's nomination, viewed as decisive in capturing the state's forty-five electoral votes.[47] From here, Archie traveled with the candidate by motorcoach on a whirlwind stump tour of northern New Jersey, where JFK bounced from the armory in Jersey City, to the Bergen Mall in Paramus, to the City Hall in Patterson, to Clifton, to the City Hall in Newark, to the County Records Building in New Brunswick, to the State Office Building in Trenton.[48]

Archie heard the candidate woo independent voters in undecided northern New Jersey towns and deftly take swipes at the Republican party without directly attacking President Eisenhower, since Ike had won the state by 756,000 votes in 1956. Kennedy spoke briskly at the Bergen Mall: "The Republicans say 'we've never had it so good,'" he blared into a microphone. "I say we could do better."[49] Cox witnessed firsthand the magnetic charm of the forty-three-year-old senator, as their caravan had to slow down or come to a halt "to avoid injury to women who rushed from curbs to try to touch his hand or sleeve."[50]

From New Jersey, the campaign assemblage jigged its way down Pennsylvania to Harrisburg, Lebanon, Reading, Columbia Park, and York, where it was joined by Pennsylvania Governor David Lawrence before winding up in Pikesville, Maryland, for tough words about Soviet Premier Nikita Khrushchev. There Archie went his own way, and the candidate flew to Greenville, North Carolina.[51] A taste of the campaign trail at least helped take Archie's mind off problems back in Washington.

The shift of influence away from Cox's operation on L Street, toward the speechwriters on the road, had become painfully obvious. Archie would occasionally attempt to "smuggle ideas" to the candidate through Joe Kraft, but this rarely worked. As Kraft recalled the unfortunate situation: "[Cox] felt that Ted was shutting him out from the candidate. Ted for his part, I think, felt that he just wasn't getting much useful stuff from Archie."[52] The two men had fallen into an "inevitable conflict of roles."[53] As Kraft assessed it, integrating the Cox operation into the campaign apparatus on the road proved to be "like trying to funnel Niagara into a hose."[54]

The files of the 1960 campaign reveal that the friction between the two camps grew, above all else, from seriously mismatched perceptions. Although Cox's group viewed itself as mandated to produce actual speeches for the candidate, this perception bore no relation to the evolution of the Kennedy campaign. Nor was it in hindsight realistic. Most of Cox's academic stable of writers had no experience in political campaigns. They were not present on the road to gauge the reactions of the press, or of crowds, as the campaign swept in unplanned gusts across the country. Explained Jim Sundquist, "Speechwriting is a special art. One has to have a feel for cadence, delivery, and applause lines. Unless you've done it, there's no reason to know how to do it."[55] Many of Kennedy's actual speeches abandoned the carefully planned script that had been laid out months in advance and focused on events in the news a day or two earlier, or on statements by Vice President Nixon the night before.

JFK looked for colorful language and short, snappy punch lines to move the crowds. The "egghead" drafts rarely delivered this quality. Arthur Schlesinger, Jr., wrote worriedly to Archie as early as August about a proposed defense speech authored by Walt Rostow. "The speech is heavy, prosy and boring," Schlesinger cautioned. "Conceivably it might be okay for the Senate, but it would be death before the American Legion."[56]

Comparing drafts prepared by Cox's group with the speeches actually delivered by the candidate on the road illustrates poignantly why Kennedy clung to speechwriters like Sorensen and Goodwin and refused to surrender to the academicians. In anticipation of the candidate's trip to Salt Lake City to deliver a critical speech on religion, Cox's group drafted a plodding address that resembled a law review essay rather than political oratory:

> Religious liberty is only one of the civil liberties which secure human freedom. By civil liberties, I mean an individual's immunity from governmental oppression. A society which respects civil liberty realizes that freedom of its people is built, in large part, upon their

privacy. The Bill of Rights, in the eyes of its framers, was a catalogue of immunities, not a schedule of claims.[57]

The speech that Kennedy actually delivered on September 23 at the Mormon Tabernacle glistened with sparkling prose and catchy phrases. It came from the pen of Ted Sorensen, who hailed from the Midwest and had developed an expertise on religion issues. The speech began by praising Utah's late Senator Reed Smoot, a Mormon, as a vehicle for springing into the more delicate religion issue:

> Tonight I speak for all Americans in expressing our gratitude to the Mormon people—for their pioneer spirit, their devotion to culture and learning, their example of industry and self-reliance. But I am particularly in their debt tonight for their successful battle to make religious liberty a living reality—for having proven to the world that different faiths of different views could flourish harmoniously in our midst—and for having proven to the Nation in this century that a public servant devout in his chosen faith was still capable of un-diminished allegiance to our Constitution and national interest.[58]

The actual function of Cox's group as it evolved, although Cox himself did not realize it, was to provide the speechwriters with a steady infusion of ideas, raw materials, and intellectual ammunition. Dick Goodwin would explain later that there was "not much by way of research facilities on the *Caroline*." With little time and less sleep, the speechwriters relied heavily on the draft speeches and position papers supplied by the Cox and Feldman organizations as a portable library. Goodwin recalled carrying around a Sears Roebuck footlocker and a suitcase jammed with papers generated in Washington. As Goodwin would summarize the importance of the Cox group's work during the campaign of 1960, "I don't know what the hell we would have talked about without it."

Kennedy's own style, moreover, was to keep himself and his writers in suspense until the final moment. Formal, prepared texts of the sort that Cox's group envisioned and methodically generated were the exception rather than the rule. Kennedy's prime concern "was to evoke a response." If there was no response forthcoming, "he would shift very very rapidly."[59] Sorensen and Goodwin would frequently stay up all night completing a final speech, only to have Kennedy "stand up at the platform and give another." After stepping down from the dais, Kennedy would enjoy quipping to his aides, "Great speech."[60] Joe Kraft would sum it up: "An awful lot of it was spitballing, it had to be spitballed."[61]

Nerves were shot and sleep was a scarce commodity on the *Caroline*. Kennedy intentionally kept Washington at bay as the campaign entered its frantic final stretch, in order to keep Sorensen and Goodwin focused. As Schlesinger would explain, "Not only were they doing a great job, but JFK felt they were rather possessive. He didn't want Galbraith and me, or Archie's group, traveling with them."[62]

None of these explanations was particularly useful or comforting to Archie. By the fall of 1960, Cox's staff and the writers he had recruited had grown increasingly frustrated, so much so that Bill Attwood packed up in midstream and left. Cox wrote a memo to Sorensen dated September 17, 1960, almost begging: "It seems to me that, if you wish any help from me or other writers here, you should sit down with me and give us some kind of indication as to what roles we are to play. I am completely up in the air, and I judge that most of my associates feel the same way."[63]

On October 1, Cox drafted another strong letter to Sorensen, complaining with uncharacteristic sharpness: "I grow increasingly concerned about the flow of material to you and the Senator. . . . It seems that there ought to be some way of getting more use out of these raw materials."[64] Archie never mailed that letter, however. Before it was proofread or posted, a "showdown" occurred.

The same day that Cox drafted that letter, he and Jim Sundquist flew out to Minneapolis through thunderstorms to meet the candidate's campaign entourage, attending the traditional "Bean Feed" sponsored by the Minnesota Democratic Farmer-Labor organization.[65] After Kennedy's speech on agriculture, a draft of which had been prepared by Cox's group but scrapped, Cox and Sundquist flew with Sorensen in the candidate's plane to the next stop, Duluth. In midflight the conflict between the two Kennedy advisers boiled over.[66]

As Sundquist recalled the encounter, Sorensen said the material produced by Cox's group "read like magazine articles instead of speeches delivered from the stump." The only "good stuff," Sorensen told Cox in a loud voice, was the work being turned out by Sundquist. He wanted Sundquist to continue on the campaign plane with the candidate; the rest of the Washington operation was virtually useless.

Archie was stunned by this "dressing down." He felt a mixture of anger and disappointment.[67] He stayed aboard the *Caroline* long enough for the day's swing up into the iron range of Michigan.[68] Then he flew back to Washington, alone. He never quite recovered from the midwestern trip. In a letter to Professor Clark Byse, a close friend at Harvard Law School, Cox wrote in confidence: "The pace of activity here is stepping up and in our view the support for the Senator is beginning rapidly to snowball. Nevertheless, I confess that political campaigns are so inconsistent with all our professional training that it will be a personal satisfaction to rejoin you all in November." Cox concluded the letter by warning Byse in parentheses: "Perhaps this last revelation is one for your eyes only."[69]

D espite Cox's despondency over his role in the Kennedy campaign of 1960, oral histories and old political files reveal that his group made significant contributions to the success of that effort. They simply were not the contributions that the Brain Trusters had envisioned themselves making.

The Democratic National Committee files show that although few speech drafts prepared by the Cox operation were delivered verbatim by the candidate, the ideas, concepts, themes, sentences, words, and turns of phrases from the Cox group all seeped into the speeches prepared by Ted Sorensen and Dick Goodwin, providing foundational materials, building blocks, cement for the joints.

In Fort Worth, on September 13, crowds jammed Burk Burnett Park as Kennedy spoke under azure skies of the city's colorful history beginning as an Indian outpost and becoming a modern builder of B-58 bombers. These words closely tracked material from the Cox speech factory.[70]

In Harrisburg, Pennsylvania, as the young Pittsburgh Pirates ball club marched toward a World Series, JFK joked that "fighting youth is winning out in the fall." He then segued into a theme of achieving full employment, following a draft authored by the Cox operation.[71]

In the sprawling Atlantic City convention hall on September 19, Kennedy drew heavily from one of Cox's labor speeches that was packed with tedious facts and figures that he had scrupulously avoided in principal addresses. Kennedy used this ammunition to expertly handle a barrage of questions from the floor at the rambunctious United Steelworkers of America Convention.[72]

Cox's speech-factory drafts showed up in chunks, pages, or snippets of the candidate's remarks in Memphis, Tennessee (dealing with the Tennessee Valley Authority); Billings, Montana (relating to Khrushchev's appearance at the United Nations); Sioux Falls, South Dakota (National Plowing Contest speech on farm policy); Syracuse, New York (Khrushchev and the Cold War); New York City (Economic Club speech drafted by Galbraith with revisions by Cox, including comments from JFK's father); Harlem (civil rights, from a draft produced by Harris Wofford); and Dayton, Ohio (world peace).[73]

The work of the Cox operation also appeared verbatim in remarks offered by Senator Kennedy in a speech delivered on the Senate floor dealing with proposed amendments to the Fair Labor Standards Act.[74] It appeared word-for-word in a press release, "News Release to America's Young Voters" issued October 5.[75] It surfaced in the form of canned packages of facts and possible questions dealing with national defense, civil rights, "birth control," and American policy on the Asian islands of Quemoy and Matsu, all used in preparing for the televised debate against Vice President Nixon.[76] The group's work was evident in broad concepts that bounced in and out of campaign rhetoric, dealing with the proposed International Youth Services (later the Peace Corps), the so-called Missile Gap, and a string of speeches dealing with America's "prestige" abroad.[77]

The Peace Corps, which many individuals have claimed as their own brainchild over the years, in fact was spun out of a last-minute memo prepared by the academic group and an impromptu speech given by JFK on the steps of the University of Michigan student union at eleven o'clock one October night. The idea of an international youth service had been in the air for some time as a result of legislation proposed by Senator Hubert Humphrey and others. It had been kicked around the Kennedy camp even before the formal campaign began. Cox had contacted Professor Wilbur Cohen at the University of Michigan asking for a speech draft on the subject; Cohen was too busy and punted the assignment to his junior colleague, Professor Samuel P. Hayes.[78]

Hayes prepared a memo entitled "A Proposal for an International Youth Service," dated September 30, which Cox forwarded to the candidate.[79] When Kennedy flew into Ann Arbor on the *Caroline* on the night of October 13, a large crowd of students spontaneously assembled at the union. Having read that memo on the pile of his briefing materials, Kennedy walked up the steps and began talking about an "International Youth Service," with Professor Hayes in the audience watching. Sargent Shriver would return to the Michigan campus years later and call Hayes the "grandfather of the Peace Corps."[80]

The Cox group made its impact through trickles, dribs and drabs, seeds of ideas that sometimes sprouted into something bigger. As well as providing a constant infusion of raw materials to Sorensen and Goodwin on the road, Cox's group produced over a hundred newspaper and magazine articles, press releases, and position papers that were printed verbatim over JFK's signature during the campaign.[81] Although this sort of work was second nature to academicians like Cox, it proved to be more valuable than they understood.

The detailed journalistic and scholarly pieces churned out by the Cox operation not only solidified Kennedy's popularity among the well educated, but won new converts among fresh groups of voters. Even more importantly, the operation began to define the candidate's policy on hundreds of issues that would form the foundation of a new Kennedy administration.[82] "The Cox operation," summarized Arthur Schlesinger, Jr., "provided an indispensable source of materials on which the Kennedy staff drew freely during the long and arduous campaign."[83]

Archie never knew this, however. He never sorted through the files to realize that his group had made such contributions. By mid-October, he had dropped the idea of redefining the chain of command. Senator Kennedy was aware of the problem between the speechwriters and the Brain Trusters, but dismissed it. The day prior to a major economic speech in New York, JFK had lunched with Schlesinger and made clear that he regretted the rift between Sorensen and Cox, but he stressed, "Ted is indispensable to me." So the subject was dropped in the candidate's preoccupied mind, just as it was dropped in Cox's mind.[84]

Archie briefly considered quitting, but it seemed pointless. It was too late, for second-rung players like Cox, to restructure the amorphous campaign operation. So he quietly counted the days until the election.

As the campaign surged to a neck-and-neck finale, Cox found himself pinch-hitting in several odd jobs that at least broke the monotony. When the first televised debate was being aired, JFK asked Archie if he would make the trip to Hyannis Port and sit with Jackie, who was pregnant with their second child, and protect her from the jostling crowd of reporters who had descended on the Kennedy compound.[85] Photographers captured a pregnant wife of the candidate sitting on a tiny couch with a tall, straight Archibald Cox. They were watching television intently, as journalists and high-society ladies in flowered hats—including the chairwoman of "Teas for Kennedy"— lined the back of the Kennedy living room for a "listening party."[86]

Despite his shrinking access to the candidate himself and the maddening pace that the campaign had reached, Cox remained on good terms with the young senator. When JFK learned that Archie and Phyllis did not own a television set, he ordered a color TV from a department store in Boston, to be shipped to Wayland so that Archie and Phyllis could watch the last debate in living color. Archie sent a brief note of thanks to Kennedy; then he made a call and canceled the shipment. It was an old New England precept that "you must never accept any money or any other material thing from anyone that will put you in debt."[87] As tired as the campaign had made him, and despite his flagging interest in politics, there was no need to abandon such basic precepts now.[88]

By the end of the draining month of October, Cox knew that he had had enough. He considered his own organization a failure. The Brain Trust that had been so highly touted in the press had "declined in stature and importance."[89] Archie was tired. Above all, it was time to go home.

The final recollection that Cox would preserve of his campaign work for John F. Kennedy was an encounter just before the election in November. The campaign was just breaking up. "I was hurting a little bit," Cox admitted.[90] The senator thanked Archie for his efforts. Shook his hand. Then added somewhat off-the-cuff, "Well, if I win, I hope maybe you'll be available to help during the transition."

Archie's response was noncommittal at best. It may have even been ungracious. All he could bring himself to say was, "Well, maybe. Let's wait and see."[91]

Archie and Phyllis Cox attended an election-night party at the home of Chester Bowles in Connecticut. At midnight they were tired; they decided to go home. "When we left," Archie remembered, ". . . it certainly was inconclusive, and it looked as if Kennedy might be going to lose.

"And then it was on our way back that the news came that Illinois had gone for Kennedy."[92]

10

THE
CELESTIAL
GENERAL

After the election of John F. Kennedy as the thirty-fifth president of the United States, Archie had no real expectation of a post in the new administration. The Brain Trust was shut down. He was back at Harvard. His only fear was that he might be asked to fill a vacancy on the National Labor Relations Board, and "how in the hell was I going to get out of it?"[1] A little voice in the back of his head told him that he was in a horrible quandary. "I was clear that I didn't want to do it. I was also clear that [if I didn't do it] I could be acting contrary to things that I had not only written for him but firmly believed—about duty to public service—and I just hoped it wouldn't happen."[2]

So when President-elect Kennedy placed the telephone call from his study in Palm Beach, Florida, to the old Evarts estate in Windsor just before Christmas, asking Archie to serve as solicitor general of the United States, Cox was "totally astounded."[3]

The events leading up to that phone call, like most events guided by politics, were completely unplanned, unscripted, and a surprise to the person in fate's path. Shortly after the election, Professor Mark De-Wolfe Howe, who had earlier lobbied for Cox to serve as head of the Brain Trust, had written to JFK urging him to push Cox as the person to fill Kennedy's own vacant seat in the U.S. Senate once he moved to the White House. On December 3, 1960, the president-elect wrote back cordially to Howe, thanking him for his advice but concluding, "I think it more probable that I will ask [Cox] to serve in another capacity in the administration."

Records now reveal that Kennedy first offered the solicitor general-ship to Paul Freund, Cox's colleague at Harvard Law School and preeminent constitutional scholar. Justice Felix Frankfurter had caught wind of Kennedy's intention and scrawled a hurried note to Freund: "I can only repeat to you what LDB [Louis D. Brandeis] said to me when I had a similar offer from Roosevelt. RIDICULOUS!"[4] Justice Frankfurter believed that Freund's life as a quiet academician was vastly superior to the encroachments of public life, at least anything short of an appointment to the Supreme Court. Freund had already committed himself to the "Holmes bequest," acting as senior editor to a multivolume work, *The History of the Supreme Court of the United States*. This was an important undertaking, was it not?

So when President-elect Kennedy telephoned Freund and asked if he would serve as solicitor general of the United States, the gentleman with gray hair "gratefully and respectfully declined" the post. Freund was worried about more than Frankfurter's note. He did not like the idea of abandoning his position at Harvard or the "in and out" government approach that was becoming common for academics. Freund was well aware that if he did become solicitor general, this would dramatically enhance his chances of being named to the Supreme Court. For a shy, principled man like Freund, however, this presented a "question of conscience." Freund did not want to accept the solicitor generalship "simply as a stepping stone to the Court."[5]

There was dead silence on the other end of the black telephone. Was there "some apprehension that he would appoint his brother as attorney general?" the president-elect asked. Was Freund concerned that he would be used to "gild" the controversial selection of Bobby Kennedy? If that was the worry, Freund could accept the solicitor generalship now without any announcement to the press. He could then withdraw if he was uncomfortable with JFK's choice for attorney general or the public reaction to that choice.[6] JFK wanted him badly. He would make accommodations for this appointee.

No, that was not the issue, Freund answered. He had other commitments that he should stick with. More silence. The president-elect seemed miffed, but it was pointless to debate the matter. Kennedy put a final question to Freund. If Freund was not going to take the post, was there someone else he could suggest? Someone who would be particularly qualified?[7]

Freund replied without missing a beat, "Archie Cox."

"And it turned out to be a very proud moment for me that I had recommended him," Freund would say, raising two great, gray eyebrows.

Before this telephone conversation, Archie was actively being considered for undersecretary of labor.[8] Ted Sorensen had listed him on another short list labeled with a general tag, "Justice Department," proof that Sorensen was nursing no hard feelings after the campaign.[9] Now that Freund had declined the offer, Archie moved into a select pool with Carl McGowan and Morris Abram as one of three candidates for the coveted position of solicitor general.[10]

Archie knew nothing of this. As Phyllis would describe her husband's frame of mind in December 1960, "You know Archie is such a humble soul really. If it had even entered his head, I think he'd have felt embarrassed even having such a thought."[11]

On December 16, the president-elect appointed Robert Kennedy as his attorney general.[12] John Kenneth Galbraith would remember being completely "surprised" the day JFK revealed his decision. John Kennedy told several close friends, "I'm going to walk out the door at about 3:00 in the morning, look up and down, and if nobody's watching I'm going to whisper: 'It's Bobby.' "[13] It was not that Kennedy lacked confidence in his brother's ability, but he knew that there would be hell to pay in the press. There was a brief debate within the Kennedy family. Father Joseph Kennedy insisted that Bobby take the job,[14] as did RFK's mentor, Justice William O. Douglas.[15] Bobby himself balked. In the end, JFK told his brother to quit protesting. "Comb your hair, Bobby!"[16] he snapped, and pushed his younger brother out the door to meet the press.

Cox would later admit that his initial reaction, when he learned that President Kennedy had appointed his brother attorney general, was one of utter "disappointment." "I had expected him to name a really first-class lawyer," he said. "By no stretch of the imagination could one characterize Bob's past experience as justifying describing him in those terms."[17] In four years' time, Cox would dramatically alter that assessment. "I lived to both admire him and love him," Cox would say, "and I think he was a great attorney general."[18] But it would take months before Cox would develop any respect for the president's younger brother. This happened only because they found themselves working in the same building.

The first hint Cox received that he might be offered the solicitor generalship came from *New York Times* reporter Anthony Lewis, a friend and former Nieman Fellow at the law school. Lewis had always been a reliable source, an astute reporter with one ear to the ground. Had the senator asked Cox to accept the position? Lewis delicately posed the question in mid-December. Archie almost dropped the phone. "Well, he's going to," Lewis blurted out. "I know it."[19]

Word arrived in short order that Cox was to call the Kennedy compound in Florida at an appointed hour just before Christmas. "And my memory is that it turned out at that hour we were driving in a wind-swept snowstorm along the shore of Lake Sunapee in New Hampshire on my way to my mother's for Christmas," Cox recalled. "I remember standing in one of those glass pay stations, with the wind and snow howling around me, putting in the call." It turned out that JFK "wasn't there at the assigned hour."[20]

One day later, the president-elect's secretary, Evelyn Lincoln, picked up the phone and dialed a Vermont number from Kennedy's book-lined study in Palm Beach. Kennedy was looking across a patio toward the Atlantic Ocean, working on his inaugural address.[21]

Molly Cox, Archie's youngest sister, remembered this Christmas vividly. The Coxes had assembled for their annual Windsor gathering, the same tea, the same stories, the same Christmas dinner with poems. "It was a very big day," Molly said. "We knew Kennedy was going to call. Bill told us so." The whole family tried to go about their ritual as usual. "We were having lunch when the phone rang. Archie told me to answer because I had the most sense. . . . I answered and it was Jack Kennedy."[22]

Before the call had arrived, Cox had informed Molly that he would have to "think it over" if the job offer came.[23] But now, there did not seem to be much thinking to do. For Cox, who had revered the image of the "celestial general" since his law school days, "there was no serious question of going ahead."[24] "The solicitor general is the 'conscience of the government,'" Cox had heard it said. He liked the ring of that phrase.[25]

Amid the Christmas decorations and stockings hung over the fireplace, in the home that once belonged to his great-grandfather William Maxwell Evarts, with a picture of his brother Rob in handsome British army attire on a desk in the sitting room,[26] Archibald Cox accepted the position "then and there."[27] He hung up the phone, talked to Phyllis quietly, and pledged the family to secrecy until the news was made official.[28]

Phyllis would recall being "almost numbed by the thought. . . . The practical side of me began to wonder what we would be doing with the animals and how it would affect all of us."[29]

In a column bearing Anthony Lewis's byline dated December 27, 1960, the *New York Times* scooped the story that President-elect Kennedy had recruited forty-eight-year-old Harvard Law Professor Archibald Cox as solicitor general over the Christmas weekend. The position paid $20,500, but more significant than the salary, which was relatively modest for a top-flight lawyer, the job was one of "unique importance" in the American legal system. The solicitor general represented the government in all cases before the U.S. Supreme Court. He enjoyed a "special relationship" with the justices. William Howard Taft had gone on from that position to become president and later chief justice. Others like Robert Jackson and Stanley Reed had moved from the solicitor generalship to seats on the Supreme Court. It was one of the greatest honors a lawyer could earn.[30]

The splash of attention was dizzying for Cox. Perhaps the average farmer in Maine or woman-on-the street in Wayland did not know who or what the solicitor general was. But much of the world knew. The *Berkshire Eagle* in Pittsfield, Massachusetts, ran a picture of Cox looking suitably erudite behind a desk, large glasses perched on his nose, a pile of law books sprawled out in front of him.[31] The *Boston Herald* showed Cox seated between his neatly posed daughters, Sally, age twenty-one, and Phyllis, age fifteen, noting that friends in Wayland referred to him affectionately as "the Perfessor."[32]

The biggest question, according to the *Boston Herald,* was whether Cox would continue to drive his half-ton pickup truck to work, or "whether this type of transportation would prove an embarrassing contrast to the rest of Washington officialdom."[33]

"You have no idea," daughter Sally coyly offered the press, "how cold and hard those seats can be on a winter morning."[34] The *Herald* went on to report that wife Phyllis was "busily feeding" the livestock when reporters called, and had no time to be interviewed. She did make it clear that the family's three horses, one dog, twelve hens, and two cats (Jimmy Skunk and Little Orphan Annie) were "absolutely essential" to the Cox family and would somehow figure into the move to Washington.[35]

Judge Learned Hand was now almost eighty-nine years old, but he had made it out to vote for John F. Kennedy in the election. He wrote to Archie from New York City on December 30, 1960: "I felt sure that you were going to get a good job in this administration, and I cannot think of anyone whom I should be more glad to see installed as Solicitor General." Hand added an aside: "I could wish that you had been selected as the Attorney General and would select judges; and, frankly, I am a little troubled at that appointment; but for one who means to stick to the law there is no job better than that of the Solicitor General."36

For Cox, accepting this new position meant, for the first time since he had joined the faculty after World War II, resigning his professorship at Harvard. University President Nathan Pusey hemmed and hawed in telling Archie that he would be required to turn in his keys; the solicitor general's post had to be viewed as "semipermanent."37 But Cox told President Pusey that he had already drafted his resignation letter. As Cox wrote privately to Learned Hand on January 12: "I leave Harvard with mixed feelings, as you will know. Harvard has been very good to me and my work suited me well. . . ." He hoped that the doors would remain open.38

It was less difficult for Archie to resign as selectman in Wayland. After two years of battles over traffic patterns and most recently a fight over a proposed "sheltering home" for two hundred cats, Cox was ready for a break. "Gentlemen," he told his fellow selectmen at their final meeting in the town hall on January 1, as he prepared to leave for Washington, "I hope that I shall never again be involved in a case so difficult as the Great Cat House Controversy."39

Archie's predecessor in the Solicitor General's Office, J. Lee Rankin, had quietly returned home as a ghost-town stillness settled upon Washington after the election. Archie claimed his key and moved into the "celestial" quarters in the monolithic Justice Department building at the corner of Tenth and Constitution Avenues. Chiseled in limestone over one door were the words "JUSTICE IS THE GREAT INTEREST OF MAN ON EARTH." At another entrance was the Latin phrase "LEGE ATQUE ORDINE OMNIA FIUNT," taken from Pliny's *Epistulae:* "Everything is created by law and order." Archie's office was furnished with ornate woodwork, paintings, a working fireplace guarded by the marble heads of four lions, a conference room, and a tiny hidden bedroom nestled atop a winding staircase.

From the window over his shoulder, Archie could see the Supreme Court and the Capitol on the rise of the hill. Across the street was the Smithsonian complex; in another direction the National Archives, where the original Declaration of Independence and the U.S. Constitution were housed in airtight encasements. It was an incredible vantage point, from this chair. It was now his own.

By January 5, Cox was meeting with outgoing Attorney General William P. Rogers and incoming Attorney General Robert F. Kennedy, discussing the transition to a new administration.[40] He also reserved time during that first week to meet with two selectmen from Wayland, who visited the capital to talk about new traffic problems. They "spread out the blueprints" on a bed at the Statler Hilton and thrashed out the problem. But now Cox had to move onto bigger subjects.[41]

Cox's confirmation hearing before the Senate Judiciary Committee was held on January 18. It lasted only ten minutes. Chairman James O. Eastland of Mississippi noted that the file on the nominee from the Federal Bureau of Investigation was unusually barren of negative comments. When Archie was questioned whether he had any holdings of stocks and securities, he replied seriously, "The only stock we have is my wife's horse." Senate Minority Leader Everett Dirksen, who had sat across the table from Cox during the Landrum-Griffin Act days, concluded the hearing by saying of the nominee, "I have been quite impressed with his abilities in the legal field, notwithstanding the fact that we have consistently and steadily disagreed on most things."[42]

Archie was sworn in on January 23 at a small ceremony presided over by his old boss from the early solicitor general days, Charles Fahy, who had become a federal judge under President Truman. Cox now joined other prominent Brain Trusters who occupied key positions in the new Kennedy administration.[43]

The inauguration of John F. Kennedy lit up the east front of the Capitol on Friday, January 20. Archie and Phyllis held tickets for the president's platform, sitting in section 2, row 11. Chief Justice Earl Warren administered the simple oath to the new president. The day was cold and blowy; a snowfall had tangled up the city the night before. Robert Frost read a brief poem, "The Gift Outright," as the wind whipped through the spectator seats. Solicitor General Cox, wearing a black formal coat accentuated with a white tie, and Phyllis Ames Cox, dressed in flowing aqua gown and fur stole, were caught in the society pages of the Boston newspapers as they arrived at the

National Guard Armory for an inaugural gala. As cold as it was, a flush of pride was captured on their faces, which summarized the high point of a long drive from Wayland to Washington, together.

Cox was pleasantly surprised as the new Kennedy Justice Department began to take shape. Although he had been skeptical of Robert Kennedy's appointment as attorney general, he was encouraged that RFK displayed a sufficiently "strong sense of inner security" to name top-flight lawyers as his chief deputies. Byron "Whizzer" White, former Rhodes scholar from Yale and professional football player, became deputy attorney general. Burke Marshall, a nationally prominent antitrust lawyer from Plainfield, who had (coincidentally) grown up with Archie's younger brother Max, was appointed to head the Civil Rights Division. Nicholas deB. Katzenbach, a Yale Law School graduate, former law professor at University of Chicago, and another prominent antitrust lawyer, was named assistant attorney general. For a non-honors graduate of Virginia Law School who might easily have felt threatened by credentials outshining his own, Robert Kennedy seemed remarkably able to suppress any ego problems and shoot for the best. Cox was impressed.

Archie also quickly came to admire RFK's "instinct for the jugular" (using Holmes's phrase) as they began to wade into messy legal problems.[44] Cox frequently found himself saying, "Now, wait a minute, Bob. Now listen." Particularly on complicated criminal and civil rights issues, the president's younger brother seemed "a little prone to jump to instinctive conclusions as to who was a white hat and who was a black hat. But he *would* wait and listen," much to Cox's surprise. In the end, Cox found "few occasions to disagree with [RFK's] judgment when he was done."[45]

Civil rights became one of the first hotbeds of action for the Kennedy Justice Department. It was an area in which RFK, the consummate pragmatist, and Cox, the stubborn adherent to detail and precedent, would frequently find themselves butting heads. As their relationship warmed, however, their divergent philosophies found gears on which to mesh. The solicitor general and the attorney general, who shared little in common superficially, would eventually coax out of the Supreme Court some of the most significant civil rights decisions of the twentieth century.

Civil rights was never a particular passion of the new president, at least not initially, not in his gut and soul. JFK had a solid record as a congressman and senator in favor of civil rights, but nothing extraordinary compared to other northern Democrats, or even compared to his opponent Richard Nixon.[46] Kennedy had taken a symbolic lead during the campaign by offering moral support to the pregnant wife of the Reverend Martin Luther King, Jr., pressuring Georgia prison officials for King's release in October 1960, when the civil rights leader was arrested and thrown in a DeKalb County jail.[47]

In general, however, Kennedy had had little contact with blacks, little deep-seated understanding of their problems. In the Boston-Irish congressional district where Kennedy had cut his teeth, the "percentage of blacks was minor," according to Dave Powers. Even after he was elected senator in Massachusetts, his constituency of what polite society called "Negroes" remained small. Not until JFK traveled around the country during the campaign did he really "become aware" of the race issue.[48]

It was only through chance, luck, and a bit of good advice that Archibald Cox happened to choose a civil rights case as his first to argue in the Supreme Court.

It was protocol that the new solicitor general should pay a visit on the chief justice and then, in descending order of seniority, visit each of the remaining justices. On February 2, Archie stepped into the chambers of his old professor, Felix Frankfurter, for their prearranged luncheon. They dined quietly, sipping on water and passing warm, buttered bread. Archie should get started on the right foot, Frankfurter told his old student, his spectacles glinting in the light. The first case would be highly symbolic; it often set the tone for a solicitor general's entire term in office. It was time, Frankfurter said, that the solicitor general took "a bigger interest in the criminal cases."[49] They finished lunch leisurely. Archie thanked his old professor for his words of advice. He decided, walking out of those magnificent chambers, that he would argue a criminal case in his first appearance before the Court.

When the news caromed back through the fifth floor of the Justice Department, lawyers on Cox's staff, including his first assistant, Oscar Davis, protested vehemently. Criminal cases were important, sure; but with marches and Freedom Riders and young blacks engaging in peaceful but explosive sit-ins at lunch counters down South, it would be a travesty—speaking of symbolism—for Cox to select anything but a civil rights case.[50]

Different strains of civil rights actions were reaching the Court from different pipelines by early 1961. A smattering of old school-desegregation cases were still grinding through the system in the aftermath of the 1954 decision in *Brown v. Board of Education*. A new group of cases involving sit-in demonstrators, black students and white sympathizers who defied local bans against "colored people" eating at lunch counters and using public accommodations, had also inched their way onto the Court's docket. Legislative reapportionment cases, laced with racial and political overtones, were making a splash. The new solicitor general vacillated. Felix Frankfurter's advice was important and valued. On the other hand, it did make sense to set a new tone for the administration, to make it clear that the U.S. government would take an active role in opposing racial discrimination across America. In the end, Archie picked *Burton v. Wilmington Parking Authority,* case number 164 on the October 1960 docket, as the one in which he would make his debut before the highest court as solicitor general.

The Eagle Coffee Shoppe was located in an off-street parking garage in Wilmington, Delaware. In 1958, William Burton, a black man, had parked his car in the state-owned parking garage, walked around to the privately owned coffee shop, and entered the front door on Ninth Street. After he was refused a menu and asked to leave, he returned to his car and drove away. Burton then filed a suit under the Fourteenth Amendment, peacefully challenging the action in a Delaware court.

On February 21, 1961, one month after occupying his new office, Cox walked into the deep-purple courtroom of the Supreme Court to present his first oral argument as the voice of the U.S. government. Phyllis sat nervously in a visitor's box, accompanied by young Phyllis and Archie, Jr.[51] They were only here for the day. Young Phyllis was still finishing up her sophomore year at the Winsor School; wife Phyllis was still looking for a home for the family pets and livestock. For the moment, Archie was living alone in the downtown University Club. The reunion was brief but welcome.

Cox was dressed in formal swallowtail, striped trousers, and pearl gray vest, an age-old tradition for attorneys representing the United States. The attire was meant to symbolize "the dignity of the United States in arguments before the Supreme Court."[52] What most observers in the courtroom did not know, however, was that it was the same formal coat and striped trousers that the solicitor general had worn when he had married Phyllis Ames in 1947.[53]

Cox straightened his cutaway coat and stepped forward on behalf of the United States as amicus curiae (friend of the court), peering over half-glasses that dated back to his eye trouble in Law School. His argument was direct. The refusal of the coffee shop in the Wilmington garage to serve Burton violated his Fourteenth Amendment rights, under these circumstances, even though it was a privately owned business ordinarily outside the sweep of the Constitution.

Cox had driven up to Wilmington on the Sunday before his oral argument to shake off his preargument jitters. As he stood before the bland edifice that had spawned his first Supreme Court case as solicitor general, Archie was immediately struck by an odd fact: the flag of the United States and the flag of Delaware were flying together over the Wilmington Parking Authority Garage, and over the Eagle Coffee Shoppe. He got into his car and drove back to Washington.[54]

Looking unusually tall in his long coat and stiff white collar, Cox now stood before the Supreme Court and invoked the imagery of the flags that he had seen waving above the parking garage. It was a gamble; he was referring to "evidence" that was not in the lower court record. But it seemed appropriate that the justices should hear about it: "On the front of the building, on the roof over the coffee shop, are two flagpoles which, on the ordinary days of the week, fly the United States flag and the flag of Delaware," Cox told the Court. "Anyone who was the victim of discrimination in this coffee shop could not escape the fact that the discrimination took place in a public building and, literally, here, under the flag of the United States and of Delaware."[55]

Perched on the edge of her chair, Phyllis Cox watched her husband as she blinked occasionally and feigned calmness. She noticed that the "timbre of his voice" started out high-pitched and unsure, as if he were reading from a script. But his voice grew stronger and more confident as he moved forward, nailing down points methodically as the justices raised them.[56]

"If the Fourteenth Amendment means anything at all," Cox said, clutching his fist in the air to drive home a point, "surely it means that all citizens shall stand alike in their relation to their government, regardless of race or color." He touched his typed speech for the feel, but did not read it. "No one looking at the problem with any human understanding, I submit, could take the view that [these Negroes] stood before the State of Delaware, in this building owned by the State of Delaware, on an equal plane with all other citizens."[57]

That night, Archie and Phyllis attended a cocktail party at the Yugoslavian consulate. The solicitor general received high praise from lawyers who had witnessed his oral argument.[58] On April 17, the Court handed down its decision in *Burton v. Wilmington Parking Authority*, finding that the state of Delaware could not escape responsibility for this discriminatory conduct, even though it was ostensibly carried out by a "private" business. Among other things, the Court observed that the parking authority flew state and federal flags from mastheads on the roof: "The State has so far insinuated itself into a position of interdependence with [the Eagle Coffee Shoppe]," wrote Justice Tom Clark, "that it must be recognized as a joint participant in the challenged activity."[59]

Three justices dissented. One of them was Archie's former professor, Felix Frankfurter.

Archibald Cox and Robert Kennedy were developing styles as different as their appearances and personalities. RFK was short and wiry and appeared to be "smaller than he was." He was "somewhat slight," with sandy hair. Friendly. "Very direct—no wasted motions," recalled Burke Marshall. He had "intense blue eyes" that could intimidate even the toughest CEO in their first encounter. "He was an intense listener," said Marshall. Yet he was charming, youthful, perceptive, a contagious source of enthusiasm once his attention was focused.[60]

Archie, on the other hand, was the personification of the blue-blooded New Englander. With his tall, patrician looks, he was a "father figure" in a young department. Cox was "stuffy in the nicest meaning of the word," Nick Katzenbach told an interviewer in 1968, and "wore his learning on his sleeve."[61] While RFK came to work in shirtsleeves, often without a tie, Cox adopted an entirely different dress code. When he was not in Court wearing a formal morning coat, he dressed impeccably in a suit jacket and bow tie.

Their offices were just as different. RFK kept a mounted swordfish above his fireplace, a stuffed Bengal tiger next to the bookcase, and drawings from his children (he had seven at the time) cluttering the office wall. He occasionally brought his dog, Brumus, a lumbering black Newfoundland known for his fits of unpredictability, to work because he worried that the dog was too lonely at home. The attorney general threw footballs in his office with Byron White and interacted with colleagues as a "warm and friendly and funny friend." Archie, on the other hand, maintained a "spartan" office. There were few "gee-gaws" or fancy trappings of power on the tables. Few valuable government oil paintings hung from the wall.[62] The solicitor general did not throw footballs; he was not someone "cuddly to a stranger." He was dignified around the office. One colleague described Cox as "somewhat austere." To the same extent that Robert Kennedy was a public person, Archibald Cox maintained a shell of privacy.[63]

It was an unlikely dynamic, but one that yielded interesting results. Archie was included early on as part of RFK's "cabinet system" of decision-making. There were regular staff lunches on Tuesdays and Thursdays in the big kitchen behind the attorney general's office. These were "fun" and "open" but "serious" times for debate among the heads of divisions and RFK's top deputies.[64] There were also lunches and swimming at Robert Kennedy's home at Hickory Hill. At times, twenty "guests" tramped onto the patio after Bobby gave his wife, Ethel, a half-hour advance warning.[65]

As Herbert "Jack" Miller, head of the Criminal Division remembered, Archie sat on the stone terrace at Hickory Hill and transformed himself into a "policy" and "legal" adviser on a wide range of subjects. Cox had good legal instincts; the younger Justice Department lawyers tapped into them freely. Even on criminal issues outside his usual sphere of expertise, Archie participated in the discussions, from wiretap issues,[66] to automobile searches, to the impending prosecution of Teamsters leader Jimmy Hoffa.[67] Those sitting around the lunch table knew that "if Archie was worried about something, then there was something to worry about."[68]

Archie's style in running his own solicitor general's office was "low key." The glass-enclosed wooden bookcases were for use, not show. Stacks of *United States Reports* and working papers sat on tables. Archie made it a point to read everything that crossed his desk. Not only did he read, but he dug into briefs, scribbling revisions on every piece of paper that required his signature. "He had the Puritan sense of duty that he ought to look carefully at anything that came out of the office under his name," said Ralph Spritzer, who replaced Oscar Davis as Cox's first assistant.[69] Cox spent so much time editing briefs that the attorney general's office had to occasionally, gently, request that he stop.[70]

Anthony Lewis of the *New York Times* had covered the Supreme Court and the Justice Department for years. What stood out about

Cox, Lewis recalled, was his enormous productivity: "He did the work. More than any other solicitor general of my time. He read every line of every brief."[71]

Hard work was exactly the image that Cox wanted to convey. Hard work and accessibility. Young lawyers could walk into Cox's door and talk to their boss directly. Washington journalists found themselves regularly interviewing the solicitor general in the high-ceilinged office trimmed in blue paint and silver stars. He may have initially come across "as a ramrod Yankee," but they found him extremely "approachable."[72]

Still, Archie lacked a certain spark in the eyes of some staff members and colleagues. Although he was brilliant and unmatchable as a lawyer, some perceived Cox as being a bit too inflexible. Even Nick Katzenbach, a close friend, admitted, "I would say that once he made up his mind about something, the idea that he could possibly be mistaken was very difficult for him to appreciate. So he could be a little rigid. In that sense, stubborn."[73]

In one criminal case, *Preston v. United States,* involving the right of officers to search automobiles brought to the police station, Cox felt there was no justification for the government's position. "He refused to make the arguments before the Court," one assistant attorney general recalled. "We lost the case."[74] Archie had so much confidence—some called it arrogance—that it was whispered around the office and among Supreme Court clerks that he occasionally "lectured" the justices, conveying the impression that he was "really looking down his nose at them."[75]

There was also a rigidity when it came to personal relations. Cox never became "one of the boys" in his own office. He never invited everyone to his home for parties and receptions, as other solicitors general did. His idea of "socializing" was having lunch in the Federal Trade Commission cafeteria. The first time Phyllis came to the office for an informal get-together, Archie "forgot to introduce her" to a group of lawyers around him. Said one staff member, "He didn't have a natural, easy social sense."[76]

But those closest to Cox understood that he was neither "contemptuous" nor "arrogant." Rather, there was "a shyness,"[77] which created a facade difficult to crack. He was "loved by his staff," insisted Katzenbach.[78] At the same time, he remained an inscrutable Boston Brahmin, whom very few lawyers in the office would ever get to know intimately.

Archie never felt the need to make excuses or offer explanations. For the first eight months there was no entertaining because the Coxes had no home in Washington. Phyllis was still raising their teenage daughter and tending to the animals in Wayland. For the remaining years there were no parties or cocktail hours, because it was not the Coxes' style. They lived in McLean, Virginia, where young Phyllis could be close to her school and Phyllis could teach second grade at the nearby Potomac School, in a house too small for a throng of visitors. Later, they would move to a stone gardener's cottage in Great Falls, even smaller quarters, so that Phyllis could keep a horse.

Despite the hard shell, Archibald Cox did have a softer side, which was visible only to a handful of people. It was within the private confines of a white sheet of paper that Archie expressed his emotions most easily and comfortably. Staff members in the solicitor general's office would never see this side of the man; nor were they intended to see it. Archie wrote to Phyllis for their anniversary on June 10, 1961, sending the letter via air mail:

> My Darling,
>
> I hope that by good luck this will reach you Monday. When we aren't together on June 12, as has been true all too often, at least I'd like to have a letter there that says, I love you.
>
> Our wedding is getting to be quite a long time ago—longer than I like to realize sometimes. Time wasn't needed to teach me how lucky for me that day was, but it has proved me wrong in anticipating too little happiness and too few joys, not too many or too much. Sometimes, if I let my mind dwell on it, I have an awfully guilty feeling of giving too little and taking too much.
>
> How can I tell you how much I love you? That my universe, despite the time we are apart and the depth of my professional interests revolves about you? That knowing that you are there and we will be together is my absolute dependence? I don't know how to say it very well. You are me, for without you there would be no me.

Archie wrote in fluid little paragraphs, on unlined University Club stationery:

> I must be getting old because thinking on our anniversary makes my mind go back. Dublin. Do you remember swimming in the quarry in Dorset? . . . But the past isn't all; with you it's only a promise of more joys, more happiness, more love together.

I'll take this to the Post Office now in the hope that it will get there
Monday. Goodnight, my darling wife.[79]

Such written displays of emotion were common for Archie and
Phyllis during their periods of separation, but only for their eyes. The
Archibald Cox who reported to the solicitor general's office for a long
day's work, seven days a week, was serious, unflappable, at times
intimidating. He sat under the carved American walnut paneling, the
silver stars painted on the high ceiling, the gold-framed portraits of
bygone American statesmen, looking every bit like one of them. The
Archibald Cox who sat in a room each night, waiting for Phyllis to
arrive and his married life to resume, was something quite different.
"Perhaps absence does not make the heart grow fonder," he wrote on
July 31, 1961, anticipating Phyllis's arrival, "but if one is happy at
home, it surely makes you appreciate your blessings. And you are the
most important of mine." Archie described a trip he was envisioning:
"It would be lots of fun to go to Lake Placid together. And I like to
have a chance to show you off." For now, he had more concrete plans:
"I expect to telephone in a few minutes and hear your voice. All my
love goes to you, my darling. I adore you."[80]

By the spring of 1961, a group of black and white civil rights activists
known as the Freedom Riders were crisscrossing the South in a
multicolored Greyhound bus, challenging segregation in public facilities. This voyage culminated in a melee in Montgomery, Alabama. A
white mob shouting, "Get those niggers!" surged forward and attacked the bus. The *New York Times* reported that "at least twenty
people [were] beaten with clubs," and some of the riders were kicked
and punched. The attorney general was forced to deputize local
officials as special marshalls to bring the crowd to order.[81] John
Seigenthaler, RFK's administrative assistant on the scene, was beaten
over the head and hospitalized, bringing the sense of trouble even
closer to Washington.[82]

By the end of 1961, a string of sit-in cases keeping pace with the
Reverend Martin Luther King's movement across the South now
buffeted the courts, forcing the Justice Department to take a stand
and take it now. Arthur Schlesinger, Jr., recalled that President Kennedy was "rather irritated" by the Freedom Riders; they were causing
turmoil just as he was preparing for a critical trip to Vienna to meet

with the Soviet premier Nikita Khrushchev.[83] Bobby Kennedy viewed the Freedom Rides and other demonstrations as a "problem for the president," which made them a "problem" for himself. Still, RFK had a raw, natural sympathy for the protesters. When it came to Negro citizens being excluded from restaurants and theaters, he drew the line. Recalled Burke Marshall: "He'd always talk about how he would feel if it were his children being excluded from these places."[84]

The National Association for the Advancement of Colored People and prominent civil rights attorneys, including Jack Greenberg, advocated a sweeping new theory: All discrimination in restaurants and lunch counters, even discrimination by private citizens and establishments, should be treated as "state action" triggering the protections of the Fourteenth Amendment. First, restaurants opened themselves to the public; they were common carriers. Second, once the state was called in to enforce trespass laws that furthered private discrimination, that was a form of state action. The Supreme Court had used a similar approach to strike down racially restrictive covenants in *Shelley v. Kraemer*[85] in 1948, but had never extended the logic to other forms of private discrimination. Finding "state action" here admittedly went beyond existing constitutional law. But RFK favored the position. If Negroes could not eat at lunch counters, in RFK's mind, it was simply wrong; end of constitutional analysis.

Cox had trouble with this kind of broad state action theory. Although he felt sympathy for the civil rights protesters on a human level, he reminded himself that he was sworn to serve two masters. He was first an advocate for the Justice Department. Because of his special role as solicitor general, however, he also had a duty to protect the Court as an institution. It was not at all clear to Cox that this kind of a sweeping view of the Fourteenth Amendment would or should fly. Precedent had been flatly to the contrary for one hundred years, ever since the *Civil Rights Cases* in the 1880s. Even if those cases were bad law, distasteful law, was there any principled basis for the Court to disregard them now?

Cox remembered a little essay written by his old boss Learned Hand and Felix Frankfurter, back in the 1930s. They had warned that judges and lawyers should never substitute their own judgment for the will of the people, expressed through an orderly system of government. Otherwise, one person's notion of a "just result" might extinguish that of the collective society.[86]

Burke Marshall observed Cox's quandary: "He wanted, to the

extent he could professionally do so, to be on the side of the civil rights movement."[87] At the same time, Cox worried about the future of the American constitutional system if he pushed bad law on the Court and they bought it. A row of bookcases outside his office containing briefs filed by the solicitor general's office dating back countless administrations served as a visible reminder of the never-ending cycle of justice. As Learned Hand had put it: "To whom am I responsible?" If the Court went down the wrong path, it could permanently damage the notion of stare decisis, the rule that courts must follow their own precedent. It could open up a can of worms in areas having nothing to do with race discrimination, allowing the Constitution to reach private activity that was never within the vaguest intention of the original framers.[88]

Cox also privately worried about the practical effect of going as far as Bobby Kennedy and the NAACP wanted. Wouldn't restaurants, bars, and private businesses quickly find ways to get around such a broad interpretation of the amendment by hiring bouncers and "security guards" to enforce their own brand of "justice," allowing violence to replace government rule?[89]

Cox agonized. He wrote out a longhand Socratic dialogue between himself and an imaginary debater, attempting to hash out the "state action" question. On some nights he went to bed thinking, "Well, if I had to decide I'd decide that we couldn't say state action." On others, the debater convinced him to go in the opposite direction.

In the end, Cox decided that he would deal with the cases one by one. He would find a narrow ground, in each case, so that the United States could come down on the side of the sit-in demonstrators in good faith. He would not, however, take a position on the broader state action issue, "until we *had* to have one."[90] Just as he had written two letters to Ropes and Gray and Palmer and Dodge back in 1938, one accepting and one rejecting a job, Archie concluded, "The important thing is which letters I mailed. And up to that point, there was no need for a decision."[91]

Bobby Kennedy was becoming more and more impatient with Cox's strategy. His own philosophy for dealing with this or any other legal issue was "There was a problem. What do we do about the problem? Who does it? And when?"[92] RFK felt strongly that blacks had to be kept "believing in their government." He wanted an open show of government support for the sit-in demonstrators. Getting all tangled up in "the law of trespass and private property," as far as RFK was concerned, "was just wrong."[93] Cox's hypercautious approach was particularly irritating to RFK because Archie insisted on delivering it like a nit-picking professor. "He had to give you a lecture with whatever advice he gave you," Burke Marshall chuckled.[94]

Still, RFK respected, almost feared, Cox's intellect.[95] He understood that if he undercut the independence of the professor from Harvard, who was highly regarded by the Court, the integrity of the briefs and oral arguments flowing from the Justice Department to the Supreme Court would be jeopardized. He waited.

The trickle of sit-in cases grew to a swift flow by November 1962. Cox's office handled a clump of challenges involving eight thousand blacks who had attempted to eat at "white" lunch counters in North Carolina, South Carolina, Louisiana, and Alabama. They took another case involving Negro children who had attempted to ride a merry-go-round at the Glen Echo Amusement Park in Maryland.[96]

The *Glen Echo* case showed how cautiously Cox was treading. Five young blacks had been evicted for trespass because management had a policy "not to have colored people on the rides, or in the park." Jack Greenberg, the NAACP's lawyer, argued strenuously that this amounted to state action. The state's trespass laws had been invoked and *enforced* by private parties, did this not make the state of Maryland an indirect accomplice? Why should they not be dragged in and made to pay for this brand of overt discrimination?

Cox remained careful. The Fourteenth Amendment was not built for such private conduct. He looked for an opening. The security guard who had evicted the five young people was an off-duty sheriff's deputy from Montgomery County. He was still wearing his badge when he arrested the youths for trespass.[97] Cox stood before the Court and argued that these unique facts justified a finding of state action.

"What you are really saying," clarified Justice Brennan, "is that we ought to consider the *Glen Echo* case as if that badge had been worn by the manager of the park." "Precisely, precisely," Cox nodded.[98]

Cox was playing a waiting game. In Congress, there was talk of civil rights legislation, the kind that would outlaw private discrimination and render these court cases moot. If he could win minor victories on slim grounds until Congress acted, Cox could keep the vigil alive. Besides, it was not at all clear to Cox that he would win if he pushed the NAACP's position to the mat. He needed five votes on the Court to buy this kind of sweeping state action theory, and he did not see five votes right now. "If we went all or nothing," he said to himself, "it would have been nothing."[99]

Jack Greenberg was irate. He accused Cox of selling out to the bigots of America and acting like a "Frankfurterian." "If you believe your position," Greenberg fumed, "write it up for the *Harvard Law Review*. But now you're the Solicitor General of the United States, and it is the policy of the Kennedy Administration to oppose discrimination wherever it can."[100] Felix Frankfurter, on the other hand, charged that his former student was coddling the civil rights activists.[101] Cox was damned either way.

RFK continued to anguish in his red chair on the fifth floor of the Justice Department over the plodding course of his solicitor general. By late 1962, RFK was finding himself increasingly drawn into the civil rights turmoil, emotionally. His brother the president, more an "evolutionist" than a "revolutionist," reassured RFK that "this will take time." But as those close to the brothers saw it, "Bobby wanted it to take time right now."[102]

Ironically, Cox's cautious, dogged approach was earning him an increased standing inside the Supreme Court. In discussions among the justices and their clerks, Cox was being compared with the finest solicitors general in history. As Justice Byron White would explain after he joined the Court, "We could always rely on what he said. He didn't try to horse around."[103] Even within the Justice Department, Cox was developing a special status and credibility. Partly because he was older than most other lawyers in the department, and partly because of his close relationship with the president, he was viewed as a star player of the administration.[104]

Robert Kennedy decided to wait the solicitor general out.[105]

The sit-in cases finally came to a head in a case called *Bell v. Maryland*. Twelve Negro students had been arrested and convicted after engaging in a sit-in protest in a Baltimore restaurant.[106] The Court directly requested briefs on the state action issue.[107] Cox took a gamble. He argued that where trespass laws were invoked to prosecute sit-in demonstrators in states like Maryland that had been segregated for years by *law and custom,* state action existed in the narrowest sense.[108] But he went no further, much to the disappointment of the NAACP and the attorney general.[109]

When the opinion came down in *Bell,* the Court accepted Cox's theory by the slimmest majority, steering clear of the difficult state action controversy. But Justice Black's dissent in *Bell* tipped the Court's hand. It revealed that at least three justices would have voted squarely against a broad state action theory, and several others sat on the fence.[110] Had the issue been pushed in the direction that the NAACP wished, the voice of hindsight whispered, the sit-in demonstrators most likely would have lost.[111]

Before each oral argument Cox prepared diligently, treating each as if it were his most pressing appearance. He rehearsed in the office and on the banks of the old Chesapeake & Ohio Canal. "Walking is a very good way to stir up your mind." He used the time to ask himself, "What questions will I be asked? How will I answer them?"[112] Cox also wrote out a prepared script in longhand, on looseleaf tablets. "It wasn't that I was going to read the argument," he would explain. "It was the self-discipline. Writing it down was a way of getting phrases, sentences that would come, more or less, spontaneously to your mind during the argument."[113] No matter how many appearances he made in the Court's sanctuary, his adrenaline still flowed. Archie always woke up "in the wee hours of any morning I was going to argue a case," heart pumping and ready to pore over pages of notes.[114]

As for Phyllis, she faithfully took her seat in the VIP section at the front of the Supreme Court chambers, wearing a freshly ironed dress, hair neatly set, watching her husband in calm suspense. She never forgot a nightmare that Archie had told her about before one oral argument. He had dreamed that he appeared in the Supreme Court chambers wearing his swallowtail and nothing else underneath, other than his boxer shorts.

Before each argument Phyllis made it a point to ask, "Are you sure you have your pants on?"[115]

11

THE
LANDMARK
CASES

I t was routine for Cox to get to work by 8:00, before the secre-taries had arrived to plug in the coffeemaker. When the phone rang, Cox would pick it up and at times the president himself would be on the other end.[1] In June 1962, JFK called Cox after the Supreme Court handed down its controversial decision in *Engel v. Vitale,* banning prayer in public schools.[2] The president was stumped. "What should I say?" he asked Archie. How should he react to the decision?

"I gave a long, professorial answer that somewhat embarrassed me even as I gave it," Cox remembered. He finally told the president, "I'll try and get back to you or Ted Sorensen later in the day when I've thought of something more suitable." Before Cox ever pulled his thoughts together, the president had released a statement in response to the school prayer ban: "The lesson is that people should pray more at home."

Concluded Cox, "There's the difference between someone who has a real political instinct and a law professor."[3]

In labor matters, Cox was a natural person for JFK to consult. When a major wage-price controversy erupted in the steel industry in April 1962, after U.S. Steel Chairman Roger Blough announced hefty price increases that threatened to blow the lid off the government's inflation controls,[4] the president tracked Archie down as the solicitor general was on his way to deliver an address to the Arizona State Bar Association. Cox reached his motel in Tucson at nearly one o'clock in the morning. When he arrived, "the receptionist or night manager—whatever you want to say—was all agog. 'The president wants you to call him as soon as you get here.' I said, 'Oh, he can't really mean that. It's three o'clock in the morning back in Washington.'" The hotel clerk looked flustered. "'Yes he *does*. He was just on the phone himself ten minutes ago.'"

President Kennedy was wide awake. He told Cox that he would have him picked up in an Air Force plane and flown back to Washington as soon as his speech was over. Archie gave his talk the next morning, then he jetted back to participate in deliberations on the steel crisis. Several days later, after a blitz by the president and his makeshift circle of advisers, U.S. Steel rescinded the increase and the crisis was resolved.[5] Cox was a bit player in these White House excursions, but he enjoyed the bit. He found Kennedy to be just as sharp as during the labor legislation days—but there was something even more impressive about him now that he was president: "His carriage was a little more assured," said Cox.[6]

Cox also gave advice to the president during the crisis at the University of Mississippi. A black man named James Meredith had been blocked from enrolling at the Deep South university by Governor Ross Barnett in defiance of a federal court order. Bricks, guns, bottles, firebombs, gas grenades, and bullets from snipers shattered the tiny Oxford campus on a Sunday night in late September 1962. Deputy Attorney General Nick Katzenbach landed in Oxford on a Jetstar to personally take charge; the situation only worsened as the Mississippi state police withdrew and the riot "waxed and thrived through the night." Robert Kennedy finally made the tough decision to dispatch the 82nd and 101st Airborne Divisions, allowing a swarm of army helicopters to take over the night and quell the violence. This was the first time the Kennedy administration had been forced to call in federal troops to keep order.[7] By the time the smoke had lifted from the campus, three rioters had been killed and six U.S. marshals shot. Archie was summoned out of the Supreme Court by the president on the following morning, October 1. The question: What legal action could be taken against the law-defying governor?

The telephone conversation, recorded on a Dictabelt machine for the White House, revealed Cox and the president interacting in their standard fashion. An obviously harried President Kennedy was attempting to obtain legal advice, while an obviously harried Cox was anxious to get back into the Supreme Court. Archie answered "right" several times to the president's questions. He said "good-bye" and "thank you." Then he hung up the phone on the chief executive.[8]

"I couldn't imagine that I could be [so] abrupt to the president of the United States," he would later say. When he looked back on the conversation, he felt "greatly embarrassed."[9] But life in Washington moved quickly. It was not all the stuff of neat quotations and careful press releases.

There were other pinch-hitting assignments. Cox teamed up with Texas lawyer Leon Jaworski to supervise the prosecution of Governor Barnett for contempt of court after the James Meredith incident.[10] He was so impressed with Jaworski, who had risked his professional reputation by taking on such an unpopular case in the Deep South, that he broke his usual rule and split his argument time with Jaworski in the Supreme Court. (They won the case.) Archie also counseled the president in an odd controversy involving submerged oil-rich mounds of land in Louisiana, known as "mudlumps," that rose up along the Louisiana coast next to public lands. Who owned them? The president told Congressman Hale Boggs of Louisiana not to worry, "my lawyer" Archie Cox would figure it out.[11]

Some felt that RFK intentionally played on the fact that Archie prized his relationship with the president, and "over-recognized it." "The President would be very grateful," RFK would pose the task, "if you can handle these Louisiana oil problems."[12] But Robert Kennedy was savvy enough to understand that Cox had direct access to the president. He also knew how heavily his brother leaned on the solicitor general. In fact, the stories of Archie's extracurricular advice to the president became so widely known that Robert Kennedy enjoyed telling a self-deprecating story at Justice Department parties and gatherings: "The president called me, as attorney general," Robert Kennedy would relate, "and wanted an opinion of the attorney general on some legal question. So, the next day or two after I had studied it I called him back and said, 'My opinion is thus and so.' " "Well, is that just what *you* think?" the president would ask. His brother would reply, "It's the opinion of your *attorney general.*" To which the president would respond by screwing up his face and saying, with a heavy Boston accent, "Bobby, ask *Ahchie.*"[13]

The most daunting challenges that faced Cox as solicitor general did not come from his moonlighting trips to the White House, but from a wave of new cases hitting the Justice Department, with the word "Reapportionment" marked on their file jackets.

A person on the street in the early 1960s would never have expected that the reapportionment cases would be among the most revolutionary constitutional decisions of modern American history. They were so revolutionary, however, that Chief Justice Earl Warren would one day call them the most important decisions of his career, even more important than the landmark desegregation case of *Brown v. Board of Education*. Reapportionment meant redrawing district lines for congressional and state legislative seats across the United States, most of which had become shockingly unbalanced in terms of population by the middle of the twentieth century. It meant wrestling power away from entrenched rural legislators, who occupied districts created before the explosion of population in urban centers, yet insisted on clinging to seats containing relatively small numbers of constituents. It meant ensuring that each citizen's vote carried roughly the same weight in the voting booth—a basic right, it seemed, but one never mentioned explicitly in the Constitution.

Cox and Robert Kennedy once again started at opposite philosophical poles on this issue. RFK had managed his brother's national campaign; he understood how the imbalance in state legislative districts tended to hurt urban areas, prime Democratic turf. Cox, on the other hand, had read and reread Felix Frankfurter's 1946 opinion in *Colegrove v. Green,* suggesting that reapportionment raised "political questions," strictly off limits to the courts.[14]

In theory, the solicitor general was not unsympathetic to the notion that each citizen's vote should count equally. Archie understood that in many parts of the country, rural voters were dominating the legislatures and "cheating" urban voters out of votes by refusing to reapportion.[15] He knew that black citizens often bore the brunt of distorted election districts.[16] On the other hand, Cox was a legal realist. To walk into the Court in early 1962 and argue that the Fourteenth Amendment of the Constitution *required* states to create voting districts of equal sizes was suicidal. As he sized it up, "I would have lost maybe seven to two."[17]

A Tennessee case called *Baker v. Carr* still posed an interesting question. A group of Tennessee lawyers came to see Archie about it, arguing that the case was so "extreme" that the government should take a stand on it. One of the lawyers was John Jay Hooker of Nashville, barely thirty years old. He had worked for the Kennedy campaign and knew Cox slightly through that link. "Archie," Hooker said in his Southern drawl, putting his boots up on the desk and looking around the stately office, "you're doing a lot better than during the campaign." Cox gave a "wan smile." He listened to the Tennessee lawyers' pitch. Boots or not, the argument sounded compelling.[18]

The facts of *Baker* were unusually strong. Although a provision of the Tennessee constitution required the legislature to redistrict itself every ten years, a new apportionment scheme had not been adopted since 1910. Some urban districts contained twenty-five times the population of rural districts. In Cox's mind, this sort of gross disparity in voting districts pushed the Constitution far beyond its limits.[19] It made no sense to say that the Court did not have the *power* to examine state apportionment maps for this type of gross inequality, under the Fourteenth Amendment. Although the assumption had been that the Court had to stay out of the business of drawing state legislative maps, based upon the old "political questions" bugaboo, the extreme *Baker* case convinced Cox that this logic had gone too far. When it came to the more iffy question of pushing *strict* equality, "one person, one vote," Archie saw no reason to worry or take a stand. That issue was light-years away.[20]

Archie walked down the hall to tell Robert Kennedy that he had decided to file an amicus brief in *Baker*.[21] The attorney general swiveled around in his giant red leather chair.

"Are you going to win?" RFK shuffled some papers.

"No, I don't think so." Archie stood up straight. "But it will be a lot of fun."[22]

Baker v. Carr was one of those rare cases that found its way onto the Supreme Court's calendar twice. The first go-round, in April 1961, was relatively uneventful. Archie dodged the one-person-one-vote issue.[23] He also tried to dodge bullets from Felix Frankfurter, who was obviously outraged by the idea that federal courts should butt into state politics. It was a draw. The Court ordered the lawyers to prepare another round of briefs.

Shortly after the first *Baker* argument, Archie and Phyllis attended a formal dinner at the Anderson House in Washington. It was an elegant affair sponsored by the American Bar Association, in honor of the Supreme Court justices. Archie sat next to the wife of Justice Potter Stewart, who complimented the solicitor general on an excellent argument in *Baker*. Attempting to make a joke of it, Archie said in a high-pitched voice, loud enough to travel across the dinner table, "I wish that you would speak to the justice about that case, Mrs.

Stewart. Here we write our briefs and go up and argue the case as best we can in February. Come May, the Court says to come back and do it all over again in October. What kind of way is that to run the Court?"

There was polite laughter. A voice trumpeted back across the table: "Archie!" The entire room fell silent. It was Justice Felix Frankfurter. "Archie!" he repeated. "I will tell you why *Baker v. Carr* was set for reargument. When the case was reached in our conference, one of my colleagues said, 'The new solicitor general doesn't argue very well in [April], does he? Let's have him come back and see if he can do better in October.' "[24]

Frankfurter squinted through his spectacles. Several guests chuckled and went back to the meal, but Archie knew that his old professor was not joking. In his own way, he was scolding Cox for what he perceived to be an attempt to pry into the justices' thinking. There would be few jokes between them when it came to the Tennessee apportionment battle.

The man who represented a common bond between Cox and Frankfurter, Judge Learned Hand, died on August 18, 1961. When the news arrived, Archie was working on the second batch of briefs for *Baker v. Carr*.[25] Stories circulated back from Windsor that Judge Hand had been a fighter until the end. When an ambulance arrived to drive him from Cornish to the hospital in New York after one setback, he had insisted on riding in the front of the ambulance with the driver, wearing a neat brown business suit, while a distraught Mrs. Hand rode in the back.[26] Archie visited Frankfurter's home at 4:30 P.M. on August 25, to discuss preparing a tribute to Judge Hand.[27] The meeting was cordial. But the bonds that had sealed their relationship for three decades now seemed to be dissolving.

In September 1961, Phyllis finally moved into the house in Virginia. Archie found time for sporadic breaks: yardwork, a trip to Lake Placid with Phyllis (as he had daydreamed), a quick weekend excursion to Windsor to visit his mother.[28] For the most part, though, the Indian summer was consumed by reapportionment.

The second argument in *Baker v. Carr* was scheduled for October 9. It was a major event for the press in Washington. All eyes were on the Supreme Court. Would it take a swat at voting maps, and risk angering the states? Cox assumed that Justice Frankfurter "had spent all summer getting ready to tear him apart."[29] He knew that he had to hold his ground against his old professor, at all costs.

"What I'm going to try and do," Archie told himself, "is come out of the argument *even* with Felix Frankfurter. . . . If I come out *even*, there may well be a majority that wants to go our way. But they've got to be convinced that there is an acceptable intellectual rationalization for what they want to do in terms of the law."[30]

When Cox stood in the Supreme Court, the jitters that he had felt as a young lawyer came back with full force. The house was packed. Cox slowly cranked down the wooden lectern as far as it would go, so that he could simultaneously see the Court and read his notes. Nine sets of eyes watched him carefully from the bench.

The assistant attorney general from Tennessee, James Glasgow, shifted in his seat. He knew that the solicitor general held a "distinct psychological advantage" in any Supreme Court argument. He remembered Cox as "tall and thin," "erect," an "imposing figure" in his cutaway.[31] Yet the Tennessee lawyer, dressed in an ordinary blue suit, could not know that Archie felt less than imposing on this day.

Cox waited for the cue from Chief Justice Earl Warren and stood up straight. He began by reminding the justices that the decision in this case would "profoundly affect the course of government in many states."[32] If federal courts entered the world of reapportionment, it would mean that the bulk of the state legislative seats in the country would have to be scrapped as unconstitutional, completely redrawn. But the Court should not cower from difficult decisions. "Judicial inaction," Cox lectured the Court, "through excessive caution or a fancied impotence in the face of admitted wrong and crying necessity, might do our governmental system, including the judicial branch, still greater damage."[33]

Justice Frankfurter pounced on Cox and asked why it made any difference that Tennessee had violated its *own* constitution in failing to reapportion? Was not that piece of Tennessee's "history" irrelevant in federal court? Did it not underscore the fact that this was a question for the state and its own elected officials?

Cox answered: "One could infer from that that this hasn't been done rationally. That's what it boils down to."

Frankfurter shot back: "History very often isn't rational."

Cox defended himself: "Well, perhaps where it's entirely irrational the results don't conform to the Fourteenth Amendment."[34]

Cox now battled back by attempting to draw a sharp line between

Frankfurter's opinion in *Colegrove* and this blatant instance of malapportionment in Tennessee. Chief Justice Warren nodded his head. Some of the other justices seemed to be swaying. Justice Charles Evans Whittaker jumped into the fray to aid Cox: "Even if you couldn't tell the legislature exactly what to do, does that mean you can't tell them that what they're doing is *wrong?*"

The question was a slow pitch down the middle. "Of course not," Cox answered reflexively. He could see the Court moving in his direction intellectually. Frankfurter sat silent, writhing in his chair.

When reporters jumped up to wire out their stories on this first day of the Court's new session, Cox felt disoriented. Unsure of what he had done. He remembered walking out of the marble Supreme Court building, kissing Phyllis and her mother, who had traveled from California to see her son-in-law argue in the Supreme Court. He remembered walking back to the office along Pennsylvania Avenue in his formal coat and striped pants to clear his head, and being struck by an ungodly fear that "maybe I was going to win."

"And I remember it was a lovely October day. I remember walking the mile back down to the Department of Justice in all of my finery, alone and sort of saying to myself, 'Young man, what have you done now?' Because I respected and still respect Felix Frankfurter and his views. It doesn't mean I think they were always right, but it meant that if you were in sharp disagreement, it was something to worry about."[35]

What Cox worried about most of all was the long-term good of the Court. The preservation of precedent for the sake of a more enduring constitutional principle. Was he betraying the Court, as an institution, by telling the justices that they could meddle with state politics? Archie had watched Learned Hand, a close friend and soul mate of Frankfurter's, anguish over these same issues. Hand was a firm believer in continuity. He felt "duty bound" to follow Supreme Court precedent, even when he clearly abhorred it.[36] "I wrap my head in my toga, like your friend, G. J. Caesar," Hand wrote in one district court opinion, "and fall before the daggers of ruthless men who do not understand the force of reason."[37] Did Cox not have a similar duty, to caution the Court against ignoring precedent that had steered them away from "political questions" for over a century?

On March 26, 1962, the Supreme Court handed down its decision in *Baker v. Carr,* holding that state legislative maps across America were subject to constitutional review under the Fourteenth Amendment. The vote was six to two, not even close.[38] Only two dissenters took issue with the majority. One was Justice John Harlan. The second was Justice Felix Frankfurter.

Burke Marshall, head of RFK's Civil Rights Division, was present in the courtroom for the reading of the decision that day; he was struck by the "vigor and vehemence" with which Frankfurter delivered his dissent from the bench.[39] "For a Court watcher," Marshall explained, summing up the powerful aftershock of the ruling, "the clear implication of *Baker v. Carr* was that every state legislature in the country was unconstitutional."[40] Anthony Lewis, writing for the *New York Times,* called *Baker* a "landmark case," a "historic decision" that represented "a sharp departure from the court's traditional reluctance to get into questions of fairness in legislative districting."[41]

For Cox, still tormented over his role in the victory, the full impact of *Baker* was summed up in one unexpected trip to the Supreme Court, which he rarely spoke about. It was the same week that *Baker v. Carr* was handed down. Archie had read in the morning paper that Justice Whittaker had notified the president that he was retiring because of "physical exhaustion"; he had not even participated in the vote on *Baker*.[42] Cox scribbled a brief note to Whittaker "telling him how sorry I was. And saying that I was sure he'd be far too busy to have time to talk to me before he left Washington. . . . But that, if he had a moment, it would be a pleasure to call."[43]

The messenger had barely returned from the Supreme Court building after delivering Cox's message when Justice Whittaker's secretary telephoned and "invited me to come right up and see him."[44] Archie buttoned his coat, called a government car, and hurried over to the sweeping marble edifice on Constitution and Pennsylvania Avenues. Inside the chambers, he found Whittaker in a "state of emotional tension that made him very talkative."[45] The justice launched into a soliloquy on *Baker v. Carr,* confessing, in effect, "It just about killed me . . . I couldn't make up my mind."

Although he had not been assigned the opinion, Whittaker confided that he had written relentlessly. Full opinions, back and forth. First on one side, then the other. He just could not make up his mind. He had followed along with Cox's logic at oral argument. But Frankfurter's position was sound, wasn't it?—the Court wasn't designed to deal with apportioning legislatures! *Baker v. Carr* had nearly torn him apart, leading to his physical and mental deterioration, leading to his resignation.

Archie quietly said farewell. He buttoned his coat and summoned the government car back to his office. The justice's mental and physical condition made Archie feel inexplicably sad, almost guilty.

After the trip to see Justice Whittaker, there was another encounter with Justice Frankfurter that Archie did not like to talk about, that gnawed at him. In April 1962, just a month after *Baker* was decided, Frankfurter's secretary had found the justice on the floor of his Supreme Court chambers. He had had a stroke. Shortly afterward Archie saw him. "He wasn't able to speak very clearly. He was weak. He was in a wheelchair. But he said something that conveyed in substance the message that it had been *Baker v. Carr* that had been responsible for the breakdown in his health. And it seemed to me . . . that somehow he linked some of that responsibility to me."[46]

The political aftershock flowing from the *Baker* case was still too mysterious to gauge.[47] Word came down from Ted Sorensen and the "Kennedys" in the White House, including Sargent Shriver and Steven Smith, that the concept of voting equality should now be pushed one step further by the Justice Department. It was time, they said, to embrace "one person, one vote."

There were exactly two openings on the Supreme Court during the truncated Kennedy presidency. Byron White's surprise appointment came when Justice Whittaker resigned abruptly in March 1962. While many other names had been floated, Cox himself had pushed the nomination of William Hastie, a black judge on the Third Circuit. RFK rejected the suggestion, saying, "Well, [Justice] Bill Douglas tells me he'd be another vote for Frankfurter so he won't do."[48] Byron White's name soon emerged. He was an insider, an attractive All-American football star who had gone to Yale Law School, played professionally for the old Pittsburgh Pirates (as they were then called) and Detroit Lions football teams, headed "Citizens for Kennedy" during the election, and was a first-rate legal mind. He also "had an ulcer," according to Burke Marshall, and wanted to get out of the political front lines in the Justice Department.[49] Byron White was a comfortable choice; he easily gained confirmation as the eighty-third associate justice of the Supreme Court.

The Coxes were invited to an elegant dinner party at the Anderson House, at which Phyllis was the partner of the newest justice as men escorted women into the dining room. They stood at the top of the

Archibald Cox, Sr. (left), took over his father's law office in New York City's Woolworth Building in 1900. With such a legacy, Cox's oldest son always expected to practice law. Archie was studying at Harvard College when his father died, leaving his mother, Frances (below, center), to finish raising their seven children: (from left) Archie, Louis, Max, Molly, Rowland, Betty, and Rob.

In the St. Paul's School class of 1930, Archie Cox stood out for both scholarship and student activities (below). While in law school Archie met Phyllis Ames, a lively young woman from a family of distinguished legal scholars. They married on June 12, 1937 (opposite), with his college friend Teddy Chase as best man and niece Fanny Perkins as flower girl.

Barclay Cooke

YALE   635 PARK AVE., PATERSON, N. J.
('24-'30) D.; H.; Simpson House Supervisor; Chest Committee '25; Flag Bearer; Lawn Tennis Association; Choir '24; Second Testimonial '28; Delphian Football '29; Delphian Hockey '29, Captain '30; Delphian Baseball '29, '30; Delphian Tennis '29, Captain '30; S. P. S. Hockey '29, '30.

Archibald Cox, Jr.

HARVARD   PLAINFIELD, N. J.
('26-'30) I.; S.; Sixth Form Councillor; Executive Committee of Missionary Society; Vice President of Cadmean Literary Society; Library Association; Dramatic Club; Scientific Association; Propylean Literary Society; Lawn Tennis Association; Squash Committee; Foster House Supervisor; Acolyte; Camp Councillor; Chapel Warden; Hugh Camp Cup; S. P. S. Debating Team '30; Second Testimonial '27, '28; First Testimonial '29, '30; Phi Beta Kappa Squad; Keep Prize in English History; Isthmian Football '29; Isthmian Baseball '29, '30; Isthmian Tennis '29, Captain '30; Isthmian Squash '29, '30; S. P. S. Tennis '30; *Magna Cum Laude.*

Benedict Crowell, Jr.

YALE   2187 OVERLOOK RD., CLEVELAND, OHIO
('26-'30) I.; H.; Concordian Literary Society; Missionary Society; Choir; Glee Club; Second Testimonial '28.

Archie and Phyllis spent their honeymoon in Europe, including several days punting on the Thames (above). Back in New York awaited a clerkship with legendary federal judge Learned Hand (right).

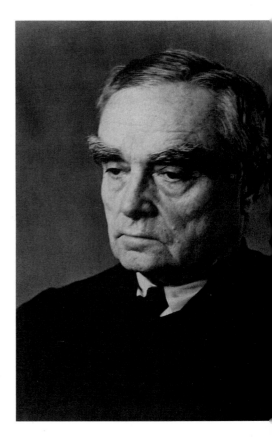

After four years in Washington during World War II, Cox accepted a faculty position at Harvard Law School (above; Cox is in back row, wearing bow tie). His specialty was labor law, and he was often called to arbitrate labor disputes, requiring investigative trips like this ride to Milwaukee in a locomotive engine cabin (below).

Professor Cox returned to Washington in 1952 to chair the Wage Stabilization Board, settling disputes between the nation's largest unions and corporations. For the first time he attracted national attention, such as this cartoon about his confrontation with United Mineworkers leader John L. Lewis, drawn by Gib Crockett for the *Washington Star*. Cox's service ended unhappily: he resigned in protest after President Harry Truman overruled the board and acceded to Lewis's demands.

k in Massachusetts, Archie and Phyllis
e raising a busy family: Sarah, young
hie, and young Phyllis (above). Another
nber of the Cox household, allowed in
kitchen only, was pony Mrs. Gregor
ht, with young Phyllis).

Senator John F. Kennedy asked Cox to advise him on labor issues, then to assemble and lead a group of academic researchers and speech writers ("the Brain Trust") for the 1960 presidential race. Another favor for the candidate: Cox sat with Jacqueline Kennedy (then pregnant with son John, Jr.) during her husband's televised debate with Richard Nixon. Cox joked that men often asked him to accompany their wives because he posed no threat.

sweeping marble staircase, where Justice White took Phyllis's arm. "It's a long way from Buffalo, Wyoming, to this," White whispered in his gruff voice.[50] Together, they walked down the steps under the glistening chandelier.

A second unexpected vacancy occurred on the Court when Felix Frankfurter stepped down in August 1962 after suffering his devastating stroke. The president strongly favored Paul Freund, who was still the nation's preeminent constitutional scholar. But Robert Kennedy reminded his brother that Freund had turned down the solicitor generalship; why should he be rewarded for such a lack of commitment? In private meetings, Robert Kennedy strongly pushed Cox for the vacancy. Edward M. Kennedy, the youngest of the brothers, recalled that RFK "admired the power of [Cox's] ideas."[51] He had worked faithfully in the campaign. Who better to symbolize the Kennedy administration on the bench?[52] As RFK himself told an oral historian in 1964, "I mean, the logical person would be, if you're going to appoint him, would be to appoint Archie Cox."[53]

The idea appealed to the president. But if he was not going to offer the post to Freund, who was in a class by himself, he felt that he had made a commitment to his secretary of labor, Arthur Goldberg, when he had offered Goldberg the cabinet post. Goldberg should be put on the Court first. Cox would follow. There would be plenty more appointments to come.[54]

Both the White House and the attorney general wanted to get behind "one person, one vote" with all of their political muscle in the next string of reapportionment cases listed on the Court's docket. Robert Kennedy was in a bind, however. The solicitor general seemed to be digging in against it. It was one thing, in Cox's mind, for him to argue that the Court had jurisdiction to hear reapportionment challenges under the Fourteenth Amendment. It was another thing to leap to the proposition that every state in the Union was required to follow *strict numerical equality* in drawing its voting districts; that was going too far.

Cox was consumed by the same doubts and fears, ironically, that had led Justice Frankfurter to dissent in *Baker*. "It didn't fit with history. It didn't fit with the federal structure. It didn't fit with the history of England. It didn't fit with anything."[55]

Cox could not lend his pen to the betrayal. He firmly believed that his job "was to protect the Court from itself."[56] The solicitor general made up his mind. He would not sign his name to any brief that embraced the one-person-one-vote principle, at least not until he was *forced* to take a concrete position. If the White House or the attorney general forced him to take a stand prematurely, Cox resolved, he would have only two choices: "Either to do it or to leave."[57]

Robert Kennedy was at times a dreamer, an idealist, but always a man of action. He could visualize "one person, one vote" in his mind's eye. It was good for the country. It was good for the Democrats politically, gearing up for the 1964 election. Yet he had no intention of forcing his solicitor general into a box. He had to proceed cautiously. Some accounts would later suggest that there was an orchestrated plan to cajole Cox into "coming around" on the reapportionment issue,[58] but none of those closest to Cox or to RFK would see it in such simplistic terms. Burke Marshall, who dealt extensively with both men, remembered that "Robert Kennedy's view was that he would not even *consider* imposing his own view on the solicitor general. He had to come to that on his own, or not at all."[59]

There were plenty of external forces pressing down on Cox. Long before he had become president, John F. Kennedy had written an article for the *New York Times Magazine* about the evils of malapportionment.[60] Now he personally conveyed the message, through his White House staff, that he was interested in these cases. The president should remain consistent, should he not? And wasn't it inevitable that the Court would have to resolve the problem, anyway? In the twenty months following *Baker,* scads of states had redistricted and lawsuits had been filed in thirty-nine states to clean up lopsided apportionment maps.[61] Cases had inched their way to the Supreme Court from New York, Alabama, Colorado, Maryland, Virginia, and Delaware, as well as federal congressional cases from Georgia and New York.[62] In the Alabama case, legislative districts had drifted into horribly unequal sizes; there had been no reapportionment in that state since 1900. Senators representing as few as 19.4 percent of the citizens controlled the Alabama Senate, a blatant dilution of voting strength.[63] The one-person-one-vote issue was ripe for political picking. The president was behind it.

A flurry of paperwork swept through Archie's office and made its way to the attorney general's desk, then onward to the White House. One of Cox's brightest assistants, Bruce Terris, wrote a long memo to the solicitor general, virtually pleading that Cox embrace the one-person-one-vote position in the round of Supreme Court briefs about to be written. Terris, a thirty-year-old Harvard lawyer known for his strong pro-civil-rights views, wrote with passion to the solicitor general: "The subject of this memorandum is of enormous importance. I doubt whether even the sit-in cases are of equal significance as the state apportionment cases." He put it on the line with Cox: "It is generally accepted, and I am sure the Court agrees, that we carried the brunt of persuading the Court to decide *Baker v. Carr* as it did."[64] Terris concluded urgently: "I think that it would be a tragedy if the great victory in *Baker v. Carr* were thrown away by our persuading the Supreme Court to accept a weak substantive standard."[65]

Cox was unmoved. In a "state constitutional convention," Cox wrote tersely in a memo to the attorney general, his vote might go the other way. But it was not the job of the solicitor general to coax the Court into rewriting the Constitution by "judicial decree." Freedom for the states to establish their own forms of government lay at the heart of American democracy.[66] The government should take a "low-key" approach, should try to knock off the most extreme reapportionment maps presented to the Court, such as Alabama's. Cox nevertheless felt strongly that the Justice Department should steer away from "one person, one vote" as a mandatory constitutional rule.[67]

Cox delivered his memo to Robert Kennedy. Several lawyers from the Civil Rights Division smuggled a copy of Terris's memo to their boss, Harold Greene of the Appellate Division, expressing "strong agreement" with Terris's position. Rural areas were being grossly overrepresented on state apportionment maps so incumbent politicians could cling to power. "We do not see why such inanimate factors as land or cows should be represented in a legislature," they effused in support of the one-person-one-vote position.[68] Bobby Kennedy shipped a copy of Terris's memo to the White House.[69] It was a complicated game of chess, among players theoretically on the same team.

As the Court's 1963 fall term swiftly approached, a meeting was set up between RFK, Burke Marshall, Ted Sorensen (who in Cox's eyes had matured greatly since the campaign days), Sargent Shriver, Steven Smith, Kenneth O'Donnell, Larry O'Brien, Bruce Terris, and Cox. The White House and the attorney general had decided to "persuade" Cox.[70] According to one version of this unusual gathering, Archie launched into a twenty-minute exposition in support of his reapportionment position. RFK poured himself a noisy glass of orange juice, then "drummed his hands on his desk and played with his tie." Finally, RFK blurted out, "Archie—isn't the real issue should some people's vote count more than other people's vote?" At this point the meeting unraveled and was adjourned.[71]

Cox agreed to go forward with the Alabama case, *Reynolds v. Sims,* but only with an understanding that he would split the difference.[72] He would argue that the Alabama districting scheme was a "crazy quilt," "irrational." At the same time, he would steer far wide of the one-person-one-vote minefield.[73] Since there were two new Kennedy appointees on the Court, Archie realized this might begin to tilt the balance in favor of the White House position. But who could predict how Justices White and Goldberg would vote? And wasn't the proper question what position the U.S. Department of Justice should take, in good conscience?[74] *Reynolds v. Sims* would one day become a landmark in the history books, although it was certainly through no plan of the solicitor general. He was too busy worrying about an obscure Colorado case on the horizon, *Lucas v. 44th General Assembly of Colorado,* which was his worst legal nightmare.

A heavy February snow blanketed Washington. Cox was tortured by the Colorado case. In 1962, the citizens of that state had overwhelmingly approved a referendum requiring the statehouse to be apportioned based strictly on population, but allowing other factors (geography, municipal boundaries, etc.) to be taken into account in drawing state Senatorial districts. This plan did not achieve perfect numerical equality; 3.6 times as many people lived in the most populous Senate district compared to the least populous district. But it was hardly horrendous. How could anyone say it was undemocratic? The voters themselves had approved it.

Cox was in a bind. He had no personal quarrel with this Colorado plan. But if the solicitor general did not actively oppose it, he might undercut the Kennedy administration, including the president who had appointed him.

Cox wrote a desperate memo to the attorney general, giving him five reasons that they should stay out of the Colorado case, some of them almost alarmist.[75] If the Supreme Court actually accepted the one-person-one-vote rule, he warned, it might trigger "a severe constitutional crisis" requiring federal troops to be called in if states like Colorado defied the Supreme Court. "Are we then to use troops to remake the state legislature," wrote Cox, "or will we ignore the defiance because the country supports it?" In twenty or thirty years the country might be ready for "one person, one vote." In 1964, however, Cox felt strongly that it would be a disaster.

Cox attached his memo to an opposing one by Bruce Terris. He delivered them both to Robert Kennedy, writing bluntly, "You know, I believe, how very strongly I feel about this view."[76] He could not stand before the Court and argue against one hundred years of constitutional history, simply because "the president wants it."[77]

Another meeting was scheduled with the White House. Archie assembled his papers and walked grimly past the secretaries. In the alcove beyond the reception room, he ran into Burke Marshall just exiting the private elevator that creaked its way between floors. Marshall, whom Archie still knew as "little Burkie" from Plainfield days, stood silently at the doorway. He was a "retiring, shy," ultraprofessional lawyer, for whom Archie had great respect. Although he was a "frail-looking" man of forty, with a "soft, creaky voice," he possessed a great "inner assurance."[78] Marshall said to Archie, "You've got us in an impossible situation. The attorney general can't say no to the one-person-one-vote people, and he equally can't instruct you to file a brief you don't believe in."[79]

Cox had already thought about his damnable position. He personally believed that the one-person-one-vote notion had some appeal. It was not a perfect solution, but it was a legitimate attempt by the Kennedy administration to solve a serious problem. At the same time, once Archie eliminated his feelings of "what do I like?" and "what do I feel is a good political solution?" he was left with a nagging question: How did he justify telling the Court that the Fourteenth Amendment *required* mathematical equality in voting districts? The entire history of the United States pointed in the opposite direction. "And history's a part of law," Cox reminded himself.[80] Was Cox supposed to transform himself into a self-appointed policy maker, and trade precedent for personal preference? Was he not supposed to be the guardian of something more important?

Marshall was still standing in front of the elevator. He understood what was troubling Cox: "He [Cox] knew perfectly well that his position would be very persuasive. It might be conclusive on which way the Court went. And so he was concerned about his responsibility to the Court. . . ."[81]

Archie finally scratched at his graying crew cut. He said that he could write a brief that supported the plaintiffs in the Colorado case, but only if he could argue the simpler point that the Colorado Senate districts were so far apart numerically that they were "irrational" under the Fourteenth Amendment. It would be the same argument he had made in the Alabama cases. It was a bit of a stretch, but he could do it.[82]

Marshall walked down the fifth floor corridor, past portraits of old attorneys general, past frescoes painted for the Work Projects Administration of the Great Depression, into the huge walnut-paneled office. He reported to the attorney general that the standoff was over. The White House advisers heaved a sigh of relief; they knew that RFK would never have overruled Cox. "I think the attorney general thought that that was not possible," Marshall said bluntly.[83] The Supreme Court would have understood that the "respected legal scholar" was being overruled by the "very political brother of the president," which would have spelled disaster.[84] At the same time, Cox realized that within the structure of the Justice Department, he had certain duties to reach practical solutions, apart from his obligations to the Court.[85]

Several paragraphs were changed in the government's brief. Cox and RFK arranged a "truce." They established ground rules, deciding what Cox would say at oral argument in response to questions from the justices so that the Court would not interpret Cox's answers to signal *opposition* to "one person, one vote." "It was a question of working out language which would satisfy [Archie's] own conscience," Robert Kennedy recalled before his death, "and yet . . . cover what I felt should be the position of the United States government."[86]

On June 15, 1964, the Supreme Court rolled six reapportionment cases into one and handed down its historic decision in *Reynolds v. Sims*, taking the name of the Alabama challenge that Cox had argued. *Reynolds* easily embraced the one-person-one-vote standard that Cox had been so reluctant to push, holding that rough numerical equality was required in both houses of the state legislature if the guarantee of equal protection was to be met. Chief Justice Earl Warren, the author of the unanimous opinion, wrote in fluid prose that sounded much like the early memo from the Civil Rights Division lawyers: "Legislators represent people, not trees or acres."

Anthony Lewis, who was seated at a tiny press desk below the justices' bench, remembered it as a "remarkable day."[87] The *Times* reporter jotted a note to Cox and slid it along the counsel table: "How does it feel to be present at the second American Constitutional Convention?" Cox scribbled back, "It feels awful."[88] Ironically, the chief justice's law clerk would later inform Cox that the historic one-person-one-vote opinion had drawn heavily from the solicitor general's brief. "I felt," Cox would sum up his misgivings, "that the Court wouldn't buy 'one person, one vote'—and if the Court bought it, the country wouldn't buy it. . . . It's been plain to me now for some years that I was all wrong."[89]

It was important, however, that Cox allow the Court to make its own break with precedent, if the shifting winds of history coaxed it in that direction.

In the troublesome world of civil rights, Cox observed the attorney general and his brother in the White House entering a period of transformation. Since the beginning of the Kennedy presidency, the White House and RFK had attempted to stay "one step ahead" of the civil rights movement. To restore blacks to the political process, the Kennedys focused on getting them registered to vote and ending illicit voting practices in the South. The Kennedys preferred this to the uncertain task of pushing legislation through Congress. RFK believed, almost unrealistically at times, that if Negro citizens could be injected into the political mainstream, many of their problems would vanish.[90] He would insist, "Isn't it best that we attempt that before we try to seek legislation?"[91]

For Robert Kennedy, ending discrimination in America was first and foremost a "moral" issue. Whites and blacks had to learn "to accept each other as brothers."[92] On the other hand, civil rights lawyers like Thurgood Marshall were tired of the missionary work of converting whites on a moral plane. The long-awaited hundredth anniversary of the Emancipation Proclamation was arriving in 1963, and still blacks faced the disturbing realization that "they were not, in fact, free."[93]

Early on, the Kennedy administration had adopted a tactic of attempting to combat discrimination through executive action, making halfhearted attempts to deal with urban problems, segregation in transportation, and housing inequities.[94] By the middle of 1963, however, this approach could be rated a colossal failure. In part, this was an inevitable result of the president's style. "The Kennedy I came to know was cautious to the point of timidity," said one adviser. "He always tested the ice first. He was very loathe to risk political capital."[95]

The unmistakable transformation began to occur, Cox and others in the Justice Department observed, when stepped-up civil rights protests unexpectedly brought pictures of brutality onto the front pages of newspapers and television screens: the Oxford, Mississippi, crisis involving James Meredith; the atrocities of Police Commissioner Bull Connor in Birmingham, Alabama; the murder of NAACP leader Medgar Evars in Jackson, Mississippi.[96] The final straw was the bombing of a small black church in Birmingham on September 15, 1963. That explosion blew out stained-glass windows and killed four little girls as they attended Sunday school class, having just sat through a lesson entitled "The Love That Forgives."

"When those four young girls were blown up," said presidential adviser Dave Powers soberly, "that was it."[97]

In February 1963, President Kennedy had proposed sweeping voting rights legislation that would end the most flagrant types of discrimination against blacks.[98] In June, after the race riots in Alabama, the voting rights provisions were rolled into a broader bill that would prohibit racial discrimination in places of public accommodations like restaurants, hotels, and lunch counters. It was a bold attempt to enact sweeping changes to the nation's civil rights laws.[99]

Cox played a small role at this stage of the stop-start work on civil rights reform. He publicly defended the proposed voting rights legislation, saying that its constitutionality "is not really open to serious doubt."[100] He appeared on the *Today Show* to put in a plug for the Civil Rights Act of 1963, and stood behind the attorney general in declaring the urgent necessity of its passage.[101] But real progress was erratic.[102] Congress was taking its cues from the American public, which remained skeptical.

On November 20, 1963, Robert F. Kennedy attended his annual birthday party in the Justice Department. Close friends, family, and coworkers crammed into the long, stately office. Those present recalled that the thirty-eight-year-old attorney general was particularly "down in the dumps" on this afternoon, almost cynical. Friends and advisers raised their glasses to drink a toast. Many of them were dressed to attend a formal judicial reception at the White House that evening, after which the president would host another birthday party for his younger brother before leaving for Texas the next day.

Spontaneously, RFK hopped onto his desk, a large wooden piece the size of a "freight car" that had been a gift from his wife, Ethel. As Assistant Attorney General Ramsey Clark described the scene, Bobby Kennedy took on a "self-mocking tone." He was sarcastic or despondent or both. Standing between the murals of "Justice Triumphant" and "Justice Defeated," RFK launched into an ironic speech about "how good he was for the president, how good his civil rights work had been for the president, how much organized labor loved him, how much the steel industry loved him."[103]

Many in the room knew that RFK had almost reached the bursting point. Nick Katzenbach explained, "I think that Bobby was concerned that he hadn't taken as much pressure off the president as he wanted to take off the president. The demonstrations kept going on, and the legislation was going to take forever."[104] Many of these friends understood the subtext of this unhappy oration: They did not expect RFK to continue as attorney general in a second Kennedy administration. "I don't think he [RFK] expected it at all," said Burke Marshall.[105]

RFK was thinking about the State Department. Ever since the Bay of Pigs and the Cuban Missile Crisis, he had developed an interest in international affairs. "Obviously, [JFK] couldn't replace Dean Rusk," aides knew. But Bobby might at least become undersecretary of state.[106] Other listeners, like Ramsey Clark, concluded that RFK might leave to run the 1964 campaign, although this seemed like a step backward.[107]

After RFK climbed down from the desk and disappeared with his wife, Ethel, Cox and Clark left the birthday party. It was time to get freshened up and take a car over to the White House. They walked down the long hallway, past the law library where staff attorneys labored under a tall lamp topped by a rearing Pegasus. Archie said in a flat tone, "I think Bob was telling us that he won't be around much longer. I think he won't be around till Christmas."[108]

Archibald Cox and Robert Kennedy had together produced many of the landmark Supreme Court decisions that had come to symbolize the Kennedy administration. Their relationship drew its vitality from their polar approaches. It was a relationship that had warmed greatly as the Kennedy Justice Department matured. Cox had introduced RFK to the Supreme Court in February of their first year, giving the fatherly advice that "a cutaway and striped trousers are de rigueur."[109] He helped the younger attorney general prepare for his first and only Supreme Court appearance in *Gray v. Sanders,* a congressional reapportionment case in which Kennedy was described by the press as looking like a "nervous and uncomfortable bridegroom."[110] Cox was well pleased after sitting in the Supreme Court gallery with an expectant clutch of Kennedys watching the oral argument. As he would assess RFK's performance, if it were any other young lawyer making his first appearance before the Court, "Well, I'd be glad to send the young man up again."[111]

Cox observed in Robert Kennedy an unusual ability to touch others through acts of kindness. At times, the solicitor general found himself on the receiving end of this special quality. Archie would never forget the day in 1962 that he delivered a speech at the Harvard Commencement. He and Phyllis were celebrating their twenty-fifty anniversary; it was their son's college graduation. How could it be a more special day? Cox's speech, cleared by the White House, advocated that U.S. government lawyers should be given a voice in resolving pivotal wage and price battles to avoid protracted strikes.[112] The solicitor general stood in the gleaming sun of Harvard Yard with his six-foot, seven-inch son dressed in cap and gown, savoring the moment. Later that day the stock market dropped like a brick. Business leaders were in a "tizzy": Cox should not have been talking about government intervention when the president had just given a speech at Yale extolling the benefits of a "free economy" in which business and labor unions freely worked out their differences.[113]

White House Press Secretary Pierre Salinger took a swipe at Cox's speech; he issued a statement that Cox was "not authorized" to issue pronouncements on behalf of the president regarding federal labor policy. This public drubbing stunned Cox. He was "hurting a little bit." After returning to Washington, Archie took a long walk along the canal near his home, trying to calm himself. He wrote to Phyllis back in Boston: "I guess my speech really made quite a stir. . . ." He nevertheless believed that it was "sheer folly to blame the decline in the stock market upon it."[114]

At work, Archie dragged himself down the hall to confide in Robert Kennedy, who knew perfectly well that the speech had been cleared. RFK pounded the desk. "Why, that's outrageous," he fumed. "You're not supposed to be making political judgments anyway, that isn't why we have you here." RFK ordered his car and drove over to the White House, where he immediately "put a stop to this."[115] For Cox, it was but one example of Robert Kennedy's nature as "an awfully compassionate, warm-hearted fellow."[116]

Cox remembered another day at the height of the Cuban Missile Crisis, when his sister Molly was visiting from New York. Molly was staying at the Coxes' rented cottage in McLean, not far from Robert Kennedy's estate. It was one of the ugliest days of the crisis, in which the entire nation seemed gripped in a silent fear. Molly was taking a walk down the road when she heard a horse gallop by. It stopped. Came back. The rider was Robert Kennedy. "You're Archie Cox's sister, aren't you?" "Yes." "Well, I just came back to tell you we think it's going to be all right." And then he went on.[117]

"So we live and learn," Cox would later say, referring to his early displeasure with Robert Kennedy's appointment as attorney general. "Whatever my initial feeling, it wasn't my final feeling."[118]

By 1963, Cox was widely regarded as one of the finest solicitors general in history. Some called him "the Willie Mays of Supreme Court lawyers."[119] He had argued more cases in that Court than had any other lawyer of his era, more than anyone since presidential candidate John W. Davis of the 1920s. He had a dazzling won-lost record, especially in critical civil rights cases.

Cox was certainly aware that more than one solicitor general had been appointed to the Supreme Court over the course of American history. He remembered a dinner party that he and Phyllis had attended when Byron White was named to the bench in 1962. Justice Stanley Reed, himself a former solicitor general, had sat next to Phyllis and chatted away. When they were driving home, Phyllis had told Archie, "Justice Reed said he had hoped that you might some day go to the Court and that not a few solicitors general had been appointed. But that the pendulum swung toward a man just once and, if it swung away without reaching him, then he would never get it."[120]

The pendulum, by late 1963, seemed to be swinging directly in Cox's direction. Chief Justice Earl Warren and Justice Hugo Black were over seventy years old. Justices Tom Clark, William O. Douglas, and John Harlan were all in their sixties. There would certainly be a retirement, or death, before long. In fact, Arthur Schlesinger, Jr., had discussed the matter directly with the president. "Had Kennedy lived," said Schlesinger, "he would have appointed [Cox] to the Supreme Court. He had it on his mind."[121]

12

NEW
PRESIDENT

On November 21, 1963, President Kennedy unsuccessfully attempted to reach Cox's home by telephone, at 5:35 P.M. White House logs indicate that President Kennedy succeeded in reaching him at 6:43 P.M., "at request [of] A.G." Cox would be unable to recall why the president called, or what they discussed. At the time, it was a perfectly unmemorable event. But it would turn out to be, according to White House telephone records, the last call that John F. Kennedy would ever make from the White House.[1]

On November 22, Cox was standing in the hall outside his office when the assistant attorney general, Ramsey Clark, came rushing up from the second floor on the private elevator. Clark's face was colorless. He had received word from Dallas that the president had been shot, badly wounded. "Maybe even critically wounded."[2] He and Archie hurried down the fifth floor corridor, past the gold-framed portraits, past the law library through the archway marked "Attorney General." The red leather chair was empty. Robert Kennedy was out of the building. Had someone reached him? There was an interminable period of waiting.

Archie sat by the phone back in his own office. The entire Justice Department building ceased moving; nobody touched a phone for fear of impeding the flow of news. They listened on radios or watched hastily hooked-up television sets. Finally the unthinkable was announced.

The "impact, the blow, the shock" of the news that the president had died were impossible to describe, as Cox later pieced it together. It was difficult for Archie to digest that an assassination had really taken place and "to separate out the president from the personal side."[3]

Hugh Sidey, a *Time* magazine journalist traveling with the president, spoke as an observer: "I heard the shots. I was in the first press bus, and I heard those, and there was that stirring inside, you know. They were sounds that could have been backfires, but you weren't quite sure. And then you saw the hysterical scene, the people on the ground and all, and then you knew something was wrong."[4]

The machinery of government faltered momentarily, as America fell into a state of shock. Then it ground on. Hugh Sidey expressed the incongruity:

> Once this kind of skipped heartbeat of the government caught itself again, then the thing just went on. There had to be the oath of office; life went on. And somehow you just wanted to stop. You didn't want to do anything; you didn't want to write; you didn't want to do anything. It was so kind of grubby—not grubby but it was so inconsequential, the place and the time and the whole thing. I could never get used to that, being told by the priest that the president was dead on a curbing of a kind of homely building in Dallas, Texas, of all places, on a hot day. There weren't even many people around, and there was still traffic on the street. . . . I never could get used to that; I probably never will.[5]

The president was pronounced dead at 2:00 P.M. eastern time. Burke Marshall received an urgent call at 4:20 P.M. from Judge Thurgood Marshall in New York, one of the first blacks named to the federal bench, appointed by president Kennedy. Was the assassination engineered by anti-civil-rights groups? They attempted to sort out the meaning, the sense of it.[6]

Cox's official diary for November 23, 1963, had only a single line: "Paid respects to the President." A cold, dark line of mourners waited to kneel, to bless themselves, at the Lincoln catafalque in the Capitol Rotunda where the president's closed coffin was displayed.[7] The funeral Mass at St. Matthew's Cathedral in Washington, the funeral procession through the streets of Washington to Arlington National Cemetery, which Archie watched anonymously from the Mayflower Hotel, were all a blur.[8]

On November 24, Cox handwrote a letter to Robert F. Kennedy on his solicitor general's stationery:

Dear Bob,

There are no words for such occasions. I write this note only to say that in this time of our country's loss of a great leader, the thoughts of Phyllis and myself are also with you in your loss of a brother. May God aid you.

Sincerely,

Archie[9]

The Department of Justice faltered like an incandescent light, then surged forward. Burke Marshall dictated bland memos to the attorney general dealing with routine office matters, not permitting himself to register that Robert Kennedy's mind was still fixed at the gravesite at Arlington National Cemetery, burying his brother the president.[10] Archie returned to work on Tuesday the twenty-sixth, attending meetings on a case involving Boeing Aircraft.[11] Outside his window the flag flew at half-mast.

For months, Robert Kennedy was depressed and disoriented. The grief-stricken attorney general took time off for a quiet trip to Florida.[12] He took his family skiing in Colorado.[13] When he sporadically appeared in the office for "an hour or two" he was "pale, subdued almost to the point of numbness."[14] His absences grew longer. Without official pronouncement or publicity, Deputy Attorney General Nick Katzenbach silently took over the office.

Shortly after Katzenbach took charge, he approached Cox with an unusual piece of news: President Johnson had decided that Chief Justice Earl Warren should head up a commission to investigate the assassination of President Kennedy. In fact, Katzenbach himself had devised the plan and convinced the president to implement it.[15] There were "all kinds of rumors," at the time, "scary ones," as Cox knew.[16] Lee Harvey Oswald, the alleged assassin, was shot dead in the basement of the Dallas police headquarters by a man named Jack Ruby on Sunday, November 24, as the nation sank deeper into panic. Was it a Soviet conspiracy? Or perhaps it was Fidel Castro. Oswald had been spotted recently at the Cuban Embassy in Mexico City, accepting money. Some implicated the Federal Bureau of Investigation or the Central Intelligence Agency in JFK's murder; others pointed to Lyndon Johnson himself.

Katzenbach wanted Cox's help in approaching Earl Warren on the president's behalf.[17] At six feet, two inches tall and 215 pounds,

Katzenbach could be persuasive. Having taught at the University of Chicago, he understood the mind of a law professor. He leaned against the desk and appealed to Archie's sense of duty. The solicitor general was "the normal channel to deal with the chief justice of the Supreme Court." Archie had the closest relationship to the Court, particularly to Chief Justice Earl Warren, of any individual in the administration. Since the president wanted Katzenbach to approach the chief justice and persuade him to head this "Assassination Commission," he gently pushed Cox, didn't Archie want to come along?[18]

Cox was unsure, unenthusiastic. "I don't think he ought to do it," he told Katzenbach. "I'm happy to come along because that is the nature of the SG's office. But I really can't help to persuade him to do it because I don't think he ought to do it."[19]

There was no precedent in American history for such a commission. Cox was well aware that Justice Owen Roberts had headed the investigation into the bombing of Pearl Harbor and (in Cox's mind) had been away from the Supreme Court far too long. He also remembered that Justice Robert Jackson had ventured off to lead the prosecution in the Nuremberg trials after World War II. Jackson's absence and the high political visibility of the task had ultimately been "terrible for the Court."[20]

Cox did not want to be responsible for prodding a sitting justice, much less the chief justice of the United States, to take on such a high-profile job. Engaging in these types of nonjudicial matters, Cox felt, would inevitably "rub off on the Court and impair its legitimacy."[21] At the same time, Archie realized that the kind of commission that Katzenbach envisioned might be good for the country, to calm the panic. He was torn.[22]

Katzenbach's appointment log for Friday, November 29, recorded numerous calls and meetings between the acting attorney general and the solicitor general.[23] Cox eventually told Katzenbach, "I won't undercut you. But I'm really not going to attempt to persuade." Although the whole plan rubbed him the wrong way, Cox reluctantly agreed, "I'll come along anyway."[24]

The meeting with Chief Justice Earl Warren, the barrel-chested former governor of California, was brief and polite. In response to Katzenbach's urging that he head the unusual commission, the chief justice shook his head no. He somberly recited all the reasons that Cox had already spelled out to Katzenbach.[25] The deputy attorney general and solicitor general rose from their chairs and thanked the chief justice for his time.

The next day, word came down that Earl Warren had accepted the position. "By hearsay," explained Cox, "I have it that LBJ got the chief down to the White House that night—I think Abe Fortas was there . . . [and LBJ] told the chief that we would have an atomic war with Russia unless he did it. The chief felt he didn't have any choice and agreed to do it."[26]

Robert Kennedy returned to the Justice Department in early 1964 after taking a trip around the world at the urging of friends. He walked around the Washington Mall with Burke Marshall and told him that "he was going to stay in the Department, for a while at least."[27]

RFK regained a lackluster interest in his former passions—organized crime and civil rights, including the last few reapportionment cases. His energy level was low, halfhearted. "I would have to say," Burke Marshall remembered, "that I don't think he ever really recovered his interest in the Justice Department."[28] RFK spent time looking at haunting letters on his desk, including one from Anne Riley, an eight-year-old girl whose younger sister had been run over by a car and killed while the two of them walked to school. "Try not to feel bad," the girl had written to the attorney general. "My mother told me in May when Beth died that some people are special and God needs them to help him in heaven. Please dont look so sad in your pictures cause you always smilled happy before."[29] RFK wrote back to Anne Riley: "I shall pray for you and Beth and I hope that you will pray for my brother and me."[30]

Entries in telephone journals showed that RFK was attending far fewer Justice Department meetings and spending far more time at impromptu family gatherings to discuss a fledgling plan to establish a special library—somewhere—to house the papers that would preserve the memory of his brother's truncated presidency. An occasional message appeared on his desk after several months of seclusion, which gave him a brief jolt of purpose: "Jackie would like to have dinner and go to the movies with you this evening."[31]

LBJ attempted to draw RFK into several projects after the assassination. But Bobby was moody and "rebuffed" the advances. RFK was interested in only one job, the vice presidency, as a way of preserving the soul of his brother's administration. There were thousands of the people who had "come into government" because of his brother. He had to keep them above water and deliver on the promises of the Kennedy administration. The vice presidency was one way to do it.

President Johnson "scoffed" at the idea, in Burke Marshall's words.[32] In a thinly veiled move to exclude RFK from the running, LBJ announced that no member of the cabinet would be eligible for the vice presidency. Rumors flew that President Johnson had attempted to have the Secret Service surreptitiously record the conversation when he broke the news to RFK. The story went that Johnson had called in the head of the Secret Service and said, "Now, I want every word of this conversation recorded. I don't trust him. I've got to be sure it's recorded right. You put in your best recording equipment. I don't want the attorney general to know about it, but put it in." The equipment was installed. Bobby Kennedy entered the new president's office in the White House for his meeting and placed his briefcase on the table as they talked. President Johnson made it clear that the younger Kennedy would not be his choice for vice president, now or ever. As soon as RFK left, LBJ called in the Secret Service and boomed, "Play me the tape back, play me the tape back. Make sure this is right." The tape was replayed—beep, beep!—and the machine did nothing but emit high-pitched noises. LBJ "flew into one of his rages, which was something of a rage according to all reports," at which time the Secret Service agent said, "Sir, that's the noise characteristic of someone who's brought in a *de*bugging device."

LBJ thundered, "Why, that little son of a bitch doesn't trust *me!*"[33]

This ugly climate could not continue. There was talk of making RFK ambassador to Vietnam, to get him out of the administration and out of the United States. RFK considered various options: teaching, a college presidency, becoming a newspaper publisher or editor, heading a foundation.[34] Finally, he left the Justice Department on September 3, 1964, accepting the encouragement of a growing national constituency to run for the U.S. Senate in New York. He joked that he knew so little about New York that he carried around a little book describing the state's history for easy reference.[35] The game plan was clear: he would launch his own run for the presidency in 1972, when President Johnson would have to vacate the office.

Archie found himself preoccupied during this uncomfortable period of transition. One day at lunchtime he walked into a sign on the street and slashed his head.[36] Another day he was mowing a wet lawn at home and cut off the tip of his middle finger on his right hand, because "I stupidly tried to clean grass out while it was still going."[37] His mind was on other things, as a new president with new priorities took over the White House.

Staff members crammed into the Great Hall, across the fountain-sprayed plaza of the Justice Department, to witness the departure of the sixty-fourth attorney general of the United States. Archie and other colleagues delivered tributes to their young boss, the last symbol of an ambitious administration that had been far too brief. There were plenty of going-away presents exchanged that day. One of them would remain in the Cox home for years, carefully stored in a dry corner of the basement. It was a large framed photograph of Robert F. Kennedy—his official portrait as attorney general—dressed in a crisp suit and striped tie, hair combed neatly (an unusual sight) to one side. RFK handed the portrait to his solicitor general before the farewell gathering broke up, scribbling a one-sentence message at the base of the picture in indelible pen: "For Archie Cox, with the appreciation and admiration of a friend—and a brother of a friend."[38]

The Kennedy administration had never established a precise "blueprint" on civil rights strategy. It had evolved on its own with the unpredictable marches, protests, and violent Southern riots in the early years of the 1960s.[39]

In October 1963, Nick Katzenbach had flown to an Army–Air Force football game with Senate Majority Leader Everett Dirksen and brought home an optimistic report that he conveyed directly to the president: Senator Dirksen had promised that the administration's civil rights bill would come up for a vote in the Senate, soon. "I think the President was pleased," Katzenbach remembered.[40] Victories would have to be slow and incremental. The mood of Congress would have to be massaged, until it was gradually changed.

After the assassination of President Kennedy, Congress's mood did change, quickly and powerfully. The Civil Rights Act of 1964 and the Voting Rights Act of 1965 allowed John F. Kennedy to accomplish more in death, ironically, than he had ever accomplished during his lifetime when it came to the broiling issue of civil rights.

Cox now became a major operator in the Justice Department machinery that would grind out fresh civil rights legislation. This legislation would finally resolve the nagging "state action" question that had dogged Cox since the earliest sit-in cases; he had a personal interest in seeing it done right.[41] If Congress itself enacted civil rights laws that applied to purely private conduct, and did so with a firm constitutional base, Archie's worries about overruling one hundred years of Court precedent would become moot. The Supreme Court could then extend its rulings to reach private conduct, including the unfair treatment of sit-in demonstrators, without any problem.

The diciest question of strategy was this: Should the crucial "public accommodations" section of the new Civil Rights Act outlawing discrimination in restaurants, motels, movie theaters, and so forth, be grounded on the commerce clause (Article 1, Section 8) of the Constitution? Or should it be hinged directly on the power of Congress to enforce the equal protection clause contained in the Fourteenth Amendment? Robert Kennedy and most prominent civil rights lawyers of the day believed that the Fourteenth Amendment provided a broader, more satisfying base.[42] The subject had even been raised with President Kennedy before his death; he himself had preferred the Fourteenth Amendment for political reasons. JFK thought that FDR had hooked so much legislation onto the commerce clause during the New Deal, that the Republicans "just never forgot it."[43] The Fourteenth Amendment was a much safer bet.

But Cox did not like this plan. He spelled out his reasons for Robert Kennedy. To find that Congress had power to act under the Fourteenth Amendment when it came to private discrimination, according to Cox, the Court would still have to overrule its nettlesome opinion in the *Civil Rights Cases* of 1883. Bad law, some might argue. But established law and precedent, nonetheless. "And here my philosophy about the role of judges and the prestige of the Court, the legitimacy of the Court's decisions, did play an important part," Cox remembered.[44]

The commerce clause, for Cox, provided a much neater solution. Based upon an old line of National Labor Relations Board cases that Cox knew from his labor days, plus the standard post–New Deal decisions of the Supreme Court, Cox felt that the Court could easily uphold broad civil rights legislation. It would be duty-bound to accept Congress's determination that a particular industry "affected" interstate commerce, unless Congress had made an "irrational" decision on this score. For Cox, it was "as easy as rolling off a log" for the Supreme Court.[45]

In October 1964, a packed Supreme Court heard Solicitor General Cox argue *Heart of Atlanta Motel* and *Katzenbach v. McClung*, two blockbuster cases that would determine the fate of the new Civil Rights Act. Moreton M. Rolleston, Jr., a prominent Georgia attorney, was retained to oppose the government on behalf of the posh Heart of Atlanta Motel. Rolleston's view of Cox was not flattering: "He was a typical Harvard Law School man who thinks they're better than everyone else in the world," said Rolleston.[46] The Atlanta lawyer was particularly miffed when he received a copy of the government's brief and realized that the solicitor general had hinged his argument on the commerce clause. It was dirty pool, in his view. Most people in the South, and most people in the country at that time, as Rolleston saw it, "still believed in segregation and supported it." Whether it was right or wrong, it was fact. If the government wanted to argue the issue fair and square, he felt, it should rely directly on the Fourteenth Amendment and force the Court to deal with its old *Civil Rights Cases* head-on. When Rolleston saw the commerce clause injected as a convenient hook, he felt hornswoggled.

The hornswoggling worked. The Supreme Court unanimously upheld the Civil Rights Act of 1964, hanging its hat primarily on the commerce clause.[47]

In January 1965, President Johnson had announced in his State of the Union address that he would send a refurbished Voting Rights Act to Congress,[48] but there was no concrete bill on the table other than bits of old Kennedy legislation. In February, Nick Katzenbach personally asked Cox to prepare a draft of a new voting rights law. It was "not at all common" for a solicitor general to sully his hands in this kind of work.[49] But Cox had experience in writing statutes from his Landrum-Griffin days. Who better than the solicitor general to construct a piece of legislation that would withstand constitutional attack in the Supreme Court?[50]

By the end of the month, Cox had turned in a rough sketch of a seven-part bill. It was a masterstroke, Katzenbach remembered thinking as he read over the proposal. The United States would be permitted to *presume* that literacy tests and other suspicious devices were intended to discriminate against blacks if the state had a history of keeping minorities from polling places, as determined by recent voting statistics.[51] This would place the burden on the *states* to justify practices that discriminated against blacks, instead of dumping the responsibility on individual plaintiffs who typically had slim financial resources and poor access to lawyers.[52] Technically, reliance upon voting statistics had nothing to do with the bill's constitutionality. They nevertheless pointed the finger at the offending states in a politically attractive way. "It was less offensive to talk about it in terms of statistics than it was in terms of discrimination," explained Katzenbach.[53] It was much easier to tell a Southern governor that voting practices had to be changed because of percentages, rather than because of gross misconduct. Said Ramsey Clark, who had become deputy attorney general, "It was really a neat piece of legislative imagination and statesmanship. It provided what we needed."[54]

Revised drafts of the bill were churned out by Katzenbach, Harold Greene in the Appellate Division, and Burke Marshall.[55] Cox continued to make revisions, laboring over the voting rights bill until he was shut off. Katzenbach had learned this trick in dealing with Cox's Supreme Court briefs. "He loved to edit," Katzenbach said deadpan. "I had to stop Archie on his editing page proofs. It cost too much money."[56]

A brand new piece of legislation finally pushed its way through the House Judiciary Committee in March 1965. It contained Cox's original "switched presumption," which became the heart of the Voting Rights Act of 1965.[57] Although Cox would never claim credit for this work, Katzenbach was specific in his recollection. "He drafted the damn thing," Katzenbach chuckled.[58]

Archibald Cox began work on the brief in *South Carolina v. Katzenbach,* which would successfully defend the voting rights legislation in the Supreme Court. Although he did not yet know it, when Cox would walk into the chambers of the Court to present this argument, he would no longer hold office in the Johnson administration.

By 1965, Cox's reputation as a Supreme Court oral advocate had placed him in an elite class. Lincoln Caplan would later call him one of the "three most respected Solicitors General" in American history, along with Robert Jackson and John W. Davis.[59] Cox had personally prevailed in over 80 percent of the cases he had argued before the Supreme Court, and his office had won 87.7 percent of the cases in which the government was amicus, many of them important civil rights victories.[60] It was Cox's extraordinary versatility, however, that put him in a class by himself.

He argued labor matters, his old expertise, with a special flair,[61] often lecturing the justices like "nine law students."[62] He prevailed in *Arizona v. California,* a complex case dealing with western water rights and the Colorado River that filled an entire room in the Supreme Court with briefs and led to the longest oral argument (a full week) in modern American history.[63] "He was the perfect picture of a solicitor general," recalled David B. Currie, then a Supreme Court clerk and later a professor at the University of Chicago Law School. "Tall and elegant. Nobody ever wore a long coat better than he."[64]

Cox handled a tough battle involving the application of the Atomic Energy Commission to build a nuclear reactor thirty miles from Detroit. The lower court viewed the reactor as a threat, as if it were a nuclear bomb. "You could practically hear it ticking in the opinion," Cox remembered. Cox concluded that if *he* could understand the reactor, in presenting the government's case, he could convince the Court that it was controllable and safe. After meeting with physicists at Argonne National Laboratories, he entered the Supreme Court on the day of the oral argument carrying a scale model of the nuclear reactor.[65] Cox spent most of his allotted time "disassembling the thing and showing how it worked." One law clerk remembered, "The chief justice was enthralled."[66] The U.S. government won the case, seven to two.

One of Cox's most legendary performances came in a giant antitrust case, *St. Regis Paper Co. v. U.S.,* in which he was not convinced that the independent government agency that he represented, the Federal Trade Commission, had a defensible position. But he did not want to undercut his client's argument. So the solicitor general stepped up to the lectern in the Supreme Court and argued both sides of the case. Justice Felix Frankfurter, then still on the Court, demanded to know why his old student could not work out the problem within the Justice Department before showing up for oral argument.

"Oh, Mr. Justice," Cox answered, "if the dispute were only inside the Justice Department, I'm sure I could settle it."[67]

If a case was an important one, whether it dealt with tax or antitrust or the most arcane area of agency law, Cox delivered the argument himself. Law clerks lined up along the wall between the large, white marble columns to watch him in action. Charles Nessen, who clerked for Justice Harlan in 1965 and went on to teach at Harvard Law School, remembered Cox's style as deadly and precise. Rather than stating his own case first, and "letting the justices poke holes in it," Cox would "flip the tables" by "stating his opponent's case very accurately." By the time Cox had shifted to his own argument, the justices would be leaning out of their chairs wondering, "Well, how's he going to do it?"[68]

Phil Heymann, who clerked for Justice Harlan before moving to the solicitor general's office under Cox, recalled the highly structured nature of his arguments. Cox would typically begin by telling the justices, "I am going to discuss three points." Invariably, he stuck to his promise. Archie took the younger Heymann aside after one argument and told him the secret: "You should always say you have three points. If you have only two in mind, a third will come to you."[69]

Cox loved his job. When not in Washington, he was giving speeches around the country or traveling abroad as a U.S. dignitary. He flew to England to study the British court system.[70] In India, he met with Indira Gandhi.[71] Back home, he gave a speech to thirty-five hundred spectators at the Masonic Temple in Detroit, on the same platform as entertainer Dinah Shore. Archie joked to Phyllis: "The arrangement is that if they will come and stay through my speech, then they will get to hear Dinah Shore put on the Chevrolet song."[72]

Everything about the solicitor general's job was perfect. Cox enjoyed working for Nick Katzenbach. But there was one hitch.

Archie still felt a nagging obligation, a certain sense of pride, that told him to submit a letter of resignation to President Johnson once LBJ's own term began in 1965. His feelings were a bit hurt that Johnson had never acknowledged his existence, let alone brought him into his own circle of advisers. On inauguration day, Archie sat in his office by himself, working on a brief.[73] His closeness with President Kennedy had spoiled him, perhaps, and made it less palatable to work for LBJ in such a distant capacity. "There were no personal overtures made to him to make him feel wanted, . . ." observed Ralph Spritzer, Cox's first assistant. There were plenty of hangers-on in the Johnson administration, but Cox did not like the idea of being one of them. "Well, you weren't there because the president wanted you there. You were there because you had been on the spot and he didn't think he ought to fire you."[74] A resignation letter would allow the president to decide if he wanted to appoint his own solicitor general or make it clear that he wanted Cox to stay.[75]

Part of Archie's ambivalent feelings at this time was also based upon the realization that he had been in Washington for four and one-half years. He asked himself, "Isn't it time to go home? Home being partly back to New England and home being partly

Harvard."[76] If President Johnson really wanted him to stay, "it was very easy for him to say so."

Nick Katzenbach strongly opposed Cox's plan; Archie should leave well enough alone. "I kept trying to talk Archie out of writing that letter to LBJ. I was afraid that what happened would happen. I was quite sure that he [could] stay on and everything would be fine."[77]

Whether Cox actually believed that the president would accept his letter of resignation is unclear. He certainly understood his own stature and enjoyed his position of strength. The glamour and importance of Washington were alluring. There would most likely be seven more years of a Johnson presidency. Perhaps another shot at the Supreme Court. Cox had met with Chief Justice Earl Warren in his chambers just months earlier, and the chief justice had confided that JFK "had plans" for him on the Court, before the president had been assassinated.[78]

Nevertheless, Cox sat down at his desk on Friday, June 25, and dutifully wrote out a letter to be delivered to the president. Cox's diary indicates that the attorney general promised to deliver "a letter" to LBJ as soon as the Coxes left for their much-awaited vacation. The next day, Archie and Phyllis loaded up their pickup truck, with horse in trailer, and proceeded to the yellow farmhouse on the coast of Maine. Two weeks later the phone rang at Bucks Harbor. It was Nick Katzenbach. President Johnson had accepted the resignation.[79]

"I think it came as a complete shock to Archie," his assistant Phil Heymann said candidly. "But he took it with complete grace."[80] On July 13, Archie's secretary wrote in his official diary: "A black day! . . . Official announcement made of resignation . . ."[81]

President Johnson issued a press statement stating that "personal affairs" had prompted Cox to give up his post, a true loss to the department. In Cox's place, President Johnson announced the appointment of Thurgood Marshall as solicitor general, the first black man ever to serve in that office. It was a good choice, as far as Archie was concerned, an excellent appointment. But Cox's proudest stint in public service, as "celestial general," was now over.[82]

Friends, well-wishers, and staff crammed into the Carlton Hotel on July 29, hosting a farewell party for the solicitor general. Justice Hugo Black, in brief remarks, stated that Cox had distinguished himself as a true "lawyer of the people of the United States." Robert Kennedy told his famous "ask Ahchie" story on himself. First Assistant Ralph Spritzer offered praise: "There is only one word that describes Archie

Cox. That is rectitude." Many heads nodded. The speakers presented Archie with a bound volume of his oral arguments, which he would keep on his shelf for the rest of his life.[83]

"I think [Cox] was very unhappy," said Katzenbach. "He loved that job. God, anybody in their right mind would."[84]

The next day, Friday the thirtieth, Phyllis and Archie set off for Maine a second time in their pickup truck. This time, there was no return date.

The *Washington Post*, in reporting Cox's exodus as solicitor general, wrote a glowing editorial: "Mr. Cox filled the office with extraordinary devotion, learning, effectiveness and style. Even in comparison with a succession of most able predecessors, his performance must be rated as genuinely brilliant."[85]

John W. Douglas, an assistant attorney general under RFK, wrote to Cox: "You have left a large, gaping hole in the Department."[86] Chief Justice Earl Warren scribbled a note after returning from a trip out west, sending it air mail: "I was both non-plussed and made unhappy by the news. Why you were not reappointed to that or a higher position is something I do not believe I will ever understand." The chief justice continued somewhat sourly, "I hope that you will someday return to the service of the government in some capacity that will bring into play to the fullest extent your great capabilities and your devotion to the cause of Justice. And when and if you do return I am confident that you will be rewarded with more than ingratitude."[87]

Harold J. Gallagher, of the prestigious New York firm of Willkie, Farr, Gallagher et al., mailed a seductive letter about career options. "I was glad to learn that you had not yet made definite plans for the future," Gallagher wrote, suggesting that a lucrative position in private practice might be a mutually attractive possibility.[88] The *Boston Globe* envisioned something quite different for Cox, suggesting that "President Johnson, who has named Federal Judge Thurgood Marshall to succeed Mr. Cox, would do well to appoint the latter to one of the existing vacancies on the court of appeals in Boston."[89]

Senator Robert F. Kennedy stood on the floor of the Capitol where his brother had once extolled Archie's work on labor legislation, and delivered a tribute for the *Congressional Record* on July 13, 1965: "Everyone who knows Archibald Cox feels that his resignation today marks in a special way the turning of a page in [history]. . . ." Senator

Kennedy added, "He is a wise and trusted counselor, and a steadfast friend.

"There have been many great Solicitors General . . . Stanley Reed, Robert Jackson, Charles Fahy, and Simon Sobeloff. To that great roll is now added the name of Archibald Cox. . . . He has earned the respect and gratitude of all [the nation's] citizens."[90]

Only one tribute meant more to Archie. It arrived by mail several days later, from Windsor, Vermont.

> Dearest Darling Bill—
>
> Just a note to tell you my heart and mind are filled with thoughts of you, and of [what] all this change means to you. I know you love Washington, all your work there, and it is hard for you to leave that position you have filled with such success—and great integrity. The ups and downs of life are strange and pleasant and painful, but through it all, the longer I live the surer I am that if one can say dispassionately 'I have given of my best,' that is all that counts. I know you can say this, and will always be able to.
>
> You know how I both love and admire you in every way—One's child is always one's child no matter how old one grows—so surely let me know how the future shapes itself. And when you get back from Washington just rest and [enjoy life] with Phyllis.
>
> All my love,
>
> Mamma

The *Boston Globe* was not far off in its prediction. Even before Archie drafted his resignation letter to President Johnson, a vacancy had developed on the First Circuit Court of Appeals, the federal appeals court that covered Massachusetts and Maine. Archie was quietly hopeful that he might have a shot at this federal appointment. His old mentor Charlie Wyzanski had been strongly pushing his name behind the scenes. By late 1964 Cox had already written privately to Wyzanski: "I am more inclined now than I was last spring to think of leaving Washington, and therefore somewhat more inclined to accept a judgeship if one were offered."[91] In November 1964 Cox again wrote to Wyzanski after learning more concretely of the vacancy on the First Circuit: "I am anxious to get the vacancy [underlining the word himself] and while I cannot bring myself to put on a campaign, I shall not be coy about it."[92]

Nick Katzenbach strongly pushed Cox's nomination in discussions with President Johnson. Although the seat was not slated to go to Massachusetts this time, Katzenbach argued, Archie's connections to Maine were close enough for him to be a legitimate nominee from that state. Even AFL-CIO leader George Meany, who had once uttered "God save us from our friends" in reacting to Cox's work on JFK's labor bill, had written a letter to President Johnson, strongly endorsing Cox's appointment.[93]

Archie, on the other hand, was not particularly built for politicking. In the final months of his solicitor generalship, while an army of would-be nominees and friends of potential nominees were busy blitzing their senators on the phone, Archie sat at his desk overlooking Constitution Avenue, finishing his work. In the end, Senator Edmund Muskie secured the nomination of Frank Coffin, former congressman from Maine and one of Cox's former students at Harvard Law School, to fill the vacancy on the First Circuit. Cox returned to Harvard, with a quick appointment as Visiting Professor to commence immediately. The pendulum of history had swung away from Cox. It would never swing back.

Nick Katzenbach cursed the horrible timing. All of this could have been avoided, he felt strongly, if Cox had held back his resignation letter to LBJ. "He was the most principled man I ever met," Katzenbach said of Cox. "He was also a bit stubborn."[94] If Cox had remained in the solicitor general's office, Katzenbach had it figured out, President Johnson would have had a powerful incentive for appointing Cox to the First Circuit, if Johnson wanted to name his own solicitor general. A little political muscle and jockeying would have been enough to turn the tide of Cox's life. "He could have traded [his job] for the court," said Katzenbach frankly.

It was not in Cox's nature to open up doors that way, however. "I respected him," Katzenbach said, nodding his bald head. "That's how he did things."[95]

There was no further discussion of Cox for a position on the First Circuit during the Johnson presidency. Nor was there any serious mention that Cox might be named to the Supreme Court. Phil Heymann summed up Cox's fortunes: "Whatever prospect there would have been of [an appointment to the Supreme Court] died when Jack Kennedy died in 1963."[96]

If fame could be visualized as a towering ladder to the stars of one's profession, Archibald Cox could now be viewed as securely perched on fame's second rung—largely by choice—losing his final chance to scale to the top. But Archie himself would choose to look at his failure to reach the federal bench in 1965 in a far more positive light. "It worked out for much the best," he would smile, opening and closing one hand reflexively. "On the whole, I've had a much more satisfying and exciting life than I would have had otherwise."

13

<hr>

STUDENT

RIOTS

After moving out of the "celestial" quarters of the solicitor general's office, Archibald Cox had every intention of resuming a quiet perch in academia. American university campuses, however, were no longer the serene places Cox had known before he left. The late 1960s would now throw Cox into the most difficult role of his career, even more agonizing on a personal level than the Watergate ordeal that was waiting around the bend. Few people outside the ivy-covered walls of Harvard, however, would ever know about this chapter of his life.

Cox had allowed himself a brief weaning period from government work. Nick Katzenbach asked the former solicitor general to ghost-write the brief in *South Carolina v. Katzenbach,* which established once and for all the constitutionality of the Voting Rights Act of 1965. Katzenbach personally argued the case as attorney general; Cox joined in the oral argument as a "Special Assistant Attorney General" from Massachusetts.[1] After a swift victory in that case, Cox found himself handling *Shapiro v. Thompson,* arguing that welfare recipients had the right to receive benefits after they moved from one state to another. John Douglas, a young friend from the Justice Department, congratulated Cox on what turned out to be another landmark victory: "Nice going on the welfare-residency decision," he wrote from Washington. "Isn't it about time for you to lose a case up there?"[2]

Cox did all of this work without pay. He submitted a bill to Neighborhood Legal Services in Washington for $474.78 to cover his expenses in the welfare case, but added a note: "I think you should knock the hotel bill down to some considerably more modest figure, even though I did use the sitting room to do a good deal of work."[3] Cox saw it as "one of the duties of a member of the bar" to accept pro bono work. Besides, when it came to an important constitutional case, Archie's philosophy was simple: "Who needs to be compensated for a case in the Supreme Court of the United States?"[4]

Cox also accepted a few assignments from Robert F. Kennedy, after the new senator had settled into his job and begun the slow transformation into a presidential candidate. Cox consulted with RFK on the New York Transit strike of 1966 and other issues, mostly labor related.[5] Archie's feeling about Robert Kennedy's candidacy and a potential position in a new Kennedy administration were "if asked then we'll see. I was well disposed."[6]

Back in Masssachusetts, Cox even dabbled in statewide politics. He helped arrange a press conference and breakfast at the Harvard Faculty Club in October 1966 for an old student, Elliot Richardson, who was leaving his post as lieutenant governor to run for state attorney general. Richardson wrote to his old professor after a victory in November: "I'm deeply grateful to you not only for your confidence in me but your willingness to express it so emphatically and so publicly. It's great to have you back in this area and I look forward to seeing much more of you in the months ahead."[7]

For the most part, however, Cox was moving away from politics, away from government, away from the marble edifice of the Supreme Court, and back into academics. In 1965 he was named the first Samuel Williston Professor of Law, a prestigious endowed chair.[8] He taught Constitutional Law, loving it. "I think his experience in the solicitor general's office was an important one," assessed Derek Bok, Cox's younger colleague who had become dean of the law school. "When he came back, his relationships with other people and students were much warmer. He placed much more store in human contacts, whether he knew it or not."[9]

Cox continued a steady pace of writing (Derek Bok now collaborated on the Labor Law text), but branched off into new subjects. In 1967 he published a book entitled *The Warren Court,* and coauthored another book with Mark DeWolfe Howe and J. R. Wiggins entitled *Civil Rights, the Constitution, and the Courts,* published by Harvard University Press. Among other issues of the day, the latter book discussed the virtues and perils of civil disobedience by young people, a growing topic of concern as sporadic protests flashed across college campuses in response to the escalating war in Vietnam. Some of the dangers posed by widespread civil disobedience were already evident at campuses like Columbia and Colgate Universities and the University of Michigan. At these institutions, recent student rebellions had led to building seizures, destruction of property, even violence.[10] "One cost we pay for all civil disobedience is the heavy damage it does to the principle of government by consent of the governed," Cox wrote in one of the book's essays, "a principle which is the surest guaranty of individual liberty devised by man."[11]

The winter of 1968 had been a particularly busy one at the Law School. During the May recess, Archie and Phyllis packed up their "Brookway Farm" truck and drove to Maine. It was time for a rest, before another summer of intense writing on constitutional subjects. The phone rang, upsetting the silence of the South Brooksville farmhouse. It was Mike Sovern, a fellow Labor Law professor at Columbia. He wanted to know if Cox would consider chairing a new but important fact-finding commission. It would deal with the recent building seizures and student riots at Columbia.[12]

The New York campus had been rocked by a series of alarming incidents, including the seizure of Low Memorial Library and Hamilton Hall by Students for a Democratic Society (SDS) and militant black students, as well as the occupation of the president's office and the imprisonment of Dean Henry Coleman for twenty-four hours by radical students. The protests stemmed from a host of flash points. One was the presence of CIA and military recruiters on campus; another was the intense racial tension generated by Columbia University's effort to buy property and build a gym in the largely black and Puerto Rican neighborhood of Morningside Heights at the rim of Harlem. The Vietnam War only seemed to be fueling anger and frustration among students, making the New York campus a tinderbox of conflicted emotions.[13]

The Columbia faculty had all but repudiated President Grayson Kirk and his administration. An "Executive Committee" had stepped in to steer the university. They sought a detached, highly regarded group of outsiders who could reduce the tension and allow Columbia to "open peacefully" in the fall.[14] Some of the biggest names on the East Coast would help Cox carry out his task: Simon H. Rifkind, former federal judge and high-powered lawyer from New York; Dr. Dana L. Farnsworth, director of the Harvard Health Services; Hyland G. Lewis, distinguished black professor of sociology at Brooklyn College; and Anthony Amsterdam, a young law professor at the University of Pennsylvania who had clerked for Felix Frankfurter.[15] It sounded interesting, different. Archie decided to do it.

The Cox Commission was instantly swamped with assignments. It scheduled hearing after hearing, twenty-one days of them, producing 3,790 pages of typed transcripts and listening to testimony from seventy-nine sworn witnesses.[16] Archie took up temporary residence at the Harvard Club in downtown New York,[17] spending long weekends in the city and shuttling back and forth from Boston. " 'Twas ever thus," Phyllis told a newspaper reporter from her distant garden in Maine.[18]

Clashes continued at Columbia. During the early testimony of Vice President David Truman, who had become the spokesman of the administration after President Kirk fell from leadership, Cox had a direct run-in with Mark Rudd, leader of the radical SDS organization at Columbia. Truman had barely begun his testimony when Rudd and a group of fifteen SDS members marched into the hearing room, forming a wedge as they swarmed into seats in the tiny auditorium. Cox viewed their arrival nervously. "I wondered," he would recall, "if they were there to disrupt. Is there going to be another building seizure?"[19]

Vice President Truman began his testimony. He recounted events of the student insurrections in a sharp tone. Mark Rudd shouted suddenly, "Liar!" His party chanted, "Liar, liar." They stopped, as if pondering how else to display their intense displeasure. "My heart went into my throat," Cox said.[20] What would happen next? What would the chairman do?[21]

A number of thoughts flashed into Cox's mind. He remembered conversations with Charlie Wyzanski as a young lawyer, about the trial of Communists in New York for violation of the Smith Act. The attorneys representing the Communist defendants had made a "shambles" out of the trial. Wyzanski had always been critical of the federal judge for letting this happen. "What's he to do?" Cox had asked Wyzanski. "Just by his presence," Wyzanski had emphasized, "he's got to dominate the scene."[22]

Cox had never been satisfied with this answer, even as a young man. But after the students' chants of "liar, liar" continued, he had few alternatives but to take Wyzanski's approach. Cox leaned forward in his chair and announced in the firmest voice he could command, "Mr. Rudd, you were invited to testify before this commission and you refused. You will be given another chance if you wish. But for now *you will keep still.*"[23] Cox sat back, nervous, surveying the crowd of SDS members.

"Well, by golly, they did keep still from then on," Cox chuckled.[24]

One of Cox's principal goals as chairman of the impromptu commission was to get inside the minds of the student protesters. He took one of the SDS leaders—who was also a member of the radical Progressive Labor movement—to dinner, hoping to sort out his complex motives and allegiances. As a graduate student in engineering on a scholarship, the young man had grown up in poverty in an industrial city in upstate New York and succeeded through sheer intelligence and drive. Cox retained an image of a "kind, almost gentle fellow,"[25] who firmly believed that the "revolution [would] come" when students and workers banded together.

After a pleasant dinner, the self-professed radical agreed to take Cox to a public meeting of the SDS, where major issues and strategies of student protesters would be debated. The scene was extraordinary. Hippies with ripped blue jeans and long beards and average-looking students with angry faces swarmed into the secret assembly spot. As soon as Cox and the young man came within sight of the building where the meeting was taking place, "the student insisted on leaving me. He wouldn't sit with me. And his whole personality changed. He became this tough, shouting, certainly aggressive [person]."[26]

Cox was sympathetic toward many of the "abstract ideals" of the student protesters. He nevertheless disapproved, more strongly than he could express, of their destructive methods. "We take seriously what we were taught at home and in Sunday School," a young man with long hair and unwashed beard told him with great sincerity.[27] Archie knew that the students believed they were acting with utmost honor and cause; they were exhibiting a higher level of morality than the putrid establishment that they sought to topple. On the other hand, Cox believed that violence and destruction were no solutions.

The Cox Commission issued a 222-page report in early October, entitled *Crisis at Columbia*. It was printed by Random House in a record eight days, with forty thousand paperback copies selling briskly at $1.95 apiece, except on the Columbia campus, where they were distributed at cost for twenty-five cents.[28]

The report amounted to a "strong indictment" of the Columbia administration. That the university leaders had been too authoritative for too long and "invited mistrust" was the thrust of the Cox Commission's findings. It charged that the police had employed "excessive force" when they cleared university buildings, and engaged in acts of "brutality" that "caused violence on a harrowing scale." The report also suggested that the administration had failed to act decisively at key junctures to defuse the student occupations. At the same time, the commission condemned the "disruptive tactics" employed by some student rebels, and warned that "the survival—literally the survival—of the free university depends upon the entire community's active rejection of disruptive demonstrations."[29]

Several weeks before the Cox Commission report was issued, perhaps in anticipation of it, President Grayson Kirk had submitted his resignation to the trustees of Columbia on August 23, 1968. Vice President Truman had also left to become president of Mount Holyoke College.[30] With a fresh semester and a new administration at Columbia, the immediate crisis had worked its way to a peaceful conclusion. But the sparks of discontent that had caught flame at this New York campus now began to rekindle themselves in a wider venue, across the nation.

Cox opened his morning paper on Wednesday, June 5, 1968, and dropped it in shock: Senator Robert F. Kennedy had been shot and gravely wounded in California, just after winning the state's presidential primary. Twenty hours later he would die. Cox placed his head in his hands and said a silent prayer. Rather than watching a young candidate capture the Democratic nomination for the presidency, as he had watched John F. Kennedy capture it in 1960, Archie found himself standing guard beside Robert Kennedy's casket on the final night that his body was laid in state in St. Patrick's Cathedral. Cox had been selected by the Kennedy family to maintain a vigil in the dark, foreboding shadows of a second Kennedy funeral assemblage.[31]

Two days after Robert Kennedy's death Archie stood in the Great Hall of the Department of Justice, staring at the blurry tile floor beneath the balcony, surrounded by faces and objects that had once been familiar, had once been part of the exciting milieu in which he and an energetic young attorney general had shared boundless ambitions. This time, on June 8, 1968, Archie returned to this old building to deliver a eulogy.

"One looks at the walls—one walks down the corridors—" Archie spoke with a halting voice as throngs of RFK's former employees and staff members huddled together in grief, "and nothing is changed. Yet inside our hearts there is aching emptiness: our leader is gone and nothing is the same." Archie spoke of Robert Kennedy's unique warmth as a human being: "Those of us who worked with him knew both the little acts of friendship and solicitude in times of strain and the steadfast loyalty that defended us even when we stumbled."[32] In the end Cox saw his younger colleague's greatest virtue in a single, unwavering conviction:

> Robert Kennedy shared with his brother, the late President, the belief that by using reason, knowledge, and intelligence men can improve the condition of men. With him the conviction burned so hot that the question often was not one of the capacity to shape our fate, but of the will to do it.
>
> In combination, these two qualities produced a restlessness of spirit, a will to drive himself still harder, and sometimes an impatience with the laggard. But in a period of stress when too many despair in the existing system—too many of the young and idealistic who felt close kinship with Bob Kennedy—it is important to recall that his impatience never led to bitterness—never produced intolerance of men of sincere good will whose judgments differed—never involved loss of confidence in the powers of reason and persuasion and the civility for which law supplies part of the formal structure.

Cox folded his notes, looking around at the faces.

> The lesson of Robert Kennedy's Attorney-Generalship is that a revolution in human and social justice can be accomplished by, and within, democratic process, the frame of law. He would deny that it was fully done, and he would be right. There is too much more to do. But the path was opened and we learned that with a will the revolution might be accomplished within the rule of law.

In the fall of 1968, sparks of campus unrest had continued to ignite student protests throughout the country: from the tiny Trinity College in Hartford to the sprawling University of Michigan in Ann Arbor, to Colgate University in New York, to Stanford University to San Francisco State College.[33] There was a great interest in Cox's book *Crisis at Columbia*. What lessons could be learned from the events at Columbia in New York City? Would such disturbances, given the mysterious insurrections that seemed to be popping up nationwide in the spring, repeat themselves at other universities that autumn?

The Harvard Faculty of Arts and Sciences invited Cox to address their meeting on October 15, 1968. His theme: "chance" had played a large role in the Columbia affair.[34] Cox believed that the "house plan" at Harvard, by which masters (many of them faculty) lived and ate alongside students in the dormitories, made the likelihood of riots and violence much more "remote" in Cambridge than at the dense urban setting of Columbia.[35]

Cox's predictions, however, quickly proved wrong. In April 1969, a noisy rally was staged to protest the presence of the Reserve Officers Training Corps on the Harvard campus. ROTC was viewed as the U.S. military's direct attempt to co-opt college campuses and drag them into an immoral and illegal war in Vietnam.[36] On Wednesday, April 9, five hundred anti-ROTC demonstrators and members of SDS convened a mass meeting on the porch of Memorial Church around noon, using bullhorns to call the crowd to action. As the warm April sun shone through the trees, sixty or eighty of the "hard-liners," mostly members of the militant Progressive Labor party, swarmed forward shouting "Fight, fight, fight!" They flooded into University Hall in the center of Harvard Yard, evicting administrative officials, deans, and staffers—some by force—and barring entry to the building.[37]

A huge granite structure with steep steps, University Hall served as the command center for the administration. In many ways it symbolized all the power and mystique of Harvard. Dean Archie C. Epps III refused to leave. "You are responsible for killing people in Vietnam," a female demonstrator shouted at him. "I am not responsible for killing people in Vietnam," Epps answered. "You are using methods here that I thought you objected to—violence and force."

"What the f—— do you know about it?" The woman screamed back. A group of protesters threw Epps backward out the east door, down the granite steps. Only luck and a dense crowd saved him.[38] Student reporters from WHRB, the campus radio station, took over the office of Dean Franklin L. Ford of the Faculty of Arts and Sciences, where they broadcast the occupation live.

"We have occupied the building," the defiant students told Dean Ford after chaining themselves inside and jeering at his request that they reconsider the seizure, "and we are going to close down the University until our demands are met."[39]

The six demands of the student occupiers were outlined in a leaflet captioned "The Time to Fight Is Now!" distributed widely on the Harvard campus. The "demands" included the abolition of the

ROTC, the replacement of ROTC scholarships with generic Harvard scholarships so that university funds would be spent productively rather than destructively, rent rollbacks in university-owned apartments, and the scrapping of plans to demolish 182 black families' homes in the Roxbury section of Boston to make room for Harvard Medical School expansion. "If we can be here in the morning," one student protester announced to the *Harvard Crimson*, "the anti-war movement at Harvard will be stronger than it ever was before."[40]

By nightfall, the crowd of students occupying University Hall had swelled to over three hundred. They carried in blankets and food and pried open locked file drawers in search of proof that Harvard was secretly connected to the government's war efforts in Southeast Asia. Hundreds more students and onlookers milled around outside, even after the gates to Harvard Yard had been locked. Some pro-administration students shouted "Out, out, out!" burning figures of SDS members in effigy. Inside, student rebels climbed onto desks in the Faculty Room amid portraits of Harvard's founders and plotted strategy around an elegant wood table, a gift to the university from a Philippine ambassador. They rearranged letters on a bulletin board in the building's foyer to read "Che Guevara Hall." The SDS flag, a black circle on a bright red background, flew prominently from a window.[41]

Harvard President Nathan Pusey convened an emergency meeting in his living room at 17 Quincy Street, behind locked gates. Along with key administration officials gathered at his stately residence, he would make a decision that would haunt the university for the rest of his presidency. "Many students were honestly concerned about the Vietnam War," Pusey said, later reconstructing his thought process, "but they were victimized by a small group of people who thought there was going to be a revolution. I thought it was nonsense."[42]

Before dawn, four hundred state troopers and local police stormed University Hall, removing hundreds of students, "sometimes violently," injuring nearly 45 and arresting 196, including 50 women. A long cordon of buses left deep tire marks in the Yard as they skidded off to the Third Middlesex District Court in East Cambridge for mass bookings. The protesters were charged with criminal trespass and locked up. An extra edition of the *Harvard Crimson* reported that the police had entered University Hall equipped with glinting blue helmets, black boots and jodhpurs, shields, billy clubs, sledgehammers, chain cutters, and a four-foot battering ram. According to eyewitnesses, some students linked arms for "nonviolent resistance." Others jumped out the first floor windows. Many were beaten or dragged away by their long hair. It was a swift and intense purging that took only twenty-five minutes, leaving a trail of blood as dawn rose over the troubled university. One observer watched police beat a handicapped student out of his wheelchair onto the ground. As an Associated Press reporter recorded from the eye of the tempest: "You can read about so-called 'police brutality' in Alabama, and even get to see it on television in Chicago, but the impact doesn't hit home until you wind up on the middle of a clash like the one that took place in Harvard Yard Thursday."[43]

Suddenly there were rumors that Cox's handiwork in *Crisis at Columbia* had influenced President Pusey's decision to launch the raid. After all, hadn't the Cox Commission report chided the Columbia administration for failing to "retake" Low Library during a lull when the SDS had temporarily abandoned the building? The police assault on University Hall seemed to be directly patterned after Cox's recommendations, the *Harvard Crimson* suggested.[44] Cox, who was never consulted before President Pusey ordered the ill-fated raid, resented these comparisons. The two situations, he believed, were "utterly different." One involved a building that was virtually empty. The other involved "hundreds of Cambridge police and the arrest of hundreds of Harvard students."[45] Cox did not condone, let alone recommend, the Harvard action—not at all.

Fallout from the University Hall debacle, whether Cox's report had anything to do with it or not, was nevertheless swift and damning. Within seven hours of the "bust," a lengthy "student strike" was announced.[46]

A swelling group of Harvard faculty, incensed by President Pusey's confrontational posture, held a four-hour closed-door meeting in Loeb Drama Center on April 11. They overwhelmingly proposed the creation of a "Committee of Fifteen," which would investigate the causes of the crisis, discipline students (and a handful of faculty members) in the University Hall seizure, and recommend changes in the governance of the university.[47]

President Pusey convened his own emergency meeting of senior faculty members in the now-reclaimed Faculty Room. Archibald Cox was among those in attendance. The precise purpose of the gathering was never clear. President Pusey was abruptly called away from the meeting. "My next memory," Cox recalled, "is that I was somehow up in front of the body presiding, having taken charge."[48]

Out in the Yard, students were busy regrouping. Picketers carried signs: "STRIKE; FIGHT THE PIGS." Copies of the underground radical newspaper *Old Mole* were distributed across campus, reporting that files taken during the occupation of University Hall proved the existence of links between Harvard and the U.S. military. One piece of damning evidence the newspaper reported was a telegram from the State Department thanking Harvard for making Professor Henry Kissinger available for a mission "of great importance" to South Vietnam in 1966. The cover of *Old Mole* blared: "Harvard = CIA = State Department = Murderers."[49]

Two thousand students, many of them self-proclaimed moderates who were shocked by President Pusey's insensitivity, gathered at Memorial Church to endorse a mass student strike. The church was the spiritual center of the campus; the name of Robert Hill Cox II, Archie's younger brother, was engraved there among the Harvard students who had given their lives during World War II. The students of 1969 perceived a new threat to their American freedom. Dissidents cut red armbands from cloth and produced strike posters (depicting a large, red fist) nonstop, even silk-screening the images onto their bodies.

Posters adorned the 333-year-old Harvard campus with a bold, red declaration: "There Is Some Sh—— We Will Not Eat. Strike." The "Harvard New College" scheduled alternative classes in abandoned university buildings, offering "Motorcycles and Sex," "Aesthetics of Revolution," and "From Chemicals to Life."[50] Rock concerts by Albatross and the underground band Far Cry took over the Yard in place of classes, complete with a "weird flickering light show." The San Francisco mime troupe Gutter Puppet and Gorilla Marching Band performed on April 16.[51]

Harvard's image worldwide was trashed. The Benton Harbor, Michigan, *News-Palladium* announced, "The Cool is missing from Harvard Yard," and "its magnificent aplomb has been tarnished." The *Enterprise* in Paris acknowledged, "Harvard n'est plus un sanctuaire."[52]

Three days after the bust, students swarmed across the Charles River into the sprawling Soldiers' Field football stadium to discuss their game plan. The first mass meeting of five thousand led to a stalemate; the strike was continued. Only after the administration acceded to several demands, including the elimination of academic credit for ROTC, did a second meeting of ten thousand students vote to "suspend" the strike and return to classes. A vote of "no confidence" in the administration was nevertheless thrown in for good measure.[53]

Harvard limped its way to the end of the 1968–69 academic year.[54] Dean Ford suffered a stroke as a result of strike-related stress. Six seniors did not receive degrees, and 135 rebels were disciplined for their involvement in the University Hall takeover.[55] Disruptions flared up even through the June commencement.[56] It was, as Pusey himself wrote in his annual President's Report, a "dismal year."[57]

In the summer of 1969, President Pusey asked Cox if he would present the university's cases to a new faculty-student disciplinary body called the Committee on Rights and Responsibilities that would succeed the Committee of Fifteen in passing judgment on student rebels in case of future disturbances.[58] "It wasn't a request that I was any too happy with," Cox admitted. "But on the other hand you owe certain obligations to an institution that you have been part of, and at a time of crisis I could sort of temper my distaste by saying, 'Well, at least I can present cases without vindictiveness—at least I think I can.' "[59] One faculty member would later describe the selection of the former solicitor general of the United States to "prosecute" student protesters as "shooting at gnats with an elephant gun."[60] Cox, however, felt that the job was important enough to the university, and important enough to the students' futures, to do it.[61]

In early September, automobiles and moving vans arrived in Harvard Yard en masse, marking the start of an uneasy fall term. The radical Weathermen quickly trashed the Center for International Affairs. President Pusey asked Cox to join a second, more policy-oriented committee, to advise the university's governing corporation, called the President and Fellows of Harvard College. The new committee would recommend appropriate responses in case of ongoing disruptions.[62]

The composition of this new unnamed committee revealed more about President Pusey's view of how to deal with student uprisings than did any official statement. Besides Cox, Pusey appointed Robert Tonis, chief of the Harvard Police and retired FBI agent; General Leonard Cronkhite, former provost marshal in charge of the military police, who now headed a teaching hospital in Boston; and Sam Williamson, a young assistant professor of history who had taught at

West Point and served in the military during the early stages of the Vietnam conflict.[63] The tenor of the appointments was clearly designed to be aggressive and quasi-military. General Cronkhite refused to accept the assignment, believing that it was "not commensurate" with his skills. Cox, Williamson, and Tonis were left to handle the job alone.

Cox and Williamson drafted a report to the President and Fellows of Harvard College in late September, recommending that a single person be named to make all decisions for the university, if future disruptions struck the campus. This person would serve in a role comparable to the "Executive Officer on a battleship."[64] The polite subtext underlying this recommendation was obvious: There was a growing sense throughout the university that President Pusey lacked the "instinct, philosophy, approach, political antenna, public relations antenna towards students that was desirable" to deal with the growing crisis.[65] At the same time, nobody felt comfortable suggesting that Harvard should "get a new president."[66]

In early October, the President and Fellows asked Cox to join them at one of their first meetings. They said in so many words, "Well, since you've made this fine report, you now carry it out."[67] Cox was asked to become the de facto president of the university in all matters concerning student disruptions. Professor Sam Williamson would become his "aide, adviser, shoulder to cry on, and everything else."[68]

With mixed feelings, Cox accepted the assignment. He walked out of the hallowed University Hall into a quiet Harvard Yard where maple trees were huddled together in a fiery display of color, preparing to shed their leaves for another cold winter.

This was a total period of alarums and excursions," Cox would recall.[69] Bomb threats became commonplace. Calls came to the Cox home at three o'clock in the morning from the night duty officer of the Harvard Police: "Shall I evacuate the building?"[70] Archie would wake up, try to get oriented, and make a decision. "Well, how did the call sound?" He would attempt to pick up clues. The most troublesome alerts were late-night bomb scares at Peabody Terrace, the graduate students' dorms along the Charles River, where spouses and children were mixed with students. If the call came at night after a string of false alarms throughout the university, Cox would usually say, "Let's chance it." It was terrible to turn entire families into the streets in the middle of the night. If the threat came in daytime, however, or near dawn, he would usually issue the order: "Evacuate the building."[71] In making these racking decisions, Cox had to take educated gambles: "I didn't think that there was any real possibility that the bomb would be enough so that people in more than one apartment, if that, could be hurt."[72]

Fortunately, "luck held."[73] Amid dozens of threats, not a single bomb exploded in university housing. Still Archie would continue to dream about the nighttime calls, no matter how he tried to block them from his consciousness. Nights and days were filled with other crises, stealing away long periods of sleep and adding new levels of tension.

On December 3, 1969, black student members of OBU (Organization for Black Unity) rallied on the steps of Memorial Church, demanding greater minority employment on Harvard construction jobs. The assassination of Dr. Martin Luther King, Jr., the previous year and the small numbers of minority students at Harvard (the freshman class of 1968 included barely one hundred black students, and previous classes had included only two dozen) gave black students an acute sense of vulnerability.[74] "Our concern really was the economic deprivation to the black working-class community," explained Raymond Jones, a law student and OBU member who went on to become a Colorado Superior Court judge. "My participation came from pride."[75]

The next day, one hundred OBU members occupied University Hall for six hours. Cox, on behalf of the university, signed an agreement with third-year law student Phillip Lee, by which Harvard agreed in principle to increase black participation in building projects. Both men stood in long winter coats in the chilly December air, signing their names to a document pressed up against the wall of the building. Said Raymond Jones, "We were angry with Cox at that time. Although he understood our issue perfectly, he was making excuses for the university."[76] The black students, many wearing Afro haircuts, beads, platform shoes, bell-bottoms, and dashikis, left the building to the sound of beating war drums.[77]

One week later, after concluding that Cox and the university were not moving fast enough on their promises, OBU members marched to a construction site at the School of Design carrying two-way radios and chains. This time they locked gates and barricaded workmen out of the job site.[78] Another swarm of OBU students moved to

University Hall, where they kicked in a panel door, took over the empty office of Dean Ernest May, and began singing and chanting. "It was like a little corner of the civil rights movement," explained one protester. The group's quest was "not to do damage, not to hurt people."[79] They nevertheless wanted action. They wanted Harvard to agree that "a minimum of 20% of the skilled and semi-skilled work force" on all construction projects be "composed of black and Third World workers."[80] The OBU members chanted and sang:

> Who's going to survive in America?
> Very few Negroes and no crackers at all.
> Power to the people—
> Black, black people—
> To the African people![81]

Dean May finally arrived. Standing outside with a bullhorn, he announced that the demonstrators were occupying the building in violation of university rules. He summarily suspended them.

Cox ran over from the Law School. Despite the growing scent of trouble, he and Sam Williamson had decided early on that if another building were occupied, the debacle of the first University Hall seizure would not be repeated. He did not want to call outside police to the scene. A college campus was not a place for police action, unless absolutely necessary. "We were prepared to wait them out" was Cox's philosophy.[82]

Cox went inside the building and talked to the OBU members personally. Jones remembered, "I felt at that time Professor Cox felt a little bit trapped. . . . Just looking at him, looking him in the eye, I felt he respected us. He told us we were wrong, and we knew it. But no one could deny the rightness of our cause."[83]

Harvard counsel hustled off to the Middlesex County Superior Court to get a temporary restraining order. As soon as the injunction was served, the black students left en masse, with fists raised, much to the relief of university officials. The *Crimson* theorized that the OBU members fled "because violation of the court order would have made them liable to jail sentences for contempt of court."[84] The truth was that Cox had negotiated a secret deal with OBU's leaders: if he got a "lawful order of court," they would leave peacefully. In return, he would hire a neutral arbitrator, a distinguished black military officer, to hash out terms for increasing minority participation in Harvard construction projects. "We had it all worked out together," said Jones, "as a way to save face."[85]

The ironies of the times would never cease to disturb Cox. He remembered walking back to the Law School with Jones that day, seeing their reflections in a window as they passed. Cox saw himself as the ugly symbol of the administration's failed mission; Jones was the angry symbol of a new generation adrift. Cox climbed the steps of Langdell Hall, to teach Labor Law. Jones sat quietly in Cox's class, taking notes.[86]

The OBU conflict died down.[87] Harvard honored the deal to bring about the hiring of more blacks on Harvard construction projects. "[Cox] came through," said Jones. "He did come through."[88] But other problems did not vanish. President Nathan Pusey, overwhelmed by the relentless upheaveal and plagued by the lack of confidence among faculty and students, announced that he was contemplating early retirement after eighteen years as president. "I was so unhappy due to the behavior of so many members of the faculty, who I felt should have helped young people through this in a sensible way," Pusey reflected decades later. "I felt I needed to get out."[89]

In the spring of 1970, antiwar protests swept across the country, erupting into a full-scale riot in Harvard Square. "Every damn window in Harvard Square was broken," Sam Williamson recalled of the April 15 melee. Three thousand peace marchers and two hundred police officers from seven municipalities clashed in the streets. The result was burned buildings, looted stores, and gutted police vehicles.[90] At the direction of Cox "acting for the President," the gates of Harvard Yard were locked.[91] Hundreds more police were called in. Protesters threw sidewalk bricks over the wall of the Yard at state police on Massachusetts Avenue. Tear gas bombs were fired back over the wall. A banner in the middle of the square proclaimed the triumph of the "Yippies-Panthers." Protesters chanted "One, Two, Three, Four, We Don't Want Your F—— War," until nearly 1:00 A.M.[92]

College campuses across the country seemed to be falling apart. Disruptions broke out at the University of Wisconsin, the University of New Mexico, Oberlin College in Ohio, Northwestern University in Chicago, University of California–Los Angeles, and dozens more.[93] A rally at Yale was staged to protest the jailing of Black Panther leader Bobby Seale. The Committee of Fifteen attempted to explain in its report what the students were experiencing during the tumultuous times: "Politically concerned students, brought up to trust their leaders and to expect good will and progress from them, have . . . undergone an experience which has been tantamount to the discovery of sin, the end of trust and an overflow of guilt for having been acquiescent or 'accomplices' for so long."[94]

Then came the devastating blow. On Friday, May 1, the *Crimson* carried a bold, blackened headline: "Nixon Announces Invasion of Cambodian Border." The president had revealed that American and South Vietnamese troops had crossed the Cambodian border to attack a central Vietcong base. American college campuses across the country churned themselves into a state of distress.[95] Four students were killed by U.S. National Guardsmen at Kent State University in Ohio. Within two weeks, two black students would be shot and nine more wounded by police at Jackson State College in Mississippi.[96] Even President Pusey softened his rhetoric, acknowledging the "dismaying turn of events in Southeast Asia." Although he could not officially endorse a student-led moratorium on classes to protest the Vietnam War, Pusey announced that all university instructors and personnel should be prepared to accommodate "acts of conscience relating to our country's involvement in the war in Southeast Asia."[97]

Although Pusey was still a Republican by registration and had supported Richard M. Nixon in the 1968 election, he now thought that the Grand Old Party was "going to hell." In Pusey's opinion, President Nixon was getting "bad advice about student disturbances," and the decision to call in troops at Kent State was a "ghastly mistake."[98] The "Establishment" itself was now splintering with self-doubt. Cox had been part of it his whole life, enjoying the ample benefits of an Ivy League education, secure finances, government contacts, and an influential position on the Harvard faculty. Now it was time to pay his dues.

Cambodia blew that campus apart," Sam Williamson would put it. On May 8, five hundred demonstrators, including SDS members, swept into Harvard Square after a massive antiwar rally at Soldiers' Field and decided to march to Shannon Hall, the ROTC headquarters near the Law School. Although the faculty had voted to end academic credit for ROTC, the organization was permitted to remain in the barn-red Shannon Hall rent-free until those already enrolled completed their training.[99] The plan of the protesters was simple and direct: burn down this symbol of the university's link to the war. It was the "diciest moment of our strategy," Williamson recalled. The university was prepared to sacrifice Shannon Hall itself, but the Mallinkrodt chemistry laboratory nearby was a powder keg that could blow up instantaneously if the fire swept in that direction.[100]

Pressure on Cox mounted, as twilight spread across the sky. Williamson recorded in his diary that at 7:15 P.M., "Chief Tonis [of the Harvard Police] wanted to continue on with his supper, that is to say he wanted to continue business as usual. This is one of the few occasions in which I have seen Mr. Cox blow his cool and slam down the telephone, telling the Chief to go on and finish his supper. The Chief was of little value to us that night."[101]

Cox had picked up advance whispers that Shannon Hall might be a target after the rally. The day before, he had met secretly with Massachusetts Governor Frank Sargent in Boston. They had discussed bringing out the National Guard to Harvard, but the killings at Kent State were barely a week old. They decided instead that the National Guard should be quietly moved to an armory near Fresh Pond, a mile or two from Harvard.[102] A large squad of Harvard Police would then be stationed around Shannon Hall as a show of force. Cox and the governor quietly agreed that if the crowd could not be kept at bay, the National Guard would be ready as a last resort, but *only* as a last resort.

Williamson and Cox set up a command post in the Harvard Police Headquarters, in the basement of Grays Hall in the Yard. Cox kept in touch with the lieutenant in charge at Shannon Hall by walkie-talkie. Events began to move quickly.

The crowd had multiplied from five hundred to several thousand as daylight vanished. They moved in a wall across the Harvard campus, fanning out toward Shannon Hall. In minutes the lieutenant's voice on the walkie-talkie turned urgent. "They've begun to throw rocks," he reported to Cox. "Somebody's going to get hurt. What shall we do?"[103]

Cox tried to focus, to stay calm. The Harvard Police had never been intended to serve as anything more than a symbol. They were not stationed at Shannon Hall to pull guns or clubs or to engage in riot control.

Cox said firmly, "Well, you'd better get the hell out of there." His voice crackled over the walkie-talkie. "But try to do it quietly."

The Harvard Police inched slowly away from the building. A rumor suddenly swept through the crowd: the Harvard Police were leaving to make room for the Boston tactical squad and the Somerville police (known for their tough riot control), who "were coming to beat them all up." Cox and Williamson, still hidden at their command post in Grays Hall, watched in amazement as the student siege of Shannon Hall ended in a trail of footsteps and whispers, as protesters "practically ran away."[104] Dean Ernest May issued a statement praising the "cool judgment and performance" of all concerned.[105] Neither the students nor the newspapers ever learned that a large detachment of the National Guard had been stationed a mile away, just in case.

But there was no time for rest. "We were having a crisis a minute," said Law School Dean Derek Bok.[106] Cox awoke one morning in May at five A.M. to the sound of a ringing phone. This time the Harvard Police had a grim announcement: "Lawrence Hall is on fire." The trip from Wayland, even at fast speeds along empty roads, took nearly twenty-five minutes. Archie arrived just in time to see a wall of Lawrence Hall, an old, abandoned building on the fringe of the university, fall over ablaze on four Cambridge firemen.[107]

Lawrence Hall had served as the home of the "Free University" run by radical students during the day; by night, approximately thirty "street people" who had become "wards" of the students had taken over its deserted halls. Before this incident, Cox and university officials had specifically discussed the danger of a fire at Lawrence Hall. He had decided to leave the squatters undisturbed, fearful of provoking a fight. "I decided that we would chance the waifs' being on drugs and doing something that started a fire. This had all been discussed. So, when you saw the wall go over [you thought] 'My God, I'm responsible for this.'"[108]

None of the firemen were killed, but some suffered serious injuries. One student was reported missing in the fire. Sam Williamson remembered Cox grimly preparing a press release, "ready to take responsibility" for the student's death. Then the missing student was found unharmed; the press release never went out. Cox's nerves were being worked raw. The fire marshal's report confirmed what Cox had feared: the blaze had been caused by "accidental ignition of a mattress via hot plate, candle or careless use or disposal of smoking materials."[109] One Cambridge fireman injured in the crumbling building brought suit against Cox and Harvard for negligence, compounding Archie's feeling of guilt.

Cox's nerves were shot. At 2:15 one night, after he decided not to evacuate for another bomb threat, Phyllis helped Archie call Williamson. Archie almost begged for assurance that he had made the right decision. "It was a low point," admitted Phyllis. "He needed it. Sam said that he had done the right thing."[110]

Williamson was impressed that Cox did not attempt to parlay his performance in any of these crises into a job promotion, even in the face of growing attention from the media and the Harvard community. As wearying as the tasks were, Cox was slowly becoming viewed as the true president of Harvard, as the student disruptions dominated the news of the University.

It was not as if Cox had never thought about opportunities for "higher" positions in government or academe. Early in his career, a push had once surfaced to have Cox named dean of the University of Pennsylvania Law School.[111] After a brief caucus with Phyllis, he turned it down. Nor had Archie ever been particularly interested in becoming dean in his own backyard at Harvard. His feelings on such an appointment were summed up in the punchline of an old New England joke about being tarred, feathered, and ridden out of town on a rail. "If it weren't for the honor of the thing," the joke went, "I would just as lief have missed it." "That summarized my feelings on becoming dean," Cox said. "I had done my share."[112]

As his exposure from handling the student disturbances spread, his name was regularly batted around to succeed Nathan Pusey as president, "but I'd think twice if anyone said that I had a serious chance."[113] In fact, the *Harvard Crimson* ran a story entitled "Seven Men Who *Won't* Become the 25th Harvard President," listing Cox among the seven. He was described as a person of great "finesse and strength," but students viewed him as an enforcer who was "aloof and evasive," and a "law and order" figure.[114] (Ironically, Cox had just agreed to represent an indigent murder defendant in the Supreme Court, a man who could find no other lawyer.[115] But Cox had no time to worry about such ironies.)

The only time Williamson saw any hint of ambition on the part of Cox, any clue that there might be a dream of advancement, came the day they stopped in Harvard Square so that Cox could pick up a copy of *Life* magazine. It contained "a list of potential Supreme Court nominees."[116] Cox never opened the magazine in front of Williamson to see if his name was on the list. These sorts of things were done in private, on one's own time.

As tensions grew in the spring of 1970, more anger was aimed at the controversial Center for International Affairs, Henry Kissinger's old base. It had come to symbolize the university's connection with travesties in Southeast Asia. After one overseers meeting at the center, an angry crowd followed Professor Robert Bowie, the center's director, and Joseph E. Johnson, president of the Carnegie Endowment for International Peace and chair of the Center's Board of Visitors, out of the building. The crowd quickly swelled to over a hundred. Bowie and Johnson attempted to shake the mob by walking a distance, then climbing into a cab at Harvard Square near the subway entrance.[117] The crowd circled the cab and created a human blockade that prevented the vehicle from leaving. Bowie, a vociferous critic of the antiwar protesters and their tactics, became enraged. He sat in the cab for fifteen minutes, then twenty minutes. The crowd was still growing.

Cox heard of the siege while sitting in his law school office. He dropped his pencil and hurried to the square. It was a clear, blue day. He recalled seeing students catching Frisbees in Harvard Yard as he hurried down the red brick walkway. Cox thought to himself, "Oh, if they could only keep the Frisbees flying."

In the square, Cox found the cab mobbed by protesters. Bowie was "sort of half in half out." He seemed "determined to provoke a confrontation." Bowie kept yelling at the driver to drive forward. "He wanted the taxi driver to get in and drive and simply force his way through the crowd. If that didn't work, he wanted the police to come and make some arrests to clear a path. And by golly he was going to have his liberty of movement sustained."[118]

Cox was worried. If the taxi began to move or if police were called in, "somebody would get hurt." So Cox told his colleague, "Oh, come on, Bob. Let's leave quietly and have an end to this."

Red in the face, the white-haired, bespectacled Bowie demanded, "Are you advising me to do this or *ordering* me to do this?" It was no secret on campus that Bowie did not approve of Cox's role as de facto president. Cox had not been appointed to replace Nathan Pusey, had he? He was just another professor; he had no official power or status in the university.

Cox stood up straight and cocked his head. "I am *ordering* you." Professor Bowie's eyes narrowed, radiating resentment. He said nothing for a minute; then he walked angrily away. Whereupon Professor Cox and Bowie's guest proceeded to a park bench in the Cambridge

Common and sat motionless until the protesters got bored and left. Robert Bowie was harassed for several more blocks until a driver gave him a lift. And the cab drove freely up Massachusetts Avenue.[119]

Cox was getting it from all directions. Students at the professional schools were starting to revolt.[120] "Moderate" students, such as Tom Gerety, who went on to become a college president, viewed Cox and the administration as "out of touch."[121] Cox's oldest daughter, Sally, who worked at the Center for International Affairs for Robert Bowie, was "beat[en] up" and "manhandled" by the radical Weathermen. The ugly sense that violence was about to happen only seemed to surge forward with a relentless pulse, as the commencement of 1970 approached.

For over three centuries, commencement had been considered a sacred event at Harvard. Its 319th commencement exercises would be the first to include female seniors from Radcliffe College in a joint ceremony. On the Wednesday night before thousands of parents and alumnae were scheduled to stream into the campus, a "strange gathering" appeared in the Yard.[122] The June 10 edition of the *Harvard Crimson* announced that a massive group of seniors planned to stage an "alternative graduation." A special "Commencement Issue" of the *Crimson* displayed a stark picture of children dressed as national guardsmen on the cover, flanked by a sign: "After Graduation WHAT?"[123]

Sam Williamson and Cox walked through the Yard, testing the atmosphere. Chaplain Charles P. Price was leading a candle-lit procession for peace, in front of the darkened statue of John Harvard. Cox stopped and whispered to Williamson, "If Pusey would only light one candle, there would be a lot fewer problems."[124] Instead, university officials were busy constructing a plan to counteract the next day's demonstration.[125]

Commencement day arrived with blue skies and noisy crowds. The academic procession flowed through the Yard, on schedule. Administrators, faculty, and graduates stepped forward in colorful, billowy gowns, marching to the ceremonial tent and stage. In a carefully choreographed move, the entire faculty stood up and placed their chairs in the aisles, blocking the path to the stage to cut off any disruption. But an unexpected countermove followed. As if perfectly rehearsed, "the graduating class all picked up their chairs and stood aside."[126] A group of black demonstrators from Cambridge led by political activist Saundra Graham "jumped onto the podium to protest

Harvard's housing policies in the nearby Riverside area." She began speaking into the microphone.

"Go home!" someone yelled.

"*You* go home. I'm home!" she shouted back. The microphone was cut off.

Only after a tense negotiation, in which the Senior Fellow allowed Graham several minutes to speak through a bullhorn about injustices in Cambridge, did the rocky commencement limp to a conclusion.[127]

Cox, in his own words, was "useless" during this episode.[128] He and Williamson had been awake for twenty-five hours straight.[129] President Pusey was forced to rush through his remarks in time for lunch. It was one of the most "terrible scenes" for Cox, in a long semester of ordeals. "I had failed in my job and I was also conscious that I had sort of gone to pieces, although I don't know how visible that was to others."[130]

For Williamson, there was only one thread of redeeming grace about that final day in the 1970 academic calendar. "We still didn't bring in the police," Williamson said, dropping his voice. "She said her piece and went on."[131] It was a small comfort in the face of a much larger failure.

Samuel Williamson was given a leave in the 1970–71 academic year to do research in Vienna.[132] Archibald Cox stayed on as trouble-shooter for Harvard University, by himself. He felt alienated from a growing segment of students. He felt desperately behind in classwork and writing projects. Mostly, he was worn out.

Nearly nine months passed without major strikes, occupations, or violence. Cold months in New England discouraged brisk student activism. The worst mischief in the fall of 1970, other than one bomb blast at the Center for International Affairs that caused no injuries, was a Halloween pumpkin placed on the head of the metal rhinoceros that guarded the front of the Harvard biology labs.[133] In 1971, Derek Bok, Archie's colleague who had impressed students and faculty in his handling of student protests at the Law School, was named as the successor to President Pusey, effective at the end of the academic year.[134] There seemed to be a moment of calm. Cox hoped that he might now be able to refocus his energy on teaching.

The Yard police still called him "the Top Cop." The *Harvard Crimson* referred to him as "the General." Some students called him "the Chief Pig."[135] Epithets notwithstanding, he was ready to turn in his keys and become regular "Professor Cox" again. The spring of 1971, however, would not be so kind. Whatever slim reserves Cox had left were entirely depleted once the month of March arrived.

On March 23, the *Crimson* announced that the Harvard-Radcliffe Students for a Just Peace, a conservative group intent on counteracting the antiwar sentiment at Harvard, planned to sponsor a "counter-teach-in" at Sanders Theatre. The controversial list of speakers would include Bui Diem, South Vietnamese ambassador to the United States.[136]

Despite a last-minute switch substituting Nguyen Hoan, counselor for political affairs at the South Vietnamese Embassy, for the more controversial Diem, the program remained on the Harvard calendar for that Friday, in the face of growing threats of confrontation. The planned speakers also included Dolph Droge, a top White House adviser on Vietnam, and other "pro-war" figures such Anand Panyarachun, Thai ambassador to the United Nations.[137] The SDS and the University Action Group, a group of radical faculty and graduate students, openly announced their intention to halt the program. They would bury the pro-war propagandists' words with deafening applause, they pledged, in honor of "the heroic struggle of the Vietnamese people" against U.S. aggression.[138]

Cox and the university faced a thorny question: how should they deal with the inevitable clash? The speakers could not be "disinvited." This was a matter of freedom of speech. The open exchange of ideas was particularly sacred on a college campus. At the same time, the guests could not be led to slaughter. There had to be a plan. Cox's plan was this: "Let them go ahead and then if, after they started, there was such hooting and noise in Sanders Theatre that they couldn't be heard, then I would emerge from the wings. . . ." He would convince the protesters to let the speakers have their say.[139]

Sanders Theatre was a steeply banked auditorium in the old red brick Memorial Hall, built after the Civil War, sitting on a far edge of Harvard Yard. Friday night, March 26, witnessed an unusual gathering. The hall was crawling with students, faculty, antiwar activists, pro-war activists, and police.

When Cox and the "pro-war" speakers arrived at 8:00 P.M., they were greeted by "shouting and bullhorns." Moderator J. Lawrence McCarthy of the American Conservative Party took the microphone, but he was "unable to make himself heard." The crowd of over a thousand shouted, stamped, booed, whooped, clapped. It was time for Cox to control the crowd. Calm them. Convince them to honor the rights of the speakers.

Footage of the Sanders Theatre pandemonium shows Cox, wearing a red bow tie and a neat gray suit, standing on the stage in front of a map of South Vietnam. Wadded papers, marshmallows, and debris were being hurled onto the dais. Students holding flags of North Vietnam jostled the camera. Signs rose and fell proclaiming "Murderer" and "*No* Freedom for War Criminals." Protesters wearing beards and long hair shouted into megaphones. The Indochinese guests on stage held up their hands, desperately trying to block the objects being thrown.[140]

There was unrelenting noise, nearly forty minutes of it. Cox finally stepped forward. Speaking loudly into the bank of microphones, he begged the audience to quiet down, to listen to his statement. The shouting and chanting continued as the protesters "hurled invective and various objects."[141] Archie clung to the microphone that was his only mooring and delivered a brief speech, "in the name of the President and Fellows of the University on behalf of freedom of speech." His address would be remembered as one of the most dramatic moments of the long period of student unrest, even though few, if any, protesters in the hall ever heard it.

Cox began his plea with a measured appeal to logic, speaking directly into the curtain of noise: "If this meeting is disrupted—hateful as some of us may find it—then liberty will have died a little. . . ." The hall was packed beyond capacity; the words vanished and bounced back in a vague echo. "Men and women whose views aroused strong emotions," Cox continued, "loved by some and hated by others—have always been allowed to speak at Harvard—Fidel Castro, the late Malcolm X, George Wallace, William Kunstler, and others." The noise pounded forward, uninterrupted. "Last year, in this very building, speeches were made for physical obstruction of University activities. Harvard gave a platform to all these speakers, even those calling for her destruction. No one in the community tried to silence them, despite intense opposition. . . ."

Cox recalled being hit by "waves of sound." It was an actual physical surge that pushed him away from the microphone. Someone yelled, "F—— you, Archie!" The chanting and shouting remained steady. Cox continued, his voice strained, the half-glasses on his nose occasionally slipping down from sweat:

The reason is plain, and it applies here tonight. Freedom of speech is indivisible. You cannot deny it to one man and save it for others. Over and over again the test of our dedication to liberty is our willingness to allow the expression of ideas we hate. If those ideas are lies, the remedy is more speech and more debate, so that men will learn the truth. . . .

Cox's plea lasted about four minutes. The protesters "chanted on"; his words went "unheeded."[142] Cox ended his speech with an impassioned finale, his face choked with emotion, almost begging. "Answer what is said here with more teach-ins and more truth," he shouted over the roaring chants, "but let the speakers be heard."

As Cox recalled that jarring night, the speech "had no effect in the hall."[143] Police Chief Robert Tonis passed a message that another crowd outside the hall was attempting to force its way in. Police were scuffling with students; one group had already scaled a fire escape and was moving closer.[144] After forty-five minutes of pounding, noise, threats, and scuffles, Cox made the decision: the "counter-teach-in" had to be aborted. But how to get the speakers out of the building?

Cox quickly ushered his guests behind the stage. Students were now pushing forward against the Harvard Police, attempting to break through the line of protection. There was little time to act. A plain clothes detective opened a locked door, and Cox and his speakers descended a little-used staircase into the steam tunnels. Unknown to most of the university, these tunnels connected the entire Harvard campus in an intricate maze of dark passageways underneath Harvard Yard, down to the Charles River. Chief Tonis had known about them from his days in the FBI, when a German spy disappeared using this secret route. The tunnels were just big enough for a human to walk through them, crouched alongside the steam pipes.[145] Cox and his visitors vanished from Memorial Hall without a trace, causing a rumble of confusion. The crowd surged aimlessly looking for its target. Finally it dispersed.

Cox's speech had been drowned out and lost to the protesters in the Memorial Hall. It was, however, carried live by the Harvard radio station and other frequencies that night and heard by students and faculty around the university. Copies were printed by the university and handed out in leaflets on the Harvard campus, then passed like curiosities through the dormitory rooms. The speech made its way into newspapers, first in Boston, and then was picked up by the wire services, flashing its way across the country the following morning.

Anthony Lewis of the *New York Times* lauded Cox's stand as an act of courage. The governor of Vermont sent a quick wire to Harvard: "Tell the General my hat is off to him. Freedom of speech is in more danger than most people think." Senator Mike Mansfield, a Democrat from Montana, who was a passionate opponent of the war in Vietnam, nevertheless inserted the entire Sanders Theatre speech into the *Congressional Record* as a model of First Amendment oratory.[146] Chief Justice Warren Burger would later describe Cox's brief plea in Memorial Hall as one of the most memorable statements in favor of free speech in modern times.[147]

It may not have caused protesters to change their views, that night or that week or that month. The speech did, however, in the view of many observers, have something to do with "the gradual change in atmosphere" at Harvard during the interminable spring of 1971.[148]

The fall brought back brilliant-colored leaves and a parade of majestic maple sugar trees in New England. The Harvard campus settled once more into tranquility. Derek Bok officially took office as the twenty-fifth president of the university. The war in Vietnam was slowly grinding to a halt, with Harvard's own Henry Kissinger, now President Nixon's assistant for national security affairs, bringing home a proposed peace plan that looked encouraging.[149] President Richard M. Nixon won a smashing re-election victory in November 1972, promising to take the country into a new era of prosperity and moral reaffirmation. Archibald Cox was finally able to return to "professoring."

Phyllis Cox would later look over her shoulder at the student riots of the Vietnam era and refer to them as the most difficult period, personally and professionally, in her husband's long career. Archie experienced a painful attack of kidney stones during this time. Some colleagues whispered gently that it was "psychosomatic." Others said it was caused by the stress of events. Derek Bok thought that Archie "kind of wore himself out."[150] Cox had endured a full load of teaching and writing, on top of the unrelenting crises. There were nights, Archie and Phyllis would both candidly confess, when Archie was unsure if he could go on. As Phyllis would say, "He felt responsible for all these people. . . ."

Sam Williamson would observe, after becoming a college president himself at the University of the South in Sewanee, Tennessee, that he learned from Cox that "a university must stay a place of civility. It can't become a political football, regardless of the pressures. . . ."

Cox himself would summarize the experience of the student riots at Harvard much more simply. "My general reaction," he concluded, "was that on the whole we kept the university from blowing up."[151]

WATERGATE
AND
BEYOND

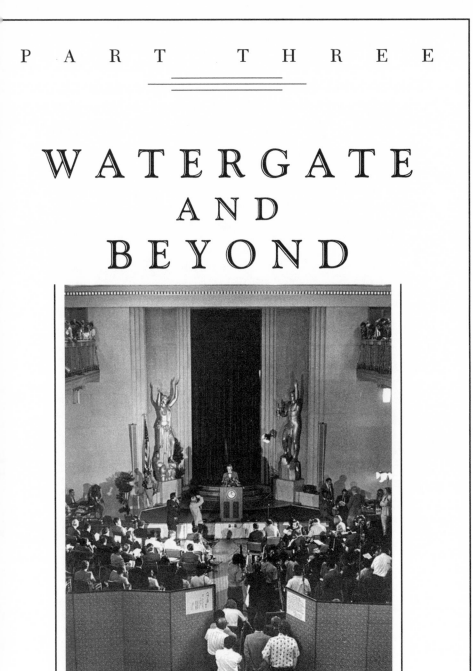

Archibald Cox, Watergate Special Prosecutor (1973)

Cox family

14

A THIRD-RATE
BURGLARY?

In June 1972, as Archie and Phyllis Cox were packing up the pickup truck and preparing their horses and trailer for the annual trek to Maine, an unusual crime was uncovered in Washington. At 2:10 in the morning on June 17, four Cubans and one American were arrested at the posh Watergate complex, which contained a hotel, apartments, shops, and offices, near the Potomac River in Washington. A security guard had spotted an apparent burglary in progress on the sixth floor and contacted the D.C. police. FBI agents were called to the scene because phone taps were involved: the burglars had broken into the headquarters of the Democratic National Committee and were installing bugging devices. The men were wearing surgical rubber gloves. They carried transmitters, photographic equipment, walkie-talkies, a radio receiver—all sophisticated electronics. When police searched the burglars, they found lock-picking devices, cans of Mace, and $2,400 in cash, including thirteen brand-new $100 bills.

One burglar, the American, turned out to be using an alias. He was quickly identified as James McCord, a former CIA employee who specialized in telecommunications assignments. More recently he had served as chief of security for the Committee to Re-elect the President, or CREEP. The four Cubans had all once worked for the CIA. At their arraignment, each burglar identified his occupation as "Anti-Communist."

The story became even more tantalizing when the FBI discovered that two men who had supervised the burglary, E. Howard Hunt and G. Gordon Liddy, worked for the White House and had monitored the break-in from a nearby Howard Johnson's hotel room. Hunt had been a White House consultant working on national security matters relating, among other things, to the Pentagon Papers case. Liddy had worked for John Ehrlichman, assistant to President Nixon for domestic affairs, as part of the Special Investigations (or "plumbers") unit, before becoming counsel to the finance committee for the president's re-election apparatus. Liddy was an offbeat character; those in White House circles "were uneasily aware that Liddy often carried a gun and was quite capable of using it."[1] When the FBI searched the hotel where Hunt and Liddy had been stationed, they found an envelope with a check written by Hunt, and notations to "W.H." and "W. Hse" in the Cubans' address books.[2] Investigative reporters Bob Woodward and Carl Bernstein of the *Washington Post* confirmed the odd link to the White House. The plan of espionage and sabotage even had its own code name, "Gemstone"—all the ingredients of a spy novel.

The Coxes, however, were too busy to pay much attention to this saga in the newspapers. Phyllis had a summer's worth of gardening and outdoor work waiting for her in Maine. Archie was committed to a heavy lineup of writing assignments and other projects that had piled high as a result of his extra duties during three years of student unrest at Harvard. The burglary at the Watergate complex in Washington occupied only a tiny window of his attention in the summer of 1972.

At Harvard, the pace was brisk. Archie had recently moved into a spacious office in a corner of Langdell Hall, an old office smelling vaguely of pipe smoke and ancient books that had once belonged to his old professors Warren Seavey and Roscoe Pound. "Being a sentimentalist," he said, "why I'm rather happy to follow in this seat."[3] The new quarters seemed to agree with him. His professional life was busy and productive.

Cox testified in Congress, at the invitation of Senator Edward M. Kennedy, concerning the constitutionality of legislation that would allow eighteen-year-olds to vote. (Congress and the states went a step further by adopting the Twenty-sixth Amendment in the summer of 1971.)[4] He scored a major Supreme Court victory in *Coolidge v. New Hampshire,* the case he had argued pro bono on behalf of an accused murderer, establishing new ground rules for police in the sensitive area of automobile searches.[5] In early 1972, he ran in Wayland as an Alternate At-Large Delegate committed to the candidacy of Senator Edmund S. Muskie of Maine, in the Democratic presidential primary. (Cox won the alternate delegate spot, but never had the time or inclination to attend the convention.)[6] Throughout 1972, Cox also served as counsel for a legislative committee in Massachusetts that investigated misconduct charges against two sitting members of the state's superior court, Judges DeSaulnier and Brogna, that ultimately led to the removal and disbarment of one and the censure of the other for fixing a stock fraud case.[7]

In early 1973, Cox published a short book, *The Role of the Supreme Court in American Government,* in which (among other things) he reacted skeptically to the Supreme Court's decision in *Roe v. Wade,* decided in January of that year. Although he passed no judgment on the moral issue posed by *Roe,* he asserted that the abortion decision read "like a set of hospital rules and regulations" rather than good constitutional law.[8]

All these activities represented Cox's own attempt to follow Oliver Wendell Holmes's admonition that lawyers should "live greatly, within the law."[9] Archie was now sixty years old. The glory days of his career were over. He was hardly a nationally known figure, other than in narrow legal circles.[10] But he had tried to follow an honorable path each time a challenge came his way.

When he was not writing or teaching, Cox plunged himself back into arbitration work. For Archie, it represented the most important "human" side of his outside activities.[11] Over a period of twenty years, Cox had amassed a long list of cases in which he felt he had brought a small measure of justice to the workplace as a labor mediator.[12] He was personally pleased that he was continuing to make a contribution in this arena; it was a perfect way to cap off his legal career, before retirement.

The only disappointing turn of events, as far as Cox saw it, was that labor arbitration had become "lawyerized to such a great extent" by the 1970s.[13] The old-fashioned system of labor justice seemed to have given way to shouting attorneys and harsh tactics designed to produce victories at any cost. It bothered Cox that by 1973, lawyers in general had begun to earn a plummeting image in the public eye.

In May 1973 Archibald Cox was presenting a series of lectures at the University of California at Berkeley. These talks explored a question that fascinated Cox: To what extent were American presidents able to successfully reshape and remake the course of constitutional law? It was a topic inspired by President Nixon's recent attacks on the Warren Court during his 1972 presidential campaign. One of the themes of

Cox's lectures was the importance of a sustained faith in the Supreme Court as an institution, regardless of one president's efforts to alter the makeup of that body.[14]

A telephone call was patched into Cox's room on the Berkeley campus on Wednesday, May 16. It was his former student, Elliot Richardson, who began the conversation by wishing his old professor a happy birthday. Archie was turning sixty-one years old the next day; he was astounded that someone on Elliot's staff had bothered to look it up.[15]

Cox had run into Richardson more than once since his former student's graduation from Harvard Law School in the late 1940s. Richardson had served as U.S. attorney in Massachusetts at the beginning of Cox's tenure as solicitor general (Richardson was later "fired" by Bobby Kennedy at the behest of President Kennedy, due to a political squabble in Boston).[16] He had been elected to office as lieutenant governor of Massachusetts and later attorney general of the state. More recently, Elliot had occupied a string of government posts in Washington under President Nixon. Cox and Richardson had led, in many ways, parallel lives on opposite sides of the political fence. They moved in the "same or similar circles professionally."[17] They were "friends" in the proper New England sense of the word, but they were not, as Cox would say, "in any sense, intimate."[18]

Richardson was now secretary of defense under President Nixon, following a stint as secretary of health, education, and welfare. Cox knew, as he cradled the phone, that Elliot had just been nominated to succeed Richard G. Kleindienst as attorney general after Kleindienst's tainted resignation (along with presidential advisers H. R. Haldeman, John Ehrlichman, and John Dean) in the swirl of the Watergate scandal. The affair had been gaining increased attention in the newspapers, as Archie knew from reading the morning *Times* with his cup of coffee. That was about all he knew, or cared to know, about this Watergate debacle.

Elliot's question took him off guard: Would Archie consider taking on the position of Watergate special prosecutor? The alleged scandal had come so close to the executive branch that it seemed wise to divorce the investigation from the Justice Department. The idea of a special prosecutor was admittedly unusual, yet it made sense to have someone oversee the case from an independent vantage point. Cox's name had surfaced as a possible candidate. This was not a formal offer. Just an exploratory phone call.

"Why me, Elliot?" Cox asked half-jokingly. "I don't think I ever defended anyone for anything more than a traffic offense, and I'm not sure that in those instances that the defendant didn't plead guilty."[19]

Richardson had already anticipated this question. Cox could hire a prosecutor to serve as the actual trial lawyer if that was a worry. He had the confidence of many senators on both sides of the political aisle, not to mention the American Bar Association, based upon his service as solicitor general.[20] His integrity would compensate for any lack of criminal trial experience.

Cox's immediate assessment was that the assignment would be "exceedingly challenging." It would also be "lots of fun. In my judgment very important to the country."[21] But he kept his reactions masked—he didn't want to rush into a bad decision. Cox knew surprisingly little about the Watergate affair, nothing more than he got from the papers and the evening news. He did know that one of the alleged burglars, James McCord, had recently written a letter to federal Judge John Sirica, suggesting that the conspiracy went much further than the original testimony let on. Cox also knew about the fresh series of resignations of presidential aides Dean, Ehrlichman, and Haldeman. He suspected that Elliot Richardson's nomination to replace Kleindienst "hung, perhaps, on his naming a special prosecutor" who was suitable to both the president and Congress.[22]

But Richardson did not seem particularly worried about his own confirmation. That did not seem to be the force motivating this phone call. In fact, Cox could not tell if Elliot really wanted the post. In Washington, Cox realized, the position of attorney general could be viewed as "a step down from secretary of defense," particularly given the importance of the defense position with the Vietnam War coming to an end, and the negative images that flowed from the recent Watergate mess.[23] Archie sympathized with his old student. This was no great promotion. Elliot was doing what he felt he had an obligation to do.

A few things worried Cox, as his mind turned around the position that Richardson had described. Why had savvy Washington insiders like Warren Christopher—the former deputy attorney general under President Johnson, who had returned to private practice in Los Angeles—rejected the offer to serve as Watergate special prosecutor, according to the newspapers? Was there some pitfall that Cox did not appreciate, other than the obvious no-win situation that any special prosecutor would face?

What Cox did not know, but what Richardson's notes would carefully preserve, was that a total of seven other candidates had already turned down the position as Watergate special prosecutor. Most of them were acting or semiretired judges who had decided that they were too old for the position or unwilling to give up a lifetime appointment for this uncertain venture.[24] These names included (in the order they turned Richardson down) Senior Judge J. Edward Lumbard of the U.S. Court of Appeals for the Second Circuit, whom Nixon himself had proposed; federal district judge Edward Thaxter Gignoux of Maine; Chief Justice Joseph Weintraub of the New Jersey Supreme Court; retired state judge David W. Peck of New York; Justice William H. Erickson of the Supreme Court of Colorado; federal judge Harold R. Tyler, Jr., of New York, rumored to be leaving the bench; and Warren Christopher, who had flown to Washington to speak to Richardson and rejected the offer before he left the airport the next day. Lawrence Walsh, a New York lawyer with a background as a prosecutor and judge, was an early front-runner who quickly faded from consideration.[25] Texas attorney Leon Jaworski was also among those considered, but was ruled out early in the process by Richardson personally, who viewed him as too much of a "wheeler-dealer."[26]

Hundreds of individuals had been contacted by Richardson's office for recommendations. Ironically, many of these individuals—Robert Bork, Charles Alan Wright, Leon Jaworski, Alexander Bickel—would play conflicting roles in Watergate themselves.[27] Confidential memos and wires containing recommendations of proposed "best candidates" inundated Richardson's office from across the United States. This list included sitting Justices Byron White and Potter Stewart of the U.S. Supreme Court, both of whom Richardson considered briefly for the job.[28] The initial "selection process" outlined by Richardson's aide in a confidential memo called for consultation with former Chief Justice Earl Warren and Chief Justice Warren Burger before a final candidate was selected.[29] It was meant to be a high-profile game, with big-name players.

By May 9, eight candidates had made Richardson's private "first cut." This list did not include Archibald Cox.[30] In fact, his name was nowhere to be found in the penciled lists of contenders. Repeat phone calls ended in more and more polite declines. Scratch marks began to cover the list. Nobody with a nationally recognized name wanted to attach that name to the Watergate special prosecutor's position. It was an untested, risky job with little chance of building a more prestigious career from it. Richardson philosophized more than once with his staff about the difficulty in finding a special prosecutor. He enjoyed philosophizing, puffing on his pipe while leaning back in his chair. "It often seemed like we had become a nation where the only heroes were rock singers and ball players," he said, "and that there were no large men of probity . . . who could be called upon for the task."[31] His aide Wilmot Hastings saw the problem in more practical terms: "The smart ones knew there was a mess of trouble in this thing."[32]

It was at this late stage of the Watergate hunt that a number of contacts, both solicited and unsolicited, recommended Archibald Cox as a dark horse. He had no prosecutorial experience; that was his "big minus." But some felt that he earned strong bonus points based upon his experience as solicitor general and his strong reputation for independence. Justice Richard Poff of the Supreme Court of Virginia, in confidential interviews with Will Hastings, ranked Cox as his "first choice."[33] Albert M. Sacks, the dean of Harvard Law School, strongly recommended Cox: "I assume others have mentioned [Archie], but I wanted to add his name myself; doesn't have the trial experience, but has everything else." Justice Paul C. Reardon of the Supreme Judicial Court of Massachusetts had some reservations but said that Cox "still looks like a very good candidate to [me]. Understands the potential liabilities of the Harvard syndrome [i.e., the New England self-righteousness that President Nixon viewed with disdain] but still think he is good."

Others saw him as a horrible candidate. Robert Meserve, a lawyer at Palmer and Dodge in Boston and outgoing president of the American Bar Association, panned Cox as a "humorless man" who was "probably not very perceptive in his dealings with people." Said Meserve, "He tends to regard people by surface impressions only." Sumner Babcock, a Boston lawyer, chimed in that Cox was "not the right kind of guy. Not experienced in fact gathering and investigation." Roswell Perkins, a New York lawyer with extensive government experience, dismissed Cox as "not an action man, did not have a style which would go over well with the press or Congress." Henry Petersen, head of the Criminal Division in the Justice Department overseeing the existing Watergate trial, which had recently come under attack for its lack of objectivity and collusion with the White House, commented flatly about Cox, "Would not recommend."[34]

All the other candidates that Richardson had previously contacted shared one common denominator: significant experience as a prosecutor or a trial lawyer. This had been a "working requirement" for Richardson's staff, in compiling names. Will Hastings remembered,

"We were looking for a 'fact man.' This was not a scholarly program. This was a question of 'who did it?' We were looking for someone who had tremendous trial experience."[35] Cox miserably failed this test. But at least he had good instincts, Richardson said. Maybe they could compensate by tacking on a deputy with courtroom know-how.

So it was from this hodgepodge of positive and negative assessments that Archibald Cox's name moved to the top of an increasingly scratched-out list. Cox had stature in Washington and a national reputation for objectivity and uprightness that would satisfy many in the fracas. His older age was a plus; it would be difficult for either side to suspect that he was taking the case to catapult himself into a new career in politics or law. President Nixon had given his new attorney general designee an open-ended instruction to "do it right." That was exactly what Elliot Richardson intended to do.

Hastings himself was not enthused with the selection. He had taken Cox's course in agency law back in 1958 and viewed Cox as an "insufferable" teacher and a stuck-up New Englander. His candid reaction was, "Not that stuffed shirt!"[36] But he understood what was driving his boss's decision. "Elliot knew he could call [Cox] down to talk honestly, and it wouldn't be in the *Washington Post* the next day," explained Hastings. "It was the old Yankee s——. There's a lot to be said against the tribe of New England Protestants who populated the Northeast. But there's a lot to be said about the old-boy network of trust."[37]

Another Richardson aide put it more bluntly. "It is a terrible thing to say, and I am [sure] Archie Cox would take it in good spirits," said J. T. Smith, "but we were getting desperate."[38]

Cox saw another problem, as his mind jolted back to the telephone and the issue of this unusual new job proposal. He would have to discuss it with Derek Bok, Harvard's new president, before he could give Elliot a firm answer. How many times could a professor make detours into public life without betraying his commitment to the university? There was a disturbing trend among younger faculty members to view academic life as a temporary perch upon which to hang one's hat while looking to jump to the next government post. In Cox's mind, this was not a proper way to view one's duty to a university, not when one held a tenured position on a major faculty. "Wasn't I setting a bad example?" Cox wondered as Elliot carefully explained the importance, to the nation and to all concerned, of his accepting the post.[39] Was Cox not betraying something just as important?

A third more puzzling issue would have to await Archie's return to Cambridge. That morning, he had climbed out of bed at his hotel, stood up, and discovered that he could not hear out of his right ear. It had "gone dead all of a sudden"—totally deaf.[40] Was this a permanent condition? Would it affect his ability to function in such a high-visibility post? Cox did not dwell on this personal problem with Richardson. He listened with his good left ear and agreed with Elliot that it was worth moving to a second level of discussions. Richardson's assistant had already hashed out a set of proposed guidelines that might govern the special prosecutor. Cox and Richardson would work through this draft, iron out details, and see if they could reach a common ground. But it would be absolutely understood that Cox was not committing himself. He had to go home, have some time for discussing the matter with Phyllis, have some time for soul-searching.

On Wednesday and Thursday, May 16 and 17, the telephone line between Washington and Berkeley stayed open at sporadic intervals during the day and night, as Richardson and Cox attempted to define a new position that had no exact counterpart in American history. Richardson felt strongly that as attorney general he should maintain some sort of "overall responsibility" for the Watergate investigation. A provision must be included in the guidelines, he insisted, that the special prosecutor could be dismissed for gross misconduct or "extraordinary improprieties."[41] Ironically, this phrase had come from Richardson's conversations with Archie's old dean, Erwin Griswold, who was finishing up his stint as solicitor general under President Nixon. Griswold had spun the language out of a 150-year-old Harvard statute governing the dismissal of tenured professors. The term "grave misconduct" appeared in the Harvard statute, but Richardson and Griswold disguised it so that the press did not perceive the guidelines as "the Ivy League trying to run the government."[42]

Archie did not know that the altered phrase had traveled from Harvard, where it already governed him, into this new document. No matter where it came from, he did not like the sound of it. At the same time, Archie "certainly didn't intend to engage in anything that anybody could possibly call gross misconduct."[43] So the language was inserted. It seemed like a distracting little detail.[44]

Cox insisted, though, that if he took the job he must have the freedom to decide what information he would report to the attorney general, and what he would keep confidential.[45] Richardson would occupy a sensitive niche, straddling the camp of the prosecutor and the nest of potential targets within the White House. Neither Cox nor any special prosecutor should be expected to disclose all details of the probe to the attorney general, Cox argued, even though the attorney general would technically be the "superior" official in any formal chain of command. This point was acceptable to Richardson. The two men agreed to leave it in the form of an unwritten understanding, as was true of many of their compromises during these two days. In Elliot's mind, hashing out the guidelines for the special prosecutor was a formality. "I never doubted that if I had responsibility for Watergate, I would do it right. I took it for granted that the person I appointed would do it right. So all of this talk about conditions of independence was for appearance."[46]

The most important revision to the charter, history would later reveal, related to the breadth of the special prosecutor's powers. As originally proposed by Richardson, the special prosecutor's ability to investigate and prosecute was sharply limited: if a crime was not directly linked to the Watergate break-in, it was off limits. This troubled Cox. Although he was largely in the dark about Watergate, he had skimmed enough in the papers to know that allegations of illegal campaign contributions by massive corporations like International Telegraph and Telephone were "in the air." There were also allegations that someone had broken into the office of a psychiatrist in California. Who was to say, at this point, whether these events might be indirectly linked to the Watergate burglary? Archie did not want to be burdened with the task of proving in advance whether a particular episode or piece of evidence was directly "connected to Watergate." Untangling big cases did not work that way. Criminals did not stop to stamp "Watergate" on each puzzle piece of proof strewn along the path. If wrongdoing by White House aides or presidential appointees came to Cox's attention, he needed to be able to plunge headlong into the investigation and worry about links to the Watergate break-in in due course. "I wanted to be damned sure that *I* was going to be the fellow who made all the decisions," he said, ". . . including the decisions about my own jurisdiction."

Having been in law enforcement in Massachusetts, Elliot Richardson understood the concern. He knew all about the booby traps that faced government prosecutors. He agreed to insert language giving the special prosecutor wide jurisdiction over allegations of criminal conduct involving White House assistants or presidential aides, past or present. This guarantee was "enormously broad," as Cox understood. It would give him "plenty of latitude."[47]

Six months later, Richardson would confess that this simple revision gave Cox much more "latitude" than he expected.[48] It created looming problems for Richardson down the road. It created even bigger problems, it turned out, for those occupying chairs within the White House.

After two days of impromptu telephone negotiations, Cox took the red-eye flight back to Boston following his last Thomas Jefferson lecture at Berkeley. It was time to talk to others, "then make up my own mind."[49]

Phyllis would think back on this blur of days, remembering only a long, serious discussion at their home in Wayland on Thursday. She and Archie hashed over the positives and negatives. Early the next morning (Friday), Archie sat in Derek Bok's office in Massachusetts Hall. They discussed many things, particularly Archie's concern about setting a poor example for younger faculty members. Cox was still haunted by the words of his old mentor Learned Hand, when Hand accepted an honorary degree from Harvard in 1939. Judge Hand had stressed the importance in a free society of maintaining purely disinterested scholars. Their job was to "lay aside all else, and seek truth," while maintaining an "aloofness from burning issues." They were not to carry swords under their gowns; rather, the scholar's duty was to avoid becoming a soldier for hire in any particular camp.[50] After years of activity in labor work and absences on behalf of John F. Kennedy, Cox's recurring fear was "whether I hadn't run off from the law school too often . . . which is not quite consistent with preserving that detached attitude of pure scholar."[51]

Derek Bok was "reassuring" on all counts. Archie should take the job; it was important to the country to have this Watergate mess concluded.[52] Besides, Archie could strive to preserve the "detachment" that Judge Hand had spoken about, by bringing true independence to the Watergate position.[53]

At 11:00 A.M., Archie was meeting with a top ear specialist in Boston. "Well, you've come to the right man," the doctor said. "I've performed eight of the only twelve autopsies that have been performed on the ear of someone who lost their hearing that way." Cox recoiled. "Nobody was going to get my ear to perform an autopsy," he would later say, only half joking.[54]

When the specialist completed his examination, he informed Cox that his hearing in one ear was lost, permanently, most likely because of a low-grade virus. Nothing could ever be done to bring it back.

Cox sat back silently. Would this deafness handicap him so much that he should not accept the special prosecutor's post? he asked the doctor in strict confidence. The specialist picked up his chart. "It will handicap you just as much as you think it will handicap you and not more."[55]

That was all Cox's good ear needed to hear. He would ignore the problem. For the rest of his life.

"Well, then I shouldn't tell the attorney general anything about it," the doctor winked, walking Cox to the door. Cox cocked his head. He replied, partly facetiously, partly not, "That would be a great way to start the Watergate investigation, wouldn't it?"[56]

"This is probably a no-win job," Archie remembered telling Phyllis when he got home. "It'll end up inconclusive—the conclusive evidence either exonerating President Nixon or damning President Nixon won't be available. Those who hate him will be saying, 'If Cox weren't so damn stupid, he would have proved that Nixon was involved personally.' Those who liked and admired Nixon would be saying, 'If Cox wasn't a prejudiced Democrat, he'd have exonerated Richard Nixon.' And I'll be damned by everybody."[57]

"True," said Phyllis. But wasn't this an important challenge, an important duty, for someone?

As they talked back and forth, a simple point lodged itself in Archie's mind. He would later reconstruct the point like this: "Somebody clearly has to do it. It's important that everything possible be done to show that a fair inquiry into wrongdoing at the very highest levels of government can be conducted under our system." And in the end, Archie concluded, "maybe there's no one better to do it than a sixty-year-old tenured law professor who isn't going anywhere [in public life] anyway."[58]

So he called Elliot Richardson that day, May 18, and accepted the post. It was the same day that one of the Watergate burglars, James McCord, testified before the Senate committee investigating the Watergate affair that he had been offered "executive clemency" if he took the fall for the break-in, and that there had been pressure on the Watergate defendants to keep their mouths shut from "the very highest levels of the White House."[59]

Richardson held a press conference at his office in the Pentagon later that afternoon, announcing that he would name Archibald Cox to the $38,000-a-year job as Watergate special prosecutor (a small pay hike from Archie's teaching salary) if the Senate approved Richardson's nomination as attorney general.[60] "This is a task of tremendous importance," Richardson told the press. "Somehow we must restore confidence, honor and integrity in government."[61]

Archie himself held a tiny news conference in the press room at Harvard, almost squinting as a handful of cameras blinked at him. "I have accepted if the Senate approves," he said tentatively, "not without an awed sense of responsibility."[62]

The press generally seemed to approve of the choice. The Framingham, Massachusetts, *South Middlesex Sunday News* lauded the selection of Cox as a man who "has the reputation of being cool under fire."[63] The Pittsfield, Massachusetts, *Berkshire Eagle* called Archie "the right man for a grim job."[64] The *Cleveland Plain Dealer* labeled Cox "ramrod straight."[65] Drawing a comparison between Cox and Elliot Richardson, the Long Beach, California, *Independent* editorialized in colorful adjectives: "The two men are very alike, self-confident, impatient of stupidity, exacting, publicly severe, perhaps snooty. They even look alike, trim, agile, similarly costumed in the casually precise garb of New England's private boys' school." One Harvard professor added, "Both treasure their independence, neither will want to surrender power to the other, but both have a tremendous sense of obligation."[66]

Phyllis Cox, who was described somewhat amusedly by the press as a "teacher and a horsewoman" (she recently taught third grade in Concord), was quoted only briefly regarding her husband's new job: "I know Archie will love it. It appeals to his old-fashioned sense of being called by the nation."[67]

In Windsor, Vermont, Archie's mother and sister Molly heard the news on the radio while sitting in the sunroom of the sprawling old family home that had once been part of William M. Evarts's estate in the 1800s. They were "quite surprised" that Archie would make the national news at this advanced stage of his career. In honor of the unusual event, they "went to the corner store to get a paper."[68]

The *Washington Post* announced the selection of Cox with high marks. It reported, however, that a number of Democratic senators still expressed grave concern about the "independence" of any special prosecutor operating under Richardson. Richardson had testified openly in front of the Senate Judiciary Committee that he intended to directly supervise the Watergate prosecution, a notion that riled Democratic lawmakers.[69] Democratic Senator Adlai E. Stevenson III of Illinois issued a strong warning signed by twenty-eight powerful colleagues, demanding stiffer guarantees of independence by Richardson if he expected to be confirmed.[70]

But Richardson was not backing down. He replied to Senator Stevenson that "the Attorney General [must] retain that degree of responsibility mandated by his statutory accountability."[71] There were now serious "questions about Richardson's own prospects for Senate confirmation."[72] Senator Edward M. Kennedy, a prime mover on the powerful Judiciary Committee and front-runner for the Democratic presidential nomination in 1976, saw it coming. Unless Richardson gave stronger guarantees of independence for the special prosecutor, "he wasn't going through."[73]

Elliot Richardson, a self-declared righteous New Englander, took affront at all this blustering. Republican or not, he thought it elementary that he would exercise his role fairly. "It's a characteristic of us upright Yankees that we tend to be oblivious to other people's worries of appearances that might affect perceptions of integrity."[74] His nomination was nevertheless "losing support rapidly" in the Senate, according to reporter James Doyle of the Washington Star.[75] The Democrats were determined not to allow the special prosecutor to be a shill position; they were not going to allow this ivy-tower professor from Harvard to be gulled by a former student turned politician. The Judiciary Committee wanted to hear from Cox, in the flesh.

On Monday, May 21, the fifth day of hearings on the appointment of Elliot Richardson and three days after he had officially nominated Cox as special prosecutor, Archibald Cox appeared before the Senate Judiciary Committee. Richardson outlined Cox's past service in government and academics. He underscored the professor's extensive service in the Kennedy administration as solicitor general, a position that Cox had occupied with impartiality and distinction. When the microphone was turned over to Cox, he responded to sharp questioning from committee members, particularly Democrats, by assuring them that he would be in a position to act independently. Using a reference to the "whip hand," a phrase that he had tried out forty years earlier in his college thesis, "The Senatorial Saucer," Cox underscored the depth of his conviction on this point. Senator Robert Byrd, the powerful Democratic whip with a strong West Virginia accent and a distinctive pompadour, laid into Cox. Over and over, he tested Cox's commitment to keeping sensitive information away from Elliot Richardson:

BYRD: You will have what?
COX: The whip hand.
BYRD: And you won't hesitate to use it?
COX: No, Sir. . . .

At Senator Byrd's suggestion that the attorney general might seek to extract confidential information from the special prosecutor, Cox refused to back down:

BYRD: What would you do if Mr. Richardson as Attorney General demanded such information under what he considers to be and what he states to be his statutory accountability?

COX: Well, I guess—if the Secretary [Richardson] will forgive me—I would revert to the role of professor and say, "Look, Elliot, that isn't the way we understood it." [*Laughter*] Second, if I had the belief . . . that it should not be given to him, I would say, "The only way to exercise your final statutory authority is fire me. It is your move."[76]

That evening, the headline of the *Washington Post* announced, "Cox Helps Richardson Nomination." The same day, the *Post* broke the news that former White House chief of staff H. R. Haldeman had allegedly instructed the CIA to block the Watergate investigation, at the urging of the president himself. Cox's strong pledge of independence in the midst of the worsening Watergate situation, the newspaper reported, had provided a major boost to Richardson's prospects.[77] Cox had promised the committee to pursue the trail of any crime, regardless of its scope or implications. Senator Byrd had pressed, "Even if that trail should lead, heaven forbid, to the Oval Office of the White House itself?" "Wherever that trail may lead," Cox had assured the senator.

This response had seemed to mollify many influential Democrats. Senator Kennedy recalled, "When Elliot Richardson said he'd give independence and Cox said he'd exercise it, that was the key understanding." The Senate was now "reluctantly" leaning toward confirming Richardson with Cox an integral part of the package.[78]

Ironically, President Nixon himself capitalized on the selection of

Cox as special prosecutor. On May 22, the president told the American people:

> The truth about Watergate should be brought out in an orderly way, recognizing that the safeguards of judicial procedure are designed to find the truth, not to hide the truth. With his selection of Archibald Cox—who served both President Kennedy and President Johnson as solicitor general—as the special supervisory prosecutor for matters related to the case, Attorney General–designate Richardson has demonstrated his own determination to see the truth brought out. In this effort he has my full support.

President Nixon went on to assure all concerned that if Richardson and Cox were approved, the White House would cooperate fully. He pledged:

> Accordingly, executive privilege will not be invoked as to any testimony concerning possible criminal conduct or discussions of possible criminal conduct, in the matters presently under investigation, including the Watergate affair and the alleged cover-up.

The president took this opportunity to state categorically that

> I had no prior knowledge of the Watergate operation.
> I took no part in, nor was I aware of, any subsequent efforts that may have been made to coverup Watergate.
> At no time did I authorize any offer of executive clemency for the Watergate defendants, nor did I know of any such offer.

President Nixon concluded firmly:

> I want the public to learn the truth about Watergate and those guilty of any illegal actions brought to justice.[79]

These strong assurances seemed to placate even a skeptical Congress. They also provided reassurance to Cox and Richardson. "The assumption [was] that there would be no withholding of any information or evidence from me," said Cox, remembering the subtext of the president's encouraging message. "The assumption was that I would get to see everything."[80]

The Senate moved rapidly. On Friday, May 26, Elliot Lee Richardson took the oath of office as the sixty-ninth attorney general of the

United States. To add to the solemnity of the occasion, the oath was administered by Chief Justice Warren Burger, President Nixon's hand-picked appointee to the Supreme Court. The formal ceremony took place in the East Room of the White House, with the president and Mrs. Nixon presiding over a guest list of three hundred.[81] "This is a time," Richardson said in brief comments, when "the institutions of our government are under stress." A "kind of sleaziness" had infected "the processes of government," Richardson told the elite audience, and he aimed to eliminate it. The new attorney general pledged to be both "fair" and "fearless" in carrying out his duties.[82]

Cox's swearing-in ceremony was much more modest, a tiny gathering in the gray-blue reception room attached to the solicitor general's office. Dean Erwin Griswold still held the keys to that office, although he was soon to be replaced by Yale law professor Robert Bork.[83] This spot on the fifth floor of the Justice Department seemed to be a perfect symbolic location to begin such a daunting new challenge. The oath was administered by Charles Fahy, who as solicitor general had employed Archie as his young assistant in the 1940s. The eighty-year-old Fahy, appointed to a federal judgeship by President Truman, presided with a flowing robe, gray hair, and slightly stooped shoulders. Archie's crew cut was also full of gray by now. But he was anxious to have some figure, some role model, to look up to. Fahy, with his principles of steel, was a perfect choice.

With Richardson at his side and Phyllis in the front row of chairs, Cox took the oath of office to carry out a previously nonexistent role in American government. He told a small group of friends and family that, by his service as special prosecutor, he hoped to emulate the qualities of Judge Fahy: "candor, honor, sensibility, dedication to justice and unswerving rectitude without a taint, I hope, of self-righteousness."[84]

Cox wore a traditional, red pin-striped four-in-hand tie that he had borrowed from his brother Louis for the swearing-in, rather than a bow tie. It was a truly serious occasion.[85]

President Nixon had never mentioned Richardson's selection for special prosecutor in the White House swearing-in ceremony that night. Shortly after Cox's makeshift induction in the solicitor general's anteroom, however, his name was on the tongues of many Nixon advisers. News swept through the White House that Cox's guest list had included Senator Edward M. Kennedy and Ethel Kennedy and that Judge Fahy had presided—all of them high-profile Democrats.

The *St. Louis Post-Dispatch* reported that RFK's widow had "sat on a couch, beaming."[86] The ugly word "conspiracy" laced many conversations on Pennsylvania Avenue. Erwin Griswold saw it coming: "There were at least ten members of the Kennedy family present. And I thought it was a terrible mistake. But I kept my mouth shut."[87]

Cox was nonplussed by the immediacy and nastiness of the reaction. The "Kennedy angle" was splashed across the morning newspapers, in bold print. The White House did not seem amused. "The porcupine had flung all of its quills into the president's face," said Leonard Garment, one of the president's lawyers.[88] Cox realized that he still had plenty to learn about politics. In his own mind, however, there was nothing that he had done wrong, nothing that he should have done differently. After all, he had worked closely with John and Robert Kennedy and had grown to know their families. He and Phyllis knew few other people in Washington. "I mean, whom do you ask to such a thing?" he explained. "You ask your friends."[89]

The swearing-in fiasco was just the beginning of an unhappy perception that slowly percolated through the White House: Cox was a patsy of the Kennedy Democrats, bent on toppling the Nixon presidency. Ironically, Cox's background as a Democrat and his work in the Kennedy administration had calmed the fears of the Judiciary Committee and allowed President Nixon's nominee to be confirmed. That Cox was "identified with the enemy" had been considered a big plus by Richardson's staff.[90] They viewed Cox as nonpartisan "even to the point of prickliness."[91] As a solid Republican fiercely loyal to the president, Richardson had selected Cox precisely because he viewed him as an apolitical creature. These details, however, like many facts of Watergate, were quickly lost to the maw of history.

Given the strong aversion to Cox's Kennedy ties within the White House, why had President Nixon approved of Cox's appointment to the post in the first place? Years later, Cox would puzzle over this issue aloud to Elliot Richardson when the two men were in England. Archie asked his old student, "How was it that Richard Nixon had approved of my appointment?"

Elliot Richardson answered, "Well, that's easy. I didn't consult him."[92]

The full story related to the day that Richardson had been asked by the president to accept the post as attorney general. Richardson had been flown by helicopter to Camp David on a beautiful spring Sunday in April to meet with President Nixon at his private retreat in the Maryland mountains. The President, he recalled, "looked sort of gray and shaken. . . . He said he had just done the hardest thing he had ever done in his life," in getting rid of Haldeman, Ehrlichman, and Kleindienst.[93] Would Elliot succeed the embattled Kleindienst as attorney general?[94] Richardson replied carefully: no, Mr. President. He was reluctant to take on the job. He would prefer to see someone *outside* the administration take the post. His independence would be questioned.

In fact, Richardson had anticipated the offer and had decided to turn it down. He loved his job as secretary of defense; he had already "done" the attorney general's job in Massachusetts. In lengthy notes written to himself that morning, he had begun in typical introspective fashion: "The more I think about it, the more the job seems to be one of real danger and risk for ELR."[95] Richardson believed that "the attitude behind what the White House has gotten itself into is worse than the actual behavior." The White House had been treating the Watergate scandal with "arrogance, contempt, and a lack of real understanding." Unless this attitude could be reformed in the president himself and his closest advisers, there could "be no real 'clean-up.' " Richardson had ended his scribbled notes with several pointed questions to himself:

1. What if the President did know about it [the cover-up]?
2. Do you have the stomach for it?

Particularly on the latter question, he had his doubts. The president had nevertheless insisted on that cloudless Sunday afternoon at Camp David that he "needed" Richardson to do the job.[96] "I had already decided," Richardson would later admit, "that if he really put it on me, I'd have no choice."[97]

It was President Nixon himself who first raised the idea of naming a special prosecutor.[98] One name the president threw out was John J. McCloy, age seventy-eight, distinguished New York lawyer and perennial presidential adviser, who had been closely associated with Felix Frankfurter. (Frankfurter had been Richardson's boss many years earlier.) Another was J. Edward Lumbard, age seventy-one, former chief judge of the Second Circuit Court of Appeals, who had taken senior status and, according to Nixon, would "bring enormous stature to the job."[99] The third choice—at the opposite end of the age spectrum—was thirty-eight-year-old Will Hastings, Elliot's former general counsel at the Department of Health, Education and Welfare and his assistant in the Massachusetts attorney general's office. Hastings was a young man with whom Elliot worked comfortably.[100] The president envisioned someone who answered directly to Richardson. The ideal person would be "somebody controlled by Elliot in charge of the case," who theoretically "would not do anything that Elliot didn't think he should do."[101]

During the course of the conversation, as Richardson sized things up, Nixon appeared a bit "flat and perhaps depressed." He was, however, in "perfectly complete control in sharpness and focus."[102]

The president made clear that Richardson "could decide whether to appoint, and if so whom." The understanding was that Richardson would be under no obligation, one way or the other. If he selected someone, he should simply "inform him [the president] who it was."[103]

"Anybody who is guilty must be prosecuted," Nixon told him, clenching his fist. "No matter who it hurts."[104] It would be a "new start," a period of "restoring trust" in the executive branch. The president leaned over and looked Elliot in the eye. The sun caused them both to blink involuntarily. "There will be nobody between you and me. That's the only way you should take the position."[105] Richardson nodded his head.

The president concluded their discussion by raising several "dark" references to "national security concerns."[106] "Be extremely careful of national security interests," Richardson's notes of the meeting record the president warning, "otherwise, I don't give a goddam. . . ." The president wanted to make sure that Richardson did not overlook the White House's critical interests. "Be evenhanded," he said.[107] Furthermore, the president would have to stand firm on a single point: "conversation[s] with the President are privileged."[108] President Nixon looked into Richardson's angular New England face and said that he should not accept the new job if he did not believe that Nixon had "not known anything about White House involvement in Watergate until he began his own investigation in March."

"Above all," Nixon said, "protect the Presidency—not the President if he's done anything wrong."[109]

The helicopter delivered Richardson back to the hulking structure of the Pentagon. In the coming months, the president would repeatedly find himself haunted by the double-edged guarantees that he had given Elliot Richardson on that pleasant Sunday in April. They were guarantees essential to attracting a person of Richardson's caliber and integrity to the broken office of the attorney general. Nevertheless, the president's own assurances of autonomy and independence would create an increasingly claustrophobic position for Richard M. Nixon in months to come.

Archibald Cox was allowed to dip into a government pool and select his own secretary, Florence Campbell, and borrow a shabby office in the Justice Department building. Two colleagues from Harvard Law School, James Vorenberg and Philip Heymann, volunteered to give up their summers to help Cox establish his office. As Heymann would joke, "You could still hear the ringing of the phone from Elliot . . . when I appeared at Archie's office suggesting that he needed help and I was the right person."[110] Heymann had been one of Cox's students and had also worked with him in the solicitor general's office. After serving in the U.S. attorney's office and the State Department, Heymann had joined the Harvard Law faculty, where Cox remained a mentor. Vorenberg had acted as chairman of the Crime Commission under President Johnson, which made him well connected with top officials in the Justice Department and the U.S. attorney's offices in Washington. Both men would be invaluable, Cox concluded, in helping him through the maze of political actors and federal bureaucrats.

The unglamorous four-room office that Cox inherited had been previously occupied not by a high-level government lawyer or adviser to the president, but by the bureaucrat whose job it was to track down vacant office space for new employees. The bureaucrat had "every incentive" to find Cox a permanent home quickly.[111] Cox and his assistants cleaned out stray boxes, climbed onto chairs, and took down pictures of former Attorneys General Kleindienst and Mitchell from the wall to give the office an air of independence. Those faces were now possible targets of the Watergate investigation.[112]

Archie shuttled between Boston and Washington, laden with top-secret papers and reports that otherwise stayed in a locked file cabinet. When Cox traveled, two federal marshals accompanied him, watching the papers' every movement. The marshals took up temporary residence at Cox's home in Wayland, their eyes glued to Archie's hands as he flipped through reports and adjusted the half-glasses on his nose. "I fed them," Phyllis explained. "And watched them watch Archie."[113]

Rumors continued to spread that the new special prosecutor was in the back pocket of Senator Ted Kennedy, the president's political nemesis. A meeting at Jim Vorenberg's Cambridge home on the Sunday before Memorial Day only intensified the speculation. One of the senator's staffers, Jim Flug, met with Cox, Vorenberg, and Heymann to review Watergate evidence accumulated to date by the Senate subcommittee chaired by Kennedy that preceded Sam Ervin's Watergate Committee. Flug turned over all of the subcommittee's documentary evidence to the new special prosecutor.[114] Nothing about the briefing seemed "startling" to Cox. He would later say that it only confirmed for him that "a good deal was surmise, not proof."[115]

The Cambridge setting for the gathering, however, only seemed to thicken the plot. As Heymann would later acknowledge, the general profile of the Cambridge liberal in 1973 was hardly a neutral or dispassionate one. Whether Cox consciously digested it or not, the Cambridge circles in which he was moving tended to be much more anti-Nixon than the country at large. "I do know that Nixon was a major villain to the crowd of liberal Democrats that Archie associated with in Washington and Cambridge," Phil Heymann would admit.[116] Political acumen, however, was never Cox's strong suit.

The day after the Flug meeting, Cox hosted a small Memorial Day press conference in the Law School faculty lounge for the elite corps of reporters who had once served as Harvard Nieman Fellows. This "backgrounder" was completely off the record: "no quote marks, no fact of meeting, no dateline." Questions were fired at Cox. Most of these he did not answer.[117] The reporters seemed "frustrated."[118] They whispered speculations as to whether a sheltered professor could deal with the political world of "knives and blackjacks" that he was entering. In Washington, being an academic meant being "soft, mushy," and "without sharp cutting edges."[119]

The notes of one reporter, James Doyle, reveal several clues about Cox's priorities in his earliest days as special prosecutor. For one, he was determined to eliminate the intentional leaks of information that had dominated Watergate before his arrival. "The country wants, and I'm inclined to think needs, info. and reasons rather than dramatic stories," Doyle's notes read. "When I decide to give things out, it will not be by leaks."[120]

When it came to the power he would soon wield in deciding who would be indicted, Cox was extremely reserved. "It's kind of an awesome thing to be called on to play God."

Vorenberg interjected, "It's sort of playing St. Peter, isn't it?"

"I'd be content to settle for that role," Cox said. "He doesn't pass the judgments."[121]

What was Cox thinking when it came to the "big" question, the possible involvement of President Richard M. Nixon in Watergate crimes? Inwardly, he would say firmly, he was hoping not to find the president guilty of any wrongdoing in the months or years ahead. He would think back and reflect, "I do know that I was not anxious to find Richard Nixon was responsible for the break-in, for a cover-up, or for any other wrongdoing. A notion that any President of the United States would engage in such things is unwelcome news to me—an unwelcome idea. I guess Richard Nixon and his intimates will never believe that but it's very clear in my mind that I was not. I was looking to get to the bottom of it."[122]

Cox's own instinct was to be wary of charges against any individual occupying the Oval Office.[123] "On the whole, I think I would have been happier with conclusive proof that he was not personally involved," said Cox, "than with conclusive proof that he was personally involved."[124]

In one limited respect, Cox turned out to be correct. President Richard M. Nixon and his intimates would never believe anything but the worst: that Archibald Cox, the newly appointed special prosecutor, was motivated by a personal desire to topple Richard M. Nixon and his presidency.

15

THE NEW
SPECIAL
PROSECUTOR

This move to Washington, like most for Archie, began with only one-fifth of the Cox family. "If I could close down the house [in Wayland] and say to the animals, 'Take care of yourself,' fine," Phyllis would reflect. "But there were horses and chickens to think of."

Archie moved to a temporary home in Washington, owned by a friend of the family traveling in India. In the fall, Phyllis planned to pull the horse back from Maine, move to Washington, and rent out their house in Wayland for an indefinite stretch. The Teapot Dome scandal, after all, had occupied Owen Roberts for six years in the 1920s in the aftermath of the Harding administration.[1] The three children were now grown. Sally was working at Harvard; Archie, Jr., was married and at thirty-two had recently been made a partner at the investment banking firm of Morgan Stanley in New York; young Phyllis was married, living in Colorado with a brand new baby, and was beginning law school at the University of Denver. Other than a collection of animals that needed to be placed, the nest was empty.

Archie wrote a letter to Dean Albert M. Sacks, formally requesting a leave from the law school for a year, but noted that the situation was "unpredictable" enough that he might have to request an extension, or eventually resign altogether. His office in the corner of Langdell Hall was cleared out. The desk that had been used by his father and grandfather and the oriental rug that had warmed the wooden floor in his office were dragged into storage.[2]

Archie's arrival in Washington on the Monday after Memorial Day was a scene of "utter chaos." Masses of television crews, print reporters, and curious citizens gathered around the Tenth and Constitution

Avenue entrance to the Justice Department to record the arrival of this unusual political, nonpolitical creature. Jim Vorenberg would savor the moment: "It felt a bit like MacArthur coming back to the Philippines."[3]

Archie shut the door and settled into his small office to read "everything he could get his hands on," mainly summaries of grand jury testimony and transcripts of the early Watergate trials.[4] The Watergate break-in case had produced plenty of mysteries. One puzzle that Archie had to address immediately was: Why had the case floundered as a prosecution?

The original criminal case had been tried by a three-man team led by Assistant U.S. Attorney Earl Silbert, Jr. Just thirty-six years old, Silbert was considered one of the top prosecutors in the office. But the case quickly hit a brick wall. The White House had downplayed the break-in as a "third-rate burglary"; the trial seemed to fulfill this advance billing.[5] Much to the irritation of Judge John J. Sirica, the prosecutors seemed to steer away from the most puzzling questions: Who had authorized the burglary, who had paid for it, and to whom did the defendants report? In Sirica's mind, "naïveté" and "inexperience" had led the young prosecutors into a dead end.[6] The burglars were convicted. The case was ready to disappear into obscurity.

That is, until James McCord blew the whistle. His final-hour letter to Judge Sirica suggested that the conspiracy went much higher than these five defendants. Evidence now surfaced that actors within the White House—H. R. Haldeman, White House chief of staff; John Ehrlichman, assistant to the president for domestic affairs; and John Dean, young counsel to the president—had used the CIA and FBI to limit the Watergate investigation by sending up "national security" smokescreens. Recent statements from McCord and Jeb Stuart Magruder, a high-placed deputy at CREEP, indicated that former campaign manager John Mitchell had participated in discussions of the Watergate bugging, including several times while he was attorney general. Their statements flatly contradicted Mitchell's public statements and testimony before the grand jury.[7] Reports appeared in the press that Mitchell and others had authorized paying hush money to the burglars, using funds secreted in the White House.[8]

The Watergate case was beginning to divide itself into two halves, equally intriguing. The first half was the "who, what, and why" of the break-in, the robbery case that had reached an unsatisfying conclusion in front of Judge Sirica. The second half was a new, more complicated issue of a cover-up. Was there a conscious plan to obstruct justice and keep the lid on the Watergate prosecution, perhaps by high-placed government officials sitting at desks within the White House?

While Archie plowed through boxes of records, Vorenberg handled administrative matters and hiring. Cox and Vorenberg settled on a $2.8 million budget, more money than they could ever need (they agreed) to prosecute one case. It was a maddeningly slow process. Heymann explained, "It was going to be a big operation. But you only had three of us. We couldn't . . . do the work of sixty or seventy people and hire sixty or seventy people at the same time."[9]

Security measures were a novelty for three professors from Harvard. The marshals at the Justice Department had asked: What security did the Special Prosecution Force need? Vorenberg had scratched his head, "Well, give us the same security as the most secret units in the FBI."[10] When Cox entered his office, he saw heavy mesh curtains over the windows. He threw open the drapes to allow light into the shadowy office and get a view of the street. Bells immediately went off and security agents rushed into the room. The curtains were the latest technology, the marshals solemnly informed Cox, to "prevent somebody who may be up in an airplane or in a window of a building across the street or on the roof from taking pictures of what's on your desk."[11]

Archie took a walk down to the Lincoln Memorial to contemplate his new position. He stood underneath the immense statue of Abraham Lincoln, where he had stood years earlier during the Wage Stabilization crisis of the Truman years. He stared at the words chiseled on marble: "that government of the people, by the people, for the people shall not perish from the earth." Archie thought to himself, "Of course, hardly anything looks as overwhelming in history as it looks at the time." Nonetheless, resolving the Watergate affair, and restoring confidence in government, might have some small significance in history some day. His goal was to forget about the usual bureaucratic habits and routines that bogged down Washington, and try to do things his own way. Otherwise, he shook his head at the statue and repeated an old expression, he ". . . will come a cropper."[12]

One of the first orders of business for the makeshift Special Prosecution Force was a meeting between Cox, Vorenberg, and Henry Petersen, the assistant attorney general heading up the Criminal

Division of the Justice Department. It turned out to be, as Cox remembered it, "an uncomfortable evening."

Petersen was the man ultimately in charge of the young assistant U.S. attorneys handling the Watergate prosecution. Both Cox and Vorenberg knew Petersen from their previous stints in Washington. An ex-Marine, Petersen had worked in the Justice Department from the ground up. He was fifty-two years old, tough-looking with a deep-lined face and raspy voice, a career Justice Department lawyer who had devoted twenty-five years to government service. Other than sailing on the Chesapeake Bay with his seven children, the Department of Justice was Henry Petersen's life. He was the first career staffer ever promoted to a presidential appointment. "He was enormously indebted to Nixon for that. Proud of the fact that he was first."[13] Petersen had been opposed to the appointment of a special prosecutor from the start and made no apologies about it.[14]

Cox and Vorenberg met with Petersen on the night of May 29, 1973. They chatted briefly. Politely. Before long, however, the mood shifted. Cox and Vorenberg pushed question after question until, in Cox's words, the encounter "border[ed] on an interrogation." A stenographer recorded the questions and answers in shorthand.[15] The most striking fact that emerged from Petersen's responses was this: On the Sunday afternoon that John Dean was fired, the same Sunday afternoon that Haldeman and Ehrlichman had resigned, President Nixon had summoned Petersen from his boat on the Chesapeake Bay to the Old Executive Office Building across from the White House. The president had confronted Petersen angrily: "How is it that you promised John Dean immunity? I issued orders that nobody in the White House was to be offered immunity."

There was a long pause. Petersen seemed uncomfortable reliving the story in front of Cox and Vorenberg.

"I cannot put the awful words in the President's mouth," Petersen told them. The gist of the story was this: President Nixon had rattled off a series of expletives and insisted that Petersen *did* promise John Dean immunity. He had spat out that John Dean "told me so himself."

In response to this presidential venting, Petersen had mustered up all the courage, respect, firmness, confidence, and deference at his command. He replied, "You must have misunderstood him, Mr. President."

Nixon leaned back and snapped, "He did. You can listen to the tape."[16]

Although the story was intriguing in itself, this last statement triggered an immediate series of alarm bells in the minds of Cox and Vorenberg. Petersen was telling them that a conversation between Dean and the president had somehow been recorded on tape. Vorenberg took copious notes. They would have to explore this lead later.

An overshadowing fact that struck Cox at this meeting was that Petersen "was sort of overimpressed by what the president wants, what the White House wants, and the obligation to do it."[17] This presented a problem, in Cox's mind. It was dangerous for any official in the Justice Department, let alone the official directly responsible for overseeing the Watergate case, to be bound so close to the president. Cox's first task would be to delicately extricate himself from the three assistant U.S. attorneys under Petersen's charge. It was a tricky maneuver. As Phil Heymann would explain: "None of us were prosecutors. It was clear we had to keep the U.S. attorney people doing their work." At the same time, Heymann admitted bluntly, "I felt we had to string them along for a while. And then . . . get rid of them."[18]

The assistant attorneys general—Earl Silbert, Jr., Seymour Glanzer, and Donald Campbell—had originally treated the Watergate break-in as a straightforward burglary case. Only the five men arrested inside the Democratic National Committee headquarters and their immediate supervisors, Hunt and Liddy, were indicted for criminal misconduct. At trial, Silbert told the jury that McCord and Liddy "were off on an enterprise of their own." He assured reporters that there was no evidence of a wider conspiracy.[19] In fact, Silbert's opening statement at trial suggested that the Cubans and McCord had committed the break-in "because they needed the money," a narrow theory that Judge Sirica found hard to swallow.[20]

With the eleventh-hour letter of McCord to Judge Sirica, however, the terrain shifted quickly. There was now evidence of a cover-up, pointing directly to presidential advisers. Silbert's team still did not budge. In their judgment as federal prosecutors who had tried dozens of street crimes, the Watergate case could be brought to conclusion in short order. They said as much in a memo to Elliot Richardson before Cox was appointed: "We are in the driver's seat; we have momentum. Consequently we urge that we be authorized to complete our investigation."[21] It was just a short road to a definitive ending of the criminal prosecution, they had insisted, thanks to their efforts in breaking the case "wide open" with McCord's surprise letter.[22]

In spite of Silbert's confidence, Cox was uncomfortable with this truncated view of the Watergate case.[23] The affair was filled with far too much intrigue and high-level finger-pointing to be that simple. Besides, as Phil Heymann put it, Archie was hired to "substitute his credibility" for that of Silbert and his team.[24] What to do with them? At first, Cox had toyed with the idea of "integrating the operation" of the U.S. attorneys into his own.[25] There was a sort of "mating dance" going on.[26] Cox had gone so far as to invite Silbert and his associates to move over to the Special Prosecution Force's new offices as soon as they were set up on K Street. It soon became clear, however, that this amalgamation would not work. Not that Cox believed that the work of the young prosecutors was "wretched." Phil Heymann had gone to school with Silbert; he had a reputation as a good, honorable prosecutor. But some of Silbert's "theories as to what lay behind the burglary" were questionable. And there seemed to be "distracting limitations being put on them by the Justice Department."[27]

Silbert himself was not happy that Cox had replaced him in the driver's seat on the Watergate case. He was tired of having his competency questioned by the press, by Judge Sirica, by Democratic National Committee lawyers. As Silbert dictated in his private diary of events on May 22, 1973, "I have had [it] with the case, I think this case is nothing but problems and we have compromised on integrity, [have] been questioned, we have no supporters, we have no credibility."[28]

Another weight around the neck of Earl Silbert was dragging him down. It was a handicap that was not, and could not be, fully revealed to the press. Nevertheless, it was making his investigation nearly impossible. It involved Henry Petersen.

It was no secret that before Cox's appointment, leaks were sprouting freely from the Justice Department. As Vorenberg put it, there was "all sorts of stuff coming out and nobody knew where it was coming from."[29] It became increasingly evident to Cox that "the White House knew what the grand jury testimony was going to be on any day before the grand jury knew it."[30] It was also evident that part of the problem was Henry Petersen. In a memo dated April 30, 1973, Earl Silbert's office informed Elliot Richardson that Petersen himself was a potential "witness" to obstruction of justice and improper links between the FBI and the White House. "Mr. Petersen cannot, accordingly, remain in charge of the Watergate investigation, examining grand jury minutes of other witnesses and making prosecutive decisions."[31]

The worries about Henry Petersen were largely kept under wraps, yet they laced Silbert and his associates in a horrible straitjacket. Petersen was their superior; he was head of the Criminal Division. In the past year, however, he had allowed himself to become much too close with the president and his advisers. The relationship was not intentional or diabolical; anyone who knew Henry Petersen knew that he was straight, honest, and professional. At the same time, Silbert knew that Petersen had a tendency to become "fearful" and "timid" when dealing with high-level "public officials" and "political figures."[32] It turned out that Petersen was especially malleable when it came to one such figure, President Richard M. Nixon.

Although Henry Petersen was a Democrat by registration, he felt an unwavering sense of loyalty to the president who had allowed him to work his way up from an FBI clerk to a top lawyer in the Department; and there came the problem.[33] As Silbert recorded in his diary even before Cox's arrival, his prosecution team was increasingly "concerned" about Petersen's close contact with the White House.[34]

In fairness to Petersen, in the year 1973, most government officials (including Justice Department lawyers) trusted their president. Government scandals at the top of the pyramid were virtually unheard of. "Trying to figure out how to deal with the president who was chief law enforcement officer, and *not* deal with him, was fairly complicated," explained one White House lawyer.[35] But the extent of the president's web around Petersen, discovered mainly through the U. S. attorneys' interviews with John Dean, was becoming both embarrassing and alarming to Silbert's group.

John Dean had known Henry Petersen since Dean was in his twenties, when he had acted as an associate deputy attorney general and had worked alongside the veteran Petersen. Dean moved from the Justice Department to the White House at the age of thirty, but stayed friendly with Petersen. "When Watergate happened," Dean explained openly, "it was very easy for me to talk to him, and get information from him."[36] Although Silbert and his team would not yet piece together all of the connections, the guts of the facts were these:

- In June 1972, shortly after the Watergate break-in, Dean met with Petersen in the office of Attorney General Kleindienst. Dean told the two government lawyers, "I don't think the White House can take a wide-open investigation." Petersen fixed himself a stiff drink and "bolted it down." Petersen then listened as

Dean requested that the two officials limit the Watergate inquiry to the burglary itself, so that the FBI did not "stumble into" other sensitive matters like campaign act violations, the break-in of Daniel Ellsberg's psychiatrist's office, and other problems. Petersen nodded his head and agreed that the investigation should be limited to Watergate. Said Dean, "I went back and reported that to my superiors. . . . We had a deal."[37]

- Dean admitted that as the 1972 election moved closer, he met repeatedly with Petersen concerning Watergate and passed along the content of these conversations to Haldeman and Ehrlichman in the White House.

- When political saboteur Donald Segretti was called before the grand jury, Petersen directed the U. S. attorneys not to ask who at the White House had hired him. In August 1972, when the White House became angry over grand jury subpoenas for various presidential aides, including Nixon's finance chairman, former Secretary of Commerce Maurice Stans, Petersen arranged (at Ehrlichman's insistence) to have these statements given privately in the Justice Department rather than before the grand jury.

- When the grand jury sought testimony from Petersen's old boss, former Attorney General John Mitchell, to whom he was fiercely loyal, Petersen called Dean and "telegraphed" the areas of questioning that the prosecutors planned to explore in front of the grand jury.[38]

- In December 1972, Dean informed Petersen that he had personally turned over material from E. Howard Hunt's White House safe, including two notebooks that set forth the names of those involved in the break-in of Ellsberg's psychiatrist's office, to acting FBI director L. Patrick Gray. Gray then burned the documents. Petersen failed to pass along this critical information to Silbert and his team until long after they had learned about it from Dean.

- Throughout the time that John Dean was engaging in damage control for the White House in the Watergate cover-up, he admitted that Petersen was his key source in the Justice Department. In Dean's words, Petersen was "an open conduit. He told me everything I needed to know. And then some."[39]

By early May, the U.S. attorneys had informed Elliot Richardson of the seriousness of the problem. Richardson's notes of May 4 indicated that "President's counsel—could have gained something from discussion with HP to help in obstruction of justice. . . ." The notes concluded, "It won't work to have the special prosecutor work for Henry Petersen."[40]

The situation had become so bad that Silbert considered asking Judge Sirica to direct that all grand jury documents remain in the courthouse, to keep them away from Petersen. That plan was scrapped as too transparent.[41] Silbert described the problem in his diary: "In our view we have trouble with Mr. Petersen because he is a witness and he is in a very delicate position."[42] Furthermore, Petersen and the Criminal Division had served to "limit somewhat our investigation," by imposing restrictions that "weren't obvious or blatant but were calculated to restrict."[43]

Silbert and his co-prosecutors knew this. John Dean, now a prosecution witness, knew this. Elliot Richardson and his staff had talked to the U.S. attorneys, and knew this. Now Cox and his closest associates found out about it.[44]

The task of severing ties with the U.S. attorney's office, however, which was strongly linked to Henry Petersen, was "immensely more difficult" than expected. The three young prosecutors were "sensitive"; they were "hurt" that the Senate had meddled in their investigation by appointing a special prosecutor.[45] As Silbert dictated in his diary, if they were going to go, it was important to go "not with your tail between your legs."[46]

As early as May 22, Silbert, Glanzer, and Campbell publicly announced that the Watergate investigation could be completed within sixty days if they remained in charge. It was a preemptive strike, designed to overpower Cox's investigation before it got started. They would be willing to advise Cox of their actions; that much was fine. But if the special prosecutor continued to ignore them and interfere with the prosecution, they would resign on the spot and the Watergate case would be set back indefinitely.[47]

The relationship between Cox and Silbert's group quickly went into a tailspin. Silbert recorded in his diary that Cox was an "arrogant man, got kind of a mean look in those eyes, smile is not really a friendly smile."[48] Cox, on the other hand, was "outraged" by what he regarded as the young prosecutors' "irresponsibility," in "trying to force my hand by going public."[49] Despite this tug-of-war, Silbert and his group knew it was impractical to stay. "I really felt that I wanted out of the case," Silbert told his diary, "tired of it, sick of it, I could see us doing the work and then getting—whatever happening Cox getting the credit for any work, having picked up the marbles and turn something the prosecutors had worked in shambles into a success where in fact we really have the case."[50]

Cox was in a quandary. He "badly needed" the cooperation of the assistant U.S. attorneys until his own investigation was up and running.[51] Silbert and his team grudgingly agreed to stay. Otherwise, Silbert recorded, "we would look like we were acting childish, like a little boy taking his football and going home."[52] At the same time, they decided to issue a public statement declaring that they had earned Cox's "confidence," and that the Watergate investigation "is substantially complete."[53]

Silbert recorded in his diary: "The press release was pretty well received, got a lot of headlines the next day and most of the newspapers—a lot of attention, it's amazing the power of the press. The attention you have to give it, the fear [that] anyone will knock you . . ."[54]

On May 29, Cox issued his own sharp press release, making clear that he—and he alone—would be responsible for making decisions about the prosecution. He warned that the assistant U.S. attorneys were to "refrain from any kind of statement, comment or speculation about any aspect of the investigation."[55] Simultaneously, Cox hired forty-three-year-old Nashville trial attorney Jim Neal as chief Watergate trial lawyer. Neal's job would be to run interference with Silbert and simultaneously build an independent trial operation within the special prosecutor's office.

Cox knew Neal from the Kennedy Justice Department days, when Neal had served as a U.S. attorney in Tennessee, helping Bobby Kennedy put Jimmy Hoffa behind bars in 1964. Since then, Neal had represented a glittering array of white-collar criminal defendants and civil clients, including country singer Johnny Cash.[56] Neal would complement Cox, making up for the professor's lack of trial experience. He would act as the actual prosecutor at the eventual Watergate trial; Cox would play a secondary, more symbolic role. "It was taken for granted there would be *some* trial," Cox said. "Who the defendants would be was still unknown."[57] Neal agreed to drop his law practice in Nashville for "several weeks" to help straighten things out in Washington. Several weeks turned into several months, with the word

"Watergate" scrawled across his calendar along with large X marks that counted off time lost from his private practice.

Jim Neal soon became the mainstay of an impressive pool of legal talent that Cox's Special Prosecution Force attracted from the most elite law firms and the most prestigious government offices across the country. The list of attorneys recruited eventually read like a *Who's Who in American Law*. Letters piled up in Cambridge and Washington. They came from top lawyers from across the country, some of whom knew Cox, Vorenberg, or Heymann from Harvard, some of whom simply wanted a taste of Washington action. Many came from lawyers with stellar credentials, who, to Cox's surprise, were willing to jeopardize successful careers to join an uncertain but exciting venture.[58]

The staff soon included Henry S. Ruth, age forty-two, who had worked with Vorenberg on LBJ's Crime Commission and taught at Penn law school. He now became Cox's deputy. On the team preparing for the cover-up trial were George Frampton, former clerk for Supreme Court Justice Harry Blackmun; Richard Ben-Veniste, former assistant U.S. attorney from the Southern District of New York; and Jill Wine Volner, a thirty-year-old trial lawyer on loan from the Justice Department's criminal division, the first woman prosecutor of organized crime in the history of the department. Joseph Connolly, age thirty-two, a Republican from a well-connected Main Line family in Philadelphia with experience in the Pentagon and solicitor general's office, would head the ITT investigation. Richard J. Davis, another assistant U.S. attorney from New York, was in charge of the unit investigating "dirty tricks" and political sabotage. William Merrill, a former aide to Robert Kennedy during his presidential campaign, would head the "plumbers" unit. Thomas F. McBride, age forty-four, with experience in the Justice Department and the New York City district attorney's office, was assigned to head the presidential campaign finances unit. Peter Kreindler, a former clerk to Justice William O. Douglas and a *Harvard Law Review* editor, would serve as Cox's executive assistant. Phil Lacovara, former counsel to the New York City Police Department, professor at Columbia, and most recently deputy under President Nixon's new solicitor general, Robert H. Bork, would become the "lawyer's lawyer," serving as Cox's aide, policy adviser, and legal counsel.[59]

Jim Doyle, a stocky, young investigative reporter from the *Washington Star*, signed on as Cox's press secretary and special assistant.

Doyle wore his sideburns thick and his ties wide in keeping with the style of the early 1970s. A Nieman Fellow at Harvard and a Pulitzer-prize-winning political journalist in Boston, he was an aggressive member of the Washington press corps on Capitol Hill.[60] Doyle's goal in teaming up with Cox was to help the special prosecutor change how Watergate information was being selectively leaked to newspapers and reporters. Doyle could establish guidelines that would ensure that all information reached the public evenhandedly.[61] Although he was hired as press adviser, Doyle eventually became Cox's closest friend, confidant, and second conscience.

The Special Prosecution Force quickly developed a rhythm, a syncopated sense of dedication, working together late hours, seven days a week. "An awful lot of it was intense, worrisome work," Cox said. On top of everything else, Archie had a stack of Labor Law examinations from Harvard that he still had not graded. He lugged these blue books around to Watergate meetings, to his Washington home, and back to work, until they finally vanished in a package to Cambridge. Professor Cox never considered allowing someone else to grade his exams, even during a time of national crisis. He did treat himself to the luxury of grading the exams pass/fail, however, a "sacrifice of principle to exigency."[62]

Office hours were around the clock. Archie would arrive at work by 7:30, after walking two miles from his temporary home on Q Street Northwest, near DuPont Circle. He would eat lunch across K Street at a greasy spoon called "Archibald's." (His young assistants sniggered about how it became a topless bar at night.) Archie would typically work until 8:00. He would then walk home and cook hamburgers and vegetables for himself or have dinner at a local Chinese restaurant or nearby eatery with his staff. Dinner always included a double shot of Tennessee bourbon, "never less, never more." He would try to squeeze in more work at home until 11:00, before excusing himself from visitors or phone callers by announcing sheepishly, "Time for beddy-bye."[63]

To the press, Cox was enigmatic, a person who did not exactly fit into the mold of the capital. *Newsweek* printed a photo of Cox sitting in a chair outside his Washington home on a sunny weekend, short-sleeved knit shirt making him look as thin as Ichabod Crane, half-glasses perched on his nose, reading yet another brief propped up against his lanky knee. One Senate Democrat complained of Cox, "He's too quiet. He just doesn't seem to be turned on to his job."[64]

But Cox was "turned on" by hard work. And he expected the same from his predominantly young staffers.

As of June 7, Cox's group had moved out of their offices in the Justice Department, where potential leaks and conflicts danced in every corner, and occupied new space on K Street at 14th. Now they were surrounded by local hookers who surfaced faithfully each night at twilight.[65] Vorenberg recalled with a smile, "I do remember Archie's first realization that I had committed us to a building that seemed to be surrounded by prostitutes . . . gave him some pause."[66]

Behind the bland concrete facade of a government passport office at 1425 K Street just off McPherson Square, a serious-minded office was taking shape. As Phil Heymann described it, it was a collection of "aggressive, prosecutorial, ambitious" young lawyers. Investigating the highest officials in the administration gave their work an aura of "dangerousness" and excitement.[67]

The metal door entering the building bore no identifying marks. On the ninth floor there was a nondescript sign: "Push Bell." Closed-circuit cameras recorded every move of people entering and exiting the corridors.[68] Yellow stickers on the phones cautioned against bugging. In the hallway, next to two policemen and a shabby wooden entrance desk, a poster showed a telephone wired to dynamite and bearing the warning "Talk is explosive."[69] A parade of famous and semifamous suspects—E. Howard Hunt, John Dean, G. Gordon Liddy, Charles Colson—were escorted daily through the halls of the obscure K Street building to be interviewed by hungry young prosecutors.[70] The office grew from three to sixty to ninety staffers (about thirty-six of these were lawyers), nearly overnight.[71] It included an "excited, frantic, self-important bunch of young prosecutors." Daily accounts of alleged criminal activity tied to Watergate were splashed across the newspapers and spurred them forward; it gave them juice for their suspicions, which in turn made them "push" constantly on Cox.[72] They were hungry, famished for action.

It was just this quality of the Special Prosecution Force that raised a brooding concern among Republicans. Some of the White House staff had early on joked with Elliot Richardson, "*Archie* Cox? I thought you said you'd picked *Eddie* Cox!" Eddie Cox was Nixon's son-in-law, who had married daughter Tricia Nixon and recently graduated from law school.[73] Now, however, the selection was becoming less of a laughing matter. The White House was "surprised and horrified" by the seeming expansion of the investigation being conducted by Cox's newly ordained prosecutorial "units."[74] "They thought that he had been appointed to investigate the break-in at the Watergate Hotel," Phil Heymann explained. "And suddenly people were looking at tax audits, electronic surveillance," and a distressingly wide range of alleged White House crimes.[75]

Criticism flew that Cox's staff was taking on the look of a liberal Democrat love fest. This was true even though Cox and Vorenberg had intentionally recruited Republicans like Joe Connolly and young assistant U.S. attorneys working under Republican appointees to defuse the "Kennedy-pawn" charges. Most of the lawyers, as Cox would point out, had never been politically active in their lives.[76] In fact, as charts and graphs showed, the only real prejudice Cox exhibited was toward Harvard Law School graduates, a valid charge, since he tended to hire people whom he knew and trusted from teaching days.

These facts did nothing to mollify the growing swarm of Republican critics, however. The clear political design of this Kennedyesque prosecution force, they concluded, was to destroy the Nixon presidency.[77] Richard Nixon himself later criticized the Cox operation in his memoirs: "No White House in history could have survived the kind of operation Cox was planning. If he were determined to get me, as I was certain that he and his staff were, then given the terms of their charter it would be only a matter of time until they had bored like termites through the whole executive branch."[78]

It was difficult to dispute that the young lawyers recruited by Cox from the Eastern Ivy League universities, most of whom had grown up during the Vietnam War era, were far from model Nixon supporters. Nor could one disagree that Cox himself, in his tweedy and professorial ways, represented the antithesis of the Southern California businessmen with whom President Nixon had surrounded himself. As one presidential aide accurately observed, "I can hardly imagine two guys less likely to hit it off than Dick Nixon and Archie Cox."[79]

On a more personal level, it is probably true that Archibald Cox the individual did not particularly like Richard M. Nixon (although he never said so publicly or otherwise).[80] Moreover, Cox probably would not have come to Washington were it not for the issue of whether the president himself had been involved in the Watergate cover-up. As deputy Hank Ruth put it, "It is clear to me that Archie's principal reason to be there was to discover if the president of the United States had committed a crime. If it was only the other issues . . . my guess is that he wouldn't have come."[81]

Yet describing the Cox operation as a partisan effort driven by politics largely reflected the age-old problem of politicians projecting their own motivations and instincts onto others, when all others do not necessarily think and act like politicians.

For every tie that bound some member of the Special Prosecution Force to a previous Democratic president, candidate, or administration, dozens of facts showed far less partisan leanings. Phil Lacovara had been chairman of Students for Goldwater while a student at Columbia in the 1960s; he was a registered Republican and had worked for Solicitor General Robert Bork. Henry Ruth also held a major appointment in the Nixon Justice Department. Joe Connolly, head of the ITT Task Force, was the son of a Republican congressman from Philadelphia and was himself a Republican. Richard Ben-Veniste, a Democrat, had been an assistant U.S. attorney in New York and had prosecuted one of the biggest public-corruption cases of the day—against a prominent Democrat. Jim Neal, who would head the trial phase of the Watergate prosecution, was a dyed-in-the-wool Southern Democrat who had voted for President Nixon over McGovern in 1972.[82]

The fact was, in every niche and corner of the Watergate landscape, actors on both sides of the case could claim ties with the Kennedy and Johnson administrations. This was the nature of the beast in Washington. Henry Petersen, whom President Nixon had handpicked to oversee the Watergate investigation, was a Democratic "lifer" in the department. John Dean's lawyer, Charles Shaffer, had served as a prosecutor in the Kennedy Justice Department and had worked with Jim Neal on the trial of Jimmy Hoffa. John Mitchell's attorney, William Hundley, was a former head of the Organized Crime and Racketeering Section of the Justice Department during the Eisenhower, Kennedy, and Johnson administrations. Herbert "Jack" Miller, who would later represent Richard Nixon personally in the tapes controversy, had headed the Criminal Division in the Kennedy Justice Department. Everyone in Washington, including the president himself, wanted experienced lawyers. Experience flowed primarily from the previous two Democratic administrations, unless it was directly linked to President Nixon, which would create an obvious conflict of interests.

The Cox-Kennedy connection, for the most part, was a convenient piece of political artillery; most Washington insiders knew this. Cox nevertheless fueled the flames with an ample dose of political naïveté, taking actions that anxious Republicans interpreted as signs of malicious purpose. Cox did nothing to downplay his old Kennedy ties. He was not particularly close with Ted Kennedy, certainly not in the sense that he had been close to JFK and RFK. They did not socialize or talk on any regular basis. As the summer wore on, Cox even declined "on several occasions to give Ted Kennedy any information." This was not because it was off limits or secret, but simply because "I [did not] want to be in communication with him." On his infrequent visits to Capitol Hill, Cox "carefully avoided" Kennedy and other liberal Democrats to prevent any impression of playing favorites. In the early months, however, he had done nothing to fend off the notion of a cozy association between himself and the "new" Kennedy political regime. Now this image stuck.

For the most part, political appearances did not even lodge themselves in Cox's consciousness. Press secretary Jim Doyle explained, "He had enormous problems, and he had little time to be viewing himself as anything other than a man who accepted the burden. He just did not have the luxury to think about whether he was or was not a Kennedy type, a liberal Democrat, a pro- or anti-Nixon or whatever."[83]

Cox himself was puzzled by all the fuss. As he stated in an off-the-record interview given shortly after Watergate, "Like many of these myths, [Nixon] probably thought of the connection with Ted Kennedy and the Kennedy family as being much closer than it is. I get to talk to them hardly at all—well, I talk to Ted now and then over the phone, but in no sense are we, you know, close. . . . I doubt whether the President perceived that."[84]

Ironically, those who worked most closely with Cox (even the Republican members of his staff) saw this special prosecutor as someone strongly inclined to give the benefit of the doubt to the chief executive.[85] When Cox was required to make legal decisions, they considered him cautious to the point of diffidence when it came to challenging the constitutional prerogatives of the president. Phil Lacovara, one of the prominent Republicans on staff, observed that Cox was "ambivalent" and "conflicted" whenever a legal theory shifted the focus toward the president. Cox's ambivalence was partly "because he knew the consequences for the country if the evidence led to Nixon's door." Lacovara saw a strict discipline in Cox, who separated personal feelings toward Richard M. Nixon from his "public duty to deal with the office of the president."[86] So strict was this separation that Cox never allowed himself to speak negatively about the president, at least that any staff member heard. Lacovara would conclude that, ironically, Cox was more deferential to the president than was his successor, Leon Jaworski. Yet in the eyes of skeptical actors in the White House, Archibald Cox possessed the silhouette of another formidable "Nixon enemy."[87]

President Nixon would record angrily in his own memoirs, despite his earlier public endorsement of Cox's appointment, "If Richardson had searched specifically for the man whom I would have least trusted to conduct so politically sensitive an investigation in an unbiased way, he could hardly have done better than choose Archibald Cox."[88]

George Bush, then chairman of the Republican National Committee, telephoned Cox directly at least twice to inquire, "Why haven't you prosecuted any Democrats?" Although they were both Eastern establishment figures with Ivy League backgrounds, the two men had little to talk about. Cox remembered, Bush "always sounded as if somebody had told him he must do it. And that he wanted to go back able to say . . . he had done it." Cox's reply to Bush in both instances was, "Well, if you had any evidence, then of course we could." Which always produced silence on the other end of the phone.[89]

Those closest to Elliot Richardson in the attorney general's office—most of whom were Republicans—dismissed the concerns about Cox as paranoia. "We didn't believe for a minute that Cox or anyone working for him were part of a partisan inquisition," said aide J. T. Smith. At the same time, he admitted that Cox was not always sensitive to the growing appearance of his link to the "enemy camp." Said Smith, "There was a problem of optics. That's a fact."[90]

16

OPENING
ARGUMENTS

Ironically, when Archibald Cox first inched out on a limb and tested his balance as Watergate special prosecutor, it was an effort that President Nixon heartily endorsed. Cox decided to challenge, head-on, the televised Senate Watergate hearings led by Democratic Senator Sam Ervin.

The Senate Watergate Committee had been set up to investigate allegations of irregularities in the 1972 presidential campaign, including the Watergate break-in, with an eye toward enacting legislation that might prevent new improprieties from occurring in the future. In reality, drafting legislation was not at the top of the list for the committee. After all, these were political animals. The Democrats who controlled Congress were interested in maximum exposure and—if they were lucky—the chance to hurl sharp spears at the Republican administration. The Republicans were interested, if they were going to have any hope in the 1976 presidential election, in blunting attacks on Richard M. Nixon.

A few aspects of the televised Senate committee hearings rubbed Cox the wrong way. He worried, first, that they would "place in doubt our ability to try any guilty actors because of the pre-trial publicity."[1] If the special prosecutor could not guarantee defendants a fair trial in front of an impartial jury, all the evidence in the world would become useless. The Senate hearings would almost certainly turn into a circus, tainting millions of potential jurors. On top of this, Cox had a nagging fear that the Senate committee would grant immunity to key witnesses like John Dean and Jeb Magruder, so that the stockpile of evidence that his office had amassed against these defendants would have to be junked.[2] Dean's lawyer was already pushing for "use immunity" from the Senate committee (a deal by which self-incriminatory testimony could not be used if Dean was prosecuted later). The Senate seemed to be biting, since Dean held the key to unlocking evidence against dozens of other defendants. Cox felt strongly that the only proper authority to grant immunity was the special prosecutor himself—not a band of legislators, however well intentioned.[3] Televised hearings spelled disaster in Cox's mind.

Cox arranged to meet with Sam Ervin and the Senate committee's chief counsel, Sam Dash. He would explain rationally why the Senate hearings should not go forward. He would stop them.

The meeting took place in Senator Ervin's Capitol Hill office on Saturday, June 2. Cox and Vorenberg took turns pleading their case. The televised hearings would interfere with the fair administration of justice and would *have* to be scratched. Witnesses like Dean and Magruder should be kept out of the public lights, Cox stated in a high-pitched voice that almost cracked with insistence. "I don't want you to put them on at all."[4]

Senator Ervin looked amused, then annoyed. He was a big man with a beefy face. His white hair was accentuated by dark, darting eyebrows. The seventy-six-year-old senator articulated his words with a broad Carolina drawl. He appeared "very impatient" with the suggestion that television cameras should be blocked from the Senate hearings, for any reason. The affable Dash, whom Cox and Vorenberg knew from academic circles, was equally unsympathetic. He became somewhat brusque, "throwing his weight around" as Vorenberg saw it.[5] Archie was "taken aback" by the tenor of the meeting.[6] The message was clear: The televised Senate hearings would continue. Just because "Mr. Clean" had come to Washington in the form of this crew-cutted professor, did not mean that everyone else had to stop and get out of his way.[7] The meeting was adjourned. As Cox walked out the door, Senator Ervin reportedly called him "arrogant" for even pressing the suggestion.[8]

Archie nevertheless pushed again, writing to Senator Ervin on June 4 to request that the Senate committee "temporarily suspend" public hearings. This was meant to be a middle ground. The Senate should halt its proceedings until the special prosecutor had a chance to "assess this enormously complex case" and determine which witnesses should be kept out of the television lights.[9]

In reality, all Cox wanted was a month or six weeks of breathing space. He needed to get familiar with the case and see if he could work something out with the Senate committee, "in a way that doesn't foul things up."[10] Archie understood perfectly well the hazards of pulling the plug on the Senate televised hearings. The greatest would be public perception—the wrath of the average citizen-television watcher, who would assume that the proceedings were being "delayed" so that wrongdoing could be swept under the carpet. He was prepared to take the responsibility for that consequence.

"I realize that this is a very trying request to put to the Select Committee," he wrote to Senator Ervin, "because granting it might give rise to unwarranted charges that the Committee was delayed or diverted in bringing out the truth. It is an even more difficult request for me to make because there will be false charges that I am attempting to cover up the truth."[11] But Cox felt compelled to insist.

Archie received a quick lesson in public relations. He was eaten alive by the Washington press corps. At a June 4 press conference, reporters swarmed in front of him to demand whether the public Senate hearings did not "eliminate some of the speculation" and "do more good than it does harm?" Cox answered meekly, "I don't think so. I think the—" One reporter quickly interrupted: Was Cox suggesting that "speculative stories" were better than those based upon fact? Cox stammered no, he didn't mean that. Another reporter shouted, "After one year of not getting any information on the Watergate, what one single reason would you give the people to deprive them of that source of information that the Senate Committee is giving them?"[12]

Of course, there was no satisfactory answer.

The Nixon White House, ironically, rushed to Cox's defense in his battle with Senator Ervin. Anxious to keep John Dean's testimony away from the already-stunned public, the White House stoutly defended Cox's rationale. Pro-Nixon writer William Safire vigorously joined in Archie's defense; columnist Joseph Alsop called Dean a "bottom-dwelling slug" and extolled the virtues of allowing Cox to pursue a thorough investigation without the disruption of circuslike Senate hearings.[13] Few other commentators agreed.

Archie's first attempt to flex his muscles, by standing up to the powerful Democratic leadership of the Senate, had proved to be a colossal failure. Senator Sam Ervin scoffed, publicly, at the suggestion. Even Jim Vorenberg admitted that trying to stand between Senator Ervin and his televised hearings was "like standing in the middle of the railroad tracks with an express train coming at you."[14]

Undeterred, Cox drafted a motion to Judge Sirica. His secretary provided him with a large supply of art gum erasers, which he kept on his desk until he had the motion letter perfect. Florence Campbell recalled that "when he drafted something and he wasn't satisfied, he didn't crumple it up. He would erase. . . . He'd erase a whole page."[15]

Cox formally requested that Judge Sirica order that the public hearings cease, or at least not be broadcast. He further insisted that the Senate committee should be sharply curtailed in its ability to grant immunity, to avoid fouling up future criminal proceedings.[16] Cox's motion was duly stamped and docketed; it was the first official act of the special prosecutor in federal court.

Phil Heymann, Phil Lacovara, and Cox all sat at a cluttered table on K Street, assessing what they had done. Lacovara was pessimistic about the odds in court. Heymann went a step further: the whole idea was a bad one. The special prosecutor should not be perceived as "the one [who] kept the country from getting the story."[17] The motion was doomed to fail, especially given the high degree of suspicion that already permeated the press and the public. What judge in his right mind would shut off the country from Watergate news even further?

"Well, I think *you* should argue it then," Archie told his assistant.[18]

All three lawyers laughed. When they finished laughing, they all nodded their heads. Cox was right. It would be a mistake to over-emphasize a losing battle by sending the special prosecutor himself up to argue the motion. No need to put the "biggest gun on the line that soon," they decided.[19] Heymann had experience. He would do a respectable job at losing.

So it was Philip B. Heymann who appeared in Judge Sirica's court-room on June 8, 1973, to represent the Special Prosecution Force in its public debut. A large crowd was present, eager to catch a glimpse of the Watergate special prosecutor. The staff lawyers for Senator Ervin's committee had gathered, smiling and confident, "anxious to beat Archie."[20] Judge Sirica, although a stern man with heavy eye-brows and dark hair, was "happy, enjoying the big crowds."[21] He hunched forward in his chair, black robe newly cleaned, surveying the packed courtroom.

Sam Dash presented the Senate committee's argument. When the forty-year-old Heymann rose to address the court, the gaggle of Senate lawyers and much of the audience appeared "put out." Heymann had longish hair and had just grown a Fu Manchu mus-tache. This surely was not Archibald Cox.

Cox had instructed Heymann before his assistant left, to "be sure not to overargue the case." With the odds stacked so strongly against them, he should not overdo the dramatics. With these words fresh in his ears, Heymann stood at the lectern and stated seriously to Judge Sirica. "I want to be careful not to overargue my case. . . ."

Judge Sirica replied tersely, "No chance of that, young man."[22]

Sam Dash made mincemeat of the Special Prosecution Force's argument. He rubbed Heymann's nose in the dirt by citing a Supreme Court case that Archibald Cox had successfully argued as solicitor general, *Hutcheson v. United States,* that established that even a pending criminal case could not justify the court's interference with public congressional hearings.[23] The special prosecutor's motion was squashed. The Senate hearings would go forward, beamed onto television screens across the country. Cox had already alienated the Republicans; now he had picked a fight with his purported Democratic allies and lost.

One of the only tangible results of Cox's first ill-fated battle in court was to create an immediate and hostile reaction from the press. They now saw the special prosecutor as arrogant, cocky, and clueless. Jim Doyle heard the scuttlebutt among his journalist friends: The Nixon administration was taking advantage of this Harvard professor's prestige as a former solicitor general and respected Kennedy Democrat "and lend[ing] it to the cover-up effort."[24]

Even Cox would second-guess his strategy on this particular issue in later years. "The Senate hearings under Senator Ervin," he conceded, "certainly were a contribution to the public good as it turned out. None of them did interfere in any way with prosecutions, and they may have produced some evidence . . . that might not otherwise have come out."[25] Still, Cox felt it was important that the special prosecutor had "showed sensitivity to the possible abuses of publicity." If defendants raised the issue down the road, a court would at least see that "the prosecutor had done the best he could" to reel in the Senate inquiry.[26]

Did his actions concerning the Senate hearings damage Cox in the eyes of the American public, in June 1973? "Well, I read so," he admitted.[27] But as Cox was adjusting to his new role, he resolved to rely on the same internal compass that had guided him since he sat in the room overlooking the East River, in the chair facing Judge Learned Hand, and learned to become a lawyer. He would stick with his own legal instincts. And leave the political calculations to others.

In hindsight, Cox's challenge to Senator Ervin's televised hearings would represent one of the strongest pieces of evidence that the special prosecutor had not aimed the prosecution, from the start, at toppling the president. Not only had Cox confronted the Democratic power brokers, but his adamant stance against granting immunity to witnesses like Magruder and Dean was flatly inconsistent with the anti-Nixon philosophy that the White House would later ascribe to him. If the principal goal of the Watergate Special Prosecution Force had been to "get Nixon if you possibly can, come hell or high water," there would have been no reason for the special prosecutor to avoid handing out immunity to a host of minor White House players to see what their testimony might unearth.[28] Cox's earliest approach, as the failed motion to block Senator Ervin revealed, was to preserve the government's position so that he could fully prosecute all defendants, even if this strategy did not blaze a trail to the White House.

In June 1973, however, the press, Congress, and Richard M. Nixon were all beginning to reach the same conclusion: Archibald Cox had been a horrible choice in the mad scramble to appoint a special prosecutor.

Henry Petersen's story about the tape continued to stick in the minds of Cox and his associates. It made them ponder strategy, backwards and sideways. On June 6, Cox and Vorenberg arranged a meeting in their cramped offices with the attorneys who had accepted the job of representing President Nixon in his personal capacity: Leonard Garment, J. Fred Buzhardt, and Charles Alan Wright.[29]

Garment had replaced John Dean as counsel to the president. Although a Democrat, Garment was a trusted ally. He had worked with Richard Nixon at the Mudge, Rose law firm in New York in the mid-1960s, helping to prepare Nixon for his one and only Supreme Court appearance in *Time, Inc. v. Hill*. Buzhardt was a Southerner who had come to Washington as a protegé of South Carolina Senator Strom Thurmond. An ardent supporter of President Nixon, Buzhardt now acted as special counsel for Watergate affairs, switching over from the Department of Defense with General Alexander Haig, who had replaced Haldeman as White House chief of staff. (Buzhardt and Haig had been West Point friends.)[30] Charles Alan Wright, the third lawyer at the meeting, was a constitutional law expert from the University of Texas and had just been appointed as a special consultant on the Watergate case. His addition to the presidential team was viewed as critical. "We could see a truckload of constitutional problems down the road," explained Garment.[31]

The meeting was guarded; both sides were tight, ill at ease. Cox made a formal request for three specific documents: the notes of the meeting between Petersen and the president on April 16, in which the subject of the tape recording of John Dean had been raised; the memo from Petersen to H. R. Haldeman summarizing the same meeting; and the actual taped conversation between Nixon and Dean that the president had mentioned to Petersen.[32] Vorenberg threw in another stray item. He would like White House logs that listed all calls and visits between key White House aides and President Nixon between June 1972 and May 1973.[33]

According to Vorenberg's notes of the meeting, Fred Buzhardt attempted to cut off these demands immediately. The president, he stated, "is being forced into the role of Defendant, and would fight that role." He rapped his large West Point ring on the table. The president, and *only* the president, would "decide what he hands over."[34]

Charles Alan Wright viewed Cox and Vorenberg as out to pick through every locked file cabinet in the White House. Wright recorded his position in an adamant memorandum the next day: "There is no possibility that the President would, could, or should accede to a request of that kind," he wrote. The president could "hardly allow others to rummage at will through his papers to see what they could find that could be used to hurt him." Wright concluded with a touch of sarcasm: Even "the meanest defendant in a two-bit criminal case cannot be subjected to the procedures that our friends would propose to use against the President of the United States."[35]

Garment and Wright took their turns at the June 6 meeting, articulating an extremely broad view of the president's privilege as chief executive. Although President Nixon had pledged in his May 22 speech not to block Cox from obtaining any "testimony" regarding possible criminal conduct in the Watergate affair, the president had quickly clarified what he meant. On the day of Elliot Richardson's swearing in, the president had told his new attorney general that he had used the word "testimony" only "advisedly"; it was meant to apply only to oral testimony, not to documents.[36]

Wright, the preeminent constitutional scholar, now insisted that much more than Richard M. Nixon's privacy was at stake. Executive privilege had to be adhered to for the sake of "future Presidents."[37]

This privilege applied not only to President Nixon's own papers, but to the files of presidential *aides* such as Haldeman and Ehrlichman.[38] Wright stressed that many of these documents were so "sensitive" that the president could not allow his own lawyers to look at them.[39] Perhaps when it came to *some* papers, the president would voluntarily choose *not* to exercise his privilege to the fullest extent permitted by the Constitution. Perhaps he would "waive" it for some items, to speed this irksome Watergate case to a conclusion. But that would be the president's decisions, nobody else's.

It was a high stakes game of chess. The president's lawyers were skilled players. Archie turned the tables by reminding them that "it's in the president's interest to say he permitted such review" of White House documents, to restore public trust and put Watergate behind the nation.[40] Wright and Garment had a quick retort that it "might not be true from the standpoint of *future* Presidents." If the president bowed to Cox's request even on a single occasion, there might be "long-term damage" to the office of the presidency. In any event, it would certainly hamstring the president for the next four years. "His ability to govern effectively until 1977," Wright pressed hard, "would be seriously hurt if every candid comment he has made to his most intimate advisers on a variety of sensitive subjects, wholly unrelated to Watergate, were now to be made common currency." Wright was unyielding: "No President in our history has ever responded to a subpoena or allowed free access to his papers by those outside the White House."[41]

Cox was unimpressed. He reminded the president's lawyers that there was a wide gulf between "what you would disclose on the Hill," and what they might give privately to a special prosecutor, who was in a unique position to review the material and maintain confidentiality.[42] Cox also explained, in his own New England way, that "he hoped that [they] regarded him as an honorable man and a man of integrity and that [they] would assume that those who would be selected for his staff, who would have to be his 'eyes and ears,' would also be carefully chosen with these attributes in mind."[43]

Wright was unmoved. Upright lawyers or not, Cox and his prosecutors had no business meddling in the president's personal papers. He dug in his heels: "I do indeed have great respect for the honor and integrity of Professors Cox and Vorenberg, but until men become angels no Republican President is going to allow Harvard Law School professors to examine records that might include blunt comments of that kind about people and events, comments of a sort that it is essential a President be able to make in free discussion with his closest advisers, but that would be enormously damaging if they ever become known generally."[44]

The issue of the tape mentioned by Henry Petersen was of critical importance to the special prosecutors at this meeting. But Cox and Vorenberg approached it gingerly. Hadn't Petersen mentioned that he had met with the president on April 18? they asked the president's lawyers. Hadn't there been some talk of a comment made by John Dean dealing with immunity, which was on tape? Buzhardt replied that the president's reference to a "tape recording" at this meeting must have referred to a Dictabelt that the president had made *after* his conversation with John Dean. It was *not* a tape recording of an actual conversation involving the president and John Dean, Buzhardt said. This was an item created by President Nixon for himself. It was irrelevant, harmless, and privileged.

This answer raised two doubts in Cox's mind. The first was "I wonder if we're getting the truth." The second was, if it was truly a harmless after-the-fact Dictabelt, "well, give us the Dictabelt then."[45] The three presidential lawyers walked out of Cox's office before the special prosecutor had a chance to frame these two questions.

It was obvious that the president's lawyers were braced for a fight. They were confident of its outcome. As Wright wrote the next day, Cox seemed to be going for "blanket access" of presidential materials. Wright was certain that the special prosecutor "cannot possibly win." Using a phrase coined by Chief of Staff Alexander Haig, Wright asserted that the American people would understand that the "Oval Office is not a goldfish bowl." The president's papers were not available for a "blanket fishing expedition." If specific documents were requested, the president would review these requests and produce documents "*if* the public interest allows this to be done." In other instances, the president might deem it necessary to convey "factual information" contained in the documents, but not the documents themselves. The special prosecutor would simply have to trust the president.

Wright wrote with a flourish of confidence, in tidying up the meeting on paper: "As was said to our forefathers gathered at Lexington Green: 'Do not fire unless fired upon. But if they mean to have a war, let it begin here!' "[46]

Shortly after the June 6 meeting, Cox scheduled a press conference without announcing its purpose. In fact, Jim Doyle had set up the meeting as a bland courtesy to the Washington press corps, a chance for Cox to introduce new members of his staff. Now Jim Vorenberg received an urgent phone call from Fred Buzhardt at the White House. What was Cox going to say at this unannounced news conference? What was he up to?

Vorenberg decided to get some mileage out of the conversation. He reminded Buzhardt about the requests for materials at the June 6 meeting. Why had Cox's office not received any of the items they had requested? Vorenberg pushed harder: there might be a legitimate dispute over materials that were arguably privileged. Buzhardt had nevertheless promised to provide the special prosecutor, at a minimum, with copies of White House logs reflecting the dates and times of meetings and telephone calls between key White House aides and the president. It was a bluff, and Vorenberg knew it as he cradled the phone to his ear. But the bluff seemed to be working.

Buzhardt said that he would send over a package containing the White House logs immediately, but only on condition that there would be *no* attacks on the White House at Cox's press conference. Vorenberg pretended to deliberate; he shuffled some papers around. Finally he agreed to the terms, trying to sound reluctant. The package arrived within an hour. It contained a fat sheaf of papers that listed dates and times—down to the minute—of telephone conversations and meetings between key advisers and President Nixon. The press conference went forward in Room 4830 of the Department of Commerce Building. As Cox introduced new members of his staff, the White House exhaled a sigh of relief. But the Special Prosecution Force now had documents that would pin down specific dates and times of conversations between President Nixon and close aides, including Haldeman, Ehrlichman, Dean, and others.[47]

As Vorenberg described the evolving strategy in the Watergate prosecution, "Not everything was brains and skill."[48]

On the morning of June 25, the historic Senate Caucus room resembled a scene from the impeachment trial of Andrew Johnson a hundred years earlier. Amid the trappings of dignity and democracy—the marble columns, the ornate chandelier, the sacred American flag—legislators of opposing political parties called on witnesses in an effort to tear apart, or staunchly defend, the president of the United States. On this day the Senate Watergate Committee had assembled to hear the testimony of John Dean, who began reading a prepared statement at 10:30 A.M. and did not conclude until 6:00 that evening.

The former White House counsel's testimony "stunned the press and the country." It painted a disturbing picture of political corruption and intrigue, with the president directly at the epicenter. Senator Howard Baker, ranking Republican on the committee, repeatedly asked Dean in a somber voice, seeking to pin him down, "What did the President know and when did he know it?" Dean's answer surprised even Baker. The president had "substantial knowledge" of the cover-up, Dean replied impassively over his tortoiseshell glasses. The president had gone as far as to say that raising a million dollars to buy off Hunt and other Watergate defendants to ensure their silence would be relatively easy. Dean had attempted to save the president and stem the tide of Watergate before it had engulfed the Oval Office. But when Dean realized that he was being left to hang out to dry as the lone Watergate "scapegoat," he had made an appointment with the U.S. attorneys and decided to tell all.[49]

As fascinating as Dean's testimony was, it complicated life immeasurably for Cox and his office. Their case was now Dean's word against a squadron of White House witnesses of considerable credibility. How to find the truth?

Not everything in Watergate, as Vorenberg had observed, was brains and skill.

The special prosecutor's office on K Street ground forward. It was not the safest neighborhood; nor was Archie's job the safest occupation. He received several death threats. An attempted mugging was thwarted at the last minute by a mysterious contingency of FBI agents who appeared out of nowhere to whisk the special prosecutor off the street. Cox's telephone number was supposed to be unlisted, but one night the D.C. Police called him: "If you see some men watching your house, we don't want you to worry. We're watching the men who are watching the house."[50] Archie had no time to dwell on such distractions. He insisted on walking to and from work through the unglamorous neighborhood each night.[51] His office operated seven days a week, twelve hours a day.

The awkward match of Silbert and the assistant U.S. attorneys was finally brought to an ungraceful ending in late June. Relations had only worsened. Silbert complained in his diary that Cox was "not standing up for us," as the original prosecutor's team continued to be attacked by the national press.[52] They wanted Cox to "examine the record" and "endorse" them, which Cox was not willing to do.[53] Not that Cox questioned the men's integrity, but there was no time for such foolishness, no time for investigations of investigations.[54]

The assistant U.S. attorneys were starting to resent Cox. They did not consider him much of a prosecutor; he had never tried a case in his life.[55] Nor did they trust his motives. At least one of them privately concluded that Cox was a publicity-seeking self-promoter who had his eye set on a Supreme Court seat if Teddy Kennedy was elected president in 1976.

At the same time, Cox and his staff were miffed that Silbert's team had virtually pledged John Dean immunity, despite Cox's vigorous opposition to such a deal. Dean's promised immunity complicated Cox's job to no end.[56] On top of this, additional details of the Watergate investigation had been leaked to the press over the summer. Cox attributed these leaks to the U.S. attorney's team.[57] This unhappy union had to come to an end.

Silbert's group had already begun writing a lengthy memorandum that spelled out all of the evidence they had gathered, to date. Part of the purpose of this memo was to help Cox make the difficult transition into the Watergate investigation. As Silbert admitted frankly in his diary, however, the other purpose was to provide tangible evidence of their own accomplishments for posterity. "No one will ever be able to claim we didn't have our case, . . ." he recorded. "At the appropriate time should anyone claim that the case was in shambles we will be able to indicate to the contrary." After working relentlessly over a long weekend, Silbert finally completed the eighty-seven-page memorandum on June 7.[58]

This lengthy report to Cox contained a list of "Witnesses To be Interviewed in This Office and/or Presented to the Grand Jury." Silbert had included his own boss, Henry Petersen, as a likely witness. The final potential witness on the list was President Nixon, but on this name Silbert hedged: "Were he not President, there is no question but that President Nixon would have to be questioned about a number of matters. . . . This is obviously a matter of such extreme sensitivity, raising Constitutional questions, that whatever steps are taken can only be by you." Cox scribbled his own notes in the margin, below the name of President Nixon: "Inclined to lay off for now—Maybe ask narrative from him after Dean."[59]

Cox directed Silbert not to turn over the confidential report to anyone, including U.S. Attorney Harold Titus. Silbert immediately turned over the document to Titus, anyway.[60] When an attorney for the Democratic National Committee and the American Civil Liberties Union issued a 106-page report blasting the work of Silbert and his prosecutors, demanding new trials for the original Watergate defendants because of alleged improprieties,[61] Cox decided to end the misery. He asked the three attorneys to withdraw from the case. Silbert and his team were angry, but also relieved. Despite the "tremendous sadness and frustration having come so close," they felt relief at no longer having to endure the criticism.[62] They haggled for several weeks over a letter that Cox would release to the press when they left,[63] that would partially vindicate their work, but nothing more.[64]

In a letter dated June 29, Silbert's team expressed their regret at "withdrawing" from the Watergate case. They indicated that the Special Prosecution Force was now in good shape, thanks to their "strategy" of convicting the seven Watergate defendants, all of whom had remained silent during trial, and attempting to extract confessions after their guilty verdicts. Hunt, McCord, and Liddy had turned down guilty pleas and refused to cooperate with the government during the prosecution, but things had shifted, had they not? "Indeed," wrote Silbert to Cox, "not until after the successful prosecution of the seven defendants did a single witness step forward with material information. . . ."[65] Silbert attempted to deflect criticism about their prosecution strategy; "We emphatically reject any allegations of impropriety or lack of diligence which have been or might be made," he wrote.

Cox accepted the withdrawal, stating that "lawyers often differ on questions of judgment, and there are points on which my judgment might have varied from yours." At the same time, there was no indication that Silbert and his men "did not pursue your professional duties according to your honest judgment and in complete good faith."[66] The U.S. attorney's office was now purged from the Watergate prosecution, for good.

In hindsight, any picture of the Watergate investigation would be incomplete without reference to the contributions of the Silbert team. The case had indeed been "broken open" before they left. Cox was reaping direct benefits from the prosecutors' work, particularly in the form of cooperation by key witnesses such as John Dean and Jeb Magruder. Silbert's eighty-seven-page memo of June 7, "Present Status of Watergate Investigation," which remained confidential for years, provided Cox with a detailed blueprint of the Watergate case. It also revealed that the U.S. attorneys were broadening their own investigation well beyond the initial Watergate burglary, into the realm of a White House cover-up.[67]

It is doubtful, however, that history would have allowed the Silbert team to cast off its heavy baggage, had they been permitted to complete the Watergate case. A continued investigation by the U.S. attorneys' office would have smacked of "more of the same" to the American public and the press; for this reason alone it was probably doomed to paralysis or extinction. On top of this, the tiny Silbert group had barely scratched the surface of the complex cover-up case.[68] "When I walked into the prosecutor's office," recalled John Dean of his initial meeting with Silbert's team in April 1973, "they had no conception or thought of [a] cover-up." Although the U.S. attorney's group did not know it, John Dean had made the decision to stop cooperating. "They had many masters they had to serve," Dean later explained. He was a friend and admirer of Henry Petersen, but he knew firsthand that Petersen was channeling information back to the White House. The U.S. attorney's office represented a dangerous harbor for a prosecution witness like himself, Dean concluded. It was only when Cox took over the case and cut ties with the Justice Department that he decided to resume his cooperation as a pivotal government witness.[69]

The latter portion of Silbert's diary, never declassified by the Nixon Project until work on this book began, further reveals that his team had become suspicious, punchy, and nearly obsessed with self-image. Seymour Glanzer had gone so far as to consider arranging a meeting with the *New York Times,* to "get our story out." A columnist friend had advised against it: "The story had to be leaked to other people if it was going to be done at all, but only carefully."[70] Even the lengthy memorandum to Cox had become an obsession—not to assist him in the transition for the good of the Watergate investigation, but as a "big trump card," which Silbert predicted would be "a thorn in the throat of Professor Cox because of tremendous danger to him and what he can later claim to accomplish."[71]

Silbert's own diary suggests that the U. S. attorneys had lost perspective of their ultimate mission by the time they packed up to leave

Cox's operation. When they had taken on the case, "they had no idea what they had hooked."[72] They had discovered—along with the rest of the country—that Watergate was a case of monstrous size and importance, bigger than all of them. So they had embarked upon a campaign to save face, an understandable turn of events given their awkward, and not altogether fair, position in the eyes of the Washington press corps. By the end, their investigation had become virtually paralyzed.

Cox was at peace with the decision. Now he could return to strategy.

When it came to his own dealings with the press and the national news media, Cox developed a simple approach. Jim Doyle had a secretary arrive at the office at 7:00 each morning and cull through five newspapers and major network television reports. Archie tried to cover at least two papers at breakfast; with Phyllis still in Maine, he had no other company. He and Doyle would sit down together at 9:00 for coffee, doughnuts, and the day's briefing. Cox's secretary would remember these conferences vividly: "The fancier the doughnut, the better," she recalled. "He was like a kid. He didn't seem like that type at all."[73] After the coffee was poured and doughnuts selected, Doyle would explain to Cox "what the stories meant; how they came to be there." If leaks had sprouted, Doyle deciphered the likely sources. A good journalist could generally track leaks backward through the network of Washington reporters. These briefings were conducted in a "rambling, political, gossipy way" that Cox seemed to enjoy. He tried to absorb the facts and players that made up the quickly spinning world of national news, and told Doyle that he did not want to "miss anything."[74]

When it came to projecting the special prosecutor's "image" in the media, the two men followed an uncomplicated rule. Archie's job was to be himself. Doyle's job was to "explain Archie Cox to the press." They both knew that Cox did not look particularly glamorous on television. When he relaxed, his voice got high and "very squeaky." Admitted Doyle, "He just looked awful on the tube." Cox also had to move questioners to his left side because of his bad ear, at times an awkward manuever. But neither of them wasted time fretting about Archie's television profile. When Doyle became frustrated by comments or photos portraying the special prosecutor poorly in the news media, Cox would have to remind his hard-driving press officer,

"You've told me yourself many times you do what you believe to be right and then you sell it afterwards."[75] It was not the usual Washington approach to public relations. But it seemed to fit.

On July 6, Cox announced in a press release that American Airlines, one of the nation's major corporations, had confessed to making illegal corporate contributions to the Committee to Re-elect the President.[76] The next week President Nixon checked into Bethesda Naval Hospital with viral pneumonia; he was described as "forlorn, his shoulders sagging."[77] There seemed to be a link, which had a whiff of legitimacy, between a slush fund of illegal cash tied to the president's election apparatus and the cover-up activities of prominent White House aides. It seemed as if nothing more startling could turn up.

Then on Monday, July 16, 1973, Alexander Butterfield, a deputy assistant to the president, testified before the Senate committee and "spill[ed] the beans" about the elaborate taping system installed in the White House by President Nixon. Ever since 1971, Butterfield testified, every conversation of the president in the White House Oval Office, in the cabinet room, and in his Executive Office Building office had been taped. Phones in the White House and at Camp David had also been monitored. The taping was done for "historical reasons," with the intention to "record things for posterity for the Nixon library."[78]

If Dean's testimony had been scorching, Butterfield's revelation amounted to a bombshell. Among other things, it told Cox that the April 15 tape mentioned by Petersen was a minor issue. It had been swallowed up by the revelation of a whole legion of tapes that could be used to determine if John Dean, or the president's men, were telling the truth.

Years later, Cox would freely admit that if Butterfield had not dropped the bomb about the "taping system," it was unclear whether the Special Prosecution Force would have ever had the nerve, or the inclination, to subpoena tapes from the president. When Cox had written a polite letter requesting the April 15 tape, Buzhardt had quickly shrugged it off, stating that the recording in question "was a tape on which the President dictated his own recollections of that conversation after it was finished."[79] Cox would later confess, "We were, to some extent, put off by the assertion that it was just a Dictabelt dictated by the President after the meeting."[80] It was far from clear whether Judge Sirica, or any other judge, would have enforced a subpoena based on such skimpy evidence. Cox later reflected, "What did it was Butterfield's statement."[81]

The important question for the Special Prosecution Force now became how to go about obtaining the tapes. And which tapes should Cox request? Or should he pursue an entirely different route?

Cox remembered musing, "Well, the time is coming, isn't it, when I'm going to have to subpoena Richard Nixon. Since he's president, I don't believe I can get him before the grand jury, but I'm going to take his deposition."[82] Cox was well aware of Chief Justice John Marshall's ruling in the *Trial of Aaron Burr* in 1807, suggesting that there might be some ability, however limited, to gather evidence from a sitting president for purposes of an existing criminal prosecution, including requiring the president to testify at trial. Remembering the president's great skill as a debater, Cox "looked forward with some nervousness to actually cross-examining Richard Nixon."[83]

By mid-July, Cox was "edging up" to the idea of a deposition. He even wrote a letter to the president's lawyers demanding it, but never mailed it. Cox's biggest concern was that the White House would immediately force a ruling on the issue by Judge Sirica, maybe even go to the Supreme Court, and the courts would say, "God, what's he going to do next?" Archie saw no reason to frighten off the judiciary this early in the skirmishing.[84]

If he did not take the president's deposition, that left only a pair of options. He could go for the Dictabelt that Henry Petersen had referred to. Or, based upon Butterfield's recent testimony, he could attempt to tap into the wider group of recordings that had been revealed. "And it seemed pretty clear to me," Cox said, "that the right one to do was to select, I think it was nine or ten, specific tapes and seek to obtain those."[85]

That is exactly what the Special Prosecution Force geared up to do. They identified eight specific tapes of meetings, using the logs that the White House itself had supplied. Archie's philosophy was simple; he believed that a smart lawyer used "neither blunderbuss nor a shot gun, but a rifle. He chooses his gauge very carefully."[86] So Cox picked precise dates and times that President Nixon had met with John Ehrlichman, H. R. Haldeman, John Mitchell, and John Dean. They included a June 20, 1972, telephone conversation between President Nixon and John Mitchell, just three days after the Watergate break-in, along with the meeting that same day between the president, Haldeman, and Ehrlichman. The request also included the

September 15 conversation in which Dean had testified that President Nixon had praised him for "containing" the Watergate investigation. Finally, Cox listed the March 21, 1973, conversation, in which Dean had testified that he told Nixon that Watergate had become a "cancer on the presidency." The subpoena would be limited to this narrow set of eight tapes, those most relevant to possible criminal wrongdoing.

Cox, unlike Jim Neal and others on the Special Prosecution Force who had actually interviewed John Dean, was still leery of the former counsel's story. Cox admitted, "It seemed to me that, on the record, he looked like a person who . . . what he said was pretty much shaped to suit the advantage of John Dean on the particular occasion."[87] But if anything would prove or disprove Dean's damning testimony concerning Richard M. Nixon, it would be the president's own tape recordings.[88]

On July 18 Cox sent a letter to J. Fred Buzhardt, counsel for the president, requesting the eight tapes he had listed: "I would urge that the tapes be furnished for use in my investigation without restriction. This procedure strikes me as the method of establishing the truth which is most fair to everyone concerned, including the President."[89]

Cox pointed out that his request presented none of the "separation-of-powers" issues that understandably troubled the president when it came to supplying presidential papers to the Senate. The Senate committee was seeking information and holding hearings "solely in order to recommend legislation." That was a broad, unpredictable forum that admittedly might set bad precedent for future presidents. Cox's request, on the other hand, involved an ongoing grand jury investigation in a pending criminal case, an unusual event in American history that "almost surely will never be repeated."[90]

The Senate committee had no interest in being outmaneuvered. Senator Sam Ervin now publicly asked the president to supply the Senate Select Committee with a wagon-load of tapes—far more than Cox had requested.[91] Both offices waited.

On Thursday, July 19, a group of Special Prosecution Force staff members gathered in Cox's office. Senator Ervin was on television announcing that he had just received a telephone call from Secretary of Treasury George Shultz. "I am pleased to announce," Ervin drawled, "that Secretary Shultz has called me and advised me that the President has decided to make available to the Committee [the] tapes. . . ." Ervin beamed into the camera. It was "a very wise decision on the part of the President."[92] Cox's staff stood paralyzed. They did not want to play "second fiddle" to the Senate. "You must do something!" they shouted to Cox. "Why aren't you getting equal answers? Call up Buzhardt. Call up the White House. Do something."

Cox was suspicious of the report. "Well, let's just simmer down," he said, "and see how this shakes out."[93]

It turned out that the voice on the phone had not been Secretary Shultz. Senator Ervin had been "hoaxed."[94] He cursed the person who would perpetrate such an un-American deed.

The president's lawyers took advantage of the chaos by swiftly rejecting both the special prosecutor's and the Senate committee's requests. Charles Alan Wright wrote a curt letter to Cox on July 23: "I am instructed by the President to inform you that it will not be possible to make available to you the recordings that you have requested."[95]

Wright did not dispute that the president had once stated, through Attorney General Richardson, that certain items of public interest dealing with the Watergate investigation "should be disclosed." But Cox's mistake, as Wright saw it, was presuming that a special prosecutor could tell the president what was in the public interest: "It is for the President, and *only* for the President, to weigh whether the incremental advantage that these tapes would give you in criminal proceedings justifies the serious and lasting hurt that disclosure of them would do to the confidentiality that is imperative to the effective functioning of the Presidency."[96]

On that same day, July 23, President Nixon personally wrote to Senator Ervin and rejected the Select Committee's even broader request for tapes, vouching that he had listened to many of the tapes and they were best kept confidential:

> The fact is that the tapes would not finally settle the central issues before your Committee. Before their existence became publicly known, I personally listened to a number of them. The tapes are entirely consistent with what I know to be the truth and what I have stated to be the truth. However ... there are inseparably interspersed in them a great many frank and very private comments, on a wide range of issues and individuals, wholly extraneous to the Committee's inquiry. ... They are the clearest possible example of why Presidential documents must be kept confidential.[97]

President Nixon ended his letter with characteristic adamancy:

Accordingly, the tapes, which have been under my sole personal
control, will remain so. None has been transcribed or made public
and none will be.[98]

Cox walked away disheartened. The tapes might not only show
criminal activity, but also allow certain defendants to prove that they
were *not* guilty. Cox's inability to obtain them meant that he had to
continue delaying the indictments of other potential defendants. If
Cox did not have *all* the evidence in his hands, as defendants' lawyers
would surely protest to the court, numerous indictments relating to
Watergate would have to be put on hold indefinitely. The government
had no right to prosecute citizens if it knew of, but did not obtain,
additional evidence that might prove their innocence. There was no
such thing as a "piecemeal prosecution."[99] Cox had been hurled into a
prosecutorial hornet's nest.

The first expedition for the tapes had proved a flop. It had also
revealed that rivalries and jealousies were starting to creep up
between the Senate Watergate Committee and the Special Prosecution Force. Cox himself had stopped worrying about the parallel
investigation in the Senate months ago. "They were created. There
they were. One accepts them."[100] Some of Cox's staff, on the other
hand, were insistent that their own office was now taking an un-
justified back seat to the Senate committee.

Jim Vorenberg, by this time, was jetting back and forth between
Cambridge and Washington, with duties piling up at Harvard and a
daughter who had been in a serious car accident.[101] He had a single
piece of advice for Cox: "Don't worry about the tapes."[102] As a
criminal law expert, Vorenberg viewed the entire tapes issue as a
diversion. It was intentionally designed by the White House to throw
the Watergate investigation off the track. "It seemed so ridiculous that
[incriminating] tapes would be left undestroyed," said Vorenberg.[103]

Cox politely listened to his assistant's expert advice. Then he set off
"like a bird-dog who had picked up a scent."[104] The tapes were
critical, in Cox's mind. The only question was whether a subpoena for
them would prevail in the courts over the president's claim of
so-called executive privilege. Cox decided to risk it. The special prosecutor and his troop sat around a table, puzzling over how to draft a
subpoena to the president. Recalled Vorenberg, "I can remember
sending somebody to look through our stack of printed forms to see if
we had anything that could be adapted." Unfortunately, there was not
a form made for the White House.[105]

On July 23, after learning that Cox intended to issue a formal subpoena for eight tapes, the Senate Watergate Committee hurriedly announced that they had voted to subpoena five conversations between President Nixon and John Dean plus a more "scattershot" request for a whole pile of presidential tapes relating to twenty-five individuals. As spotlights gleamed down on the Senate conference table at 3:30 in the afternoon, the white-haired Senator Ervin was captured on national television placing his signature on a duly formalized subpoena.[106] The Senate committee was now ahead of the Special Prosecution Force, by hours.

This fact did not bother Cox. After patiently researching the law, he added a ninth tape to his list. He included a request for several memos. Then he issued his own subpoena to the president later that same day, July 23. It was wholly immaterial that the Senate committee had "beat me to the punch."[107]

"When we were ready," Cox would say, ". . . then we went ahead."[108]

The evening papers and television broadcasts directed all their attention to the Senate committee's subpoena. It was viewed as a constitutional milestone. There were pictures of Senator Ervin signing his historic subpoena, footage of Ervin's staff speeding across Washington in an unmarked capital police car to deliver the document to the Executive Office Building, coverage of the event from all angles in living color. *Time* magazine called it a "historic vote," with pictures of members of the Senate Watergate Committee raising their hands somberly, Senator Ervin's hand raised the highest.

The Special Prosecution Force was all but forgotten. There was a sense of "tremendous disappointment" among Cox's staff. As a legal document, they felt, their subpoena was far more significant. A command issued to the president in connection with a pending criminal investigation was much more monumental—in a constitutional sense—than a subpoena issued by Congress as part of its routine work in drafting laws. But the Senate subpoena had captured the evening news and splashed its way onto the pages of *Time*. Jim Doyle complained to Archie that his own colleagues in the media had "misread" this one.

Archie looked over his half-glasses. He put down a pencil that he had been writing with, next to his supply of art gum erasers. He raised his heavy eyebrows and dismissed Doyle with an old New England expression: "I guess all we can do is keep chopping wood."[109]

17

BATTLE
FOR THE TAPES

It was a fortunate quirk of history that J. Fred Buzhardt, special counsel to the president, agreed to accept service of the subpoena on behalf of Richard M. Nixon. Behind closed doors, Cox and his staff were pacing with worry. What would they do if their lawyers "were turned away at the White House gate?"[1] In hindsight, Cox would say that accepting the service may have been a strategic blunder for the president, if he truly wanted to conduct a stonewall defense. He should have treated Cox "like a fly or a mosquito" and "kind of laugh[ed] him off," citing Jefferson and Lincoln as models, never allowing the special prosecutor or his lawyers to go to court.[2] "I think one would say that he never should have submitted to the question of whether the tapes could be subpoenaed as evidence to the Court. He should have simply stood on the fact that 'I am president. I have my independent responsibilities. I have great respect for Judge Sirica but I've got to do my job and if that's inconsistent with his conception of his job, I'm sorry but that's the way it is.' "[3]

But the president did accept service of the subpoena, a simple form directed to "Richard M. Nixon, The White House, Washington, D.C. . . ." neatly signed by Cox and stamped "Filed" by James F. Davey, Clerk of Court.[4] Buzhardt wrote scrupulously in ink on the marshal's return form, "Received on July 23, 1973 at 6:20 P.M.," and noted "on behalf of the President."[5] With this signature Cox's group avoided the first potential constitutional crisis of the Watergate affair.

Why did President Nixon allow the subpoena to pass so easily through the doors of the White House? Len Garment later explained that the idea of refusing to accept service "seemed kind of grotesque."[6] But there was a more pragmatic reason. The president's counsel felt strongly, Cox's sources told him, that they would prevail on the tapes matter. "I'm just short of knowing," Cox later explained, "that Charlie Wright gave a categorical opinion, 'I will win.'" Cox knew that this was "Charlie Wright's style." The battle with the president's lawyers would be fierce, exact, and conclusive.[7]

Various options had been kicked around the White House before the subpoena entered its portals, some less palatable than others. The White House lawyers themselves were not permitted to listen to the tapes. They were told to "stay away from them." Garment admitted: "We knew it wasn't going to be altogether happy listening."[8] Nevertheless, the veil of uncertainty worked to their advantage in many ways. Patrick J. Buchanan, speechwriter, journalist, and Nixon loyalist, had written a memo the day the subpoena was issued, advising the president to destroy insignificant tapes and be done with them forever: "If there are conversations with confidential aides . . . that are better left confidential forever—what then is the sense of their preservation?" Buchanan's advice was candid and bold: "Perhaps the President should be provided with a day-by-day log of his tape library, and himself separate the wheat from the chaff—from his own recollection—and have the latter burned."[9]

But this was easier said than done. Some in the White House worried that the mere act of destroying the tapes might be considered an impeachable offense. On a more practical level, who would do it? Robert Bork had been asked by the president's chief of staff, General Alexander Haig, to resign his solicitor generalship and come over to the White House to represent the president personally in Watergate. Bork turned Haig down because he was told he would not be permitted to hear the tapes. He considered the idea of destroying them dangerous. "You can't call the Secret Service and tell them to burn those tapes," said Bork. "You're ruined if you're anyone who does that."[10] H. R. Haldeman, in exile in California after his resignation, was allowed to listen to one tape for the president and advised Nixon to hang onto the recordings "for historical value." Selectively using some portions and invoking executive privilege as to others could turn them into the White House's "best defense." If the tapes were considered in their entirety, Haldeman believed, they would vindicate the president.[11]

Now President Nixon had to answer Cox in court. On July 25, the president himself wrote to Judge Sirica. Citing an 1865 opinion by

Abraham Lincoln's Attorney General James Speed, President Nixon proposed that "It would be inconsistent with the public interest and with the Constitutional position of the Presidency to make available recordings of meetings and telephone conversations in which I was a participant and I must respectfully decline to do so."[12] The next day, the *Bangor Daily News*—the newspaper that Phyllis read to keep abreast of her husband's Watergate activities while she tended to the horses, barn, garden, tractor, and other chores in Maine—reported that the president had "defied demands" from both Cox and the Senate committee. The president appeared to be succeeding in his stonewall defense. Deputy White House Press Secretary Gerald L. Warren informed news reporters that President Nixon "would abide by a definitive decision of the highest court," but nothing less. "The President is very confident of his constitutional position, . . ." Warren announced with firm chin. He dismissed the two subpoenas as wishful fishing expeditions.[13]

The Senate Select Committee unanimously voted to enforce their subpoena by suing the president.[14] Cox's team pondered its next move and chose a different path. It was not particularly wise to go after the president head-on, they decided. Far more prudent, far more discreet, would be a Rule to Show Cause: a polite legal document that essentially said, "Tell us why you are not obeying the subpoena." Although nonaggressive and almost painfully deferential, the tactic might force the president's hand in a more judicious way. Some of Cox's staff pushed for a more vigorous move. Why not seek a contempt order against Richard Nixon? Cox discussed the matter with his closest advisers and decided it was far wiser to do it "in as low-key, responsible way as possible."[15]

Issuing a Rule to Show Cause to the president of the United States was still unprecedented and fraught with danger. On that afternoon of July 26, Cox walked into the grand jury room on the third floor of the federal courthouse. It was sparse, barren of windows. A U.S. marshal was posted at the door to prevent spying and the use of long-distance microphones. Cox met with the nineteen ordinary citizens who made up the Watergate grand jury (three were absent). They sat uneasily in their small wooden chairs as the special prosecutor read the White House letter and explained why these nine specific tapes and two memos were crucial to his investigation. After deliberating several minutes, this random collection of citizens of the District of Columbia unanimously voted to seek an order from Judge Sirica directing the president of the United States to "show cause why there should not be full and prompt compliance."[16]

Judge John J. Sirica assembled the grand jury in his courtroom. He wanted to hear the words himself before signing such an extraordinary document. Sirica's chambers swarmed with reporters and lawyers. Judge Sirica was a "severe, remote" man.[17] The grand jurors lined up uncertainly along one of the spectators' benches.[18]

"I was sort of nervous," Cox remembered. "It's one thing for the grand jury in the privacy of the grand jury room to say, 'Yes, go ahead. We want you to subpoena the president of the United States.' It's another when called upon in public in the crowded courtroom."[19]

The judge began to poll the jurors. The foreman, Vladimir Pregelj, a thin, forty-six-year-old man with a graying beard, stood up and answered yes, it was his intention for the court to issue an Order to Show Cause to the president. After the second or third juror had stood up in turn, Cox wiped away a bead of perspiration.[20] A group of ordinary men and women from the District of Columbia, black and white, educated and uneducated, employed and unemployed and retired, had quietly made one of the most important decisions in the constitutional history of the nation.[21]

Judge Sirica gave the White House until August 7, at 10:00 A.M.— just under two weeks—to provide the documents or respond to Cox's Rule to Show Cause.[22] It was Cox's first victory, but far from a conclusive one. He told reporters that he "did not consider the White House refusal to be final." He still "held out hope of obtaining the documents, eventually."[23]

President Nixon, meantime, responded like a solid rock to early murmurs of impeachment, predicting that any such attempt would "collapse before it gets very far." He declared, "What we were elected to do, we are going to do and let others wallow in Watergate."[24]

Richard Nixon's popularity was sinking to the lowest level for any president in two decades, according to an August Gallup poll. His ability to govern was likewise suffering. In July he had attempted to persuade Congress not to cut off funds for bombing raids in Cambodia, but was rebuffed. As six hundred thousand people were pouring into Watkins Glen, New York, for a muddy summer rock concert featuring the Grateful Dead and the Band, the mood of the country was becoming noticeably more impatient and skeptical of politicians.

House Minority Leader Gerald R. Ford of Michigan, a longtime supporter of the president in the Watergate tangle, attempted to calm the national discontent by explaining that President Nixon had spent ten to twelve hours at his Camp David retreat listening to the tapes, before overriding two high-level advisers who had urged him to release the recordings.[25] One White House spokesman defended Nixon: "He feels that people are looking for strength from the President, and he intends to make a show of strength."[26]

The game of hot potato over the tapes became front-page news in August 1973, as the deadline on Judge Sirica's order ticked away. The *Akron Beacon Journal* ran a cartoon depicting Cox and Sam Ervin attempting to tackle the president on a playing field as Nixon gleefully hurled a reel of tape through the air like a football.[27] *Time* magazine ran a cover story about the tapes crisis, entitled "Historic Challenge." Senatorial leaders, including Republicans, publicly urged the president to agree to a compromise. Perhaps he should permit the special prosecutor, along with Senators Ervin and Baker, to privately review the Watergate tapes; perhaps they could do it in a nonconfrontational setting and make this nightmare go away.[28] Roderick MacLeish of the *Christian Science Monitor* wrote: "The period immediately ahead holds little of bright promise for Mr. Nixon. The guns of August will be booming all around him as he embarks upon his high-risk strategy for survival."[29]

Elliot Richardson had issued a press release announcing that the president's and Cox's positions both had merit. Richardson urged the parties to work harder to hash the dispute out.[30]

This was not the attorney general's first attempt at mediation. Richardson had dropped out of Watergate strategizing early on, largely because the White House had shut him out. During his first press conference, Richardson had told reporters that if a conflict ever presented itself between the president and the special prosecutor, he would be forced to remain neutral. The president would have to "hire a lawyer" for legal advice on Watergate. This comment had "irritated" President Nixon and led to Richardson's increased ostracism.[31] As a result, Richardson would observe drolly, "I never did know much about Watergate."[32]

His assistant J. T. Smith described Richardson as a man of "large ambitions and large capacities." In his sprawling Justice Department office, aides saw disappointment in the attorney general. He had left a Defense Department job that he loved, only to be dragged into a position strewn with scandal and wrecked careers in which the biggest challenge, resolving the Watergate mess, had been placed into the hands of someone else. Elliot went home often at 6:30 (very early for him) during the first weeks of his new job. It had not been a happy promotion.[33]

Richardson nevertheless engaged in loose, informal chats and power brokering with his old labor law professor, as he had done since Cox's arrival in Washington. A number of flaps arose in which the White House pointedly questioned the scope of Cox's inquiry, and these inevitably landed in Richardson's lap.

On July 3, General Alexander Haig had telephoned Richardson and informed him that the president was furious. The *Los Angeles Times* had just reported that Cox was investigating President Nixon's homes in San Clemente and Key Biscayne. Allegations abounded that there had been large, hidden government expenditures on the properties, that the president had accepted unusual "loans" from his millionaire friends Charles "Bebe" Rebozo (a Miami banker) and Robert Abplanalp (a New York businessman), and that he had not paid enough taxes on the properties. Wasn't this kind of personal investigation into Nixon's affairs going *far* beyond the special prosecutor's charter relating to Watergate?[34]

Elliot Richardson called Cox to vent the White House's steam. Archie explained that he had assembled press clippings on the San Clemente matter, only because the subject had come up at a recent press conference and he felt inadequately prepared. There was no investigation involving San Clemente or Key Biscayne, Cox assured Richardson. It might technically be within the special prosecutor's charter, but he was not pursuing it. He had put that one "on the back of the stove."

Richardson called Haig back. Everything was under control, he reported.

No, it wasn't, Haig shot back angrily. The president might "move on this to discharge Mr. Cox." Elliot picked up the phone again and asked Archie if he would issue a statement to clarify that he was *not* investigating the president's homes. The White House was insisting on it. Cox did not like the command, but he agreed to do it because Elliot Richardson was asking. Richardson called Haig back to report that he had ironed out the problem. Now Haig snapped that even this sort of proposed statement was probably "inadequate." Suddenly the president himself "broke into the conversation" on the telephone line and insisted that "he wanted a statement by Mr. Cox making it clear that Mr. Cox was not investigating San Clemente, and he wanted it by two o'clock."[35] Otherwise, Cox was going to be fired. Richardson's scribbled notes of his conversation with the president indicate the insistent tone of the phone call: "You have exactly 30 minutes."[36]

Cox did issue his press release that afternoon, on time. Press Secretary Ronald L. Ziegler distributed the statement to the media,[37] concluding with the sour admonition that the president was "appalled by the consistent effort being undertaken in a malicious—I don't know if you can use libelous in terms of the President—but these constant, malicious efforts to suggest there was wrongdoing in the purchase of this property."[38]

Another conflict erupted on July 23, when General Haig called Richardson and informed him that the "boss" was very "uptight" about a move that Cox had pulled involving wiretaps. The special prosecutor's office had sent out questionnaires to the Internal Revenue Service, the Secret Service, the FBI, and other agencies asking for information about their use of electronic surveillance to determine if it had been employed for "political intelligence rather than governmental security," which might be linked to Watergate.[39] Haig warned Richardson, "If we have to have a confrontation we will have it." The president wanted "a tight line drawn with no further mistakes." He also wanted it understood that "if Cox does not agree, we will get rid of Cox."

When Richardson raised the matter with Cox, Cox reviewed the letters. He agreed that "the requests for information" sent by his office to the Secret Service and others had been "over-broadly stated." Cox made sure, personally, that letters of correction went out.[40]

Short-term solutions to such problems, however, did little to mollify those who saw Cox as a ballooning menace. The White House increasingly shouted that Cox had gone "off the reservation." In the words of Len Garment, Watergate had become a "large, man-eating shark" that "now threatened to [bite] everyone on the beach." There was the suggestion, as Richardson's aide J. T. Smith heard it, that Cox was "trying to set up some kind of perpetual inquisition that is going to plague the Republican party until Teddy Kennedy runs in '76."[41] Richardson would tell the president's lawyers, "Well, Cox isn't a demon. He is a good man. Why don't you call him up and talk to him about it?" Such comments only rankled the White House more.[42]

The president's lawyers were convinced that the special prosecutor had set out to accomplish "the death of a thousand cuts." Cox's office was going to "defeat the physical and emotional strength of the defense," and "mix everything up so 'Watergate' stood for many things." The lawyers in the White House felt as if there were "three or four of us" facing "hundreds of lawyers. Plain weariness broke the back of the thing."[43] Richardson, they believed, was playing directly into Cox's scheme.

The truth was, Elliot Richardson was hemmed into a box. The charter that he had so anxiously hashed out with his old professor via telephone, back in May, now revealed itself to be extremely generous toward Cox. Richardson dug through his files and reread the broad directive that he himself had issued to all Justice Department personnel when Cox was appointed. This vested Cox with "full authority for investigating and prosecuting" not only the Watergate case but all "allegations involving the President, members of the White House staff, or Presidential appointees." There was no time limitation, backward or forward, on the order. Cox could write his own ticket. The attorney general himself had spelled out the ground rules.[44]

Not that this was so horrible, as Richardson mulled over his situation. The Senate had insisted on giving Cox a broad mandate to restore public confidence. If there were allegations of wrongdoing even remotely linked to Watergate, Richardson concluded, "it could be investigated by me and the Criminal Division, or it could be investigated by the Special Prosecutor, but there is no question that it is going to be investigated." Given the prevalent winds of public mistrust, he felt, it was better to "err on the side of referring matters to the Special Prosecutor."[45]

This logic did not play well, however, in the Oval Office.[46] Elliot Richardson sensed an increasing personal hatred developing toward Cox. He worried about how it was affecting the president. When President Nixon checked into Bethesda Naval Hospital on July 12, Richardson feared "it might well be something other than pneumonia."[47]

Each time a complaint or worry reached the attorney general's office from the White House, Elliot would call Archie or invite him over to the Justice Department and lay out the matter forthrightly. Cox observed several things: Richardson never hid the ball; he seemed to trust Cox; but at the same time, the attorney general remained consistently loyal to the president's position.[48] He would talk about the matter openly and candidly and give Cox a chance to state his case, without tipping his own hand. Richardson's goal was simple. He wanted to understand how Cox would defend his position, so that he could, in turn, "give the White House a defensible answer when they pressed him on Cox's actions."[49] Cox was struck by Richardson's doggedness. "I do think," Cox later observed, "that Elliot Richardson was convinced, practically up to the moment of his resignation, that Richard Nixon was innocent of any criminal wrongdoing."[50]

Throughout their meetings, Elliot and Archie remained odd exceptions to the norm of Washington politics. The professor and his former student operated under an unspoken code different from that governing most politicians swarming across the Watergate landscape. The press explained it by calling them two "ramrod-straight" New England Brahmins: they both talked with a certain air of affectation; they were both cultured, intellectual, upper crust. The two men shared a precision among people who had followed the affluent path from New England prep schools to the Ivy League to successful positions in law and government, a precision of thought, of expression. Exaggeration of any kind was frowned upon. Trust in another person's word, even with no tangible assurance in writing, was mandatory.

There was more that drove the relationship, however. Even Fanny Cox bristled when her son was tagged a Boston Brahmin.[51] Although a New Englander herself, she was "very conscious of the fact Archie was a *Cox*."[52] He had inherited his father's legal talent and respect for government service, along with his name. Much of the silent language that Cox and Richardson spoke came not from the geographic region of the country that produced them, but from a common vision of government. Both had clerked for Learned Hand; both had learned to treat the law like a religious creed. Cox and Richardson had entered Washington life in the first half of the twentieth century, as young lawyers, when government was smaller and basic codes of decency were assumed. In their world, government officials of high principle—people like Henry L. Stimson, Charles Fahy, John McCloy, Charles Wyzanski, Frances Perkins, Harold Ickes, Dean Acheson—did (and were meant to) populate cabinet posts and positions of impact in the capital. Although the mold seemed to be vanishing by 1973, that was part of the problem. If government was going to become strong again, if society was to become revitalized, they believed that it was imperative that such qualities "come back on a wide scale."[53]

And so the two men continued to communicate in their archaic language. Richardson passed along objections and gripes from the White House whenever a jurisdictional issue like the San Clemente flap arose. Cox never took it personally. He "assumed that Elliot was thinking, 'Archie will do me the credit of knowing that all I'm doing is passing on what I have to pass on, and that he will understand that and make up his own mind without feeling that I'm pressuring him.' "[54]

On Richardson's scorecard, the exchange of gripes between the White House and Cox was "more or less even."[55] Richardson saw himself fulfilling a role that Louis Brandeis, before his appointment to the Supreme Court, had once described as "lawyer for the situation," in performing various thankless tasks of public service. It was a stop-gap role, beating out brushfires and hoping to avoid the one giant, fatal conflagration.[56]

As the relationship of mutual trust between Cox and Richardson grew and wrapped them like ivy tighter together, it began to raise a grave skepticism among Archie's own staff. They were unsure that Richardson could be trusted as a safe conduit of information. Wasn't Richardson beating a direct path between their office and the White House? He was a politician after all, a savvy one. Cox was nothing but a sheltered law professor. He should not be so naive; nothing good would come of this.

Cox listened to these concerns, but brushed them off. This was no time to second-guess his own judgment about the strengths and foibles of Richardson's character. He had made an assessment about Elliot Richardson and his integrity years ago, whether his staff re-mained skeptical or not. So "we went on as before as we thought proper."[57]

The day that President Nixon refused to honor the subpoena issued by the Special Prosecution Force, Elliot Richardson initiated a more aggressive campaign to work out an accommodation between Cox and the White House. In the summer of 1973, all of the players knew that the issue of whether tapes and documents could be subpoenaed from the president "wasn't an easy question" at all.[58]

"I told [the President] more than once," Richardson said, "that he ought to invite Archie Cox to bring a truck over to Pennsylvania Avenue and haul away everything, including the tapes. If Cox found something, [President Nixon] should say 'Ah shucks, I apologize, it must have been under the stress of work,' " and the matter would be done.[59] But the president did not seem interested in this advice, or many other gems of wisdom imparted by Elliot Richardson, during that summer of 1973.

On the day of the deadline set by Judge Sirica, President Nixon's attorneys instead filed their response to Cox's Rule to Show Cause, refusing to turn over any documents or tapes.[60]

The first round of the Watergate showdown thus went to federal district court on August 22. The courthouse was a nondescript building between the Capitol and the Justice Department, guarded by a statue of Blackstone, the English lawgiver. The *Akron Beacon Journal,* which an Ohio friend was faithfully clipping apart and shipping to Phyllis at her farmhouse in Maine, reported: "The institution of the presidency will be pitted against another branch of government—the grand jury and the courts—in the kind of titanic struggle that is rare, though not unknown, in American history."[61]

The oral argument in front of Judge Sirica, on the question of producing nine White House tapes, required an intense period of strategizing. Cox wanted to make "the most reasoned argument I could," as if he were standing in front of the Supreme Court wearing the formal attire of the solicitor general. At the same time, he realized that district court judges sitting in the trenches of the American legal system were not in the habit of dealing with monumental constitutional issues that might change the face of history. This meant that Cox had to be concerned with "bucking up the judge's courage to do what reason told him he ought to do."[62]

The son of an immigrant Italian barber, Judge John J. Sirica had been a semipro boxer who had put himself through law school with his fists. He was an old-time Republican politico who had written speeches for the Republican National Committee in the 1930s and 1940s. Now he was viewed as "nobody's man" on the federal bench. The criminal defense bar called him "Maximum John." He was nononsense; he did not tolerate foolishness or wasted remarks.[63]

Cox was well aware that in the sixth-floor ceremonial courtroom on Constitution Avenue, Judge Sirica maintained a physical line that kept attorneys a certain distance from the bench in case he lost his temper.[64] Cox had no intention of crossing that line. But he realized that he needed to pluck the judge out of his day-to-day role as trial judge presiding over drug cases, street crimes, and contract battles, and fill him with an appreciation of the incredibly high stakes. Cox's job was to evoke "a certain historic sense—almost reverence for the law."[65]

Charles Alan Wright, polished courtroom advocate who had appeared frequently in the Supreme Court, sat grim-faced at a walnut counsel table opposite from Cox. He was an expert in federal court

procedures, a consummate lawyer with a "prodigious, almost photographic memory and an eloquent tongue."[66] As a distinguished professor of law at the University of Texas, Wright was in many ways Cox's
Republican counterpart. He had taken on this controversial role as
special Watergate counsel for the bargain price of $150 per day, not
for the money but for the satisfaction of wrangling with complex
constitutional issues. So impeccable was Wright's reputation that Cox
himself had recommended him to his brother Max's law firm the
previous year to handle a complicated Supreme Court argument on
behalf of millionaire Howard Hughes's corporation.[67] The two lawyers now sat before the square-jawed Judge Sirica in the same majestic courtroom where the original Watergate case had been tried. It was
packed with over 350 spectators and a gaggle of the nation's press
corps. Both lawyers sat up stiffly in their blue leather chairs. Wright
adjusted his tweed vest. Scanning his notes and fiddling with his
spectacles, Cox reached for a water glass. His hand slipped and he
knocked it over. He nervously mopped up the water with a handkerchief and tried to keep his notes from running. The bailiff entered
the room promptly at 10:00, bellowing, "God save the United States of
America and this honorable court."[68]

Wright was first to address the court. One *Newsweek* magazine
reporter described him as a "towering, stiff-backed constitutionalist."
He straightened his coat as he rose. At the lectern, he adjusted a sheaf
of papers with a confident but solemn air and referred to the sunken-
eyed Sirica as "Mr. Chief Judge." The crowd had become so quiet that
the squeaking of shoes could be heard on the cork floor as late arrivals
searched for seats. Judge Sirica rocked back in his red leather chair,
high on the bench.

"It is a simple fact of history," Wright told Sirica pointedly, "that in
184 years of this republic no court has undertaken to do [any] of the
things that the Special Prosecutor contends here that this Court ought
to do." Wright emphasized the danger of loose precedent when it
came to the critical powers of the presidency. "This is not a unique
case," he insisted. Watergate might be unique, but there were four
hundred federal district judges in the United States. Wright looked
directly at Sirica. A free pass on the president's most private papers
would make it open season for all four hundred judges, for the next
hundred years.[69]

With eloquent turn of the phrase, Wright insisted that the concept
of executive privilege *of necessity* had to guard against the surrender

of the tapes. "We must leave it to the good judgment of the President of the United States," Wright concluded expertly, his voice slowing for dramatic impact, "to determine whether the public interest permits disclosure of his most intimate documents."[70]

Cox leaned back pensively in his chair. When he received the brusque nod from Judge Sirica, the special prosecutor rose to his full six feet, two and one-half inches and walked briskly up to the lectern. "May it please the Court," he began. "This is a grave and dramatic case."

The necessity of seeking a subpoena against the president, Cox reminded the court, had not arisen since the treason trial of Aaron Burr in 1807. Contrary to what Cox's esteemed opponent had suggested, Watergate was indeed a unique case. "The issues have sometimes seemed to be obscured," Cox told Sirica, "at least in some quarters, by shrouding the term 'Executive Privilege' in a sort of false mystique." But the beauty of the American legal system lay not in drama or mystique, but in the fact that "judges apply the same law whether the case is great or small."[71] There was a slight hitch in Archie's voice; he involuntarily jangled the change in his pocket.

Cox threw in a gentle legal tweak, citing Wright's own treatise on civil procedure in support of the proposition that executive privilege issues were traditionally left to the courts, *not* to the president himself.[72] Already, the likelihood of criminality was apparent; all the more reason to lift the privilege. "There is not merely accusation," he told the hushed courtroom, "but strong evidence to believe that the integrity of the Executive offices has been corrupted." He paused and added, "Although the extent of the rot is not yet clear."[73]

Cox clutched his notes with his right hand. He concluded his argument by referring to the famous scene in seventeenth-century England where King James took offense at the independence of his judges and cried out, "That I am to be under the law, that is treason to aver." Chief Justice Coke had replied by quoting Bracton, *"Non sub homine sed sub Deo et lege"* ("Not under man, but under God and the law").[74] Cox had selected this image intentionally as his way of reminding Judge Sirica of the "traditions of the law and the duty of judges to enforce the law despite the views of those who, in a way, were more powerful."[75]

Cox's argument seemed to draw in the audience, but it also angered Wright. Some of the special prosecutor's points had "stung" him. He appeared "vaguely off stride," *Newsweek* reported, when he reclaimed the lectern for rebuttal. This was too important a case to make ad hominem arguments scoring two-bit brownie points by citing his opponent's book, Wright shot back.[76] What his "friend" Mr. Cox had lost sight of was this: Richard M. Nixon was president of the United States. The man, Nixon himself, was not "above the law." But the American constitutional system limited the extent "to which the law can make its force felt against the person who currently holds the office."[77]

Wright now shifted arguments. There were things in the tapes that the special prosecutor sought, he revealed somberly, that the president could not confide even to his attorney, despite his confidence, despite the "full field security clearance" to which Wright had been subjected. "I unavoidably breach the confidentiality of Presidential conversations to say even this," Wright declared, staring directly at Sirica. "The President has told me that in one of the tapes that is the subject of the present subpoena, there is national security material so highly sensitive that he does not feel free even to hint to me what the nature of it is."[78]

Cox felt "outraged" at this puffing. He twitched in his chair, wishing he had time for fresh rebuttal. His mind raced with arguments. It was hard to believe that conversations between the president and his re-election chairman, John Mitchell, on the morning after the arrest of the Watergate burglars, for instance, would have focused on "the nation's greatest national security secrets."[79] "That was an awfully likely time for there to be some conversation about the burglary," Cox scribbled a note to himself.[80]

The battle lines were sharp; the stakes were extraordinarily high. What happened, under the American constitutional system, when the rule of law clashed with the interests of national security? The president had warned Elliot Richardson that there were "sensitive" security matters intertwined with the Watergate investigation, from the moment he had offered him the post as attorney general. Who was going to decide whether law or national security concerns should prevail? Was it the courts? Or was it the president himself?[81]

As extraordinarily complex as the issue was, Phil Heymann would later sum up, the president had still made a major concession when he permitted the case to move through the courts at all. "He's conveying to the American people that he was accepting [this process]. One thing the American people know is that you can't play a game without following the rules."[82]

At the end of the 2½-hour oral argument, Judge Sirica praised both lawyers for a "masterful exposition of the issues." Judge Sirica's law clerk, D. Todd Christofferson, remembered that "it was one of those moments when you were glad to be in the legal profession." At Sirica's instruction, his clerk began writing the opinion "both ways," to see which was most persuasive on paper.[83]

That same day, August 22, President Nixon held his first news conference in five months. Standing on the hot, paved parking lot of the Coast Guard complex adjoining his California home, he brushed off the arguments in front of Judge Sirica and pronounced the Watergate case "water under the bridge." "For a President to conduct the affairs of this office effectively," Nixon said in the broiling California sunshine, "he must be able to do so with the principle of confidentiality intact." He looked resolutely at the cameras. "Otherwise people can't talk to him . . . they will always be speaking in a eunuch-like way rather than laying it on the line."[84]

Buzhardt, Garment, and Wright wrote a memo to their boss: "Congratulations from all your lawyers on a superb press conference which we believe will go far to put Watergate to bed. Not only was the press conference a full answer to public demands but it should also provide the frosting on the cake for our legal cases."[85]

The frosting was difficult to taste, however. Just as the president was taking this outwardly firm stance, he allowed himself to be drawn into a sharp exchange with his perennial enemy, the press. When Dan Rather of CBS raised his hand at the press conference and stated that he wished to pose a question to the president with all "due respect," Nixon snapped back sarcastically, "That would be unusual." Newspapers reminded readers of an episode from a week earlier, filmed on network TV, in which an "obviously irritated" president had displayed a "rare flash of public anger" by giving press secretary Ronald L. Ziegler a "hard shove" in the midst of confusion over which door the reporters should use at a convention in New Orleans.[86] Deputy Press Secretary Gerald L. Warren admitted that "the past few months have been periods of pressure on the President."[87]

Also on August 22, Vice President Spiro T. Agnew was reported fighting for his political life, based upon allegations that he had accepted kickbacks from contractors during his term as governor of Maryland.[88] The press also reported that the White House had finally turned over its "secret file" on the ITT antitrust settlement, which the Special Prosecution Force had been encircling for months. The criminal charge in the ITT case was disturbing and serious: perjury and obstruction of justice by "high-level" White House officials, with respect to settling three massive antitrust suits against ITT in return for campaign cash.[89]

The Special Prosecution Force machinery kept whirring, with separate sections of lawyers simultaneously investigating Watergate, the ITT matter, illegal campaign financing, political sabotage and espionage ("dirty tricks"), and the increasingly bizarre activities of the special White House investigations unit known as the "plumbers."[90]

It was a week that even a determined president could not make vanish.

On August 30, Judge Sirica issued a twenty-three-page opinion that momentarily stunned the world. He directed the president of the United States to turn over the nine tapes and other materials that Cox had subpoenaed, to be reviewed by Sirica himself privately, "in camera."[91] Sirica wrote in forceful language: "The grand jury has a right to every man's evidence and that for purposes of gathering evidence, process may issue to anyone." In rejecting the president's claim of executive privilege, Sirica dug back into historical evidence, concluding that the constitutional framers never intended to create an "executive fiat," at least not in the blanket form that the president had urged. "It is emphatically the province and duty of the judicial department," Sirica wrote, quoting Chief Justice John Marshall's landmark opinion in *Marbury v. Madison* (1803), "to say what the law is."[92]

In public, Cox's team was jubilant with Judge Sirica's ruling. Cox issued a statement that he was "very pleased." "If appellate review is sought," he told the press, "we will do everything possible to expedite the proceedings."[93]

In private, however, Cox and his staff were "dissatisfied." Why had Sirica insisted on reviewing the tapes himself, rather than allowing the special prosecutor to handle the matter directly? Neither side had anticipated this; they had never even briefed or argued it as a possibility. Cox was never given a chance to address how the review should take place. "We thought it a serious mistake for anyone to review the tapes without any of the context of other evidence," Cox explained.[94] Sirica may have presided over the original Watergate burglary case nearly two years earlier, but that was ancient history. He had not heard volumes of new grand jury testimony. How could he know the details of piles of recent evidence? Under Sirica's method of review, Lady

Justice would be partially blind to important details in the prosecutor's case, not a happy posture for the special prosecutor.[95]

Cox nevertheless kept his concerns masked. In the press and public eye, Judge Sirica's order was being touted as a "big win" for the Special Prosecution Force. Sam Ervin, head of the Senate Select Committee, hailed the ruling as "a great victory in the search for truth."[96] Cox had no intention of making readers of the *Washington Post*, including those in the White House, think otherwise.

It was a lucky break for Cox, then, that the day Judge Sirica handed down his ruling, the president vowed to file an appeal. By now the White House viewed Sirica, although a lifelong Republican, as "practically an arm of the prosecution in the Watergate case."[97] The executive mansion stated belligerently that President Nixon "will not comply with this order."[98] Had the president not appealed, Cox might have been forced to surrender his psychological edge and file his own appeal head-on.[99] But now that the president had publicly proclaimed that he was taking his case to the court of appeals, Cox was able to sit back quietly. He could file a low-profile writ of *mandamus* requesting clarification of Judge Sirica's order on several key points, hoping to produce a more definitive victory in the court of appeals.[100] And watch.

Not all onlookers were pleased with the victories Cox's team were beginning to score in Washington. The American public was increasingly angry and divided. When Archie stepped off a Delta jet at Bangor International Airport at the end of August to meet Phyllis for a much-needed weekend of rest and chopping wood at their farm in Maine, a well-dressed man standing in the airport terminal gave Cox the "raspberries." Pursued by reporters, the man climbed into a late-model Cadillac convertible and snapped, "You're damn right I gave that guy the bird." He explained, "All these self-seeking guys have done is to try to make it [Watergate] into a big thing, and a stupid naive public just gobbles it right up."

When pressed by reporters for a comment, Archie scanned the line of cars for Phyllis and disappeared inside their pickup truck. "This is supposed to be a holiday," he said somberly.[101]

Did Cox suspect, by this point in August, that President Nixon was attempting to hide damning evidence? As Cox would later admit, it "seemed that he wasn't pressing a point of abstract principle just for the sake of the abstract principle." At the same time, there might be a host of different explanations for the president's refusal to hand over the nine tapes. John Dean might be lying, as Nixon claimed. Nixon might wish to protect someone else. There could be politically damaging material in these specific reels of evidence that had nothing to do with the criminal investigation. There were countless possibilities, many of which did not point to the incrimination of Richard M. Nixon. Only one thing was abundantly clear to Cox: "The central thing was, we needed the tapes."[102]

F all was always a welcome sight to a professor. It meant a return to the classroom and the start of a promising new year. September 1973, however, was a particularly attractive month for Professor Archibald Cox. Phyllis finally packed up the horses and dogs and moved to Washington from Maine. The Coxes rented a small "caretaker's house" on the edge of a large estate in Virginia as they had done in the later solicitor general years. The sound and smells of the country provided a happy escape from the travails of Watergate.

Watergate still had a way of dogging the Coxes at home. Shortly after Phyllis's move, she was troubled by "bad connections" on the telephone. She called the telephone company to report her complaint. "It almost sounds as if the phone is bugged," she explained to the operator.[103] After being transferred to a chain of different supervisors, Phyllis finally received a simple message from a senior phone company official: "I would not advise Mr. Cox to make any confidential calls on this line."[104] At work, the ears of Watergate were always open. The government security force directed that all calls coming into Cox's office be tape-recorded, after Cox's secretary gave due warning to the caller. Archie finally could not bear the intrusion. "I've taken the thing off," he said one day. "It got to be a damn nuisance."[105]

The unglamorous offices on K Street were routinely "swept" for electronic bugging devices. Even the tightest measures were not foolproof. In late August, an internal memo discussing ultrasensitive legal strategy appeared big as life in the *Washington Post,* apparently dug out of the Special Prosecution Force trash bin by an "outside source." Cox quickly ordered burn bag procedures for every scrap of paper on the premises. On weekends, all personnel were instructed to "collect your waste material and carry it to the file room" to be locked up.[106]

By September, the tension was mounting at a dizzying pace. Vice President Agnew, speaking at a Kane County Republican rally in Illinois, criticized the "persecutorial atmosphere" generated by the special prosecutors.[107] The president's lawyers filed documents in the U.S. Court of Appeals, challenging Judge Sirica's ruling as "clearly erroneous."[108]

One worry nagged Cox as he returned to the tiny caretaker's house each night in September, to collapse into bed next to Phyllis. What happened if he won the battle in the courts, but lost the war because the president simply refused to obey the federal courts? What happened if Cox gambled and lost, and ended up permanently damaging the institution of American law? "Should one start down this road," he asked himself, "only to end up revealing the weakness, even the futility, of the law when it confronts power?"[109] During these introspective moments, Cox had flashbacks to his walks with David Cole in Rock Creek Park during the mine workers' controversy of the Truman years. Cole had quoted Churchill, reminding Cox that "a democracy should never reveal its weakness."[110] In other words, without the cooperation of the executive branch, there was no way to enforce many of society's most urgent and important rules. Cox's greatest fear was that he might "end up damaging the rule of law by playing the role of the little boy who pointed out that the emperor had no clothes."[111]

So when the time came, Archie was "anxious to explore ways that would serve the needs of the special prosecutor qua prosecutor and at the same time let the president off the hook and meet any legitimate objections he had."[112] As Elliot Richardson's penciled notes record, Cox told him at a meeting on September 6: ". . . thinking down the road—one has to give a little thought to Q[uestions] of avoiding a constitutional crisis. If time ever comes when important to try to find a way out, would be glad to explore."[113]

On September 12, Archibald Cox and Charles Alan Wright appeared before the Court of Appeals for the District of Columbia Circuit to argue the tapes issue again, now just one step away from the U.S. Supreme Court.[114] The court of appeals heard argument *en banc,* with chairs set up for seven of the nine judges. The White House was not particularly pleased: two of the more conservative judges on the court, Edward Allen Tamm and Roger Robb, had disqualified themselves because of conflicts. This reduced the number of conservative Republicans on the court to two and lowered the chance of a "close" decision that the president could deem "nondefinitive."

Nonetheless, Wright remained confident of his legal position; he strode tall through the wooden doors. A hand-lettered sign in the corridor outside the courtroom read "Tapes Trial Line." But the seats were already crammed with a cavalcade of friends, relatives, law clerks, and assorted friends-of-friends-of-VIPs who had been allotted special green or white admission tickets. Among them was Senator John Stennis, the seventy-two-year-old Democrat from Mississippi. Unnoticed by Cox, he stood near the jury box, talking to his friend and fellow Southerner, J. Fred Buzhardt. Said Stennis to reporters, "I'm very much interested as a lawyer and as a senator—it's one of the most far-reaching cases we've had in a long time."[115]

White House lawyer Len Garment summarized the day's oral argument in a memo to the president: "Cox was unusually long-winded and rather dull," he reported.[116] In the special prosecutor's opinion, however, his court of appeals argument went just fine. The judges adjourned. Reporters streamed out of the courtroom. The spectators lingered briefly to compare notes, then vanished.

Cox considered it a good day. But he would later say that if he had known that Senator Stennis was present in the courtroom that day, standing next to J. Fred Buzhardt, he would have found it "quite startling."[117]

Two days later, the Special Prosecution Force received a call that the court of appeals was handing down an order. Cox panicked. "This does not seem good," he told Jim Doyle. It was much too early for it to be a win. He paced the floor, biting at fingernails. He told Doyle that he was going to bite all ten of them—or at least nine. Archie held up the middle finger of his right hand, the tip of which had been cut off in the lawn mower accident during his solicitor general years.

A short time later, the order came down.[118] Both sides were puzzled by the brief directive. The court of appeals instructed the White House and the special prosecutor to work out their differences. This was not a request; it was an order. If the parties failed to resolve their disagreements within one week, by September 20, the court would move forward and issue a binding decision, which one side or another would inevitably consider a big loss. It was a "hazy, almost plaintive" document.[119] Cox, oddly enough, felt energized by it. It was a tantalizing game of brinkmanship. He had a fifty-fifty chance of survival.

The entire country was watching, taking sides. Ninety-four-year-old James J. Monteith of Minnesota wrote to the president that he still had "most of my marbles" and urged the president to "stand your ground."[120] Adele Lovelace typed a note on University Club station-ery from Washington: "We think the President is magnificient . . . we hope that he stands pat on his tapes. The absurdity of anybody expect-ing him to turn over the private papers of the highest office in the land to every tom, dick and harry to paw over, you have to stop and pinch yourself and ask 'Is this for real?' "[121] Mrs. John J. Mahler of Argos, Indiana, agreed: "There are still many people in this great nation who have faith in their leaders. We believe there should be some 'secrets' in the White House that do not have to be shared with the whole nation. We elected you to serve as our president, so why don't people let you do your job?"[122] A. E. Wilson of California, a lawyer who had been admitted to the Supreme Court bar on the motion of Archibald Cox, also supported the president: "If it is any consolation, most of the big newspapers called President Lincoln a baboon and a gorilla in 1861. He weathered the storm and those same newspapers hail him today as one of our great Presidents. . . . Hang on to those tapes and records. Some future President will thank you."[123]

Not everyone agreed with those sentiments. Keith A. Hanger of Richmond, Virginia, mailed a postcard: "No! It cannot stand. Refusal to allow the American public and Mr. Cox access to the relevant tapes & papers is tantamount to taking the 5th Amendment, forcing one to the conclusion that they are indeed incriminating."[124] Richard T. Lewis, an "anguished American" living abroad in Japan, told the president: "I am sure the Founding Fathers did *not* intend their doctrine of separation of powers to be used as a cloak for skulldug-gery." He reported that he had heard two young Japanese men dis-cussing Watergate, and one of them had said, "If it were Japan, he would commit suicide!" Concluded Mr. Lewis, "As a Christian, I would not recommend suicide for Mr. Nixon, but I would not rule out the possibility of a resignation."[125]

Slowly, proposals were exchanged between Cox's office and the White House. The president's lawyers offered to provide written "summaries" of the tapes. This was wholly unacceptable to Cox. Among other problems, summaries could never be used as evidence in criminal trials.[126] It was, in Cox's words, a "trust us" approach. "I was not in a trusting mood," he said later, "quite apart from whether such a thing would have been of any use to the grand jury, or in a possible prosecution."[127]

Much to the horror of a number of his staff members, however, the special prosecutor drafted a lengthy counterproposal. Most of the nation would never learn of Cox's "compromise." Yet it predated any serious offer by the White House to resolve the tapes controversy during this frantic week, and it undercut later claims that Cox had refused to negotiate in good faith.[128] The terms of this secret proposal were these:

As step one, the president, or his high-level delegate, would prepare a transcript of the controversial tapes, omitting any "continuous portion of substantial duration" that related to matters outside the jurisdiction of the special prosecutor. A neutral third party would then be appointed as "special consultant"; he would listen to each tape and certify that he had followed the proper procedures. As step two, the special prosecutor would receive verbatim copies and transcripts of those portions of the tapes that were not off limits. He and the president's counsel would sit down and attempt to omit embarrassing, prejudicial, and irrelevant portions of the tapes, and paraphrase wherever possible. The materials would then be provided to the grand jury. Those portions deleted would be forever off limits. Cox settled on J. Lee Rankin, his predecessor in the solicitor general's office and a well-respected Republican, as the person whom he would propose as the neutral special consultant.

Cox had his secretary type up his proposal. With the document in his inside coat pocket, he set out to an unpublicized meeting with the president's lawyers. He was accompanied only by Phil Lacovara. The day was September 20, the last day before the court of appeals "grace period" was set to expire. Cox hoped to pull off a surprise settlement in the wearying Watergate case by settling for half—or perhaps three-quarters—of the loaf.[129]

Cox's staff was deeply distressed; some felt betrayed. Their boss was giving away the store. Why was this compromise any better than Judge Sirica's original offer? "The difference," Cox explained years afterward, "was that one was a way out of a very critical situation. . . . You weren't going to get everything if you compromised."[130] Richard Ben-Veniste, a member of the cover-up task force, found the idea of the compromise "appalling."[131] Jim Neal was also worried. "Remember, I was going to try this son of a gun," he explained. It was essential for a prosecutor to have the "best evidence," if a court demanded it. Neal told Cox, "You have got to preserve us the right to get these tapes if we have to."[132] Jim Doyle counseled Cox that "public and press reaction would be bad" if he went ahead with the deal. It was not that Doyle opposed the compromise, if Cox felt it was a fair one. "The public reaction could be handled."[133] But Doyle had an obligation to give Cox his honest assessment: the fallout from the press would be hell.

Cox walked up the steps of the Executive Office Building shortly before 11:00. He entered the building, checked in with a receptionist, then proceeded to a room where he shook hands with President Nixon's lawyers. Charles Alan Wright seemed particularly uninterested in discussions this day. Cox and Lacovara spent a good hour listening to reasons why the White House could not budge. "Who's going to go in and tell the President that he won't be believed? Nobody's going to do that," Wright said, chain-smoking cigarettes.

Cox finally pulled the proposal from his pocket. He asked the lawyers if they had considered that a third party might act as an arbiter and listen to the tapes. The men seemed surprised. Yes, they had. They had kicked around the idea of either John Sherman Cooper, retired U.S. senator from Kentucky, or Earl Warren, former chief justice of the Supreme Court. At the latter suggestion, Len Garment "rolled his eyes."[134] Cox handed over the written copy of his proposal and summarized the specifics. He was suggesting J. Lee Rankin; the name was tentative, of course, and subject to negotiation. But it was a name Cox could live with.

The president's lawyers sat back in their chairs and smiled faintly. Archie had been "busier drafting than they had thought." They would take the proposal "under consideration" and get back to him.[135]

Cox left the Executive Office Building at approximately 1:15. He retraced his steps across Lafayette Park, walking slowly enough to admire the trees draped in Indian summer foliage. He had settled into his desk for less than an hour when the telephone rang. It was one of the president's lawyers, who informed the special prosecutor that "the answer is no."[136] Cox's compromise was dead, before it took its first breath.

Since Wright and his associates had insisted that all negotiations remain "confidential," Cox could not make his proposed compromise public, not even to the court of appeals.[137] Nor did the president's lawyers offer any counterproposal. This was baffling to Cox, since he viewed his offering of Rankin (a Republican, no less) as a "major concession."[138] The president's counsel seemed increasingly confident of a win in the courts—this was the only explanation Cox could imagine, unless they were beginning to suspect that the tapes were incriminating. The White House lawyers still had the court of appeals and one shot at the Supreme Court. So, as Cox interpreted the lawyers' mindset: "If you're feeling pretty stubborn or if you're worried about what's on the tapes, you aren't going to budge very far."[139]

Cox filed a short report with the clerk of courts, stating that several meetings had taken place with the president's representatives but "I regret to advise the Court that these sincere efforts were not fruitful." The president's lawyers filed a report using identical language. There was nothing more Cox could say.[140] The matter was thrown back into the hands of the court of appeals. Cox's secret proposal went into a locked file drawer, where it remained for the duration of Watergate.

October 1973 brought with it the smoldering threat of war in the Middle East, a volatile situation caused by the increasingly shrinking pool of Arab oil in the United States. October also brought the resignation of Vice President Spiro T. Agnew, after he acknowledged accepting bribes and kickbacks as governor of Maryland and later as vice president. Elliot Richardson had taken the lead in thrashing out a difficult and distasteful compromise, by which Agnew would plead "no contest" to one felony count and be spared the disgrace of going to prison.

Cox saw his former student a good bit during this time. "One couldn't help being aware that Elliot Richardson was in an exceedingly delicate position and that pressures on him were multiplied."[141]

On October 12, the court of appeals did what it had warned. It rendered a decision that one side found appalling. By a five-to-two vote, it swept aside the president's blanket claim of executive privilege. Although presidential conversations were normally protected, the court wrote in its two hundred pages of opinion, that privilege would have to give way "in the face of the uniquely powerful showing made by the special prosecutor" that the tapes were necessary to the grand jury's investigation.[142] Although the president had been elected by nationwide ballot to "represent all the people," the court warned that "He is not above the law's commands. Sovereignty remains at all times with the people, and they do not forfeit through elections the right to have the law construed against and applied to every citizen."

In the court's eyes, the president's claim for executive privilege was dramatically weakened by the public testimony of top aides, including H. R. Haldeman, about the contents of certain White House tapes. The dispute had come down to a naked assertion of power, that the president could pick and choose his "privileges," granting or denying access to whatever documents he wished. "Support for this kind of mischief," the court of appeals wrote, "simply cannot be spun from incantation of the doctrine of separation of powers."[143]

President Nixon would be required to surrender the tapes. There was one important safety valve, however. The president could withhold those portions that squarely dealt with national security matters and foreign affairs. If the White House and special prosecutor could not agree on what qualified, Judge Sirica would have to review all nine tapes "in camera," and make the determination himself.[144] The president would have five working days, if he wished to appeal this order to the Supreme Court.[145]

As a legal matter, the court of appeals decision was more deferential to the president than some expected. The two conservative judges appointed by President Nixon who had not recused themselves, George E. MacKinnon and Malcolm R. Wilkey, had written a blistering dissent arguing in favor of absolute executive privilege. Even the five Democrat appointees who signed the majority opinion, led by noted liberals David L. Bazelon and J. Skelly Wright, remained "remarkably cautious" in tone. They were careful to suggest that the president *did* enjoy executive privilege, as a general rule. It was only under the "unique circumstances of this case," that Cox had overcome that privilege. Moreover, the procedure for screening out national security matters was fairly generous to the president.[146]

As a legal pronouncement, the opinion contained its share of minor consolation prizes for President Nixon. As a practical matter, however, the opinion was publicly viewed as another smashing victory for the special prosecutor.

Fred Graham on CBS's *Evening News* called the court of appeals decision a "crushing blow to President Nixon . . ." On NBC's *Nightly News,* John Chancellor announced that the president had lost the case "and seems to have lost it definitively." Harry Reasoner, speaking on ABC's *Evening News,* noted that the decision seemed to "broaden the original lower court ruling against Mr. Nixon," and strengthened Cox's argument that "no man, not even a President, has the right to withhold evidence in a criminal investigation."[147] The scuttlebutt among the Washington press corps was that the president would immediately appeal his loss to the Supreme Court.[148]

Just three hours after the court of appeals decision was handed down, President Nixon stepped into the East Room amid fanfare and television cameras and cheering congressmen to announce Gerald Ford as his selection for new vice president. The timing was not coincidental; the president needed desperately to blunt the force of another staggering loss by diverting the public's attention from what had happened up the street in the court of appeals. The choice of Ford, a staunch supporter of the president throughout Watergate, and a longtime friend,[149] was a brilliant and shrewd selection.[150] Impeachment proceedings, if they were ever to begin, would have to start in the House where Ford, the Republican House minority leader, held powerful sway. If the president chose to defy the courts at any stage and Congress responded with impeachment action, a strong foothold in the House might allow Richard Nixon to protect the tapes and escape with the presidency intact. Ford, perhaps more than any other political leader, could calm and control agitated representatives on behalf of the president, as the president's direct emissary.[151] The puzzle confronting Archie was becoming more, not less, complicated. All these events were "very much a part of the atmosphere and tension in the Capitol." They were cause for "intensity, worry, tension."[152]

Cox's big win stared at him from newspaper boxes on every street corner in Washington. The *Washington Evening-Star* proclaimed: "Cox 2, Nixon 0."[153] It brought back the question that had gnawed at Cox since his appointment. What if the president simply did not comply with the court order? What if he challenged the law?[154] What if he simply said, "I won't turn over the tapes"?[155] All these questions, in Cox's words, "ate at my insides."[156]

Cox met with his senior lawyers. What were the options that the president might consider? Mr. Nixon might refuse to seek certiorari to the Supreme Court and attempt to stonewall. Then what? "We'll seek a citation for contempt," one lawyer volunteered.

"Okay, then what do we do?" Cox asked.

"We'll move to have the name Richard M. Nixon stricken from lawyers authorized to practice," another voice chirped up.

"We'll get the court to impose a fine of so many dollars a day," said a third.

"It seems to me that would cheapen the whole thing," Cox answered. "And there's no more chance of enforcing that."

Another voice suggested, "We'll get a squad of deputy marshals to go over."

"They'll be met by the White House guards."

"By the marines in those fancy dress uniforms."[157]

Cox conjured up visions of a colorful Gilbert and Sullivan production breaking out in the midst of the pandemonium. He allowed himself to laugh. "Sometimes things are funny," Cox would say, "because what you're worrying about is serious."

Cox had been a reader of history since his childhood summers in Windsor. He knew about the famous standoff between John Marshall and Thomas Jefferson in *Marbury v. Madison,* in which the Federalists tried to push President Jefferson into handing over commissions to justices of the peace appointed by the outgoing president, John Adams. Chief Justice Marshall had come dangerously close to issuing an order that President Jefferson would be in a position to disobey; Marshall had wisely taken another path. Cox also knew about the famous *Prize Cases* that his great-grandfather, William Maxwell Evarts, had argued on behalf of the United States, after the government had seized Confederate blockade-runners at the start of the Civil War. Abraham Lincoln had directed a general in command of the Baltimore region to disregard a writ of habeas corpus issued by the chief justice of the United States, in order to declare the blockade valid and protect the Union.[158] The court had dealt with this political powder keg by suggesting that President Lincoln possessed sweeping powers as commander in chief, particularly during a state of emergency. Cox knew about the fireside chat that Franklin D. Roosevelt had *almost* delivered in 1935, in which the president made clear that he was prepared to ignore the Supreme Court if it invalidated his decision to scrap the gold standard.[159] Cox remembered the words of President Andrew Jackson, shortly after the Marshall Court's controversial holding in *Worcester v. Georgia,* that the state of Georgia had no legislative authority over Cherokee lands. "John Marshall has made his decision," President Jackson spat. "Now let him enforce it!"[160] American history made clear that any time a president and the courts decided to butt heads, the outcome was unpredictable, a toss-up. "I thought if *I* knew this history," Cox said, "Richard Nixon probably knew it."[161]

Again, Cox thought back to the walks with David Cole in 1952 before the bituminous coal strike that led to Cox's resignation. "You can't mine coal with bayonets," Cole had reminded him. What did one do if achieving the "right result" threatened to trigger a nightmarish chain of political consequences that prevented the country from functioning properly? "Do you provoke a confrontation? That's one way.

Or do you avoid it at all costs? That's another way. Or do you try to negotiate an accommodation?" These questions swirled through Cox's mind.[162] He could not shake a passage from Robert Bolt's play *A Man for All Seasons:* "And when the last law was down, and the Devil turned round on you—where would you hide . . . the laws all being flat?"

The answer was delivered in the play: "Yes, I'd give the Devil benefit of law, for my own safety's sake."[163]

18

SHOWDOWN

WITH THE

PRESIDENT

As the pressure mounted from all sides, Cox found himself in increasing contact with Elliot Richardson, under their informal code. When the *Washington Post* reported that Cox's team was about to indict presidential advisers Charles Colson and John Ehrlichman for the break-in of the Fielding psychiatric office in California, Richardson raised an immediate concern—an unusually strong concern— about the potential danger to national security. Although Richardson did not tell Cox, the president himself had warned of the domestic security implications lurking behind the Ellsberg matter. President Nixon's warnings "were so portentous that I more than half believed him," Richardson recalled.[1] So Cox did Richardson the courtesy of informing him that he had no plans to indict Colson and Erlichman, at least not yet.[2] He would throw no surprise punches.

Later Cox was summoned to the attorney general's office when the newspapers reported that the special prosecutor had indicted Egil Krogh for perjury. Krogh was a key actor in the White House's "plumbers unit" accused of breaking into the office of Daniel Ellsberg's psychiatrist. The *Washington Post* reported that Krogh and other potential defendants intended to release national security information as part of their defense. "I think you broke an agreement with me," Richardson began the conversation, his usually resonant voice subdued. The agreement, as Elliot recalled it, was that Archie would not indict *any* of the Watergate actors in areas involving national security, without consulting him first.

Cox was "frightfully worried." Had he slipped? He *thought* that their "indictment agreement" did not apply to charges of perjury. He had been aware of the impending Krogh indictment even when he and Elliot had made the original agreement. But he had no notes, nothing to prove it in black and white. Had he breached Elliot's trust?[3] "I think you'll find," Cox replied half hopefully, "that I said that our understanding did not apply to perjury."

Richardson pulled out his notes, flipped through pages. In the midst of elaborate doodles he found his own summary of the meeting with Archie; he had scribbled the notation "doesn't apply to perjury."[4] Cox sat back in his chair and exhaled. The two men's relationship of mutual trust worked well, even as the rest of the nation—when it came to things concerning Watergate—was becoming increasingly distrustful.

J. T. Smith, one of Richardson's closest associates, was struck by the unusual bond that cemented the two men. Neither was a "cozy, back-slapping type," according to Smith. It was "hard to think of them as bowling or drinking buddies." But somehow they were able to operate based upon mutual respect. It was anything but a typical twentieth-century Washington relationship. As Smith observed, it seemed a hundred years out of date.[5]

The Krogh conversation came one day after Elliot Richardson had gone to court to witness Vice President Agnew's nolo contendere plea and resignation. Late in his meeting with Cox, Richardson fell into one of his philosophical moods. "Well," Richardson said to Cox, "it's better to lose your job than it is to have your head cut off."[6]

Cox sat forward, puzzled. He wondered, "What signals is he sending to me?" Archie allowed his mind to explore the question. Was Elliot talking about what he had just confronted in the Agnew affair? Or was he attempting to comfort Cox by suggesting that even if Archie lost his job, this "wouldn't be as bad as having my head cut off"?[7] Cox left the meeting that day, October 12, "totally mystified."[8] He went back to the office and told Jim Doyle, "I just had the most Byzantine discussion with Elliot."[9]

Richardson sent other odd signals around this time at the two men's informal get-togethers. On one occasion, Elliot groaned spontaneously about President Nixon, "Oh, if I could only convince him that you are the best *possible* man to conduct the Watergate investigation from *his* point of view."[10] Archie took the opportunity to remind Elliot that under the terms of his original departmental order, only he could fire the special prosecutor; the president could not. Cox was intrigued when Elliot blinked his eyes and replied, "Yes, that's what the Office of Legal Counsel here in the Department tells me." So Elliot, too, had been looking into the question.[11]

It was amid these private conversations, undetected by the nose of the press, that Cox determined that "it seemed wise to explore the possibility of finding an accommodation."[12] Both men knew what a difficult maneuver this would be. Elliot remembered thinking about D day in 1944, when he was a medic in the army, landing with troops at Utah Beach. There was "a guy whose foot had been blown off by an antipersonnel mine lying in a field of barbed wire behind the top of the dunes." Richardson was his platoon's leader; he decided there was nothing for him to do "but to go in and pick him up and carry him out." With the sand blowing, it was impossible to see where there might be another mine. "So I just walked in putting one foot in front of the other. I picked him up and carried him out trying to put one foot as near as possible on where I had stepped on the way in."

As he sat in the room with his old professor, the sands of Watergate blowing fiercely in their eyes, "I tried to convey to Archie, without going into all that . . . that he and I were going to have to navigate carefully from day to day."[13]

Even Cox's own staff was cut off from this new tier of personal negotiations.[14] Cox remained acutely aware that Elliot Richardson was, "by virtue of his position, in the camp of the parties being investigated."[15] Yet their old-fashioned approach and all of its "corny" notions of trust had become one of the most important crutches upon which he allowed himself to lean. In Washington, it was becoming increasingly difficult to know who, if anybody, was acting based upon conviction, and who was acting to save, or make, a career. Cox was willing to bank on his confidence in Richardson during the following weeks, in making the most critical decisions of the Watergate investigation.

On Monday, October 15, when Richardson conveyed a new proposal from the White House designed to resolve the tapes crisis just four days before the deadline for the president to file an appeal to the Supreme Court, Cox took the matter more seriously than the outside world would ever know.[16] He was "definitely anxious," he would admit, to strike up a new level of negotiations and "find some way out of this impasse."[17]

Cox knew that the constitutional issue underlying the tapes controversy was far more complex and knotty than most onlookers—even his staff—appreciated. Austin lawyer James P. Hart, a Democrat and former justice of the Texas Supreme Court, had handwritten a note to Charles Wright on September 22: "For whatever encouragement it may be to you, I want to say that my opinion is that you are entirely correct in your position that any confidential tapes or documents in the possession of the President, relating to the conduct of his office, are privileged against compulsory disclosure. . . . I believe that it begs the question to argue that the President is not above the law; the question is whether the presidential privilege is a part of our constitutional law."[18] Learned minds differed on the question; Cox was acutely aware that there were no reliable soothsayers in this business.

As Cox fretted over constitutional issues, the weight of Elliot Richardson's problems was steadily multiplying. In the early months of Watergate, Elliot had viewed himself as "strictly a bystander."[19] Now Richardson's meetings with the White House were becoming increasingly frequent. On several occasions Richardson had assured President Nixon that he was dead wrong to view Cox as a biased Kennedyite. "Archie would rather cut off his right arm," Richardson told the president more than once, "than take any action inconsistent with his duties."[20] Yet this assurance did little to sweeten the president's taste for the special prosecutor.

What bothered the president and his advisers most about Cox was that he had extended Watergate into a "hydra-headed" investigation that now dealt with issues of money, property, campaign donations, and tax deductions. Len Garment perceived that the sentiment in the White House was that Cox's staff was bent on getting rid of Nixon, but "with all due process." The special prosecutor's office was slowly undermining the president's ability to function, even though many charges would eventually be dropped for lack of proof. The operation would "eviscerate Nixon organ after organ, limb to limb, until he fell to the ground."[21] Elliot Richardson was their single hope to stop the dismemberment.

Watergate and the Agnew debacle were both unwelcome distractions for Richardson. He was more interested in the criminal aspects of his job—running the FBI, and the Drug Enforcement Administration and drug prosecutions.[22] But there was no escaping it. After Agnew's resignation in early October, Richardson attended a session in the Oval Office. The president walked Richardson to the door. In an uncharacteristic burst of enthusiasm he blurted, "Now that we have disposed of that matter, we can go ahead and get rid of Cox!"[23] Richardson had seen the president "rambling" and "disorganized" on several occasions recently. But he observed him to be perfectly in command on this day.[24] Richardson said nothing as he left the office.

Although the two subjects had little in common on the surface, the president clearly had linked the expungement of Spiro Agnew with the expungement of Archibald Cox. In part, as Richardson's closest aides saw it, it was a sense that "Gee, Elliot's doing such a good job with the Agnew thing, wouldn't it be great if Elliot was handling Watergate instead of Archie Cox?" In part, it was a waiting game. The White House wanted Richardson to get Agnew "out of the line of succession to the Presidency." But as soon as this was taken care of, the White House lawyers felt it was time to return to the "other basket of eggs."[25]

The early weeks of October became intensely dominated by Watergate for Elliot Richardson. On Sunday night, October 14, Alexander Haig telephoned Richardson at home. "He had something important to talk to me about . . . it sounded as if it might have something to do with the Middle East."[26] Haig said that he wanted Richardson to meet him in the White House early the next morning. Richardson's handwritten notes of the call underscore in bold letters: "Middle East."[27]

When Elliot arrived early that Monday morning, at 9:00 sharp, General Haig ushered him into his neatly appointed office. As Richardson would describe the president's chief of staff, who now dressed strictly in civilian clothes, he was a "sort of square, ready, energetic, blue-eyed, square-jawed, tough-minded, two-fisted, practical guy." He had fought in Korea and Vietnam, earning a Distinguished Service Cross; he had bypassed 240 army officers with more seniority to become a four-star general and vice chief of staff before moving to the White House.[28]

The discussion between the two men initially danced around the growing crisis in the Middle East. The Yom Kippur War had broken out on October 6, the Jewish Day of Atonement. Egyptian soldiers had surged across the Suez Canal, and Syrian troops had moved into Israel over the Golan Heights cease-fire line. The situation had gone from volatile to explosive. On October 12, the same Saturday night that the court of appeals had rendered its decision, President Nixon had acted to "slash through red tape and bureaucratic timidities" and ordered an American airlift of supplies to Israel, to blunt the Soviet Union's airlift of aid to the Arabs. "Everything that flies" had been ordered into the air. U.S. Air Force planes and C-130 transports flew overseas carrying ammunition, fuselage parts, even tanks.[29]

Richardson had "an intense" interest in these events, based upon his past service in the State Department and as secretary of defense.[30] Haig knew this; the two men had frequently chatted about the Mideast during idle moments when Richardson was waiting to see the president. Today, October 15, Haig gave the attorney general a "graphic description of the battlefield situation." As the conversation wound forward, Richardson said only half-facetiously, "Al, I'm ready to go. Should I go home and tag my bags?"[31]

Haig immediately shifted gears and answered tensely, "No, Elliot, that's not really what I called you about."[32] The purpose of the meeting, it turned out, was to inform Richardson that the "problems generated by Cox's investigation were causing an intolerable diversion of the President's time and energy from far more important matters" like the Middle East.[33] The White House had developed a "plan" to deal with the tapes.[34]

The plan, as it was presented to Elliot Richardson, was this: first, the president would personally prepare an authenticated version of what was contained in the nine subpoenaed tapes, for Judge Sirica to review; second, the tapes themselves would remain the president's private property and would not be released; and third, the president would then fire Cox as his way of "mooting the case." This last step was in line with the so-called Bickel theory advanced in a widely discussed article in *The New Republic* written by Professor Alexander Bickel of Yale.[35] Bickel had posited that "Cox has no constitutional or otherwise legal existence except as he is a creature of the attorney general, who is a creature of the President." He had no "standing" to sue the president in court, because the president, as chief executive, could dismiss the special prosecutor at will. Bickel argued that if the president wished to moot the case at any moment, "he can discard his mask of Archibald Cox. He can discharge Mr. Cox and appoint someone else . . . who will follow his direction to abandon the demand for the White House tapes."

"What do you think of that?" Haig asked.

Richardson looked at Haig stoically. "If you do that, Al," he said, "I'd have to resign."

Haig backed off. "Maybe we can re-examine that," he cut off the conversation. "I'll talk to the President again."[36]

Later in the day, just after noon, General Haig called Richardson with a new proposal, which Haig identified as his own. U.S. Senator John Stennis of Mississippi, rather than the president, would prepare an authenticated summary of the tapes for Cox and Sirica. That would be it. The special prosecutor's office would get nothing else; it was far better than they deserved. Stennis was a former judge and an honorable man. What about it?

Three more phone calls bounced back and forth between Richardson in the Justice Department and Haig's office in the White House. The president would agree to this deal, Haig reported in the tone of someone who had just made a tough sell, but the boss had made clear that "this was it" in terms of access to presidential materials.[37] Richardson's meeting notes showed Haig saying, "[I don't] have to tell you this is very bloody for me, probably terminal." Haig said that he had twisted the president's arm. "If Cox refuses to go along with this," Haig told Richardson, "the President wants your support in dismissal of Cox."

Richardson stopped Haig; he did not think anything so drastic would be necessary. "If it is as reasonable as I think it is, Cox [is] likely to go along," Richardson said.[38] The attorney general was generally supportive of the new plan. "I can only tell you that I had as much confidence in Stennis as I did in Cox," Richardson would say.

Elliot Richardson had known Senator John Stennis for a long time, ever since Richardson had worked as a young legislative assistant for the chairman of the Armed Services Committee, Senator Leverett Saltonstall of Massachusetts, during the Eisenhower administration.[39] "I thought that Stennis was a very honorable man," Richardson stated.[40] Stennis was seventy-two years old and had recently suffered gunshot wounds from a burglary in front of his northwest Washington home. Richardson had visited him in the hospital and believed that despite Stennis's injury, he was "very vigorous mentally," perfectly capable of culling through national security secrets and separating impermissible information from matters germane to Watergate.[41] "My then-premise was that we really *were* looking for a compromise on the tapes," said Richardson. "I was willing to support and defend the Stennis proposal."[42]

Haig called Richardson back and informed the attorney general that he "just had a good discussion with John Stennis." Stennis thought he would accept, "but wants to sleep on it." The ball was squarely in Elliot's court.[43] Richardson agreed to "put" the Stennis plan to Cox.[44]

In retrospect, it is clear that the president had already approved the Stennis compromise—if not originated it in conjunction with Fred

Buzhardt—before any phone calls between Haig and Richardson occurred that Monday. General Haig was a veteran of hard bargaining in the military; he knew how to make his side's goal seem like an excruciating concession through timing, endurance, and guts. Richard Nixon's memoirs confirm that he himself had met with Senator Stennis briefly after the White House prayer service the day before Haig's call, Sunday, October 14. The president had used this opportunity to ask the elderly senator if he would consider verifying the accuracy of tape summaries.[45] This was not a chance encounter. Stennis's closest aide, William "Eph" Cresswell, explained that Stennis would have attended the White House prayer service only "by invitation of the president."[46] President Nixon had been in seclusion at Camp David. He had not attended church in six months, because he felt angered by a preacher's sermon in Key Biscayne on Easter, which he deemed critical of his presidency. He nevertheless helicoptered back to Washington on that Sunday, October 14, in time for the service where he spoke to Senator Stennis.[47]

As Len Garment saw the president's mind ticking inside the White House, Nixon was "feeling presidential; he was feeling his oats." The president had just taken decisive action in the Middle East; Vice President Agnew had just been removed from the White House without a bloody fight. It was time to act. "It was like surfing—catching a big wave, and he was going to ride it," said Garment.[48] The Stennis plan was the wave, and Elliot Richardson was intended to ride alongside the president.

Archie knew none of the details of Elliot's busy morning when he met informally with Richardson in his majestic attorney general's quarters at 6:00 that evening. He walked through the large conference room that had once served as Robert Kennedy's sprawling office. He sat down in Richardson's back office. A large globe from Richardson's days as undersecretary of state sat in the corner. Elliot limited his chat to the end product of the day's discussions. As they spoke, Elliot changed into formal attire for a black-tie dinner at the White House, his first such invitation during his many years in the cabinet.[49] The deal on the table, at least as Elliot understood it, was as follows. The president was willing to agree that a neutral party proposed by the White House, Senator John Stennis, would serve as "verifier." Stennis's "wide experience, strong character, and established reputation for veracity" would make him a good choice.

Stennis would be given a "preliminary record" of the nine tapes subpoenaed by Cox, as prepared by the White House. It would consist of verbatim transcripts of the tapes, except (a) it would omit chunks that were "not pertinent" to the Watergate investigation, and (b) it would be transposed into the third person. Senator Stennis would be permitted to listen to the actual tapes in part or in whole, "as often as necessary." He would be free to paraphrase language that might be "embarrassing to the president," and delete material related to "national defense" if it might "do real harm." There would be no provision for sound-enhancement devices, but if Stennis could not understand the recording, he would so indicate. The newly edited record would then be provided by Stennis to the special prosecutor, along with a signed affidavit "attesting to its completeness and accuracy and to [the verifier's] faithful observance of the procedure set forth above."[50]

Cox had serious misgivings about this plan. For one, it was unclear how much of the transcript would be "paraphrased" and how much of it would be "verbatim." He still found it significant enough as an opening bid—and the situation sufficiently urgent—that he asked Elliot to reduce the whole proposal to writing.[51]

Archie returned to his office at 8:00 that night. Phyllis had been feeling sick during the past months, due to a summer alone in Maine, the jolting move to Washington, and the tension that seemed to stalk their lives. She never objected; she was like Ruth in the Old Testament: "Whither thou goest, I shall go. Whither thou lodge, I shall lodge."[52] But there were limits even for Biblical characters. Jim Doyle was in the office that night when Archie unlocked the door to pick up his briefcase. "What's up?" Doyle asked. Cox looked worn out. He said that nothing was up; he had to hurry home because Phyllis was "saving dinner for me." Doyle observed that the special prosecutor seemed oddly worried on this night as he closed the door behind him.[53]

The next day, rested from his presidential dinner, Elliot Richardson scribbled with a pen. He turned over drafts and corrections to his typist until the document was ready on Wednesday morning, October 17. The finished product summarized the Stennis plan as he understood it, in a memo marked "A Proposal—ELR #1." It would become significant that this draft included a section titled "Other Tapes and Documents," which provided that "the proposed arrangement would undertake to cover *only the tapes* heretofore subpoenaed by the Watergate grand jury at the request of the special prosecutor."[54] As

Richardson understood it, the Stennis proposal would relate to the nine subpoenaed tapes, and nothing more. The agreement would not bar Cox's access to *future* materials.

Later that morning, Richardson's draft was submitted to J. Fred Buzhardt in the White House. Buzhardt rewrote the document. He omitted the section entitled "Other Tapes and Documents." This was because, Buzhardt told Richardson, "the proposal *on its face* dealt only with the subpoenaed tapes" and "the paragraph was therefore redundant."[55] The final draft, "ELR #4," omitted the key paragraph about future access to documents. It was submitted to Cox on late Wednesday afternoon.[56]

Cox had two goals in attempting to hash out a compromise: first, to ensure that he got usable evidence for the grand jury; second, to give the president an opportunity to "save face."[57] In his reply to Richardson drafted on Thursday, Cox sounded an optimistic note. The "essential idea" of using impartial outside parties to review the tapes and resolve the impasse, he wrote, "is not unacceptable." In an unabashedly conciliatory tone, Cox continued, "There should be no avoidable confrontation with the President. And I have not the slightest desire to embarrass him. Consequently I am glad to sit down with anyone in order to work out a solution along this line if we can."[58]

Cox listed eleven distinct concerns with the "Stennis Compromise," as it was initially placed on the negotiating table. The biggest problem was that the American people "cannot be fairly asked to confide so difficult and responsible a task to any *one* man operating in secrecy, consulting only with the White House."[59] Cox was willing to accept the general concept of injecting neutral parties into the process to resolve the Watergate stalemate. But the twist would be this. *Three* "special masters" should be named, rather than one. One could be Senator Stennis, as the White House wished. The other two names should be true "impartials," selected by both sides working together. Two possibilities might be J. Lee Rankin and retired Senator John Sherman Cooper of Kentucky, men of impeccable integrity whose names had already been tossed around in earlier negotiations. The three "special masters," whoever they were, should be made officers of the court. They would hold an elevated, quasi-judicial status. In this way, Cox hoped, the final transcripts that they verified would be admissible as evidence before the grand jury and in any future Watergate trial. This modified plan would allow Cox to remain true to his oath as special prosecutor and to his pledge to the Senate.[60] It would simultaneously accomplish the White House's goal of reducing the universe of people exposed to the documents to a small set of trusted individuals.

In the same letter, Cox dismissed any "suggestion" that there may have been "tampering" with the president's tapes. However, since the topic had been mentioned in Elliot's proposal, why not go one step further "to dispel cynicism" by making provision for the use of "skilled *electronic assistance* in verifying the integrity of the tapes and to render intelligible, if at all possible, portions that appear inaudible or garbled"?[61]

In a phone call to Richardson late that evening, Cox repeated his conciliatory tone: "I'm not saying I must . . . see the tapes," Richardson's notes reveal Cox telling him. "The idea of a third person or third persons," he said, "is not out."[62]

The attorney general passed along Cox's reply to the president's advisers at a meeting held in Haig's office in the White House that Thursday night. Richardson was puzzled that none of them—Haig, Buzhardt, Garment, or Wright—seemed interested in a panel of three "masters," whoever they were. The president's lawyers "construed the Cox comments as tantamount to rejection of the proposal." All three thought that if Cox refused to accept the Stennis compromise as is, "he should be fired."[63] They were satisfied that the American people would understand. They had faith in the "President's ability to be persuasive with the American public."[64]

Richardson was nonplussed. If Wright felt so strongly that he could sell the Stennis compromise, the attorney general countered, maybe he should "have a crack at Archie," make his own effort to convey the plan to Cox. Maybe Wright could have more luck, since he obviously felt passionately about the Stennis proposal. But there was absolutely no basis for firing Cox; there was no "extraordinary impropriety" or anything approaching it.[65]

Richardson was disturbed by Wright's aggressive stance at this meeting. The Texas scholar was a "biggish guy with blondish hair." He was "blue-eyed, vigorous, cogent, clear-headed," a "smart guy."[66] Wright had been a fan of Richard Nixon since his bid for the vice presidency in 1952. As a young professor, Wright had written Nixon to tell him that he respected and supported the vice presidential nominee, despite their differences of opinion on certain subjects.[67] On this evening, seated in the White House at the center of Nixon's efforts to salvage his presidency, Richardson perceived that Wright had the "tone of a Plaintiff's lawyer who conveys to his client that he was screwed by the other side."[68] Wright was not, as he should have been in Richardson's mind, acting as a person brought in to serve as "wise counsel."[69] The whole situation was being handled "clumsily." Nothing positive would come of it, not if Wright continued down this path.

The pulse of Watergate beat faster. It was on this same day, Thursday, October 18, that Judge Sirica ruled that he had no jurisdiction over the lawsuit filed by the Senate Watergate Committee. Senator Sam Ervin's push for the tapes was now officially dead.[70] With only one day left for the president to file an appeal in the U.S. Supreme Court, Cox's court battle was the only game in town.

If there was any doubt that Cox's office considered accepting some form of the White House compromise transmitted by Elliot Richardson, documents in Cox's files now make clear the seriousness of those efforts.

An internal memo shows the Special Prosecution Force grappling with its own conscience, spelling out various pros and cons of accepting the initial Stennis proposal. Although most of the staff were flatly opposed to the idea, they knew Cox was deeply committed to finding a resolution, so they went forward. The pros were short but important. They included the chance to "avoid the risk of a constitutional crisis," obtaining "portions of the nine tapes several months quicker than [through] litigation," preventing "struggle over impeachment," and avoiding the "break-up of Special Prosecution Force and dismissal of Attorney General."[71]

On the con side of the balance, the memo listed eight risks and costs. Chief among these was the permanent loss of evidence. Any lawyer worth a nickel knew that summaries of transcripts, especially when prepared by interested parties, would probably be useless in a court of law. "There is *no* reason to believe that an edited transcript would meet the needs of prosecution at the trial," the memo noted. "Would we proceed without them? Apparently. Would that be responsible and diligent? No."

A second major concern was the reaction of the American public—not just their immediate reaction, but their inevitable loss of faith in an already-suspect process. If a single man (a politician, no less) was permitted to circumvent the courts and decide the entire Watergate case, wrapped up in a cocoon of secrecy, what would the country think? No matter how honest the man chosen to listen to the tapes, such a course would "leave too many suspicions that once again the politicians had 'taken care of' a situation outside of the normal institutional framework."

Finally, the individual selected by the White House, Senator John Stennis, brought his own set of question marks. He had a well-deserved reputation for "probity" in government circles. But given his strong views in favor of the military and the presidency, "one could expect the decision to be in favor of secrecy and innocence wherever there was room for judgment." Furthermore, in light of Stennis's age and his recent gunshot wounds, "there is question about his time and energy, and availability for later court proceedings."[72]

Cox's staff respected their boss enormously. Stephen Breyer, who worked on the ITT arm of the investigation and later became a Supreme Court Justice, remembered feeling an unwavering sense of confidence in Cox's "diligence and judgment."[73] With the average age of his lawyers at thirty or less, Cox was twice their age. He operated by what he referred to as "Lincoln's Rule": "everyone on his staff got one vote, but his vote counted one more than everyone else's put together."[74] In difficult moments, few were prepared to second-guess the special prosecutor. Even if his staff complained, "Archie, prosecutors do this all the time," he would answer, "Yes, but is it fair?" Richard Ben-Veniste, who vigorously opposed the Stennis compromise in any form, understood that Cox had to make the decision in the end, and trusted him to do it. "If you wanted to provide the American public with a figure of decency and probity, and didn't have Archibald Cox for this job," said Ben-Veniste, "you'd have to invent him."[75]

So despite all the concerns swimming around privately in the Special Prosecution Force office, the group was prepared to defer to Cox and accept some offshoot of the Stennis plan. On Wednesday, October 17, Cox's assistant Peter Kreindler had completed a memo to his boss entitled "Possible Settlement." The memo reflected a silent acceptance that Cox was bent on achieving a compromise; it offered him advice in bargaining. Kreindler counseled Cox to avoid slippery definitions of "state secrets," which might be used by the White House to gobble up all meaningful evidence. He pushed for an agreement that the special prosecutor would receive *portions* of tape recordings once "national security" and other "sensitive" materials were deleted, if the trial judge insisted on this form of evidence in lieu of transcripts. Kreindler urged Cox, foremost, to preserve evidence at all costs.[76]

The October 17 memo reveals that it was not only possible, but likely, that some variation of the initial Stennis plan could have been worked out by the special prosecutor and the president. Cox had moved into "settlement" mode, despite the intense disappointment of his staff. Richardson did not seem opposed to turning over verbatim transcripts of those portions of the subpoenaed tapes that were within the special prosecutor's domain. The general reluctance on both sides to face a constitutional showdown made the tapes issue ripe for resolution. As Cox would later tell Walter Cronkite of CBS News, "I wasn't in any mood to break off discussions. We could have talked that through, I think."

One critical factor, however, irreversibly turned the tide of Watergate. "When Mr. Wright came into the picture," Cox said, ". . . that really cut off the discussion."[77]

Archie took refuge on Thursday night at his younger brother Louis's home outside Washington, where he "sought relief in cocktails and dinner."[78] Louis lived in McLean, Virginia, just across from Robert Kennedy's old estate at Hickory Hill, a welcome retreat from Watergate. It had been a busy, draining week. The family had just sat down at the long table for supper when the phone rang. It was Archie's deputy Hank Ruth: Cox was to call "Marshall Wright" immediately at the White House. Confusion followed at the White House switchboard. There *was* a Marshall Wright on staff . . . but he had not called Cox. Was it someone in the Pentagon? "I didn't think our military had gone in for that title," Cox would say.[79] After much clicking of telephone lines, Cox was finally put through to a familiar voice, Charles Alan Wright, the president's special counsel.[80]

Since the chairs had all been pulled into the dining room, Cox had nowhere to sit but on the floor. His eight-year-old niece, Kathy, climbed across his lap and tugged at the telephone as Wright began speaking to Cox in a serious tone. "Is it the president?" Kathy pulled at the receiver. "Let me hear, Uncle Archie, let me hear." Uncle Archie was feeling somewhat benumbed.[81]

Charles Wright proceeded to outline a "final" proposal that Cox *had* to accept, with no qualifications. The nub of the proposal was that Senator Stennis *alone* would listen to the tapes. No portion of the actual tapes would be provided to Judge Sirica or the court. Cox would have to agree not to subpoena any further presidential tapes, papers, or documents, in the future. This last condition was *non*negotiable.[82]

The purported compromise sounded to Cox's ears "more like an ultimatum than a proposal."[83] His overpowering thought was "What's Charlie expect to do by attaching even *tougher* conditions than Elliot had proposed when I'd explained to Elliot that I wasn't buying *his*?"[84]

With his niece still climbing over him, Archie replied, "Well, Charlie, this is too important to do over the phone sitting here." Although he did not mention it, "the cocktail hour had been pretty long," and Cox could not help feeling that he was not in the best circumstances "under which to start a war."[85] Cox suggested that Wright put his proposal in writing.

Even as this conversation unfolded, Cox sensed that something ominous was brewing in the White House. Archie viewed the selection of Stennis as "a fiendishly clever move." Stennis was a godlike figure in the Senate. "I had no doubt whatsoever of John Stennis's personal integrity," Cox would say. At the same time, the conservative Southern Democrat would surely hold "expansive notions" concerning the scope of executive power, as well as what a president could withhold for "national security" purposes. The president might be able to manipulate these qualities to his advantage.

On top of this, Cox understood that the president's personal counsel, J. Fred Buzhardt, was the individual who would prepare the transcript for Stennis. Buzhardt had worked with Stennis on Capitol Hill for a number of years, when Buzhardt had served as a staff member for Senator Strom Thurmond, who was a friend and former law partner of Buzhardt's father. Later, Buzhardt worked in various capacities for the Department of Defense;[86] he and Stennis had shared secrets and strategies on sensitive matters such as the My Lai massacre and the Pentagon Papers, situations in which keeping one's lip buttoned was held at a high premium. The two men were both Southerners transplanted in Washington, and good friends.[87] All that heightened the danger that Stennis might rubber-stamp the transcript without a meaningful review if prodded gently and skillfully by Buzhardt.

Added to this was the bizarre fact that the elderly Stennis was just getting back on his feet after having been shot. There were also reports that his hearing was bad. Would any of this affect his ability to do the job properly?[88] Whatever the answer to these questions, Cox knew that it was not particularly "wise to be taking on John Stennis."[89] Stennis was a powerful force on both sides of the congressional aisle. The special prosecutor was in a difficult bind. How to extricate himself from it?

The next morning, Friday the nineteenth, Wright delivered a one-page letter to Cox ostensibly drafted the night before, to "confirm our conversation of a few minutes ago." Wright began by stating that "The fundamental purpose of the very reasonable proposal that the Attorney General put to you, at the instance of the President," was to provide Cox the material he requested in a nonconfrontational fashion.[90]

Wright continued: "The President was willing to permit this unprecedented intrusion into the confidentiality of his office in order that the country might be spared the anguish of further months of litigation and indecision about private Presidential papers and meetings." Wright now completely glossed over the four demands that he had delivered so adamantly the night before. Instead, he cut directly to a self-absolving close: "If you think that there is any purpose in our talking further, my associates and I stand ready to do so. If not, we will have to follow the course of action that we think in the best interest of the country."

Cox realized what Wright was trying to do with these select bits of recollections assembled on paper. Wright was trying to hopscotch over the demands that he had issued the night before and make it appear as if *Cox* were the person refusing to act reasonably.

Archie picked up a number two pencil and began writing hurriedly on a yellow pad, extra art-gum erasers within reach. He reminded Wright of the four points that Wright had "categorically" insisted that Cox accept over the phone the night before. Point one was that the tapes must be submitted to only a *single* person, operating in secrecy, "and the President had already indicated the only person in the country [Senator John Stennis] who would be acceptable to him." That choice posed problems enough, Cox wrote. But point four, that Cox must accept these "edited transcripts" and then provide a blanket pledge that he would not subpoena any further White House tapes or documents in the future, would amount to an open breach of his oath to the Senate. Wright *certainly* knew that this would be impossible. "I categorically assured the Senate Judiciary Committee that I would challenge such claims so far as the law permitted," Cox wrote. "The Attorney General was confirmed on the strength of that assurance. I cannot break my promise now."[91]

Archie realized full well, as he wrote out this letter in careful cursive, that he was preserving points for a record in the future. He did not realize, though, that the future was now breathing down his neck.

Wright sent a second "Dear Archie" letter later that same Friday, backpedaling on his fourth demand. When he had suggested the night before that Cox could subpoena no further tapes or documents, Wright said, he had been referring only to "private presidential papers and meetings" (although he had defined "presidential papers" extremely broadly in previous meetings). Wright wrote this second letter on White House stationery, making clear that his words carried the weight of the executive branch. "It is my conclusion," Wright stated, ". . . that further discussions between us seeking to resolve this matter by compromise would be futile, and that we will be forced to take the actions that the President deems appropriate in these circumstances." He concluded: "I note these points only in the interest of historical accuracy, in the unhappy event that our correspondence should see the light of day."[92]

The clock ticked closer to the deadline for the president to file an appeal with the Supreme Court. His lawyers had only several hours left until the Court closed its doors.

Cox was baffled by a number of wrinkles in the White House strategy. First, why were the president's lawyers not asking the court of appeals for an extension of time? "It would have been damned hard to oppose," he would later admit.[93] Second, why had Charles Alan Wright suddenly injected himself into the negotiations as an agitating force? Archie had done just fine dealing with Elliot Richardson; they had begun discussing concrete compromises, as the White House well knew. As Archie saw it, "What's the point of getting someone who's been a pure and simple protagonist in this when the attorney general—who has a personal relationship on both sides . . . has been functioning as something of a mediator?" Unless Wright was prepared to make a major new concession, which would be a brilliant move on the part of the White House, Cox viewed this shift as a potentially disastrous one.[94]

That same Friday, an anxious press corps had huddled in Judge Sirica's courtroom. The Special Prosecution Force had announced an impromptu appearance that morning. Jim Doyle had made it a policy not to disclose the purpose of court appearances in advance, but the whispers said that there would be a major showdown between President Nixon and Archibald Cox on the tapes. The oddsmakers were wrong, at least for the moment.

Instead, John Dean surprised the country by pleading guilty to one count of conspiracy to obstruct justice and to defraud the United States in the Watergate affair. He placed his hand (at first the wrong hand) on the Bible as he swore to tell the truth, putting an end to a racking year in which he had become the "Watergate scapegoat."[95] This was not, Cox would later insist, a "surprise move" orchestrated by the Special Prosecution Force to throw the president off guard on the final day of his deadline. Rather, as an internal memo confirmed, Dean's guilty plea "came along in due course," after lengthy negotiating. If anything, it exerted pressure on *both* the White House and the special prosecutor to reach a final-hour compromise.[96]

Still, the White House did not appreciate the added dose of pressure. The Special Prosecution Force had cut a deal with Fred LaRue, aide to John Mitchell, on June 28. On August 16 top CREEP director Jeb Stuart Magruder had entered a guilty plea. On September 17, "dirty trickster" Donald Segretti rolled over for the government. Now John Dean had copped a guilty plea. It was a classic example of "dealing up." It seemed to be leading directly into the inner sanctum of the White House.[97]

After packing up his briefcase and wading through reporters and photographers mobbing Judge Sirica's courtroom, Archie retreated to his K Street office, lowered the blinds, and cracked open the window. He would wait until the Supreme Court closed its doors. He would see what the president's lawyers decided to do.

The Clerk's Office in the Supreme Court completed an ordinary day of business. It closed its docketing office at 5:00 P.M.[98] No certiorari petition had been filed by the president of the United States.[99] No action had been taken whatsoever. Archie assumed that the clerk had the power to keep someone at the Court until midnight under such unprecedented circumstances, especially if asked to extend that "courtesy" by the president. He did not allow himself to go home until 7:00. The lights of Washington were just beginning to blink out around him.[100]

Cox's five months of conflicted feelings since his appointment as Watergate special prosecutor had now risen to a head on this uncertain Friday in October. Archie's mind flashed back to 1963, when Robert Kennedy had walked into his office after the Supreme Court held that public schools could not require students to begin the day reading the Bible or reciting the Lord's Prayer. Governor Wallace had already refused to abide by a federal court order enforcing that decision. He had fired off a telegram to the attorney general: "I am ordering the teachers in the Alabama schools to begin the day with prayer. Are you going to send the troops down to stop us from prayer?" RFK had asked Archie, "What do I do? What's my answer?"

Much to his own embarrassment, Cox gave a typical professorial answer. He had "lamely murmured" something to the effect that "the problem was a long way off, that there was no case actually involving Alabama, and that perhaps the question would never arise."

The incident had stuck in Cox's mind, and it came back to him now. What power ultimately existed to enforce the nation's laws and compel anyone—even the president—to obey them? "The answer is," Cox said, "if they're going to be effective they have to rest upon something which one's tempted to describe as reverence for the law . . . the Court's legitimacy, the sense that it's the citizen's obligation to comply with the law."[101] Cox's old nightmares were now looming dangerously close to reality. He was boxing the president into a corner. Would Cox "be the one who revealed the fakery of law in terms of power, physical power?"[102] If he pushed the president too far over the precipice so that he defied the Supreme Court, how would the damage ever be repaired?

Phil Heymann had flown down to Washington during this final week. He visited Archie and Phyllis at their little cottage in Virginia to offer support. As Heymann remembered the scene, Cox was becoming almost desperate. If he rejected the compromise and the president thumbed his nose at the final court order, Cox worried, "Presidential defiance of the Supreme Court might become habitual."

Heymann tried to reassure him. Cox's concerns were all legitimate. Nevertheless, Heymann told Archie that he was "extremely nervous" with the idea of the special prosecutor negotiating secret compromises with Richardson under any circumstances. "Everybody would blame him for all of the deception and failure to reveal the truth that would come out," Heymann worried, if he struck a deal behind closed doors and the American public did not buy it.[103]

Archie had not found many chances to escape Washington during these frenzied months. He had made one trip earlier in the fall, which he now replayed in his mind. It had been a quick trip to Windsor to visit his mother; on the way, he had made a stopover at St. Paul's School, his old alma mater. Cox had made other trips to this tiny New

England campus during other moments of crisis in his life. The New Hampshire prep school always refreshed him, gave him a feeling of hope, a new perspective. This was one time he needed it desperately.

Mosquitoes and black flies were there to greet him, hovering around the pond at the far edge of the school; they were the same ugly pests that had multiplied in the stagnant, green waters when he was a boy. Archie began his walk around the Lower Pond, which was surrounded by drooping New Hampshire hemlocks. Here he had once rowed canoes in the fall and knocked hockey pucks around in the winter. The reflection of the red chapel, expanded in 1928 when he was a fourth former, now shimmered from across the pond. Its spire bent with the ripples, and the bells in the tower rang on the quarter hour.

Archie walked through the woods at the east edge. He kicked a pathway through the blackberry brambles and overgrown evergreen branches. Then he stopped in front of a cross-shaped stone marker. He stood, read the inscription, then walked back, got into the pickup truck where Phyllis was waiting behind the wheel, and drove quietly on to Windsor. He remembered the inscription still, five decades later: "REMEMBER NOW THE CREATOR IN THE DAYS OF THY YOUTH."

19

THE
SATURDAY NIGHT
MASSACRE

Throughout the fall, Archie felt desperately in need of an "elder statesman." Someone to confide in, to seek advice from.[1] First he sought out John Douglas, his "slightly younger" friend in the Justice Department. Douglas was the son of the late Senator Paul Douglas, for whom Cox had great respect dating back to the Landrum-Griffin years. He and John Douglas talked over lunch at the Capitol Hilton. Douglas thought that too much of a compromise was a "poor idea."[2] At the same time, if the White House put a legitimate peace offering on the table and Cox turned it down, "you'll be dead."[3]

Cox was gripped in an inner turmoil. "Gosh, John," he said, "I need a good gray eminence to advise me." Douglas shook his head and smiled powerlessly. He pointed back at Cox. "I don't know anyone around any grayer."[4]

Cox next spoke with Senator Robert Byrd, Democratic leader from West Virginia. Byrd gave him a "perfect hard-lined, conventional Democratic attack on the president." As Cox described it, "That was a bust."[5]

His final call was to his old mentor and friend, Judge Charles Fahy, the man who had groomed him as a young lawyer in the solicitor general's office and had sworn him in as Watergate special prosecutor. "I suppose," Cox recalled, "I was too old really to be looking for somebody older to lean on. But I was."[6] So the sixty-one-year-old Cox telephoned his eighty-one-year-old mentor and asked if he could talk to him about the Watergate mess. Perhaps meet with him?

Fahy was momentarily quiet. He answered softly, "Archie, I'm still a senior judge on this Court and the matter is one that clearly could come before this Court. And I think . . . while I have no reason to think that I would sit, I might be called to sit. I think I'm disqualified."[7]

Cox quietly hung up the phone. He was "embarrassed that I had, in my desperation, put this to him."[8] Twenty or twenty-five minutes later the telephone rang again: "Archie, this is Charles Fahy. Could you give me a little more time to think about you and your problem? I've been worrying about it for the last twenty minutes, as to whether maybe I shouldn't see you, but give me a little more time to think about it."[9]

Cox said that he appreciated the call. But that Judge Fahy had been right the first time. Archie softly put down the phone.

"But that second call," Cox would remember, "was almost as good as advice. It was good to know that someone you respected as I did him was worrying about your position."[10]

Archibald Cox now realized that there was nobody else in the United States who could help him. The decision was left to him. And President Richard M. Nixon.

In the White House on Friday, October 19, the critical day of the Supreme Court deadline, there was a flurry of activity. The familiar cast of presidential lawyers had assembled shortly after 10:00 A.M. in General Haig's office, in the West Wing of the White House. Elliot Richardson entered and joined them. Someone handed Richardson a copy of the first letter Wright had sent to Cox that morning, presumably to bring him up to speed. Elliot was floored.[11] For the first time, Richardson understood what was going on: Wright had added a demand that Cox swear off any *future* access to tapes and presidential materials as a condition of the Stennis compromise.

Richardson became "annoyed, angry and concerned." "I made [it] as explicit as possible," he later recounted, "that this was a proposition that had never been put to Cox. That I had never put it to him."[12] He chastised Wright for sending out the letter in the first place, *particularly* on White House stationery, *especially* "without my being informed of it or involved in it."[13] This letter, and its inflexible demand about no future tapes, "muddied the record and put the President's position in an unnecessarily bad light."[14]

The White House lawyers agreed that this point should be "cleared up." But they quickly shifted back to the topic they had been discussing before Elliot arrived—Judge Sirica's probable reaction to the

Stennis proposal. Charles Wright rated the chances of Sirica accepting it as "good." "What would Cox do," the presidential lawyers seemed to want to know from the attorney general, if some form of the Stennis compromise were forced upon Cox? "Would he resign?"[15] They apparently had researched Cox's history as head of the Wage Stabilization Board back in the 1950s. When President Truman had reached a decision that he could not live with, Cox—out of conscience—had resigned. Would his response be the same if he received a condition that he could not accept here? Richardson collected himself. Yes, he probably would, Richardson replied. Next, the president's lawyers wanted to know what *Elliot* would do in the event Cox refused to accept the Stennis proposal but did *not* resign? Would he carry out the president's order and dismiss him?

Richardson hesitated. He had not thought this one through. It was no secret among those who knew Elliot Richardson that he "harbored national political aspirations."[16] In politics, one had to be a team player. Elliot muttered some jumbled, indecisive words.

Some attending that meeting would later interpret Richardson's signals as indicating that the president should go ahead and "give Cox an order." This would effectively rid the administration of the special prosecutor without having to fire Cox.[17] Len Garment concluded that it was Richardson's "fervent prayer" that Cox would resign, so that he would not have to fire him, so that he could maintain his job.[18]

One of Richardson's closest advisers would admit that as of this Friday, Elliot "was not clear in his own mind what he would do" if the Stennis plan was limited to the nine subpoenaed tapes, if it did *not* limit future access to additional tapes, if Senator Stennis signed a complete verification that the transcript was accurate and could be submitted in federal court, if the proposal went directly from the White House to Cox, and if Cox rejected it. In that case, the special prosecutor "might be at risk."[19]

In defense of the president's position, Richardson knew, the war was still raging in the Middle East. By the end of the week, 550 American supply missions would be flown into the Mideast. Secretary of State Henry Kissinger was already on his way to Moscow for cease-fire talks. From the White House perspective, pushing the president to meet court deadlines for a two-bit criminal case in the midst of a worldwide crisis only highlighted the folly of this Watergate stand-off.[20] Richardson understood this argument. On the other hand, how could one stop the wheels of justice from spinning at home, in the name of overcoming enemies abroad?

Elliot sat in his chair, troubled and uncertain. It was not completely clear which form of the Stennis plan the White House lawyers were talking about. He certainly could not endorse blocking access to future tapes; this would directly contravene his pledge to the Senate. But the focus at the meeting "kept shifting on and off the other material."

Richardson went back to his office utterly frustrated. He had left the Justice Department "cranked up" to persuade the president's lawyers to work the matter out. Now his aides observed a strange look on his face, as if their boss suddenly felt like "an inner tube that someone has let the air out of." Elliot Richardson told his staff that he had lost his will for mediating and negotiating. He had "run out of imagination."[21]

Later that Friday afternoon, Richardson picked up the phone in his Justice Department office. He called Haig and Buzhardt at 2:25 and 4:30, respectively, to make his position clearer. He had thought over the questions they had asked him, and he did not want any misunderstanding. The Stennis plan should *not* be linked to a "no future access" pledge. First of all, after reflecting on it, he did not believe that this ploy would lure Cox into resigning. Such a course was "ill advised," he said, and "the President should be so informed."[22] Second, he would not support it. Under the circumstances, even if Cox did refuse to accept the Stennis proposal, this could in no way be regarded as an "extraordinary impropriety."[23] "My position was noted and I was told that there would be further consultation before any decision was reached."[24]

Early that evening, Richardson received a telephone call from Alexander Haig from within the White House. The clock on Richardson's desk showed approximately 7:00 P.M. General Haig informed him that a letter was being drafted as they spoke. It would be a letter from the president, directing Richardson to inform Cox that the president would *not* file an appeal with the Supreme Court. Cox, in turn, would be required to accept the "Stennis compromise" and seek no further presidential tapes or papers. If he did not agree to these terms, Cox would be fired. Richardson was stunned. Haig explained calmly that he had "twice done his best in communicating the Richardson position to the President," but "he had not been successful."[25] The letter was in the works. It would be delivered to Richardson's office soon.

"Soon" turned out to be twenty minutes. Richardson dialed Cox at his unlisted number in Virginia. It was approximately 7:45 P.M.; Richardson read portions of the White House draft to his old professor. "I am reading you this letter *for your information,"* Elliot emphasized. He was not carrying out the White House's order, just serving as a conduit of facts. The letter from President Richard M. Nixon read as follows:

Dear Elliot:

You are aware of the actions I am taking today to bring to an end the controversy over the so-called Watergate tapes and that I have reluctantly agreed to a limited breach of Presidential confidentiality in order that our country may be spared the agony of further indecision and litigation about those tapes at a time when we are confronted with other issues of much greater moment to the country and the world.

As a part of these actions, I am instructing you to direct Special Prosecutor Archibald Cox of the Watergate Special Prosecution Force that he is to make no further attempts by judicial process to obtain tapes, notes, or memoranda of Presidential conversations. I regret the necessity of intruding to this very limited extent, on the independence that I promised you with regard to Watergate when I announced your appointment. This would not have been necessary if the Special Prosecutor had agreed to the very reasonable proposal you had made to him this week."[26]

Richardson told Cox that he would schedule an appointment with the president first thing in the morning. Elliot would have "a chance to get a fresh look at the situation" by then.[27] He still wanted to act as "lawyer for the situation"; he would attempt to beat out this brushfire and avoid the final conflagration. He would convince the president to reconsider.[28] "I thought I had time," Richardson recalled. But time seemed to spin in funny directions on that unusual night in October.[29]

Meanwhile, Cox hurried back to Washington. The streets were half-deserted as the weekend enveloped the capital. Archie tracked down his press secretary, Jim Doyle, and drove quickly to the K Street office. It looked unusually dark under starless skies. Cox and Doyle turned the key, flicked on lights. An old pot of coffee sat on a burner. They waited an eternity for the Associated Press wire machine, which rattled and jangled at maddeningly long intervals in the storage room of the Special Prosecution Force office, to spit out official news of the president's actions. The wait became unbearable. Doyle suggested calling the *Los Angeles Times.* If the White House wanted to issue a statement anywhere, it would be on the West Coast, where they could still get it out in time for the morning papers.

Doyle dialed the *Los Angeles Times* Washington Bureau. He hit pay dirt on the first call: an editor confirmed that White House Press Secretary Ron Ziegler had issued an announcement at 8:18 P.M. eastern daylight time. Doyle read the wire over the phone: a "compromise" had been reached with all relevant parties in the Watergate affair. The Stennis deal was now *finalized* according to the White House press release. The White House would prepare a *summary* of the content of the tapes, and this summary would be verified by Senator Stennis. There would be no further attempts to subpoena tapes or personal presidential papers by the special prosecutor or anyone else. The president had met with Senators Ervin and Baker for over forty minutes in the Oval Office that night; they had given their blessing to the plan. Senator Stennis had commented that "he had not been told exactly what his role would be," but pledged to "render the service the best I can." The president was now directing that the special prosecutor "make no further attempts by judicial process to obtain tapes, notes, or memoranda of Presidential conversations." Although he did not wish to "intrude upon the independence of the Special Prosecutor," the statement indicated that the president felt comfortable that this unprecedented compromise was more than generous.[30]

Cox listened to the news in shock. Part of the president's directive was that Cox would receive summaries—not actual transcripts—and that he would not be permitted to subpoena any further evidence from the White House. This was not a "generous" offering at all.

Archie hurriedly began to prepare a press release for the morning papers. He dictated, while Jim Doyle banged out words on a typewriter. "We were scrambling to get in our word that it was *not* a true compromise between the parties, and we thought the court would have a lot to say about it," Cox explained.[31] The revised Stennis plan, he dictated, "would deprive prosecutors of admissible evidence" that Judge Sirica had "ruled necessary to a fair trial." Cox could not accept this and remain true to his pledge to the Senate. "I shall bring these points to the attention of the Court," he stated. He would seek to have the matter resolved by Judge Sirica as quickly as possible, in the upcoming week, "and abide by [his] decision."[32]

Jim Doyle quickly circulated the news release to the wire services and major papers. If it did not go out fast enough, the "Stennis compromise" story would hit the wires by itself, and they would be dead. The headlines would say, "John Stennis Resolves an Impasse." The special prosecutor's office would be viewed as the stubborn spoiler; they would never "catch up."[33] Archie made a hasty decision: he would hold a press conference the next day and fully explain to the American public why he could not accept the "Stennis compromise."

At the Justice Department, Elliot Richardson met with his closest advisers—Bill Ruckelshaus, Jonathan Moore, J. T. Smith, and Dick Darman—to draft his own news release. The bottom line was that he could not carry out the president's order. Although the Stennis plan was a reasonable enough concept, it was "inconsistent" with the "explicit understandings on which I was confirmed" to tell Cox that he could not subpoena tapes in the future. Richardson concluded with a final jolt of optimism: "I plan to seek an early opportunity to discuss these matters with the President."[34]

Archie was still hunched over his desk, making final revisions to his own press release, when Elliot called again. "Where's my letter?" Elliot asked. He was noticeably agitated. "I haven't got my letter from the White House yet." Richardson and Cox understood the ramifications. The formal letter from President Nixon instructing Richardson to present the ultimatum to Cox had never arrived. Elliot was now "out of the loop."[35]

Senator Stennis, according to news reports picked up by Doyle, was already en route from somewhere down south to Washington in a government plane. The White House plan was rolling forward and becoming irreversible by design.

Richardson's assistant J. T. Smith received an urgent call from Jim Woolsey at the Senate Armed Services Committee. Stennis's aides were confused. The senator had never agreed to any deal that would interpose himself between the president and Cox or Judge Sirica. They wanted to get this clarified "so that this terrible historical disaster could be reversed." Smith walked in the doorway to see his boss. "You're not going to believe this, . . ." Smith began.

Richardson looked up, tired. "It's too late," he answered, "leave me alone."[36]

Elliot Richardson returned home that night, jotting down thoughts on a piece of paper as they swam into his head. It was a damnable position. He was a politician, after all. In his own way, his aides knew, he "had it on his agenda to go as high as he could."[37] If one was a politician in Richardson's position, "as high as one can get is President of the United States."[38] The current situation would obliterate his own political future. Still, he felt tremendous loyalty to President Nixon. This was the president who had plucked him out of Massachusetts politics and placed him in three different U.S. cabinet posts. This was the president at whose international political skills he marveled. If Elliot resigned, President Nixon might be damaged permanently. On a more personal level, the president was acting in such an aberrant way that he might be in more serious trouble than Watergate; he might be "on the edge of sanity."[39] On the flip side, there were his pledges to the Senate, his obligations to treat Cox fairly, his own sense of integrity. "Integrity" was a word (he remembered from long-ago prep school days at Milton Academy) that derived from the Latin *integritas,* meaning "wholeness."

Perhaps there was an avenue that he had not explored. Elliot talked over the options, all of which sounded unpalatable, with his wife, Anne. She mused out loud that he should at least insist on being buried in a "mahogany coffin." It was an old New England phrase for a fancy burial.[40] If he were going to be swept out of government and politics forever, he should at least "go out in style."[41] At the top of his notes Elliot Richardson scribbled "The Mahogany Coffin." On one random page of notes, Richardson hurriedly worked out some logic:

> a) if you fire Cox and then resign you will do two things you had *no* reason to do;
> b) if you refuse to fire Cox and then resign you will do two things you had reason to do.

He also wrote in scratchy pen, almost angrily: "if the Middle East is that important then the Cox order should be held off by the W.H. [White House]." Though he scribbled quite a few notes before he went to bed, Elliot Richardson already knew that he had only one option remaining.

The following morning, Richardson rewrote his notes from the night before and captioned them "Summary of Reasons Why I Must Resign—ELR Oct. 19, 1973." Among the points he listed in a clear hand were the following:

> • While Cox has rejected a proposal I consider reasonable, his rejection of it cannot be regarded as being beyond the pale as would justify my own exercise of my reserved power to fire him. He is, after

all, being asked to accept a proposition that would give him significantly less than he has won in two court decisions. Besides, I really believe that in all my dealings with him he has been honest and fair.

- I do not believe the President's attitude toward Cox's role is fundamentally valid: many problems and headaches could have been avoided by cooperating with him more and fighting him less.

- In short: since I appointed Cox on the understanding that I would fire him only for "extraordinary improprieties" on his part, and since I cannot find him guilty of any such improprieties, I cannot stay if he goes.[42]

Richardson threw the handwritten pages in his leather briefcase. He snapped it shut and dressed himself for the office. Saturdays were always the worst days to go to work in Washington.

The previous night, as Archibald Cox prepared for his Saturday press conference, he had few thoughts about the personal consequences of losing his job. When asked by a United Press International reporter over the phone if he planned to resign, he replied with uncharacteristic impulse: "No—hell no."[43] The legal issue was much more pressing: How to deal with the president's outright refusal to abide by the law? It had become a constitutional dare. Senators Ervin and Baker, according to advance press accounts, had endorsed the Stennis plan and were backing the president.[44] The pressure on Cox to cave in was mounting.

At home, Phyllis offered no advice, just comfort. She was "supportive, encouraging, affectionate."[45] Other than Archie's near breakdown during the student uprisings at Harvard, Phyllis had never seen her husband so terribly agitated. "Archie was beside himself for fear that he would bring down the republic," she remembered. "Our whole republic might be in tatters, and he might be the one to do it."[46]

Archie was literally in tears. He complained to Phyllis, "I can't fight with the President of the United States. I was brought up to honor and respect the President of the United States."[47] At the same time—he shared this with Phyllis but could not disclose it to the rest of the world—his staff had prepared a massive memo dated August 24, which discussed the possible involvement of the president in a host of illegal activities, including the payment of hush money to former advisers swept up in Watergate. How could Archie ignore such evidence, make it go away?[48] Phyllis helped her husband pull himself together.[49] He took two sleeping pills that night, an unusual act. He desperately needed to calm himself.

The following morning, Saturday, October 20, Archie was "white as a sheet." He dressed in a brown-gray tweed suit and serious four-in-hand tie. Phyllis got him into the white Ford Falcon at approximately 8:50 A.M.[50] She squeezed his hand; she would drive the pickup truck into Washington before noon. He nodded his head and put the car in gear.

At work, staff members were assembled in the special prosecutor's office. Jim Doyle's assistant, John Barker, had brought in doughnuts; he knew that they were a choice delicacy for Cox. But today, the special prosecutor did not touch them. As Cox remembered the disjointed scene: "I got all sorts of conflicting advice . . . calling on me to be an actor in this role or that role or some other role; things that I knew perfectly well that I wouldn't be able to do."[51] Various staff members advised, "Don't be arrogant. Be tough. Smile often." Cox came to one conclusion from this barrage of scattered instructions: "The one thing that was perfectly clear was that it was beyond my power to be anything but myself, whatever that might be."[52]

Cox held an "intensely emotional" meeting with his staff in the small library of the special prosecutor's office. Panic had begun to creep over them; Archie could sense it even through his own exhaustion. He pleaded with the assembly of lawyers and staffers—people he had recruited—to stay on the job "regardless of what happened." If they did that, he said, his voice cracking, "there couldn't be any stopping of the investigation."[53] Most of the staff did not know that Cox had already prepared for the worst. He had sent Barker to set up a secret lockbox account at the Madison National Bank, two doors down from the K Street office, and to secure copies of key documents, particularly Cox's correspondence with Elliot Richardson. He would need these to prove what had transpired in the past week, if anything went wrong.[54]

Cox now asked to be left alone. He sat down quietly in his office, attempting to focus his mind, as if he were preparing for a critical Supreme Court argument. "What do I want to say? In what sequence? What questions am I likely to be asked? How will I answer them?"[55] Unlike preparing for a Supreme Court argument, though, he had little time to labor over a written script until the words flowed effortlessly. This time, he only had time to think.

In Boston, Phil Heymann had caught the news that Senators Ervin and Baker were publicly supporting the Stennis plan. He flew back to Washington on the first available flight. "It certainly was clear to me that Nixon had set the stage for firing Cox," Heymann remembered. He wanted to alert Archie, make him understand that he would lose the battle unless Elliot Richardson publicly supported him. He arrived in the office that Saturday morning. "I remember lots of people milling around outside not quite knowing what was going to happen," recalled Heymann. "I went in to Archie and tried to tell him that the crucial question was going to be whether Elliot stood by him. I mean, I sort of had this picture that the Senate had betrayed him. That at least the Watergate Committee had. And I also wanted to know where the Judiciary Committee was going to be."[56]

Cox's office was quiet. Heymann knocked softly and pushed open the door. "Archie was very nice and I went in and saw him and tried to give him some advice," Heymann remembered. He delivered his spiel and asked, did Archie want him to write something up for the press conference? Archie was polite yet subdued. No, he said. He was better left alone.

"But he obviously knew exactly what he was doing and where he was and where Elliot was," Heymann would smile. "He was way ahead of me."[57]

NBC and CBS had called Jim Doyle an hour earlier with the news that the press conference would be broadcast live, nationwide. (ABC was not covering it, because it had already committed to televising the NCAA football games.)[58] These calls from the networks were a boost, Doyle reassured Cox. It was not clear who, if anyone, would be watching television on a Saturday afternoon in October, especially with college football on the schedule. But at least there was a chance that Archie's message would reach a small portion of the American public.

A government car was supposed to drive Archie, Phyllis, Jim Doyle, and John Barker to the National Press Club. It got lost in the confusion and never arrived. "Let's walk," Archie said. Cox had never allowed his staff to see him "upset or nervous" during the five months that he had occupied the position of Watergate special prosecutor. On this Saturday, however, his face looked lifeless. "He was plenty upset," remembered Barker.[59]

The four of them walked in silence, up Vermont through McPherson Square, across I Street, H Street, New York Avenue. They glanced momentarily at the White House glinting under the ultrablue October sky. The president of the United States sat inside that building, they knew, thinking strategy, waiting pensively for the same press conference. The country was in a precarious position. Vice President Agnew had resigned in disgrace. Gerald Ford had not yet been confirmed by the House or Senate. Speaker of the House Carl Albert was next in line to succeed to the presidency, but there were rumors circulating that he had been drunk at the time of a 1972 automobile accident in front of a Washington bar, and did not seem particularly interested in the job.[60] Would this press conference throw the country into more of a confused state? Cox and his group walked past the Department of Treasury, turning left onto F Street. It was a crisp, sunny day. The trees were turning yellow, not red and orange and rainbow as in New England, but a chilly yellow in anticipation of another bleak winter. Past the Hotel Washington and the Willard Hotel.

Archie used the time to compose himself while Phyllis held tightly onto his arm. "For me it was not an easy trip to make," Cox would later admit. There was no doubt that he had to "insist on the President's compliance with the court order." He had a duty to adhere "to the terms of the Departmental Order by which I'd been appointed." At the same time, the prospect of going "eyeball to eyeball" with the president of the United States scared him.[61] Cox thought back to his days as a young boy, age eleven, learning that a friend of his father's had been asked to take a position in the Coolidge administration that involved a major sacrifice to his family. A young Archie had said to his father, "Why did Mr. Jones agree to do this?" His father's firm answer was, "When the President of the United States asks you to do it, you *do* it."[62] This ancient memory swept back into Cox's mind as he got closer. Who was he to be defying, challenging, the president of the United States?

All of a sudden, too much seemed to be expected of him. One of the reasons that he had loved and revered his job as solicitor general was that he had heard that office called the "conscience of government." Now, however, it seemed that his staff and Washington newspapers and Democratic senators and too many others expected him to stand up and represent the conscience of the entire American people. How could any one man or woman serve as the conscience of a nation? They couldn't, at least not any mortal Cox had ever met. The only hope, Cox thought vaguely to himself as he placed one shoe in front of another, was to somehow arouse the conscience that already existed in each citizen, awaken a collective sense of principle that had been lost in this city of grand marble edifices. If that happened, maybe the hulking machinery of government that was built to represent them would eventually respond. But how did one do this? Cox had no idea.[63]

The walk to the National Press Club seemed to last an eternity. "I don't know how I ever got there," Cox said. "It was only with my wife's help."[64]

The National Press Club building sat at the corner of F and Fourteenth Streets. A U.S. flag snapped high above on a silver pole, catching the October wind. The group waited for the light to change. They crossed. Inside, a Press Club staff member ushered them to a bank of elevators to the right. There they were whisked up to the thirteenth floor, then routed to the back entrance of the ballroom so that they would not be mobbed by reporters.

Elliot Richardson placed a hurried phone call; he caught Archie just in time, before the special prosecutor left his holding room for the ballroom. Richardson spoke quickly: he had drafted a new letter to the White House. It stated, in short, that Richardson had never endorsed the most recent conditions attached to the Stennis plan. In fact, he had disavowed them. The special prosecutor, according to the terms of the charter they had worked out, could only be removed for "extraordinary improprieties." In Richardson's mind, Cox's conduct was far from that, and he had "serious difficulty" with the president's most recent instruction in the letter dated the previous night.[65]

This phone call was critical; if at this moment Richardson had hesitated to side with Cox, the tumblers of public sentiment might have fallen into a wholly different sequence. At the moment, however, these terse words from the attorney general seemed like a small comfort. Cox took a breath. He pushed himself into the mobbed ballroom, almost in a daze, nervously holding hands with Phyllis. He carried only a notepad. Phyllis disentangled herself to find a seat, like any other guest. Archie walked forward. By himself.

The special prosecutor sat down uncertainly at a long table draped in a yellow tablecloth. In front of him was a single microphone. To one side was an American flag that John Barker had hurriedly arranged to have set up. The packed hall stopped as if in a freeze-frame, riveted at attention. The news conference was now ready to be carried live, broadcast at 1:00 P.M. eastern standard time. The lights of the network television cameras bore down. The green lights flashed to cue Cox.

"I am sorry to have had to bring you in on such a lovely day." Archie groped nervously at his pad. The room fell silent. A reporter coughed—this was no time for small talk about the weather. "I read in one of the newspapers this morning the headline 'Cox defiant,'" Archie began his talk in a high-pitched tone. "I do want to say that I don't *feel* defiant." Cox's voice cracked slightly. "In fact, I told my wife this morning I hate a fight."

Rows of journalists on foldout chairs furiously scribbled notes. "I'm not looking for a confrontation," Cox stated into the single microphone. He clenched and unclenched his large right hand. "I've worried a good deal through my life about the problems of imposing too much strain on our constitutional institutions, and I'm certainly not out to get the President of the United States."[66]

He was now feeling more composed. He spoke louder. Ever since his debating days at St. Paul's and again during his years as solicitor general, friends had always told him that his voice was strongest when he got over the introductions and moved into the thick of his argument. "I'm even worried, to put it in colloquial terms, that I'm getting too big for my britches, that what I see as principle could be vanity. I hope not." Cox peered out from under his shaggy eyebrows, two shades darker than his crewcut. "In the end I decided I had to try to stick by what I thought was right."

Cox slipped on a pair of half-glasses and glanced at his notes; the glasses now slid partway down his nose. Phyllis sat in one of the rows against the windows, watching impassively.

For the better part of an hour, Cox explained his position to the American public. As Phil Heymann would remember watching the scene from inside the ballroom, Cox started out nervous, but after the first few minutes, the "adrenaline got to him." He became "confident, enjoying exchanges with the press. Very comfortable with what he was doing."[67] The ultimatum presented by the White House, Cox said, was simply not something that he could embrace, given his oath to the Senate.

Now came a blizzard of questions about the attorney general's conduct. Archie tilted his head to hear the questions with his good ear. At times it was difficult to tell where sounds came from in such a big room, but he watched the journalists' movements and hand gestures. Elliot Richardson had acted "honorably" at all times throughout the affair, Cox replied forcefully to the first questions. If they were looking for a scapegoat, Richardson was the wrong person. He had in no fashion violated his pact with the Senate. More questions. Of course,

Cox responded, he realized that *someone* could fire him. But it was unclear if the attorney general would be willing to take that step. They would have to ask Mr. Richardson directly.

What was Cox going to do, a reporter asked, while he waited for the president to make his next move? Archie held up his head, gripped his eyeglasses, and answered firmly, "I'm going to go about my duties under the terms of which I assumed them."[68]

The press conference broke up almost abruptly. Sarah McClendon, a prominent but tough Washington correspondent, pushed forward. "I wanted to shake your hand," she blurted out to Cox as the television lights were unplugged. "You are a great American."[69] Archie shook her hand, half shy, half embarrassed. It seemed to have gone fine, but Cox and his staff had no way of knowing. The room emptied out swiftly.

By the time Archie's entourage escaped onto the street, they felt the sense of a "big letdown." On such a gorgeous fall day, who would be inside watching a dry speech by the special prosecutor? Not to mention the football games; it had been foolish to think that they could compete for national attention. "Well, we did it," Archie said matter-of-factly.[70] At least they had accomplished their goal, rebutting the misleading press reports of the previous day.[71]

Archie, Phyllis, Doyle, and Barker walked back to 1425 K Street. This time they took the route up Fourteenth, under the majestic umbrella of gingko trees. When they reached the intersection of New York Avenue, Archie suddenly stopped. "I'd like some beer," he said. None of them drank beer much, but it seemed like the appropriate thing to want.

John Barker spotted a liquor store across the street. They waited in front of the wide glass window while Barker walked inside. Three or four employees, "working-class" men, stood with their backs to the counter watching television. Barker motioned that he needed some beer. The cashier turned around, irked. "Go away," he grunted. "We're watching something important here. Come back later."

Barker looked up at the screen. The men were watching reruns of the press conference. Archie's face was flickering on the television screen. "It's for him," Barker said, pointing out the window. The men turned. Looked at Archie. Looked at the television screen. Looked back at Archie. Then hurriedly bagged up three six-packs of Budweiser. "No charge," they grunted, and pushed their way out onto the sidewalk to shake the hand of the Watergate special prosecutor.

"That's when we realized that something had happened," Barker smiled.[72]

The reaction to Cox's press conference, as reporters rushed out to send their stories flashing across the wires, was one of absolute confidence in Cox's integrity. Sympathy with his unwinnable position. The *Boston Globe* began the presses rolling on a story that would portray Cox as the "mediator who lectured President." "The press conference was a perfect illustration of his personality," Harvard colleague Frank Michelman told the *Globe*. It demonstrated his "evident sincerity."[73] *New Yorker* writer Elizabeth Drew called Cox a "folksy, tentative, Jimmy Stewart–like character" whose manner had been "disarming" and "devastating."[74] Members of the Washington press corps commented that it was the first press conference in American history that had changed public opinion in a major way.[75]

"I remember how excited I was when I watched the press conference on television," recalled Teddy Chase, Archie's longtime friend from Harvard College. "He was steadfast in every sense of the word. . . . His whole character was like his carriage. Straight and true."[76] John Kenneth Galbraith watched the showdown from a small hotel in Vermont. "I thought it was the most expressive, calm press conference I've ever listened to," said Galbraith, a veteran of national political oration.[77] Gerald Gunther, a Stanford law professor who had clerked for Learned Hand and was now writing the legendary judge's biography, watched the news conference in a basement cafeteria at the law school. He recalled hearing "the echo of Learned Hand's traits in Cox's performance."[78]

Archie's cousin Bertha "Bert" Perkins Frothingham, who still lived on the old Evarts estate in Windsor, saw an entire family history flash before her eyes: the steady hand of Roger Sherman, who had helped forge the Connecticut compromise that saved the Constitution; the independent spirit of her father, editor Max Perkins, who was constantly "searching for the truth" in literature; the unflappable adherence to the spirit of the Constitution displayed by their great-grandfather William M. Evarts, who had defended Andrew Johnson during his impeachment trial. "I think they were all . . . men of integrity," Bert Frothingham remembered thinking as she watched the screen, "who believed in their country and what their country stood for." She recalled staring at the television after it went dark, and thinking: "I [am] very proud of Bill."[79]

Journalist Clark Mollenhoff had yelled a final query at Cox, as he walked away from his news conference: Wouldn't it be useful for the American people to send cards and letters to the White House, to let the president know where they stood on the matter?[80]

It turned out to be a rhetorical question.

An avalanche of telegrams, mailgrams, and "rush" letters were already being composed at desks and kitchen tables across the country, addressed to the White House, Congress, the Justice Department, and Archibald Cox personally. Switchboards and Western Union lines were soon choked with messages. Elliot Richardson's office at the Justice Department began receiving a steady stream of wires, most of which Richardson would never have a chance to read:

"DUMP COX AND YOU'VE KILLED THE COUNTRY LET THE CHIPS FALL WHERE THEY MAY," came a telegram from L. Patton in Nokesville, Virginia. "YOU PROMISED SPECIAL PROSECUTOR PLEASE STAND BY COX OUR LAST HOPE FOR TRUTH ABOUT WATERGATE," wired Barbara Potter from Winchester, Massachusetts. "Will President Nixon achieve 'executive privilege' by default? Will he be successful in achieving immunity from the judgment of the courts by withholding evidence through legal maneuvering? . . ." wrote Mrs. Stanley K. Norton of Normal, Illinois. "I, a fellow Unitarian, a 60-year-old mother, grandmother, and college professor, hope that you, like Mr. Cox, will not fail our nation in this hour of greatest need." Charles H. Bradford, M.D., wrote a more personal note from his desk in Boston:

> Dear Elliot,
>
> I knew your father and grandfather and many of your family who lived next door to me at 222 Beacon Street in my boyhood.
> I can hardly believe that you would disgrace them by breaking your word to Cox, and by covering up Nixon's crimes.[81]

Archie knew nothing of this cavalcade of correspondence. He felt only "a large element of emotional letdown," a real sense of "exhaustion."[82] He and Phyllis went home. They would rest. And wait.

Elliot Richardson had watched the press conference in his office in the Justice Department. He found Cox's position "unassailable."[83] Several minutes after the television was switched off, he received a call from Alexander Haig. The chief of staff was highly agitated. Haig told Richardson that he had an immediate duty to perform as attorney general: he had to fire Cox.[84]

"Al, when can I see the President?" was all Richardson could say. "How about 3:30 this afternoon?" Haig replied flatly.[85]

Richardson's official limousine took him for what turned out to be his final ride. Alexander Haig met him first in the White House. He spoke of future roles Elliot might play in the administration. Perhaps ambassador to London. "And he talked about how highly the President regarded me." He even mentioned the prospect of a spot "on the national ticket after the expiration of Nixon's present term."[86]

Richardson replied in a dead tone, "Al, there's no way I can move forward with firing Cox. . . ."

Throughout their many conversations during good and bad times in the White House, Haig had always stressed his commitment to the presidency as an institution. As Richardson would recall, "It was very obvious that he was not particularly interested in or loyal to Nixon, as such. . . . But he talked quite a bit about the damage being done to the President by the corrosion of Watergate."[87] In fact, during one discussion, Haig admitted that he thought the president "could well be guilty," or at least that "he needed to be prepared for that possibility which was at least a fifty-fifty possibility."[88]

As they stood together uncomfortably at a constitutional crossroads, Haig now pushed another idea. "Well, you can submit your letter of resignation now," he told Richardson. "And date it today and then release it . . . perhaps a week later."[89] The idea was that Richardson should gauge the public reaction first; he could consider his letter effective retroactively if he still wanted to resign.

"C'mon, Al," was the extent of Elliot's guttural response.[90]

The White House had given Elliot Richardson slack, let him struggle over the Stennis plan, let him become part of the plan, so that he would "feel better about finally carrying out the President's order." The president's lawyers and chief of staff had gambled everything on a single assumption, "that they could fire Cox and Richardson would be enough of a team player and stay aboard." In the end, concluded aide J. T. Smith, "they fundamentally miscalculated."[91]

It was time for him to go in and see the president, Richardson said. Haig's face was gray. He pushed open the door to the Oval Office. Richard Nixon was seated at his desk, wearing a dark suit. "He seemed under more strain," Richardson would remember, "than I had seen him in previous years."[92]

Elliot sat at the president's right side. Richard Nixon began by talking about the dire situation in the Middle East, about the explosion of tensions between the United States and Soviet Union arising from the Yom Kippur War. "And about U.S. forces being placed on alert. How real the potential of nuclear escalation was."[93] The president painted a grim picture of the U.S. position on the international scene as a result of the turmoil of Watergate. There was a "serious possibility" that the Soviets "could very well miscalculate and have the belief that Nixon had lost control over his own administration."[94] Kissinger was in Moscow at this very moment, meeting with Leonid Brezhnev in an effort to shut down the confrontation in the Middle East. "Brezhnev would never understand if I let Cox defy my instruction," the president said icily.[95]

Richardson considered all of this "far-fetched even at the time." Still, this was the commander in chief talking, head of the most sophisticated armed forces in the world. He was speaking from first-hand knowledge that nobody else could possibly possess. Richardson had great respect for Nixon as a global military leader, and for his "geo-strategic capacity."[96] The attorney general was shaken.[97]

The president now switched to the backup position offered by Haig. Elliot should submit his resignation today, if he felt compelled to do it. But he should "have it held."

Richardson shook his head. He could not do this in good conscience. According to the terms of the special prosecutor's charter, he reminded the president, he was only permitted to fire Cox for "extraordinary impropriety." How could he possibly fire Cox "without violating my commitment to his independence?"

The president seemed aggravated. He would later mutter to Len Garment, "That's typical of Elliot. He'd rather cover his ass than protect his country."[98]

To Richardson, the president said, "I'm sorry, Elliot, that you choose to put your purely personal obligations ahead of the national interest."

Richardson felt a surge of blood rushing to his face. He would remember this last exchange of words with brilliant clarity, years after Richard M. Nixon was gone. "Mr. President," he said, keeping his voice as level as possible, "it would seem we have a differing view of the national interest."[99]

That would be their final meeting as president and attorney general.

Archie and Phyllis waited at home for the phone to ring. "It was a matter of settling down and waiting for the axe to fall."[100] Elliot Richardson called late Saturday afternoon and informed Archie, "Here's what's going to happen. I've been asked to dismiss you and resigned. Bill Ruckelshaus has resigned. And Bob Bork . . . is going to dismiss you."[101]

Cox knew Ruckelshaus was the deputy attorney general and next in command after Elliot. Bork was solicitor general, third in the hierarchy. Cox knew him only as an extremely conservative Yale law professor who "drove the liberal Yale law students up the wall by arguing that everything that happened after January 1, 1937 [the beginning of the Supreme Court's liberal New Deal decisions] was outrageous."[102] Cox had met Bork only once at a meeting with the president's counsel. He had been singularly struck by the "vehemence" in Bork's voice when he accused Cox of going outside his charter, in conducting various aspects of the Watergate investigation.[103]

That Bork would be the one who agreed to carry out Nixon's order came as no great surprise. Bork was an outspoken advocate of the theory advanced by his former colleague and best friend at Yale, Alexander Bickel. Even beyond that, the idea of an independent special prosecutor "was all wrong anyway," from Bork's perspective.[104]

Did Cox feel anger at this moment toward the man who would fire him? "I think probably my dominant sense at the time was one of inevitability," Cox would reconstruct. "Passing judgment on Bork was beside the point."[105]

Before Elliot hung up the phone, he lingered long enough to recite to Archie the words that Learned Hand, the man for whom they had both clerked early in their careers, had once inscribed on a photo for him. The phrase was taken from the *Iliad*, written in Greek. Elliot recited the original text before giving a loose translation:

> Now, though numberless fates of death beset us which no mortal
> can escape or avoid, let us go forward together, and either we shall
> give honor to one another, or another to us.[106]

Several minutes after Elliot Richardson's call, Archie's oldest daughter, Sally, who was visiting from Massachusetts for the weekend, walked to the ringing phone and picked it up. "That was the White House for you, Dad," she reported. "I should have told them that you had left town and I didn't know where you are." They all smiled.[107] The White House had asked for an address. They were sending over a messenger to deliver a letter. "And so one settled down for it to happen."[108]

Twenty minutes went by. An hour. Archie's younger brother Max called to tell him how proud he was of his performance during the press conference and to offer support. Archie thanked Max, but told him he had to hurry off the line. "The White House is calling and I'm about to be fired," Archie said.[109] Shortly after he hung up, a "bedraggled" young man rapped on the Coxes' door. The young man apologized; he had driven around for a long time, lost. It was dark and there were a lot of trees in this neighborhood of McLean. "I have a letter from the White House," he said.[110]

Archie thanked the messenger graciously. His only comment years later in discussing the manner of his dismissal was, "Couldn't they have sent a chap with a proper necktie?"[111]

Cox picked up the phone and dictated a one-sentence statement to Jim Doyle, who typed it on his manual typewriter. It would be Cox's final statement as Watergate special prosecutor:

"Whether ours shall continue to be a government of laws and not of men is now for Congress and ultimately the American people."[112]

20

WHITE HOUSE
MYSTERIES

That Saturday night, as Archie and Phyllis retired to bed in Virginia, a specter of government run amok took over the office of the special prosecutor in Washington, D.C.

White House Press Secretary Ronald Ziegler appeared "grim-faced" in the White House press room at 8:30 P.M. He declared that "President Nixon has tonight discharged Archibald Cox, the Special Prosecutor in the Watergate case." He went on to announce, "The office of the Watergate Special Prosecution Force has been abolished as of approximately 8:00 P.M. tonight. Its function to investigate and prosecute those involved in the Watergate matter will be transferred back into the institutional framework of the Department of Justice, where it will be carried out with thoroughness and vigor."[1]

FBI agents immediately sealed off the offices of Richardson and Ruckelshaus in the Justice Department, along with Cox's headquarters at 1425 K Street. This action was taken, the FBI stated, "at the request of the White House."[2] In fact, the order had come directly from Chief of Staff Alexander Haig, with acting Attorney General Robert Bork standing at his side.[3]

John Chancellor, in a special report on NBC television, announced soberly to the nation, "The country tonight is in the midst of what may be the most serious constitutional crisis in its history."[4] UPI teletypes clattered with the news: "8:31. BULLETIN. WASHINGTON (UPI) — PRESIDENT NIXON ACCEPTED ATTORNEY GENERAL ELLIOT L. RICH- ARDSON'S RESIGNATION SATURDAY NIGHT AND FIRED WATERGATE PROSECUTOR ARCHIBALD COX . . ."[5]

Haig was holed up in the White House, trying to control the

situation. An emergency phone call was patched in from Secretary of State Kissinger in Moscow, furious about his imprecise marching orders from President Nixon on the Middle East cease-fire talks. "Will you get off my back?" Haig snapped at the secretary of state. "I have troubles of my own." Kissinger's voice crackled back over the telephone: "What troubles can you possibly have in Washington on a Saturday night?"[6]

Shortly after 9:30 P.M. members of Cox's staff began to gather in a wakelike congregation at the K Street office. The assembly included not just lawyers, but secretaries, photocopy machine operators, messengers, and assistants. Some were "moist-eyed," "drawn together by word of mouth"; they had received phone calls or heard "broadcast reports that they no longer had a job." One staff member was reportedly weeping. Members of the press arrived to record the disjointed scene. At first, the FBI blocked staff members from entering the offices. Eventually agents allowed limited access, but the Special Prosecution Force staffers were told to remove nothing, "not even pictures of their wives and children." All documents were to be sealed in the building. "They're now Justice Department files," Cox's deputy Hank Ruth told a reporter grimly, "and we're told we have no authority over them whatsoever."[7]

Archie's secretary, Florence Campbell, silently cleaned out her exboss's desk, packing his papers into a locked file cabinet. "Common sense told me 'hang in there,' " she recalled that surreal night.[8] Press secretary Jim Doyle, "his composure shattered," tried to leave the offices with a pile of pictures and a copy of the Declaration of Independence that had hung in his office. "It's the Declaration of Independence, Angie," he told FBI Agent Angelo Lano, his voice quivering. "Just stamp it 'VOID' and let me take it home."[9]

James Vorenberg received a call at home that night from Hank Ruth in the special prosecutor's office. "There was a real sense [that] . . . there was sort of a danger of a fascist takeover," said Vorenberg.[10] Peter Kreindler, Cox's executive assistant, had hidden a copy of all key prosecution memos during this week of uncertainty. Now he dialed his sister's home and instructed her to move the papers to another location; he worried about an FBI search. "That was our level of fear," he said.[11] "A lot of things happened to make it look like a government under siege," recalled outgoing Deputy Attorney General William Ruckelshaus, who had resigned along with Richardson.[12] "The problem was fundamentally that Cox was getting too close."[13]

Judge Sirica sat in front of his television that night, watching the FBI seal off the special prosecutor's office. He thought to himself that it looked like a Latin American coup: "What the hell is this crowd doing?" Sirica muttered angrily at the television.[14]

Was the Special Prosecution Force office really in danger of a paramilitary takeover that night, as some of the more dramatic Watergate accounts have suggested? Robert Bork and Alexander Haig would later admit to making the decision to send in FBI agents to seal off the office. They defended that decision, however, as a snap "security" judgment. Having witnessed chaos and confusion at the White House and in the Justice Department, they were concerned about mass resignations and sensitive files walking out the door of the Special Prosecution Force headquarters in the sudden hysteria of the Cox firing. If this happened, "where the hell will we be?"[15]

Reports of a "siege" at the special prosecutor's office that Saturday night are perhaps overblown. Encounters between FBI and staffers showed a confused, almost apologetic attempt by federal agents and Watergate personnel to maintain the status quo in the storm of institutional chaos. At the same time, the sealing off of the Special Prosecution Force offices summarized the White House impulse in general: shut down the Cox machinery, make it go away, and replace it with new machinery back in Nixon's own Justice Department. As President Nixon himself stated in his memoirs, getting rid of Cox "seemed like the only way to rid the administration of the partisan viper we had planted in our bosom."[16] Although Robert Bork, by all accounts, was "deeply upset" by the role he had been thrust into and had no prearranged plan to abolish the special prosecutor's office, he was being swept along in a White House tidal wave.[17] It was only the events of the following day that made the president's plan unachievable.

A "firestorm" of public opinion, as General Haig later termed it, began to erupt once dawn unveiled itself in Washington on Sunday, October 21. The protest was so intense and dramatic that no single participant in the Watergate affair could have ever predicted its fury. The press dubbed the previous night's events "The Saturday Night Massacre." Telegrams piled up at the White House and in the special prosecutor's office, expressing outrage at President Nixon's decision to fire Cox. In Congress, clerks made room for piles of mail and Western Union wires that were then thrown into bundles and organized according to names of states. The bundles portrayed a massive testament of the depleted American trust. A total of 450,000 Mail-grams and telegrams would reach the Capitol and White House in the following days, nearly quadruple the previous record.[18] The *Boston Globe* called on President Nixon to resign. The *Washington Post* headline blared: "Pressure for Impeachment Mounting." "Impeach Nixon" hats were huckstered on the sidewalk in front of the Treasury Building. Demonstrators carried signs in front of the White House: "Honk If Nixon Should Be Impeached." The blare of horns inter-rupted the president's sleep for days.

Clergymen around the country expressed shock during Sunday sermons, with the Reverend Dr. Ernest Campbell of the Riverside Church in New York telling his faithful, "The very future of this Republic is at this moment up for grabs." The little-known governor of Georgia, Jimmy Carter, who had been named the 1974 Campaign Committee chairman for the National Democratic Committee, held a news conference to state that the president "has suffered a mental breakdown."[19] George Bush, head of the Republican National Com-mittee, rushed over to the White House to propose that Elliot Rich-ardson be rehired in the administration as damage control, perhaps as "Ambassador to USSR." Over the long weekend, Congress reacted with "shock and confusion."[20]

Historian Theodore White later wrote that the explosion of public sentiment after the Saturday night firing of Archibald Cox was as fierce and instantaneous as the day Pearl Harbor had been attacked, or the day John F. Kennedy had been assassinated.[21] Even the core of President Nixon's support began to crumble. Edward J. Domaleski, Jr., a former Nixon fan in Atlanta, implored the president: "I feel that your recent actions concerning the dismissal of several persons within your administration, [have] confused a lot of people within the United States. Therefore I respectfully request that you account to the people of the United States for these actions. I am not saying that you have done anything wrong, it is just that many of us are confused. . . ."[22] Chet Long of Berkeley, California, urgently counseled the president that the only way to regain the respect of the American people was for "Attorney General Richardson, his Assistant Mr. Ruckleshouse [*sic*] and Mr. Cox, [to be] restored immediately, and for you to return them to office on prime-time TV." He added that the president should "present the tapes to Mr. Richardson, and he—hand them to Mr. Cox—*on live TV*. . . . Otherwise the Democrats will run this into the ground for 3 years, so PLEASE."[23]

McGuire/The Boston Globe

President Kennedy appointed Professor Archibald Cox of Harvard Law School to serve as Solicitor General in 1961. Reporters visited the Coxes' home in Wayland, Massachusetts, to find out more about the nation's leading Supreme Court lawyer. For the first time since he began teaching, Archie and Phyllis would set up house outside snowy New England.

U. S. Department of Justice Archives

Cox had long enjoyed his friendship with John F. Kennedy (at a May 1963 ceremony, top). Initially skeptical of Robert F. Kennedy as Attorney General, Cox developed a strong respect for the President's younger brother as they worked together. The Kennedy Justice Department had a family atmosphere, as evident at this birthday party for the attorney general (bottom).

the election of President
on B. Johnson (with Cox
Judge Leon Higginbot-
right), Cox returned to
ard in 1965. Expecting
ve calm, he found him-
t the center of campus
sts (below).

Cox family

Preston/The Boston Globe

May 26, 1973, as new Attorney
eral Elliot Richardson looked on,
ze Charles Fahy swore in the spe-
prosecutor for the Watergate case
osite, top). Cox's investigation
rseded the troubled efforts of
ry Petersen and Earl Silbert
osite, bottom left and right) of
Justice Department. Assisted by a
ng staff (exemplified by volunteer
ip Heymann, a fellow Harvard
· professor, below), Cox began to
d criminal cases to try before
ze John J. Sirica (right).

ard Nixon insisted that only ailing
tor John Stennis (opposite, top)
ld hear the White House tapes in
 entirety. For weeks Cox debated
utive privilege with (from left)
te House counsels Charles Alan
ht, J. Fred Buzhardt, and Leonard
nent, and new chief of staff Alex-
r Haig. On Saturday, October 20,
, the President told the attorney
ral to fire Cox; Richardson and his
nd-in-command, William Ruckel-
s, resigned in protest. The recently
inted solicitor general, Robert
, issued the decree dissolving the
ial prosecution office (right). After
'Saturday Night Massacre," time
ted to run out on the Nixon
idency.

For two decades after "retireme[
Cox stayed active as a profes[
lawyer, and public servant. [
1980 he became chairman of C[
mon Cause, a Washington gr[
that lobbied for campaign fina[
reform, among other issues (l[
In 1991 he and Phyllis revie[
the highlights of a long caree[
the opening of a Harvard I[
School exhibit titled, "That Jus[
Be Done: Archibald Cox's Lif[
the Law" (below).

Archie himself spent Sunday quietly. He hiked the goat trail along the banks of the Potomac River between Little Falls and Great Falls. During this solitary trek he ran into Tom McBride from the Special Prosecution Force. Archie said hello, but kept on walking.[24] A spokesman from his office described the former special prosecutor's mood as "somber."[25]

Members of Cox's staff, in the meantime, announced that they "intend[ed] to keep pursuing their investigations involving the Nixon Administration."[26] Jim Doyle held an emergency press briefing on Sunday. "The White House announced we were abolished," he told reporters, "but, you know, if they announce the sky is green and you look up and the sky is blue . . ."[27]

On the Monday holiday, a series of meetings that could only be described as "chaotic" occurred. Robert Bork and Henry Petersen arrived at the Watergate Special Prosecution Force office to meet with Cox's staff amid a sense of "widespread revolt." Staff members were in a "terrible emotional state." They made no effort to hide their anger toward the man who had fired Cox.[28] At 11:30 A.M., Bork pulled the FBI off duty and replaced them with ordinary Justice Department guards, since the "security" of files was no longer at risk.[29] This did little, however, to placate the swarm of unhappy Special Prosecution Force members.

Cox received a call from the Justice Department. He recognized the woman's voice immediately; she had been Elliot Richardson's secretary. Archie said hello, but the secretary sounded distant. She announced, "The acting attorney general wishes to speak to you."[30] An unfamiliar voice then came on the line. Archie did a mental double take. It was not Elliot Richardson but Robert Bork, who began haltingly, "This is a very difficult conversation to begin."

"I couldn't resist it," Cox would later muse. "I just sat there and didn't say a damn thing."

As difficult as it was to say, Bork continued, he would like Cox to drive into Washington and brief him on Watergate. Archie paused. He said that he was sure Henry Ruth and others "could tell him everything there was to know." If *they* concluded that there was something only Cox could fill Bork in on, Bork could "get in touch with me" then. But, of course, there was no such thing. Robert Bork never called again.[31]

Cox would never reach a firm conclusion about his own feelings on Bork's decision to execute the order of President Nixon. Erwin

Griswold, who had served as Nixon's solicitor general before Bork, believed that his successor had made a colossal mistake. If Bork had resigned rather than fire Cox, insisted Griswold, it might have been difficult for the president to find someone to do the deed. "It is not at all clear, after the solicitor general, what the line of succession is in the Department of Justice," explained Griswold. Had Bork followed the lead of Richardson and Ruckelshaus in refusing to carry out the president's order, it might have brought a swifter end to Watergate. "Among other things, it might have been a very sobering thing for Nixon and have calmed him down so he didn't do a lot of fool things after that."[32]

Cox nevertheless reserved judgment on Bork's action. "It was clear that he was in a bind. On the one hand there was the question of principle on which Elliot Richardson and Bill Ruckelshaus acted, on which it was certainly arguable that Robert Bork and anyone else ought to act. On the other hand, it was almost perfectly clear . . . that Nixon would work his will by appointing an acting attorney general who would do what he wanted. And one could reasonably, seriously say to himself if he were in Robert Bork's position, 'What's the use in further tearing down the structure of the department when sooner or later President Nixon's going to do what he wants?' "[33] In fact, this was the same logic that had led Charles Killingsworth, Cox's vice chairman on the Wage Stabilization Board, to remain at his post after Cox had decided to resign in protest back in 1952. Preserving the machinery of government was important, Archie understood.

Richardson and Ruckelshaus would both admit, as they reconstructed the events of that infamous Saturday night, that they had stood behind Bork's decision and did nothing to dissuade him from firing Cox. In fact, they had encouraged him. Ruckelshaus would remember that night in vivid detail. He had been sitting in the attorney general's corner office overlooking Constitution Avenue with Richardson and his top aides, after Elliot's trip to the White House. Elliot Richardson was still shaken from his conversation with the president; his face was still "ashen." Ruckelshaus's secretary knocked and came in. She was unusually serious. Al Haig was on the phone, she said. "He wants to talk to you."[34]

Ruckelshaus walked down the private stairway one floor and picked up his telephone. General Haig got right to the point: he wanted Ruckelshaus "to fire Cox." It was not a gentle request, as Ruckelshaus remembered. Haig put it in terms of what "your commander in chief" was directing, "as if he [the president] was going to bring a tank over there and blow me out of my office if I didn't do it." Ruckelshaus had been thinking about the possibility of such a call all week. He was a lifelong Republican. He understood the concept of loyalty; he had been appointed by President Nixon to serve as acting director of the FBI before being named Richardson's top deputy. As head of the FBI, however, he had seen more than his share of Watergate, and "my assessment, having spent three months running the investigation, was that the president was involved." He had watched Cox carefully over the past months and had seen no shred of impropriety. So Ruckelshaus told Haig, "I really didn't agree with him." Ruckelshaus concluded, "I wouldn't do it."[35]

Haig now attempted to persuade Ruckelshaus that he should accept the alternate plan that had been proposed to Richardson. "Why don't you fire him," Haig said, "and if it bothers you, wait a week and then resign?" Ruckelshaus got the distinct impression that the president was standing beside Haig as he spoke. Ruckelshaus replied, "Well, why don't you wait a week to fire him? Then I won't resign for a week."[36]

At this point Haig became cold. He asked "if Bob Bork was around."[37]

Robert Bork, age forty-six, was pacing the floor in Elliot Richardson's office. He was new to the Justice Department. Although he had been confirmed as solicitor general in early winter, he had waited for classes to end at Yale before moving to Washington, and had held the post for barely four months.[38] Bork had wandered into work that night to polish up a memo regarding the next step to take in the Watergate tapes case. He had taken a break to write a letter to a third-grade class on the importance of the Bill of Rights. Now, out of nowhere, he found himself swept into an ugly constitutional crisis. Bork "looked like somebody had hit him in the face with a bucket of wet shrimp," remembered Ruckelshaus.

"Haig wants to talk to you," Ruckelshaus told Bork. Bork looked up in shock. His hair and beard looked redder than usual. "What are you going to do?" Ruckelshaus asked directly. "Well, I'm not going to carry it out," muttered Bork. "I'm going to resign as well."[39]

Bork was annoyed, "frustrated" by all these events. As Richardson would recall, Bork honestly seemed to believe "that the president was justified in asking the attorney general to fire Cox. And thought that Cox deserved to be fired."[40] But Bork didn't want to be the one to do it. If anything, he would fire Cox and submit his own resignation to the president. Otherwise, Bork worried, his friends would view him as an "apparatchik," someone blindly devoted to his superiors. If the job had to be done, he would make it a "murder-suicide."[41]

Both Richardson and Ruckelshaus actively attempted to talk Bork out of his "fire and resign" plan. If he was going to do the deed, he should do it, follow his conscience, fire Cox, and stay. Bork was in a different moral position than they were, they reasoned it out. First, he had made no pledge to the Senate not to fire Cox. He had been nominated and confirmed before Watergate had become a major issue. Second, he held a different set of convictions about the propriety of the president's actions. "We were telling him that given his view on the matter," Richardson would acknowledge, "he should recognize it as being in the interest of the department and do it. I think it's fair to say, yes. We were trying to persuade him to do it."[42]

Bork's "mind was in a whirl." He was new to Watergate. "I really hadn't thought of the God damn thing," he recalled. As he paced, he knew in his gut that "all hell was going to break loose." He wondered if he would survive, professionally, if he committed this act. "Good Christ," he muttered to himself. "It is a crisis."[43]

Bork felt that the president's lawyers were partly to blame for advising Nixon that Cox was going to resign if pushed to the wall. Said Bork, "Nobody asked the question 'what happens if Cox refuses the order?' " But now that the special prosecutor had defied the president, Bork felt that Nixon had no option but to "follow it through," and terminate Cox. It was "better to do it and stop the bleeding right now," was the gist of his fast-moving conversation with Elliot Richardson. Who was he, Robert H. Bork, a Yale professor new to Washington, to second-guess the White House? As a legal matter, how could anyone in the executive branch, including Cox, be insulated from the will of the president, the chief executive? "I didn't think it was a function of a subordinate officer to go around bringing down presidents," he said, piecing together his thoughts. "You know, we have constitutional processes for that."[44]

Bork walked down the corridor to the solicitor general's office. Lights were still ablaze where he had been working on his memo about the Watergate tapes appeal. He called his wife, Claire. "I think I have to fire Archibald Cox," he blurted out. "If you have something to say, say it now." Before his wife had a chance to formulate a response, a White House car arrived to pick Bork up.[45]

Ruckelshaus analyzed the odd decision made in Elliot Richardson's office that night: "I think in listening to what Bork was saying he believed that aside from whether the President was right or not the President had the power to [fire Cox]. And that it really wasn't his role to question the exercise of that power, but rather to carry out the President's wishes." Ruckelshaus added, "I think Bork was sincere."[46]

"I don't think I ever resolved it in my mind," Cox said. "Richardson and Ruckelshaus came out of it looking like and being men with principle. Giving up their office rather than violate a principle and rather than aid in the President's violation of the old precept about 'government under law.' Robert Bork comes out, at best, looking pretty pragmatic."[47]

Bork himself would later insist, both in testimony before the Senate Judiciary Committee and in personal interviews, that he fully intended to establish a new independent special prosecutor's office from the moment he fired Cox. President Nixon, sitting alone in the Oval Office with the lights dim that Saturday, had said to Bork, "I want a prosecution, not a persecution." This was a Kennedy investigation, in the president's mind; Cox needed to be purged so that a truly fair-minded prosecutor could be installed.[48]

Bork would later ruminate that the only serious mistake he made in carrying out the president's order was failing to announce immediately that the special prosecutor's office would remain intact. "What I should have done was walk out and hold a press conference," Bork said, "and explain that while Cox was gone, the Special Prosecution Force was still in effect. I think people thought there was going to be a general purge—which there wasn't going to be."[49]

Cox, however, would remain puzzled when it came to Bork's true intentions: "If that was his aim, he certainly didn't let any of it be known by the Watergate Special Prosecution Force."[50]

Part of the confused signals undoubtedly flowed from the fact that Robert Bork's ill-defined plans and the White House's plans were not the same. Len Garment, who paced the floors of the Oval Office that night with the president, saw that his boss was feeling "up and strong": "I think he felt he was going to close up the damn office."[51] The official statement issued by the White House clearly indicated that the Special Prosecution Force had been "abolished." Department Order No. 546-73, which Robert Bork signed as acting attorney general on October 23, 1973, just three days after the Saturday Night Massacre, was entitled "Abolishment of Office of Watergate Special

Prosecution Force." The first paragraph of that order stated plainly: "This order abolishes the Office of Watergate Special Prosecution Force." The order was made retroactive, effective October 21.[52]

In defense of Bork's position, however, his October 24 press release and press conference made clear that the Special Prosecution Force would not vanish entirely, but return to the Criminal Division of the Justice Department under Henry Petersen.[53] In many ways, as Bork himself would explain, it was simply a "paper move"; there was no longer a special prosecutor to which the staff could be attached.[54] Yet Robert Bork, new to the department, did not understand all that the special prosecutor's office understood about such a "paper move." In the minds of Cox's already horrified staff, a return of the Special Prosecution Force to Assistant Attorney General Henry Petersen amounted to the death knell.

Robert Bork would later admit that he "didn't know anyone was accusing [Petersen] of leaking or creating problems. No."[55] The special prosecutors, on the other hand, were acutely aware that placing Henry Petersen back in charge of the Watergate investigation meant a return to the Criminal Division, where massive leaks had sprouted before Cox's appointment, and where there had been regular contacts with the White House. Even worse, the Special Prosecution Force now had evidence of a channel of information from Petersen to the White House more extensive than Earl Silbert and his team had initially guessed:[56]

- Beginning on April 15, 1973, when then Attorney General Richard Kleindienst removed himself from the Watergate investigation because of mounting conflicts, Henry Petersen and President Nixon had engaged in a "series of daily conversations" about the Watergate case, in which Petersen spelled out what the federal prosecutors knew. In the next two weeks, Petersen and the president talked "at least daily," usually more often.

- During their frequent meetings, the president told Petersen that he had become "my adviser" on Watergate, and was "special counsel to the president." The president assured Petersen that information he provided about "developments" in the grand jury "will not be passed on."

- On April 16, the president and Petersen held a lengthy meeting in which Petersen reviewed with the president what he and the grand jury knew about the involvement of a wide array of actors—including Haldeman, Ehrlichman, and Dean—in the Watergate matter.

- The next day, after learning that Petersen might be moving to grant Dean immunity, the president invited Petersen to the Oval Office to help him draft a public statement—delivered that afternoon—that would foreclose government prosecutors from granting immunity to top White House aides. The president was particularly adamant that John Dean not receive immunity.

- On April 18, Petersen told the president that he had learned from John Dean about a possible break-in at the office of Daniel Ellsberg's psychiatrist in Los Angeles in 1971. The president replied, "Damn it, I know about that, and you stay the hell out of it; that's a national security matter and none of your business. You stick to Watergate."

- At one point in the spring, the president considered setting up a new grand jury and "get[ting] Petersen as special prosecutor." The president envisioned that White House aides would be paraded before the new grand jury, testify "I don't remember, I don't recall," and that would be the end of Watergate.

- On April 27, the president directed Petersen to call Silbert's prosecutors and demand to know if any of their conversations with Dean or others "implicate the President." The president ended, "Now dammit, I want to know . . ."[57]

Not only was Cox's organization horrified by the prospect of an investigation returned under Henry Petersen, but John Dean, the government's chief witness and Petersen's friend, was equally alarmed. "It wasn't the condition on which I had agreed to plead," Dean stated emphatically. "To me it was a huge problem. They would have put boundaries on this. There was no question the cover-up was still going on. There was just a new round of players."[58]

Oddly enough, Henry Petersen seemed to understand his damnable predicament. Behind closed doors, he wanted nothing to do with the Watergate prosecution after Cox was fired. In a private conversation with J. T. Smith, while Smith was packing up boxes in the attorney general's office after Richardson's resignation, Petersen cursed President Nixon's decision to throw Watergate back onto his shoulders.

"He was in extreme distress," recalled Smith. "Practically in tears. He could be emotive. I remember him saying, 'The bastards, the bastards.' " The message was clear: Petersen did not want to be dragged back into this snake pit.[59] He even told Robert Bork, shortly after Cox's firing, that he had met with the president several times and found him "dishonest." "It was like three-card monte," Petersen said of the president's approach to resolving Watergate problems.[60]

Nor was the president particularly complimentary of Petersen in private. When Cox was fired, the president asked Bork, "Who will it go back to?" Bork replied, "Henry Petersen." The president "made a face" and told Bork, "You know he's not too bright."[61]

Yet in public, Petersen remained the true-blue institutionalist, backing the president despite strong signals that he (Petersen) had been duped. After the Saturday Night Massacre, Petersen announced that he had no intention of keeping the Special Prosecution Force alive as an autonomous body. He dismissed the idea of hiring another special prosecutor to fill Cox's shoes, tossing "cold water on the idea."[62] Explained Smith, "He thought he was responding to the authority for whom he worked."[63]

Cox's deputy Henry Ruth would later describe Henry Petersen as a man plagued by conflicting loyalties. He was "a very devout Roman Catholic" who had "grown up with authority and who believed in authority, and believed in the presidency of the United States—and loved this president."After Cox's firing, Petersen seemed to know that he had not "pushed his suspicions far enough." The following week Petersen worked closely with the Special Prosecution Force and even signed a letter demanding more papers and tapes from the White House. He carried a resignation letter in his pocket, prepared to quit if the president did not comply with the court of appeals order.[64] But he still resisted turning over the reins of the investigation to anyone else. When it came to Richard M. Nixon, Petersen was trying mightily to do the right thing, but he had a "blind spot."[65]

Robert Bork did not fully grasp the significance of his decision to transfer the Watergate investigation back into the Criminal Division during those chaotic October days. It was, however, more than Bork's failure to hold a press conference that created a nightmare for the Special Prosecution Force. Whether he understood it or not, Robert Bork had embarked on a path that most of those inside the Special Prosecutor's Office feared would effectively kill the existing cover-up investigation. As Cox would later summarize it, a Special Prosecution

Force reconstituted under Petersen, as initially announced by the White House and sealed by the signature of Robert Bork on Order No. 546–73, "would have a very hard time maintaining its independence."[66]

All the debate about Robert Bork's original intention soon became moot, however. "The public reaction just blew the top off the whole thing," explained Len Garment.[67]

As the president attempted to recover from an intense pounding of public disapproval, the press reported that "Archie's Army" in the Special Prosecution Force remained "intact and undeterred." If anything, the "pace has quickened" with a sort of commitment to "finish the job for Archie."[68] Cox returned to K Street long enough to give a brief farewell speech to his staff. Leaning against a white post outside his old office, hands in pocket, bow tie knotted crisply, he ended with a quiet "God bless you."[69] Some clapped, some cried. A few women rushed up to kiss the sixty-one-year-old Cox on his gray crew cut.

Archibald Cox now stood as a symbol, a collective expression of something deep within the nation, binding it together. Harvard's President Derek Bok led a spontaneous morning prayer session at the Appleton Chapel in Harvard Yard, announcing from the pulpit that Cox's actions exemplified "the truth embedded in Aristotle's *Ethics*: if you would understand virtue, observe the conduct of virtuous men."[70] Archie's eighty-one-year-old mother minced no words in commenting on the events of that long October weekend. "I am glad," Fanny Cox told newsmen from her home in Windsor, "that I am not Richard Nixon's mother."[71]

Elliot Richardson would look upon the rubble left by the Saturday Night Massacre with mixed emotions. "From my point of view," he said, "it was my biggest failure. I always took a certain amount of pride in heading off foreseeable trouble. I still do." As a "lawyer for the situation," Richardson was haunted by the belief that "it shouldn't have happened."[72]

At the same time, years of reflection would lead Richardson to conclude that "if it hadn't happened this way, it would have happened anyway." From the first day at Camp David when he had looked President Nixon in the eye and accepted the job as attorney general, Richardson had operated based upon the premise that the president and his closest aides were "seriously seeking a compromise."[73] He would later conclude that this was not the case; he had been "set up."[74]

As Richardson would later piece the facts together: "I think the only way of accounting for the sequence of events was on the premise that they were looking for some formula that I would support that Cox would reject, that would precipitate the firing of Cox, which I would then defend." Richardson would reach the unpleasant conclusion that "the name of the game was to get rid of Cox but to do it in some way that I would assume responsibility for."[75]

Richardson's analysis of the "formula" that led to Cox's firing, in hindsight, seems accurate. The notes of Len Garment's secretary in the White House reveal that a plan to fire Cox was in the works well before his refusal to obey the president's order. Charles Alan Wright canceled a scheduled trip to Kansas City on Friday, October 19, because "something [was] obviously happening." The entry of Len Garment's secretary for that day reads: "On either Thursday afternoon or Friday morning saw paper on CAW's [Wright's] desk . . . referred to dismissal of Cox, abolishing Special Prosecutor's office . . . whose papers it was don't know . . . it was I believe destroyed by CAW after Sat. Night Massacre. . . ."[76] The plan to fire Cox was not nearly as spontaneous as President Nixon would portray it to the American public on that Saturday night. It had been carefully calculated, in advance, to keep Elliot Richardson on board.

One critical piece of the president's strategy was related to the Stennis compromise, a largely forgotten aspect of the White House's plan to save itself from Watergate. How did President Nixon and his closest advisers, in selecting Senator John Stennis as the sole individual who would listen to and "verify" the accuracy of the tapes, intend to salvage the Nixon presidency? Why did they consider the Stennis plan critical enough that it was worth rejecting Cox's own compromise proposal, worth risking the resignation of a highly respected attorney general, and worth forcing a showdown on the eve of their final appeal to the Supreme Court?

Did President Nixon strike a "deal" with John Stennis, by which the senator would intentionally overlook damaging portions of the president's conversations and bury the secrets of the Watergate tapes forever? On Stennis's first overnight leave from the hospital, on April 27, the two men had flown together on Air Force One to Meridian, Mississippi, for the dedication of the Stennis Naval Technical Center and the celebration of "John Stennis Day." They had spoken privately in the president's airborne office, while H. R. Haldeman and John Ehrlichman sat quietly in the rear cabin. When the two political leaders arrived in Stennis's home state, they had "heaped praise on each other." Had the president exacted some sort of promise from Stennis en route?[77]

Extremely unlikely. Stennis represented integrity incarnate. He was the first and most ardent chairman of the Senate Ethics Committee. He bristled even when "white lies" were told. Those who knew the senator considered it impossible that he would intentionally skew the facts, president or not.

Did President Nixon count on Stennis's hearing problem to make the senator miss out on damaging portions of the tapes? *Time* magazine pictured a thin Senator Stennis with one hand cupped over his ear, as if straining to hear. "Stennis Listens to a Question— Technical Help Needed?" the caption read.[78] The magazine's speculation was clear: Senator Stennis's auditory problems were so acute that he would have trouble hearing *anything*. But this worry is most likely apocryphal. Those who worked daily with Stennis, as well as his treating physician, saw no such handicap in 1973. Stennis did not wear a hearing aid until years later. Even then, he had few problems except when in a crowded room. R. James Woolsey, general counsel to the Senate Armed Services Committee and later director of the Central Intelligence Agency, dismissed the whole theory as bunk.[79]

Still, Senator Stennis had other health problems that were far from imagined. When the senator was shot by robbers at point-blank range in front of his Washington home on January 30, 1973, he sustained serious injuries.[80] One bullet traveled through his stomach twice, struck his pancreas, pierced his intestines, then lodged itself in his back.[81] "His chance of surviving that injury was less than five percent," said his surgeon, Dr. Robert Muir, chief of general surgery at Walter Reed Army Medical Center.[82] Senator Stennis did survive, but only after an ileostomy to open the lower bowel that was a "disaster," and a lengthy stint on "death's doorstep." One of his first visitors in the hospital was President Richard M. Nixon, who announced, "I think he's going to make it. . . . Senator Stennis has got that will to live in spades."[83] For six months, other than the trip to Mississippi on April 27 and a few short excursions, the seventy-one-year-old Stennis remained confined to his hospital bed.[84] He did not return to his Senate office until August 7, and then only for "limited duty." He continued to receive outpatient treatment at the hospital.[85] Not until September 5 did Stennis resume his seat in the Senate chamber, amid a standing ovation from emotional colleagues.[86]

In October 1973, when White House lawyers first publicly unveiled the Stennis plan, the senator had been back to work for barely a month. Stennis's face was thin, and aides whispered that he "never got his jowls back." Although the extent of Stennis's limitations was kept hidden from the public, the president and his advisers understood the seriousness of his condition. Dr. Muir, who had become Stennis's personal physician, would remember an early discussion of the Stennis plan even before October. There was talk of Senator Stennis getting a VIP suite in the hospital where he and someone from the White House would listen to tapes. Said Muir, "I told him that he should not do that. It was a lose-lose. He was not physically capable of listening to the tapes."

When the idea resurfaced with more urgency in late October, Dr. Muir did his best to dissuade Stennis. "He was sharp, in terms of mentally sharp, . . . " said Muir. "But he wasn't up to any big decision-making when they asked." In fact, although these details were not available for public consumption, Stennis was taking "fairly large doses of codeine for short bowel syndrome [to slow down the bowel]." When the White House approached him in mid-October about the Stennis plan, the senator was taking a prescription of "six to eight to ten half-grain codeine tablets" per day. "As a practical matter, he may not have been impaired," said Muir. "But he knew it would give the appearance of impairment. . . . He implied he didn't want to do it."[87]

The White House understood what listening to the tapes meant. The recordings were lengthy, maddeningly unclear; they required perfect attention even from the strongest listener. Speakers talked over each other. Voices were garbled and covered with echoes. At times, the president's voice was barely audible. Single sentences would have to be rewound and replayed dozens of times. White House lawyer Fred Buzhardt, one of the few people whom Nixon trusted to listen to the tapes, declared that he could only endure an hour at a time of deciphering them before he had to quit from exhaustion.[88]

The lawyers in Cox's operation were intensely aware of the hazards of the Stennis plan. Any lawyer or stenographer who had dealt with transcribed tapes understood that an elderly man on medication recovering from gunshot wounds and an ileostomy would not have the physical endurance to nitpick through hours of garbled conversations.[89] Even Robert Bork would be incredulous when it came to the proposed Stennis compromise: "He'd still be listening to those tapes." Bork shook his head.[90]

Documents now make clear that the White House had directly planned to capitalize on Senator Stennis's frailties, in more than one way. Stennis had intended to have his administrative assistant and closest adviser, attorney William "Eph" Cresswell, listen to the tapes alongside him.[91] Elliot Richardson's notes, however, reveal that the White House had different plans. On October 15, Alexander Haig explained the White House agenda for Stennis: "Take him up to Camp David. Set up tapes . . . Have Fred there. Fred will prepare report for him." Richardson's notes went on: "Stennis says wants someone he knows—will accept Buzhardt." As to the format, it would not be a verbatim transcript, but a third-party summary that would be verified by Stennis: "Report in 3rd person. No quotation marks . . ." "Buzhardt will prepare that before he goes up. Have it in front of him." Stennis would then listen to the tapes with Buzhardt and provide an "ex post facto certification."[92]

Fred Buzhardt was the logical man to sit alongside the senator. Elliot Richardson's staff often joked that "Fred's your man if you want a body buried six feet under and want it to look like no spade of earth had been moved." Buzhardt was an adept political animal and a seasoned Washington operator. He was a skilled Southern lawyer, who would "negotiate and litigate by trying to con the opposition rather than shout him down."[93] "He had a lot of moves," said one Richardson aide.[94]

When the Camp David plan was unveiled by the White House on October 16, notes reveal that Elliot Richardson raised an immediate concern: The entire procedure, by which Stennis and Buzhardt would be isolated together at the presidential retreat, would smack of a setup. Haig told the attorney general not to worry. "We're dealing with a judge," Haig insisted, referring to Stennis's early stint as a Mississippi circuit court judge. Haig quipped that Stennis was "no Boy Scout. He's willing to do it. . . ."[95]

It is virtually certain that Senator Stennis himself had no inkling of what the White House had in store for him. Stennis reacted with surprise and confusion to the Saturday Night Massacre. He was never told that his work product would be offered to Judge Sirica. He believed that he would be authenticating the transcripts solely for use by the Senate Watergate Committee: "There was never any mention about the court," he insisted. "I wouldn't have done it if there was. No, no, no. I was once a judge and the courts can ask for what they want."[96] But the White House had mapped out its own strategem; the "verified summaries" would go to both the Senate and Judge Sirica, and Watergate would be over forever. "There were a lot of fastballs and sliders," one White House lawyer put it.[97]

Even if Senator Stennis doggedly listened to the tapes and somehow discovered a smoking gun, the White House still had room to maneuver. President Nixon knew that Stennis had a strong record of supporting the president, especially when it came to national security matters and the president's power as commander in chief.[98] It was part of Stennis's personal creed not to "second-guess" a president on foreign policy or military matters.[99] Stennis had stated as much in March 1972, in debate over the War Powers Act: "I lean that way. That is my 'theory of government.' "[100] He was one of only two senators whom the president had told about the secret bombing of Cambodia in March 1969; Stennis had kept the silence.[101]

The president also knew that Senator Stennis had an extremely broad view of executive privilege and "separation of powers" that would work strongly to the president's advantage. Back in 1962, when Stennis served as head of a Senate subcommittee investigating charges that the Kennedy administration had restricted military leaders in their efforts to speak out against communism, Stennis had immediately backed off when President Kennedy wrote a letter invoking executive privilege. The president had made clear that the disclosure of certain information to the subcommittee would be "contrary to the public interest."

"I am convinced this executive plea applies," Stennis had declared, noting that the assurance of the president of the United States was good enough for him.[102] President Nixon surely knew about Stennis's 1962 ruling as he sat in the Oval Office in October 1973. In fact, he cited it at length in a letter to the House Judiciary Committee, not long after the Stennis compromise fizzled out.[103]

President Nixon was taking a calculated gamble on Senator Stennis. There was a war going on in the Middle East. The White House had floated serious "national security concerns" from the start, in chasing the Justice Department off the trail of Watergate. If Fred Buzhardt or the president himself told Stennis that certain portions of the tapes had been deleted from the third-person summaries because they involved "national security" matters that might weaken the U.S. position in the Middle East, how could the Senator question such a portentous warning? If a single respected lawmaker could be trusted to sit alone in a room at Camp David and give every benefit of the doubt to the president, it was Senator John Stennis.

Said one Cox aide, who went through the "tedious and painstaking job" of listening to the tapes: "I can tell you unequivocally that Richard Nixon would have been successful with the Stennis compromise."[104]

Elliot Richardson was undoubtedly correct. The White House had devised a complex but fairly watertight plan to get rid of Cox, keep Richardson on board, entrust the tapes to Stennis alone, and provide the senator with a watered-down summary that he would quickly "verify" and turn over to Judge Sirica as substitute evidence in place of the tapes themselves. To the extent that the White House had carried Richardson along as a loyal participant until that final Saturday in October, it is fair to say that he was "set up."

Archibald Cox would still look with admiration at the role Elliot Richardson played during those difficult months. In a reunion twenty years after the Saturday Night Massacre, Cox spoke with emotion at a candlelit table while seated next to Richardson. The former special prosecutor wondered "how different things might have been if someone other than Elliot Richardson was attorney general, someone whom I could not deal with on an absolute level of trust. I'm not sure things would have worked out the same at all."[105]

The precise details of the White House strategy during those final months leading up to Cox's firing are now buried with key actors. However, one fact remains absolutely certain: The Saturday Night Massacre was the single event in his long and controversial political life from which Richard M. Nixon, president of the most powerful nation in the world, would never recover.[106]

21

THE
WATERGATE
CLEANUP

As he prepared to leave Washington, Archie found particular solace in the outpouring of support from ordinary citizens across the United States and beyond. A dentist from Jamestown, North Dakota, posted a letter dated October 20:

> Dear Mr. Cox,
>
> God bless you and keep you, sir.[1]

A carefully printed note from a young admirer read:

> Dear Mr. Cox,
>
> I am a youth of eight years old. My name is Jonathan Soroff. I wrote you this letter to tell you I use to have a hamster named after you. He died, but I will get a new one and call him Archibald Cox III.[2]

A French citizen wrote in distress: "Porquoi NIXON, doit s'en aller?"[3] Fans sent sheet music with original lyrics about Watergate.[4] Schoolchildren composed class reports about the former special prosecutor.[5] "TRB" in *The New Republic* wrote of Archie: "Put him in knee britches and he would have done well among those Forefathers in Philadelphia, in 1787. He brought a bit of nobility to Washington."[6] *Newsweek* pictured Cox on the cover, wearing a neatly knotted bow tie. *Time* ran portraits of the president and the special prosecutor facing each other with the ominous caption "Nixon on the Brink."[7] Admirers sent bow ties in boxes from as far away as Nigeria; Cox scrupulously shipped them back with thanks, if there was a return address.[8] Photographs in papers around the world captured Archie busily chopping wood at his farm in South Brooksville, Maine, with Phyllis's tractor parked behind him.[9]

Five days after the Saturday Night Massacre, Archie was asked to deliver the 1974 commencement address at Stanford University, where Phyllis's grandfather Nathan Abbott had served as the first dean of the law school. "The annual selection of the Commencement speaker is the singular tribute accorded to distinguished individuals," wrote President Richard W. Lyman in extending the invitation.[10]

Publisher Alfred A. Knopf penned a succinct note from New York: "Three cheers for Harvard and, this time at least, to hell with Yale!"[11] The Yale band, playing at halftime during a game against Cornell, formed an "H" on the field to honor the victims of the Saturday night purge.[12]

A sixth-grade girl from Longmeadow, Massachusetts, sent a card with an "apology for what Mr. Nixon did to you. I know I do some things I am not supposed to but I don't get kicked out of my house or get suspended."[13]

The most special note of all, however, came from Windsor. The envelope was marked with a return address "Not Nixon's Mother!"

> Darling Bill—
>
> All these past days I've been trying to put in words how I feel about you. And about our country. To my mind—also my heart—you've been just perfect—noble in your courage and noble in your complete lack of vindictiveness, a quality you certainly didn't inherit from me—as my blood pressure rises every time I think of Nixon and I would just love to give him a piece of my mind. Bill, there's no sense in giving in to that. People keep asking me if I'm not proud of you, and of course I am, and always have been, and will be proud of you not only because you're my son—also because, as that woman reporter said, you're a great American. This is banality, but I keep thinking of Kipling's 'If,' and I think it says almost all I feel.
>
> Billy dear, I do love you so—Phyllis is great . . . love to her always.
>
> Mamma

Within three days of the Saturday Night Massacre, the president's lawyers did an about-face on the tapes. On Tuesday, October 23, Charles Alan Wright appeared on the *Today Show* at 7:30 A.M. to vigorously defend the Stennis plan. Afterward he attended a brief White House meeting, walked into the federal courthouse at 2:00 looking subdued, gulped down several cups of water, and stood uneasily.[14] "This President does not defy the law," Wright quietly told a bespectacled Judge Sirica, "and he has authorized me to say he will comply in full with the orders of the court."[15]

Immediately upon returning from the long weekend, House members introduced twenty-two separate bills calling for the impeachment of the president or investigation into impeachment proceedings. Another avalanche of bills was introduced to create a new special prosecutor's office that would be wholly independent of the executive branch.[16] Republican Senator Barry M. Goldwater of Arizona, one of President Nixon's staunchest supporters throughout Watergate, declared that President Nixon's credibility "has reached an all-time low from which he may not be able to recover."[17] *The Economist* referred to Richard M. Nixon as "A Shrunken President."[18]

Even in his field of perceived strength, foreign affairs, the president's grasp had slackened. When the nation awakened on October 25 to discover that President Nixon had placed the U.S. military on "worldwide nuclear alert" because of purported cease-fire violations in the Middle East, the public reaction was widespread skepticism. Although the president held an urgent press conference and described the averted superpower collision as "the most difficult crisis we had since the Cuban missile crisis in 1962," there were few takers. "Hardly anyone believed the crisis was real," wrote one commentator.[19] Some would later contend that Henry Kissinger had made the decision to call a worldwide alert unilaterally, because the president had been of no help that night. Several Kissinger aides said that President Nixon had been drinking.[20]

The House Judiciary Committee geared up for impeachment proceedings for the first time in 105 years.[21] At a news conference on October 26, the president attempted a preemptive strike by promising to appoint his own new special prosecutor, but he blurted out that he had no intention of turning over any further documents or tape recordings to this prosecutor. "The tougher it gets, the cooler I get," President Nixon announced, perspiring noticeably.[22]

When White House lawyers were forced to inform Judge Sirica on November 1 that two of the Watergate tapes subpoenaed by Cox simply "don't exist," the frenzy reached a peak.[23] Fighting for his life, the president agreed to the appointment of a new special prosecutor,

Texas lawyer Leon Jaworski, who could not be fired without the approval of a special group of Congressional leaders. Jaworski had supported Nixon's re-election and seemed like a safe bet.[24] But there was no stopping the momentum. Jaworski would ironically possess even greater independence and power than Cox ever had.[25]

Archie, in the meantime, testified for several days in front of the Senate Judiciary Committee regarding the need for special prosecutor legislation, before packing up his boxes and preparing for the welcome sight of Interstate 95 North.[26]

Archie and Phyllis had rented out their home in Wayland; they could not return there. It was midsemester, there was no job at Harvard at the moment. So they allowed themselves a little impulse: they planned to gas up the blue pickup and drive to their farm in South Brooksville, Maine. In their "wistful" moments they had always talked about staying there for the winter. They would enjoy quiet snowfalls next to the ocean, surrounded by spruce trees and sleeping lupines.

Just as Archie sealed the final cartons with tape, ready for the swift exodus to Maine, he came to the horrible conclusion that he had thrown away everything that he had ever accomplished during his tenure as Watergate special prosecutor.

He went directly to the Senate Judiciary Committee with a terrible admission: he had given away confidential information about the ITT investigation to two Democratic senators. He had sat down with Senators Ted Kennedy and Phil Hart, both friends, both members of the Judiciary Committee, during a final "debriefing" session. In this wide-ranging discussion he had mentioned that former Attorney General Richard G. Kleindienst's lawyer had told him months earlier, in "strict confidence," that "President Nixon had called Kleindienst and ordered him to settle the ITT affair."[27] Specifically, Nixon's language was, "Listen, you son of a bitch, don't you understand the English language? Don't appeal that case, and that's all there is to it."[28] Cox, believing this information relevant to the Senate inquiry, had passed it along to Kennedy and Hart as part of his final Watergate "wrap-up." Now it was all over the newspapers.

Cox was devastated. "Was I responsible for this leak? I had been struggling all summer to prevent leaks, to be discreet myself," Cox recalled. "Here I suspect a lot of emotional tension had piled up. And it had all sort of come to 'Oh my God, now here at the very end, I've blown it.' "[29]

Archie had been riding high on public support and trust. Now he had betrayed it. He felt disgraced. Cox sought out Senator James O. Eastland, chairman of the Judiciary Committee, and told him the only thing to do "was to have it all out in public." Eastland arranged to have Cox testify before the Judiciary Committee so that he could admit (with great emotion) that he was guilty of an "inexcusable" breach of confidence as the White House had charged.[30] Cox told the committee, "It's quite clear that I broke Kleindienst's confidence. . . . I feel very badly this morning." He confessed that in meeting with Senators Kennedy and Hart after he was fired, "I babbled on a little thoughtlessly. If I were sophisticated, perhaps I wouldn't have. But this has been a rough time and you like to be with your friends."[31]

Republican Senator Strom Thurmond pounced on Cox and charged that his leak violated federal law, as well as various codes of legal ethics. Democratic Senator Birch Bayh shot back that Thurmond should stop browbeating Cox. His jowls shaking, Thurmond retorted that Bayh had "gone below a snake and had no right to be a senator." Archie watched quietly. He left the hearing demolished.

The White House viewed Cox's admission as "political manna from heaven." White House spokesman Gerald Warren pointed to the Kleindienst indiscretion as proof positive that Cox had been running a "partisan" investigation for months.[32] Newsweek showed a parting photo of Cox, captioned "A hint of . . . tarnish for Mr. Clean."[33] Cox's own deputy, Henry Ruth, made clear that he "didn't appreciate" Archie's blunder. "This was a case where we couldn't make a single mistake."[34] Archie felt he had "behaved without honor." When he surrendered his keys for the little cottage in McLean, he gave it a long, tragic look beneath his thick eyebrows. "I've ruined everything, haven't I?" were his parting words to Phil Heymann.[35]

Cox later learned "for certain" that his conversation with Senators Hart and Kennedy was not the source of the leak to the newspapers. Two different contacts within the New York Times confirmed that someone else—not the Judiciary Committee or Cox—had purveyed the information.[36] Cox was interviewed briefly by the Massachusetts Bar Council on charges of "professional ethics" violations, but the matter was quickly dropped. The Massachusetts ethics investigators took the opportunity to ask Cox if he would serve as their special counsel, a minor boost to his damaged self-respect.[37] Cox was hardly interested in a new job; he wanted to wash his hands of this Watergate debacle.

On November 15, Federal Judge Gerhard A. Gesell in Washington declared that Cox's firing "was in clear violation of an existing Justice Department regulation having the force of law and was therefore illegal."[38] This ruling came in response to a lawsuit filed by consumer advocate Ralph Nader, seeking to nullify Bork's dismissal of the special prosecutor. Cox was "annoyed" by the Nader litigation and disavowed any connection with it. He refused to seek any remedy in connection with Judge Gesell's ruling, illegal conduct or not. "The issue wasn't one of whether Cox has a job or not," he said. "What happened to Cox was of no importance. The issue was whether the president of the United States was going to be subject to the law as declared by the courts of the land. And I thought Ralph Nader was just distracting attention from the real issue."[39]

Archie had plenty of time on his hands after his dismissal. His sister Molly saw "Bill" in Windsor quite a bit, grappling with conflicting emotions. He was "quite angry at being fired," she admitted. He planned to return to Harvard, but it was already November and he had not been worked into the winter teaching schedule. Although he exhibited no outward "jealousy" toward Leon Jaworski, Molly perceived confusion and turmoil on the inside. "I got the feeling he still wished he was running the show instead of Jaworski, yes," she said.[40]

Reporters arrived in lost detachments, wondering what an ex–special prosecutor did in seclusion. In the cold November winds, they "slapped their hands to restore circulation to frigid fingers." Archie stood in front of his barn in South Brooksville, Maine, "decked out in downeast Maine garb of blue denims and orange hunting jacket," searching for a silver lining in the events that had displaced him as special prosecutor. At least it had confirmed the "dedication" of the American people, he told reporters. It had reaffirmed "the extent of their commitment to the proposition that no man is above the law," and their "determination and ability to make that commitment plain to anyone."[41]

As December shook at the Cox farmhouse, the local *Ellsworth American* reported that Archie was making the most of his "unemployment" in South Brooksville. In fact, he was making excellent use of the time:

> He has been working with a chain saw cutting wood for the stove in the living room and for the wood stove in the kitchen of the farm house. And he has been cutting alders with a brush hog. He has piled some baled hay around the foundation of the house [in approved

Maine fashion]. And he has readied the barn and outbuildings for the
coming snowstorms.[42]

The country braced itself for its own bleak season. In Judge Sirica's
courtroom it was revealed that an 18½-minute gap had obliterated a
critical portion of a June 20 conversation between Nixon and chief of
staff H. R. Haldeman, just three days after the Watergate break-in.
Haldeman's notes indicated that the meeting had included a long
discussion of Watergate.[43] A team of experts determined that the gap
was caused by at least five separate erasures, performed manually.[44]
The *Washington Post* announced: "GLOOM GRIPS REPUBLICAN SENA-
TORS." Senator James B. Pearson of Kansas blurted out, "I'm shocked.
I'm surprised—I thought all the surprises were out of me."[45] Hanoi
radio reported that President Nixon was "out of his senses."[46]

Even more disturbing than the missing tapes and gaps were the
tapes the president *did* produce. Richard Ben-Veniste was one of
the first lawyers on the Special Prosecution Force team to listen to the
subpoenaed tapes. "I was dumbfounded," he recalled.[47] He replayed
the March 21, 1973, recording of a 10:12 meeting in the Oval Office on
the Sony 800B reel-to-reel several times, to make sure he was hearing it
correctly. It was a meeting of Nixon, Dean, and Haldeman, which
included passages in which the president of the United States talked
about paying hush money to silence Watergate defendants who had
already been sentenced. The reel-to-reel player amplified these words:

> PRESIDENT: How much money do you need?
> DEAN: I would say these people are going to cost a million
> dollars over the next two years.
> PRESIDENT: We could get that. On the money, if you need the
> money you could get that. You could get a million
> dollars. You could get it in cash. I know where it
> could be gotten. It is not easy, but it could be done.
> But the question is who the hell would handle it?[48]

Ben-Veniste was stunned. "One could not expect to hear more of a
smoking gun than this conversation," he said.[49] There were other
damning passages, amid expletives and startling exchanges involving
President Nixon and his closest associates. George Frampton of the
Special Prosecution Force exhaustively summarized the tapes in a
128-page document.[50] The nine tapes that Cox had subpoenaed back

in July now provided the smoking guns—or at least the smoldering pistols—necessary to galvanize the prosecution and point it for the first time directly at the president.[51] After Leon Jaworski heard those tapes, said Ben-Veniste, "he realized that Nixon could not continue as president."[52]

By May 1974, the new special prosecutor had won an order from Judge Sirica directing that the president surrender sixty-four additional recordings.[53] When the president filed an appeal, Jaworski went directly to the U.S. Supreme Court, which accepted the extraordinary case so that it could end the torment before its summer recess.

On July 8, 1974, the day the tapes case was argued by Leon Jaworski and Phil Lacovara in the Supreme Court, Cox was the "most frustrated man on earth." He wanted "very much to go down and hear the oral argument." But he feared that the press might have "misunderstood my being there," and his staff might think "I was sort of looking over their shoulder," so he decided to "throttle my curiosity." He chopped wood in Maine instead.[54]

Barely two weeks later, on July 24, Chief Justice Warren Burger stoically announced the Court's decision in *U.S. v. Nixon.* He had written the decision himself; it was unanimous. The president was required to turn over the subpoenaed tapes, just as Cox had urged nearly a year earlier, because of the pressing need to guarantee that justice be done in the criminal courts. "The generalized assertion of [executive] privilege," the chief justice read soberly, "must yield to the demonstrated, specific need for evidence in a pending criminal trial. . . ."[55]

Was it difficult for Chief Justice Warren Burger to sign his name to an opinion that would almost certainly topple the president? Burger had been handpicked by President Nixon to fulfill a campaign pledge of appointing a "conservative" and "strict constructionist" to head the Court. He had appealed to Nixon's image of strength: he was "middle-class, middle-aged, middle-of-the-road, middle Western, Presbyterian, orderly and handsome."[56] Burger had been Nixon's single greatest hope on the Court. Did he feel a sense of having betrayed the man who put him on the nation's highest tribunal? "It was painful," the former chief justice later reflected, "because I knew it was likely to produce terminal results for *a* president. But I couldn't have come out any differently."

Even the president, seated at his desk in the Oval Office, could not have suspected that the chief justice had already spent decades worrying about the issue of executive privilege that would decide *U.S. v. Nixon.* As a young night student at St. Paul College of Law (now the William Mitchell College of Law) in Minnesota, in the late 1920s, Warren Burger had belonged to a "smokers" club, an informal group that argued mock trials on Friday nights to perfect their oral argument skills. The exercises that Burger had been assigned during that year consisted of three historic cases: the trial of Warren Hastings in the British House of Commons (relating to his abuse of power as governor-general of India), the impeachment trial of President Andrew Johnson, and the trial of Aaron Burr for treason.[57]

When Burger became a mature lawyer, these cases continued to leave an imprint in his mind. In his forties, Burger, who was also a talented artist, had painted an oil painting that hung in a massive wooden frame in his office. It was a still-life picture of a candle and two law books. The first book, bound in red, depicted Cummings and McFarland's *Federal Justice,* which dealt with the "History of Justice and the Federal Executive," including passages about William M. Evarts and the impeachment trial of President Andrew Johnson. The second brown book, marked "4 Cranch," represented the volume of the early U.S. Supreme Court Reports that contained an opinion dealing with the trial of Aaron Burr, authored by Chief Justice John Marshall riding circuit as presiding justice.[58] One of Justice Marshall's most eloquent and compelling pronouncements in that case, which had always lodged itself in young Burger's memory, was that evidence in the possession of the president that was ordinarily off limits to the courts *might* be reachable if it became necessary to ensure the fair administration of an ongoing criminal trial. When he moved to the Supreme Court at age sixty-two, Warren Burger moved the painting with him. Years later, he reflected on his arduous decision in *U.S. v. Nixon:*

> Chief Justice John Marshall had written it all in the *Aaron Burr* case. . . . The details of how Marshall handled that case made it almost an exact duplicate. The idea was that the *defendant* Burr couldn't see the evidence, have access to it. In our case the *prosecution* wanted it. Yet in each case it was necessary to have in order to produce a just result—in order to ensure the fair administration of justice.
>
> I spent a long time sweating over this issue, in ways that never appeared in the written opinion. It didn't matter whether it was the

defendant or the prosecution. It was the *people* who [necessitated] making this evidence available.[59]

Much of the chief justice's initial draft in *U.S. v. Nixon* would be scrapped and rewritten by other justices.[60] But the essence, relating to the Aaron Burr trial, would be carefully preserved in *U.S. v. Nixon*. Even Burger's law clerks, who observed their boss laboring in isolation in his chambers, did not know that his pen was guided by a painting displaying two books and a candle in dark, oily hues, hanging on the wall. Chief Justice Burger explained, softening his deep voice, "I wrote [that opinion] forty years ago."[61]

The president's lawyers had been slammed by setback after setback. They felt as if it were "six of us against the world." Charles Alan Wright had returned to Texas on October 27, the week after the Saturday Night Massacre. Although his doctor avoided such "old-fashioned terminology," in Wright's own words he was on the "verge of a nervous breakdown." From Austin, he continued to serve as a consultant to the president's lawyers, but he admitted to friends in a round-robin letter the following year, "The moment I get into the White House grounds I start trembling and have to reach for a tranquilizer."[62] Fred Buzhardt suffered a heart attack in June 1974 from the stress and fourteen-hour days and was forced to cut back his duties.[63] Len Garment, a long-time personal friend of Nixon, sensed that the "die of disaster was cast." He had very little advising to do in the White House anymore, because "circumstances removed me, and most everyone else" from contact with the president.[64]

By the end of July, the true "smoking gun" had surfaced in the batch of tapes turned over to Leon Jaworski; it was a June 23, 1973, conversation (six days after the Watergate break-in), in which President Nixon was heard conspiring to use the CIA to block an FBI investigation of Watergate, directly participating in the cover-up. The House Judiciary Committee had recommended impeachment of the president on three separate charges.[65] Criticism in both houses of Congress by both political parties had reached a crescendo. The president had been pushed to the brink of his resources. He had no more room to manuever.[66]

At 11:35 A.M. on August 9, 1974, Richard M. Nixon, dressed in a navy suit, white shirt, and a tiny flag-pin on his lapel, stood saluting in front of a helicopter, the first chief executive in American history to resign from the presidency. He thrust both hands in the air, fingers in his trademark V for victory, and disappeared into the green chopper. It lifted off and circled over the Washington Monument briefly before vanishing in a jerky shadow into the sky. W. Thomas McGough, Jr., a Princeton student interning in Washington that summer, remembered the sense of confusion among government workers who populated the endless marble buildings of the capital. "Everyone just kind of quit," said McGough. "We wandered over to the White House. Wondered what to do now."[67]

Archie happened to be walking past the dean's office at Harvard Law School at the moment of President Nixon's resignation. He stopped long enough to watch a small, portable television with a group of secretaries and staff. "He was quiet," remembered Donna Chiozzi, a secretary to Dean Albert M. Sacks. "He didn't say a whole lot. He just watched."[68]

Cox's inner feeling on that day in August, less than a year after his own firing, was one of "great satisfaction" that the system had worked.[69] But he made no public statement on the occasion. As Phyllis would explain, "He wouldn't rejoice at someone else's personal sorrow."[70] In fact, Cox indicated his displeasure with the 1976 publication of *The Final Days* by reporters Bob Woodward and Carl Bernstein, which chronicled Nixon's last weeks in office. "I see no useful purpose to be served by relating gossip about the disintegration of any human being, . . ." Cox remarked stiffly at a news conference. "It's not surprising any man would disintegrate under those circumstances and I don't see any gain in peddling those stories in books and news magazines."[71]

Only when President Gerald Ford granted a full pardon to his predecessor on September 8, 1974, did Cox break his silence. He issued a brief statement, indicating his "regret" that President Nixon had been given such preferential treatment. Cox would never believe that there was a prearranged "deal" by Ford to pardon Nixon in advance. "I'm a trusting soul. I don't go for thinking people are doing improper things."[72] Cox saw Ford as "an honest man of good will."[73] At the same time, unless the pardon was necessary because of the former president's health, which had never been verified by impartial medical experts, Cox believed that Richard Nixon should have been tried in court like any other citizen. The appropriate time to exhibit leniency—as in any other criminal prosecution—would be at the time of sentencing the former president. "There is room for mercy and no room for vindictiveness in American justice," Cox stated in a press release on September 8.[74] However, the criminal justice system, in his view, should have been permitted to run its course first.[75]

President Ford would later express admiration for Cox's role in Watergate, despite his own unyielding loyalty to the former president throughout the dismal affair. Two decades after granting the pardon, President Ford would say of his own decision to pardon Richard M. Nixon: "I would do it with even more confidence today than I did then."[76] He emphasized a point that the press seemed anxious to overlook, that a 1915 opinion of the Supreme Court involving George Burdick of the *New York Tribune* made clear that the acceptance of a pardon "carries an imputation of guilt, acceptance, a confession of it."[77] President Ford and his legal advisers viewed Richard Nixon's acceptance of the pardon as tantamount to a public admission of guilt. In fact, Ford had insisted that his lawyers specifically spell out this "consequence" to the former president in California before he was allowed to accept the presidential absolution.[78] In Ford's mind, he had extracted the "confession" that the country so desperately wanted.[79]

Despite Ford's apparent good intentions, Cox would never come to agree that the pardon of Richard Nixon was good or healthy for the American system of justice. Cox's fundamental difference was that he did not, and could not, share the view that "it was important for the country to put Watergate behind it."[80] To the contrary, he said, "I think the important thing for the country was and still is to remember it. To remember the dangerous consequences of not forcing adherence to the traditional principle that even the highest government authorities must comply with the law."[81]

In Cox's mind, the average citizen said it best. The foreman of the Watergate grand jury, Vladimir Pregelj, born in Yugoslavia and a naturalized citizen, told the press that he felt stunned by President Ford's decision. "I'm not prone to outrage," he said, "but possibly I am outraged. . . . I feel almost betrayed." Pregelj struggled to express his feelings: "We weren't able to finish our job—either indict him or not indict him."[82]

A specific incident in 1974 at O'Hare Airport in Chicago summarized all of Cox's discomfort with the Nixon pardon. It was three o'clock in the morning. Cox was returning from an American Bar Association meeting in Honolulu. The airport was deserted, except for four or five baggage handlers and a handful of taxi drivers. Cox stood near the conveyor belt waiting to find his luggage, which he had to transfer to another plane. Out of nowhere he heard, "Hey, Archie!" Cox looked around. He did not see anyone he knew. Then he realized that it was one of the baggage handlers speaking. Before long a cluster of taxi drivers and airport workers had surrounded him. "Do you think he'll be indicted? Do you think he'll be indicted? Will they get him?" They peppered him with questions. Cox answered, "Look, fellows, I don't know any more about it than you do. I got fired." There was laughter. One of the baggage handlers said, "Well, if it was me, they'd put me in the pen."

This simple comment would trouble Cox for years. "And I think of the lack of equal justice: The high and mighty aren't required to answer at the bar of a court for crimes when taxi drivers and baggage handlers *are*. It's a very dangerous message to send out."[83]

On October 14, 1974, the young lawyers recruited by Cox to litigate the Watergate cover-up case, led by Jim Neal, presented their testimony to Judge Sirica. On New Year's Day of 1975, as if beginning a clean chapter in the nation's history, a jury convicted three major figures in the Nixon administration—John Mitchell, H. R. Haldeman, and John Ehrlichman—of criminal wrongdoing. All three men were sentenced to prison terms.[84]

Archibald Cox had returned to the Harvard Law School faculty and reclaimed his old corner office in Langdell Hall. Although he was anxious to resume teaching as usual, some things would never be the same. Phil Heymann observed of his old mentor and colleague, after the winds of Watergate had blown across the country and dissipated: "Something amazing happened to Archie's life. He became a permanent American hero."[85]

He was placed in the company of Winston Churchill, Salvador Dalí, Walter Pidgeon, Abraham Lincoln, and Fred Astaire, in a newspaper feature discussing famous men who had made bow ties a popular fashion. (Archie politely declined comment: "I don't see any reason to appear in print on the subject of bow ties . . . forgive me.")[86] Along with George Gobel and 1950s movie idol Tab Hunter, Cox was cited in 1976 as one of the reasons crew cuts and "flat tops" were making a comeback in the United States.[87]

Flying on planes, Archie would inevitably be moved to first class.

Taxi drivers and students wanted to shake his hand in Harvard Square. Hallmark Cards asked permission to use a quotation from his Stanford Phi Beta Kappa address for a graduation greeting card.[88] Grade school children wrote from across the country, asking for articles of Cox's clothing to auction off at fund-raisers. Dr. Susan Ferraro of Hartsdale, New York, wrote in a letter: "I think you are the only person I could vote for with enthusiasm and commitment for President in 1976."[89] Deirdre Henderson, who had worked with Cox on the Kennedy Brain Trust, informed Archie that there were "a large number of people who were very enthusiastic about starting a draft movement to persuade you to run for governor."[90] Alice Fisher of Rochester, New Hampshire, wrote a spontaneous note to Cox: "I am going to pay you what seems to be the highest compliment in America today . . . I would definitely buy a used car from you."[91]

Archie was the same person he had been before Watergate. The principles he had exhibited were no different from those that had guided him when he quit President Truman's Wage Stabilization Board in 1952, or resisted the Kennedy administration's theories in the sit-in cases or one-person-one-vote controversy in the early 1960s. Something intangible had changed, however. Heymann described Cox's unexpected quandary, "Archie had to adjust to becoming a symbol." He had become "a symbol of American rectitude."[92]

Robert Bork, the man who fired Archibald Cox, later declared that "Cox did absolutely the right thing" in doggedly seeking the Nixon tapes.[93] President Ford praised the fact that Cox had "carried out his responsibilities without any critic saying he was unfair."[94] Chief Justice Burger would extol Cox, saying that he distinguished himself even in the dreadful aftermath of Watergate. "Some people [in that position] sometimes exploit it. He did not. He took his position and that was it. He's a fellow who knows what he wants to do and ought to do, and gets right at it."[95]

Elliot Richardson would insist that he himself received too much credit for one easy decision during Watergate, when he resigned. Learned Hand had always taught him as a clerk that there came a time when one simply said "oh sh—," and made the decision that had to be made. On the other hand, Richardson believed that Cox had been faced with a much more difficult task. "In Watergate, his greatest contribution was in the demonstration of character and integrity in the fulfillment of responsibilities," Richardson said, "despite an attempt to derail, intimidate, and deter him from the performance of his duty."[96]

Elliot Richardson, like Archibald Cox, faded in and out of the public limelight after Watergate. Political opportunities in the Republican party waned rather than multiplied.[97] The pendulum of history had placed both men in a unique position to make contributions to the American system of government during six brief months in the year 1973. Neither man dwelled on the fact that, for better or worse, the pendulum of history would now inevitably swing away.

22

SEMIRETIREMENT

Archibald Cox's productive life after Watergate would span as many years as some lawyers' careers. It brought so many honors and new enterprises that it might rightly fill numerous chapters of a biography. The essence of Cox's life, however, as he moved from active status to compelled retirement, from graying hair to white, from brisk gait to slow but erect walk (especially when the pain in his legs flared up), still followed the pattern of the first six decades.

The period immediately after returning from Washington was disjointed. How did one make the transition back from a person whose face was on *Time* and *Newsweek,* to an ordinary classroom professor? How did one transform unexpected fame into something that accomplished good, at the age of sixty-one?

As an escape from the spotlight of attention, the Coxes embraced an opportunity to vanish into the English countryside for a year. Cox had accepted an offer, even before his Watergate appointment, to serve as the prestigious Visiting Pitt Professor of American History and Institutions at the University of Cambridge. In the hubbub of his move to Washington, he had forgotten to cancel the commitment. Now it seemed like a welcome escape from the pessimism that had engulfed America in the final months of the Nixon presidency. It was also a chance to return to the quiet sites—the medieval castles, the bicycle trails in the Cotswolds, the punting boats along the Thames—where Archie and Phyllis had spent their honeymoon nearly forty years earlier.

So Cox turned down an invitation by the Major League Baseball Players Association to act as a salary arbitrator for the 1975 season[1] and instead chose from among a half-dozen invitations from the colleges making up the University of Cambridge, before settling upon the smallest, Sidney Sussex College.[2] Between a partial Harvard salary and his stipend of five thousand pounds, he and Phyllis could live comfortably in their flat within bicycle-riding distance of the university and still afford some sightseeing.[3]

By happy coincidence, President Ford had appointed Elliot Richardson as ambassador to the Court of St. James in London, shortly after Watergate. Now the Coxes and Richardsons could get together under less stressful circumstances. In March 1975, Cox invited Richardson to attend the Foundation Feast at Sidney Sussex, a black-tie affair that allowed him to show his old student around the stately gardens, courtyards, and Tudor buildings of Cambridge.[4] On April 24, Cox paid a visit to Ambassador Richardson's turf, serving as the guest of honor and principal speaker at an American Chamber of Commerce meeting at the Savoy Hotel in London. Cox told the polite luncheon gathering, "Only Pollyanna could blink [away] the trauma inflicted by Watergate. . . ." The former special prosecutor nevertheless held out hope that the end result "gives more reasons for confidence in our political system than despair." Americans had been forced to look in the mirror and confront the truth. "We have lost our innocence and have learned our capacity for evil. It takes honesty and courage to face those facts. . . ."[5]

The pace at Cambridge was restorative. Archie and Phyllis allowed themselves to sleep until 7:30 in their little flat on Chaucer Road. "Glory!" Cox told an American reporter about his new lifestyle. "Well, at least I still get up and work a regular week."[6] They traveled throughout England, visiting prominent judges, barristers, and members of Parliament. They stopped over at Oxford, where Cox gave the annual Chichele Lectures, under the auspices of All Souls College, on the subject of American constitutional law. They traveled to Edinburgh, Dublin, and Wales, where Cox delivered lectures to packed halls. The Coxes even managed to spend a cloudless week on the Isle of Skye, off the west coast of Scotland, along with David Graham-Campbell, the man who had been the commanding officer of Archie's brother Rob in the British Rifle Corps during World War II.[7]

When Archie and Phyllis returned home to Massachusetts in the late spring of 1975, America had slowly begun to push Watergate out of its weary consciousness. Yet the nation, and Cox, would never be able to shake the memories entirely.

On the second anniversary of the Saturday Night Massacre, October 20, 1975, Elliot Richardson dictated an urgent letter from the American Embassy in London to Cox's office at Harvard. Richardson was stunned by the brutal reaction of the English press to the recently published Report of the Watergate Special Prosecution Force. This was the official, 277-page document issued by Henry Ruth, Cox's former deputy, and the remaining Special Prosecution Force staff. The report left no sacred cows; it took sharp issue with Attorney General Richardson's efforts on behalf of the White House and insinuated that he had tried to derail the special prosecutor.

According to Nigel Wade, writing for the *Daily Telegraph* in London, "Mr. Elliot Richardson, white knight of the Watergate scandal and now American Ambassador to Britain, emerges with tarnished armor."[8] Simon Winchester for the London *Guardian* described Richardson as an attorney general "who was constantly peering over Archibald Cox's shoulder, interfering with his work, trying to limit the scope of his inquiry, relaying messages of imperial displeasure from the Oval Office." Elliot Richardson's resignation, Winchester observed in hindsight, now looked "more expedient than ennobling." Richardson's own ambitions for the presidency "may possibly have clouded his judgment." "Truly it was a time totally without heroes," the *Guardian* declared, "when all America was shamed."[9]

Stung by these accounts, Richardson wrote to Cox on October 20: "I had long thought that I got more credit for my part in the Watergate affair than the situation merited. But I never thought I had made any attempt to cover up a bit of it." Richardson concluded nonplussed: Was there something Cox would or could do? Or was it futile? "Perhaps we [can] just let it all rest and leave this as a sort of unhappy memorial letter on a date of some significance in our lives."[10]

Cox sat in his Harvard office and responded on October 31, attempting to put an old ghost back into the ground. He was certainly unhappy with the Special Prosecution Force report. He had been shown drafts of several chapters, including those that dealt with Richardson, and had told his former staffers that he disapproved of the language and tone vigorously: "I expressed many criticisms and said that I thought any such effort to discuss the relationship between the Attorney General and Special Prosecutor without their [participation] would be highly misleading."

True, there had been plenty of times that Richardson had passed along gripes from the White House. But this was his *job;* always he had done it with a tone and demeanor that indicated sensitivity to Cox's position. Cox felt strongly "there was no occasion on which you put any pressure on me or about which anyone would be warranted in raising the slightest question."

Still, the report had been issued. Now the question remained: What to do? As far as Cox could tell, the reaction back in the States was "quite mild." Much of the voluminous report was undoubtedly good and accurate; he did not want to excoriate the whole thing. He made this proposal to Elliot: If anyone asked, Cox was prepared to "make my disagreement with any adverse commentary upon your role very plain." But unless pressed on the subject, he felt that the most prudent course would be to let the story die of natural causes. Certainly, he could hold a press conference or write a provocative letter to the British press. "All it could do would be to arouse controversy," Cox wrote to his old student in London, "and controversy would be the best way to get the original point of view of the British reporters back into newspaper columns."[11]

Richardson telexed a response from the U.S. Embassy ten days later: "Thank you for the kind letter. I agree that the moving finger writes and having writ moves on."[12] He decided to drop the matter. Cox sent no scorching letters to the press. The report was soon forgotten.

After his period of rejuvenation abroad, Cox found himself marching in a commencement procession in his own backyard, as a recipient of an honorary degree from Harvard, a coveted honor that even Learned Hand had considered a crown on his illustrious career. Cox's citation was high praise: "High principled civil servant, thoughtful and generous teacher, staunch defender of the rights and privileges of academic society."[13] Cox was also named University Professor in 1976, one of only nine faculty members to receive Harvard's highest recognition for scholars "working on the frontiers of knowledge."[14]

Cox's teaching and writing had shifted almost entirely to Constitutional Law, with an occasional course in Labor Law thrown in to prevent total rustiness.[15] He added an undergraduate class in American Constitutional History to his repertoire, delivering lectures to a packed hall of political science and history majors. Professor Cox happily wrote letters of recommendation for aspiring Rhodes scholars, graduate students, and a swarm of new faces who appeared haltingly at his Langdell Hall office looking for guidance in charting out hopeful careers.

Cox's transformation as a teacher, which had begun after the solicitor general years, had now reached its completion. Evaluations published by the Board of Student Advisors gave Cox "rave reviews." One evaluation of his year-long Constitutional Law course read: "As a teacher, he was repeatedly praised for his analytical clarity and his ability to share his practical knowledge with the class." A review of Cox's advanced seminar in First Amendment noted that "nearly all those who took this course recommended it to other students. The main object of their praise was Professor Cox himself, whom students described as 'fascinating, interesting, kind, decent, an excellent teacher, and a gentleman.' "[16]

Even Archie's colleagues and former students noticed the metamorphosis. President Derek Bok, who had known Cox as an "austere" professor of Labor Law back in 1952, referred to Cox as "a different person in the classroom." As Bok sized it up, "He developed an affection towards people."[17] Roland S. Homet, Jr., who had taken Cox's course in Agency Law back in 1959 and viewed Cox as a stuffed shirt, ran into his old professor frequently in Washington. Homet was struck by "how remarkably he had changed. I was struck by the rise of the humility quotient. . . . He seems to be a simpler man in recent years."[18] Dean Harry Wellington of Yale, who had received guidance from Cox in his early teaching days, marveled, "The transformation to the Archibald Cox of the Watergate and student unrest periods shows an interesting, adaptable person."[19]

Even the secretaries found him to be approachable. "He would bring in great big baskets of tomatoes," said long-time Harvard secretary Helen Sorrentino. "Bushel baskets full. I would have to dole them out to everyone."[20]

When he walked outside the gates of Harvard, however, Cox still struggled with the aftereffects of fame. He had scores of opportunities to lend his name to matters of public importance. But he worried that he should not risk trading his reputation for money or publicity. He participated in the bicentennial celebration of Vermont in 1977, held in Windsor, with flags and banners and booming cannons bringing to life the little New England town where he had spent his boyhood summers. He gave a graduation speech at Miss Porter's School in Farmington, Connecticut, where his mother and sister Betty had attended "finishing school" during an earlier era.[21] Other than such family-related appearances, though, Cox remained cautious about celebrity status.

There was particular pressure from friends, family, and publishers to write a book about his Watergate experiences. Clark Byse at the Law School, a friend and colleague for decades, pestered Cox that he had a *duty* to write an autobiography for future generations. Publishers chimed in that significant royalties and speaking fees could flow from such a venture. Alfred A. Knopf, Jr., wrote to Cox on behalf of Atheneum Publishers: if Cox decided "to write a book about you-know-what," he should not sign any deal until he talked to that publishing house. Elizabeth Knappman of Doubleday and Richard B. McAdoo of Houghton Mifflin added their names to the list.[22] Even Phyllis nudged her husband gently about the idea, suggesting that it might be better to tell his own story rather than leaving it to someone else's pen. "We all talked to him about writing a book about himself," said eldest daughter, Sarah.[23]

But the idea did not appeal to him. Cox did not subscribe to "self-analysis," picking apart influences upon people's lives and "seeing what effect [they had] on you." Nor did he like the idea of "cashing in" on his public service. Writing about himself and events in the past was not something that naturally "stirred his interest." He would rather spend his time thinking about the present.[24]

When the "Talk of the Town" column in the *New Yorker* magazine gave a tongue-in-cheek award for the most important "Book Not Written," bestowing the honor on Archibald Cox for *not* having written a book about Watergate, Archie and Phyllis telephoned the author, Jonathan Schell, and asked him to join them for lunch. The little article "struck a chord" with them.[25]

One assignment that Cox did deem worthwhile was heading up the Select Committee on Judicial Needs, appointed by Governor Michael Dukakis, a former student. This "blue ribbon" panel issued a thick report that eventually contributed to the reform and modernization of the "notoriously slow" Massachusetts courts, a tough feat in the old-boy network of state politics. "It would be easy to beat this by attacking Dukakis," one state legislator said of the governor's court-reform plan, "but how do you go back to the voters and explain why you're against Archie?"[26]

Cox also found himself increasingly drawn to the candidacy of Arizona Congressman Morris K. Udall during the 1976 presidential race. Cox had first known Udall's older brother Stewart, a congressman in the 1950s who participated in the Landrum-Griffin debates and later served as President Kennedy's secretary of the interior. Cox had come to know Mo Udall in later years and greatly respected him. After initially hesitating, Cox publicly endorsed Udall and decided to do some campaigning for him. Udall was a folksy character with the wit of Will Rogers. Although he hailed from the Southwest, Udall represented for Cox many of the simple virtues that one would find in Vermont or Maine. "New England people, there's an awful lot in Mo they would have been greatly attracted to," explained Cox. "The down-to-earth, simple Udall."[27] Udall possessed an appreciation for the land, for the fruits of its fields, as well as a genuine humility that seemed rare in Washington anymore. In this candidate, Cox saw an old-fashioned instinct for the best in government service.[28] So Cox spoke at a fifty-dollar-per-plate fund-raising dinner in Tucson, shook hands at a railroad station in Trenton, lent his name and face (complete with half-glasses and bow tie) to a full-page ad in the *New York Times,* declaring: "If we act now, a man of uncommon moral strength can become our President."[29]

At a Mo Udall rally at the Sheraton Hotel in Boston, just as the candidate's New England campaign had kicked off, Archie accompanied Udall for some local politicking. The press noted that Udall was dressed in his usual shirtsleeves, while Cox was wearing "a pleasantly wrinkled pinstripe suit, a white shirt with a red paisley bow tie and sensible shoes," and was dressed "for all the world like the night manager at L. L. Bean's." One onlooker shouted, "What would you think of Elliot Richardson as President?"

Cox cocked his head; he was in a political quandary. "Well, I'm very fond of Elliot," he replied as he stood up straight. "If you have to have a Republican, Elliot would make a good President."[30]

Young people followed Cox onto the stage to take a picture, shake his hand, or ask for an autograph. Many seemed just as interested in seeing the former Watergate prosecutor as meeting the presidential contender.

By July, Mo Udall's candidacy had fizzled out in a string of primaries against a little-known peanut farmer from Georgia, Governor Jimmy Carter. It was clear that Carter would win the nomination at the Democratic Convention in New York City. So the Democratic National Committee worked out a deal by which Udall would receive his moment "in the sun," having his name placed in nomination, at which point he would make a "brief and graceful speech praising

Jimmy Carter" and the campaign would be over. Cox was selected to give the nominating speech at Madison Square Garden on Udall's behalf. He was given exactly one minute and fifty-six seconds.

The speech was carried live on national television on the evening of July 14, 1976. Cox was waved onto the back of the platform by noted criminal lawyer Edward Bennett Williams, counsel to the Democratic National Committee. "Archie, I don't think you've ever addressed the Democratic National Committee before," Williams said as he greeted him over the roar. Cox admitted as much; in fact, he had never *been* to a convention. "You're a lawyer and you're accustomed to the court paying attention and you're probably accustomed as a professor to at least some of your classes paying attention," Williams shouted into Cox's good ear. "When you get up there," he pointed to the speaker's lectern some distance away, "you will look out and you will see there isn't anybody looking at you, and you will find that the noise of people conversing with each other paying no attention to you is so great that you won't even be able to understand your own thoughts. The one thing for you to do is to fasten your eye on those cameras way up there," Williams pointed toward the most distant seats, "and hope that there is [one] man somewhere sitting alone in his living room listening to you."

Cox stepped up. He gave his one minute, fifty-six second speech nominating Mo Udall for the presidency, keeping his eyes fixed on an unseen television camera. He reminded the roaring crowd that Udall embodied a simple proposition that was meant to define American government: "That open-mindedness is consistent with conviction; that civility can accompany tenacity; and that humility should go hand in hand with power." With a stiff wave to the crowd, Cox ended his brief return into national politics.[31]

Phyllis considered it an important enough event to keep the full-page *New York Times* advertisement, featuring Archie's face along with Mo Udall's, tacked up in the horse shed in Wayland for years.

C ox remained more comfortable in the world of ideas and written articles than in the world of hand-shaking and autograph-signing. He attempted to follow the creed, in the mold of teachers like Felix Frankfurter, that the best way to prepare to teach a course in Constitutional Law was to help make it. And that meant working on important constitutional issues in the Supreme Court.

In late 1975, Cox argued *Buckley v. Valeo* in the Supreme Court as amicus, responding to a call from Senators Hugh Scott (a Republican from Pennsylvania) and Edward M. Kennedy to help defend the Federal Election Reform Act of 1974.[32] The case appealed to Archie. The act had been designed to restore public confidence in elected officials by striking at longstanding corruption in electoral practices. It sharply limited the amount of contributions that could be made to candidates and limited expenditures in primary and general elections. The act also authorized public financing for presidential elections and set up a Federal Election Commission to police violations. In Cox's mind, it was the best sort of post-Watergate legislation.[33]

During the lengthy oral argument in the Supreme Court, with multiple lawyers arguing on each side,[34] Cox told the Court that Congress had every right to concern itself with "the arms race of political contributions." The obsession with "ever-increasing amounts of campaign money," he warned, "was driving candidates to wealthy special-interest contributors." Cox pounded the justices over and over with a simple message: Although campaign contributions and expenditures were linked to political expression in one sense, they were "conduct, not speech." Congress should have wide latitude to regulate them without violating the First Amendment.[35]

It was not a home run. But when the complex per curiam decision of the Supreme Court was handed down in *Buckley v. Valeo*, it was at least a double for Cox's side. Although the Court ruled that spending money on campaigns was political "speech," and thus protected by the First Amendment, it upheld key provisions of the federal election law, including ceilings on political contributions, public financing of presidential elections, and tough financial disclosure requirements.[36] John Gardner, chairman of the citizen action group Common Cause, called *Buckley* a big win "for all those who have worked so hard to clean up politics in this country."[37]

In the winter of 1977, an even bigger challenge came Cox's way. A lawyer for the University of California at Berkeley asked Cox if he would consider handling a case called *Regents of the University of California v. Bakke*. Allan Bakke was a thirty-seven-year-old engineer who had been denied admission to the University of California's medical school at Davis two different times. Bakke, a white man, had sued the university, claiming that his Fourteenth Amendment "equal protection" rights had been violated because the medical school had allocated sixteen of the hundred entering slots to "disadvantaged minorities," most of whom were admitted with lower entering scores than his own. Bakke charged that he would have certainly earned a spot in the class, if it were not for this "racial quota" system.[38]

Over 130 organizations, from the American Federation of Teachers to the Sons of Italy, filed amicus briefs in the *Bakke* case, taking wildly opposing positions. It became an instant cause célèbre, with the philosophical clashes defying traditional liberal-conservative boundary lines. Martin S. Goldman, New England education director of the B'nai B'rith, assailed the California medical school scheme: "The evil is discrimination. One does not end discrimination by discriminating." Vernon Jordan, head of the National Urban League, countered sharply: "Opponents of affirmative action programs live in some kind of dream world where people truly advance on their merits and all is efficiently governed by a neutral merit system. That world does not exist."[39]

Time magazine called *Bakke* an "exquisitely complicated" case. Only 2 percent of the nation's doctors were black. That number had not changed for twenty-five years. *Brown v. Board of Education* had commanded that state-sanctioned discrimination in education cease "with all deliberate speed." But did that command authorize affirmative action plans that gave an extra boost to minorities?[40]

The University of California lawyers, who had lost *Bakke* in the state courts, saw Cox as their best hope for a win.[41] Not only did he have great stature with the nine justices, but he had written an amicus brief back in 1974 for Harvard in an affirmative action case, *DeFunis v. Odegaard,* that had raised many of the same issues, before the case was dismissed as moot.[42]

On the day that Allan Bakke's case came to Washington— Wednesday, October 12, 1977—spectators had been lined up all night to get seats, some toting sleeping bags, "eager to glimpse history." A throng of ninety newspaper and broadcast reporters muscled their way onto the Supreme Court steps for interviews. A small group of protesters marched into Capitol Park across the street, denouncing Bakke's attack on affirmative action. By 10:00 A.M. the spectators' line had swelled to nearly four hundred. Mrs. Earl Warren, the widow of the late chief justice who had written *Brown v. Board of Education,* was escorted to a special visitor's box. Many rickety wooden seats inside the courtroom were taken up by members of Congress; there was a strong showing by black representatives and minority leaders from across the nation.[43] Democratic Senator Tom Eagleton from Missouri, an old student from Cox's Labor Law class, waved to his former professor from the gallery.[44] To avoid the heavy crush of spectators, chairs were lined up in the halls outside.

Cox was "topside"; he argued first. He cranked up the old, wooden lectern contraption to match his height. Cox wore his old swallowtail, still the one that he had been married in.[45] At sixty-five, his hair was almost white now, not gray. He cocked his left ear toward the bench to be certain that he heard clearly. It was a good feeling to be in the Court again.

Phyllis sat in the special boxes reserved for justices' spouses and dignitaries. She was accompanied by young Phyllis, now a graduate of the University of Denver Law School, and Fanny Cox, now eighty-four years old. Mrs. Cox had made the trip from Windsor to Washington to watch her son argue his eighty-sixth case in the Supreme Court. It would be his next-to-last.[46]

"Mr. Chief Justice, and may it please the Court," Cox began. He drove immediately to the heart of the constitutional issue:

> This case ... presents a single vital question: whether a state university, which is forced by limited resources to select a relatively small number of students from a much larger number of well-qualified applicants, is free, voluntarily, to take into account the fact that a qualified applicant is black, Chicano, Asian, or native American in order to increase the number of qualified members of those minority groups trained for the educated professions.

Cox peered over his half-glasses at the nine justices. Many of them had been familiar faces for much of his career: Byron White; William J. Brennan, Jr.; Potter Stewart; Thurgood Marshall; Chief Justice Warren Burger. "The answer which this Court gives," Cox addressed the Court, "will determine, perhaps for decades, whether members of those minorities are to have the kind of meaningful access to higher education in the professions which the universities have accorded them in recent years, or are to be reduced to the trivial numbers which they were prior to the adoption of minority admissions programs."[47]

Cox carefully framed the argument in broad terms, so that it covered the affirmative action programs of schools like Harvard, Stanford, Columbia, and Penn, who had joined him as amicus.[48] He quickly steered the Court away from the term "quota," or even "target," in describing the University of California plan. This was not a rigid allotment that would haunt minorities as a stigma, "pointing a finger in the way the old quotas against Jews were stigmatizing," insisted Cox. Rather, the California Medical School's plan was similar to deciding that there was a shortage of doctors in rural communities in northern California, and making it a priority to admit qualified applicants from those towns so they could return home and take care of the sick. "How important do you think it is?" Cox challenged the Court.[49]

Justice Blackmun leaned over from the bench: "Mr. Cox, is it the same thing as an athletic scholarship?"

The question threw Cox off guard, for reasons that Justice Blackmun could never have anticipated. In rehearsing the case for oral argument, Cox had wanted to draw direct comparisons between "affirmative action" plans and admitting students on football scholarships. In both cases, he felt, the university was giving preference to students based upon diverse backgrounds and talents they could bring to the institution. But the University of California lawyers had protested vigorously: "Oh no!" they told Cox. "You must *not* bring that up. You'll trivialize it."[50]

Cox did not want to betray the university's lawyers. At the same time, the justice had raised the issue fair and square, had he not? Blackmun leaned forward in his seat, waiting for an answer.

Cox clenched and unclenched his fist at his side.

"Well, I come from Harvard, sir." He stood erect. "I don't know whether it's our aim, but we don't do very well."

The bench erupted into laughter. Justice Blackmun, a Harvard alum himself, shook his head knowingly. He got the joke; the Crimson football team was not doing very well recently. Cox skirted onto another point, and left the issue of athletic scholarships behind. Oral argument was a series of land mines. One defused them through logic, reason, and an occasional feat of prestidigitation.[51]

Justice Blackmun, four years older than Cox, considered it a stellar performance by the former solicitor general in *Bakke*. He could nevertheless tell that Cox, like himself, was beginning to show his age. "His increasing deafness could be detected," admitted Blackmun.[52]

Reynold H. Colvin of San Francisco, lawyer for Allan Bakke, took over the lectern in his dark three-piece business suit and quickly personalized the issue. "This is a question of getting Mr. Bakke into medical school," Colvin announced bluntly. "That's the name of the game. Race should not be a factor."

The bottom line, Bakke's lawyer told the Court, was that the universities had become "quota happy." Although the California Medical School's motive may have been pure, it was a fundamental flaw to assume "that intelligence, that achievement, that ability are measured by skin pigmentation." Increasing the number of "disadvantaged" doctors and assembling a more diverse student body might be a noble goal. But race was still an "improper basis," an impossible basis, for making this judgment.[53]

After thirty years, Phyllis Cox could take in oral arguments with a more relaxed eye. A law clerk stepped over from behind a purple curtain to pass a note to her in the VIP section.

"Welcome and greetings! It's good to see you here." It was signed "Potter."

Another slip of paper made its way to Mrs. Cox from behind the justices' bench, via messenger:

Phyllis—

Byron and I are just delighted to see you there—it's like old times & should happen much, much more often.

Bill Brennan[54]

When Archie reclaimed the lectern for rebuttal, his final message to the Court was simple yet powerful. Every tiny college, every university nestled in the vastly different geographic and cultural terrain making up the United States, Cox told the attentive courtroom, represented the "greatest source of creativity" when it came to fashioning ways to bring diversity to education. If the Court attempted to use the Fourteenth Amendment to ban all forms of "reverse discrimination," he warned quietly, it would win the battle but lose the war. It would lose the "search for justice for all, to which this country has always been committed, and which I'm sure it still is."[55]

Drew S. Days III, assistant attorney general for Civil Rights who watched the *Bakke* case from the government's seat, observed a powerful symbolism in Cox's presence: "He was a symbol of the 'establishment' speaking to the Court. This was not someone asking them to do something outlandish."[56]

After the argument, the Coxes hailed a cab in front of the Supreme Court in time to catch an afternoon flight back to Massachusetts. Phyllis disliked flying, but she endured it for special occasions like this. Although he made no predictions about the outcome of the case, Archie smiled when asked how the day went. "There's nothing quite like being back before the Supreme Court," he told a reporter from the *Boston Globe*.[57]

On June 28, 1975, the Supreme Court issued 154 pages of opinion in the historic *Bakke* case. A school group happened to be touring the Court, finding itself in the middle of the scramble. Students and teachers joined journalists in leafing through copies of the decision on the marble steps outside the Court.[58] The decision was a splintered one; the Court had split four to four to one, with Justice Powell casting the decisive vote and writing alone. Allan Bakke was admitted to the California Medical School because the program was too close to a "quota" for comfort. The school should not have established a fixed number of seats for minorities. Justice Powell's patchwork opinion, however, seemed to authorize more flexible affirmative action plans, like the one at Harvard that Cox had defended in *DeFunis,* as long as they considered race a simple "plus" in order to achieve diversity in the student body.[59] "A farm boy from Idaho can bring something to Harvard College that a Bostonian cannot offer," Justice Powell wrote. "Similarly, a black student can usually bring something that a white person cannot offer."[60]

By most Court watchers' accounts, *Bakke* was a big win for Cox's clients. The *Washington Post* announced: "Affirmative Action Upheld."[61] Attorney General Griffin B. Bell told reporters, "This is what we thought the law was." Educators expressed "relief" that the decision was consistent with their existing college admissions policies. Said John Harding, counsel to Columbia University, "It's music to our ears. Now we can continue doing what we are already doing."[62]

Cox's personal view of affirmative action, as it spread across the land in fits and starts after *Bakke,* was as guarded as his view in the old reapportionment cases of the 1960s. At some stage, he suspected, affirmative action would have to be phased out in order to bring unity to American society. "I think in the ideal world all race, age, et cetera, is irrelevant," he reflected fifteen years after *Bakke.* At the same time, Cox felt strongly that in order to achieve the ideal, "one must first be race and origin conscious." The hardest question for Cox to answer was, For how long? He would scratch his eyebrows, and consider the appropriate answer. "About all you could say is, 'At least for now.' "[63]

Archie and Phyllis were grandparents now, receiving birthday cards addressed to "Gaga and Grandpa," and notes from grandchildren in Denver conveying important messages such as "I love you. . . . All my

baby gerbils got eaten. I feel very sorry for them. Don't you?"[64] Young
Phyllis was busy practicing law in Denver and raising two girls. Archie,
Jr., was living in England as head of Morgan Stanley's London office.
He kept busy with his three children, one of whom was Archibald III.
"I could think of better names," he joked, "but not so much better that
I chose a different one for Archie."[65] Sarah was still working in Boston
but contemplating pursuing an executive master's degree in business
administration at Northeastern University. The children were moving
on, the grandchildren were growing. New responsibilities replaced
old ones. Fanny Cox required more attention now that she had
reached her mid-eighties; Archie and Phyllis made the trip to Windsor
more regularly. Elsewhere in New England, Archie's younger brother
Rowland, an Episcopal minister who had recently been named head-
master at Groton prep school, died unexpectedly of cancer (multiple
myeloma) at the age of forty-nine. Rowland's death was a sobering
reminder that the bounties of life did not last forever.[66]

Still, Cox continued to work as if there were no end to it. At the age
of sixty-six, he kept up a full load of teaching, labor arbitrations,
speaking engagements, and writing projects. He remained coauthor
on the *Labor Law* casebook with Derek Bok. He enjoyed good success with a little book, *The Role of the Supreme Court in American
Government,* that flowed from his lectures given at Oxford during the
year in England.[67] Cox's writings were being printed as far afield as
Europe and Japan. He was named a "Knight of Mark Twain" by the
Mark Twain Society in Missouri.[68] He was awarded the first annual
Justice William O. Douglas Award by the Beverly Hills Bar Foundation for service to public interest law, entitling him to twelve highbush
blueberry plants of a breed named "Patriot" in honor of the bicentennial year in which they were introduced. Phyllis personally claimed
this award, driving the bushes home in her pickup truck from a drop-
off spot in Maine.[69] Mountains of medals and honorary degrees piled
up in Cox's basement and office file cabinet, from Amherst to Harvard
to Loyola to the University of Michigan to Wheaton College to Rut-
gers to Northeastern.[70]

It therefore came as no surprise to many legal pundits that in March
1979, a panel appointed by President Jimmy Carter unanimously
recommended Archibald Cox to fill a new seat on the U.S. Court of
Appeals for the First Circuit, the appellate court just one level below
the Supreme Court, that encompassed Massachusetts and Maine.
Although the panel was not supposed to rank its choices, it broke with

protocol and placed Cox first on a list of five, making clear that Cox was its runaway choice.[71]

Senator Edward Kennedy, head of the Judiciary Committee, was strongly backing Cox. With President Carter and Senator Kennedy competing as front-runners in a race for the Democratic presidential nomination in 1980, an appointment to the First Circuit not only presented a significant honor, but (as most Court watchers understood), looked like a natural springboard to the Supreme Court. Although Cox was honored by the selection, his attitude toward the proposed appointment—unlike in 1965 when he left the solicitor generalship—was otherwise guarded. His frame of mind was "I don't know if I want it at this point. I like things as they are. And anyway, I know damned well he won't appoint me."

Cox could not believe that President Carter would send his name to the Senate after he had championed Mo Udall for president in 1976. If President Carter did not personally block him, he felt certain that Hamilton Jordan and others in the White House would do it. At the same time, he could not "decently refuse" the appointment if it came.[72]

Cox meticulously filled out the twenty-eight-page questionnaire that would be forwarded to the Justice Department along with his nomination. Under "health," he disclosed that he had undergone an inguinal hernia operation in 1977, but otherwise suffered from nothing worse than a "common winter virus." When it came to the question whether the nominee had ever been "arrested or charged with a federal or state crime," Cox was more troubled. His old friend from Gas House days, Teddy Chase, remembered receiving an urgent telephone call from Archie: "Remember when you and I were driving from Maine to Concord during first year of Law School, and you and I were arrested? Were you driving or was I?"

Chase covered the mouthpiece and chuckled. He remembered the incident perfectly. He had been stopped for a minor traffic violation on the way back to Cambridge. The two of them had gone to a remote district magistrate's office to pay a fine. Cox had been nothing more than a witness to Chase's first speeding ticket. But Cox now insisted on going over the facts two or three times, to make sure they were accurate. "Archie was quite intent on filling out this questionnaire correctly," Chase laughed.[73]

What did Cox hope to accomplish if he became a federal judge, at a time in life when many his age were retiring? There were two qualities of good judges that Cox valued, which he hoped he could still bring to the bench in order to make a final contribution to the legal profession. The first was a quality that he had admired greatly in Learned Hand: No matter what one's personal opinions, one tried to stick to precedent, one interpreted statutes and case law cautiously, so that society's law reflected the "reasoned elaboration from the cases in history."[74]

Yet there was a competing, almost contradictory quality that Cox respected in judges like Chief Justice Earl Warren. No matter how principled one became in adhering to precedent, one could never forget the "simple human questions" that underlay the law. Cox had learned over the past six decades that it was important not to become so "enthralled by the fascination with the technical side of the law"— the codes, the language, the statutes—"that we forget its ultimate purposes." The ultimate goal of the legal system was to help organize human social life in a way that was the best in the year 1912, or 1940, or 1979. One had to periodically ask, What is fair? What is the "American way"? On the other hand, too much emphasis on the Warren perspective might lead to a sort of "lawlessness." It had to be gently kneaded into Learned Hand's world of principled reason.[75] This is what Archibald Cox hoped to accomplish, if he embarked upon a judicial career at the age of sixty-seven.

If it had been any other year but 1979, Cox's appointment might have sailed through as a routine bureaucratic act. This year, however, the jockeying had already begun for the presidential election of 1980. The *New York Times* reported that the Cox nomination was "stalled in a quiet, three-way tug-of-war among the White House, the Department of Justice and Senator Edward M. Kennedy."[76] President Carter's attorney general, Griffin Bell, was reportedly squelching the Cox nomination because the American Bar Association had a rule that it would not "evaluate" any first-time judicial candidate over the age of sixty-four, and Bell felt bound to follow this policy. Other sources said that Bell was merely "carrying the political water for the White House," and that the real stumbling block lay in President Carter's "Kennedy paranoia."[77]

Charlie Wyzanski, Cox's old mentor at Ropes and Gray and now a senior federal district judge in Boston, chastised the attorney general in writing: "I need not remind you that at [age 67] Charles Evans Hughes was nominated as Chief Justice of the United States, and for over a decade thereafter was one of the nation's greatest judges."[78]

Senator Kennedy attempted to address Bell's concern more directly. "You don't have to worry about him being too old," he told the attorney general. "These Yankees live forever."[79]

The lobbying did not work, however. Senator Kennedy got the word directly from the horse's mouth. "I saw President Carter," he recalled. "He told me he wouldn't appoint Cox." Kennedy concluded that President Carter opposed the nomination because Cox had placed Mo Udall's name in nomination in 1976. Kennedy also sensed that the White House feared giving him (Kennedy) a boost in the 1980 presidential primary, which seemed to be a groundless concern. "I told President Carter that it would be a 'ten' for him if he appointed Cox," he said, explaining the politics of the equation. "It would only be a 'seven' for me."[80] But President Carter would not budge.

Internal memos from the Jimmy Carter Library reveal a fierce internal debate over the Cox nomination within the White House. Griffin Bell wrote a terse memo to the president on May 8: "I believe that you would be well advised to hold to the rule of sixty-four. It would be extremely difficult to administer exceptions on an ad hoc basis."[81]

Counsel to the President Bob Lipshutz dictated a memo to President Carter on the same day, flatly rejecting the attorney general's logic. First, he reminded the president, the sixty-four-year-old limit was an American Bar Association rule, not a Justice Department mandate, and "you have specifically rejected it in our own guidelines." Second, several federal judges had been elevated to the court of appeals from the district court after the age of sixty-four, and it was absurd to make the distinction between "first-time" appointees and those elevated from existing judgeships. Third, the Carter administration had been at the forefront of reforming the laws dealing with age discrimination and mandatory retirement. Lipshutz wrote to the president firmly: "I urge you not to reject a candidate because of an arbitrary age rule set by the ABA."[82]

The "off-the-record" notes of one adviser in the White House indicated that the bar association's concern was not a serious one: "Believe A.B.A. would heartily endorse Cox," the lawyer scribbled, ". . . every rule has its exception."[83] Another set of notes termed Cox a "folk hero," and indicated that the bar association "will not contest, even tho it will state its rule; will walk a line . . ."[84] Ken Feinberg, special counsel to the Senate Judiciary Committee, directly informed the White House that the American Bar Association had given Cox the "green light": "They made it clear informally to me if it was Archie Cox, they wouldn't stand in the way."[85] Despite the green light, President Carter turned the Cox nomination down.

The reaction across the country was one of unhappy astonishment. Stephen Wermeil, writing for the *Boston Sunday Globe,* pointed out that Louis Brandeis had served on the Supreme Court until he was eighty-two, Oliver Wendell Holmes until ninety, and Hugo Black until eighty-five.[86] Florence Rubin, who had headed the special nomination panel assembled by the president, declared angrily, "If there was an age limit, it should have been stated." Another panel member insisted that the commission had carefully checked out the age question before approving Cox, and was "infuriated" that the White House had submarined them.[87] One Carter adviser later called it a "mistake [made] during our macho period."[88]

While Senate Judiciary staffers and White House aides bickered, Cox wrote to a lawyer friend in Phoenix who had expressed outrage at the president's decision: "Happily, no one who is fortunate enough to teach at Harvard Law School has any occasion to feel sorry for himself."[89]

When President Carter assembled a new U.S. Circuit Judge Nominating Commission the following year, Cox was asked if he would apply. He quickly declined. Cox wrote to the new chairman: "I find it distasteful to apply for an office when, in my old-fashioned view, the public interest is best served if the office seeks the appointee, rather than the appointee seek the office."[90]

In September 1980, Stephen Breyer, a friend and colleague of Cox's on the Law School faculty who was working as chief counsel to the Senate Judiciary Committee, appeared at Cox's door. Breyer felt "awkward" and "embarrassed" to tell Cox that the committee and Senator Kennedy had decided to forward Breyer's own name to the president to fill the vacancy. Having been a student of Cox's and having worked for Cox on the Watergate Special Prosecution Force, Breyer had admired Archie his entire professional life. With considerable discomfort, Breyer now asked his old professor if he minded "if [I] tried to get the nomination?"[91] "I knew what he would say," said Breyer. "But I didn't want to take it for granted what he would say."[92]

Cox stood up at his desk. "Don't worry," he assured Breyer. He never seriously thought that President Carter would appoint him in the first place. His younger colleague would make an excellent federal appeals judge; he should try hard to get the nomination.

Shortly afterward, President Jimmy Carter appointed Stephen Breyer to the First Circuit Court of Appeals. Republican presidential candidate Ronald Reagan trounced Jimmy Carter in the November 1980 election. The American Bar Association rule against appointments after the age of sixty-four was abolished.[93] Archie gave up any notion of becoming a judge. And Stephen Breyer eventually moved to the U.S. Supreme Court.

"I was very pleased," said Cox.[94]

Just after the final nails were hammered into the coffin of his proposed judicial appointment, Archie and Phyllis sat in the reserved section at the dedication ceremony for the dazzling new John F. Kennedy Library at Columbia Point, overlooking the blue waters of Dorchester Bay in Boston.[95] It was sixteen years since John F. Kennedy had been removed from the presidency by an assassin's bullet. Cox listened to toasts and speeches; he remembered the day when he had sat in Chief Justice Warren's chambers at the Supreme Court, and Warren had confided that John F. Kennedy "had plans" for him on the Court.[96] The pendulum of history had swung away years ago. Neither Cox nor JFK had lived out the plans that the young president had mapped in the early 1960s. They had nevertheless accomplished other things, perhaps more useful things, in the periods left to each of them. Archie creaked backward in his chair next to Phyllis, applauding softly.

Age, or at least age rules, continued to trip up Archie. Although Cox was largely unfazed by his missed judgeship in 1979, he was disappointed, even shaken up, when it came to retiring from full-time teaching at Harvard in 1984. The university had adopted a mandatory policy that all tenured professors retire at the age of seventy. Despite Archie's prolific output and international fame, rules could not be ignored.[97] President Derek Bok had massaged the guidelines and allowed Archie to continue teaching two extra years since Cox held the special status of University Professor. "We kind of stretched the rules a little bit," admitted Bok.[98] But the stretching room had vanished. Cox began teaching a Constitutional Law course at Boston University Law School, a new haven across the Charles River, so that he could remain active in the classroom. John J. McCloy, distinguished New York lawyer, wrote a letter of condolence from his Manhattan office:

Dear Archie,

I read in this morning's *Times* that you were being forced into retirement at Harvard Law School as a mere child.

I have recently had my 89th birthday and I am now in my 90th year, commuting from Stamford to my Wall Street office every day.

Harvard's loss is Boston University's gain and I send you my best wishes and congratulations on the height of the career you have already achieved.[99]

In leaving behind the familiar routine of classrooms, schedules, and daily interchange with students at Harvard, Cox's principal sadness was that his own opportunity to transmit experiences to a new, idealistic generation was slowly drying up. His goal had been to allow students to take with them "not so much learning itself but the spirit of learning."[100] There was still much to teach. But the stage and the audience were vanishing.

Derek Bok wrote a long, handwritten letter to Cox from the president's office in Massachusetts Hall, expressing his discomfort at carrying out the "unwelcome task" of terminating Cox's teaching duties at Harvard. "No one at Harvard has meant more to me or had a greater influence on how I have thought and acted. If that strikes you as small praise, it is because you do not know what sort of unformed, wayward creature I was when I sat in your Labor Law Class in 1953—or started teaching five years later, for that matter."[101]

Cox tried to take his departure from the full-time Law School faculty gracefully. "I had plenty of warning it was coming," he admitted.[102] When the night arrived for his "Elegant Dinner," the age-old tradition by which outgoing members of the faculty were honored with speeches, toasts, and fond remembrances, colleagues were startled when the guest of honor arrived with a guest. By tradition, the Elegant Dinner did not include spouses. But when Archibald Cox walked in the door, Phyllis Ames Cox was on his arm. "Most [colleagues] were taken aback," smiled Professor Clark Byse. "We had never seen much of her."[103] From that point forward, the Elegant Dinner would include spouses of the honorees.

As professor emeritus, Cox was entitled to keep his office in Langdell North, where framed pictures of his father and grandfather, sitting behind their law firm desk; William M. Evarts; and Charlie Wyzanski all adorned the walls. He reported to work six days a week, cranking open the window each night and opening the blinds, a ritual that he followed religiously (except in cold months or if the weather report called for rain) to allow fresh air to circulate through the office. "The practice of the generation of my mother and grandmother was to open the window at night and shut it tight in the morning [as the sun grew hot]," Cox explained. "It's best when there's an east wind, that's likely to cool."[104]

To compensate for reduced duties at Harvard, Cox increased his activities outside the Law School. He now took on a full-time teaching load at Boston University, adding a second layer of commitments to his busy schedule. According to David Seipp, a legal historian at the school across the Charles River, Cox faithfully met with a new collection of students in his B.U. office, judged moot court arguments, participated in faculty workshops, commented on manuscripts and briefs written by colleagues, and made B.U. his second home. On regular days, Archie tried to get to B.U. in time for early morning conversation—and an occasional doughnut—in the faculty lounge, so he could participate in "the give and take inevitably sparked by the morning's *New York Times*."[105]

Cox also broadened his activities beyond the walls of Harvard by becoming chairman of the board of the Health Effects Institute, a group funded jointly by the Environmental Protection Agency and the motor vehicle manufacturers in order to gather data on the health effects of automobile emissions.[106] Perhaps most important to Cox in the 1980s, he became active in a group called Common Cause.

This self-styled citizens' lobbying group, the largest in the United States, had caught Cox's eye in the early 1970s, when it was founded by John Gardner, a dynamic Stanford professor who had headed the U.S. Department of Health, Education, and Welfare under President Johnson. Gardner had become "greatly concerned that the ordinary citizen was losing touch with his government, largely, but not exclusively, because he was losing confidence in the government." He had formed an organization "with its central purpose to make government more open, honest and accountable."[107]

Common Cause took off in the tumultuous years of the 1970s, attracting an "extraordinarily loyal and persevering" group of members.[108] It was active in lobbying Congress to end U.S. involvement in the Vietnam War. The organization put great stock in reforming federal campaign finance laws and in redefining ethical standards in Congress. John Gardner had been personally "interested [in] and supportive" of Cox after the Saturday Night Massacre, a touch of human kindness that meant a great deal to Archie during a difficult time. Fred Wertheimer, then director of legislation (later president) of the organization, had provided valuable assistance on *Buckley v. Valeo* when Cox had argued the campaign reform case in the Supreme Court.[109]

Cox was elected to the governing board in the American bicentennial year, 1976, because "I thought it was a highly effective organization in the area. And it was an opportunity to try, at least, to be one of those influencing the course of events."[110] Gardner attempted to entice Cox into accepting a leadership position, but Cox declined. "All he wanted to do was teach at Harvard Law School, and argue an occasional case in the Supreme Court," said Gardner. "It didn't look too promising to me."[111]

John Gardner retired as Common Cause's chairman in the late 1970s. After three years of service by Nan Waterman, Cox was named to the committee charged with recommending a new chairperson to the Governing Board.[112] There was not "enormous enthusiasm" for any of the candidates who had submitted their names. Cox lectured the committee: "This isn't the way to get the strongest person. You decide whom you *want* and then you go and tell him that he's got to do it; that you want him badly and that he'd be wonderful and he's got to do it."

Shortly afterward, the group came to Cox. They said forcefully, "You've got to do it."[113]

"I think this really wasn't on his menu," smiled John Gardner. "But when he took it, I think it really gave him a lift that he hadn't fully expected."[114]

Dorothy Cecelski, secretary of the National Governing Board, recalled sitting in the Common Cause third-floor lunchroom with a group of staffers, "quite in awe of this man who was going to be chairman." They wondered what they should call him when he arrived. Some suggested "Professor Cox." Others said "General Cox." One person proposed "Archibald." As they were discussing their quandary, the elevator doors opened and Cox stepped off. Said Cecelski, "He was immediately recognizable with his crew cut and bow tie."

Cox saw the group through the glass lunchroom windows. He walked over seriously. He straightened his shoulders and poked his head through the door. "Hello," he said. "I'm Archie." The staff members looked at each other. "It was forever thus," laughed Cecelski.[115]

By 1980, Common Cause had more than 200,000 members and a budget of nine million dollars. The chairmanship was nearly a full-time job. With its headquarters in Washington and offspring organizations in forty-eight states, there was plenty of travel and widely divergent philosophies to reconcile. Cox's personal goal was to prevent Common Cause from becoming an impulsive "liberal" organization with too many issues piled onto its plate. Cox wanted to remain focused on two or three concrete goals and work toward them until they yielded fruits.[116]

Dorothy Cecelski saw Cox as "a consensus builder. He felt you had to have most people in agreement if you were going to be strong."[117] Fred Wertheimer viewed Cox as the symbol of what Common Cause stood for; he was a person who could make things happen: "Archie was a larger-than-life figure in the nation as a result of his service as Watergate Special Prosecutor, and at the same time he had the touch of a common man, making everyone around him feel comfortable. As a result he was a tremendous public spokesman for the organization and a tremendous unifying force within the organization—when he spoke people listened."[118]

A primary goal throughout Cox's tenure was to keep up pressure on campaign finance reform in Congress. Common Cause worked to ban the acceptance of honoraria for speeches by senators and representatives, a goal that it met by the end of the 1980s. It also worked to abolish the practice by which congressmen were permitted to keep their war chests of campaign money for personal use after retirement. The group pushed doggedly, but not always successfully, to restrict large contributions from political action committees to fund congressional and presidential campaigns. In 1982, Cox argued his final case in the Supreme Court, *Common Cause v. Schmitt,* unsuccessfully attempting to defend a federal law that would have prohibited political committees from spending over $1,000 in presidential elections.[119]

On other fronts, however, victories were more decisive. In 1982, Common Cause lobbied successfully to extend and broaden the Voting Rights Act that Cox had helped draft in his final year as solicitor general.[120] Common Cause also worked to renew the Independent Counsel law that Congress had enacted after Cox's firing in Watergate, that compelled the attorney general to seek a special prosecutor appointed by the courts when sufficient credible evidence existed to suggest that the president or other high executive officials had committed a crime. Common Cause played a role in defeating the so-called Helms Amendments, which would have limited the power of the federal courts to hear abortion and school prayer cases. In the early 1990s, the organization pushed the Senate Ethics Committee to investigate the conduct of the "Keating Five," five senators allegedly involved in the "multibillion dollar meltdown" of the federal savings and loan industry.[121]

Not all Common Cause work was pleasant politicking. When the Senate Ethics Committee issued the results of its Keating Five investigation, with a mild slap on the wrists to the offending senators without imposing serious sanctions (particularly with respect to the most serious violations), Common Cause issued two sharp press releases decrying the committee's actions as a "sophisticated whitewash."[122] Just as quickly Senator Terry Sanford, a Democrat from North Carolina and a member of the Ethics Committee, wrote to Fred Wertheimer declaring that he was "shocked" by the press releases and labeling them acts of a "lynch mob."

Cox had the duty of responding to letters like this. He wrote to Senator Sanford that he had "long admired your public service," but having read "your own sorry letter to Common Cause," was forced to reply in kind:

> You rush to use words like "lynch mob" and to impugn my motives and those of my associates. In this instance, the strong editorial condemnation of the Senate Ethics Committee in newspapers throughout the country suggests that what you hear is not a lynch mob but the sober voice of the American people.

To this Senator Sanford replied with a curt "Dear Archibald" letter: "You impugn my honor, sir, and if you think I do not resent it you are dead wrong."

As if to dilute the vitriol, Senator Stanford scribbled a hasty, "facetious" postscript at the bottom in pen: "Too bad duels have been outlawed!"[123]

Even some close to Cox in the academic community were not enamored with his work on Common Cause and felt free to take potshots at him. Charles Fried, who served as solicitor general under President Ronald Reagan before returning to Harvard Law School and (later) a seat on the Supreme Judicial Court of Massachusetts, commented of his elder, retired colleague: "Why has Archie Cox been picked on by the right? He's been very partisan lately. At Common Cause, he's Mr. Clean turned into a regular pol running a nickel-and-dime lobby."[124]

Cox understood that he had to endure such scrapes if he was to command respect in the rough business of lobbying Washington. He flew at a dizzying clip between Logan Airport in Boston and National Airport in Washington, attempting to keep up his chores at home.[125] When it was time for important dinners and Common Cause functions, Phyllis would often remind her husband to put on a bow tie before he rushed out the door. "People expected it," she would tell him.[126] Cox had become a symbol of something in Washington. He tried to fulfill his role and meet the expectations of a growing organization, however exhausting the pace.

There was one cause that Archie refused to join, however, Common Cause or not. Nearly fifteen years after the Saturday Night Massacre, that controversial event managed to rear its head one final time in Cox's life.

In July 1987, President Ronald Reagan nominated Robert Bork to the Supreme Court after the retirement of Justice Lewis Powell. By this time, Bork was sitting as a federal appeals judge in Washington. After a long internal debate, Common Cause cautiously joined forces with a stampede of other organizations to halt the ultraconservative Bork from gaining confirmation in the Senate.

As the Bork issue slowly came to dominate political debate in Washington, Cox "steadfastly refused" to take part in discussions within the governing board of Common Cause, or to engage in outside commentary concerning the "merits or demerits of the nomination." When the issue of the Bork nomination came up for consideration at a board meeting, Cox absented himself, much to the dismay of some Common Cause colleagues. He could not be shaken from his reasoning. "I thought it was a clear case of 'one who was sensitive to ethical considerations should disqualify himself,' " Cox said. If he opposed Bork, after having been fired by him during Watergate, "there was the danger that I would be, or seem to be, prejudiced against him. . . ." If he defended Bork, on the other hand, it would appear that he was "leaning over backwards so as to avoid the first charge." Concluded Cox, "The right thing to do is to get firmly rooted on the sidelines."[127]

The battle over Robert Bork became fierce and bloody. Not only was Bork notorious in some circles for firing Cox on that infamous Saturday night, but the bearded former Yale law professor from a small Pittsburgh river town was considered the potential vote that could lock in a conservative majority on an ideologically split Court. He was the extreme embodiment of the conservative mantra of "judicial restraint," who believed in adhering firmly to the "original intent" of the framers of the Constitution. Bork had been an outspoken critic of the one-person-one-vote decisions, as well as of the Court's constitutional right to privacy and *Roe v. Wade*. He had opposed court-ordered school busing as a remedy for public school segregation. He had supported the right of state legislatures to impose the death penalty and had expressed doubts about the Court's exclusionary rule as part of the Fourth Amendment.[128]

President Reagan hailed Judge Bork as a powerful intellectual force. He announced that Bork "shares my view that judges' personal preferences and judges' values should not be part of their constitutional interpretations."[129] Former President Gerald Ford, who introduced Bork to the Senate Judiciary Committee, stated that Judge Bork "may well be the most qualified nominee to the Supreme Court in more than half a century." Others on a different end of the political spectrum called Bork an "ideologue." Democratic Senator Howard M. Metzenbaum of Ohio described the nominee's views as "frightening." "We're in trip gear," announced Nan Aron, executive director of the liberal lobbying group Alliance for Justice, which was braced to oppose Bork's appointment.[130] Millions of dollars were poured into ad campaigns for and against Bork as the forces geared up. "We are standing at the edge of history," declared the Reverend Jerry Falwell, leader of the Moral Majority and a staunch Bork supporter.[131] Senate Minority Leader Bob Dole, a Republican from Kansas who likewise backed Bork, promised reporters that the confirmation hearings would be "the main event of this Congress."[132]

The governing board of Common Cause cast a formal vote to oppose Bork's confirmation, by a slim margin of four votes, the first time that group had ever challenged a Supreme Court nominee head-on.[133] Still Cox did not budge. "I didn't, behind the scenes, depart from my public stance, . . ." he insisted.[134] But Washington scuttlebutt said otherwise. When Elliot Richardson appeared at the Senate hearings to testify in favor of Bork's nomination, Committee member Ted Kennedy got into a verbal sparring match with Richardson over the propriety of Bork's actions during the Saturday Night

Massacre. If Bork believed so firmly that he had been in a different "moral" position from Richardson and Ruckelshaus when it came to firing Cox, Senator Kennedy needled Richardson, why didn't Bork just do the deed and "resign"? Wouldn't that have been "a more satisfactory way of proceeding"?

Richardson replied in a gravelly voice, "With respect, Senator, it seems to me a silly suggestion. Why would the best possible man to be Acting Attorney General quit after having gone through the most distasteful and painful part of the job? . . . Bill Ruckelshaus and I talked him out of that."

Senator Kennedy pressed harder: a ruling by federal Judge Gerhard Gesell had held that the firing of Cox was "illegal." A departmental regulation published in the Federal Register had established the special prosecutor's office in the first place. This meant that nobody— not even the president—had the right to fire Cox "except for extraordinary improprieties."

Richardson quickly countered that he found this interpretation "excessively legalistic." There was no question in anyone's mind, on that Saturday night in 1973, that *somebody* could fire Cox. "I already had had, as I said, an opinion of the Office of Legal Counsel of the Department of Justice, to the effect that the President could have fired Cox himself at any time," said Richardson. "He was certainly entitled to get it done." At these words, Senator Kennedy grimaced.[135]

The grueling confirmation hearings brought the ghosts of Watergate back into the marbled Senate Caucus Room. Some in Washington whispered that Cox must be feeding Senate Democrats ammunition in their attack on Judge Bork. This speculation reached a crescendo on September 19, as the vote drew closer, when Senator Kennedy personally grilled nominee Bork by quoting directly from the mouth of Archibald Cox. The senator told Bork that Cox could not be present at these hearings, "because he does not want this to appear to be a personal contest between himself and Judge Bork." Yet Cox's *views* were present at the hearings, and these were in the public domain. Senator Kennedy produced a copy of Cox's newly published book, *The Court and the Constitution*,[136] and read a passage to Judge Bork in a scolding tone:

> To pack the bench with men and women of a single narrow political ideology has a tendency to erode long range public confidence in judicial institutions. . . . The farther a President goes in proclaiming

an intent to predetermine the course of decisions, the more he will undercut the foundations of legitimacy.

Judge Bork scratched his beard. He responded, "I agree with [Cox's point] entirely. I wish I could write it that well."

At this, Senator Kennedy held the book in midair: "I think that most Americans would agree with Archibald Cox, and I think that most Americans would agree that the man who fired Archibald Cox does not deserve to be promoted to Justice on the Supreme Court."[137] Images of Senator Kennedy holding Cox's book aloft and chastising the Supreme Court nominee appeared on television networks across the country.

Had Cox departed from his public stance of noninvolvement in the Bork hearings? Had he worked behind the scenes against the man who had fired him as Watergate special prosecutor? Preserved in a file tucked away in Senator Kennedy's Capitol Hill office, an exchange of correspondence demonstrates the intensity of the senator's battle to convince Cox to oppose Bork, and Cox's private response.

Senator Kennedy and his staff had been in touch with Cox by telephone several times during the Bork confirmation hearings, urging him to come out against Bork. When these calls proved fruitless, the senator took a more direct approach. On August 7, 1987, Senator Kennedy sent a personal letter to Cox's home in Wayland:

Dear Archie:

It was good to talk with you on Wednesday, and I'm reluctant to press the point further in light of your obviously strong feeling.

We may be able to defeat Bork without you, but the outcome is by no means certain, and the Senate verdict on that Saturday Night in 1973 could well make the difference. . . .

The White House is vigorously pressing its view that Bork acted reasonably in the Saturday Night Massacre, and Elliot and Phil Lacovara are lending their support. So far, we have no one of their stature to refute them. If you don't in some way indicate your opposition, then Bork may well prevail by default on this issue.

The even greater danger is that your silence will be construed as consent. It would be tragic if Bork's appointment to the Supreme Court is Watergate's most lasting legacy.

Senator Kennedy concluded with a firm plea:

America still remembers you from that day, Archie, and will not ask
you to do something that you feel will tarnish the incredible lesson in
integrity that you have given the country. But even Yankees come
down from Olympus sometimes.[138]

To this personal appeal from Senator Edward M. Kennedy, whose
family had figured prominently in much of his own career, Cox carefully scribbled out a reply on a piece of Law School stationery. The
note was written at home, for the eyes of nobody else, without copy
machines or secretaries producing duplicates:

Dear Senator,

I have read and thought about your letter. I remain convinced
that I ought not to express an opinion upon a matter on which there
is a risk that reaching fair judgment could all too easily become
embroiled in purely personal feelings.

With warm regards,

Archie[139]

On October 23, 1987, the full Senate rejected the nomination of
Robert H. Bork for a seat on the Supreme Court, amid a firestorm of
controversy over his conservative views. The vote was fifty-eight to
forty-two, the largest margin of defeat for any Supreme Court nominee in American history.[140] When the news was announced that
Friday, the phones began to ring in Cox's Harvard office. Reporters
were looking for a comment on the Bork vote.

Cox opened his windows a crack, allowing the air to circulate
through his open blinds. He turned out the lights and locked the door.
Then he went home, early.

EPILOGUE

HOME
TO
NEW ENGLAND

Phyllis A. Cox

Archibald Cox, Maine Gentleman Farmer

Along life brings with it the occasion to witness many passings. The longer the life, the more funerals become inevitable. Not long after Cox earned positive reviews in 1988 for *The Court and the Constitution*,[1] a sturdy, readable book that his mother kept on a table beside her in a Woodstock, Vermont, nursing home, Fanny Cox passed away, just four days before her ninety-sixth birthday. Bishop Paul Moore of New York, a St. Paul's classmate of Archie's brother Rob, presided over services at the red brick Episcopal church in Windsor, where countless generations of Evartses, Perkinses, and now Coxes had been ushered out of the world with the soft chords of an organ.

Frances Perkins Cox was buried next to Archibald Cox, Sr., in Ascutney Cemetery, where for fifty-seven years his clean marble stone had awaited a new inscription to make their union complete. At St. Paul's School, where Fanny Cox had remained an active supporter until the end, a file contained a note scribbled at the bottom of an obituary clipping that read: "This was a remarkable woman . . . alert, canny, in total control of this huge, sprawling SPS-related [St. Paul's School–related] family."[2]

Teddy Chase could not help thinking about the last time he had seen Fanny Cox, at a picnic lunch in Windsor. "It hailed," he recalled. "It was in the fall. It was very cold. Mrs. Cox sat there with a great, big woolen scarf, smiling." "Teddy," she said to him, looking up at the sky as it dumped buckets of rain onto Paradise, "Isn't it wonderful?"[3]

Three years after Fanny Cox's death, in 1991, Cox stood before a gathering at Harvard Law School paying tribute to Austin Wakeman

Scott, his teacher, mentor, and friend who had helped bring Phyllis and him together as a young couple. Mr. Scott had died at the age of ninety-six, a gentle man with a gentler soul. Cox thought back to the day he had walked alongside Mr. Scott through Harvard Yard and the subject of religion had come up. "I suppose that the Harvard Law School is my religion," Scott had said quietly. The elder Mr. Scott had lived out this faith, in a way that Cox greatly admired. At his ninetieth birthday party, Mr. Scott had encapsuled his own life by quoting *The Canterbury Tales*: "And gladly would he learn, and gladly teach." But Cox thought of a different line when he summarized Mr. Scott's life in the law. It was also from Chaucer: "He taught, but first he followed it himself."[4]

On April 22, 1994, former President Richard M. Nixon died in New York; his body was flown to Yorba Linda, California, for burial. The day of the funeral, Cox was working quietly in his office at Harvard. His secretary poked her head into the dim room in Langdell North. She wanted to let Professor Cox know that he was still being deluged with phone calls from reporters and television stations. Cox nodded and went back to work; there would be no public comment on this occasion. Nor would Cox say any more in private. "At a time like this," was all he said, "one tends to think first of all of the sadness for his family. . . ." To persistent reporters he quoted a single phrase in Latin: *"De mortuis nihil nisi bonum."* Of the dead speak kindly or not at all.[5]

Old age brought with it the slow extinction of names and friendships and identities that had once formed a busy part of Cox's life. Yet it also brought with it unexpected milestones that he could never have imagined in the thick of living, however successful his career.

Archie and Phyllis celebrated their golden wedding anniversary on June 12, 1987, spending the day quietly at their farm in Maine. A card from their fifteen-year-old granddaughter, Melissa Hart, made its way from Denver:

> Dear grandma and grandpa,
>
> Happy 50th Wedding Anniversary!! It's really an exciting day— particularly in the modern world where the 5th anniversary sometimes seems like a miracle of slow divorce courts!
> . . . I love you both very much.[6]

In September 1991, Archie celebrated a different anniversary with Harvard University: the forty-fifth year since his appointment as professor. To coincide with the occasion, the Treasure Room in the Langdell Library blazed with lights and memories, as the exhibition "That Justice Be Done: Archibald Cox's Life in the Law" opened at Harvard Law School. Glimmering display cases were filled with photos, yellowing legal briefs, original water-stained correspondence between Cox and historical figures including Learned Hand, John F. Kennedy, Robert Kennedy, Richard M. Nixon, Harry Truman, and others. Within the climate-controlled repositories of the Special Collections, Cox's papers would now be housed along with those of Oliver Wendell Holmes, Jr., Felix Frankfurter, and James Barr Ames (Phyllis's grandfather), for use by scholars and historians of future generations.

Dean Robert Clark, the new head of the Law School who was a teenager when Cox became solicitor general, welcomed guests by observing that Cox's long-running career encompassed "achievements that most of us can only dream about." These included "appearing in a *New York Times* crossword puzzle" (three letters for "important figure in Saturday Night Massacre") and "appearing in a Doonesbury cartoon."[7] The invitation-only crowd of dignitaries, judges, senators, alumnae, faculty colleagues, and friends laughed, as Cox smiled and cocked his left ear to hear clearly. "No one exemplifies more fully and more effectively the best of the legal profession and the best of the Harvard Law School," Clark told the Treasure Room audience. "Archibald Cox has set the standard for excellence and achievement."[8]

In 1992 Cox retired from the chairmanship of Common Cause, ending his last full-time job. Although the bylaws of Common Cause provided that a chairman would only serve for two terms (four years), the governing board had amended its bylaws four times in order to allow Cox to stay. "Where are you going to get anyone better?" was the general sentiment among board members and constituents.[9] This time, however, Cox requested that there be no amendment. After twelve years as chairman, he felt that he should make room for younger blood. It was healthy for the institution, healthy for himself.

"He made sure it [the organization] was rooted in some very important principles," said Dorothy Cecelski. "And he established us, really. It was a very steady course."[10]

Retirement from Common Cause allowed Archie and Phyllis to drive out to Boulder, with their large golden retriever, Misty, sitting in the front seat of the pickup truck between them, so that Archie could teach a course at the University of Colorado. Not only was the two-thousand-mile voyage a relaxing change of scenery and a beautiful trip in the snow, but it allowed the grandparents to spend time with young Phyllis's family, wandering through the Flatirons and the Rocky Mountains on weekends.[11] Now that he had reached his eightieth birthday, he took the walks slower.

Some transitions were less voluntary. The Coxes were forced to sell the sixteen-acre Ames homestead in Wayland, where Phyllis had grown up and where the Cox children had passed into adulthood, because of dwindling funds that came with a fixed income. There had been plenty of pro bono work during Archie's career, but pro bono cases did not pay taxes and upkeep on a big place in Massachusetts, and on a second farm in Maine. "So we had to downsize," said Phyllis matter-of-factly.[12]

The Coxes moved into a tiny white house on Old Connecticut Path, further on the outskirts of Wayland. It was big enough for "Grandpa" the clock to fit inside, a big vegetable garden out back, and space to build (according to the Wayland Zoning Board permit) "a horse stall plus storage place for hay, grain and tools."[13] Even with a horse and the smell of the country, though, Phyllis's children observed that the move from the old family homestead was "traumatic" for their mother.[14] " 'Place' is extremely important to her," young Phyllis explained. "One reason she's offered so much support to father is that she's grounded. The fact that her children grew up in the house she was born in gave great pleasure to her."[15] The children watched their mother struggle to adapt: she could not bring herself to drive past the old Ames house and confront how time had changed the place. Although the old and new homes were separated by only two miles and several stoplights, "She's never gone back there," said Sarah Cox. "I'm inclined to say she never will."[16]

Archie's luck in freezing the past was no better. In 1996, the same year that he celebrated his fiftieth year as professor at Harvard Law School, Cox found himself displaced from his old office on the second floor of Langdell Hall. Much of the faculty had moved to new quarters in the elegant, high-tech Hauser Hall that had risen in the field where oak trees had once formed a backdrop for Cox's corner office. The old wing of Langdell Hall where Cox had faithfully cranked open the window each evening to let in the easterly breeze was now gutted to make room for new library space wired with computer cabling. Cox waited until construction began and the corridors were blocked with red "WARNING" tape, before moving into a smaller office in the International Legal Studies building. It was further away from most of his colleagues, he worried, but on the positive side, it was closer to the parking lot where he parked his truck six days a week, seven if he checked his mail on Sunday.

No shrine was immune from the stealthy tricks of time. Molly Cox, Archie's younger sister, died of respiratory problems in 1995. The homestead on William M. Evarts's old "Runnemede" estate, which had been the cornerstone of family life for over a hundred years, was now without an Evarts, Cox, or Perkins to occupy it. The sagging white house was placed on the real estate auction block to be sold.

There were also breakdowns of the Coxes' physical health, which had once seemed impervious to the passage of time. Archie suffered two hip replacements. He endured a radiating pain in his legs that doctors could not diagnose or cure. He experienced increasing deafness in his "good" left ear that required constant help from a hearing aid. "I might just as well not go to cocktail parties," he explained. "I can smile and nod. In fact, I've gotten pretty good at it."[17] In the summer of 1994, he suffered a mild stroke that sent a scare through the family. Cox had been scheduled to teach a course at Boston University Law School in the fall, and a second one at the University of Colorado at Boulder in the spring. He called the respective deans (with a slight slur in his voice) and promptly withdrew; he did not want to risk teaching if he was not fully recovered. Friend and colleague Clark Byse advised him, "Why don't you wait a while, Archie? You like to teach. You like Colorado. You may be better." But he made the call, anyway. He would be selling the students short, he worried aloud to the family, if he drove to Boulder and found that he had problems speaking or preparing for classes.[18] As luck would have it, Cox was fully recovered within a month—after the Boulder law school had hired a replacement.

Phyllis suffered her own setbacks. She was thrown from a horse in Maine in 1994 and broke a vertebra when a deer jumped out during their morning ride. "It was a question of who was jumping the highest," she reconstructed the accident. "It was totally unexpected, for both me and the horse. But it didn't slow me down. I was picking peas the next day."[19] That same year, Phyllis was pinned under a pile of plasterboard while repairing the inside of the farmhouse in Maine. She was trapped under the heavy load for hours until Archie found her. With his hearing aid turned off, Archie had not heard her calls. By the time he took her to the hospital, Phyllis was "pretty well bruised up."[20] In the summer of 1996 Phyllis endured more bad luck. She broke her hip while stepping over the dog in Wayland, then cut her leg on a piece of barbed wire while picking raspberries in Maine. The latter injury required pills for the infection that cost five dollars each. "I felt nauseous," she said of her injury. "It's not from the pain, as much as the price of the pills."[21]

Archie and Phyllis were now grandparents six times over; they were waiting to become great-grandparents.[22] Their own children were successful in their respective careers: Sarah had become a business executive in New England.[23] Archie, Jr. (taller than his father at six foot, seven) had moved back from London as an internationally renowned investment banker and was tackling new challenges in the United States.[24] Young Phyllis practiced law in Denver, doing a wide range of pro bono work and producing two daughters, one of whom— Melissa Hart—graduated from Harvard Law School and earned the Sears Prize for academic excellence, like her grandfather sixty years earlier.[25]

Cox himself continued to teach constitutional law at Boston University one semester a year, neatly dressed in a suit (with an old red parka over it in cold weather) and still sporting a crew cut and bushy gray eyebrows. "Whenever the barber wants to trim them," he explained, "I tell him no, I keep them to scare the students with."[26]

At home in Wayland, Cox busied himself sawing and chopping logs for the woodstove and fireplace. He played "very bad chess" against a computer. He watched New England Patriots football games on the television on Sunday afternoons and an occasional college game if Notre Dame was playing ("I have an honorary degree from there").[27] He attended meetings of the Cambridge Scientific Club, an assortment of law clubs,[28] and the Saturday Club, the Boston literary/intellectual organization that dated back to the days of Emerson and Thoreau.[29] He read by the fireplace while "Grandpa" the clock ticked noisily in the living room. He took leisurely breaks for lunch with Phyllis: a whole can of soup, or a turkey sandwich with a thin spread of butter (not mayonnaise). Then he returned to his reading pile, which included David Herbert Donald's biography of Lincoln, Stephen Ambrose's account of the Lewis and Clark expedition, Tom Wolfe's *Bonfire of the Vanities*, Catherine Drinker Bowen's biography of Sir Francis Bacon, and a growing collection of John le Carré's spy thrillers.[30]

"I think they do what they used to do," said Sarah Cox of her parents' activities after they had passed the age of eighty, "and occasionally take a little longer time doing it."[31]

Archie was awarded the Founders' Medal at Boston College Law School and the Harvard Medal for "extraordinary service" at his own university that had spanned over half a century.[32] Phyllis was honored at a dinner hosted by the University of Massachusetts in the fall of 1996, for fifty years of service to the 4-H organization and lifelong commitment to youth programs.[33] The best part of this award, Phyllis commented, was that she did not have to give a speech. "I don't think I have to sing for my supper, which is good."[34]

The Cox children considered it fitting that recognition came to their parents as a pair. As daughter Sarah described her mother's influence on her father during their half-century of marriage, "On a purely practical level, as I told my father in Mother's presence, Dad owes a great deal of his success to his support system—specifically his wife. Mother took care of every day-to-day worry. This gave him the freedom to devote his time outside. Mother kept it all together."[35] Daughter Phyllis described the support system on another level: "To know there's unconditional love has to be a support that most people don't have, in a way they have had each other."[36]

Although Archibald Cox was no longer a participant in events making national headlines, he made it a point to think about them as if they were his own. Although he still reported to Boston University or Harvard by 7:45 each morning, he tried to linger over the *Times* with his coffee and reflect over the day's news while driving to work in the pickup truck or digging asparagus trenches in the garden on late afternoons.

On a recent afternoon, he sat in his small Harvard office, leaning back at the old desk that had belonged to his father and grandfather, and discussed some legal controversies of the day with an old student. The framed pictures of William M. Evarts and Charlie Wyzanski that had hung on the walls of Langdell North for so many years were now facedown on a file cabinet collecting dust, for lack of space. Otherwise, the books and papers and rug and piles of folders were all the same.

The independent-counsel law that had grown out of Watergate had found new targets in the Reagan, Bush, and Clinton administrations.

What was Cox's reaction to this evolution of the special prosecutor law? He had developed ambivalent sentiments about it.[37] Although he thought that the Iran-Contra investigation of the Reagan-Bush years was "a very important one to have conducted" because it dealt with alleged abuses of power by the president and his closest advisers while in office, he felt that it had led to disappointing results. Congress had hamstrung the independent counsel, Lawrence Walsh, and made it "very difficult for [him] to do the job right."[38] Important national security issues were never sorted out. Congress had granted waivers to key witnesses and allowed them to testify in return for immunity, something that Cox had worked hard to prevent during Watergate. Even more disturbing for Cox, politicians on both sides of the aisle had learned from Watergate that scandal could become a sure ticket to publicity. "Unhappily," said Cox, "the principal attractive figures on television [like Oliver North] turned out to be on the side of those who had violated the law."[39]

When it came to the Whitewater investigation of the Clinton years, Cox developed a different set of concerns. In his mind, "the real question is, how much time and effort should be spent chasing down remote leads to possible misconduct of some kind by a president years before he became president, not an abuse of power while in the White House?" Cox did not quarrel with the propriety of allowing and even encouraging that law enforcement officials examine charges of past crimes levied against the president from pre–White House days, as they would do with any other citizen. His problem came when the alleged wrongdoing was transformed into grist for the extraordinary apparatus of a special prosecutor and his nearly limitless resources. "There is a need to think of how far that is the proper subject of a federal investigation and the appointment of independent counsel," he mused.

A large measure of the problem surrounding the runaway application of the independent-counsel statute, Cox would reluctantly conclude, related to the transformation of the press into a hungry beast that stalked government wrongdoing. He perceived a trend "that seems to have grown in recent years," by which the press would "turn every little charge into 'This leads to a major scandal.' " Observed Cox, leaning back in his worn chair, "It's become a fad. I think it's had bad consequences."[40]

Yet Cox still believed in the importance of the independent-counsel law. "The simple fact is that one cannot count on the Department of

Justice to carry out a vigorous, fair, and publicly credible investigation of senior members of the same administration," he concluded. "It just isn't the way the world works, unfortunately."[41]

Cox remembered the suggestion being tossed around, early in the congressional debate over the law, that the solicitor general should appoint the special counsel rather than the courts doing so. "So I began thinking, would I really have trusted myself to be uninfluenced by my friendship with Arthur Goldberg or 'Bill' Wirtz, each secretary of labor, in choosing an independent counsel to investigate them? It was quite clear to me, no. I wouldn't possibly have been able to forget who they were investigating or forget my confidence in the people they were investigating. Which also made it clear it would be wrong to have me choose the investigator, if there was any basis at all for conducting the investigation."[42]

"I think we do need some such statute," Cox insisted. But he felt lawmakers should raise the "threshold" of evidence necessary before unleashing the extraordinary powers of the special prosecutor's office. Requiring only "reasonable grounds" to believe that further investigations were warranted had led to the appointment of too many special prosecutors. "A more stringent formula should be developed," Cox believed.[43] Also, the "time line" of the alleged crime should be considered. Alleged wrongdoing before an individual occupied the White House or ran for president might be fine for the ordinary machinery of state or federal investigations. It would debase the office of the special prosecutor, however, to get into these matters. They would make investigations of presidents almost perpetual.[44] "The benefits of allowing investigation of earlier wrongdoing are outweighed by the risk of encouraging opposing politicians to dig for stories of past misdeeds," Cox concluded.[45]

Finally, Cox believed that the independent counsel position should be a full-time job, to keep the investigation moving, and should be as much concerned with "public exoneration of the innocent as for indictment of the guilty." Cox explained: "Even if the individual under investigation is never convinced that the spirit of the inquiry was truly evenhanded, the American people will sense and honor the truth."[46]

What did Cox foresee in the future of the Supreme Court, where he had invested so much of his professional life? Cox rocked backward in his chair. He anticipated few surprises on the horizon. It was unlikely, as the nation turned the corner into the twenty-first century, that there would be dramatic developments "of the magnitude of the shift that took place after 1937 [in the midst of the New Deal], or with the Warren Court." Although it was conceivable that a succession of "like-minded presidents" could make a "series of conservative appointments who might achieve somewhat of a counterrevolution," Cox did not anticipate such a radical shift. The Burger and Rehnquist Courts had admittedly "toughened up" in some areas, such as the rights of the criminally accused and habeas corpus. In other areas, however, like the First Amendment, the Rehnquist Court seemed "even more enthusiastic than the Warren Court" to expand the rights of the individual. Most likely, any changes would be incremental, as had been the case throughout most of American history. "The Court is in the hands of the middle-of-the-roaders," Cox said, gripping a pencil firmly in his hand. "Their votes are necessary, and they have had an impact."[47]

Whatever the conservative justices of the Court believed personally when it came to the controversial landmarks of the latter half of the twentieth century—school desegregation, "one person, one vote," even the early privacy cases of *Griswold* and *Roe,* which dealt with contraceptives and abortion—Cox believed that these decisions would be difficult to scrap. The conservative "counterreformers" had publicly criticized the Warren Court by asserting that "the judge is limited—he mustn't put into the Constitution his vision of society, he must follow the law." That same creed would make it difficult for the justices to overrule well-entrenched precedent, even if they found it personally distasteful.[48]

"Obviously there's room for some overruling [while] still being loyal to these books about us," Cox would reflect, invoking the lesson of Learned Hand, "but I think that may well greatly temper majority votes. Marginal cutting back with fairly wide margins? Yes. But radical changes—I don't think so. Pressures for an old-fashioned view of law will remain. . . ."[49]

When it came to a final question, Cox momentarily blinked his eyes, perplexed. His cousin Bert Frothingham, the eighty-four-year-old daughter of editor Max Perkins who still occupied a home on the old Evarts estate in Windsor, had passed along this message: "Ask Bill about the future of American democracy." Bert herself believed that democracy was in a state of decline in the United States, considering how politicians were routinely attacking the president; how medicine and law were becoming money-making industries rather than caring professions; how education was no longer taken seriously for its own sake. Was it possible, she wondered, for the nation to recover from this decline?[50] Cox mulled over cousin Bert's question. He had no precise answer.

In Cox's eyes, the United States had undoubtedly endured a decline in the "spirit of community," in the sense that citizens no longer believed that they had "a *duty* to members of a community." It worried Cox to say it, but he did smell trouble in the wind. For Cox, a shared notion of community was the "sine qua non" of a healthy democracy. "How do you hope to recover it?" he asked, straightening his leg. Given the "mobility of society," and "the fact that most enterprises are now not nationwide but worldwide," it seemed doubly "hard to rebuild." America's new generations needed to discover ways to replicate the spirit of side-by-side cooperation that had once thrived in small towns like Brooksville, Maine; Windsor, Vermont; and other communities across America that prized loyalty and continuity. Without this dedicated, cooperative spirit, it would be (as Cousin Bert had warned) difficult to create a twenty-first-century version of democratic values that could sustain the nation.[51]

Part of the threat to the moorings of American democracy, Cox believed, also flowed from the diminished emphasis on the search for knowledge as a serious enterprise. "People don't believe in ideas anymore," Cox shook his head. There was a pervasive trend, not only in government, but in academia, business, and government, to assume that "one idea is as good as another." Rather than doing the hard work of picking apart competing ideas and carefully scrutinizing them with the conviction that some ultimate "truth" exists toward which humankind should ultimately move, citizens and leaders were becoming increasingly sloppy. People tended to avoid criticizing any idea, for fear of offending its owner. Everyone from town mayors to governors to teachers to church committee members to business leaders to legislators to law professors to community activists felt inclined to give equal time to each notion thrown out on the table, rather than doing the hard work to separate the gold from the feldspar.[52]

Where would all of this bring the country in the next century? Cox had difficulty envisioning the United States in fifty years. "Part of my problem," he admitted, "is I've never learned to run a computer." (Nor did he type.) "Much will develop along these lines," he expected. But Cox could see the danger that the high-tech age might contribute to a wider decline in education, for which there had to be some corrective plan. "I think one of the costs of the computer and related developments—the Internet—more and faster information, is that it discourages reflection. In the legal world, I think it discourages good writing, clear and thoughtful analysis."[53] Although information highways would certainly define America in the twenty-first century, Cox saw an urgent need to shore up and revitalize those basic human skills that had invented this technology in the first place: careful thought, creative but precise logic, the patient anguishing over sentences, paragraphs, books, statutes, judicial opinions, and other forms of communication that brought order to a society.

Cox had not lost his faith in the system that he and Americans of earlier generations, including his great-grandfather William M. Evarts, had staked their careers upon. "I was born an optimist," he smiled, glancing at a picture of his father and grandfather sitting at the same desk that he still occupied. "I have confidence that a way that's good enough for a while will turn up, and a way that's good enough for another while will turn up."[54]

Although life in modern America had become much more "confrontational"; although cooperation and consensus were giving way as men and women dropped out "to press their separate aims"; although old voluntary civic associations were shriveling up; although the Boy Scouts, Red Cross volunteers, labor unions, the Lions Club, the Elks, PTAs, and other hallmarks of twentieth-century American life were becoming slowly extinct; although ethical standards in society at large were still "frighteningly low"; Cox still saw ample room for hope. Major reforms had been implemented in American government in the last quarter of the twentieth century. In all strata of society, a concern for family and community and a broader concern for humanity even spilling across national borders was slowly on the rise. America was reinventing itself again. Although Cox did not expect to live to see its new face, he trusted that it would take on a heartening new look.

As he had told a group of Chicago dignitaries in 1995, when he received the Senator Paul H. Douglas Medal for Ethics in Government:

> I find guidance in the words of my great teacher, Judge Learned Hand, speaking of the path of mankind from the dark swamp in which our remote ancestors blundered. "Day breaks forever, and above the eastern horizon the sun is now about to peep. Full light of day? No, perhaps not ever. But yet it [has] grown lighter and the paths that were so blind will, if one watches sharply enough, become hourly plainer. We shall always learn to walk straighter. Yes, it is always dawn."[55]

Archibald Cox had risen high in the world of name recognition and national acclaim, but he would never quite receive the top prizes of his profession. He would remain a footnote in American history, one short line in the encyclopedias that recorded the leading figures of twentieth-century American life. Was there a touch of tragedy in his seemingly uncapped career? "Heavens, no," Cox shook the question off. "Would I have liked to be on the Supreme Court? The answer is yes. But it never seemed to me to be seriously in the cards." Besides, missed opportunities after he left the solicitor general's office in 1965 had produced surprise calls in their place. "Look at all the good, fun things I have been able to do since then. I would never have been able to play a role in Watergate or head up Common Cause if I had been appointed to the bench. These things have been so interesting—I'm not sure I can picture my life without them."

"Would I do anything different if I had to live life over again?" Archie clenched and unclenched his fist. "Nothing major. There is surely a list of things—if I could Monday-morning quarterback—I might do differently. But I don't think about those things."[56]

Cox adjusted the hearing aid in his left ear. "At my age, you say, 'When will you be forced to stop?'" He wiped away a tear that came with hay fever. "I just try not to think about it and keep working because I enjoy it. I have to say I'm not looking forward to retiring. Perhaps I won't."[57]

Archibald Cox carried a worn edition of the *Home Book of Verse* to the Wayland Public Library. It was a spring night in April; retirement provided time for such excursions. A small crowd of townsfolk had gathered at the old building, built around 1845, the first tax-supported library established in Massachusetts. They were here for a read-aloud program, sponsored by the American Library Association and designed to promote reading as a family pastime. Retirees, parents with children, and college students all crowded into the main level of the library to hear prominent Wayland residents recite their favorite verses. The speakers included the chief of police, the junior high school principal, a town selectman, and a local radio station announcer. But the person most of the audience had come to hear was the oldest: Archibald Cox, onetime Watergate special prosecutor.[58]

For his reading, Cox had selected the poem about the wreck of the *Prairie Belle* steamship on the Mississippi River. It was the same poem that Archie used to recite as a boy while gathered with his brothers and sisters at their grandmother's home in Windsor. The hero of the poem, and still one of Archibald Cox's heroes in old age, was the colorful character Jim Bludso. "He weren't no saint," the poem recited. But he had two principles in life that had guided him faithfully as a riverboat captain. First, he would never let another steamboat pass him on the Mississippi; he wanted to be the best at what he did. Second, if the *Prairie Belle* ever took fire, he swore that he would deliver each passenger safely to the shore, no matter what the personal costs. He'd "hold her nozzle agin the bank," recited the poem, "Till the last galoot's ashore."

Cox adjusted his half-glasses. He stood underneath the gentle lights of the public library's reading room, reciting the verses with voice rising and plummeting in an odd mixture of New England and New Jersey accents, just as he had done a lifetime ago with his brothers and sisters, under the flicker of a single kerosene lamp before lights went out:

> *Whar have you been for the last three year*
> *That you haven't heard folks tell*
> *How Jim Bludso passed in his checks*
> *The night of the* Prairie Bell?

Jim Bludso had no specific ambition designed to bring himself fame and wealth. His life on the Mississippi was spartan compared to many of those scurrying around on the bank. Yet Cox had always felt that Bludso possessed a certain durability of character. In dedicating his life to guarding the ship and its passengers from a single moment of peril, if it ever came, he had followed a calling as valuable as that of any person whose face appeared in the biographies of great men and women. He had surrendered success, as it was defined in the prevailing lexicon of American life, for his own vision of how one contributed to the common good.

Phyllis sat in the front row of wooden chairs. She shut her eyes to listen to her husband's voice, still a pleasant sound after so many decades. It was a "good read," she felt.[59] Archie slowly closed the worn blue book. He delivered the ending of the poem slowly, by memory, just as he had done sitting at the edge of his bed in the old Evarts homestead in Windsor. The words had a stirring effect on him, even eight decades later:

He weren't no saint,—but at judgment
I'd run my chance with Jim,
'Longside some pious gentlemen
That wouldn't shook hands with him.
He seen his duty, a dead-sure thing,
And went for it thar and then;
And Christ ain't a going to be too hard
On a man that died for men.[60]

Or, as Phyllis thought to herself as they walked arm-in-arm through the chilly April drizzle, across the parking lot outside the tiny Wayland Public Library, and climbed into their blue pickup truck, "a man who lived for men."[61]

Sources

Author's Interviews

James Barr Ames, Boston, Mass., June 20, 1994.
°John F. Barker, Washington, D.C., October 25, 1995.
Griffin B. Bell, Atlanta, Ga., September 23, 1996.
Richard Ben-Veniste, Washington, D.C., October 16, 1995.
°Elizabeth "Betty" Cox Bigelow (sister), New York, N.Y., July 9, 1991.
Derek C. Bok, Cambridge, Mass., July 20, 1994.
°Robert H. Bork, Washington, D.C., June 12, 1991.
T. Edward Braswell, Jr., Arlington, Va., October 20, 1995.
°William J. Brennan, Jr., Washington, D.C., March 29, 1991.
Stephen Breyer, Washington, D.C., January 11, 1995.
Louise Brown, Wayland, Mass., December 17, 1996.
Victor Brudney, Martha's Vineyard, Mass., July 19, 1995.
Rex G. Buffington, Starkville, Miss., October 18, 1995.
°Warren E. Burger, Washington, D.C., June 11, 1991.
Clark Byse, Cambridge, Mass., June 14, 1995.
Donald E. Campbell, Washington, D.C., October 13, 1995.
Florence L. Campbell, Danvers, Mass., October 13, 1995.
Ronald A. Cass, Boston, Mass., December 29, 1996.
Dorothy Cecelski, Washington, D.C., August 13, 1996.
Theodore Chase, Dover, Mass., June 23, 1994.
Donna Chiozzi, Cambridge, Mass., October 4, 1995.
D. Todd Christofferson, Mexico City, Mexico, October 31, 1995.
Warren Christopher, Washington, D.C., August 15, 1994.
Ramsey Clark, New York, N.Y., September 11, 1995.
Thomas W. Clark, Bass Harbor, Maine, May 13, 1994.
Archibald Cox, Jr. (son), Anderson, Ind., December 17, 1995.
Louis A. Cox (brother), Martinsburg, W.Va., June 9, 1995.
°Mary "Molly" Cox (sister), Windsor, Vt., August 15, 1990; May 27, 1994.

441

Maxwell E. Cox (brother), New York, N.Y., June 12, 1995.
Phyllis Cox (daughter), Denver, Colo., October 19, 1995.
°Phyllis Ames Cox (wife), Wayland, Mass., December 7, 1991.
Sarah "Sally" Cox (daughter), Wolfeboro, N.H., November 29, 1995.
William "Eph" Cresswell, Philadelphia, Miss., October 17, 1995.
David B. Currie, Chicago, Ill., September 8, 1995.
Drew S. Days III, New Haven, Conn., August 21, 1996.
John W. Dean III, Beverly Hills, Calif., June 22, 1996.
Joseph F. Dolan, Englewood, Colo., September 14, 1995.
°John W. Douglas, Washington, D.C., June 12, 1991.
Ralph A. Dungan, St. John, Barbados, October 8, 1993.
John T. Dunlop, Cambridge, Mass., December 29, 1994.
Peter B. Edelman, Washington, D.C., September 5, 1995.
Anna Ela, Bolton, Mass., August 9, 1996.
Philip Elman, Truro, Mass., September 1, 1995.
Harold L. Enarson, Boulder, Colo., May 2, 1995.
Kenneth R. Feinberg, Bethesda, Md., December 15, 1996.
Myer Feldman, Washington, D.C., June 3, 1991.
Robben W. Fleming, Ann Arbor, Mich., May 3, 1995.
James Flug, Washington, D.C., August 5, 1994.
°Gerald R. Ford, New York, N.Y., March 23, 1992.
William G. Foulke, Philadelphia, Pa., May 13, 1994.
John D. French, Minneapolis, Minn., September 8, 1995.
°Paul A. Freund, Cambridge, Mass., March 8, 1991.
Charles Fried, Cambridge, Mass., June 14, 1995.
°Bertha Perkins Frothingham, Windsor, Vt., February 8, 1994.
°John Kenneth Galbraith, Cambridge, Mass., August 31, 1995.
John W. Gardner, Stanford, Calif., September 23, 1996.
Leonard Garment, Washington, D.C., September 14, 1994; October 19, 1994.
Harris A. Gilbert, Nashville, Tenn., September 5, 1995.
Seymour Glanzer, Washington, D.C., October 10, 1995.
James M. Glasgow, Union City, Tenn., September 1, 1995.
Richard N. Goodwin, Concord, Mass., July 20, 1992.
°Erwin N. Griswold, Washington, D.C., June 11, 1991.
Gerald Gunther, Palo Alto, Calif., March 24, 1997.
°Alan N. Hall, Concord, N.H., May 30, 1994.
Melissa Hart, New Haven, Conn., September 6, 1995.
Floyd Haskell, Washington, D.C., September 14, 1995.
Wilmot Hastings, Worthington, Mass., August 3, 1994.
Samuel P. Hayes, Washington, D.C., June 29, 1994.
Susan Lawrence Hazard, New York, N.Y., June 20, 1994.
°Deirdre Henderson, Cambridge, Mass., March 8, 1991.
David R. Herwitz, Cambridge, Mass., June 15, 1995.
°Philip B. Heymann, Cambridge, Mass., March 7, 1991.
Roland S. Homet, Jr., Washington, D.C., September 8, 1995.
Jim Jeffords, Washington, D.C., September 8, 1995.
E. Dudley Johnson, Princeton, N.J., May 13, 1994.

Raymond Dean Jones, Denver, Colo., September 28, 1995.
°Nicholas deB. Katzenbach, Morristown, N.J., July 8, 1991.
Milton P. Kayle, New Rochelle, N.Y., May 3, 1995.
John C. Keeney, Washington, D.C., August 22, 1996.
°Edward M. Kennedy, McLean, Va., October 23, 1995.
Charles C. Killingsworth, Holt, Mich., May 3, 1995.
Charles Kirkland, Englewood, N.J., June 16, 1994.
Thomas C. Korologos, Washington, D.C., November 21, 1995.
Peter M. Kreindler, Morristown, N.J., October 20, 1995.
Philip Allen Lacovara, New York, N.Y., October 12, 1995.
Philip Landrum, Jr., Washington, D.C., August 23, 1995.
Richard A. Lester, Hightstown, N.J., August 5, 1994.
Anthony Lewis, Boston, Mass., September 18, 1995.
Evelyn Lincoln, Chevy Chase, Md., July 22, 1992.
Frank Lorson, Washington, D.C., January 19, 1995.
°Burke Marshall, New Haven, Conn., July 5, 1991; July 22, 1991.
Daniel K. Mayers, Washington, D.C., September 6, 1995.
°James H. McConomy, Pittsburgh, Pa., July 11, 1995.
Myres S. McDougal, New Haven, Conn., September 7, 1994.
W. Thomas McGough, Jr., Pittsburgh, Pa., September 22, 1995.
Herbert "Jack" Miller, Jr., Washington, D.C., September 19, 1995.
Adelia Moore, Hartford, Conn., October 7, 1996.
Charles Morgan, Jr., Destin, Fla., September 5, 1995.
Mary Roberts Morgan, Gladwyne, Pa., June 20, 1994.
Robert Warren Muir, Reading, Pa., November 7, 1995.
James F. Neal, Nashville, Tenn., October 9, 1995.
Charles R. Nesson, Cambridge, Mass., July 14, 1995.
Louis F. Oberdorfer, Washington, D.C., September 14, 1995.
Harriet Kennedy Parker, Bass Harbor, Maine, May 6, 1995.
°David F. Powers, Boston, Mass., July 1, 1993.
Vladimir Pregelj, Washington, D.C., September 22, 1995.
Nathan M. Pusey, New York, N.Y., September 28, 1995.
Lucian W. Pye, Cambridge, Mass., June 29, 1994.
Lloyd G. Reynolds, Washington, D.C., July 5, 1994.
°Elliot L. Richardson, Washington, D.C., September 28, 1992;
    October 16, 1992; November 25, 1992.
Moreton M. Rolleston, Jr., Atlanta, Ga., September 12, 1995.
Walter A. Rosenblith, Cape Cod, Mass., July 14, 1994.
Walt W. Rostow, Austin, Tex., July 25, 1994.
James R. Rowan, Millbrook, N.Y., May 2, 1995.
William D. Ruckelshaus, Washington, D.C., July 24, 1991.
Henry Ruth, Tucson, Ariz., October 9, 1995.
Paul A. Samuelson, Cambridge, Mass., June 29, 1994.
°Arthur M. Schlesinger, Jr., New York, N.Y., July 9, 1991.
Louis B. Schwartz, San Francisco, Calif., June 14, 1995.
Richard H. Seeburger, Pittsburgh, Pa., October 4, 1996.
John Thomas Smith, Washington, D.C., October 17, 1995.

°Theodore C. Sorensen, New York, N.Y., July 8, 1991.
Helen Sorrentino, Marblehead, Mass., December 12, 1996.
Ralph S. Spritzer, Tempe, Ariz., September 1, 1995.
John Hampton Stennis, Jackson, Miss., May 12, 1994.
Edgar "Buddy" Stillman, New York, N.Y., June 20, 1994.
Rufus Stillman, Litchfield, Conn., June 20, 1994.
David H. Stowe, Catonsville, Md., May 31, 1995.
James Sundquist, Arlington, Va., July 20, 1994.
°Robert Tonis, Cambridge, Mass., August 9, 1995.
Nina Totenberg, Washington, D.C., September 14, 1995.
David J. Vann, Birmingham, Ala., August 28, 1995.
Arthur T. Von Mehren, Cambridge, Mass., June 14, 1995.
°James Vorenberg, Cambridge, Mass., March 8, 1991.
Harry H. Wellington, New York, N.Y., August 24, 1995.
Fred Wertheimer, Washington, D.C., April 17, 1997.
Daniel L. Wessels, Pittsburgh, Pa., February 11, 1997.
°Byron R. White, Washington, D.C., September 25, 1992.
William G. Wigton, Plainfield, N.J., June 20, 1994.
Samuel R. Williamson, Jr., Sewanee, Tenn., July 26, 1991.
R. James Woolsey, Washington, D.C., October 13, 1995.

° Indicates interview in person. All other interviews were by telephone, with interviewee at location indicated.

Unpublished Sources

MANUSCRIPT COLLECTIONS

Harvard Law School Library, Special Collections, Cambridge, Massachusetts
    Archibald Cox papers
    James Doyle papers (unprocessed)
    Learned Hand papers (courtesy of Gerald Gunther and Jonathan Hand Churchill)
    Mark DeWolfe Howe papers
    Charles E. Wyzanski papers
    W. Barton Leach papers
    Felix Frankfurter papers
    Austin Wakeman Scott papers

St. Paul's School, Concord, New Hamsphire
    Cox family alumni files, Alumni Office (with special permission)
    Archives, Ohrstrom Library

Harvard University Archives, Cambridge, Massachusetts
    Harvard Crimson, Harvard University Gazette
    Harvard Yearbooks, Harvard Class Reports, Reports of the Presidents of Harvard College
    General History Collection (1968–71)

National Archives
   Records of the Wage and Salary Stabilization Boards of the Economic Stabili-
   zation Agency (at archives in Washington, D.C.)
   Richard M. Nixon Presidential Materials (at archives in College Park, Md.)
   Records of Watergate Special Prosecution Force (at archives in College Park,
   Md.)

Manuscript Collections, Harry S. Truman Library, Independence, Missouri
   Harry S. Truman papers
   Harold L. Enarson papers
   Charles S. Murphy papers
   John T. Dunlop papers

John F. Kennedy Library, Boston, Massachusetts
   John F. Kennedy papers
   Robert F. Kennedy papers
   Democratic National Committee 1960 Campaign papers
   Theodore C. Sorensen papers
   Richard Goodwin papers
   Burke Marshall papers
   Nicholas deB. Katzenbach papers (with permission)
   Victor Navasky papers (with permission)
   U.S. Department of Justice files

Jimmy Carter Library, Atlanta, Georgia
   Carter Presidential papers

U.S. Department of Justice Archives, Washington, D.C.
   Solicitor General papers

Supreme Court of the United States Library
   Transcripts of Oral Arguments

Library of Congress, Washington, D.C.
   William M. Evarts papers
   Elliot L. Richardson papers, with permission
   Leonard Garment papers (with permission)

Catholic University, Department of Archives and Manuscripts, Washington, D.C.
   John Brophy papers

Common Cause Archives, Washington, D.C.
   Miscellaneous papers

Special Collections, Mississippi State University
   John C. Stennis papers

ORAL HISTORY TRANSCRIPTS

Harry S. Truman Library
   Ewan Clague, David L. Cole, Milton P. Kayle, William S. Tyson

John F. Kennedy Library
    William Attwood, Richard Bolling, Chester Bowles, Abram Chayes, Alexander
    K. Christie, Archibald Cox, Joseph F. Dolan, Paul H. Douglas, William O.
    Douglas, Ralph A. Dungan, Frederick G. Dutton, Peter Edelman, Felix Frank-
    furter, Milton S. Gwirtzman, Seymour E. Harris, Nicholas deB. Katzenbach,
    Robert F. Kennedy, Joseph Kraft, Phil M. Landrum, Anthony Lewis, Lee
    Loevinger, Burke Marshall, Thurgood Marshall, Samuel V. Merrick, Jac-
    queline Kennedy Onassis, David F. Powers, Walt W. Rostow, Leverett Sal-
    tonstall, Hugh Sidey, James Sundquist, Arthur T. Thompson, Donald M.
    Wilson, Robert C. Wood, Adam Yarmolinsky

DISSERTATIONS AND THESES

Cox, Archibald. "Senatorial Saucer." Honors thesis in history, Harvard University,
    1934.
Hutton, Sister M. George Bernard. "William M. Evarts: Secretary of State, 1877–
    1881." Ph.D. dissertation, Catholic University of America, 1966.
Shurbet, Joanna Healey. "John L. Lewis: The Truman Years." Ph.D. dissertation,
    University of Michigan, 1976.

AUDIOVISUAL SOURCES

Dictabelt transcripts, Presidential Recordings, John F. Kennedy Library.
Nixon White House Tapes, National Archives.
Archibald Cox, Sanders Theatre Speech (video), Harvard University Archives.
"The Saturday Night Massacre: A Twenty-Year Retrospect." Program featuring
    Archibald Cox, Elliot L. Richardson, Philip B. Heymann, and James Doyle, at
    University of Pittsburgh School of Law, December 3, 1993. Video donated to
    Harvard Law School Library, Special Collections.

COX FAMILY PAPERS

Letters (1941–43) of Robert Hill Cox II, ed. Maxwell Perkins, (privately printed,
    n.d.), contained in Bertha Perkins Frothingham, private papers.
Unpublished interviews, Frances Bigelow Krause (a.k.a. Nancy Bigelow Krause) and
    Frances Perkins Cox, "Grandma's Memories," 1983, contained in Phyllis Ames
    Cox, private papers.

Published Sources

OFFICIAL PUBLICATIONS

Congressional Record. Washington, D.C.: U.S. Government Printing Office.

Ford, Gerald R. *Public Papers of the Presidents of the United States, Gerald R. Ford.* 4
    vols. Washington, D.C.: U.S. Government Printing Office, 1975–79.

Johnson, Lyndon B. *Public Papers of the Presidents of the United States, Lyndon B. Johnson.* 10 vols. Washington, D.C.: U.S. Government Printing Office, 1965–70.

Kennedy, John F. *Public Papers of the Presidents of the United States, John F. Kennedy.* 3 vols. Washington, D.C.: U.S. Government Printing Office, 1962–64.

Massachusetts, Governor's Select Committee on Judicial Needs. *Report on the State of the Massachusetts Courts.* Boston: Commonwealth of Massachusetts, 1976.

Nixon, Richard M. *Public Papers of the Presidents of the United States, Richard M. Nixon.* 6 vols. Washington, D.C.: U.S. Government Printing Office, 1971–75.

Nomination of Robert H. Bork to Be Associate Justice of the Supreme Court of the United States. Washington, D.C.: U.S. Government Printing Office, 1987.

Report of the Joint Special Committee Established to Investigate and Study the Matter of Justices De Saulnier and Brogna (Senate No. 1253). Boston: Commonwealth of Massachusetts, 1972.

Roosevelt, Franklin D. *Public Papers and Addresses of Franklin D. Roosevelt.* 13 vols. New York: Random House, Macmillan, and Harper (Samuel I. Rosenman, ed. 1938–50).

Trial of Andrew Johnson, President of the United States Before the Senate of the United States, on Impeachment by the House of Representatives for High Crimes and Misdemeanors. 3 vols. Washington, D.C.: U.S. Government Printing Office, 1868.

Truman, Harry S. *Public Papers of the Presidents of the United States, Harry S. Truman.* 8 vols. Washington, D.C.: U.S. Government Printing Office, 1961–66.

U.S. House Committee on the Judiciary. *Impeachment of Richard M. Nixon, President of the United States. Report of the Committee on the Judiciary, House of Representatives.* Washington, D.C.: U.S. Government Printing Office, 1974.

———. *Hearings before the Committee on the Judiciary, United States Senate, on Archibald Cox, Solicitor General–Designate, Eighty-seventh Congress, First Session, January 18, 1961.* Washington, D.C.: U.S. Government Printing Office, 1961.

———. *Hearings before the Committee on the Judiciary, United States Senate, Ninety-third Congress, First Session, on Nomination of Elliot L. Richardson, of Massachusetts, to Be Attorney General.* Washington, D.C.: U.S. Government Printing Office, 1973.

———. *Hearings before the Committee on the Judiciary, United States Senate, Ninety-third Congress, First Session, on Special Prosecutor.* 2 vols. Washington, D.C.: U.S. Government Printing Office, 1973.

U.S. Senate Subcommittee on Constitutional Rights. *Hearings before the Subcommittee on Constitutional Rights of the Committee on the Judiciary, United States Senate, Ninety-first Congress, First and Second Session.* Washington, D.C.: U.S. Government Printing Office, 1970.

U.S. House Subcommittee on Criminal Justice. *Hearings before the Subcommittee on Criminal Justice of the Committee on the Judiciary, House of Representatives, Ninety-third Congress, on H.J. Res. 784, A Joint Resolution to Provide for the Appointment of a Special Prosecutor, and for Other Purposes.* Washington, D.C.: U.S. Government Printing Office, 1973.

U.S. Senate Subcommittee of the Subcommittee on Communications. *Freedom of Communications, Final Report of the Committee on Commerce, United States Senate, Prepared by Its Subcommittee of the Subcommittee on Communications, Pursuant to S. Res. 305, Eighty-sixth Congress. Part 1: The Speeches, Remarks, Press Conferences, and Statements of Senator John F. Kennedy, August 1 through November 7, 1960.* Washington, D.C.: U.S. Government Printing Office, 1961. (Abbreviated *Freedom of Communications* in notes.)

Watergate Special Prosecutor Force Report. Washington, D.C.: U.S. Government Printing Office, 1975.

Weekly Compilation of Presidential Documents. Washington, D.C.: Office of the Federal Register, 1973.

BOOKS

AMBROSE, STEPHEN E. *Nixon.* Vol. 3, *Ruin and Recovery, 1973–1990.* New York: Simon and Schuster, 1987.

———. *Undaunted Courage: Meriwether Lewis, Thomas Jefferson, and the Opening of the American West.* New York: Simon and Schuster, 1996.

AVORN, JERRY L. *University in Revolt: A History of the Columbia Crisis.* London: Macdonald, 1968.

BARROWS, CHESTER L. *William M. Evarts: Lawyer, Diplomat, Statesman.* Chapel Hill: University of North Carolina Press, 1941.

BARTLETT, JOHN. *Familiar Quotations: A Collection of Passages, Phrases, and Proverbs Traced to Their Sources in Ancient and Modern Literature.* 13th ed. Boston: Little, Brown and Company, 1955.

BEATTY, JACK. *The Rascal King: The Life and Times of James Michael Curley, 1874–1958.* Reading, Mass.: Addison-Wesley, 1992.

BELLACE, JANICE R., and ALAN D. BERKOWITZ. *The Landrum-Griffin Act: Twenty Years of Federal Protection of Union Members' Rights.* Philadelphia: University of Pennsylvania, Industrial Research Unit, Wharton School, 1979.

BEN-VENISTE, RICHARD, and GEORGE FRAMPTON, JR. *Stonewall: The Legal Case against the Watergate Conspirators.* New York: Simon and Schuster, 1977.

BENEDICT, MICHAEL LES. *The Impeachment and Trial of Andrew Johnson.* New York: W. W. Norton, 1973.

BERG, A. SCOTT. *Max Perkins: Editor of Genius.* New York: E. P. Dutton, 1978.

BERGER, RAOUL. *Impeachment: The Constitutional Problems.* Cambridge, Mass.: Harvard University Press, 1973.

BERNSTEIN, IRVING. *Promises Kept: John F. Kennedy's New Frontier.* New York: Oxford University Press, 1991.

BEVERIDGE, ALBERT J. *The Life of John Marshall.* 4 vols. Boston: Houghton Mifflin, 1919.

BLAIR, JOAN, and CLAY BLAIR, JR. *The Search for J.F.K.* New York: Berkley Publishing, 1976.

BLUM, JOHN MORTON. *Years of Discord: American Politics and Society, 1961–1974.* New York: W. W. Norton and Company, 1991.

BOLLING, RICHARD. *House Out of Order.* New York: E. P. Dutton, 1965.

BOLT, ROBERT. *A Man for All Seasons.* New York: Random House, 1962.

BOWEN, CATHERINE DRINKER. *Francis Bacon: The Temper of a Man.* New York: Fordham University Press, 1993.

BRAUER, CARL M. *John F. Kennedy and the Second Reconstruction.* New York: Columbia University Press, 1977.

BRINKLEY, DAVID. *Washington Goes to War.* New York: Ballantine Books, 1988.

BURNS, JAMES MACGREGOR. *John Kennedy: A Political Profile.* New York: Harcourt, Brace, 1960.

BUSHNELL, ELEANORE. *Crimes, Follies, and Misfortunes: The Federal Impeachment Trials.* Urbana: University of Illinois Press, 1992.

CAPLAN, LINCOLN. *The Tenth Justice: The Solicitor General and the Rule of Law.* New York: Vintage Books (Random House), 1988.

COCHRAN, BERT. *Harry Truman and the Crisis Presidency.* New York: Funk and Wagnalls, 1973.

COLODNEY, LEN, and ROBERT GETTLIN. *Silent Coup: The Removal of a President.* New York: St. Martin's Press, 1991.

CONLIN, KATHERINE E., WILMA BURNHAM PARONTO, and STELLA VITTY HENRY. *Chronicles of Windsor: 1761–1975.* Taftsville, Vt.: Countryman Press, 1977.

COOK, FRED J. *The Crimes of Watergate.* New York: Franklin Watts, 1981.

COX, ARCHIBALD. *The Court and the Constitution.* Boston: Houghton Mifflin, 1987.

———. *Crisis at Columbia: Report of the Fact-Finding Commission Appointed to Investigate the Disturbances at Columbia University in April and May 1968.* New York: Vintage Books, 1968.

———. *The Role of the Supreme Court in American Government.* New York: Oxford University Press, 1976.

———. *The Warren Court: Constitutional Decision as an Instrument of Reform.* Cambridge, Mass.: Harvard University Press, 1968.

COX, ARCHIBALD, MARK DEWOLFE HOWE, and J. R. WIGGINS. *Civil Rights, the Constitution, and the Courts.* Cambridge, Mass.: Harvard University Press, 1967.

CRANE, CHARLES EDWARD. *Let Me Show You Vermont.* New York: Alfred A. Knopf, 1945.

CUMMINGS, HOMER S., and CARL McFARLAND. *Federal Justice: Chapters in the History of Justice and the Federal Executive.* New York: Macmillan, 1937.

DASH, SAMUEL. *Chief Counsel: Inside the Ervin Committee—The Untold Story of Watergate.* New York: Random House, 1976.

DEAN, JOHN W. III. *Blind Ambition: The White House Years.* New York: Simon and Schuster, 1976.

DEWITT, DAVID MILLER. *The Impeachment and Trial of Andrew Johnson.* New York: Macmillan, 1903.

DONALD, DAVID HERBERT. *Lincoln.* New York: Simon and Schuster, 1995.

DONOVAN, ROBERT J. *Tumultuous Years: The Presidency of Harry S. Truman, 1949–1953.* New York: W. W. Norton, 1977.

DOYLE, JAMES. *Not Above the Law: The Battles of Watergate Prosecutors Cox and Jaworski.* New York: William Morrow and Company, 1977.

DREW, ELIZABETH. *Washington Journal: The Events of 1973–1974.* New York: Random House, 1974.

DRURY, ROGER W. *Drury and St. Paul's: The Scars of a Schoolmaster.* Boston: Little, Brown and Company, 1964.

DUBOFSKY, MELVYN, and WARREN VAN TINE. *John L. Lewis: A Biography.* New York: Quadrangle, 1977.

DUNLOP, JOHN T., and ARTHUR D. HILL. *The Wage Adjustment Board: Wartime Stabilization in the Building and Construction Industry.* Cambridge, Mass.: Harvard University Press, 1950.

DYER, BRAINERD. *The Public Career of William M. Evarts.* Berkeley: University of California Press, 1933.

EDMONDS, JOHN B., ed. *St. Paul's School in the Second World War.* Concord, N.H.: Alumni Association of St. Paul's School, 1950.

EICHEL, LAWRENCE E., KENNETH W. JOST, ROBERT D. LUSKIN, and RICHARD M. NEUSTADT. *The Harvard Strike.* Boston: Houghton Mifflin, 1970.

EISENHOWER, JULIE NIXON. *Pat Nixon: The Untold Story.* New York: Simon and Schuster, 1986.

EVARTS, SHERMAN, ED. *Arguments and Speeches of William Maxwell Evarts.* 3 vols. New York: Macmillan, 1919.

FAIRLIE, HENRY. *The Kennedy Promise: The Politics of Expectation.* Garden City, N.Y.: Doubleday, 1973.

FERRELL, ROBERT H. *Harry S. Truman and the Modern American Presidency.* Edited by Oscar Hanlin. Boston: Little, Brown and Company, 1983.

———. *Harry S. Truman: A Life.* Edited by William E. Foley. Columbia: University of Missouri Press, 1994.

FORD, GERALD R. *A Time to Heal: The Autobiography of Gerald R. Ford.* New York: Harper and Row, 1979.

FRANK, JEROME, and BARBARA FRANK. *Not Guilty.* New York: Da Capo Press, 1971.

FRIED, CHARLES. *Order and Law: Arguing the Reagan Revolution—A Firsthand Account.* New York: Simon and Schuster, 1991.

GALBRAITH, JOHN KENNETH. *The Liberal Hour.* Boston: Houghton Mifflin, 1960.

———. *A Life in Our Times: Memoirs.* Boston: Houghton Mifflin, 1981.

GITLOW, ABRAHAM L. *Wage Determination under National Boards.* New York: Prentice-Hall, 1953.

GOLDEN, CLINTON S., and HAROLD J. RUTTENBERG. *The Dynamics of Industrial Democracy.* New York: Harper and Brothers, 1942.

GOODWIN, RICHARD N. *Remembering America: A Voice from the Sixties.* Boston: Little, Brown and Company, 1988.

GRAHAM, GENE S. *One Man, One Vote: Baker v. Carr and the American Levellers.* Boston: Little, Brown and Company, 1972.

GREENBERG, JACK. *Crusaders in the Courts: How a Dedicated Band of Lawyers Fought for the Civil Rights Revolution.* New York: Basic Books, 1994.

GRIFFITH, KATHRYN. *Judge Learned Hand and the Role of the Federal Judiciary.* Norman: University of Oklahoma Press, 1973.

GUNTHER, GERALD. *Constitutional Law.* 12th ed. New York: Foundation Press, 1991.

————. *Learned Hand: The Man and the Judge.* New York: Alfred A. Knopf, 1994.

GUTHMAN, EDWIN O., and JEFFREY SHULMAN. *Robert Kennedy in His Own Words: The Unpublished Recollections of the Kennedy Years.* New York: Bantam Books, 1989.

HAGAN, HORACE H. *Eight Great American Lawyers.* Oklahoma City: Harlow Publishing, 1923.

HAIG, ALEXANDER M., JR., with CHARLES MCCARRY. *Inner Circles: How America Changed the World. A Memoir.* New York: Warner Books, 1992.

HALDEMAN, H. R. *The Haldeman Diaries: Inside the Nixon White House.* New York: G. P. Putnam's Sons, 1994.

HAMBY, ALONZO. *Beyond the New Deal: Harry S. Truman and American Liberalism.* New York: Columbia University Press, 1973.

HAND, LEARNED. *The Spirit of Liberty: Papers and Addresses of Learned Hand.* 3rd ed. Edited by Irving Dilliard. Chicago: University of Chicago Press, 1977.

HARBAUGH, WILLIAM H. *Lawyer's Lawyer: The Life of John W. Davis.* New York: Oxford University Press, 1973.

HECHLER, KEN. *Working with Truman: A Personal Memoir of the White House Years.* New York: G. P. Putnam's Sons, 1982.

HECKSCHER, AUGUST. *St. Paul's: The Life of a New England School.* New York: Scribners, 1980.

HENTY, GEORGE ALFRED. *Under Drake's Flag: A Tale of the Spanish Main.* New York: Scribners, 1925.

————. *With Lee in Virginia: A Story of the American Civil War.* New York: Scribners, 1921.

ICKES, HAROLD L. *The Autobiography of a Curmudgeon.* New York: Reynal and Hitchcock, 1943.

JAWORSKI, LEON. *The Right and the Power: The Prosecution of Watergate.* New York: Gulf Publishing, 1976.

JENKINS, ROY. *Truman.* New York: Harper and Row, 1986.

KAHN, E. J., JR. *Harvard: Through Change and Through Storm.* New York: W. W. Norton, 1969.

KAHN, ROGER. *The Battle for Morningside Heights: Why Students Rebel.* New York: William Morrow and Company, 1970.

KIMBALL, PENN. *Bobby Kennedy and the New Politics.* Englewood Cliffs, N.J.: Prentice-Hall, 1968.

KISSINGER, HENRY A. *Years of Upheaval.* Boston: Little, Brown and Company, 1982.

KURLAND, PHILIP B., and GERHARD CASPER, EDS. *Landmark Briefs and Arguments of the Supreme Court of the United States: Constitutional Law.* (243 vols.) Arlington, Va.: University Publications of America, 1975.

KUTLER, STANLEY I. *The Wars of Watergate: The Last Crisis of Richard Nixon.* New York: Alfred A. Knopf, 1990.

LASH, JOSEPH P. *Dealers and Dreamers: A New Look at the New Deal.* New York: Doubleday, 1988.

LASKY, VICTOR. *J.F.K.: The Man and the Myth.* New York: Macmillan, 1963.

LAWFORD, PATRICIA KENNEDY, ed. *That Shining Hour.* New York: Halliday Lithograph, 1969.

LEE, R. ALTON. *Eisenhower and Landrum-Griffin: A Study in Labor-Management Politics.* Lexington: University Press of Kentucky, 1990.

———. *Truman and Taft Hartley: A Question of Mandate.* Lexington: University of Kentucky Press, 1966.

LEUCHTENBURG, WILLIAM E. *Franklin D. Roosevelt and the New Deal, 1932–1940.* New York: Harper and Row, 1963.

LINCOLN, EVELYN. *My Twelve Years with John F. Kennedy.* New York: David McKay, 1965.

LUKAS, J. ANTHONY. *Nightmare: The Underside of the Nixon Years.* New York: Viking Press, 1976.

MANKIEWICZ, FRANK. *Perfectly Clear: Nixon from Whittier to Watergate.* New York: Quadrangle, 1973.

———. *U.S. v. Richard M. Nixon: The Final Crisis.* New York: Quadrangle, 1975.

MARQUIS, DON. *archy and mehitabel.* New York: Anchor Books (Doubleday), 1990.

MATUSOW, ALLEN J. *The Unraveling of America: A History of Liberalism in the 1960s.* New York: Harper and Row, 1984.

MCADAMS, ALAN K. *Power and Politics in Labor Legislation.* New York: Columbia University Press, 1964.

MCANDREWS, LAWRENCE J. "Broken Ground: John F. Kennedy and the Politics of Education." Printed in Robert E. Burke and Frank Freidel, *Modern American History: New Studies and Outstanding Dissertations.* New York: Garland Publishing, 1991.

MCCULLOUGH, DAVID. *Truman.* New York: Simon and Schuster, 1992.

MCKITRICK, ERIC L. *Andrew Johnson and Reconstruction.* Chicago: University of Chicago Press, 1960.

MOLLENHOFF, CLARK R. *Game Plan for Disaster: An Ombudsman's Report on the Nixon Years.* New York: W. W. Norton and Company, 1976.

MORGAN, CHARLES, JR. *One Man, One Voice.* New York: Holt, Rinehart and Winston, 1979.

MORISON, SAMUEL ELIOT, ed. *The Development of Harvard University since the Inauguration of President Eliot, 1869–1929.* Cambridge, Mass.: Harvard University Press, 1930.

MORRIS, EDMUND. *The Rise of Theodore Roosevelt.* New York: Coward, McCann and Geoghegan, 1979.

NAVASKY, VICTOR S. *Kennedy Justice.* New York: Atheneum, 1971.

NELSON, MARCIA, ED. *The Remarkable Hands: An Affectionate Portrait.* New York: Foundation of the Federal Bar Council, 1983.

NIXON, RICHARD M. *RN: The Memoirs of Richard Nixon.* New York: Touchstone, 1990.

O'DONNELL, KENNETH P., and DAVID F. POWERS with JOE MCCARTHY. *"Johnny, We Hardly Knew Ye."* Boston: Little, Brown and Company, 1972.

OSBORNE, JOHN. *The Fifth Year of the Nixon Watch.* New York: Liveright, 1974.

OUDES, BRUCE, ed. *From: The President: Richard Nixon's Secret Files.* New York: Harper and Row, 1989.

PAPER, LEWIS J. *The Promise and the Performance. The Leadership of John F. Kennedy.* New York: Crown Publishers, 1975.

PARMET, HERBERT S. *Jack: The Struggles of John F. Kennedy.* New York: Dial Press, 1980.

PERKINS, MAXWELL E. *Editor to Author: The Letters of Maxwell E. Perkins.* Edited by John Hall Wheelock. New York: Scribners, 1950.

PRICE, RAYMOND. *With Nixon.* New York: Viking Press, 1977.

REHMUS, CHARLES M., and DORIS B. MCLAUGHLIN. *Labor and American Politics: A Book of Readings.* Ann Arbor: University of Michigan Press, 1967.

REHNQUIST, WILLIAM H. *Grand Inquests: The Historic Impeachments of Justice Samuel Chase and President Andrew Johnson.* New York: William Morrow, 1992.

RICHARDSON, ELLIOT L. *The Creative Balance: Government, Politics and the Individual in America's Third Century.* New York: Holt, Rinehart and Winston, 1976.

ROSS, EDMUND G. *History of the Impeachment of Andrew Johnson, President of the United States by the House of Representatives, and His Trial by the Senate, for High Crimes and Misdemeanors in Office, 1868.* New York: Burt Franklin, 1965.

SAKI. *The Best of Saki (H. H. Munro).* 2nd ed. London: Bodley Head, 1952.

SALOKAR, REBECCA MAE. *The Solicitor General: The Politics of Law.* Philadelphia: Temple University Press, 1992.

SANDEL, MICHAEL J. *Democracy's Discontent: America in Search of a Public Philosophy.* Cambridge, Mass.: Belknap Press of Harvard University Press, 1996.

SCHICK, MARVIN. *Learned Hand's Court.* Baltimore: Johns Hopkins Press, 1970.

SCHLESINGER, ARTHUR M., JR. *Robert Kennedy and His Times.* Boston: Houghton Mifflin, 1978.

———. *A Thousand Days: John F. Kennedy in the White House.* Boston: Houghton Mifflin, 1965.

SCHWARTZ, BERNARD. *The Ascent of Pragmatism.* Reading, Mass.: Addison-Wesley, 1990.

SHANKS, HERSHEL, ed. *The Art and Craft of Judging: The Decisions of Judge Learned Hand.* New York: Macmillan, 1968.

SIDEY, HUGH. *John F. Kennedy, President.* New York: Atheneum, 1964.

SIRICA, JOHN J. *To Set the Record Straight: The Break-In, the Tapes, the Conspirators, the Pardon.* New York: W. W. Norton and Company, 1979.

SORENSEN, THEODORE C. *Kennedy.* New York: Harper and Row, 1965.

STEVENSON, BURTON EGBERT. *The Home Book of Verse, American and English.* 7th ed. New York: Henry Holt, 1945.

———. *The Home Book of Verse, American and English.* 9th ed. 2 vols. New York: Holt, Rinehart and Winston, 1953.

———. *The Home Book of Verse for Young Folks.* New York: Henry Holt, 1929.

SULZBERGER, C. L. *The World and Richard Nixon.* New York: Prentice Hall, 1987.
SUSSMAN, BARRY. *The Great Coverup: Nixon and the Scandal of Watergate.* New York: Thomas Y. Crowell, 1974.
SUTHERLAND, ARTHUR E. *The Law at Harvard: A History of Ideas and Men, 1817–1967.* Cambridge, Mass.: Belknap Press of Harvard University Press, 1967.
TREFOUSSE, HANS L. *Impeachment of a President: Andrew Johnson, the Blacks, and Reconstruction.* Knoxville: University of Tennessee Press, 1975.
TROWBRIDGE, EUNICE, and APRIL RADBILL. *Dr. Josephine Evarts: A Tribute.* Windsor, Vt.: privately printed, 1981.
TRUMAN, HARRY S. *Memoirs.* Vol. 1, *Year of Decisions.* Garden City, N.Y.: Doubleday, 1955.
Watergate: Chronology of a Crisis. 2 vols. Washington, D.C.: Congressional Quarterly, 1973.
WATKINS, T. H. *Righteous Pilgrim: The Life and Times of Harold L. Ickes. 1874–1952.* New York: Henry Holt, 1990.
WELLMAN, FRANCIS L. *The Art of Cross-Examination.* 1904. Reprint, New York: Macmillan, 1928.
The White House Transcripts, Submission of Recorded Presidential Conversations to the Committee on the Judiciary of the House of Representatives by President Richard Nixon. New York: Bantam Books, 1974.
WHITE, THEODORE H. *The Making of the President, 1960.* New York: Atheneum, 1961.
———. *Breach of Faith: The Fall of Richard Nixon.* New York: Atheneum, 1975.
WILLS, GARRY. *The Kennedy Imprisonment: A Meditation on Power.* Boston: Little, Brown and Company, 1982.
WOLFE, TOM. *The Bonfire of the Vanities.* New York: Farrar, Straus and Giroux, 1987.
WOODWARD, BOB, and CARL BERNSTEIN. *The Final Days.* New York: Simon and Schuster, 1976.
WYZANSKI, CHARLES E., JR. *A Trial Judge's Freedom and Responsibility.* New York: Association of the Bar of the City of New York, 1952.

SCHOLARLY ARTICLES

BURKOFF, JOHN. "Appointment and Removal Powers under the Federal Constitution: The Impact of *Buckley v. Valeo." Wayne Law Review* 22 (1976): 1336.
COX, ARCHIBALD. "Judge Learned Hand and the Interpretation of Statutes." *Harvard Law Review* 60 (1947): 370.
———. "Some Aspects of the Labor Management Relations Act, 1947." *Harvard Law Review* 61 (1948): 1.
———. "The Influence of Mr. Justice Murphy on Labor Law." *Michigan Law Review* 48 (1950): 767.
———. "The Right to Engage in Concerted Activity." *Indiana Law Journal* 26 (1951): 319.
———. "Current Problems in the Law of Grievance Arbitration." *Rocky Mountain Law Review* 30 (1958): 247.
———. "The Landrum-Griffin Amendments to the National Labor Relations Act." *Minnesota Law Review* 44 (1959): 257.
———. "Reflections upon Labor Arbitration." *Harvard Law Review* 79 (1959): 1482.

————. "Poverty and the Legal Profession." *Illinois Bar Journal* 54 (1965): 12.

————. "Foreword: Constitutional Adjudication and the Promotion of Human Rights." *Harvard Law Review* 80 (1966): 91.

————. "More Learned Than Witty." *Harvard C.R.C.L. Review* 7 (1972): 501.

————. "Federalism and Individual Rights under the Burger Court." *Northwestern University Law Review* 73 (1978): 1.

————. "The Lawyer's Independent Calling." *Kentucky Law Journal* 67 (1978–79): 5.

————. "Recent Developments in Federal Labor Law Preemption." *Ohio State Law Journal* 41 (1980): 277.

————. "Congress and the Supreme Court." *Mercer Law Review* 33 (1982): 707.

————. "Constitutional Issues in the Regulation of the Financing of Election Campaigns." *Cleveland State Law Journal* 31 (1982): 395.

————. "Freedom of the Press." *University of Illinois Law Review* 1983 (1983): 3.

FREUND, PAUL. "Charles Evans Hughes as Chief Justice." *Harvard Law Review* 81 (1964): 4.

HAND, LEARNED. "Mr. Justice Cardozo." *Harvard Law Review* 52 (1939): 361.

HAND, LEARNED, and FELIX FRANKFURTER. "How Far Is a Judge Free in Rendering a Decision?" National Advisory Council on Radio in Education, Law Series, vol. 5, 1933, quoted in Archibald Cox, "Reflections upon Labor Arbitration," *Harvard Law Review* 79 (1959): 1506–7.

LEWIS, ANTHONY. "Legislative Apportionment and the Federal Courts." *Harvard Law Review* 71 (1958): 1057.

SEGAL, JEFFREY A. "Amicus Curiae Briefs by the Solicitor General during the Warren and Burger Courts: A Research Note." *Western Political Quarterly* 41 (1988): 135.

————. "Supreme Court Support for the Solicitor General: The Effect of Presidential Appointments." *Western Political Quarterly* 43 (1990): 137.

SELIG, JOEL L. "Book Reviews." *Land and Water Law Review* 25 (1990): 625.

SHANE, PETER M. "Presidents, Pardons, and Prosecutors: Legal Accountability and the Separation of Powers." *Yale Law and Policy Review* 11 (1993): 361.

WECHSLER, HERBERT. "Toward Neutral Principles of Constitutional Law." *Harvard Law Review* 73 (1959): 1.

POPULAR ARTICLES

"Anarchy Spreads in U.S. Colleges." *U.S. News & World Report,* May 6, 1968, 65.

"At War with War." *Time,* May 18, 1970, 6.

"Battle over Presidential Power." *Time,* August 6, 1973, 8.

"The Bazelon Court Awaits the Case." *Time,* September 10, 1973, 15.

BICKEL, ALEXANDER M. "The Tapes, Cox, Nixon." *New Republic,* September 29, 1973, 13.

"Birmingham, U.S.A.: 'Look at Them Run.' " *Newsweek,* May 13, 1963, 27.

"Black October: Old Enemies at War Again." *Time,* October 15, 1973, 30.

"The 'Bust' at Harvard." *Newsweek,* April 21, 1969, 102.

"The Campus Spring Offensive." *Newsweek,* April 28, 1969, 66.

"Chairman of Weaker WSB Picks His Way Carefully." *Business Week,* September 6, 1952, 168.

COHEN, RICHARD E. "Another White House Folly." *National Journal*, September 8, 1979, 1492.

"The Congress: Nine Days of Labor." *Time*, May 9, 1959, 11.

"The Court's Middle Man." *Newsweek*, October 15, 1973, 20.

"Cox at Cambridge." *New Yorker*, January 20, 1975, 25.

COX, ARCHIBALD. "Campus Unrest—Why?" *Williston Bulletin* (Williston Academy, Easthampton, Mass.) spring 1969, 4.

———. "More Reasons for Confidence Than Despair." *Anglo American Trade News*, June 1975, 6.

———. "Reflections on a Firestorm." *Saturday Review*, March 9, 1974, 12.

"Crackdown on Campaign Gifts from Big Firms." *U.S. News & World Report*, October 29, 1973, 28.

"Days of Violence in the South." *Newsweek*, May 29, 1961, 21.

"Explosion in Alabama." *Newsweek*, May 20, 1963, 25.

"Exposing the Big Cover-Up." *Newsweek*, May 28, 1973, 26.

"The Fall of Spiro Agnew." *Time*, October 22, 1973, 19.

"Famous Friends." *Harvard Magazine*, September-October, 1996, 80.

"For All the Marbles." *U.S. News & World Report*, September 21, 1987, 20.

GERSCHENKRON, ALEXANDER. "The Most Unbelievable Thing." *Harvard Magazine*, April 28, 1969, 43.

"A Good Lineman for the Quarterback." *Time*, October 22, 1973, 16.

"The Great Tapes Crisis." *Newsweek*, October 29, 1973, 22.

"Harvard and Beyond: The University under Siege." *Time*, April 18, 1969, 47.

HECHINGER, GRACE, and FRED M. HECHINGER. "Election Cry: 'Win with Harvard.' " *New York Times Magazine*, October 9, 1960, 26.

"The Historic Duel for the Nixon Tapes." *Newsweek*, September 3, 1973, 37.

"The Idea Men around Kennedy." *U.S. News & World Report*, December 5, 1960, 51.

"Instant Replay—the ITT Case." *Newsweek*, October 12, 1973, 29.

"Investigations: Last Go-Round." *Time*, July 27, 1959, 13.

"Judge Sirica: The First Test." *Time*, August 13, 1973, 8.

KARNOW, STANLEY. "Elliot Richardson: Dreaming of the Presidency." *New Republic*, May 17, 1975, 14.

KENNEDY, JOHN F. "The Shame of the States." *New York Times Magazine*, May 18, 1958, 18.

KRAMER, MICHAEL. "The Brief on Judge Bork." *U.S. News & World Report*, September 14, 1987, 18.

"Labor Reform Act of 1959." *Time*, September 14, 1959, 25.

"Labor—the Sound and the Fury." *Newsweek*, August 11, 1958, 15.

LATHAM, AARON. "Seven Days in October." *New York*, April 49, 1974, 41.

LEWIN, NATHAN. "Gross Miscalculation." *New Republic*, November 3, 1973, 12.

———. "Who Gets the Tapes?" *New Republic*, October 27, 1973, 14.

"The Man behind the Subpoena." *Newsweek*, August 6, 1973, 16.

"The Mideast Erupts." *Newsweek*, October 15, 1973, 38.

"The Miners' Milk Money." *Journal of Commerce*, October 24, 1952, 1.

"Mississippi: The Sound and the Fury." *Newsweek*, October 15, 1962, 23.

"The Mystery of the Missing Tapes." *Time*, November 12, 1973, 22.

"A New Board Takes Over." *Business Week,* August 2, 1952, 101.

"The New Style at Morgan Stanley." *Business Week,* January 9, 1974, 47.

"New White House Blast." *Time,* November 12, 1973, 78.

"The Nixon Tapes: Round Two to Cox." *Newsweek,* October 22, 1973, 43.

"Nixon's Tapes: How to Settle Out of Court." *Newsweek,* September 24, 1973, 33.

"The Occupation, the Bust, the Aftermath." *Harvard Alumni Bulletin,* April 28, 1969, 20.

"The Other Investigator." *Time,* July 16, 1973, 71.

PINCUS, WALTER. "The Cox Investigation." *New Republic,* December 8, 1973, 10.

———. "The Silbert-Petersen Puzzle." *New Republic,* July 6 and 13, 1974, 15.

———. "Who Dunnit: The Rose Mary Woods Mystery." *New Republic,* February 2, 1974, 14.

"Prosecutor vs. President: The Role of Archibald Cox." *U.S. News & World Report,* August 20, 1973, 47.

QUEIJO, JON. "Witness to Justice." *Bostonia,* September/October 1987, 49.

RASKIN, A. H. "Secrets of John H. Lewis' Great Power." *New York Times Magazine,* October 5, 1952, 15.

"Richard Nixon Stumbles to the Brink." *Time,* October 29, 1973, 12.

RICHARDSON, ELLIOT. "The Saturday Night Massacre." *Atlantic Monthly,* March 1976, 40.

"Rosemary's Boo-Boo." *Newsweek,* December 10, 1973, 26.

"Schools Hit by New Violence." *U.S. News & World Report,* October 28, 1968, 32.

"The Secretary and the Tapes Tangle." *Time,* December 10, 1973, 15.

"The Senate: Labor and a Candidate." *Newsweek,* April 7, 1958, 22.

"A Shrunken President." *The Economist,* October 27, 1973, 13.

"The South: Dark Day in Jackson." *Newsweek,* May 25, 1970, 35.

"The South: Death in Two Cities." *Time,* May 25, 1970, 22.

"State of Business: The Hot-Air War." *Time,* August 18, 1952, 77.

STEIN, JACOB. "Four Probes Endanger the Executive Branch." *National Law Journal,* June 19, 1995, 21.

"Struggle for Nixon's Tapes." *Time,* September 3, 1973, 3.

TRB. "Supreme Performances." *New Republic,* November 10, 1973, 4.

"Wage Price Action? Cox Asks for New Formula." *U.S. News & World Report,* June 25, 1962, 28.

"What Right for White?" *Time,* October 24, 1977, 95.

"Whose Labor Reform Bill? Candidate's Aches." *Newsweek,* September 7, 1959, 31.

Newspapers Consulted

Akron Beacon Journal
Albuquerque Tribune
Arizona Republic
Bangor (Maine) Daily News
Benton Harbor (Mich.) News-Palladium
Biddeford-Saco (Maine) Journal
Blue Hill (Maine) Weekly Packet

Boston American
Boston Globe
Boston Herald
Boston Herald Traveler
Boston Phoenix
Boston Record-American
Butte Montana Standard
Charlotte (N.C.) Observer
Chicago Sun-Times
Chicago Tribune
Christian Science Monitor
Cincinnati Post & Times-Star
Cleveland Plain Dealer
Columbia Daily Spectator
Concord (N.H.) Monitor
Daily Telegraph (London)
Detroit News
Ellsworth (Maine) American
Enterprise (Paris, France)
Erie (Pa.) News
Fort Worth Star-Telegram
Framingham (Mass.) South Middlesex News
Guardian (London)
Harrisburg (Pa.) Patriot News
Hartford Courant
Harvard Crimson
Harvard Law Record
Harvard University Gazette
Long Beach (Calif.) Independent
Los Angeles Times
Lynchburg (Va.) News
Maine Sunday Telegram
Miami Herald
Minneapolis Sunday Tribune
Nashua (N.H.) Telegraph
Nashville Tennessean
New Haven Register
New York Daily News
New York Herald Tribune
New York Post
New York Times
Observer (London)
Old Mole (radical underground)
Ottowa Citizen
Pelican (St. Paul's School, Concord, N.H.)
Philadelphia Evening Bulletin
Philadelphia Inquirer

Pittsfield (Mass.) Berkshire Eagle
Providence Bulletin
St. Louis Post-Dispatch
St. Petersburg Times
Tallahassee Democrat
Tucson Star
United Mine Workers Journal
Valdosta (Ga.) Daily Times
Village Voice
Wall Street Journal
Washington Evening Star
Washington (D.C.) National Observer
Washington Post
Waterville (Maine) Sentinel
Wayland (Mass.) Town Crier
Yale News

Notes

Notes on Source Materials

A principal source of material for this biography was a series of transcribed interviews conducted by the author with Archibald Cox over a period of three years. The first set of interviews took place at Cox's office at Harvard Law School in Cambridge, Massachusetts, and at his farm in South Brooksville, Maine, in the summer of 1990. The second major set of interviews took place while Cox was teaching a course at the University of Colorado School of Law in Boulder, during the spring of 1993. These interviews, recorded on 37 tapes, span over 1,500 pages in transcribed form. In the source notes, the author's interviews with Archibald Cox are designated "AC," along with the tape number and page, for easy reference in the transcripts. (Thus, AC 3:15 indicates transcribed interview with Archibald Cox, tape 3, page 15.) The author's less formal interviews with Cox over the seven-year span of work on this book are designated "AC follow-up interview," along with date. The author's interviews with all other individuals are indicated by name of interviewee. Follow-up interviews are so designated. Dates are listed at the beginning of these source materials. Transcribed interviews and the author's original notes have all been donated to the Harvard Law School Library, Special Collections, where they will be open to researchers.

The bulk of Archibald Cox's papers are housed at the Harvard Law School Library, Special Collections. Throughout these source notes, they are designated "AC papers," along with the appropriate box and folder numbers. References to Cox's "personal papers" indicate those papers that are still in the possession of the Cox family.

Several other collections require a special note. Elliot Richardson's papers, which are used extensively in the Watergate chapters, are located at the Library of Congress, Washington, D.C. These are designated "ELR papers." The large press file of James Doyle, Cox's Watergate press spokesman, occupied space in the author's attic for four years and was used extensively in researching the Watergate chapters. This significant collection has now been donated to the Harvard Law School Library to be housed with Cox's papers. For purposes of writing this book, the author organized the

461

materials in Doyle's file into temporary folders so that they could be retrieved in an organized fashion. In future years, researchers will have access to these materials at the Harvard Law School Library, undoubtedly with a more permanent index system. For now, however, the author's temporary folder numbers have been noted. All materials in this collection are designated "James Doyle papers."

A significant amount of source material for this biography was obtained from presidential collections, particularly the John F. Kennedy Library in Boston, Massachusetts; the Harry S. Truman Library in Independence, Missouri; and the Nixon Project at the National Archives in College Park, Maryland. Additional materials came from a wide array of repositories, including the Harvard University Archives, the Harvard Law School Library, and the Library of Congress. To simplify the researcher's job of locating material, the author has followed the citation form recommended by each particular library for its own source materials. Thus, citation forms may vary in the notes from library to library. However, this hopefully will achieve a broader consistency and allow documents to be retrieved easily in the future.

The following abbreviations are used throughout the source notes:

AC:	Archibald Cox
HLS:	Harvard Law School
HLSL:	Harvard Law School Library
JFK:	John F. Kennedy
JFKL:	John F. Kennedy Library
RFK:	Robert F. Kennedy
DNC:	Democratic National Committee
ELR:	Elliot L. Richardson
RN:	Richard M. Nixon

Prologue

1. Bushnell, *Crimes, Follies, and Misfortunes,* p. 137.
2. Hagan, *Eight Great American Lawyers,* p. 270; Rehnquist, *Grand Inquests,* pp. 224–25.
3. Evarts was assisted by the recuperating Henry Stanberry, as well as former Supreme Court Justice Benjamin R. Curtis and two Democratic former congressmen. See Trefousse, *Impeachment of a President,* p. 150.
4. Bushnell, *Crimes, Follies, and Misfortunes,* p. 129; Barrows, *William M. Evarts,* p. 138.
5. Hutton, "William M. Evarts: Secretary of State," pp. 14–15; Barrows, *William M. Evarts,* pp. 97–99.
6. Evarts, ed., *Arguments and Speeches of William Maxwell Evarts,* 1:3–4. The Lemmons, citizens of Virginia, had arrived in New York with eight black slaves. They planned to stay in New York only briefly before embarking for Texas, another slave state. The New York Court of Appeals held that the slaves were free by virtue of entering free territory, agreeing with Evarts's position.
7. Ibid., 1:214. After the Civil War, in 1867, the federal government again hired

Evarts to prosecute the Confederate President Jefferson Davis for treason. See ibid., 3:460; Barrows, *William M. Evarts,* pp. 171–75. Although Jefferson Davis was indicted and held in jail for two years, he was eventually released on bail and never tried. See Barrows, *William M. Evarts,* pp. 171–75.

8. Barrows, *William M. Evarts,* pp. 124–25.

9. Ibid., p. 142.

10. Evarts, ed., *Arguments and Speeches of William Maxwell Evarts,* 1:340; Barrows, *William M. Evarts,* p. 139; Rehnquist, *Grand Inquests,* pp. 210–11.

11. Hutton, "William M. Evarts: Secretary of State," p. 21. Stanton was a holdover from the Lincoln administration and had a running history of confrontations with President Johnson. See Burkoff, "Appointment and Removal Powers under the Federal Constitution," *Wayne Law Review* 22 (1976): 1388–89. Congressman Boutwell and other radical Republicans had an obvious axe to grind with the president. They had gone so far as to float the "dark suspicion" that President Johnson was linked to the murder of Abraham Lincoln. See Berger, *Impeachment: The Constitutional Problems,* p. 270.

12. Barrows, *William M. Evarts,* pp. 285–87.

13. Hagan, *Eight Great American Lawyers,* p. 255; James Doyle interview with AC, circa 1975, pp. 1–3, James Doyle papers, Harvard Law School Library, Cambridge, Massachusetts (hereinafter cited as James Doyle papers).

14. Hutton, "William M. Evarts: Secretary of State," p. 3.

15. Ibid., p. 23.

16. Hagan, *Eight Great American Lawyers,* p. 274.

17. Barrows, *William M. Evarts,* p. 157. In fact, the Tenure of Office Act was repealed in 1887. See Burkoff, "Appointment and Removal Powers under the Federal Constitution," *Wayne Law Review* 256 (1976): 1393. Another variation of that act (dealing with the appointment and removal of postmasters) was later found unconstitutional in *Myers v. U.S.,* 272 U.S. 52 (1926).

18. *Trial of Andrew Johnson,* 2:271; Evarts, ed., *Arguments and Speeches of William Maxwell Evarts,* 1:350.

19. *Trial of Andrew Johnson,* 2:270; Evarts, ed., *Arguments and Speeches of William Maxwell Evarts,* 1:348.

20. Barrows, *William M. Evarts,* p. 283.

21. Ibid., pp. 285–87.

22. Ross, *History of the Impeachment of Andrew Johnson,* pp. 98–99; Evarts, ed., *Arguments and Speeches of William Maxwell Evarts,* 1:396–98; Barrows, *William M. Evarts,* pp. 156–57.

23. Evarts, ed., *Arguments and Speeches of William Maxwell Evarts,* 1:386 (emphasis added).

24. Ibid. 1:525.

25. Hutton, "William M. Evarts: Secretary of State," p. 24.

26. Ibid.; Barrows, *William M. Evarts,* pp. 158–59.

27. Trefousse, *Impeachment of a President,* pp. 165–66; Rehnquist, *Grand Inquests,* pp. 232–35.

28. Rehnquist, *Grand Inquests,* p. 233.

29. Bushnell, *Crimes, Follies, and Misfortunes,* p. 139.

30. Trefousse, *Impeachment of a President,* p. 167. As historians would later replay the events, critical votes were cast by Senator Edmund G. Ross of Kansas and,

after him, by the more obscure Senator Peter G. Van Winkle of West Virginia. See ibid., pp. 165–68; Bushnell, *Crimes, Follies, and Misfortunes,* p. 157. Ten days later the same vote was recorded on a second article of impeachment.

31. Hutton, "William M. Evarts: Secretary of State," p. 25.

32. Ibid., pp. 24–25 n. 53.

33. C. F. Adams to William M. Evarts, July 24, 1868, William M. Evarts papers, box 1, Correspondence of William M. Evarts, January 26, 1842–June 20, 1872 (bound volumes), Library of Congress.

34. Barrows, *William M. Evarts,* p. 164.

35. Ibid., pp. 182–83.

36. Hagan, *Eight Great American Lawyers,* p. 290.

37. Evarts had secured the wildly disputed election of 1876 for the Republican Party by negotiating electoral college votes in four states that gave the election to Rutherford B. Hayes. See Evarts, ed., *Arguments and Speeches of William Maxwell Evarts,* 2:246–50. The election dispute occurred because conflicting certificates were submitted from electors in Florida, Louisiana, South Carolina, and Oregon, allowing both Democrats and Republicans to claim victory. A special Electoral Commission was established by Congress to resolve the dispute; Evarts represented the Republican Party before that commission and prevailed. Southern Democrats in Congress may have agreed not to challenge the decision of the commission in return for an agreement by congressional Republicans to withdraw federal troops from the South and end Reconstruction. But there was no indication that Evarts, an ardent Reconstructionist, was a party to any such "agreement." See Hutton, "William M. Evarts: Secretary of State," pp. 36–41.

38. Hagan, *Eight Great American Lawyers,* p. 289.

39. Evarts, ed., *Arguments and Speeches of William Maxwell Evarts,* 3:458.

40. Barrows, *William M. Evarts,* p. 54.

41. Ibid., p. 47.

42. Ibid., p. 97.

43. Dyer, *The Public Career of William M. Evarts,* p. 263.

44. Barrows, *William M. Evarts,* p. 485.

45. Ibid., p. 493.

46. Evarts, ed., *Arguments and Speeches of William Maxwell Evarts,* pp. xxiv–xxv.

Chapter 1

1. Harriet Parker, author's interview; Mary "Molly" Cox, author's interview, August 15, 1990.

2. *National Cyclopedia of American Biography,* 4 (1916):76–77.

3. Archibald Cox, interview by author, tape 1, page 1 (hereinafter cited as AC 1:1).

4. AC 1:2.

5. AC 2:20; Mary "Molly" Cox, author's interview, August 15, 1990.

6. William G. Wigton, author's interview.

7. AC 2:35.

8. Harvard Class Report, Class of 1896, Report no. 4, 1911, Harvard Archives, Cambridge, Mass.

9. Mary "Molly" Cox, author's interview, August 15, 1990.
10. Frances Bigelow Krause (a.k.a. Nancy Bigelow Krause) and Frances Perkins Cox, "Grandma's Memories," unpublished oral history, 1983, p. 125; Elizabeth Cox Bigelow, author's interview. Ms. Krause was the eldest of the grandchildren, and was named after her grandmother. A copy of "Grandma's Memories" is deposited with the Cox papers at Harvard Law School Library, Special Collections (hereinafter cited as HLSL).
11. Evarts was called "Bill" and "Billy" as a child. See Barrows, *William M. Evarts*, p. 9.
12. Frances Cox recalled that "Billy" spoke early as an infant. When she said, "Call Father, Bill!" Archie screwed up his face and yelled, "Atchy! Atchy!" His mother was extremely pleased. "Now, I always felt that was terribly smart," she explained. "You see, he'd worked it out. This person that I called 'Archie' was the same as 'Father.'" See Krause and Cox, "Grandma's Memories," p. 128.
13. Guest book, June 12, 1912, private papers of Bertha Perkins Frothingham.
14. AC 2:19. Some family history is recounted in Trowbridge and Radbill, *Dr. Josephine Evarts: A Tribute*.
15. Hemingway would one day dedicate *The Old Man and the Sea* to Perkins. Wolfe would dedicate *Of Time and the River* to him. Perkins also served as editor to Ring Lardner, Marjorie Rawlings, and other noted authors. His full name was William Maxwell Evarts Perkins, but he quickly shucked the formalities to become plain old "Max Perkins." See Berg, *Max Perkins*, pp. 27–29.
16. William M. Evarts, who was then a U.S. senator, was riding in the carriage with Perkins and was seriously injured. Dyer, *Public Career of William M. Evarts*, p. 266; Mary "Molly" Cox, author's interview, May 27, 1994.
17. Elizabeth Cox Bigelow, author's interview.
18. Hay, "Jim Bludso of the *Prairie Belle*," in Stevenson, *Home Book*, 7th ed., pp. 3342–44.
19. Bertha Perkins Frothingham, author's interview.
20. Maxwell Cox, author's interview. The formal, given names of the seven Cox children were Archibald, Elizabeth, Mary ("Molly"), Robert, Maxwell, Louis, and Rowland.
21. The Cox children also played "private school." Archie was the principal; his sisters were the pupils. Maxwell Cox, author's interview.
22. AC 3:32.
23. Mary "Molly" Cox, author's interview, May 27, 1994.
24. Elizabeth Cox Bigelow, author's interview.
25. Mary "Molly" Cox, author's interview, May 27, 1994.
26. Ibid.
27. AC 3:24; Krause and Cox, "Grandma's Memories," p. 160.
28. Krause and Cox, "Grandma's Memories," pp. 132–33.
29. Mary "Molly" Cox, author's interview, May 27, 1994.
30. Mary "Molly" Cox, author's interview, August 15, 1990; Krause and Cox, "Grandma's Memories," p. 186.
31. AC 3:2, 3.
32. AC 3:3.
33. Krause and Cox, "Grandma's Memories," p. 221.
34. AC 3:3.

35. Archibald Cox, Sr., to C. C. Monie, April 12, 1926, St. Paul's School Alumni file, Archibald Cox folder, St. Paul's School, Concord, N.H.

36. C. C. Monie to Archibald Cox, Sr., April 15, 1926, St. Paul's School Alumni file, Archibald Cox folder.

37. Meredith, "Farragut," in Stevenson, *Home Book for Young Folks,* pp. 504–5.

38. Thomas W. Clark, author's interview; William Foulke, author's interview.

39. William G. Foulke, author's interview.

40. Thomas W. Clark, author's interview.

41. William G. Foulke, author's interview.

42. To counteract mischievous urges in the boys, Dr. Drury would intercede "in loco parentis" and attempt to hammer in good behavior and manners. He lined up all the boys in the Big Study one day and taught them how to shake hands. "We had to stand up straight and look him in the eye as we walked by, . . ." one classmate remembered, "where he warned us not to be too hearty ('the athlete's handshake' and thump on the back) or too insipid ('the dead fish' or 'milking the cow')." See William G. Foulke entry, Sixty-fifth Reunion Booklet, 1930 Form, St. Paul's School (1995).

43. Mary "Molly Cox, author's interview, May 27, 1994.

44. *Horae Scholasticae,* March 22, 1927, St. Paul's School Archives.

45. Charles M. Kirkland entry, Sixty-fifth Reunion Booklet, 1930 Form, St. Paul's School (1995).

46. Thomas W. Clark, author's interview.

47. Ibid.

48. AC, author's follow-up interview, August 25, 1994; Mary "Molly" Cox, author's interview, August 15, 1990.

49. Thomas W. Clark, author's interview; William G. Foulke, author's interview.

50. *Horae Scholasticae,* November 24, 1927.

51. Ibid., June 6, 1929.

52. Marquis, *archy and mehitabel,* pp. 53–54.

53. AC 3:38.

54. *Horae Scholasticae,* June 6, 1928.

55. Ibid., June 19, 1928.

56. Frances Cox to Dr. Samuel S. Drury, undated, St. Paul's School Alumni file, Archibald Cox folder.

57. *Horae Scholasticae,* December 17, 1929.

58. Ibid., May 3, 1930.

59. Paul deGive, letter to author, July 12, 1995.

60. *Horae Scholasticae,* June 18, 1929.

61. Charles Kirkland, author's interview.

62. *Horae Scholasticae,* May 3, 1930.

63. Charles Kirkland, author's interview; J. Randall Williams III, letter to author, June 27, 1995.

64. *Horae Scholasticae,* June 4, 1930.

65. Krause and Cox, "Grandma's Memories," p. 221.

66. *Horae Scholasticae,* June 19, 1930.

67. Dr. Samuel S. Drury to Henry Pennypacker, Certificate of Honorable Dismissal, February 27, 1930, Harvard Archives, Archibald Cox undergraduate folder.

68. AC 17:18.
69. William G. Foulke, author's interview.
70. AC 3:18.
71. Alan N. Hall, author's interview.
72. Cox even toyed briefly with the notion of returning to the school as a master.
73. AC 3:18.

Chapter 2

1. AC 3:16.
2. AC 32:21; Wellman, *The Art of Cross-Examination.*
3. AC 3:37.
4. Ibid.
5. Gunther, *Learned Hand,* p. 139.
6. Krause and Cox, "Grandma's Memories," p. 153.
7. Learned Hand to Henry Pennypacker, March 31, 1930, Harvard Archives, AC undergraduate folder.
8. Archibald Cox, Sr., to A. C. Hanford, August 12, 1930, Harvard Archives, AC undergraduate folder.
9. Krause and Cox, "Grandma's Memories," p. 218.
10. AC 4:2.
11. Thomas W. Clark, author's interview.
12. AC 4:5.
13. AC 4:5–10.
14. Charles Kirkland, author's interview.
15. Ibid.
16. AC 4:18.
17. Ibid.
18. Thomas W. Clark, author's interview; Charles Kirkland, author's interview.
19. AC 4:13.
20. AC 4:16.
21. Theodore Chase, author's interview.
22. Mary "Molly" Cox, author's interview, August 15, 1990; Krause and Cox, "Grandma's Memories," p. 129.
23. Krause and Cox, "Grandma's Memories," p. 189.
24. Mary "Molly" Cox, author's interview, August 15, 1990; AC 4:20.
25. AC 4:20.
26. Mary "Molly" Cox, author's interview, August 15, 1990.
27. Maxwell E. Cox, author's interview.
28. Mary "Molly" Cox, author's interview, August 15, 1990.
29. Louis A. Cox, author's interview.
30. Susan Lawrence Hazard, author's interview; Louis A. Cox, author's interview; Thomas W. Clark, author's interview.
31. AC 4:20.
32. Mary "Molly" Cox, author's interview, May 27, 1994.

33. Frances B. Cox to R. W. Drury, March 10, 1931, St. Paul's School Alumni file, AC folder.
34. Ibid.
35. Permanent grade record, March 6, 1931, entry, Harvard Archives, AC undergraduate folder.
36. AC 4:21; Rufus Stillman, author's interview.
37. Notation, Concord Academy to Radcliffe, Radcliffe Archives, Harvard University, Cambridge, Mass.
38. AC, author's follow-up interview, August 25, 1994.
39. Elizabeth Cox Bigelow, author's interview; Mary "Molly" Cox, author's follow-up interview, June 20, 1994; Elizabeth Cox Bigelow, author's follow-up interview, July 17, 1995; AC, author's follow-up interview, September 11, 1996.
40. AC, author's follow-up interview, August 25, 1994; Charles Kirkland, author's interview; Elizabeth Cox Bigelow, author's follow-up interview, July 17, 1995; Maxwell E. Cox, author's interview.
41. AC 4:17; Cox, "Senatorial Saucer." p. 1.
42. AC 4:17.
43. Cox, "Senatorial Saucer," pp. 119–22.
44. In large part, the Democrat-Republicans were angered by the Federalists' move to make the federal judiciary strong and independent. Chief Justice Marshall's historic ruling in *Marbury v. Madison* in 1803, giving the federal courts power to determine the constitutionality of acts of Congress, only enraged them further.
45. Cox, "Senatorial Saucer," pp. 28–32.
46. AC 4:26.
47. AC 4:27, 28.
48. AC 4:26.
49. AC Transcript, 1934–37, Office of the Registrar, Harvard Law School.
50. AC 4:33.
51. AC 4:33.
52. AC 4:32.
53. Berg, *Max Perkins*, p. 36.
54. Roscoe Pound to AC, June 22, 1935, Phyllis Ames Cox, personal papers.
55. Theodore Chase, author's interview.
56. Cox's roommates would remain friends for years: Teddy Chase from college; Nat Winthrop, of the well-known Boston Winthrop family; and Sandy Choate, the grandson of the distinguished New York lawyer and ambassador Joseph H. Choate. Choate's grandfather, by pure coincidence, had been a law partner of William M. Evarts in the late 1800s. See Evarts, ed., *Articles and Speeches of William Maxwell Evarts* 1:xii; AC 4:28, 29. The firm was Evarts, Southmayd and Choate.
57. Theodore Chase, author's interview.
58. Ibid.; AC 5:33–35.
59. Floyd Haskell, author's interview; Nina Totenberg, author's interview.
60. AC, 3:33–36; 4:22, 23.
61. AC 4:22, 23.
62. AC 1:3.
63. AC to Mr. Monise, April 12, year unknown, and Frances B. Cox to Dr. Drury, July 15, year unknown, St. Paul's School Alumni file, Robert Cox folder.

64. Susan Lawrence Hazard, author's interview; Susan Lawrence Hazard, letter to author, June 20, 1994.
65. Theodore Chase, author's interview.
66. Phyllis Ames Cox, author's interview.
67. Ibid.
68. Ibid.
69. Theodore Chase, author's interview.
70. Ibid.; Mary "Molly" Cox, author's interview, August 15, 1990.
71. Anna Ela, author's interview.
72. Ibid.
73. James Barr Ames, author's interview.
74. AC 6:1. Nathan Abbott had graduated from the Boston University School of Law.
75. AC 6:2.
76. Another ancestor was Stephen Field from Vermont, who served on the U.S. Supreme Court. Cyrus West Field lay the first telegraph cable across the Atlantic Ocean. See James Doyle interview with AC, circa 1975, pp. 1–4, 5, James Doyle papers.
77. *Boston Post,* July 2, 1935; *Boston Herald,* July 2, 1935; *New York Times,* July 3, 1935. The story of Phyllis's cousins, the Ames brothers, is told every year on Class Day just before Harvard commencement, during the awarding of a prize in their memory.
78. Phyllis Ames Cox, author's follow-up interview, September 25, 1996.
79. Phyllis Ames Cox, author's interview; AC 2:5, 6.
80. Phyllis Ames Cox, author's interview.
81. AC 5:35, 36.
82. Phyllis Ames Cox, author's interview, and author's follow-up interview, October 12, 1994; Clark Byse, author's interview; AC follow-up interview, August 25, 1994.
83. Archie himself was a hopelessly "un-musical" person. But Phyllis's mother felt that Archie should attend at least one opera before he and Phyllis got married. For an engagement present, she picked Wagner's *Tristan and Isolde,* a heavy opera that overlay a beautiful love story. "He sat through that," Phyllis said, nodding her head, "but that was about it." Phyllis Ames Cox, author's follow-up interview, October 12, 1994.
84. AC 6:3; Phyllis Ames Cox, author's interview.
85. Phyllis Ames Cox, author's interview.
86. *New York Times,* March 15, 1936.
87. AC 32:10.

Chapter 3

1. AC 5:9.
2. Leuchtenburg, *Franklin D. Roosevelt and the New Deal,* p. xii.
3. Lash, *Dealers and Dreamers,* pp. 112–13.
4. AC 5:9, 10, 30.
5. AC 5:14, 15.
6. Theodore Chase, author's interview.
7. AC 5:28.

8. AC 5:18, 19.
9. AC 5:19.
10. AC 5:37.
11. James Barr Ames, author's interview.
12. AC 6:8.
13. AC, author's follow-up interview, June 5, 1995.
14. AC 34:6.
15. AC 34:5.
16. Griffith, *Judge Learned Hand and the Federal Judiciary,* p. 9.
17. AC 33:3, 4. For a lively discussion of the religious beliefs of Judge Hand and the senior Cox, see AC 29:22–27.
18. AC 6:11.
19. Ibid.
20. AC 6:12.
21. See miscellaneous correspondence in Learned Hand papers, box 1, folder 4, HLSL.
22. AC to Learned Hand, December 31, 1936, Learned Hand papers, box 51, folder 23, HLSL.
23. AC 32:25, 26.
24. Phyllis Ames Cox, author's follow-up interview, December 3, 1995.
25. Louis A. Cox, author's interview.
26. Phyllis Ames Cox, author's follow-up interview, December 3, 1995; *New York Times,* June 13, 1937; family photos and clippings, undated; Phyllis Ames Cox, author's follow-up interview, December 3, 1995; Mary "Molly" Cox, author's interview, August 15, 1990.
27. Phyllis Ames Cox, author's follow-up interview, December 3, 1995.
28. Phyllis Ames Cox, author's interview.
29. AC 6:13.
30. Phyllis Ames Cox, author's interview.
31. Ibid.
32. Learned Hand to Walter S. Smeaton, August 2, 1941, Archibald Cox papers, Harvard Law School Library (hereinafter cited as AC papers), box 37, folder 15.
33. AC 6:17.
34. Ibid.
35. AC 6:19; Cox, "More Learned than Witty," p. 502 n. 1. For another amusing bench memo authored by Hand during Cox's tenure as a clerk, see the memorandum to fellow Judges Hand and Clark in *Quinn v. Kungsholm,* May 25, 1938, AC papers, box 37, folder 15.
36. AC 6:20.
37. AC 6:21.
38. AC 6:24.
39. Gunther, *Learned Hand,* p. 301.
40. AC 6:23.
41. AC 6:26.
42. AC 6:25.
43. AC 6:25, 26.
44. AC 6:26.
45. AC 6:26, 27.

46. AC 6:26. The full segment of the song from *Iolanthe,* which Hand sung, went like this:

> The law is the true embodiment.
> Of everything that's excellent.
> It has no kind of fault or flaw,
> And I, my Lords, embody the Law.
> The constitutional guardian I
> Of pretty young Wards in Chancery,
> All very agreeable girls—and none
> Are over the age of twenty one.
> A pleasant occupation for
> A rather susceptible Chancellor!

See Sir William Schwenck Gilbert and Sir Arthur Seymour Sullivan, *Iolanthe* (1882).

47. AC 6:30.
48. AC 33:8, 9; *New York Times,* January 11, 1938.
49. AC 33:11. Hand was seriously considered for the Court and passed up at least three different times: in 1922, 1930, and 1942. See Gunther, *Learned Hand,* pp. 274–75, 418–28, 569–70; Nelson, *The Remarkable Hands,* pp. 13, 18–19.
50. Gerald Gunther's biography confirms that Hand wrangled with powerful conflicting emotions when it came to his failed promotions to the Supreme Court. After Hughes was selected in 1930, Hand wrote to his wife, Frances, on one of her many trips abroad: "Really, I am not so sorry about the closing of the door for me to Washington. That damned thing was in my thoughts all the time; it made a kind of coward of me. After the first, which I will agree was a little of a dasher, I began to feel as though something had been lifted from my spirits and now I feel freer." See Gunther, *Learned Hand,* pp. 427, 569–70.
51. AC 33:11, 12.
52. Ibid.
53. AC 6:28.
54. Ibid. In other words, Hand wished he had been a "bon vivant." He felt "rankled" to the end of his life that he missed this opportunity. For a lively discussion of this topic, see Gunther, *Learned Hand,* pp. 26–31.
55. AC 6:29.
56. For a list of Hand's clerks through 1959, see Louis Henkin to Mrs. Curtis, November 19, 1954, Learned Hand papers, box 234, folder 18, HLSL.
57. AC 6:35, 36.
58. AC 6:29.
59. AC 7:4, 5.
60. AC 7:6.
61. Ibid.
62. Ibid.
63. AC 7:6, 7.
64. Phyllis Ames Cox, author's interview.
65. AC 7:6.

Chapter 4

1. Phyllis Ames Cox, author's interview.
2. The firm was now Ropes, Gray, Best, Coolidge and Rugg. Charles Rugg was the

son of Arthur P. Rugg, former chief justice of the Supreme Judicial Court of Massachusetts.

3. AC 7:12.

4. AC 7:15.

5. AC 7:12, 13; Lash, *Dealers and Dreamers,* pp. 430–33; *Associated Press v. Labor Board,* 301 U.S. 103 (1937). The principal case that sustained the National Labor Relations Act and led FDR to abandon his court-packing plan was *NLRB v. Jones & Laughlin,* 301 U.S. 1 (1937).

6. Lash, *Dealers and Dreamers,* p. 431.

7. AC 7:13.

8. AC 34:20.

9. Lash, *Dealers and Dreamers,* p. 110.

10. AC 7:20; Lash, *Dealers and Dreamers,* pp. 110–111.

11. Phyllis Ames Cox, author's follow-up interview, December 20, 1994.

12. The oldest child's given name was "Sarah." But her birth certificate mistakenly recorded her name as "Sally," a nickname that followed her throughout childhood.

13. James Doyle interview with AC, circa 1975, pp. 1–8, James Doyle papers.

14. *Public Papers and Addresses of Franklin D. Roosevelt,* vol. 10, item 103, pp. 435–38, and item 116, pp. 490–95; Shurbet, "John L. Lewis," p. 49.

15. *Public Papers and Addresses of Franklin D. Roosevelt,* vol. 10, item 103, pp. 435–38, and item 20, pp. 76–80.

16. Learned Hand to Francis Biddle, November 17, 1941, box 49, folder 19, Learned Hand papers, HLSL.

17. This term dated back to Robert Jackson's tenure, prior to his appointment to the Supreme Court. During Jackson's years as solicitor general, a letter mailed with only the address, "The Celestial General, Washington, D.C.," made its way to his office. See Caplan, *Tenth Justice,* p. 171.

18. AC, author's follow-up interview, June 5, 1995; AC 15:29–32; *Weber v. United States,* 315 U.S. 787 (1942); *Weber v. United States,* 119 F.2d 932 (9th Circuit 1941).

19. AC 15:30.

20. Ibid.

21. Krause and Cox, "Grandma's Memories," pp. 230–32.

22. Molly Cox, author's interview, August 15, 1990.

23. Robert Cox to Frances Cox, undated, following May 3, 1943, letter, *Letters (1941–43) of Robert Hill Cox II,* ed. Max Perkins, (privately printed, n.d.), contained in Bertha Perkins Frothingham private papers (hereinafter cited as *Letters*). A copy of these letters has been provided to the Harvard Law School Library, AC papers.

24. AC 35:5, 6.

25. Robert Cox to Frances Cox, August 25, 1942, *Letters.* Jalna refers to the series of novels by Canadian writer Mazo de la Roche about the mythical Whiteoaks family. *Jalna* itself was published in 1927; the series continued through the mid-1940s. Forsyte refers to John Galsworthy's saga about the upper-middle-class Forsyte family in London. This series of books was published in the early 1900s.

26. Mary "Molly" Cox, author's interview, May 27, 1994.

27. Krause and Cox, "Grandma's Memories," p. 235.

28. AC 7:42, 43.

29. For an account of how the United States geared up for battle in World War II, see Brinkley, *Washington Goes to War.*
30. Robert Cox to Frances Cox, June 4, 1943, *Letters.*
31. AC 8:13, 14; Lieutenant G. A. Lyon to Frances Cox, August 21, 1943, *Letters;* John B. Edmonds, ed., *St. Paul's School in the Second World War,* pp. 108–9.
32. Lieutenant G. A. Lyon to Frances Cox, August 21, 1943, *Letters.*
33. AC 35:6.
34. AC 35:6, 7.
35. Lieutenant G. A. Lyon to Frances Cox, August 21, 1943, *Letters;* Mary "Molly" Cox, author's interview, May 27, 1994.
36. Mary "Molly" Cox, author's interview, May 27, 1994.
37. George R. I. VI (king of United Kingdom) to Frances Cox, May 19, 1943, Mary "Molly" Cox, private papers; Mary "Molly" Cox, author's interview, May 27, 1994.
38. Phyllis Ames Cox, author's interview.
39. Louis A. Cox, author's interview.
40. Robert Cox to Frances Cox, undated, *Letters.*
41. Frances Cox to Learned Hand, June 14, 1943, Learned Hand papers, box 69, folder 19, HLSL.
42. The Lend-Lease Administration, the Department of Justice, and the Department of Treasury all resisted being integrated into Finletter's operation in the State Department when it came to coordinating aid to the Allied powers abroad. Myres S. McDougal, author's interview.
43. AC 8:4.
44. AC 8:5, 6.
45. AC 8:8.
46. AC 8:9, 10.
47. AC 8:16.
48. Watkins, *Righteous Pilgrim,* pp. 813–14.
49. AC, author's follow-up interview, June 5, 1995. There was also a new man appointed by President Truman to become solicitor of labor, William S. Tyson, who did not impress Cox. The feeling was apparently mutual. See oral history interview, William S. Tyson, October 6, 1977, p. 8, Truman Library; AC, author's follow-up interview, June 5, 1995.
50. AC 22:26.
51. AC, author's follow-up interview, June 5, 1995.
52. AC 8:17, 18.
53. Phyllis Ames Cox, author's follow-up interview, December 20, 1994.
54. Phyllis Cox (the mother) would enjoy poking fun at the name for years: "There hasn't been another Phyllis named, I think, since we named our daughter that. You know how old a person is, if they're a Phyllis. You know they're at least forty-five or over." Phyllis Ames Cox, author's interview.
55. AC 1:8.
56. AC 8:20, 21.
57. AC 8:21, 22.
58. AC 8:28.
59. AC 8:23.
60. AC 8:24.

61. AC 8:25.
62. AC 8:26.
63. AC 8:27.
64. Maxwell E. Cox, author's interview.
65. AC 8:31–34. Cox's salary is recorded in his personnel file at the Harvard Law School.
66. AC 8:36, 37.
67. AC 6:34.
68. AC 8:38.
69. AC 8:39.

Chapter 5

1. Lee, *Truman and Taft Hartley*, p. 17.
2. McCullough, *Truman*, pp. 480–81, 492–506; Truman, *Memoirs*, pp. 500–503; Cochra, *Harry Truman*, pp. 205–6.
3. This board was headed by Cy Ching of U.S. Rubber Company, a man widely regarded as the granddaddy of industrial relations in the United States.
4. *New York Times*, June 14, 1951.
5. Robben W. Fleming, author's interview.
6. Cox had done a little of this sort of work as associate solicitor of labor, dabbling in Davis-Bacon Act cases. But for the most part it was new terrain. See AC 9:12–14.
7. For a discussion of the events leading up to the *Steel Seizure* case, see Donovan, *Tumultuous Years*, pp. 383–85; Hamby, *Beyond the New Deal*, p. 455; Gitlow, *Wage Determination under National Boards*, p. 184; *New York Times*, April 2, 3, 5, and 8, 1952; Radio Address, April 6, 1952, Wage Stabilization Proposals, 1950–52 folder, Enarson papers, Harry S. Truman Library, Independence, Mo. (hereinafter cited as Truman Library). The Wage Stabilization Board had recommended higher wages and fringe benefits for the steelworkers, prompting the industry members of the board to resign en masse. The steel companies then refused to pay the wage increases, and the Steelworkers' union declared their intention to strike.
8. Donovan, *Tumultuous Years*, p. 387; McCullough, *Truman*, pp. 897–99. White House advisers recall that the Defense Department bluntly warned President Truman that a shortage of steel supplies would threaten thousands of American troops on the battlefield in Korea. As overblown as these warnings may have been in hindsight, they prompted President Truman to take decisive action. See Harold L. Enarson, author's interview; Milton P. Kayle, author's interview.
9. The Taft-Hartley Act, the Court held, was the only proper vehicle for resolving labor disputes in the case of a national emergency.
10. Donovan, *Tumultuous Years*, p. 390; *New York Times*, July 30, 1952; Gitlow, *Wage Determination under National Boards*, pp. 180–88.
11. Phyllis Ames Cox, author's follow-up interview, December 20, 1994.
12. Frances Cox to Learned Hand, May 15, 1952, Learned Hand papers, box 86, file 16, HLSL. *Spirit of Liberty* generated wide acclaim and propelled Hand into the unexpected status of "American folk hero." Gunther, *Learned Hand*, p. 639.

13. "Chairman of Weaker WSB Picks His Way Carefully," *Business Week*, September 6, 1952, p. 169.
14. Hechler, *Working with Truman*, pp. 45–49; Ferrell, *Harry S. Truman: A Life*, p. 189.
15. Appointment papers, July 30, 1952, WHCF:OF, 2900B (Jan.–Nov. 1952 folder), Truman papers, Truman Library; *New York Times*, July 31, 1952.
16. *New York Times*, August 1, 1952.
17. Ibid.
18. Phyllis Ames Cox, author's interview.
19. Sally Cox, author's interview.
20. Harold L. Enarson, author's interview.
21. *New York Times*, July 31, 1952.
22. The guidelines established a formula for determining what level of increases were permissible. AC 9:20, 21; News Release, September 10, 1952, Comparative Wage Movements—WSB folder, Enarson papers, Truman Library.
23. AC 9:21.
24. AC 9:21, 22.
25. News Release, September 10, 1952, Comparative Wage Movements—WSB folder, Enarson papers, Truman Library.
26. Harold L. Enarson, author's interview.
27. Ibid.
28. Ibid.
29. Shurbet, "John L. Lewis," pp. 6–10, 100–108.
30. Jenkins, *Truman*, p. 84.
31. *New York Times*, September 26, 1952.
32. *United Mine Workers Journal*, October 1, 1952.
33. *New York Times*, October 11, 1952.
34. Ibid., October 11 and 14, 1952.
35. Ibid.
36. AC 9:23.
37. The other public members consisted of Harold Enarson from the Bureau of Budget; Charles Killingsworth, an economics professor from Michigan; and Herman Lazarus, a lawyer from Philadelphia.
38. *New York Times*, October 19, 1952.
39. Ibid.
40. Ibid.; Press Release, October 18, 1952, Records of the Wage and Salary Stabilization Boards of the Economic Stabilization Agency, RG 293, Box 136, National Archives.
41. *New York Times*, October 21, 1952.
42. *New York Times*, October 26, 1952.
43. Ibid.
44. AC 9:23; "The Miners' Milk Money," *Journal of Commerce*, October 24, 1952.
45. *Washington Post*, October 23, 1952.
46. John L. Lewis to Harry M. Moses, October 21, 1952, WHCF:OF, 407-B Coal Strike (1950–53) folder, Truman papers, Truman Library.
47. *New York Times*, October 26, 1952.

48. AC 34:18.
49. Old Ben Coal Corp. to R. L. Darby, October 23, 1952, and R. L. Darby to Harry S. Truman, October 24, 1952, WHCF:OF 407-B Coal Strike, D folder, Truman papers, Truman Library.
50. Hazel Sholenberger to Harry S. Truman, August 27, 1952, WHCF:OF, 407-B Coal Strike, S Folder, Truman papers, Truman Library.
51. John J. Holloran to Harry S. Truman, October 22, 1952, WHCF:OF, 407-B Coal Strike, H folder, Truman papers, Truman Library.
52. John DeVito to Harry S. Truman, October 21, 1952, WHCF:OF, 407-B Coal Strike, U folder, Truman papers, Truman Library.
53. Harold L. Enarson, author's interview.
54. AC 9:26.
55. Ibid.; Bolt, *A Man for All Seasons*, p. 66.
56. AC 9:23–26, 34:15.
57. President's appointments, November 12, 1952, PSF, Presidential Appointment File, Memorandum re: Appointment File, Daily Sheets—1952—November folder, Truman papers, Truman Library.
58. AC 34:16.
59. President's appointments, November 12, 1952, PSF, Presidential Appointment File, Memorandum re: Appointment File, Daily Sheets—1952—November folder, Truman papers, Truman Library.
60. AC 9:27.
61. Harold L. Enarson, author's interview.
62. *New York Times,* October 26, 1952.
63. Transcript of Proceedings, November 17, 1952, Economic Stabilization Agency Bituminous Coal Appeal, November 12, 1952, folder, Enarson papers, Truman Library. See also *United Mine Workers Journal,* November 15, 1952, which referred to Roger Putnam as "Pussyfooter Putnam."
64. Charles C. Killingsworth, author's interview.
65. AC 34:12.
66. Oral history interview, David L. Cole, September 20, 1972, pp. 28–30, Truman Library; *Washington Post,* October 27 and December 5, 1952; *United Mine Workers Journal,* November 1, 1952; Shurbet, "John L. Lewis," p. 306. Within weeks the two would be good friends, with the president inviting Lewis to serve as a trustee of the proposed Truman Library in Independence, Missouri. Lewis wired his acceptance and later made a contribution of ten thousand dollars to the library. See Shurbet, "John L. Lewis," pp. 306–7; McCullough, *Truman,* p. 962.
67. Gitlow, *Wage Determination under National Boards,* p. 188.
68. Harry S. Truman to Roger L. Putnam, December 3, 1952, WHCF:OF, 407-B Coal Strike (1950–53) folder, Truman papers, Truman Library.
69. AC 34:17.
70. John T. Dunlop, author's interview.
71. Harold L. Enarson, author's interview. Enarson joined the other two public members of the board, Killingsworth and Lazarus, in issuing a news release that summarized their view: "In our judgment, this is not an appropriate time or way to terminate the stabilization program. Nor can we in good conscience assume responsibility for destroying the program that we were appointed to administer."

See News Release, December 3, 1952, WSB-Memos and Clippings re: the Coal Industry—1952, Enarson papers, Truman Library.

72. AC 9:24.
73. Ibid.
74. Harold L. Enarson, author's interview.
75. James Doyle interview with AC, circa 1975, pp. 1–22, James Doyle papers.
76. Harold L. Enarson, author's interview.
77. AC 9:28.
78. Ibid. (emphasis added).
79. Harold L. Enarson, author's follow-up interview, January 26, 1996.
80. As one board member described the dangerous game that Putnam had played, "You try to hold the line. You use oblique language. Before long the game is gone." See Harold Enarson, author's interview.
81. AC 9:32. Murphy even suggested that he should write the letter of resignation for Cox. See James Doyle interview with AC, circa 1975, pp. 1–35, James Doyle papers.
82. PSF, Longhand Notes (Harry S. Truman), Longhand Personal Memos, 1952 (folder 2), December 5, 1952, Truman papers, Truman Library.
83. AC 9:30, 31.
84. *Washington Post,* December 4, 1952.
85. Appointments, December 4, 1952, WH-Record of Telephone Calls and Appointments—1952 (June–Dec.) folder, Murphy papers, Truman Library.
86. AC to Harry S. Truman, December 4, 1952, AC papers; WHCF:OF, 2900-B (Dec. 1952–53) folder, Truman papers, Truman Library.
87. Harry S. Truman to AC, December 4, 1952, WHCF:OF, 2900-B (Dec. 1952–53) folder, Truman papers, Truman Library.
88. *New York Times,* December 5, 1952.
89. AC 34:11; AC, author's follow-up interview, July 15, 1996.
90. Edward H. Collins to AC, December 11, 1952, AC papers, box 36, folder 1.
91. Undated poem, author "wbn," Economic Stabilization Agency (transcript of proceedings) Bituminous Coal Appeal, November 17, 1952, folder, Enarson papers, Truman Library.

Chapter 6

1. AC 22:38, 29, 30.
2. AC 22:30–32. Material regarding Cox's work as a labor arbitrator can be found in AC papers, boxes 63–70, HLSL.
3. AC 22:32, 33; *New York Times,* April 29 and August 14, 1954.
4. *New York Times,* August 14, 1954.
5. Ibid., June 4, 1960.
6. AC 22:33, 34.
7. AC 22:29, 30; *Boston Herald,* December 3, 1949.
8. AC 10:9–17; *Gryger v. Burke,* 334 U.S. 728 (1948). This was before the days when indigent parties were entitled to lawyers as a matter of course. See *Gideon v. Wainright,* 372 U.S. 335 (1963).
9. AC 10:9–17; *Townsend v. Burke,* 334 U.S. 736 (1947). Cox scrupulously avoided

making direct reference to the "saxophone" crack, since Judge McDevitt had corrected this error. But the court still concluded that McDevitt had been too "facetious" during sentencing, and made specific reference to the saxophone comments. See *Townsend v. Burke*, 334 U.S. 736 (1947).

10. See also *Keenan v. Burke*, 342 U.S. 881 (1951) (per curiam).

11. AC 10:12.

12. AC 10:12, 13.

13. AC 10:13.

14. Louis B. Schwartz, author's interview. For a full account of Sheeler's case, see Frank and Frank, *Not Guilty*, pp. 167–86.

15. AC 10:13.

16. AC 5:6.

17. AC 5:5.

18. Cox, "Some Aspects of the Labor Management Relations Act, 1947," *Harvard Law Review* 61 (1948): 1; Cox, "Reflections upon Labor Arbitration," *Harvard Law Review* 72 (1959): 1482.

19. Cox "Some Aspects of the Labor Management Relations Act, 1947," *Harvard Law Review* 61 (1948): 1; Cox, "Reflections upon Labor Arbitration," *Harvard Law Review* 72 (1959): 1482; Cox, "Current Problems in the Law of Grievance Arbitration," *Rocky Mountain Law Review* 30 (1958): 247.

20. Cox, "Judge Learned Hand and the Interpretation of Statutes," *Harvard Law Review* 60 (1947): 370.

21. James R. Hoffa to AC, November 2, 1960, AC papers, box 38, folder 13; AC to James R. Hoffa, November 22, 1960, AC papers, box 38, folder 13.

22. The list of Cox's publications is contained in his Personal Data Questionnaire submitted to the U.S. Circuit Judge Nominating Commission in early 1979. See AC to Florence R. Rubin, January 26, 1979, and accompanying Questionnaire, AC personal papers.

23. W. Willard Wirtz to AC, February 22, 1955, AC papers, box 42, folder 8.

24. Philip B. Heymann, author's interview. Cox also did his share of committee work whenever Dean Griswold asked him to take on an assignment. Among other assignments, he served on a major committee with A. J. Casner, Kingman Brewster (later president of Yale), and other faculty colleagues charged with recommending curriculum reform in the late 1950s. David R. Herwitz, author's interview; AC, author's follow-up interview, June 12, 1995.

25. Milton P. Kayle, author's interview.

26. Harry H. Wellington, author's interview.

27. Cox himself described his teaching philosophy in the *Harvard Law School Record*, October 30, 1946, shortly after he was hired.

28. See, for example, *New York Times*, February 29, 1960.

29. The accounts of former students are not attributed to specific sources, in order to avoid embarrassment to individuals who have requested anonymity. However, they are documented in the author's interview notes relating to Cox's teaching, which have been donated to the Harvard Law School Library.

30. Another day in Labor Law, Cox called on a string of students, all of whom were unprepared. Recalled Richard H. Seeburger, who later became a law school dean in Pittsburgh, "He simply folded up his book and walked out of the classroom." Richard H. Seeburger, author's interview.

31. Daniel K. Mayers, author's interview.
32. Maxwell E. Cox, author's interview.
33. On the other hand, Cox could at times be sharp and unflattering in his commentary. He wrote one note to the Board of Students Advisors about an agency case he had judged, and stated that the problem was "unsatisfactory" and parts of it "absurd." See AC to Board of Student Advisors, March 14, 1960, AC papers, box 84, folder 21.
34. AC to George Goldberg, October 5, 1956, AC papers, box 37, folder 16.
35. Harry H. Wellington, author's interview.
36. AC 22:27; Elliot L. Richardson, author's follow-up interview, May 2, 1995.
37. Elliot L. Richardson, author's follow-up interview, May 2, 1995.
38. Phyllis Cox, author's interview.
39. Sally Cox, author's interview.
40. Phyllis Cox, author's interview.
41. Ibid.; Archibald Cox, Jr., author's interview; Stevenson, *Home Book of Verse,* 7th ed., p. 176; Bartlett, *Familiar Quotations,* p. 658.
42. Maxwell E. Cox, author's interview.
43. Wayland United Nations correspondence is contained in AC papers, box 42, folder 4. Two successful programs dealt with the "Suez Canal Crisis" and "Security in the Atomic Age."
44. Phyllis Ames Cox, author's follow-up interviews, July 23 and August 21, 1996.
45. Sally Cox was pictured on the cover of *Morgan Horse Magazine* in 1954, in a neat riding jacket, after winning first prize in the "fitting and showmanship" class of a national competition with her horse Townsend MacArthur. See *Morgan Horse Magazine,* 1954, Phyllis Ames Cox personal papers.
46. Phyllis also judged 4-H youth presentations. One year, she watched stoically as a seven-year-old boy with thick eyeglasses demonstrated with intensity and thoroughness "how you tell a mommy rabbit from a daddy rabbit," in order to win his year's achievement award. See Phyllis Ames Cox, author's follow-up interview, September 11, 1996.
47. Phyllis Ames Cox, author's follow-up interview, December 13, 1995.
48. Archibald Cox, Jr., author's interview.
49. AC to Archibald Cox, Jr., undated, Phyllis Ames Cox personal papers.
50. The name "Brookway Farm" was created by the children.
51. AC to Phyllis Ames Cox, undated, Phyllis Ames Cox personal papers.
52. Sally Cox, author's interview; Archibald Cox, Jr., author's interview; Phyllis Cox, author's interview; family photos.
53. Rufus Stillman, author's interview.
54. Adelia Moore, author's interview. Bishop Paul Moore had been a classmate of Rob Cox's at St. Paul's School.
55. Rufus Stillman, author's interview.
56. Krause and Cox, "Grandma's Memories," pp. 112, 121–22; Mary "Molly" Cox, author's interview, May 27, 1994.
57. Frances Cox to Matthew Warren, December 4, 1963, and Matthew Warren to Frances Cox, December 9, 1963, St. Paul's School Alumni file, Robert Cox folder.
58. Sally Cox, author's interview; Phyllis Cox, author's interview; Archibald Cox, Jr., author's interview.
59. Archibald Cox, Jr., author's interview.

60. See "The Coxes' Christmas Rhymes," foreword and p. 16, Phyllis Ames Cox personal papers. A copy of this typed collection of the Cox family poems has been deposited with the Cox papers, Harvard Law School Library.
61. "The Coxes' Christmas Rhymes," p. 36, Phyllis Ames Cox personal papers.
62. Phyllis Ames Cox, author's follow-up interview, August 21, 1996; Archibald Cox, Jr., author's interview.
63. Sally Cox, author's interview.
64. "The Coxes' Christmas Rhymes," foreword, Phyllis Ames Cox personal papers.

Chapter 7

1. AC 9:34.
2. Ibid.
3. AC 9:36, 10:1; *Wayland (Mass.) Town Crier,* October 9, 1958. The Cochituate end of Wayland, on the other side of town from the Coxes, was once part of the old shoe center at Natick.
4. AC 10:19, 20.
5. Blair, *The Search for J.F.K.,* pp. 365–67.
6. JFK to AC, March 24, 1953, April 18, 1953, and April 27, 1953, Senate Files Correspondence, "C" (Cox–Cri) folder, Pre-Presidential Papers, box 416, John F. Kennedy Library (hereinafter cited as JFKL). See also white copies of same letters in Senate Files General, "C" (CL–CO) folder, Pre-Presidential Papers, box 479, JFKL; AC to JFK, April 21, 1953, and attached undated memorandum, Senate Files General, "C" (CL–CO) folder, Pre-Presidential Papers, boxes 416 and 479; *New York Times,* May 27, 1953.
7. Evelyn Lincoln, author's interview.
8. JFK to AC, June 1, 1953, Senate Files General, "C" (CL–CO) folder, Pre-Presidential Papers, box 479, JFKL.
9. AC to JFK, June 18, 1953, Senate Files General, "C" (CL–CO) folder, Pre-Presidential Papers, box 479, JFKL.
10. Bellace and Berkowitz, *The Landrum-Griffin Act,* pp. 2–3.
11. Ibid., p. 3.
12. "Investigations: Last Go-Round," *Time,* July 27, 1959, p. 13.
13. AC 10:21, 22.
14. This informal advisory group included Lloyd Reynolds, economics professor at Yale; J. Douglass Brown, labor economist at MIT; Richard Lester, arbitrator and professor of economics at Princeton; Philip Taft, labor expert at Brown; Harry H. Wellington, former student of Cox's and then professor at Yale Law School; and Sumner H. Slichter, Harvard economics professor. See AC 10:22; Memorandum, Ralph A. Dungan to Lloyd G. Reynolds et al., November 4, 1957, Senate Files Legislation, Labor 10/4/57–11/14/57 folder, Pre-Presidential Papers, box 696, JFKL; Ralph A. Dungan to AC, November 5, 1957, and November 6, 1957, Pre-Presidential Papers, box 437, JFKL; Ralph A. Dungan to AC, October 15, 1957, November 19, 1957, and December 4, 1957, Senate Files Correspondence, "C" (CO–CY) folder, Pre-Presidential Papers, box 437, JFKL.
15. AC 10:24; oral history interview of AC by Richard A. Lester, November 25, 1964, pp. 3–4, JFKL.

16. See Memo to Mssrs. Brown et al., January 15, 1958, AC papers, box 88, folder 12.
17. AC 35:13; oral history interview of AC, pp. 4–5, JFKL.
18. AC 10:29.
19. Lee, *Eisenhower and Landrum-Griffin*, p. 97.
20. AC 10:29, 30.
21. Oral history interview of Seymour Harris by Arthur Schlesinger, Jr., June 16, 1964, and June 17, 1964, p. 8, JFKL.
22. Oral history interview of Ralph A. Dungan by Larry J. Hackman, December 9, 1967, p. 53, JFKL; Ralph A. Dungan, author's interview.
23. Press Release, March 28, 1958, Senate Files Legislation, 85th–2nd Labor: S 3974 Kennedy-Ives Bill 3/11/58–6/10/58 folder, Pre-Presidential Papers, box 623, JFKL.
24. Burns, *John Kennedy*, p. 225.
25. Senate Report 1684, 85th Cong., 2d sess., Serial 12062, March 27, 1958; "The Senate: Labor and a Candidate," *Newsweek*, April 7, 1958, 24; Lee, *Eisenhower and Landrum-Griffin*, p. 82.
26. Lee, *Eisenhower and Landrum-Griffin*, p. 81.
27. Press Release, June 12, 1958, Senate Files Legislation, 85th–2nd Labor: S 3974 Kennedy-Ives Bill 6/12/58–6/19/58 folder, Pre-Presidential Papers, box 623, JFKL.
28. Ralph A. Dungan to AC, March 10, 1958, Senate Files Correspondence, COR–CZ 1958 folder, Pre-Presidential Papers, box 451, JFKL.
29. JFK to AC, February 5, 1958, Senate Files Correspondence, COR–CZ 1958 folder, Pre-Presidential Papers, box 451, JFKL.
30. AC 10:33.
31. AC 10:33, 34.
32. Oral history interview of Ralph A. Dungan, pp. 16–17, JFKL.
33. Evelyn Lincoln, author's interview.
34. Ibid.
35. Ibid.
36. Oral history interview of Ralph A. Dungan, pp. 38–39, JFKL.
37. Ibid., pp. 55–56; oral history interview of Alexander K. Christie by John F. Stewart, December 6, 1966, p. 56, JFKL.
38. Oral history interview of Ralph A. Dungan, p. 56, JFKL.
39. Ibid., p. 38.
40. Oral history interview of AC, p. 10, JFKL.
41. Oral history interview of Ralph A. Dungan, p. 44, JFKL.
42. Ibid., p. 46.
43. Ralph A. Dungan, author's interview.
44. Ibid.
45. Oral history interview of Ralph A. Dungan, pp. 1–16, JFKL.
46. *Wayland (Mass.) Town Crier*, May 22, 1958; Clark Byse, author's interview.
47. Evelyn Lincoln, author's interview.
48. AC 10:33.
49. AC 10:31, 32.
50. *Christian Science Monitor*, June 19, 1958.
51. JFK to Erwin N. Griswold, June 6, 1958, General Files, "G" folder, Pre-Presidential Papers, box 697, JFKL.

52. Erwin N. Griswold to JFK, June 12, 1958, Senate Files Legislation, Labor 6/9/58–6/16/58 folder, Pre-Presidential Papers, box 697, JFKL.

53. *Congressional Record* 104 (1958): 15419–28; "Labor: The Sound and the Fury," *Newsweek,* August 11, 1958, 15; Lee, *Eisenhower and Landrum-Griffin,* pp. 85–88; Burns, *John Kennedy,* p. 225–26; Bellace and Berkowitz, *The Landrum-Griffin Act,* p. 5.

54. AC to Ralph Dungan, August 29, 1958, Senate Files Legislation, Labor 10/9/58–10/22/58 folder, Pre-Presidential Papers, box 699, JFKL.

55. Press Release, August 18, 1958, Senate Files Legislation, 85th–2nd Labor: S. 3974 Kennedy-Ives Bill 6/17/58–8/18/58, Pre-Presidential Papers, box 623, JFKL.

56. Lee, *Eisenhower and Landrum-Griffin,* pp. 96–97.

57. Oral history interview of Ralph A. Dungan, p. 37, JFKL.

58. JFK to AC, January 31, 1959, Senate File Correspondence, COR–CZ 1958 folder, Pre-Presidential Papers, box 451, JFKL; JFK to AC, December 31, 1958, Senate Correspondence Copy file, Pre-Presidential Papers, box 451, JFKL.

59. Lee, *Eisenhower and Landrum-Griffin,* p. 99.

60. Ralph A. Dungan, author's interview.

61. Press Release, April 14, 1959, Senate Files Legislation, 86th–1st Labor Management Reform Material 2/12/59–4/15/59 folder, Pre-Presidential Papers, box 632, JFKL.

62. *Erie (Pa.) News,* January 27, 1959; *Lynchburg (Va.) News,* January 26, 1959; *Charlotte (N.C.) Observer,* January 29, 1959.

63. *Nashville Tennessean,* January 23, 1959.

64. Oral history interview of Alexander K. Christie by John F. Stewart, December 6, 1966, pp. 7–8, JFKL; oral history interview of AC, pp. 13–14, JFKL; Lee, *Eisenhower and Landrum-Griffin,* p. 99.

65. C. F. Early to JFK, March 13, 1959, Senate Files Legislation, Labor 3/17/59–3/31/59 folder, Pre-Presidential Papers, box 721, JFKL.

66. Lee, *Eisenhower and Landrum-Griffin,* pp. 100–101.

67. AC 10:6.

68. Ibid.

69. Lee, *Eisenhower and Landrum-Griffin,* pp. 102–8; Cox, "The Landrum-Griffin Amendments to the National Labor Relations Act," *Minnesota Law Review* 44 (1959): 257; oral history interview of AC, pp. 14–16, JFKL. The pro-labor "sweeteners" were added to Title VI of the bill.

70. Lee, *Eisenhower and Landrum-Griffin,* p. 112. The McClellan "Bill of Rights" would have allowed the federal government to heavily regulate internal union affairs.

71. *New York Times,* April 23, 1959; "The Congress: Nine Days of Labor," *Time,* May 9, 1959, p. 11; Burns, *John Kennedy,* p. 227.

72. AC 11:14.

73. AC 35:15, 16.

74. AC 11:14.

75. Oral history interview of Ralph A. Dungan, p. 51, JFKL.

76. Senator Hill et al. to AC, April 29, 1959, Senate Files Correspondence, CI–CZ folder, Pre-Presidential Papers, box 458, JFKL; *New York Times,* April 25 and April 26, 1959.

77. Oral history interview of Paul H. Douglas by John Newhouse, June 6, 1964, p. 26, JFKL.

78. Dick Lynch to JFK, July 1, 1959, Senate Files Legislation, Labor 7/2/59–7/16/59 folder, Pre-Presidential Papers, box 721, JFKL.

79. Cox, "The Landrum-Griffin Amendments to the National Labor Relations Act," *Minnesota Law Review* 44 (1959): 257, 259.

80. These included a significant proposal drafted by Carl Elliot of Alabama, dubbed the "Elliot bill," that was fairly sympathetic to labor. See Bellace and Berkowitz, *The Landrum-Griffin Act,* pp. 6–7; Lee, *Eisenhower and Landrum-Griffin,* pp. 138–51; *New York Times,* August 14, 1959.

81. Oral history interview of Richard Bolling by Ronald J. Grele, November 1, 1965, p. 12, JFKL. See also *New York Times,* August 18, 1959.

82. McAdams, *Power and Politics in Labor Legislation,* pp. 248–49; Lee, *Eisenhower and Landrum-Griffin,* p. 152.

83. Lee, *Eisenhower and Landrum-Griffin,* p. 153; Bellace and Berkowitz, *The Landrum-Griffin Act,* p. 7.

84. Oral history interview of AC, pp. 29–31, JFKL; Burns, *John Kennedy,* p. 228; "Whose Labor Reform Bill? Candidate's Aches," *Newsweek,* September 7, 1959, 31.

85. AC 11:11; James Doyle interview with AC, circa 1975, pp. 1–28, James Doyle papers.

86. AC 11:11; *New York Times,* August 25, 1959.

87. Philip Landrum, Jr., author's interview.

88. Oral history interview of AC, p. 29, JFKL.

89. AC 11:11, 12.

90. AC 11:10.

91. AC 13:6.

92. AC 11:1.

93. AC 10:34.

94. Ibid. Kennedy's Republic opponent in 1958 was Vincent Celeste. One academic adviser recalled the story that JFK got on the phone to a friend in Boston and said, "Can't we get a stronger Republican candidate against me in Massachusetts? I need a lot of votes and if they put up some bum, who is going to come out and vote?" Oral history interview of Walt W. Rostow, pp. 5–6, JFKL.

95. Lee, *Eisenhower and Landrum-Griffin,* pp. 111–12, 149.

96. Ralph A. Dungan, author's interview.

97. Oral history interview of Phil M. Landrum by Ronald J. Grele, October 20, 1965, p. 7, JFKL.

98. Ralph A. Dungan, author's interview.

99. AC 11:3, 4.

100. Lee, *Eisenhower and Landrum-Griffin,* p. 143.

101. AC, author's follow-up interview, October 17, 1996.

102. *Congressional Record* 105 (1959): 17719–30; *New York Times,* September 4 and September 5, 1959; Lee, *Eisenhower and Landrum-Griffin,* pp. 154–56.

103. Lee, *Eisenhower and Landrum-Griffin,* pp. 157–58; Cox, "The Landrum-Griffin Amendments to the National Labor Relations Act," pp. 260–74.

104. Lee, *Eisenhower and Landrum-Griffin,* p. 154. Pro-union measures included

expedited elections, a ban on non-Communist elections, and other measures. As an example of political deal-making, one House conference member insisted on a revision to the bill because, as drafted, it might adversely affect department stores, like the one his family owned in Canton, Ohio. See AC 12:3–5.

105. Burns, *John Kennedy*, p. 228.
106. "Labor Reform Act of 1959," *Time*, September 14, 1959, 25; Burns, *John Kennedy*, p. 228.
107. Learned Hand to AC, November 5, 1959, Learned Hand papers, box 86, folder 16, HLSL.
108. Lee, *Eisenhower and Landrum-Griffin*, p. 158. The quote is attributed to George Reedy, Lyndon Johnson's legislative aide.
109. Memorandum on Labor-Management Reform Legislation (undated, 1959), Senate Files Legislation Labor 11/9/59–11/20/59 folder, Pre-Presidential Papers, box 722, JFKL.
110. *Cincinnati Post & Times-Star*, September 21, 1959.
111. *Albuquerque Tribune*, September 28, 1959.
112. Oral history interview of AC, p. 33, JFKL; AC 10:36; 11:16, 17.
113. AC 10:36; oral history interview of AC, pp. 33–34, JFKL.
114. AC 10:37. Additional material on Cox's work on the legislation that culminated in the Landrum-Griffin Act can be found in AC papers, boxes 59–61 and 88.
115. Ralph Dungan, author's interview.

Chapter 8

1. AC 12:1, 2.
2. AC 12:7.
3. *Wayland (Mass.) Town Crier*, October 9, 1958.
4. AC 10:2, 3; *Wayland (Mass.) Town Crier*, October 23, 1958.
5. *Wayland (Mass.) Town Crier*, March 5, 1959.
6. Theodore C. Sorensen, author's interview; Notes, Academic Advisory Board Meeting, February 15, 1959, 86th Cong. 1st, Labor Management Reform Material 2/12/59–4/15/59 folder, Pre-Presidential papers, box 632, JFKL.
7. Oral history interview of Seymour E. Harris by Arthur Schlesinger, Jr., June 16–17, 1964, p. 13, JFKL.
8. *Boston Sunday Globe*, December 13, 1959.
9. David F. Powers, author's interview.
10. These names included John Kenneth Galbraith and Arthur Schlesinger, Jr., of Harvard; Henry Kissinger, an international affairs scholar at Harvard; Walter W. Rostow of MIT, a prominent expert on Russia; Robert G. Wood, an authority on urban affairs; Mark DeWolfe Howe, civil liberties specialist from Harvard Law School; General James M. Gavin, former army chief of staff; Lucian Pye, expert on Southeast Asia; and others. See *Boston Sunday Globe*, December 13, 1959.
11. Ibid.
12. *New York Times*, March 11, 1960.
13. Ibid.
14. Richard N. Goodwin to Mark DeWolfe Howe, January 5, 1960, and Mark

DeWolfe Howe to Richard N. ("Dick") Goodwin, January 9, 1960, Mark De-Wolfe Howe papers, box 13, folder 7, HLSL.

15. Mark DeWolfe Howe to Richard N. ("Dick") Goodwin, January 9, 1960, Mark DeWolfe Howe papers, box 13, folder 7, HLSL.

16. JFK to AC, January 18, 1960, AC papers, box 58, folder 2.

17. AC to JFK, January 22, 1960, AC papers, box 58, folder 2.

18. AC 35:15.

19. For a general account of the Democratic primaries of 1960, see Sorensen, *Kennedy*, pp. 122–53.

20. Oral history interview of Archibald Cox by Richard A. Lester, November 25, 1964, p. 38, JFKL.

21. JFK to AC, January 18, 1960, AC papers, box 58, folder 2.

22. Memo, Richard N. Goodwin to Deirdre Henderson, January 29, 1960, Sorensen Campaign Files, 1959–60, box 21, Academic Advisory Com. folder, Theodore C. Sorensen papers, JFKL. The guests in attendance included from MIT, Professors Jerome Wiesner, Walt W. Rostow, Paul Samuelson, Lucian Pye, and Walter Rosenblith; from Harvard Law School, Professors Mark DeWolfe Howe, Paul Freund, and Abram Chayes; and from Brandeis University, Professor Edward L. Katzenbach, Jr.

23. Theodore C. Sorensen, author's interview.

24. AC 12:11.

25. Walter A. Rosenblith, author's interview.

26. Walt W. Rostow, author's interview.

27. Paul A. Samuelson, author's interview.

28. Walter A. Rosenblith, author's interview.

29. Lucian W. Pye, author's interview.

30. Walter A. Rosenblith, author's interview.

31. Paul A. Samuelson, author's interview.

32. Walter A. Rosenblith, author's interview.

33. AC 12:11, 12.

34. *Boston Sunday Globe,* December 13, 1959.

35. James Doyle interview with AC, circa 1975, pp. 1–30, James Doyle papers.

36. Deirdre Henderson, author's interview.

37. *Wall Street Journal,* August 4, 1960; Lasky, *The Man and the Myth,* p. 415.

38. Oral history interview of Archibald Cox, pp. 43–44, JFKL. For instance, in the spring of 1960 when there was talk of a Russian proposal on nuclear test bans, a swarm of professors called Cox with ideas and advice. Although the influence of any one of them was "probably fairly small," the ideas went to JFK and there was a sense of input. Ibid.

39. Deirdre Henderson, author's follow-up interview, July 3, 1995.

40. *New York Times,* February 8, 1960.

41. Mary "Molly" Cox, author's interview, August 15, 1990.

42. *Wayland (Mass.) Town Crier,* October 31, 1957.

43. AC 12:8, 9.

44. David F. Powers, author's interview; *New York Times,* October 13, 1959.

45. Oral history interview of Walt W. Rostow by Richard Neustadt, April 11, 1964, pp. 21–22, JFKL; oral history interview of Robert C. Wood by John F. Stewart,

January 29, 1968, p. 3, 6, JFKL; Deirdre Henderson, author's interview. Rostow also provided Kennedy with the phrase "The New Frontier" that came directly from his book *The Stages of Economic Growth*, published in 1960. Although Kennedy openly gave credit to Rostow for that phrase that came to define the Kennedy administration's domestic program, Rostow would say: "The man who gets credit for a political phrase should not be the inventor but the politician who takes the risk." Walt W. Rostow, letter to author, February 27, 1997.

46. Oral history interview of Robert C. Wood, p. 7, JFKL.
47. Oral history interview of Ralph A. Dungan, p. 114, JFKL.
48. AC, author's follow-up interview, March 8, 1991.
49. Oral history interview of Robert C. Wood, p. 5, JFKL (emphasis added).
50. John Kenneth Galbraith had actually come out publicly for Kennedy in an *Esquire* magazine interview in 1958. He reaffirmed this support in June 1960, just before the convention, in a joint statement with Arthur Schlesinger, Jr., Arthur Goldberg, Henry Commager, and others. Schlesinger was a good friend of Eleanor Roosevelt, who was a strong Stevenson supporter, which made the defection particularly difficult for him. See John Kenneth Galbraith, author's interview; Arthur M. Schlesinger, Jr., author's interview; Paul A. Samuelson, author's interview; Arthur M. Schlesinger, Jr., letter to author, August 14, 1995. See also AC, 10:35.
51. As early as the winter of 1958–59, Galbraith and Schlesinger met at Locke-Ober's, Kennedy's favorite restaurant in Boston, to discuss economic matters and how the campaign was shaping up. See John Kenneth Galbraith, author's interview; Arthur M. Schlesinger, Jr., letter to author, August 14, 1995; John Kenneth Galbraith, author's follow-up interview, January 26, 1996. According to Galbraith, they always ate the same dinner: lobster stew "with plenty of what Kennedy called 'knuckle meat.' " "Famous Friends," *Harvard Magazine*, September–October 1996, p. 82.
52. Arthur M. Schlesinger, Jr., author's interview.
53. Ibid.
54. AC 12:16.
55. AC 12:16, 17.

Chapter 9

1. *New Yorker*, September 17, 1960.
2. Hechinger and Hechinger, "Election Cry: 'Win with Harvard,' " *New York Times Magazine*, October 9, 1960, 26.
3. Memo, AC to J. Kenneth Galbraith et al., August 25, 1960, J. Kenneth Galbraith folder, Democratic National Committee (hereinafter cited as DNC) 1960 Campaign papers, box 199, JFKL.
4. *Wall Street Journal*, August 4, 1960.
5. Paul A. Samuelson, author's interview.
6. Oral history interview of Seymour Harris, p. 10, JFKL.
7. Ibid.; oral history interview of Archibald Cox, p. 59, JFKL.
8. Paul A. Samuelson, author's interview.
9. AC 13:12, 13; oral history interview of Archibald Cox, p. 57, JFKL.

10. AC 12:14.
11. AC to Phyllis Ames Cox, August 8, 1960, Phyllis Ames Cox personal papers.
12. AC 22:24.
13. Memo, AC to Steve Smith, August 12, 1960, Smith, Steve, folder, DNC 1960 Campaign papers, box 203, JFKL.
14. *New York Times*, April 6, 1960.
15. Ibid.
16. *Butte Montana Standard*, September 18, 1960.
17. *Vogue*, September 15, 1960; *Il Globo*, September 1960; Deirdre Henderson personal papers.
18. *St. Louis Post-Dispatch*, August 23, 1960.
19. *Wall Street Journal*, August 4, 1960.
20. Robert Kennedy had held a completely invisible post in the Stevenson campaign of 1956, doing nothing of consequence but taking copious notes. The exercise would now come in handy, as RFK himself would joke: "I was learning what *not* to do in a presidential campaign." See oral history interview of David F. Powers by Larry J. Hackman, April 3, 1969, p. 7, JFKL.
21. Oral history interview of Frederick G. Dutton by Charles T. Morrissey, May 3, 1965, pp. 29–30, JFKL.
22. AC 13:7.
23. AC 13:6–8.
24. Oral history interview of Joseph Kraft by John F. Stewart, January 9, 1967, p. 1, JFKL.
25. John Kenneth ("Ken") Galbraith to Theodore C. ("Ted") Sorensen, undated, and attached confidential memorandum, Campaign Strategy, 1960 Campaign Files, Richard Goodwin Files, Speech Writing Strategy folder, Pre-Presidential Papers, box 996, JFKL.
26. Memo, John Bartlow Martin to Robert F. Kennedy, June 13, 1960, Campaign Strategy, 1960 Campaign Files, Richard Goodwin Files, Speech Writing Strategy folder, Pre-Presidential Papers, box 996, JFKL.
27. Memo, AC to Senator JFK, June 17, 1960, Campaign Strategy, 1960 Campaign Files, Richard Goodwin Files, Speech Writing Strategy folder, Pre-Presidential Papers, box 996, JFKL.
28. Memo, Speech-Writing for the 1960 Post-Convention Campaign (by Theodore C. Sorensen), undated, Campaign Strategy, 1960 Campaign Files, Richard Goodwin Files, Speech Writing Strategy folder, Pre-Presidential Papers, box 996, JFKL.
29. Memo, AC to Myer ("Mike") Feldman, July 29, 1960, Feldman, M., folder, DNC 1960 Campaign papers, box 199, JFKL.
30. AC 12:20.
31. Ibid.
32. AC 13:24.
33. AC 13:25.
34. AC to Senator JFK (via Sorensen), September 6, 1960, Sorensen, T. C., folder, DNC 1960 Campaign papers, box 203, JFKL.
35. *New York Times*, September, 1960; *Freedom of Communications*, pp. 109, 915; oral history interview of AC, p. 53, JFKL; Labor Day Speech, undated, Detroit— Labor Day 9/1/60 folder, DNC 1960 Campaign papers, box 214, JFKL. See also *Detroit News*, September 5, 1960.

36. AC 13:2; Memorandum Re: Cuba, undated, Cox folder, DNC 1960 Campaign papers, box 214, JFKL.

37. As adviser Abram Chayes would later say, it was a position that ultimately "made it very hard for him [JFK] to take any different stand than he did in the Bay of Pigs business." See oral history interview of Abram Chayes by Eugene Gordon, May 18, 1964, pp. 75–76, JFKL.

38. AC 35:18.

39. AC 12:18; oral history interview of AC, p. 55, JFKL.

40. Cox would later conclude that Kennedy intentionally withdrew from this battle because he embraced FDR's method of "encouraging his advisers to disagree and fight and engage in jurisdictional conflicts with respect to their turf." See AC 12:18. Others believed that there was no such plan; rather, it was an utter lack of organization that caused the crossed signals.

41. AC to Mrs. Archibald Cox, August 8, 1960, Phyllis Ames Cox personal papers.

42. James Doyle interview with AC, circa 1975, pp. 1–36, James Doyle papers; AC 13:16.

43. AC 13:16.

44. James Sundquist, author's interview.

45. Oral history interview of James Sundquist by Charles T. Morrissey and Ronald J. Grele, September 13, 1965, pp. 13–14, JFKL.

46. Oral history interview of Joseph Kraft, p. 12, JFKL.

47. *New York Times,* September 15, 1960; AC 13:11–14; Schlesinger, *A Thousand Days,* p. 70.

48. U.S. Senate Subcommittee of the Subcommittee on Communications, *Freedom of Communications, Final Report* (hereinafter cited as *Freedom of Communications*), pp. 238–49; *New York Times,* September 15, 1960.

49. *New York Times,* September 15, 1960.

50. Ibid.

51. *Freedom of Communications,* pp. 249–61; *New York Times,* September 16 and 17, 1960; *Harrisburg (Pa.) Patriot News,* September 16, 1960.

52. Oral history interview of Joseph Kraft, p. 4, JFKL.

53. Ibid.

54. Ibid., p. 17.

55. James Sundquist, author's interview.

56. Arthur M. Schlesinger, Jr., to AC, August 22, 1960, Schlesinger, Arthur, folder, DNC 1960 Campaign papers, box 203, JFKL.

57. Salt Lake City draft, September 20, 1960, DNC 1960 Campaign Research Materials (Cox) file, Salt Lake City—Civil Liberties folder, DNC 1960 Campaign papers, box 215, JFKL. A second, somewhat livelier draft, which was never used, appears in the Salt Lake City (Freedman) folder, box 216, JFKL.

58. *Freedom of Communications,* p. 346; *New York Times,* September 24, 1960. For another example of the dramatic difference between the Cox group's drafts and the final speeches of Sorensen's team, see Warm Springs draft (Cox), October 10, 1960, Warm Springs, Georgia, 10/5–10/10 folder, DNC 1960 Campaign papers, box 215, JFKL. See also *Freedom of Information,* pp. 543, 1104.

59. Oral history interview of Joseph Kraft, p. 12, JFKL.

60. Richard N. Goodwin, author's interview.

61. Oral history interview of Joseph Kraft, p. 16, JFKL.
62. Arthur M. Schlesinger, Jr., author's interview.
63. AC to Theodore C. Sorensen, September 17, 1960, Sorensen, T. C., folder, DNC 1960 Campaign papers, box 203, JFKL.
64. AC to Theodore C. Sorensen, October 1, 1960, Sorensen, T. C., folder, DNC 1960 Campaign papers, box 203, JFKL.
65. *Minneapolis Sunday Tribune,* October 2, 1960; *New York Times,* October 2, 1960; James Sundquist, author's interview.
66. James Doyle interview with AC, circa 1975, pp. 1–36, James Doyle papers.
67. AC, author's follow-up interview, October 17, 1996.
68. Ibid.; oral history interview of AC, p. 61, JFKL; *Freedom of Communications,* pp. 416–42.
69. AC to Clark Byse, October 1, 1960, Clark Byse folder, DNC 1960 Campaign papers, box 198, JFKL.
70. *Fort Worth Star-Telegram,* September 13, 1960; *Freedom of Communications,* p. 221; Fort Worth Speech, September 6, 1960, Forth Worth (M. S. Gwirtzman) folder, DNC 1960 Campaign papers, box 216, JFKL; *New York Times,* September 14, 1960.
71. *Freedom of Communications,* pp. 249, 1019; Harrisburg Speech, September 9, 1960, Harrisburg (Sundquist) folder, DNC 1960 Campaign papers, box 215, JFKL; *New York Times,* September 16, 1960.
72. *Freedom of Communications,* p. 281; Atlantic City speech, September 17, 1960, Atlantic City, N.J.—Steelworkers folder, DNC 1960 Campaign papers, box 214, JFKL.
73. Memphis, Tennessee: *Freedom of Communications,* p. 305, 1042; Memphis speech, September 20, 1960, Memphis (Kraft) folder, DNC 1960 Campaign papers, box 215, JFKL; *New York Times,* September 22, 1960; Billings, Montana: *Freedom of Communications,* p. 331; Memorandum for Mr. Cox (Billings speech), September 20, 1960, Billings, Montana, (Sundquist) folder, DNC 1960 Campaign papers, box 214, JFKL; Sioux Falls, South Dakota: *Freedom of Communications,* pp. 319, 1044; Plowing Match speech, September 19, 1960, Sioux Falls, S.D., Plowing Contest (Cochrane) folder, DNC 1960 Campaign papers, box 216, JFKL; memo from AC to Theodore C. Sorensen re: Plowing Contest Speech, September 19, 1960, Sorensen, T. C., folder, DNC 1960 Campaign papers, box 203, JFKL; Syracuse, New York: *Freedom of Communications,* pp. 408, 1067; draft of address by Sen. John F. Kennedy (Syracuse), September 29, 1960, Syracuse, N.Y., folder, DNC 1960 Campaign papers, box 216, JFKL; Warm Springs, Georgia: *Freedom of Communications,* p. 542; Warm Springs speech, October 10, 1960, Warm Springs, Georgia, folder, DNC 1960 Campaign papers, box 216, JFKL; New York City (Economics Club): *Freedom of Communications,* p. 557; AC to RFK and Sargent Shriver, October 7, 1960, and attached speech, October 6, 1960, Kennedy, Robert, folder, DNC 1960 Campaign papers, box 200, JFKL; AC 13:11–14; oral history interview of AC, p. 52, JFKL; Harlem, New York: *Freedom of Communications,* p. 580; draft for Harlem talk, October 12, 1960, Harlem (Wofford) folder, DNC 1960 Campaign papers, box 215, JFKL; Dayton, Ohio: *Freedom of Communications,* pp. 575, 623, 1147; Dayton speech, October 15, 1960, Dayton, Ohio (Kraft) folder, DNC 1960 Campaign papers, box

214, JFKL; "Talk to Conference on Constitutional Rights and American Freedom," October 12, 1960, Harlem (Wofford) folder, DNC 1960 Campaign papers, box 215, JFKL.

74. Press Release on "Fair Labor Standards" Amendments, August 8, 1960, 10-60, Fair Labor Standards—Senate Speech folder, DNC 1960 Campaign papers, box 214, JFKL; Senate Floor Speech (Second Draft—James L. Sundquist), August 28, 1960, Senate Floor Speech (Sundquist) August 28, 1960, folder, DNC 1960 Campaign papers, box 215, JFKL.

75. *Freedom of Communications*, p. 1080; Message of Senator John F. Kennedy to the Nation's New Voters, October 5, 1960, Youth folder, DNC 1960 Campaign papers, box 209, JFKL.

76. Notes for October 7 TV Debate (Harris Wofford), undated, and Possible Questions in Foreign Policy and Defense, undated, Debate Material, 9/26–10/7/60 folder, DNC 1960 Campaign papers, box 214, JFKL; AC to Mike Feldman (and attached memo re: birth control), October 17, 1960, Position and Briefing Papers: Birth Control folder, Pre-Presidential Papers, box 991, JFKL.

77. "A Proposal for an International Youth Service" (Samuel P. Hayes), September 30, 1960, 1960 Campaign file, Peace Corps folder, JFK Pre-Presidential Papers, box 993, JFKL; "Missile Gap": Providing for the Common Defense October 15, 1960, Defense, Providing for the Common, folder, DNC 1960 Campaign papers, box 214, JFKL. There were apparently several drafts of the "Common Defense" paper, which included significant input from Jerome B. Wiesner and Lucian Pye at MIT, as well as Ed Katzenbach, Paul Nitze, and Walt Rostow. See Deirdre Henderson, author's interview; AC to Theodore C. Sorensen, February 16, 1960, Academic Advisory Committee folder, Theodore C. Sorensen papers, box 21, JFKL; Arthur Schlesinger, Jr., to AC, August 22, 1960, Schlesinger, Arthur, folder, DNC 1960 Campaign papers, box 203, JFKL. Finally, with respect to the "prestige" issue, see Prestige speech, October 18, 1960, Prestige (Cox) folder, DNC 1960 Campaign papers, box 216, JFKL.

78. Samuel P. Hayes, author's interview; Richard N. Goodwin to AC, March 12, 1960, Sorensen Campaign Files 1959–60, Peace Corps folder, Theodore C. Sorensen papers, box 24, JFKL.

79. "A Proposal for an International Youth Service" (Samuel P. Hayes), September 30, 1960, 1960 Campaign file, Peace Corps folder, JFK Pre-Presidential Papers, box 993, JFKL.

80. Samuel P. Hayes, author's interview; Goodwin, *Remembering America*, p. 120; oral history interview of Frederick G. Dutton by Charles T. Morrissey, May 3, 1965, pp. 30–34, JFKL; Sorensen, *Kennedy*, p. 184. In early November, JFK gave a more formal speech on the subject at the San Francisco Cow Palace. See *Freedom of Communications*, pp. 862, 1237. Samuel Hayes later produced a sixty-four-page pamphlet on the subject, which was passed along to Sargent Shriver and others in the Kennedy operation and which helped form the bedrock of the Peace Corps.

81. The work of Cox's group included a book review of *Deterrent or Defense* for the *Saturday Review;* an article on religion in the *Cathedral Age;* "The Challenge of Education" in the *Michigan Education Journal;* a piece for Americans abroad in the *London American;* "American Prestige Abroad" in the *Akron Beacon Journal;*

commentary in the United Presbyterian Church's *Social Progress* entitled "A New Mission for America"; "The Farm Problem" in the Salt Lake City *Deseret News;* "Senator Kennedy's Replies to Questions from the Board of Editors of the *Bulletin of Atomic Scientists*"; and dozens more like these. See miscellaneous articles and statements in Articles and Statements written for Senator Kennedy in Prof. Cox's office I: 6/20/60–9/10/60 folder and Articles and Statements II 9/21/60–10/18/60 folder, DNC 1960 Campaign papers, box 204, JFKL.

82. Richard N. Goodwin, author's interview.
83. Arthur M. Schlesinger, Jr., letter to author, February 12, 1996.
84. Schlesinger, *A Thousand Days*, p. 70.
85. AC 13:17.
86. *Boston Globe,* September 27, 1960; Wide World Photo, Associated Press.
87. AC 22:23.
88. Phyllis would conclude the story: "We did finally get [a television], but it was not from JFK, it was from ourselves." Phyllis Ames Cox, author's interview.
89. Oral history interview of Abram Chayes, p. 93, JFKL.
90. AC 13:18.
91. AC 14:20.
92. Ibid. According to Kennedy campaign adviser Dave Powers, the key state was Michigan rather than Illinois. "It really wasn't Illinois. We could have given that to Nixon. It was Michigan that really shifted it." David F. Powers, author's interview.

Chapter 10

1. AC 35:22.
2. AC 14:23.
3. Ibid.
4. Paul A. Freund, author's interview.
5. Oral history interview of Abram Chayes, p. 90, JFKL; Paul A. Freund, author's interview.
6. Oral history interview of Abram Chayes, pp. 94–95, JFKL; Paul A. Freund, author's interview.
7. Paul A. Freund, author's interview.
8. Oral history interview of Abram Chayes, p. 93, JFKL.
9. Theodore C. Sorensen, author's interview.
10. Oral history interview of Abram Chayes, p. 92, JFKL.
11. Phyllis Ames Cox, author's interview.
12. *New York Times,* December 17, 1960.
13. John Kenneth Galbraith, author's interview; Joseph F. Dolan, author's interview.
14. Arthur M. Schlesinger, Jr., author's interview.
15. Oral history interview of William O. Douglas by Roberta Greene, November 13, 1969, p. 6, RFK oral history program, JFKL.
16. John Kenneth Galbraith, author's follow-up interview, August 31, 1995.
17. AC 15:8, 9.
18. AC 15:9.

19. AC 14:24.
20. Ibid.; James Doyle interview with AC, circa 1975, pp. 1-32, James Doyle papers.
21. Evelyn Lincoln, author's interview.
22. Mary "Molly" Cox, author's interview, August 15, 1990.
23. Ibid.
24. AC 14:25.
25. AC 14:26.
26. Mary "Molly" Cox, author's interview, August 15, 1990.
27. AC 14:26.
28. AC 15:1.
29. Phyllis Ames Cox, author's interview.
30. *New York Times,* December 28, 1960.
31. *Pittsfield (Mass.) Berkshire Eagle,* December 24, 1960.
32. *Boston Herald,* December 29, 1960.
33. Ibid.
34. Ibid.
35. Ibid.; Sidey, *John F. Kennedy, President,* p. 47.
36. Learned Hand to AC, December 30, 1960, Learned Hand papers, box 86, folder 16, HLSL.
37. AC 15:2, 3.
38. AC to Learned Hand, January 12, 1961, Learned Hand papers, box 86, folder 16, HLSL.
39. This story is recounted in the *Boston Globe,* December 5, 1973.
40. *New York Times,* January 5, 1961.
41. This story is told in *Framingham (Mass.) South Middlesex Sunday News,* May 20, 1973.
42. U.S. Senate Committee on the Judiciary, *Hearing before the Committee on the Judiciary, United States Senate, on Archibald Cox, Solicitor General-Designate,* 87th Cong., 1st Sess., January 18, 1961 (Washington, D.C.: U.S. Government Printing Office, 1961), p. 3. The story about stocks and securities is from Ramsey Clark, author's interview.
43. Among others, Arthur M. Schlesinger, Jr., was special assistant to the president; John Kenneth Galbraith was ambassador to India; Walt W. Rostow was assistant adviser on foreign affairs; Abram Chayes was legal adviser in the State Department; Paul A. Samuelson was chairman of the Council of Economic Advisors; Paul Nitze was assistant secretary of defense.
44. AC 15:9.
45. AC 15:10.
46. Campaign Bulletin, October 1, 1960, Civil rights and Liberties folder, DNC 1960 Campaign papers, box 204, JFKL. At times JFK leaned on Professors Paul Freund and Mark DeWolfe Howe, of Harvard Law School, for speech material or advice on civil rights matters. See, for example, Memorandum to Mssrs. Freund, Howe and Saltonstall (from AC), January 26, 1960, Mark DeWolfe Howe papers, box 13, folder 8, HLSL.
47. Regarding JFK's record, see Record of Senator JFK (Dem.—Mass.) on Civil Rights, undated, Civil Rights Kennedy Record (Speeches, statements, and sections) folder, 1960 Campaign files, Pre-Presidential Papers, box 1028, JFKL.

Miscellaneous speeches of JFK, as a congressman, on civil rights are contained in Miscellaneous Speeches folder, Speech Files 1947–52, House Files, Pre-Presidential Papers, box 93, JFKL. Regarding the King incident, see *New York Post*, October 28, 1960; oral history interview of Thurgood Marshall by Berl Bernhard, April 7, 1964, p. 3, JFKL; Brauer, *John F. Kennedy and the Second Reconstruction*, p. 46–50.

48. David F. Powers, author's interview. See also oral history interview of Paul H. Douglas by John Newhouse, June 6, 1964, pp. 31–32, JFKL.
49. AC 16:17; National Diary, February 2, 1961, AC personal papers.
50. AC 16:7, 8.
51. National Diary, February 20 and February 21, 1961, AC personal papers.
52. *New York Times*, July 14, 1965.
53. Phyllis Ames Cox, author's follow-up interview, December 3, 1995.
54. AC 17:23.
55. Kurland and Casper, *Landmark Briefs and Arguments*, 55:495.
56. AC 18:22.
57. Kurland and Casper, *Landmark Briefs and Arguments*, 55:491–92.
58. National Diary, February 2, 1961, AC personal papers.
59. *Burton v. Wilmington Parking Authority*, 365 U.S., pp. 720, 725.
60. Burke Marshall, author's interview.
61. Nicholas deB. Katzenbach interview, December 13, 1968, p. 6, Katzenbach folder, box 29, Victor Navasky papers, JFKL.
62. Ralph Spritzer, author's interview.
63. Burke Marshall, author's interview; Nicholas deB. Katzenbach, author's interview; John W. Douglas, author's interview.
64. Louis F. Oberdorfer, author's interview; Burke Marshall, author's interview; oral history interview of Lee Loevinger by Ronald G. Grele, May 13, 1966, p. 15, JFKL; Nicholas deB. Katzenbach, author's interview.
65. For examples of dates on which Cox visited Hickory Hill for lunch and/or swimming with RFK and advisers, see the following entries in Cox's diaries: National Diary, August 21, 1961, and July 31, 1962; Standard Diary, July 19, 1963, and January 4, 1965, AC personal papers.
66. During his first year in office, RFK endorsed a bill that gave virtually unlimited wiretapping power to police. He felt that it was impossible to launch an assault on large-scale organized crime "without some ability to monitor the communications channels." But with the invention of technology like "spike mikes" that could be driven into walls and radiators and allow the government to bug citizens at will, RFK developed a growing concern about privacy. By 1962, he shifted toward legislation that allowed wiretape only under strict controls. Cox advised RFK that some reasonable wiretap legislation could be adopted without violating the Fourth Amendment. Their views were fairly consistent on this issue. See oral history interview of Lee Loevinger, pp. 35–36, JFKL; oral history interview of Anthony Lewis by Larry J. Hackman, July 23, 1970, p. 9, RFK oral history program, JFKL; Lawford, *That Shining Hour*, p. 103; Schlesinger, *Robert Kennedy and His Times*, p. 290.
67. Herbert J. Miller, author's interview.
68. Burke Marshall, author's interview, July 5, 1991.

69. Ralph Spritzer, author's interview.

70. Nicholas deB. Katzenbach, author's interview.

71. Anthony Lewis, author's interview.

72. Ibid.

73. Nicholas deB. Katzenbach, author's interview.

74. This story is recounted in the *Cleveland Plain Dealer*, May 19, 1973. See *Preston v. United States*, 376 U.S. 364 (1964).

75. *Cleveland Plain Dealer*, May 19, 1973; oral history interview of Peter Edelman (no. 7) by Larry J. Hackman, February 13, 1973, p. 21, RFK oral history program, JFKL.

76. Ralph Spritzer, author's interview.

77. Ibid.

78. Nicholas deB. Katzenbach, author's interview.

79. AC to Mrs. Archibald Cox, June 10, 1961, Phyllis Ames Cox personal papers.

80. Ibid., July 31, 1961.

81. Oral history interview of Joseph F. Dolan by Charles T. Morrissey, December 4, 1964, pp. 111–16, JFKL; *New York Times*, May 21, 1961; "Days of Violence in the South," *Newsweek*, May 29, 1961, 21; Brauer, *John F. Kennedy and the Second Reconstruction*, pp. 100–103.

82. Guthman and Shulman, *Robert Kennedy in His Own Words*, pp. 84–87.

83. Arthur M. Schlesinger, Jr., author's interview; Burke Marshall, author's interview, July 5, 1991.

84. Oral history interview of Burke Marshall, p. 46, RFK oral history program, JFKL. See also oral history interview of Nicholas deB. Katzenbach by Anthony Lewis, November 16, 1964, pp. 9–12, JFKL.

85. *Shelley v. Kramer*, 334 U.S. 1 (1948).

86. Hand and Frankfurter, "How Far Is a Judge Free in Rendering a Decision?" *National Advisory Council on Radio in Education, Law Series* 1 (1933): 5, quoted in Cox, "Reflections upon Labor Arbitration," *Harvard Law Review* 79 (1959): 1506–7.

87. Burke Marshall, author's interview.

88. AC 17:24, 25. Cox would talk about the "private citizen sitting in his living room in Vermont," in discussing the subject with Burke Marshall. If the private homeowner chose to exclude guests from his home based upon color, or religion, or political affiliation, would the Constitution prohibit it? Cox would insist that as reprehensible as the conduct might be morally, the answer as a legal matter was certainly no. See Burke Marshall, author's interview, July 22, 1991.

89. Burke Marshall, author's interview, July 22, 1991. In effect, the NAACP and other civil rights groups advanced two different positions. The strongest was that a restaurant's actions, because it was a common carrier, amounted to "state action" by definition. The second was that once a state was called in to enforce its trespass laws to further private discrimination, state action was present. Marshall was here talking about the second form of state action.

90. AC 18:1.

91. AC 18:2.

92. Oral history interview of Burke Marshall by Larry J. Hackman, January 19–20, 1970, p. 7, RFK oral history program, JFKL.

93. Ibid., p. 11.

94. Ibid., p. 10.
95. Ibid.
96. *New York Times,* November 8, 1962; *Peterson v. Greenville,* 373 U.S. 244 (1963) (consolidated sit-in cases); *Lombard v. Louisiana,* 373 U.S. 267 (1963) (sit-in case); *Wright v. Georgia,* 373 U.S. 284 (1963) (playing basketball in public park); *Griffin v. Maryland,* 378 U.S. 130 (1964) (Glen Echo amusement park, and other consolidated cases).
97. *Griffin v. Maryland,* 378 U.S. 130 (1964).
98. Cox emphasized that the Court had no reason to go further and make sweeping pronouncements about private conduct under the Fourteenth Amendment. On this issue, the solicitor general himself took "no position." See Transcript of Oral Argument, *Griffin v. State of Maryland,* no. 26 of 1962, pp. 393–400, U.S. Supreme Court Archives, Washington, D.C.
99. AC, author's follow-up interview, September 5, 1995.
100. Navasky, *Kennedy Justice,* p. 289; Greenberg, *Crusaders in the Courts,* pp. 309–10.
101. Frankfurter told an oral historian in 1964 that Cox "has in some ways disappointed me because he's allowed himself to be too much in alliance to the NAACP. Therefore, he's making political decisions instead of legal decisions in deciding whether he should go into a case." See second oral history interview of Justice Felix Frankfurter by Charles McLaughlin, June 19, 1964, p. 53, JFKL.
102. Evelyn Lincoln, author's interview.
103. Byron R. White, author's interview.
104. AC 15:15.
105. Burke Marshall, author's interview, July 5, 1991.
106. *Bell v. Maryland,* 378 U.S. 226 (1964). At the direction of the restaurant chain's president, the hostess had refused to serve the students. The students remained peacefully for an hour and a half until warrants were sworn out. They were then hauled off to jail and convicted in a Maryland state court.
107. Greenberg, *Crusaders in the Courts,* p. 312.
108. This position was spelled out at length in a memo written by Cox to Burke Marshall and others. The theory was that "The practice of segregation as a mark of inferiority was fostered by State action in the narrowest sense of the term," because in such cases, state custom and statutes had directly endorsed "the notion that Negroes should be treated as an inferior caste." See Memo, AC to Mssrs. Marshall, Spritzer, Greene and Claiborne, December 18, 1963, Sit-Ins folder, box 32, Victor Navasky papers, JFKL.
109. Cox had already made this argument at a Princeton speech in 1962. "The refusal of department store owners to allow Negro customers to break bread together is the product of a social system," Cox had told the audience. "The community shares the responsibility." See AC, "Racial Equality and the Law," Princeton University, April 28, 1962, Material Collected: CL–CO folder, Burke Marshall papers, box 35, JFKL. Cox and Burke Marshall signed a special supplemental brief to the Supreme Court in *Bell,* essentially embracing this argument as the position of the U.S. government.
110. *Bell v. Maryland,* 378 U.S., p. 318 (Black, J., dissenting). It is clear that several justices were "on the fence," based on the majority's explicit disclaimer of the broad state action theory in deciding the cases. See ibid., p. 228.
111. As Harold Greene, the head of the Appellate Section of Robert Kennedy's Civil

Rights Division told an interviewer in 1968, "As it turned out, probably the Solicitor General was right." Interview of Harold Greene by Victor Navasky, spring 1968, Greene, Harold, folder, box 27, Victor Navasky papers, JFKL.

112. AC 35:29.
113. AC 35:30.
114. Ibid.
115. Phyllis Ames Cox, author's interview.

Chapter 11

1. AC 16:19, 20.
2. *Engel v. Vitale*, 370 U.S. 421 (1962).
3. AC 16:20.
4. Sorensen, *Kennedy*, pp. 447–59.
5. AC 16:23; National Diary, April 12, 1962, AC personal papers; oral history interview of AC, pp. 66–67, JFKL; Bernstein, *Promises Kept*, pp. 142–43; Fairlie, *The Kennedy Promise*, at 202–3.
6. Oral history interview of AC by Richard Lester, p. 72, JFKL.
7. Oral history interview of Nicholas deB. Katzenbach by Anthony Lewis, November 16, 1964, pp. 20–21, JFKL; second oral history interview of Nicholas deB. Katzenbach by Anthony Lewis, November 29, 1964, pp. 91–123, JFKL; oral history interview of Joseph F. Dolan, pp. 111–17, JFKL; Report, N. L. Alldredge, Administrator of Correctional Service, to J. V. Bennett, Director, October 9, 1962, microfilm copies of records of the Department of Justice, roll 33, JFKL; Memorandum of Argument before Supreme Court by Solicitor General *(U.S. v. Barnett)*, undated, microfilm copies of records of the Department of Justice, roll 33, JFKL; "Mississippi: The Sound and the Fury," *Newsweek*, October 15, 1962, 23; *New York Times*, October 1, 1962.
8. Item 4G.4, October 1, 1962, Dictabelt Transcripts (Integration of the University of Mississippi), Presidential Recordings, JFKL.
9. AC 16:19.
10. The president and the attorney general had initially backpedaled on the prosecution, worrying about the messy political consequences of indicting a sitting governor. Cox, on the other hand, insisted that the Court would have little respect for the administration if they took no action, and prevailed. See Burke Marshall, author's interviews, July 5 and July 22, 1991; AC 16:25, 26, 36:5; Nicholas deB. Katzenbach, author's interview; Nicholas deB. Katzenbach interview, February 12, 1968, Katzenbach, Nick, folder, Victor Navasky papers, box 29, p. 8, JFKL.
11. AC 16:21; President's Engagements, August 27, 1963, Schedules—President's Daily 6/1–11/20/63, Desk Copy folder, Personal Secretary's Files, President's Office Files, box 134, JFKL. There were numerous conversations and meetings between the president and Cox on the "mudlumps" issue. See Standard Diary, January 29, March 4, May 21, and August 27, 1963, AC personal papers. Cox eventually determined, on behalf of the government, that the oil-rich mudlumps belonged to the states. *New York Times*, December 31, 1963.

12. Nicholas deB. Katzenbach interview, December 13, 1968, Katzenbach folder, Victor Navasky papers, box 29, p. 6, JFKL.
13. AC 15:16; Philip B. Heymann, author's interview; Louis Claiborne interview no. 2, undated, Claiborne, Lewis, folder, Victor Navasky papers, box 25, p. 5, JFKL. Cox also advised the president on the politically sensitive subject of proposed legislation that would provide low-interest federal loans for building Catholic and other religious schools. See Memorandum for the President, March 31, 1961, Education and Religion 3/16/61–4/10/61 folder, Theodore C. Sorensen papers, box 33, JFKL. See also McAndrews, "Broken Ground," in Burke and Freidel, *Modern American History,* pp. 72–79.
14. AC 18:5.
15. One of the leading articles on the subject had been written by Anthony Lewis of the *New York Times* while a Nieman Fellow at Harvard. See Anthony Lewis, "Legislative Apportionment and the Federal Courts," *Harvard Law Review* 71 (1958): 1095–96.
16. In the South, however, other obstacles still prevented many blacks from voting.
17. AC 18:4.
18. Graham, *One Man, One Vote,* pp. 209–17; Harris A. Gilbert, author's interview.
19. *New York Times,* April 20, 1961, emphasis added.
20. Cox, *The Court and the Constitution,* pp. 288–304.
21. Cox's predecessor in the Eisenhower administration, J. Lee Rankin, had already signed off on the certiorari petition in *Baker* on behalf of the United States, although this piece of paper got lost in the shuffle of the transition.
22. Ibid., p. 289.
23. *New York Times,* April 20, 1961.
24. Cox, *The Court and the Constitution,* p. 295; National Diary 1961, April 15, AC personal papers.
25. National Diary 1961, August 18 and August 19, AC personal papers.
26. Mary "Molly" Cox, author's interview, May 27, 1994; Krause and Cox, "Grandma's Memories," p. 123.
27. National Diary August 25, 1961, AC personal papers.
28. Ibid., September 14 and September 16, 1961.
29. Graham, *One Man, One Vote,* p. 248.
30. AC 18:6, 7.
31. James M. Glasgow, author's interview; Harris A. Gilbert, author's interview.
32. *New York Times,* October 10, 1961.
33. Ibid.
34. Kurland and Casper, *Landmark Briefs and Arguments,* 56:571.
35. AC 18:8.
36. Gunther, *Learned Hand,* p. 298.
37. Ibid., 299.
38. *Baker v. Carr,* 369 U.S. 186 (1962). Justice Charles Whittaker had become ill and was unable to cast a vote in the decision.
39. Burke Marshall, author's interview, July 5, 1991.
40. Ibid., July 22, 1991.
41. *New York Times,* March 27, 1962.

42. Ibid., March 29, 1962; *Washington Post,* April 1, 1962.
43. AC 29:17.
44. Ibid.
45. AC 29:18.
46. AC 29:16.
47. Cox told a Bar Association group in Portland, Oregon, "Whether the decision is right will depend upon the degree of assent which it commands from State legislatures, other public officials and the general public." See Address, "Law and the People" May 1, 1962, Material Collected: CL–CO folder, Burke Marshall papers, box 35, JFKL.
48. AC 15:33.
49. Burke Marshall, author's interview, July 5, 1991; Byron R. White, author's interview; oral history interview of Joseph F. Dolan by Charles T. Morrissey, December 4, 1964, pp. 98–102, JFKL. For a fuller account of Byron White's appointment, see oral history interview of Nicholas deB. Katzenbach by Anthony Lewis, November 16, 1964, pp. 56–75, JFKL.
50. Phyllis Ames Cox, author's interview.
51. Edward M. Kennedy, author's interview.
52. Caplan, *The Tenth Justice,* p. 191; Salokar, *The Solicitor General,* p. 148.
53. Oral history interview of Robert F. Kennedy and Burke Marshall by Anthony Lewis, December 4, 1964, p. 414, JFKL.
54. Arthur M. Schlesinger, Jr., author's interview. Regarding the commitment to Arthur Goldberg, see also oral history interview of Nicholas deB. Katzenbach by Anthony Lewis, November 16, 1964, pp. 58–59, 72–73, JFKL. Katzenbach recalled that there was really no question in President Kennedy's mind that the seat "belonged" to Arthur Goldberg based upon the president's promises when Goldberg accepted the post as secretary of labor. Nicholas deB. Katzenbach, author's follow-up interview, February 16, 1996. Justice Frankfurter, still outspoken after his stroke, criticized the selection of Goldberg. He said of Robert Kennedy, who was advising the president, "What does Bobby understand about the Supreme Court? He understands about as much about it as you understand about the undiscovered 76th star in the galaxy." See second oral history of Felix Frankfurter, June 19, 1964, pp. 51–55, JFKL.
55. Oral history interview of Robert F. Kennedy and Burke Marshall by Anthony Lewis, December 12, 1964, p. 573, JFKL.
56. Ibid.
57. AC 17:37.
58. See Navasky, *Kennedy Justice,* pp. 277–323. This was far from Cox's favorite book, because he felt it gave too much credence to the views of several young staff lawyers, and oversimplified the complex relationship between himself, Robert Kennedy, Nick Katzenbach, and other central players in the Kennedy Justice Department. In fairness to the author of that book, however, Cox was able to spare little time to be interviewed for *Kennedy Justice;* it was written during a period of student disturbances at Harvard, a time that proved intensely busy for Cox. Thus, he provided little input.
59. Burke Marshall, author's interview, July 5, 1991.
60. Kennedy, "The Shame of the States," *New York Times Magazine,* May 18, 1958,

18; oral history interview of Robert F. Kennedy and Burke Marshall, December 4, 1964, p. 575, JFKL.

61. *New York Times,* November 13, 1963.

62. Ibid., November 13 and December 10, 1963; *Reynolds v. Sims,* 377 U.S. 533, 589 n. 1 (1964).

63. Kurland and Casper, *Landmark Briefs and Arguments,* 58:885.

64. Memorandum, Bruce J. Terris to AC, July 3, 1963, private papers of Bruce J. Terris, p. 1.

65. Ibid., p. 10. By "weak standard," Terris was referring to Cox's recently conceived idea that he might support a middle ground, endorsing strict population equality for *one* house of the state legislature when it came to voting districts, but recognizing that there might be a "substantial deviation" from rigid numbers in the other house (i.e., the state Senate).

66. Memorandum, AC to the Attorney General, August 19, 1963, private papers of Bruce J. Terris, pp. 17–20.

67. Ibid., pp. 17, 20, 22–28, 33.

68. Memorandum, David Rubin and Howard A. Glickstein to Harold H. Greene, undated, private papers of Bruce J. Terris, p. 1.

69. Oral history interview of Robert F. Kennedy and Burke Marshall, December 4, 1964, pp. 575–76, JFKL.

70. Ibid., p. 573; oral history interview of AC, p. 65, JFKL; Navasky, *Kennedy Justice,* p. 314.

71. Navasky, *Kennedy Justice,* pp. 314–15.

72. Cox, *The Court and the Constitution,* pp. 296–99. The consolidated cases argued by Cox were *Reynolds v. Sims,* 377 U.S. 533 (1964) (Alabama); *WMCA, Inc. v. Lomenzo,* 377 U.S. 633 (1964) (New York); *Maryland Committee v. Tawes,* 377 U.S. 657 (1964) (Maryland); and *Davis v. Mann,* 377 U.S. 679 (1964) (Virginia). Cox also argued the Delaware case as amicus in December of that year: *Roman v. Sincock,* 377 U.S. 695 (1964) (Delaware).

73. Anthony Lewis picked up the subtle message in the *New York Times,* noting that "Mr. Cox did not argue that there could *never* be any significant departure from population equality. . . . He said the Court need not decide that ultimate question now." *New York Times,* November 14, 1963 (emphasis added).

74. AC, author's follow-up interview, October 17, 1996.

75. Cox urged instead that the government press for dismissal based on a somewhat obscure doctrine, "want of equity," that would allow the Court to avoid the ultimate question and put it on the shelf. See Navasky, *Kennedy Justice,* pp. 318–23.

76. Memorandum, AC to the Attorney General, February 2, 1964, private papers of Bruce J. Terris; Bruce J. Terris to AC, February 3, 1964, private papers of Bruce J. Terris.

77. Burke Marshall, author's interview, July 5, 1991.

78. Oral history interview of Anthony Lewis by Larry J. Hackman, July 23, 1970, p. 14, JFKL; *Washington Post,* May 11, 1963.

79. AC 18:15.

80. AC 29:14.

81. Burke Marshall, author's interview, July 22, 1991.

82. AC 18:15, 16. Nick deB. Katzenbach, the new deputy attorney general who had

replaced Byron White, had proposed a compromise like this as early as February. See Nicholas deB. Katzenbach to RFK, February 11, 1964, private papers of Bruce J. Terris.

83. Burke Marshall, author's interview, July 5, 1991.
84. Philip B. Heymann, author's interview. In past administrations, the attorney general had on occasion filed a brief that the solicitor general had refused to sign. Those who worked with RFK, however, knew that he had no intention of doing this with Cox. Burke Marshall, author's interview, July 22, 1991.
85. Cox discussed his dilemma in a letter to a friend in 1968. See AC to Prof. Robert G. Dixon, Jr., October 1, 1968, AC papers, box 44, folder 7. See also oral history of AC, p.66, JFKL.
86. Oral history interview of Robert F. Kennedy and Burke Marshall, December 4, 1964, p. 579, JFKL.
87. Anthony Lewis, author's interview.
88. Ibid.; Navasky, *Kennedy Justice*, p. 321.
89. AC 18:14.
90. Oral history interview of Thurgood Marshall, pp. 5–7, JFKL; oral history interview of Anthony Lewis, RFK oral history project, p. 11, JFKL.
91. Oral history interview of Anthony Lewis, RFK oral history project, p. 11, JFKL.
92. Transcript of "Voice of America" Program, June 4, 1963, p. 8, Press Conference, USA Voice of America, 6/4/63 folder, Attorney General's Files, Speeches 1961–1964, RFK papers, box 2, JFKL.
93. Oral history interview of Thurgood Marshall, pp. 5, 7, 9, 16, JFKL.
94. The administration tried, and failed, to set up the Department of Urban Affairs. It also issued a much more successful edict that the Interstate Commerce Commission desegregate bus terminals in the wake of the Freedom Riders' beatings in Montgomery. There were also partially successful efforts to deal with housing discrimination. These slow gains had the advantage of not jeopardizing other priorities in Congress that might be sunk if a civil rights bill were introduced and filibustered. See oral history interview of Thurgood Marshall, pp. 8–9, JFKL; Arthur M. Schlesinger, Jr., author's interview; oral history interview of Nicholas deB. Katzenbach, p. 21, JFKL; Brauer, *John F. Kennedy and the Second Reconstruction*, pp. 126–31, 205–10, 230–37.
95. Paul Samuelson, author's interview.
96. All these events clearly had an impact on the president: the James Meredith affair in 1962, in which rocks and homemade bombs and ugly racial invectives were hurled at an articulate young Air Force veteran in an attempt to block him from registering for college, because he was black; the shocking actions of Police Commissioner Bull Connor in Birmingham, who unleashed police dogs and fire hoses and cattle prods in the spring of 1963 to battle civil rights activists to the pavement; and the murder of NAACP leader Medgar Evers on June 12, 1963, in Jackson, Mississippi. See *New York Times*, May 21, 1961; "Days of Violence in the South," *Newsweek*, May 29, 1961, 21; "Mississippi: The Sound and the Fury," *Newsweek*, October 15, 1962, 23–29; *New York Times*, October 1, 1962; "Explosion in Alabama," *Newsweek*, May 20, 1963, 25; "Birmingham, U.S.A.: 'Look at Them Run,' " *Newsweek*, May 13, 1963, 27; *New York Times*, May 12, 1963; *New York Times*, September 16, 1963.
97. David F. Powers, author's interview; Arthur Schlesinger, Jr., author's interview;

Theodore C. Sorensen, author's interview; oral history interview of Thurgood Marshall, p. 15, JFKL; *New York Times*, September 16, 1963; Brauer, *John F. Kennedy and the Second Reconstruction*, pp. 285–98.

98. This legislation would outlaw the arbitrary application of literacy tests to blacks, create a presumption that anyone who had passed sixth grade was qualified to vote in federal elections, and establish a mechanism for speeding voting suits through the federal courts. It borrowed from earlier (failed) legislation drafted in 1962 by Burke Marshall working under the direction of Robert Kennedy. See Kennedy Administration Accomplishments in Civil Rights, June 1963, Year-End Reports 1961–64 folder, Civil Rights Division Files, Burke Marshall papers, box 16, JFKL; Introductory Statement, April 2, 1963, 4/2/1963–4/25/1963 folder, Attorney General's Files, Speeches, 1961–1964, RFK papers, box 2, JFKL; Department of Justice Press Conference, April 2, 1963, Attorney General, April–June 1963 folder, Special Correspondence files, Burke Marshall papers, box 8, JFKL; Brauer, *John F. Kennedy and the Second Reconstruction*, pp. 221–22, 265–72; oral history interview of Burke Marshall, p. 63, RFK oral history project, JFKL.

99. Statement of Attorney General, July 1, 1963, Public Accommodations, Senate Commerce Committee 7/1/63 folder, Attorney General's Files, Speeches 1961–1964, RFK papers, box 2, JFKL; Kennedy Administration Accomplishments in Civil Rights, June, 1963, Year-End Reports 1961–64 folder, Civil Rights Division Files, Burke Marshall papers, box 16, JFKL; Brauer, *John F. Kennedy and the Second Reconstruction*, pp. 265–310. Drafting of the Civil Rights Act began immediately after Burke Marshall returned from the Alabama race riots in the spring of 1963. Nicholas deB. Katzenbach, author's interview.

100. *New York Times*, April 29, 1962.

101. Standard Diary, July 17, 1963, AC personal papers. The existing injustice in public accommodations was both obvious and inexcusable for Cox. As Robert Kennedy had testified passionately during the summer months, in front of the Senate Judiciary Committee, tourist guidebooks of the South revealed that "there was only one establishment where a Negro could obtain overnight lodgings in Montgomery, Alabama, and none in Danville, Virginia." Yet the same guidebooks indicated that "a dog, traveling with a white person, was welcome to stay in five places in Montgomery and four in Danville." See Brauer, *John F. Kennedy and the Second Reconstruction*, p. 279.

102. In part, the failure of President Kennedy's legislative initiatives in Congress were a product of his own tenuous relationship with that body. His relations with his former Senate colleagues were "good and friendly." But as a young senator he had bucked "the Senate club," and some of his colleagues "never forgot it." See oral history interview of Walt W. Rostow, p. 7, JFKL.

103. Ramsey Clark, author's interview.

104. Nicholas deB. Katzenbach, author's interview.

105. Burke Marshall, author's interview, July 22, 1991.

106. Nicholas deB. Katzenbach, author's interview; oral history interview of Nicholas deB. Katzenbach, RFK oral history project, p. 11, JFKL; oral history interview of William O. Douglas by Roberta Greene, November 13, 1969, pp. 7, 12, RFK oral history project, JFKL; oral history interview of Burke Marshall, p. 13, RFK oral history project, JFKL.

107. Ramsey Clark, author's interview; Burke Marshall, author's interview, July 22, 1991; Nicholas deB. Katzenbach, author's interview.
108. Ramsey Clark, author's interview.
109. Memo, AC to RFK, February 9, 1961, Kennedy, Robert F., 1961–1964 folder, Attorney General's Personal Correspondence File, RFK papers, box 14, JFKL.
110. Navasky, *Kennedy Justice*, p. 277; National Diary, January 17, 1963, AC personal papers. Robert Kennedy also moved the admission of his younger brother, Senator Edward M. Kennedy, at the Supreme Court on this day.
111. AC 16:30, 31; Navasky, *Kennedy Justice*, pp. 304–6.
112. Address, "Wages, Government and Lawyers," June 13, 1962, Phyllis Ames Cox personal papers; *New York Times*, June 14 and June 15, 1962; "Wage Price Action? Cox Asks for New Formula," *U.S. News & World Report*, June 25, 1962, 28; National Diary, June 13 and June 14, 1962, AC personal papers.
113. *New York Times*, June 14 and 15, 1962; "Wage Price Action? Cox Asks for New Formula," *U.S. News & World Report*, June 25, 1962, 28; *New York Herald Tribune*, June 14 and June 15, 1962.
114. AC to Mrs. Archibald Cox, June 18, 1962, Phyllis Ames Cox personal papers.
115. AC 15:11.
116. Ibid.
117. AC 15:12.
118. Ibid.
119. This nickname is recorded in the *Cleveland Plain Dealer*, May 19, 1973.
120. AC 15:5.
121. Arthur M. Schlesinger, Jr., author's interview.

Chapter 12

1. Telephone Memorandum, November 21, 1963, Misc. files—Telephone Memos folder, Presidential Office Files, box 34, JFKL.
2. AC 18:30.
3. AC 19:36.
4. Oral history interview of Hugh Sidey by Fred Holborn, April 7, 1964, p. 52, JFKL.
5. Ibid., p. 53.
6. Daily Telephone Log (Burke Marshall), November 22, 1963, Telephone Logs: November 1963 folder, Burke Marshall papers, box 11, JFKL.
7. Oral history interview of Milton S. Gwirtzman by Roberta W. Greene, December 23, 1971, p. 44, RFK oral history project, JFKL.
8. Standard Diary 1963, November 25, 1963, AC personal papers.
9. AC to RFK, November 24, 1963, Attorney General Correspondence—Condolences folder, RFK papers, box 2, JFKL.
10. See, for example, Memorandum for the Attorney General, December 2, 1963, Robert F. Kennedy October–December 1963 folder, Alphabetical File, Burke Marshall papers, box 3, JFKL.
11. Standard Diary November 22 and November 26, 1963, AC personal papers.
12. Oral history interview of Milton S. Gwirtzman, p. 11, RFK oral history project, JFKL.

13. Oral history interview of Nicholas deB. Katzenbach by Larry J. Hackman, October 8, 1969, p. 1, RFK oral history project, JFKL.

14. Ibid., p. 4; *New York Times*, January 9, 1964.

15. An excellent account of the conception of the Warren Commission is contained in a retrospective piece in the *Washington Post*, November 14, 1993.

16. AC 35:33.

17. Philip B. Heymann, author's interview.

18. AC 35:34.

19. Ibid.

20. AC 35:34, 35.

21. AC 35:35, 36.

22. Philip B. Heymann, author's interview.

23. Appointments, November 29, 1963, Appointments File, Calls and Callers, 10/1/63–12/31/63 folder, Nicholas deB. Katzenbach papers, box 3, JFKL; *Washington Post*, November 14, 1993.

24. AC 35:34.

25. Ibid.

26. AC 35:34. See also *Washington Post*, November 14, 1993.

27. Oral history interview of Burke Marshall, p. 54, RFK oral history project, JFKL.

28. Ibid., p. 92.

29. Anne Riley to RFK, undated, Condolences, Special for RFK: Attention folder, Attorney General's—Correspondence Condolences, 1963–1964 File, RFK papers, box 9, JFKL.

30. RFK to Anne Riley, April 20, 1964, Condolences, Special for RFK: Attention folder, Attorney General's—Correspondence Condolences, 1963–1964 File, RFK papers, box 9, JFKL.

31. Telephone messages (RFK), April 4, 1964, Telephone Messages 1/64–9/3/64 folder, Attorney General files, RFK papers, box 1, JFKL. Regarding the formation of a Kennedy Library, see RFK telephone messages on January 13, January 29, February 3, February 28, March 5, and March 9, 1964.

32. Oral history interview of Burke Marshall, p. 54, RFK oral history project, JFKL; oral history interview of Donald M. Wilson by Roberta W. Greene, June 19, 1970, pp. 2–3, RFK oral history project, JFKL; oral history interview of Milton S. Gwirtzman, p. 13, RFK oral history project, JFKL.

33. AC 19:27, 28. Whether or not this story is apocryphal is not clear. However, there is ample evidence that the two men did not trust or respect each other. RFK frequently compared Johnson with his brother, and was not impressed. For instance, Robert Kennedy wrote a personal memo to himself following a luncheon with Russian Ambassador Anatoly Dobrynin in July 1964, complaining about the shallowness of recent cabinet meetings led by President Johnson dealing with overflights in Cuba and civil rights. "None of the questions were raised that would ordinarily be raised by President Kennedy at those kind of meetings, searching analytical questions which people would have to come up with the answers to," RFK wrote sharply. "In fact, in my judgment, in many of these meetings we don't get really to the heart of the problem." See RFK on Luncheon with Ambassador Anatoly Dobrynin, July 7, 1964, Robert F. Kennedy 1961–1964 folder, Attorney General's Personal Correspondence File, RFK papers, box 14, JFKL.

34. Oral history interview of Burke Marshall, p. 55, RFK oral history project, JFKL; oral history interview of William O. Douglas by Roberta W. Greene, November 13, 1969, p. 14, RFK oral history project, JFKL.

35. RFK to Lyndon B. Johnson, September 3, 1964, Attorney General's Personal Correspondence folder, RFK papers, box 9, JFKL; oral history interview of Donald M. Wilson by Roberta W. Greene, June 19, 1970, p. 1, RFK oral history project, JFKL; *New York Times,* September 4, 1964.

36. Standard Diary May 4, 1964, AC personal papers.

37. Standard Diary, May 13, 1964, AC personal papers; AC, author's follow-up interview, September 5, 1995.

38. The photograph is contained in the personal papers of AC and Phyllis Ames Cox.

39. As journalist Anthony Lewis would write in a tribute to Robert Kennedy after his death: "Over those years he learned about the injustice to Negroes and the poor and other social victims, and he understood. Many politicians, perhaps most, become hardened or cynical over time. Bobby became warmer, more sympathetic, more understanding of humanity's imperfections." Lawford, *That Shining Hour,* p. 104.

40. Oral history interview of Nicholas deB. Katzenbach by Anthony Lewis, pp. 168–69, November 16, 1964, JFKL.

41. AC 17:8, 9.

42. AC 17:8.

43. Oral history interview of Burke Marshall, pp. 4–5, RFK oral history project, JFKL.

44. AC 17:8.

45. Ibid. For Katzenbach, it was particularly appropriate to rely upon the Commerce Clause because the history of the Constitution revealed that the Commerce Clause had been agreed to (by the Southerners) only in exchange for an explicit recognition of slavery. So "it was a nice ironic twist that we use[d] the Commerce Clause to get rid of the last vestiges of slavery." See Nicholas deB. Katzenbach, author's interview.

46. Moreton M. Rolleston, Jr., author's interview.

47. *Heart of Atlanta Motel v. United States,* 379 U.S. 241 (1964); *Katzenbach v. McClung,* 379 U.S. 294 (1964). For an interesting discussion of the debate between those who favored relying upon the Commerce Clause and those who felt that the Fourteenth Amendment was the proper base, see Gunther, *Constitutional Law,* pp. 148–49.

48. Ramsey Clark, author's interview.

49. Nicholas deB. Katzenbach, author's follow-up interview, August 31, 1995.

50. As Nick deB. Katzenbach (author's interview) explained, "It was important both that it [the Voting Rights legislation] be right, and that he [Cox] be totally committed to supporting it. And, what better way to get him totally committed to supporting it than to have him draft it?"

51. Memorandum for the Attorney General, February 23, 1965, Civil Rights file, 1965–66 Voting Rights folder (no. 5), Nicholas deB. Katzenbach papers, box 8, JFKL. In other words, a low percentage of voter turnout coupled with a suspect device such as a "literacy test" would trigger a presumption that the state had intentionally denied the right to vote based upon race or color.

52. AC 17:6, 7; Nicholas deB. Katzenbach, author's interview; Burke Marshall, author's interview, July 5, 1991.

53. Nicholas deB. Katzenbach, author's interview.

54. Ramsey Clark, author's interview.

55. Marshall had left the Johnson administration after RFK's departure, but participated in the Voting Rights Act work as a consultant.

56. Nicholas deB. Katzenbach, author's follow-up interview, August 31, 1995.

57. Nicholas deB. Katzenbach, author's interview; Burke Marshall, author's interview, July 22, 1991; Ramsey Clark, author's interview. For an example of other work by Cox on the Voting Rights Act, see Memorandum for the Attorney General, March 23, 1965, Civil Rights file, 1965–66 Voting Rights Legislation folder (no. 2), Nicholas deB. Katzenbach papers, box 8, JFKL.

58. Nicholas deB. Katzenbach, author's interview.

59. Caplan, *The Tenth Justice*, p. 10.

60. Segal, "Amicus Curiae Briefs by the Solicitor General," *Western Political Quarterly* 41 (1988): 139, 148. Of the sixty-seven cases Cox argued in the Supreme Court as Solicitor General, he won fifty-one (76 percent), lost thirteen (19 percent), and split decisions in three (5 percent). He therefore prevailed in a total of 81 percent of the cases. These figures come from the author's review of Supreme Court records and *United States Reports*.

61. See, for example, *Fireboard Corp. v. Labor Board*, 379 U.S. 203 (1964), dealing with the National Labor Relations Act; *Brown Shoe Co. v. United States*, 370 U.S. 294 (1962), dealing with corporate mergers under the Clayton Act.

62. *Cleveland Plain Dealer*, May 19, 1973.

63. Ramsey Clark, author's interview; *New York Times*, November 15, 1962.

64. David B. Currie, author's interview; see *Arizona v. California*, 373 U.S. 546 (1973).

65. *Harvard Law Record*, October 7, 1965; *Power Reactor Development Corp. v. International Union of Electrical Workers*, 367 U.S. 396 (1961).

66. John D. French, author's interview.

67. *Washington Post*, July 14, 1965; AC, author's follow-up interview, October 17, 1996; Caplan, *The Tenth Justice*, pp. 189–90; Navasky, *Kennedy Justice*, pp. 286, 296. See also *St. Regis Paper Co. v. U.S.*, 368 U.S. 208 (1961).

68. Charles R. Nessen, author's interview.

69. Philip B. Heymann, author's interview.

70. AC to Phyllis Ames Cox, undated (London), Phyllis Ames Cox personal papers.

71. AC to Phyllis Ames Cox, undated (Calcutta), Phyllis Ames Cox personal papers.

72. Phyllis told Archie: "Make sure that Dinah Shore doesn't speak and you try to sing." National Diary, May 1, 1961, AC personal papers; Cox, "More Reason for Confidence Than Despair," *Anglo American Trade News*, June 1975, p. 8.

73. Standard Diary, January 20, 1965, AC personal papers.

74. AC 36:6.

75. AC 19:29; Ralph Spritzer, author's interview.

76. AC 36:6.

77. Nicholas deB. Katzenbach, author's interview.

78. Standard Diary, March 8, 1965, AC personal papers.

79. Standard Diary, June 25 and July 8, 1965, AC personal papers.

80. Philip B. Heymann, author's interview.
81. Standard Diary, July 13, 1965, AC personal papers.
82. LBJ to AC, July 13, 1965, and AC to LBJ (undated) White House Press Release, July 13, 1965, Phyllis Ames Cox personal papers.
83. Standard Diary, July 29, 1965, AC personal papers; Caplan, *The Tenth Justice,* p. 159; Burke Marshall, author's interview, July 5, 1991.
84. Nicholas deB. Katzenbach, author's interview.
85. *Washington Post,* July 14, 1965.
86. John W. Douglas to AC, July 14, 1965, Phyllis Ames Cox, personal papers.
87. Earl Warren to AC, October 20, 1965, Phyllis Ames Cox personal papers.
88. Harold J. Gallagher to AC, July 14, 1965, Phyllis Ames Cox, personal papers.
89. *Boston Globe,* July 22, 1965.
90. *Congressional Record* 111 (1965): 16700.
91. AC to Charles E. Wyzanski, October 31, 1964, Charles E. Wyzanski, Jr., papers, box 3, folder 6, HLSL.
92. AC to Charles E. Wyzanski, Jr., November 3, 1964, Charles E. Wyzanski, Jr., papers, box 3, folder 6, HLSL.
93. George Meany to LBJ, April 21, 1965, Phyllis Ames Cox personal papers.
94. Nicholas deB. Katzenbach, author's follow-up interview, August 31, 1995.
95. Ibid.; Nicholas deB. Katzenbach, author's interview.
96. Philip B. Heymann, author's interview.

Chapter 13

1. *South Carolina v. Katzenbach,* 383 U.S. 301, 306 (1966); Nicholas deB. Katzenbach, author's interview.
2. John Douglas to AC, April 23, 1969, AC personal papers; *Shapiro v. Thompson,* 394 U.S. 618 (1969).
3. AC to Peter S. Smith, October 29, 1968, AC personal papers.
4. AC 20:6.
5. Seventh oral history interview with Peter Edelman by Larry J. Hackman, February 13, 1973, pp. 1–4, 16–17, RFK oral history project, JFKL.
6. AC 36:7. Robert Kennedy did not view himself as a presidential candidate for the 1968 election until fairly late, after the Vietnam War worsened and President Johnson announced his intention not to run. Most observers had assumed that RFK would run in 1972. See oral history interview of Peter Edelman by Larry J. Hackman, July 15, 1969, pp. 1–4, RFK oral history project, JFKL.
7. Elliot Richardson to AC, December 7, 1966, AC papers, box 47, folder 4, HLSL; Jonathan Moore to AC, October 24, 1966, AC papers, box 47, folder 4. Another person who helped Richardson in his campaign was former Vice President Richard M. Nixon. Cox and Nixon, however, did not attend the same fund-raising event. Elliot L. Richardson, author's interview, September 28, 1992.
8. News Release, October 22, 1965, AC personnel file, Harvard Law School.
9. Derek C. Bok, author's interview. Cox's ample Washington contacts made him a sought-after reference by students. Laurence Tribe, who had taken his constitutional law class, reported on December 16, 1966, that he had obtained a clerkship

with Justice Stewart on the Supreme Court: "I am confident that your comments played a vital role in his decision to offer me a clerkship, and I want you to know how deeply grateful I am for your assistance." Laurence H. Tribe to AC, December 16, 1966, and AC to Laurence H. Tribe, December 20, 1966, AC papers, box 47, folder 12.

10. "Anarchy Spreads in U.S. Colleges," *U.S. News & World Report,* May 6, 1968, 65.

11. Cox, Howe, and Wiggins, *Civil Rights, the Constitution, and the Courts,* pp. 14–15, 29. This book was originally presented as a series of lectures at the Massachusetts Historical Society in 1965–66.

12. *New York Times,* October 6, 1968.

13. Avorn, *University in Revolt;* Kahn, *The Battle for Morningside Heights;* "Anarchy Spreads in U.S. Colleges," *U.S. News & World Report,* May 6, 1968, 65.

14. AC 20:12–17; *New York Times,* October 6, 1968. The committee was chaired by Mike Sovern and included Fred Friendly, who had left CBS and knew Cox from his Washington days.

15. Avorn, *University in Revolt,* p. 235 n. 4.

16. *New York Times,* October 6, 1968.

17. Kahn, *The Battle for Morningside Heights,* p. 29.

18. *Nashua (N.H.) Telegraph,* May 16, 1968.

19. AC 20:14.

20. James Doyle interview with AC, circa 1975, tape 3, page 1 (hereinafter designated 3:1), James Doyle papers.

21. AC 20:14.

22. AC 20:14, 15.

23. AC 20:15.

24. Ibid.

25. AC 20:20.

26. Cox, "The Challenge of the College Generation" (speech at Roger Baldwin Foundation Award Dinner, Chicago, July 9, 1969), p. 6, AC personal papers; James Doyle interview with AC, circa 1975, pp. 2–44, 45, James Doyle papers.

27. Cox, "The Challenge of the College Generation," p. 4, AC personal papers; Cox, "Campus Unrest—Why?" *Williston Bulletin,* Spring 1969, 7–8.

28. Proceeds were donated to a fund for the benefit of Columbia students. See *New York Times,* October 6, 1968; *Columbia Daily Spectator,* October 7, 1968. Materials concerning the publication of the Cox Commission Report can be found in AC papers, box 54.

29. Cox, *Crisis at Columbia.*

30. Kahn, *The Battle for Morningside Heights,* p. 19.

31. AC 35:32, 33; *New York Times,* July 8, 1968; newspaper clipping on RFK funeral (undated), Phyllis Ames Cox personal papers; Ethel Kennedy to AC, October 25, 1968, Phyllis Ames Cox personal papers.

32. Cox, "Robert F. Kennedy" (speech at U.S. Justice Department, July 8, 1968), AC personal papers.

33. "Anarchy Spreads in U.S. Colleges," *U.S. News & World Report,* May 6, 1968, 65; *New York Times,* October 28, 1968.

34. Minutes of October 15, 1968, Meeting of the Faculty of Arts and Sciences, Harvard Archives.

35. AC 20:28.
36. *Harvard Crimson,* April 9, 1969; "The 'Bust' at Harvard," *Newsweek,* April 21, 1969, 102; "The Occupation, the Bust, the Aftermath," *Harvard Alumni Bulletin,* April 28, 1969, 19–20. For a discussion of the symbolism of ROTC in the minds of the protesters, see Eichel et al., *The Harvard Strike,* pp. 51–76.
37. *Harvard Crimson,* April 10, 1969; "The 'Bust' at Harvard," *Newsweek,* April 21, 1969, p. 102; News Release, "Events of Wednesday, April 9, 1969," General History, 1969, box 178, HUA 969.23.5, Harvard Archives; "The Occupation, the Bust, the Aftermath," *Harvard Alumni Bulletin,* April 28, 1969, 20–21.
38. "The Occupation, the Bust, the Aftermath," *Harvard Alumni Bulletin,* April 28, 1969, 22; Robert Tonis, author's interview.
39. News Release, "Events of Wednesday, April 9, 1969," General History, 1969, box 178, HUA 969.23.5, Harvard Archives.
40. "The Time to Fight Is Now," April 9, 1969, General History, 1969, box 182, HUA 969.100, Harvard Archives.
41. "The 'Bust' at Harvard," *Newsweek,* April 21, 1969, 102–3; "The Occupation, the Bust, the Aftermath," *Harvard Alumni Bulletin,* April 28, 1969, 22.
42. Nathan M. Pusey, author's interview.
43. *Harvard Crimson,* April 12, 1969; "The 'Bust' at Harvard," *Newsweek,* April 21, 1969, 102–3; "Harvard and Beyond," *Time,* April 18, 1969, 47–48; "The Occupation, the Bust, the Aftermath," *Harvard Alumni Bulletin,* April 28, 1969, 28–30. The story about the student being beaten out of a wheelchair comes from Raymond Dean Jones, author's interview.
44. AC 20:28; *Harvard Crimson,* March 21, 1971.
45. AC 20:28, 29.
46. Statement, April 9, 1969, General History, 1969, box 178, HUA 969.23.5, Harvard Archives.
47. The Committee of Fifteen was also designed to mediate immediate matters relating to the University Hall sit-ins, thus wrestling away control from the president. See *Boston Globe,* April 12, 1969; "The 'Bust' at Harvard," *Newsweek,* April 21, 1969, 103; *Harvard Crimson,* April 30, 1969; Progress Report of the Committee of Fifteen, General History, 1969, box 180, HUA 969.35.2, Harvard Archives.
48. AC 20:30, 31. This meeting probably took place on April 14, 1969, when Pusey met with an ad hoc committee of advisers and was summoned to leave for a meeting with the Board of Overseers. See Memo, "FYI," April 14, 1969, General History, 1969, box 183, HUA 969.100, Harvard Archives.
49. *Old Mole,* April 11 to April 24, 1969, General History, 1969, box 197, HUA 969.100.65, Harvard Archives.
50. *Harvard Crimson* Photo Annual, 1968–69, General History, 1969, box 178, HUA 969.23.5, Harvard Archives; Strike posters, circa 1969–1970, General History, 1969, HUA 969.82 pf.; "Harvard New College," General History, 1969, box 184, April 18, 1969, folder, HUA 969.100, Harvard Archives.
51. *Harvard Crimson,* April 18, 1969; Poster, General History, 1969, box 183, April 16, 1969, folder, HUA 969.100, Harvard Archives.
52. *Benton Harbor (Mich.) News-Palladium,* April 14, 1969; *Enterprise* (Paris, France), May 3, 1969. The French phrase translates as "Harvard is no longer a sanctuary."

53. *Harvard Crimson,* April 14, 1969; "The Occupation, the Bust, the Aftermath," *Harvard Alumni Bulletin,* April 28, 1969, 36–46; "Harvard and Beyond," *Time,* April 18, 1969, 48; "The 'Bust' at Harvard," *Newsweek,* April 21, 1969, 103. The two mass meetings occurred on April 14 and April 18, 1969. Reports on the number of students present at each meeting varied, ranging from five thousand to ten thousand.

54. *Harvard Crimson,* April 30, 1969. President Nixon, on his one hundredth day in office, declared that professors and administrators must not "surrender to force." He warned: "It is the time for the faculty and boards of trustees and school administrators to have the backbone to stand up." California Governor Ronald Reagan stated that the campus movement against ROTC was part of a national campaign led by persons loyal to America's enemies. See ibid.

55. *Harvard Crimson,* June 10, 1969. A total of 170 individuals were also found guilty of criminal trespass in the Middlesex County Third District Court and fined twenty dollars each. See ibid., May 2, 1969.

56. President Pusey was forced to give the SDS fifteen minutes to address the commencement crowd in order to diffuse a skirmish. See *Boston Globe,* June 11 and June 12, 1969; *Boston Herald Traveler,* June 13, 1969.

57. Official Register of Harvard University, October 30, 1970, "Report of the President of Harvard College and Reports of Departments, 1968–1969," p. 5, Harvard Archives.

58. The original Committee of Fifteen had decided that it should no longer take responsibility for disciplinary matters. See Progress Report of the Committee of Fifteen, October 24, 1969, General History, 1969, box 180, HUA 969.35.2, pp. 9–10, Harvard Archives. The Committee of Fifteen also adopted a Resolution on Rights and Responsibilities on June 9, 1969, setting forth certain rights and responsibilities that applied to all members of the academic community, students and faculty alike. In September 1969, it recommended the formal creation of the Committee on Rights, and Responsibilities (CRR), which would serve as a successor body with respect to handling disciplinary matters. The faculty later ratified both committee actions. See Official Register of Harvard University, Report of the President of Harvard College, 1969–1970, pp. 61–62, Harvard Archives. James Q. Wilson, distinguished Professor of Government, was named chairman of CRR.

59. AC 20:34.

60. Eichel et al., *The Harvard Strike,* pp. 298–99.

61. AC 20:35.

62. AC 20:38, 39.

63. Ibid.; Robert Tonis, author's interview.

64. AC 21:1, 2.

65. AC 21:2.

66. Ibid.

67. AC 21:3. Derek C. Bok, dean of the Law School, was among those who pushed Cox's name. It was "a hell of a thing to do to your friend," he later said. Derek C. Bok, author's interview.

68. AC 21:2, 3. The sequence of these events is clarified by Samuel R. Williamson, Jr., letter to author, March 1, 1996.

69. AC 21:4.

70. AC 21:5.

71. AC 21:5, 6.

72. Ibid.

73. AC 21:6.

74. Raymond Dean Jones, author's interview; Epps, "The 1969 Rebellion: Through Change and Through Storm" (paper delivered at Massachusetts Historical Society, Boston), April 1995.

75. Raymond Dean Jones, author's interview.

76. Ibid.

77. *Harvard Crimson*, December 6, 1969; *Harvard University Gazette*, December 5, 1969; Memo, December 15, 1969 (author unknown), Samuel R. Williamson, Jr., personal papers; Raymond Dean Jones, author's interview.

78. General Fact Statement on the Occupation of University Hall, December 11, 1969, Samuel R. Williamson, Jr., personal papers; *Harvard Crimson*, December 11, 1969; *Harvard University Gazette*, December 12, 1969; Raymond Dean Jones, author's interview.

79. Raymond Dean Jones, author's interview.

80. *Harvard Crimson*, December 11, 1969; *Harvard University Gazette*, December 5, 1969. See also the following items from the personal papers of Samuel R. Williamson, Jr.: A. Tillman Merritt, letter to Professor James Q. Wilson, January 8, 1970; General Fact Statement on the Occupation of University Hall, December 11, 1969; News Release, December 12, 1969; Memo (author unknown), December 15, 1969.

81. Epps, "The 1969 Rebellion: Through Change and Through Storm" (paper delivered at Massachusetts Historical Society, Boston), April 1995, p. 18.

82. Samuel R. Williamson, Jr., author's interview.

83. Raymond Dean Jones, author's interview.

84. *Harvard Crimson*, December 11, 1969. See also the following items from the personal papers of Samuel R. Williamson, Jr.: News Release, December 12, 1969; General Fact Statement on the Occupation of University Hall, December 11, 1969; Memo (author unknown), December 15, 1969.

85. Raymond Dean Jones, author's interview.

86. AC 21:9.

87. Most of the OBU students involved in the incidents received mild warnings. Those suspended were generally given a second chance by the university. See *Detroit News*, January 23, 1970; *Harvard University Gazette*, January 23, 1970. However, the Law School imposed its own discipline on several students who participated in the OBU occupation. See Raymond Dean Jones, author's interview.

88. Raymond Dean Jones, author's interview.

89. Nathan M. Pusey, author's interview. Pusey's contemplated retirement was announced on February 15, 1970, and appeared in the *Harvard University Gazette* the same day. He remained president, however, until July 1971.

90. *Harvard Crimson*, April 16, 1970.

91. Samuel R. Williamson, Jr., author's interview; "Statement: 11:40 P.M., Wednesday," April 15, 1970, General History, 1969, box 177, HUA 969.2, Harvard Archives; *Harvard University Gazette*, April 17, 1970.

92. *Boston Record-American*, April 16, 1970; *New York Times*, April 17, 1970; *Boston Globe*, April 16, 1970; "Statement: 11:40 P.M., Wednesday," April 15, 1970, General History, 1969, box 177, HUA 969.2, Harvard Archives; Memo, Chief Robert Tonis to AC, April 16, 1970, Samuel R. Williamson, Jr., personal papers.
93. "At War with War," *Time*, May 18, 1970, 7–12.
94. Report, June 9, 1969, the Committee of Fifteen, Harvard University, p. 5, John Dunlop personal papers.
95. *Harvard Crimson*, May 2 and May 4, 1970.
96. "At War with War," *Time*, May 18, 1970, 6; "The South: Dark Day in Jackson," *Newsweek*, May 25, 1970, 35; "The South: Death in Two Cities," *Time*, May 25, 1970, 22.
97. Statement by President Nathan M. Pusey, May 5, 1970, General History, 1969, box 177, HUA 969.2, Harvard Archives.
98. Nathan M. Pusey, author's interview.
99. Eichel et al., *The Harvard Strike*, pp. 54, 328.
100. Samuel R. Williamson, Jr., author's interview; *Harvard University Gazette*, May 8, 1970; *Harvard Crimson*, May 9, 1970.
101. "Memorandum for the Record" (diary), May 23, 1970, p. 17, Samuel R. Williamson, Jr., personal papers.
102. AC 21:17.
103. AC 21:18, 19.
104. AC 21:19; *Harvard Crimson*, May 9, 1970; "Memorandum for the Record," Samuel R. Williamson, Jr., personal papers, p. 18.
105. *Harvard Crimson*, May 9, 1970.
106. Derek C. Bok, author's interview.
107. *Harvard Crimson*, May 8, 1970, *Harvard University Gazette*, May 8, 1970.
108. AC 21:7.
109. *Harvard University Gazette*, May 22, 1970.
110. Phyllis Ames Cox, author's interview.
111. Justice Roberts of the U.S. Supreme Court had retired in 1945 and had taken over the deanship from 1948 to 1951; he called Cox and asked if he was interested in the permanent spot.
112. AC 21:37, 38; 36:9.
113. AC 21:38.
114. *Harvard Crimson*, Registration Issue, Fall 1970.
115. *Harvard Crimson*, October 13, 1970, and January 13, 1971. The case of *Coolidge v. New Hampshire*, 403 U.S. 443 (1971), became an important one curtailing the ability of police officers to search and seize parked automobiles without a warrant. The case involved the gruesome kidnapping and murder of a fourteen-year-old girl who was on her way to a babysitting job in Manchester, New Hampshire. Because of the horrible nature of the crime and public unpopularity of the case, New Hampshire attorneys had carefully avoided it. Material relating to Cox's work on the *Coolidge* case is contained in AC papers, boxes 54 and 55.
116. Samuel R. Williamson, Jr., author's interview.
117. Report of Disciplinary Action in Cases Arising Out of the Disruption at the Center for International Affairs, May 20, 1970, Samuel R. Williamson, Jr., personal papers; News Release, April 28, 1970, General History, 1969, box 177, HUA 969.2, Harvard Archives; *Harvard University Gazette*, April 10, 1970.

Regarding a previous attack on the Center for International Affairs, see *Harvard University Gazette,* September 26, 1969.

118. *Harvard University Gazette,* April 10, 1970; AC 21:29–33.

119. AC 21:33–35. See also Samuel R. Williamson, Jr., letter to author, March 1, 1996.

120. Angry Medical School students staged a game of "Capture the Flag," hoisting a large Bike athletic supporter and a flag of the NLF (National Liberation Front) atop the building's roof until Cox dragged the items down. See "Memorandum for the Record" (diary), May 18, 1970, p. 31, Samuel R. Williamson, Jr., personal papers. These offending items are housed in the Harvard Archives, General History, 1971, HUA 971.2. See also AC to Harley P. Holden, November 24, 1975, AC papers, box 84, folder 19.

121. Tom Gerety was then a first-year Harvard law student who had engaged in peaceful protests, but opposed the violent abduction of administration officials by the Progressive Labor Party. He was almost prosecuted by the university for his involvement in a melee, even though he was actually attempting to set free a university official who had been taken hostage by PLP members. The Harvard authorities saw photos of Gerety in the middle of the scuffle and filed charges against him for obstructing the university. It was only after the full story came out that Gerety became a "begrudged hero." Cox was "agitated" with the student protesters, and they were agitated with him. Ironically, in 1972 Tom Gerety married Adelia Moore, the god-daughter of Archie's mother, Fanny Cox. Gerety went on to become the president of Trinity College and later of Amherst College. See Mary "Molly" Cox, author's interview, August 15, 1990; Tom Gerety, letter to author, September 23, 1995.

122. AC 21:21.

123. *Harvard Crimson,* June 10, 1970.

124. Samuel R. Williamson, Jr., author's interview.

125. AC 21:21.

126. AC 21:22.

127. *Harvard Crimson,* June 11, 1970; *Harvard University Gazette,* June 19, 1970.

128. AC 21:22.

129. Samuel R. Williamson, Jr., author's interview.

130. AC 21:22.

131. Samuel R. Williamson, Jr., author's interview.

132. Ibid., author's follow-up interview, August 16, 1996. Williamson spent most of the fall in Cambridge, assisting in some of the student prosecutions, and left for Vienna in the winter of 1971.

133. *Harvard University Gazette,* October 30, 1970.

134. *Harvard Crimson,* January 11, 1971.

135. Robert Tonis, author's interview; *Harvard Crimson,* March 21, 1971; Phyllis Ames Cox, author's interview.

136. *Harvard Crimson,* March 23, 1971. The "Students for a Just Peace" included the Young Americans for Freedom, another well-known conservative group.

137. *Harvard Crimson,* March 26, 1971; *Boston Herald,* April 21, 1971.

138. *Boston Herald,* April 21, 1971.

139. AC 21:12.

140. "Counter Teach-In, Film of March 26, 1971," film no. 140, Harvard Archives; *Boston Herald Traveler,* March 27, 1971.
141. *Harvard University Gazette,* April 2, 1971; *Boston Herald,* April 21, 1971.
142. *Harvard Crimson,* March 27, 1971.
143. AC 21:13.
144. *Harvard Crimson,* March 27, 1971; *Harvard University Gazette,* April 2, 1971.
145. AC 21:14; Robert Tonis, author's interview.
146. Governor Deane C. Davis wire, March 31, 1971, Phyllis Ames Cox personal papers; *Congressional Record* 92, S. 117 (1971): 10299–300 (statement of Senator Mansfield).
147. Warren E. Burger, author's interview.
149. AC 21:13. The dissipation of anger and unrest was gradual; many students remained frustrated. The 1971 Harvard Yearbook panned the newly released movie *Love Story,* starring Ryan O'Neil and Ali McGraw, because it portrayed Harvard "sans rock, sans dope and sans worry." The caption read: "Even My Mommy Didn't Like It." See Harvard Yearbook, 1971, pp. 23–24, Harvard University Archives. By commencement of 1971, however, the campus had settled down.
150. Nixon, *RN,* pp. 691–707.
150. Derek C. Bok, author's interview. Cox was so busy he did not even have time to talk to a young professor from Stanford and former clerk to Judge Learned Hand, Gerald Gunther, who was beginning research on a biography that he planned to write about their old boss. The correspondence between Gunther and Cox is contained in AC papers, boxes 44 and 45.
151. AC 21:35.

Chapter 14

1. Drew, *Washington Journal,* p. 12.
2. Earl J. Silbert to AC, June 7, 1973, Watergate Special Prosecution Force, Special Prosecutor's Files—General Correspondence, box 6, U.S. Attorney—Dist. of Col. folder, National Archives; Kutler, *The Wars of Watergate,* pp. 187–89; Dash, *Chief Counsel,* p. 4; Mankiewicz, *U.S. v. Richard M. Nixon,* p. 12.
3. James Doyle interview with AC, circa 1975, p. 39, James Doyle papers.
4. Cox had first expressed his belief that the voting age could be reduced from twenty-one to eighteen by statute, rather than through the more laborious constitutional amendment process, in Cox, "Foreword: Constitutional Adjudication and the Promotion of Human Rights," *Harvard Law Review* 80 (1966): 91. Cox testified on the subject, at Senator Kennedy's invitation, in February 1970. See U.S. Senate Subcommittee on Constitutional Rights, *Hearings,* February 24, 1970. The original federal legislation that Cox supported, in the form of the 1970 amendments to the Voting Rights Act, was upheld as it applied to federal elections but was held invalid as it applied to state elections. See *Oregon v. Mitchell,* 400 U.S. 112 (1970). Additional material on Cox's participation in this matter can be found in AC papers, box 62, folder 1. See also Edward M. Kennedy, author's interview.

5. *Coolidge v. New Hampshire*, 403 U.S. 443 (1971). *Coolidge* held that where no "exigent circumstances" existed at the time of defendant's arrest in his home, police had to obtain a warrant before searching and seizing a parked automobile in defendant's driveway.

6. Edmund S. Muskie to AC, February 14, 1972, AC papers, box 62, folder 15; Town of Wayland, Massachusetts, "Results of Presidential Primary," April 25, 1972, Democratic Ballot. Cox did not, in later years, recall running for the position.

7. *Chicago Sun-Times*, May 19, 1973; *Boston Globe*, February 17 and June 10, 1973; Massachusetts, Governor's Select Committee on Judicial Needs, "Report."

8. AC, *The Role of the Supreme Court in American Government*, pp. 113–14. *Roe* held that the Fourteenth Amendment notion of privacy was broad enough to include a woman's right to choose whether or not to have an abortion. Cox did not argue, as his old boss Judge Learned Hand might have argued, that the due process clause of the Fourteenth Amendment was devoid of "substantive rights" of a fundamental nature. Rather, Cox's quarrel with *Roe* was that the substantive rights identified in that case were too ambiguous: "Constitutional rights ought not to be created under the Due Process Clause," he wrote, "unless they can be stated in principles sufficiently absolute to give them roots throughout the community and continuity over significant periods of time, and to lift them above the level of the pragmatic political judgments of a particular time and place." See ibid., pp. 113–14, 52–53. Cox later softened his view on *Roe* after it had been in place for nearly two decades. At that point, he felt that "[it] has been the law in the sense that people have acted on it and it's been the predicate of all kinds of action." See AC 30:16.

9. Cox, *The Lawyer's Profession* (lecture delivered at Boston College Law School, November 7, 1965), AC personal papers.

10. For example, in late 1972 Cox wrote to the publisher of *U.S. Law Week* stating that he had paid his annual subscription fee of $158, only to discover that professors were supposed to receive a 50 percent discount. A representative of the publication, H. Burl, wrote back promptly, stating that professors were indeed entitled to a 50 percent discount, but "there was no indication as to whether or not you were a professor or a student." See AC to Bureau of National Affairs, November 30, 1972 and December 11, 1972, and H. Burl to AC, December 8, 1972, AC papers, box 43, folder 13.

11. AC 22:35.

12. AC 22:31, 32.

13. AC 22:35.

14. AC 23:3, 4.

15. Interview with AC by Phil Heymann et al., February 19, 1974, p. 2, AC papers, box 24, folder 1.

16. Richardson had been "asked" to resign so that Kennedy could appoint his own U.S. attorney in Massachusetts, in part as a result of pressure exerted by Massachusetts politicians. See Joseph F. Dolan, author's interview. Richardson liked to joke that he was "fired" by Bobby Kennedy; in fact, he was given no choice but to resign or be fired. See Joseph F. Dolan, author's interview; Press Conference of Elliot L. Richardson, October 23, 1973, p. 12, James Doyle papers, temporary folder 155.

17. AC 23:8. Ironically, Richardson's great-grandfather, Dr. George Shattuck, Jr., had founded St. Paul's School, where the Coxes and Evartses were leading families. But Richardson attended Milton Academy rather than St. Paul's and never encountered Coxes at this stage of his life. Elliot L. Richardson, author's follow-up interview, February 3, 1997.
18. Ibid.
19. Ibid.
20. Ibid.
21. "The Saturday Night Massacre," program, December 3, 1993.
22. AC 23:10.
23. Ibid.
24. Elliot L. Richardson, author's interview, September 28, 1992.
25. *New York Times,* May 5, 1973, May 6, 1973; *Washington Post,* May 4, 1973.
26. Elliot L. Richardson, author's interview, September 28, 1992. Judge Erickson was never formally offered the job, although Richardson discussed it seriously with him. See interview with Elliot Richardson by James Doyle, May 3, 1975, pp. 1–4, James Doyle papers.
27. Memo, Wilmot R. Hastings to Elliot L. Richardson, May 9, 1973, box 231, Watergate SP—search for special prosecutor, first ranking, Hastings memos folder, Elliot L. Richardson papers, Library of Congress (hereinafter cited as ELR papers).
28. Memo, "MM—Thoughts, Etc.," May 8, 1973, box 229, Watergate SP—search for special prosecutor, Candidates—Cox folder, ELR papers.
29. Draft memo, "Description of Selection Process," Wilmot R. Hastings to ELR, May 7, 1973, box 231, Watergate SP—search for special prosecutor, description of process folder, ELR papers.
30. Memo, Wilmot R. Hastings to ELR, May 9, 1973, box 231, Watergate SP—search for special prosecutor, first ranking, Hastings memos folder, ELR papers.
31. Typed notes of J. T. Smith (undated, 1974), John T. Smith personal papers.
32. Wilmot Hastings, author's interview.
33. Misc. Memos, box 229, search for candidates—Cox folder, ELR papers.
34. Ibid.
35. Wilmot Hastings, author's interview.
36. Ibid.
37. Ibid.
38. Interview with John T. Smith by Phil Heymann et al., April 22, 1974, p. 58, John T. Smith personal papers.
39. AC 23:12.
40. Interview with AC by Phil Heymann et al., February 19, 1974, p. 3, AC papers, box 24, folder 1.
41. AC 23:17; Doyle, *Not Above the Law,* p. 44.
42. Erwin N. Griswold, author's interview.
43. AC 23:17.
44. Draft Charter, "Duties and Responsibilities of the Special Prosecutor," May 17, 1973, AC papers, box 21, folder 8. It is highly probable that Senator Kennedy's office, through conversations with Elliot Richardson's staff, had also suggested

the "extraordinary improprieties" language, or at least insisted that the attorney general, rather than the president, have the ability to determine what an extraordinary impropriety was. See James Flug, author's interview.

45. AC 23:17, 18.
46. Elliot L. Richardson, author's interview, September 28, 1992. Cox also insisted that it be written directly into the guidelines that the special prosecutor have independent power to decide when to go public with information flowing from the Watergate investigation. Cox believed that "the ability to explain yourself in the world of Washington politics and the press is one of greatest importance." See AC 23:15; Draft Charter, "Duties and Responsibilities of the Special Prosecutor," May 17, 1973, AC papers, box 21, folder 8.
47. Interview with AC by Phil Heymann et al., February 19, 1974, pp. 7–9 and 13–15, AC papers, box 24, folder 1.
48. Ibid., p. 7.
49. AC 23:18.
50. AC 34:1; Learned Hand, *The Spirit of Liberty,* pp. 134–39.
51. AC 34:1.
52. AC 23:19; Doyle, *Not Above the Law,* p. 46.
53. AC 34:2, 3.
54. AC 23:23.
55. Ibid.
56. AC 23:23, 24.
57. AC 23:11, 12.
58. Ibid.
59. Mollenhoff, *Game Plan for Disaster,* p. 297; "Exposing the Big Cover-Up," *Newsweek,* May 28, 1973.
60. Statement, May 18, 1973, Watergate—SP: Special prosecutor, announcement of Cox file, box 227, ELR papers.
61. *Washington Post,* May 19, 1973.
62. *Harvard University Gazette,* May 25, 1973; *Harvard Law Record,* May 19, 1973.
63. *Framingham (Mass.) South Middlesex Sunday News,* May 20, 1973.
64. *Pittsfield (Mass.) Berkshire Eagle,* May 21, 1973.
65. *Cleveland Plain Dealer,* May 19, 1973.
66. *Long Beach (Calif.) Independent,* May 24, 1973.
67. Ibid.
68. Mary "Molly" Cox, author's interview, August 15, 1990.
69. *Washington Post,* May 19, 1973; Doyle, *Not Above the Law,* p. 40.
70. Adlai E. Stevenson III to ELR, May 3, 1973, Administrative Files of the Watergate Special Prosecution Force, RG 460, BSD-1 Authority & Establishment, National Archives.
71. ELR to Adlai E. Stevenson III, May 17, 1973, ibid. Richardson sounded a similar theme in the press. See Memo, May 7, 1973, box 229, ELR papers.
72. *Washington Post,* May 19, 1973.
73. Edward M. Kennedy, author's interview.
74. Elliot L. Richardson, author's interview, September 28, 1992.
75. *Washington Star,* May 14, 1973.
76. U.S. Senate Committee on the Judiciary, *Hearings before the Committee on the*

Judiciary, United States Senate, Ninety-third Congress, First Session, on Nomination of Elliot L. Richardson, of Massachusetts, to Be Attorney General, May 1973, pp. 148–49.

77. *Washington Post*, May 21, 1973.
78. Ibid.; Edward M. Kennedy, author's interview.
79. Press Release, May 22, 1973, Memoranda to Cabinet folder, box 232, ELR papers; Mollenhoff, *Game Plan for Disaster*, p. 299; Sussman, *The Great Cover-up*, p. 231; Ambrose, *Nixon*, 3:147.
80. Interview with AC by Phil Heymann et al., February 19, 1974, p. 4, AC papers, box 24, folder 1.
81. *Los Angeles Times*, May 26, 1973.
82. Ibid.; *New York Times*, May 25, 1973.
83. *New York Times*, May 25, 1973; *Los Angeles Times*, May 26, 1973. Cox had originally recommended Griswold to Attorney General Ramsey Clark for the post after Thurgood Marshall left for the Supreme Court, although Griswold never knew this.
84. *Washington Post*, May 26, 1973.
85. Ibid.
86. *St. Louis Post-Dispatch*, May 26, 1973; *New York Times*, May 26, 1973.
87. Erwin N. Griswold, author's interview.
88. Leonard Garment, author's interview, September 14, 1994.
89. AC 23:28.
90. Wilmot Hastings, author's interview.
91. Interview with AC by Phil Heymann et al., February 19, 1974, p. 33, AC papers, box 24, folder 1.
92. AC 23:21.
93. "The Saturday Night Massacre," program, December 3, 1993.
94. Richardson, *Creative Balance*, pp. 4–5.
95. Notes, April 29, 1973, box 229, Watergate SP—Notes of Conversation w/ Nixon, 29 April 1973 folder, ELR papers.
96. "The Saturday Night Massacre," program, December 3, 1993.
97. Ibid.
98. Ibid.
99. "RMN Notes," April 29, 1973, box 229, Watergate SP—Notes of Conversation w/ Nixon, 29 April 1973 folder, ELR papers.
100. Ibid.; Elliot L. Richardson, author's interview, September 28, 1992; Richardson, *Creative Balance*, pp. 4–5. Hastings's reaction was not positive when Richardson informed him that the president had suggested his name: "I was not proud. It meant I was regarded as a friendly patsy." See Wilmot Hastings, author's interview.
101. Interview with John T. Smith by Phil Heymann et al., April 22, 1974, pp. 41–42, John T. Smith personal papers.
102. Elliot L. Richardson, author's interview, September 28, 1992.
103. Ibid.
104. "RMN Notes," April 29, 1973, box 229, Watergate SP—Notes of Conversations w/ Nixon, 29 April 1973 folder, ELR papers.
105. Ibid.

106. "The Saturday Night Massacre," program, December 3, 1993.
107. "RMN Notes," April 29, 1973, box 229, Watergate SP—Notes of Conversations w/ Nixon, 29 April folder, ELR papers.
108. Ibid.
109. Richardson, *Creative Balance,* p. 5; "RMN Notes," April 29, 1973, box 229, Watergate SP—Notes of Conversations w/ Nixon, 29 April 1973 folder, ELR papers.
110. "The Saturday Night Massacre," program, December 3, 1993.
111. Philip B. Heymann, author's interview.
112. James Vorenberg, author's interview.
113. Phyllis Ames Cox, author's follow-up interview, May 15, 1996.
114. James Flug, author's interview. The original subcommittee chaired by Senator Kennedy was the "Administrative Practice and Procedure" subcommittee of the Senate Judiciary Committee. See ibid.
115. AC 23:32.
116. Philip B. Heymann, author's interview.
117. James Vorenberg, author's interview.
118. Ibid.
119. Philip B. Heymann, author's interview; "The Saturday Night Massacre," program, December 3, 1993.
120. Notes on "backgrounder," May 28, 1973, James Doyle papers, temporary folder 9.
121. Ibid.
122. AC 23:33.
123. Cox's old friend and colleague Clark Byse would recall having lunch with the new special prosecutor in the faculty dining room in Pound Hall at Harvard Law School just before Cox left for Washington. Archie had confided to him, "I certainly hope the President didn't do anything wrong—it would be bad for the country." See Clark Byse, author's interview.
124. AC 23:33.

Chapter 15

1. *Washington Post,* May 24, 1973.
2. AC to Albert M. Sacks, June 7, 1973, and Albert M. Sacks to AC, September 10, 1973, AC personnel file, Office of the Dean, Harvard Law School.
3. James Vorenberg, author's interview.
4. Ibid.
5. Drew, *Washington Journal,* p. 15; Mankiewicz, *U.S. v. Richard M. Nixon,* p. 13.
6. A detailed account of the original Watergate trial and Judge Sirica's frustration with the young prosecutors' limited theories (which he attributed to "naïveté" and "inexperience") is set out in Sirica, *To Set the Record Straight,* pp. 40–83. See also Mankiewicz, *U.S. v. Richard Nixon,* p. 17.
7. Mitchell had been a partner of Nixon's at a New York law firm before heading Nixon's 1968 campaign. He was appointed attorney general after the successful campaign, but left the Justice Department in March 1972 to run the president's re-election campaign. He quit three months later, two weeks after the Watergate

break-in, saying his wife Martha encouraged him to leave. See *New York Times,* May 11, 1973. Jeb Stuart Magruder was apparently the first to implicate Mitchell in conversations with the original Watergate prosecutors. See *Washington Post,* April 19, 1973. McCord then implicated Mitchell in his testimony before the Senate committee on May 18. See "Exposing the Big Coverup," *Newsweek,* May 28, 1973, p. 26.

8. Richardson, *The Creative Balance,* p. 3.

9. "The Saturday Night Massacre," program, December 3, 1993.

10. AC 24:19.

11. AC 24:19, 20.

12. *Maine Sunday Telegram,* June 10, 1973.

13. AC 23:35.

14. Meeting notes, April 30, 1973, Administrative Files of the Watergate Special Prosecution Force, RG 460, BSD-1, Authority & Establishment, National Archives.

15. AC 23:35. Earl Silbert may have also attended a portion of this meeting, although Cox did not recall him being present for the questioning.

16. AC 23:35, 36.

17. AC 23:35.

18. Philip B. Heymann, author's interview.

19. Sirica, *To Set the Record Straight,* pp. 42–43; Rebuttal to Earl Silbert's Reply to Morgan Report, p. 191, discussed in James Doyle notes, temporary folder 22, James Doyle papers. For a discussion of the limited view of the original Watergate case that Silbert had conveyed to reporters, see also an article written by Walter Pincus of the *New Republic,* "A Promotion for Earl Silbert?" which appeared in the *Washington Post,* July 11, 1974, when Silbert was nominated by President Nixon to become U.S. attorney.

20. Sirica later wrote: "I don't think that it ever occurred to him that people like John Mitchell, Jeb Magruder . . . would lie before a grand jury." See Sirica, *To Set the Record Straight,* pp. 61, 42–63.

21. Memo, Harold H. Titus et al. to Elliot L. Richardson, April 30, 1973, box 228, Cox liaison materials folder, ELR papers.

22. Ibid. Judge Sirica's account of receiving the letter from McCord indicates no participation of the young assistant U.S. attorney's team in bringing about this event. See Sirica, *To Set the Record Straight,* pp. 68–83.

23. Judge Sirica had publicly "snapped" at the assistant U.S. attorneys at the end of March for not calling back key witnesses before the grand jury "in view of substantive developments." See *New York Times,* March 31, 1973.

24. Philip B. Heymann, author's interview.

25. James Vorenberg, author's interview.

26. Peter M. Kreindler, author's interview; James Vorenberg, author's interview.

27. AC 23:36, 36:26, 27.

28. Earl Silbert's diary, Watergate Task Force, US Attorney Files, May 22, 1973 (entry 108), National Archives (hereinafter cited as Silbert diary).

29. James Vorenberg, author's interview.

30. AC 36:27.

31. Memo, Harold H. Titus et al. to Elliot L. Richardson, April 30, 1973, box 228, Cox liaison materials folder, ELR papers.

32. Silbert diary, April 29, 1973 (entry 97).
33. Pincus, "The Silbert-Petersen Puzzle," *New Republic,* July 6 and 13, 1974, pp. 15–16; "Agnew's Nemesis at Justice," *Time,* October 8, 1973, pp. 16–17.
34. Silbert diary, undated (entry 101).
35. Leonard Garment, author's interview, September 14, 1994.
36. John W. Dean III, author's interview.
37. Ibid.
38. Ibid.
39. Ibid.
40. The unusual links between Henry Petersen and the White House are generally documented in the following sources: Pincus, "The Silbert-Petersen Puzzle," *New Republic,* July 6 and 13, 1974, pp. 15–16; Memo, Earl J. Silbert to AC, June 5, 1973, James Doyle papers, temporary folder 74; Harold H. Titus et al. to Elliot L. Richardson, April 30, 1973, James Doyle papers, temporary folder 74; Henry Petersen, D.C. Grand Jury No. 2, August 23, 1973, James Doyle papers, temporary folder 74; "Agnew's Nemesis at Justice," *Time,* October 8, 1973, pp. 16–17; Mollenhoff, *Game Plan for Disaster,* p. 295; Meeting Notes (ELR), May 4, 1973, Administrative Files of the Watergate Special Prosecution Force, RG 460, BSD-1, Authority & Establishment, National Archives.
41. Silbert diary, May 8, 1973 (entry 100).
42. Ibid., May 10, 1973 (entry 103).
43. Ibid., April 29, 1973 (entry 97).
44. AC 24:2, 3.
45. AC 23:26.
46. Silbert diary, April 29, 1973 (entry 97).
47. *Washington Post,* May 25, 1973; Doyle, *Not Above the Law,* pp. 51–54; Silbert diary, undated (entry 110).
48. Silbert diary, May 25, 1973 (entry 111).
49. Interview with AC by Phil Heymann et al., February 19, 1974, pp. 56–57, AC papers, box 24, folder 1.
50. Silbert diary, May 25, 1973 (entry 111).
51. Doyle, *Not Above the Law,* p. 52; Press Release, Harold H. Titus, Jr., May 24, 1973, AC papers, box 21, folder 9; interview with AC by Phil Heymann et al., February 19, 1974, p. 57, AC papers, box 24, folder 1.
52. Silbert diary, May 25, 1973 (entry 111).
53. Press Release, Harold H. Titus, Jr., May 24, 1973, AC papers, box 21, folder 9; Silbert diary, May 25, 1973 (entry 111).
54. Silbert diary, May 25, 1973 (entry 111).
55. News Release, May 29, 1973, box 228, Cox liaison materials folder, ELR papers.
56. James Vorenberg, author's interview; Ben-Veniste and Frampton, *Stonewall,* p. 25.
57. AC 23:37, 38.
58. Notes on "backgrounder," May 28, 1973, James Doyle papers, temporary folder 9.
59. AC 24:9–13. Doyle, *Not Above the Law,* pp. 61–64.
60. Doyle later turned up on President Nixon's "enemies list," as a Washington journalist whom the president considered unfriendly toward the Nixon administration.

61. Press Release (Newsscope), undated, James Doyle papers, temporary file 16; Doyle, *Not Above the Law,* pp. 66–68.
62. AC 24:15.
63. "The Man Behind the Subpoena," *Newsweek,* August 6, 1973, p. 16; "The Other Investigator," *Time,* July 16, 1973, p. 71; John F. Barker, author's interview; James F. Neal, author's interview; Richard Ben-Veniste, author's interview.
64. "The Man Behind the Subpoena," *Newsweek,* August 6, 1973, p. 16.
65. James Vorenberg, author's interview.
66. Ibid.
67. Philip B. Heymann, author's interview.
68. "The Saturday Night Massacre," program, December 3, 1993.
69. Lukas, *Nightmare,* p. 440; *U.S. News & World Report,* August 20, 1973, p. 47.
70. Philip B. Heymann, author's interview.
71. Ibid.
72. "The Saturday Night Massacre," program, December 3, 1993; Philip B. Heymann, author's interview.
73. Price, *With Nixon,* p. 236.
74. Philip B. Heymann, author's interview.
75. Ibid.
76. AC 24:9, 10; Memorandum, John Barker to Jim Doyle, August 28, 1973, James Doyle papers, temporary folder 11.
77. *Washington (D.C.) National Observer,* August 18, 1973. A summary of the connections between members of the Special Prosecution Force and previous Democratic administrations is contained in Memo, John Barker to James Doyle, November 6, 1973, James Doyle papers, temporary folder 184.
78. Nixon, *RN,* p. 912.
79. Lukas, *Nightmare,* p. 418.
80. Philip Allen Lacovara, author's interview.
81. Henry Ruth, author's interview.
82. Cox viewed Neal as someone who was "brought up, and continued to want to trust, his President." Interview with AC by Phil Heymann et al., February 19, 1974, pp. 26–27, AC papers, box 24, folder 1.
83. Interview with James Doyle by Phil Heymann et al., May 1, 1974, p. 46, temporary folder 214, James Doyle papers. The Special Prosecution Force's own biggest "image" concern was that they had recruited no black lawyers and almost no women, despite hasty efforts to do both. They feared backlash on this issue, but the press never picked up on it. The "Kennedy" tie, on the other hand, continued to dog them. See ibid.
84. Interview with AC by Phil Heymann et al., February 19, 1974, pp. 26–27, 34, AC papers, box 24, folder 1.
85. Philip Allen Lacovara, author's interview.
86. Ibid.
87. Julie Nixon Eisenhower, the president's daughter, later wrote that her family was "particularly upset by the unabashed partisanship of Cox's prosecutors." Eisenhower, *Pat Nixon,* p. 382.
88. Nixon, *RN,* p. 910.
89. AC 24:12.
90. John Thomas Smith, author's interview.

Chapter 16

1. AC 24:27. The U.S. Attorney's office had raised this concern even before Cox was appointed. See Harold H. Titus, Jr., to Elliot L. Richardson, May 15, 1973, and attached memo by Earl J. Silbert, May 11, 1973, AC papers, box 21, folder 8.
2. AC 24:27, 28.
3. AC 24:32.
4. Dash, *Chief Counsel*, p. 141.
5. James Vorenberg, author's interview.
6. AC 24:28.
7. Dash, *Chief Counsel*, p. 144.
8. James Vorenberg, author's interview.
9. AC to Sam J. Ervin, June 4, 1973, box 228, Cox liaison materials folder, ELR papers.
10. Interview with AC by Phil Heymann et al., February 19, 1974, pp. 44–45, AC papers, box 24, folder 1.
11. AC to Sam J. Ervin, June 4, 1973, box 228, Cox liaison materials folder, ELR papers.
12. Transcript of Press Conference, June 4, 1973, James Doyle papers, temporary folder 19.
13. Dash, *Chief Counsel*, p. 145.
14. James Vorenberg, author's interview.
15. Florence L. Campbell, author's interview.
16. AC 24:28; *Bangor (Maine) Daily News*, June 7, 1973.
17. Philip B. Heymann, author's interview.
18. Ibid.
19. James Vorenberg, author's interview.
20. Philip B. Heymann, author's interview.
21. Ibid.
22. Ibid.
23. Dash, *Chief Counsel*, p. 146.
24. Interview with James Doyle by Phil Heymann et al., May 1, 1974, pp. 4–5, James Doyle papers, temporary folder 214.
25. AC 24:29. At the same time, history would prove that some of the concerns of Cox's group were not farfetched. As Philip Lacovara, Cox's legal counsel, would point out, the refusal to take certain immunized testimony privately in executive session, as Cox had urged in Watergate, was what led to the reversal of several criminal convictions in the Iran-Contra affair, two decades later. See Philip Allen Lacovara, author's interview.
26. Telephone interview notes, June 9, 1973, James Doyle papers, temporary folder 30; interview with AC by Phil Heymann et al., February 19, 1974, AC papers, box 24, folder 1.
27. AC 24:33.
28. AC 24:31, 32. In fact, Cox went as far as to place his evidence against Dean under seal with Judge Sirica, prior to Dean's testimony before the Ervin Committee, to ensure that he was not immune from prosecution for any crimes that Cox could prove independently, without using the Senate testimony. Richard Ben-Veniste,

who would later serve as a trial lawyer in the Watergate cover-up case, explained that "Archie felt it was critical that John Dean should not escape, when we were punishing others." See Mankiewicz, *U.S. v. Richard M. Nixon,* pp. 19–21; Richard Ben-Veniste, author's interview.

29. Doyle, *Not Above the Law,* p. 82.
30. *New York Times,* June 29, 1973.
31. Leonard Garment, author's interview, September 14, 1994.
32. James Vorenberg, author's interview.
33. Ibid.
34. Ibid.
35. Memo, Charles Alan Wright to J. Frederick Buzhardt and Leonard Garment, June 7, 1973, box 9, Chronology, 1969–74, March–July 1973 folder, Leonard Garment papers, Library of Congress.
36. Sussman, *The Great Coverup,* p. 263.
37. James Vorenberg, author's interview.
38. Ibid.; AC 25:5.
39. James Vorenberg, author's interview.
40. Ibid.
41. Memo, Charles Alan Wright to J. Frederick Buzhardt and Leonard Garment, June 7, 1973, box 9, Chronology, 1969–74, March–July 1973 folder, Leonard Garment papers, Library of Congress.
42. James Vorenberg, author's interview.
43. Memo, Charles Alan Wright to J. Frederick Buzhardt and Leonard Garment, June 7, 1973, box 9, Chronology, 1969–74, March–July 1973 folder, Leonard Garment papers, Library of Congress.
44. Ibid.
45. AC 25:6, 7.
46. Memo, Charles Alan Wright to J. Frederick Buzhardt and Leonard Garment, June 7, 1973, box 9, Chronology, 1969–74, March–July 1973 folder, Leonard Garment papers, Library of Congress.
47. James Vorenberg, author's interview; Press Briefing, June 18, 1973, James Doyle papers, temporary folder 13; Doyle, *Not Above the Law,* pp. 15, 96. Another package of such White House logs, supplied several weeks later, can be found in James Doyle papers, temporary folder 51. Correspondence between Cox and Buzhardt relating to White House logs and other material is contained in James Doyle papers, temporary folder 52.
48. James Vorenberg, author's interview.
49. Dash, *Chief Counsel,* pp. 162–63; Ambrose, *Nixon,* 3:157–63, 190.
50. AC 24:21.
51. James Vorenberg, author's interview.
52. Silbert diary, June 6, 1973 (entry 114).
53. Ibid., May 25, 1973 (entry 111).
54. Philip B. Heymann, author's interview; James Vorenberg, author's interview.
55. Donald E. Campbell, author's interview. Campbell recalled that Cox suggested that he himself might try a case in the local D.C. court to "get his feet wet," which the U.S. attorney's team considered a horrible idea that would underscore his inexperience.

56. Interview with AC by Phil Heymann et al., February 19, 1974, p. 94, AC papers, box 24, folder 1.

57. One involved a leak to the *New York Times* in late May that the Watergate prosecution team had evidence directly linking H. R. Haldeman and John Ehrlichman to the illegal break-in of Daniel Ellsberg's psychiatrist's office. Ellsberg was a prominent critic of President Nixon's Vietnam War policy, a key individual responsible for releasing the so-called Pentagon Papers, and a general thorn in the president's side. See Memo, AC to Silbert et al., undated, AC papers, box 21, folder 9. The second was a leak to CBS in July, disclosing that the original prosecutors had recommended indicting Mitchell, Haldeman, Ehrlichman, and Dean. Cox called this a "gross breach." See *Washington Evening Star,* July 5, 1973.

58. Silbert diary, May 25, 1973 (entry 111), June 6, 1973 (entry 114), June 11, 1973 (entry 115).

59. Memo, Earl J. Silbert to AC, June 7, 1973, "Present Status of Watergate Investigation Conducted by United States Attorney's Office for the District of Columbia," Watergate Special Prosecution Force, Special Prosecutor's Files—General Correspondence, RG 460, box 6, U.S. Attorney—Dist. of Col. folder, National Archives.

60. Silbert diary, June 11, 1973 (entry 115).

61. Noted trial attorney Charles Morgan, Jr., filed the so-called Morgan Report on behalf of the ACLU. See Morgan, *One Man, One Voice,* pp. 252–53; "Response for the Senate Judiciary Committee to 'A Report to the Special Prosecutor on Certain Aspects of the Watergate Affair,' " James Doyle papers, temporary folder 23.

62. Silbert diary, June 22, 1973 (entry 117), undated (entry 118), July 4, 1973 (entry 119).

63. Doyle, *Not Above the Law,* pp. 79–81; *New York Times,* June 30, 1973.

64. AC to Earl J. Silbert, June 29, 1973, box 228, Cox liaison materials folder, ELR papers; *New York Times,* June 30, 1973.

65. Earl J. Silbert et al. to AC, June 29, 1973, box 228, Cox liaison materials folder, ELR papers.

66. AC to Earl J. Silbert, June 29, 1973, box 228, Cox liaison materials folder, ELR papers.

67. Memo, Earl J. Silbert to AC, June 7, 1973, "Present Status of Watergate Investigation Conducted by United States Attorney's Office for the District of Columbia," Watergate Special Prosecution Force, Special Prosecutor's Files—General Correspondence, RG 460, box 6, U.S. Attorney—Dist. of Col. folder, National Archives; Sussman, *The Great Coverup,* p. 264.

68. For an interesting discussion of the failed nature of the Silbert team's prosecution by a reporter who followed the original Watergate trial, see Pincus, "The Silbert-Petersen Puzzle," *New Republic,* July 16 and 13, 1974, pp. 15–16.

69. John W. Dean III, author's interview. The U.S. attorney's team had promised Dean a sort of "transactional immunity," by which none of the information he divulged could be passed along or used against him. Dean was particularly upset that this "deal" had been quickly broken when Silbert's office reported Dean's conversations to Petersen, who in turn made them known to the White House. See ibid.

70. Silbert diary, June 17, 1973 (entry 116). Silbert and his team also tried to appear on the CBS program *Face the Nation* to justify their investigation and answer questions. This plan likewise backfired. Attorney General Richardson summoned the three prosecutors into his office and warned that it was contrary to Justice Department regulations (and perhaps American Bar Association standards) for government lawyers to appear on television and comment on pending cases. See Silbert diary, undated (entry 118); *Washington Post,* July 5, 1973. Earl Silbert next revealed that he had kept his personal "diary" on the Watergate case, and "made contacts" about writing a book on the material, which further "nettled" Cox. The idea was dropped when Silbert was cautioned that departmental regulations barred him from publishing information gained in his official duties without express permission from the Justice Department. See *Los Angeles Times,* August 29, 1973; *Washington Evening Star,* August 31, 1973.

71. Silbert diary, July 4, 1973 (entry 119).

72. James Vorenberg, author's follow-up interview, August 7, 1996.

73. Florence L. Campbell, author's interview.

74. Interview with James Doyle by Phil Heymann et al., May 1, 1974, pp. 24–27, 76–77, James Doyle papers, temporary folder 214; interview with AC by Phil Heymann et al., February 19, 1974, p. 78, AC papers, box 24, folder 1.

75. Interview with James Doyle by Phil Heymann et al., pp. 13, 18, 32, James Doyle papers, temporary folder 214.

76. News Release, July 6, 1973, box 228, Cox liaison materials folder, ELR papers.

77. *Time,* July 23, 1973, 15; *Washington Post,* July 13, 1973.

78. *Christian Science Monitor,* July 20, 1973; *Akron Beacon Journal,* July 17, 1973.

79. AC to J. Fred Buzhardt, June 15, 1973, and J. Fred Buzhardt to AC, June 16, 1973, James Doyle papers, temporary folder 52.

80. AC 36:27, 28.

81. AC 36:28.

82. AC 25:8.

83. Ibid.

84. Interview with AC by Phil Heymann et al., February 19, 1974, p. 90, AC papers, box 24, folder 1.

85. AC 25:8.

86. Interview with AC by James Doyle, circa 1975, pp. 2–34, James Doyle papers.

87. AC 25:12.

88. Peter M. Kreindler, author's interview.

89. AC to J. Fred Buzhardt, July 18, 1973, box 228, Cox liaison materials folder, ELR papers; ibid., AC papers, box 21, folder 11.

90. AC to J. Fred Buzhardt, July 18, 1973, AC papers, box 21, folder 11.

91. Dash, *Chief Counsel,* pp. 185–88.

92. Teletype, July 19, 1973, James Doyle papers, temporary folder 104; AC 25:15; Doyle, *Not Above the Law,* p. 98.

93. AC 25:16; interview with AC by James Doyle, circa 1975, pp. 2–37, James Doyle papers.

94. Teletype, July 19, 1973, James Doyle papers, temporary folder 104.

95. Charles Alan Wright to AC, box 228, Cox liaison materials folder, ELR papers; ibid., AC papers, box 21, folder 10.

96. Charles Alan Wright to AC, box 228, Cox liaison materials folder, ELR papers, emphasis added.
97. Richard Nixon to Sam J. Ervin, Jr., July 23, 1973, box 228, Cox liaison materials folder, ELR papers.
98. Ibid.
99. Henry Ruth, author's interview.
100. AC 25:18.
101. James Vorenberg, author's interview.
102. Ibid.
103. Ibid.
104. Ibid.
105. Ibid.
106. Doyle, *Not Above the Law,* p. 103; Lukas, *Nightmare,* p. 385; Dash, *Chief Counsel,* p. 188; "Battle Over Presidential Power," *Time,* August 6, 1973, 8. The White House lawyers viewed the Senate subpoena as "sweeping" and unlikely to stick, under any circumstances. See Memo, J. Fred Buzhardt et al. to RN, July 24, 1973, box 2, Memoranda for President folder, Leonard Garment papers, Library of Congress.
107. AC 26:2.
108. Ibid.; *Subpoena duces tecum* and attached schedule, July 23, 1973, AC papers, box 21, folder 10.
109. Interview with James Doyle by Phil Heymann et al., May 1, 1974, pp. 88–89, James Doyle papers, temporary folder 214.

Chapter 17

1. AC 26:2.
2. Interview with AC by James Doyle, circa 1975, pp. 2–35, 36, James Doyle papers.
3. AC 26:2, 3.
4. *Subpoena duces tecum,* July 23, 1973, AC papers, box 21, folder 11.
5. Marshall's Return, July 23, 1973, James Doyle papers, temporary folder 87.
6. Leonard Garment, author's interview, September 14, 1994.
7. AC 26:3.
8. Leonard Garment, author's interview, September 14, 1994.
9. Associated Press Teletype, July 23, 1974, James Doyle papers, temporary folder 107. On the surface, Buchanan's memo apparently excluded "the so-called Watergate tapes." However, the decision as to which tapes related to Watergate seemed to rest with the president, when it came time to burn the "chaff." Lukas, *Nightmare,* p. 384. It was widely known that several Nixon aides suggested burning the tapes.
10. Robert H. Bork, author's interview.
11. Haldeman, *The Haldeman Diaries,* pp. 677–78.
12. Richard Nixon to Judge Sirica, July 25, 1973, AC papers, box 21, folder 11.
13. *Bangor (Maine) Daily News,* July 27, 1973.
14. Ibid.
15. AC 26:3, 4.

16. Transcript of Proceedings, Grand Jury Presentment, July 26, 1973, AC papers, box 22, folder 10; Vladimir Pregelj, author's interview; Doyle, *Not Above the Law*, pp. 105–6; *Bangor (Maine) Daily News*, July 27, 1993.

17. James Vorenberg, author's interview.

18. Cox, *The Court and the Constitution*, p. 5; Doyle, *Not Above the Law*, pp. 105–6.

19. AC 26:5.

20. Ibid.; Transcript of Proceedings (polling the grand jury), July 26, 1973, James Doyle papers, temporary folder 87; Verified Petition for an Order Directing Richard M. Nixon or any Subordinate Officer Whom He Designates to Show Cause Why Certain Documents or Objects Should Not Be Produced in Response to a Grand Jury Subpoena Duces Tecum, July 26, 1973, James Doyle papers, temporary folder 87.

21. Cox, *The Court and the Constitution*, pp. 5–6.

22. *Bangor (Maine) Daily News*, July 27, 1973.

23. Ibid., July 29, 1973.

24. *Akron Beacon Journal*, July 28, 1973.

25. *Washington Post*, August 15, 1973; "Battle over Presidential Power," *Time*, August 6, 1973, 8; Ambrose, *Nixon*, 3:204.

26. *Washington Post*, August 15, 1973; "Battle over Presidential Power," *Time*, August 6, 197, 8; Ambrose, *Nixon*, 3:204.

27. *Akron Beacon Journal*, August 4, 1973.

28. *Bangor (Maine) Daily News*, July 30, 1973.

29. *Christian Science Monitor*, August 3, 1973.

30. News Release, July 24, 1973, box 229, Watergate SP: Nixon Statements, August 15, 1973 folder, ELR papers; Doyle, *Not Above the Law*, p. 106.

31. Interview with Elliot Richardson by James Doyle, June 3, 1975, pp. 1–12, James Doyle papers; "The Saturday Night Massacre," program, December 3, 1993; *Washington Post*, June 5, 1973.

32. "The Saturday Night Massacre," program, December 3, 1993.

33. John T. Smith, author's interview; transcribed interview with J. T. Smith by Phil Heymann et al., April 22, 1974, p. 37, John T. Smith personal papers.

34. Philip B. Heymann, author's interview; Affidavit of Elliot Richardson, June 17, 1974, box 229, Richardson Affidavit, Executive Privilege folder, ELR papers; Osborne, *The Fifth Year of the Nixon Watch*, pp. 115–16; Ambrose, *Nixon*, 3:205–6.

35. Affidavit of Elliot Richardson, June 17, 1974, ELR papers.

36. Memoranda of Conversations, May–October 1973, July 3, 1973, box 205, Nixon folder, ELR papers.

37. Press release (ELR), July 3, 1973, box 229, Richardson release re: Nixon's statement, 16 August 1973 folder, ELR papers; Memo, Conversation between ELR and AC, July 3, 1973, James Doyle papers, temporary folder 3; Cox press release, July 3, 1973, James Doyle papers, temporary folder 15.

38. UPI teletype, July 3, 1973, James Doyle papers, temporary folder 15; interview with AC, February 19, 1974, p. 83, AC papers, box 24, folder 1. For a discussion of the allegations concerning the renovations on the San Clemente property, as well as its acquisition, see Osborne, *The Fifth Year of the Nixon Watch*, pp. 115–16.

39. Philip B. Heymann, author's interview.
40. Affidavit of Elliot Richardson, June 17, 1974, ELS papers; Lukas, *Nightmare,* p. 422; Pincus, "The Cox Investigation," *New Republic,* December 8, 1973, 10–11.
41. Interview with J. T. Smith by Phil Heymann et al., April 22, 1974, pp. 66, 71, John T. Smith personal papers; Leonard Garment, author's interview, September 14, 1994.
42. Interview with J. T. Smith by Phil Heymann et al., April 22, 1974, pp. 66, 71, John T. Smith personal papers.
43. Leonard Garment, author's interview, September 14, 1994.
44. Interview with AC by Phil Heymann et al., February 19, 1974, p. 16, AC papers, box 24, folder 1; Directive of the Attorney General, May 31, 1973, Administrative Files of the Watergate Special Prosecution Force, RG 460, BSD-1, Authority & Establishment, National Archives.
45. Interview with J. T. Smith by Phil Heymann et al., April 22, 1974, p. 62, John T. Smith personal papers.
46. Interview with Elliot Richardson by James Doyle, June 3, 1975, pp. 1–10, 11, James Doyle papers.
47. Interview with J. T. Smith by Phil Heymann et al., April 22, 1974, p. 69, John T. Smith personal papers; *New York Times,* July 13, 1973.
48. AC 24:36, 25:1, 2.
49. "The Saturday Night Massacre," program, December 3, 1993.
50. AC 25:1, 2.
51. In some circles, "Boston Brahmin" was a pejorative phrase. As brother Louis Cox explained to the author, it sometimes referred to the fictitious old aunt who lived on Beacon Hill, belonged to the Somerset Club or some other stuffy association, and upon meeting a cousin from Ohio gushed, "Ohio, Ohio, I always thought you pronounced it Iowa!"
52. Maxwell E. Cox, author's interview. According to Maxwell Cox, "Mother hated Archie being viewed as a New Englander. He was from New Jersey." In other words, he was very much his father's son. Ibid.
53. AC, letter to author, July 1, 1996.
54. AC 25:1.
55. Elliot L. Richardson, author's interview, October 16, 1992.
56. "The Saturday Night Massacre," program, December 3, 1993.
57. AC 25:2.
58. AC 26:8.
59. "The Saturday Night Massacre," program, December 3, 1993.
60. Brief in Opposition, August 7, 1973, James Doyle papers, temporary folder 89; *Akron Beacon Journal,* August 8, 1973. Cox's brief on the subject, Memorandum in Support of an Order, August 13, 1973, can be found in James Doyle papers, temporary folder 89.
61. *Akron Beacon Journal,* August 22, 1973.
62. AC 26:8.
63. "Judge Sirica: The First Test," *Time,* August 13, 1973, 8.
64. AC 25:14.
65. AC 26:9.
66. *Akron Beacon Journal,* August 22, 1973; Charles Alan Wright to AC, September 27, 1972, AC papers, box 47, folder 21.

67. Charles Alan Wright to AC, September 27, 1972, AC papers, box 47, folder 21.
68. "The Historic Duel for the Nixon Tapes," *Newsweek*, September 3, 1973, 37; *Akron Beacon Journal*, July 25, 1973; Philip Allen Lacovara, author's interview.
69. Transcript of proceedings, "In the Matter of a Grand Jury Subpoena Issued to Richard M. Nixon," August 22, 1973, pp. 1–5, AC papers, box 21, folder 11.
70. Ibid., p. 11.
71. Ibid., pp. 22–23; *Christian Science Monitor*, August 23, 1973; *Bangor (Maine) Daily News*, August 23, 1973.
72. Transcript of proceedings, "In the Matter of a Grand Jury Subpoena Issued to Richard M. Nixon," p. 25.
73. Ibid., p. 28; Doyle, *Not Above the Law*, p. 111.
74. Transcript of proceedings, "In the Matter of a Grand Jury Subpoena Issued to Richard M. Nixon," p. 49.
75. AC 26:9.
76. Transcript of proceedings, "In the Matter of a Grand Jury Subpoena Issued to Richard M. Nixon," p. 63; "The Historic Duel for the Nixon Tapes," *Newsweek*, September 3, 1973, 37; AC 26:9; "The Saturday Night Massacre," program, December 3, 1993.
77. Transcript of proceedings, "In the Matter of a Grand Jury Subpoena Issued to Richard M. Nixon," p. 58.
78. Ibid., p. 56.
79. AC 26:10.
80. "The Saturday Night Massacre," program, December 3, 1993.
81. Ibid.
82. Ibid.
83. D. Todd Christofferson, author's interview.
84. *Bangor (Maine) Daily News*, August 23, 1973.
85. Memo, J. Fred Buzhardt et al. to the President, August 22, 1973, box 2, Memoranda for President folder, Leonard Garment papers, Library of Congress.
86. Lukas, *Nightmare*, p. 393; *Bangor (Maine) Daily News*, August 22, 1973.
87. Lukas, *Nightmare*, p. 393; *Bangor (Maine) Daily News*, August 22, 1973.
88. *Bangor (Maine) Daily News*, August 22, 1973.
89. *Akron Beacon Journal*, August 6, 1973, August 13, 1973, August 20, 1973, August 22, 1973; *Bangor (Maine) Daily News*, August 22, 1973.
90. *Akron Beacon Journal*, August 13, 1973.
91. *Washington Post*, August 30, 1973; *In re Subpoena to Nixon*, 360 F. Supp. 1 (D.C. Circuit 1973).
92. *Washington Post*, August 30, 1973; *In re Subpoena to Nixon*, 360 F. Supp. 1 (D.C. Circuit 1973). Opinion and Order (Sirica, C. J.), August 29, 1973, AC papers, box 21, folder 13.
93. *Washington Post*, August 30, 1973.
94. AC 26:11; Lewin, "Who Gets the Tapes?" *New Republic*, October 27, 1973, 14.
95. Cox also worried that Judge Sirica would have to make snap judgments as to the relevance and admissibility of evidence at trial as he listened to the tapes. Cox considered this a dangerous proposition when Sirica only had a tiny piece of the complex Watergate puzzle in front of him. See AC 26:12.
96. *Washington Post*, August 30, 1973.

97. Price, *With Nixon,* pp. 249–50.
98. *Washington Post,* August 30, 1973; Writ of Mandamus, *Nixon v. Sirica and Cox,* September 6, 1973, James Doyle papers, temporary folder 97.
99. AC 26:12.
100. Doyle, *Not Above the Law,* p. 114; Petition for a Writ of Mandamus, *U.S. v. Sirica and Nixon,* September 7, 1973, AC papers, box 22, folder 2. Specifically, Cox wished to clarify Sirica's order with respect to the procedures the judge would follow in reviewing the tapes.
101. *Bangor (Maine) Daily News,* August 31, 1973.
102. AC 26:13.
103. Phyllis Ames Cox, author's interview; Mary "Molly" Cox, author's interview, August 15, 1990.
104. AC 24:25.
105. "The Man Behind the Subpoena," *Newsweek,* August 6, 1973, 16.
106. Memo, AC to staff, August 23, 1973, Administrative Files of the Watergate Special Prosecution Force, RG 460, BSD-4 Policy and Procedure, National Archives.
107. *Washington Post,* September 9, 1973.
108. This special writ named Judge Sirica himself as a party, requiring the sixty-nine-year-old judge to find his own lawyer and file a brief. See *New York Times,* September 7, 1973.
109. AC 26:15.
110. Ibid.
111. AC 26:16.
112. Ibid.
113. ELR meeting notes, September 6, 1973, box 228, Cox notes folder, ELR papers.
114. Judge Sirica took the unusual step, just before the day set for the Court of Appeals argument, of making a public statement welcoming "a court order permitting Watergate Special Prosecutor Archibald Cox to join him in listening to President Nixon's Watergate tapes." See *Washington Post,* September 11, 1973.
115. *New York Times,* September 12, 1973; Doyle, *Not Above the Law,* p. 117.
116. AC Oral Argument (final draft), August 22, 1973, AC papers, box 22, folder 1; Transcript of Proceedings (oral argument), September 11, 1973, James Doyle papers, temporary folder 102. The memo from Garment to the president, dated September 11, 1973, is contained in box 2, Memoranda for President folder, Leonard Garment papers, Library of Congress.
117. AC 26:18.
118. Notes of taped recollections, September 16, 1973, James Doyle papers, temporary folder 109.
119. Memorandum Opinion, September 13, 1973, AC papers, box 22, folder 5; "Nixon's Tapes: How to Settle Out of Court," *Newsweek,* September 24, 1973, p. 33; Doyle, *Not Above the Law,* p. 120.
120. James J. Monteith to Richard M. Nixon, July 27, 1973, box 30, Criminal Matters, August 8, 1973, folder, Richard M. Nixon Presidential Materials Project, National Archives.

121. Adele Lovelace to Rose Mary Woods, undated, Criminal Matters, box 33, October 3–17, 1973, folder, ibid.
122. Mrs. John J. Mahler to Richard M. Nixon, August 7, 1973, Criminal Matters, box 32, August 23, 1973, folder, ibid.
123. A. E. Wilson to Richard M. Nixon, August 29, 1973, Criminal Matters, box 32, August 28–September 4, 1973, folder, ibid.
124. Keith A. Hanger to Richard M. Nixon, undated, Criminal Matters, box 32, September 4, 1973, folder, ibid.
125. Richard T. Lewis to Ron Ziegler (press secretary), June 7, 1973, Criminal Matters, box 28, June 20–27, 1973, folder, ibid.
126. Doyle, *Not Above the Law*, p. 120.
127. AC 26:20.
128. Proposal Submitted to the White House by Archibald Cox, September 20, 1973, AC papers, box 22, folders 5 and 6 (with notations).
129. Ibid.; AC 26:20; Doyle, *Not Above the Law*, pp. 121–22.
130. AC 26:22.
131. Richard Ben-Veniste, author's interview.
132. James F. Neal, author's interview.
133. Notes, Meetings between Cox and White House, September 15, 1973 to September 20, 1973, James Doyle papers, temporary folder 118.
134. Ibid.
135. Ibid.
136. Ibid.; Doyle, *Not Above the Law*, p. 122; "The Saturday Night Massacre," program, December 3, 1993.
137. In fact, the White House refused to disclose details of Cox's proposed compromise even after he had been fired. Feeling "bound" by the informal agreement with the president's lawyers, Cox declined to tell the press about it. See *St. Louis Dispatch*, October 25, 1973.
138. "The Saturday Night Massacre," program, December 3, 1993.
139. AC 26:23, 24.
140. AC to Hugh E. Kline (clerk), September 20, 1973, AC papers, box 22, folder 6.
141. AC 26:29.
142. Cox, *The Court and the Constitution*, p. 12; *Nixon v. Sirica*, 487 F.2d 700 (D.C. Circuit 1973).
143. "Rejecting Nixon's Absolutes," *Time*, October 22, 1973, p. 25; "The Nixon Tapes: Round Two to Cox," *Newsweek*, October 22, 1973, p. 43; *Nixon v. Sirica*, 487 F.2d 700 (D.C. Circuit 1973).
144. *Washington Post*, October 13, 1973; *Nixon v. Sirica*, 487 F.2d 700 (D.C. Circuit 1973).
145. Judgment, October 12, 1973, James Doyle papers, temporary folder 129; Cox, *The Court and the Constitution*, p. 17.
146. Lewin, "Who Gets the Tapes?" *New Republic*, October 27, 1973, 16; "The Nixon Tapes: Round Two to Cox," *Newsweek*, October 22, 1973, 43.
147. Television report transcripts, October 12, 1973, James Doyle papers, temporary folder 130.
148. "Rejecting Nixon's Absolutes," *Time*, October 22, 1973, 25.
149. Ford had known Nixon since 1948, when they were both young congressmen

who belonged to "The Chowder and Marching Club," a group of junior Republican members of the House that Nixon helped organize. See Ambrose, *Nixon,* 3:236.

150. "The Fall of Spiro Agnew," *Time,* October 22, 1973, 19; "A Good Lineman for the Quarterback," *Time,* October 22, 1973, 16; Cook, *The Crimes of Watergate,* pp. 142–43.

151. According to his own autobiography, Ford was also selected because President Nixon and his advisers felt he could be speedily confirmed in Congress and was therefore the "safest choice." See Ford, *A Time to Heal,* p. 107 n.

152. AC 26:28.

153. *Washington Evening Star,* October 14, 1973.

154. AC 26:29.

155. AC 36:31.

156. "The Saturday Night Massacre," program, December 3, 1993.

157. Ibid.

158. *Prize Cases,* 67 U.S. (2 Black) 635 (1863).

159. AC 26:30, 36:31; Cox, *The Court and the Constitution,* p. 16.

160. The case was *Worcester v. Georgia,* 6 Peters 515 (1832). See Gunther, *Constitutional Law* (12th ed. 1991), p. 25.

161. AC 26:30.

162. AC 26:31.

163. Bolt, *A Man for All Seasons,* p. 66; AC 9:26.

Chapter 18

1. Richardson, *The Creative Balance,* p. 19.

2. AC 26:34, 35.

3. AC, letter to author, May 1, 1995; "The Saturday Night Massacre," program, December 3, 1993.

4. AC 25:36, 27:1; Doyle, *Not Above the Law,* pp. 133–34; *Washington Post,* October 19, 1973, December 1, 1973. Material on the Krogh case can be found in James Doyle papers, temporary folder 73.

5. John T. Smith, author's interview. Some later questioned whether Richardson had allowed himself to fall into a conflict by seeking to act simultaneously as attorney general and "mediator." See "The Saturday Night Massacre," John F. Kennedy School of Government, Case Program, Case #C-14-77-150.0, 542.0, 543.0 and 544.0 (1977), Harvard University. Cox, on the other hand, saw no such conflict. He could no longer imagine "being aided by outside mediators." See AC 37:11.

6. AC 27:1.

7. AC 27:2.

8. Ibid.; Doyle, *Not Above the Law,* p. 134.

9. Doyle notes re: meeting, December 12, 1973, James Doyle papers, temporary folder 73; Doyle, *Not Above the Law,* pp. 134–35.

10. AC 27:2.

11. AC 27:3.

12. AC 27:4.
13. Interview with Elliot Richardson by James Doyle, June 3, 1975, pp. 1–31, 32, James Doyle papers.
14. "The Saturday Night Massacre," program, December 3, 1993.
15. AC 27:4.
16. Cox, *The Court and the Constitution*, p. 17.
17. "The Saturday Night Massacre," program, December 3, 1993.
18. James P. Hart to Charles Wright, September 22, 1973, attached to Charles Alan Wright to Leonard Garment, September 25, 1973, box 8, Charles Alan Wright 1973–74 folder, Leonard Garment papers, Library of Congress.
19. "The Saturday Night Massacre," program, December 3, 1993.
20. Elliot L. Richardson, author's interview, October 16, 1992.
21. Leonard Garment, author's interview, October 19, 1994.
22. Elliot L. Richardson, author's interview, September 28, 1992.
23. Ibid., October 16, 1992; Richardson, *The Creative Balance*, p. 38; Affidavit of Elliot Richardson, June 17, 1974, box 229, Richardson Affidavit, Executive Privilege folder, ELR papers.
24. Elliot L. Richardson, author's interview, October 16, 1992.
25. Interview with J. T. Smith by Phil Heymann et al., April 22, 1974, pp. 89, 135–37, John T. Smith personal papers.
26. Elliot L. Richardson, author's interview, September 28, 1992.
27. Memoranda of Conversations, May–October 1973, October 14, 1973, box 205, Haig folder, ELR papers.
28. Elliot L. Richardson, author's interview, October 16, 1992; Lukas, *Nightmare*, pp. 438–39.
29. "The Mideast Erupts," *Newsweek*, October 15, 1973, 38; "Black October: Old Enemies at War Again," *Time*, October 15, 1973, 30; White, *Breach of Faith*, pp. 257–58, 260–61; Price, *With Nixon*, p. 254; Ambrose, *Nixon*, 3:240.
30. "The Saturday Night Massacre," program, December 3, 1993.
31. Ibid.; interview with Elliot L. Richardson by James Doyle, June 3, 1975, pp. 4-12, James Doyle papers.
32. "The Saturday Night Massacre," program, December 3, 1993; interview with Elliot Richardson by James Doyle, June 3, 1975, James Doyle papers.
33. Richardson, *The Creative Balance*, pp. 39–40.
34. "The Saturday Night Massacre," program, December 3, 1993; Richardson, *The Creative Balance*, p. 40; Elliot L. Richardson, author's interview, October 16, 1992.
35. Memo, "Summary Chronology re: Cox Firing, Richardson-Ruckelshaus Resignation," undated, box 227, Watergate SP—Chronological File of events, 15–20 October 1973, ELR papers; Bickel, "The Tapes, Cox, Nixon," *New Republic*, September 29, 1973, 13–14.
36. "The Saturday Night Massacre," program, December 3, 1993; Memo, "Summary Chronology re: Cox Firing, Richardson-Ruckelshaus Resignation."
37. Memo, "Summary Chronology re: Cox Firing, Richardson-Ruckelshaus Resignation."
38. Memoranda of conversations, May–October 1973, October 15, 1973 (multiple sheets), box 205, Haig folder, ELR papers; John T. Smith, author's interview.

Elliot Richardson's handwriting is particularly difficult to read. Portions of his notes were "translated" by his former aide, John T. Smith, in interviews with the author.

39. "The Saturday Night Massacre," program, December 3, 1993.

40. Elliot L. Richardson, author's interview, October 16, 1992.

41. Ibid.

42. Elliot L. Richardson, author's interview, November 25, 1992.

43. Memoranda of Conversations, May–October 1973, October 15, 1973 (sheet 2), box 205, Haig folder, ELR papers; John T. Smith, author's interview.

44. Memo, "Summary Chronology re: Cox Firing, Richardson-Ruckelshaus Resignation."

45. Nixon, RN, p. 929.

46. William "Eph" Cresswell, author's interview; Thomas C. Korologos, author's interview.

47. White, Breach of Faith, p. 259.

48. Cox, The Court and the Constitution, p. 17; Attorney General's Schedule, October 15, 1973, box 227, Watergate SP—Chron. file 15–20 October 1973 folder (tab A), ELR papers. The dinner was for outgoing Secretary of State Williams P. Rogers, who had been displaced by Henry Kissinger.

50. U.S. Senate Committee on the Judiciary, in "A Proposal—ELR October 17, 1973," Hearings before the Committee on the Judiciary, United States Senate, Ninety-third Congress, First Session, on Special Prosecutor, 1 (tab D): 280–81; AC 37:5; Washington Post, October 21, 1973.

51. Memo, "Summary Chronology re: Cox Firing, Richardson-Ruckelshaus Resignation"; Cox, The Court and the Constitution, p. 18, emphasis added.

52. Interview with AC by James Doyle, circa 1975, pp. 2–15, James Doyle papers; Ruth 1:16.

53. Interview with James Doyle by Phil Heymann et al., May 1, 1974, pp. 67–68, James Doyle papers.

54. Memo, "Summary Chronology re: Cox Firing, Richardson-Ruckelshaus Resignation," emphasis added.

55. Ibid., emphasis added.

56. U.S. Senate Committee on the Judiciary, "A Proposal—ELR October 17, 1973," 1 (tab D): 280–81; AC 27:5.

57. "The Saturday Night Massacre," program, December 3, 1993.

58. "Comments on Attorney General's Proposal by Archibald Cox," October 18, 1973, AC papers, box 22, folder 5; Washington Post, October 21, 1973.

59. "Comments on Attorney General's Proposal by Archibald Cox," October 18, 1973, AC papers, box 22, folder 5.

60. AC 27:8, 37:5, 6.

61. "Comments on Attorney General's Proposal by Archibald Cox," October 18, 1973, AC papers, box 22, folder 5.

62. Memoranda of conversations, May–October 1973, October 17, 1973, box 205, Cox folder, ELR papers.

63. Memo, "Summary Chronology re: Cox Firing, Richardson-Ruckelshaus Resignation."

64. Ibid.

65. Ibid.; interview with Elliot Richardson by James Doyle, June 3, 1975, pp. 1–35, James Doyle papers.

66. Elliot L. Richardson, author's interview, October 16, 1992.

67. Charles Alan Wright to Richard M. Nixon, July 26, 1952, and Nixon to Wright, September 15, 1952. These letters are attached to a letter from Wright to Leonard Garment, October 29, 1973, box 8, Charles Alan Wright 1973–74 folder, Leonard Garment papers, Library of Congress. Wright disagreed with Nixon's "conclusions" in the controversial Alger Hiss case, in which Hiss (a diplomat) was accused of spying for the communists. Yet Wright applauded Nixon for "soberly and devotedly" seeking to get at the truth "without thought of political gain."

68. Elliot L. Richardson, author's interview, October 16, 1992.

69. Ibid.

70. Washington Post, October 18, 1973; New York Daily News, October 18, 1973.

71. Memo, undated, AC papers, box 23, folder 8.

72. Ibid., emphasis added; Philip Allen Lacovara, author's interview.

73. Stephen Breyer, author's interview.

74. Peter M. Kreindler, author's interview.

75. Richard Ben-Veniste, author's interview.

76. Memo, Peter M. Kreindler to AC, October 17, 1973, AC papers, box 23, folder 13; typed transcript "An Interview with Archibald Cox" (CBS), October 24, 1973, James Doyle papers, temporary folder 157.

77. "An Interview with Archibald Cox" (CBS), October 24, 1973, James Doyle papers, temporary folder 157. Charles Alan Wright declined to be interviewed for this book. In reply to the author's letter seeking an interview, Mr. Wright's secretary responded that "he took a vow many years ago not to discuss anything to do with Watergate." Kathy R. Bartsch, secretary to Charles Alan Wright, letter to author, May 21, 1991.

78. Cox, The Court and the Constitution, p. 19.

79. "The Saturday Night Massacre," program, December 3, 1993.

80. AC 27:5.

81. Cox, The Court and the Constitution, p. 20; Louis A. Cox, author's interview.

82. Cox, The Court and the Constitution, p. 20. Wright remembered the phone call to Cox differently. He took the position that he never told Cox that he had to abandon all future efforts to obtain further tapes or evidence from the White House; rather, he refused to give an advance commitment on the matter and left it open for negotiation. See Lukas, Nightmare, p. 429.

83. Cox, The Court and the Constitution, p. 20.

84. AC 37:9.

85. AC 27:10.

86. New York Times, June 29, 1973. Buzhardt first worked as special assistant to the assistant secretary of defense, then became general counsel for the Department of the Defense.

87. Ben-Veniste and Frampton, Stonewall, p. 165; Doyle, Not Above the Law, pp. 145, 159; Colodny and Gettli, Silent Coup, p. 344. Buzhardt had come to Washington as an aide to Senator Strom Thurmond, his father's friend.

88. AC 27:7, 8; "The Saturday Night Massacre," program, December 3, 1993.

89. AC 27:8.

90. Charles Alan Wright to AC, October 18, 1973, AC papers, box 22, folder 5; U.S. Senate Committee on the Judiciary, *Hearings before the Committee on the Judiciary, United States Senate, Ninety-third Congress, First Session, on Special Prosecutor,* 1 (tab E): 282.

91. AC to Charles Alan Wright, October 18, 1973, AC papers, box 22, folder 5; U.S. Senate Committee on the Judiciary, *Hearings before the Committee on the Judiciary, United States Senate, Ninety-third Congress, First Session, on Special Prosecutor,* 1 (tab E): 283.

92. Charles Alan Wright to AC, October 18, 1973, AC papers, box 22, folder 5; U.S. Senate Committee on the Judiciary, *Hearings before the Committee on the Judiciary, United States Senate, Ninety-third Congress, First Session, on Special Prosecutor,* 1 (tab E): 283-84.

93. AC 27:11, 12.

94. AC 27:13.

95. "The Saturday Night Massacre," program, December 3, 1993; *Washington Post,* October 20, 1973; Kutler, *The Wars of Watergate,* p. 415.

96. AC 27:12; Memo, James F. Neal et al. to AC, September 28, 1973, James Doyle papers, temporary folder 45; AC to Charles Norman Shaffer, October 18, 1973, James Doyle papers, temporary folder 137.

97. Lukas, *Nightmare,* p. 422; Ben-Veniste and Framptom, *Stonewall,* pp. 61-63.

98. Frank Lorson (Supreme Court clerk), author's interview.

99. Cox, *The Court and the Constitution,* p. 21.

100. "The Saturday Night Massacre," program, December 3, 1993.

101. AC 36:32, 33. This story is told in various places and relates to the Supreme Court's decision in *Abington School District v. Schempp,* 374 U.S. 203 (1963). See Cox, Howe, and Wiggins, *Civil Rights, the Constitution, and the Courts,* pp. 16-18; *New York Times,* April 16, 1964.

102. AC 27:14, 15; Cox, *The Court and the Constitution,* p. 15.

103. Philip B. Heymann, author's interview.

Chapter 19

1. AC 26:31.

2. John W. Douglas, author's follow-up interviews, September 15, 1995, October 10, 1995.

3. Interview with AC by Phil Heymann et al., February 19, 1974, AC papers, box 24, folder 1, p. 87.

4. AC 26:31, 32.

5. Ibid.

6. Ibid.

7. AC 26:32, 33.

8. Ibid.

9. Ibid.

10. Ibid.

11. Elliot L. Richardson, author's interview, November 25, 1992; Richardson, *The Creative Balance,* p. 41.

12. "The Saturday Night Massacre," program, December 3, 1993.
13. Elliot L. Richardson, author's interview, October 16, 1992; Memo, "Summary Chronology re: Cox Firing, Richardson-Ruckelshaus Resignation."
14. Richardson, *The Creative Balance*, p. 41.
15. Memo, "Summary Chronology re: Cox Firing, Richardson-Ruckelshaus Resignation"; "The Saturday Night Massacre," program, December 3, 1993; interview with Elliot Richardson by James Doyle, June 3, 1975, pp. 1–36, 37, James Doyle papers.
16. John T. Smith, author's interview.
17. Interview with Robert Bork by James Doyle, circa 1975, pp. 1–35, 36, James Doyle papers; interview with Elliot L. Richardson by James Doyle, June 3, 1975, pp. 4–23, 24, James Doyle papers.
18. Leonard Garment, author's interview, October 19, 1994. Richardson remembered having no such thought, but he admitted it might have been true that "I would rather have had Cox resign than to deal with *the question of whether or not to fire him.*" Elliot L. Richardson, letter to author, February 27, 1997, emphasis in original.
19. John T. Smith, author's interview.
20. Price, *With Nixon,* p. 254; Ambrose, *Nixon,* 3:240.
21. John T. Smith, author's interview, and author's follow-up interview, September 18, 1996; interview with John T. Smith by Phil Heymann et al., April 22, 1974, pp. 92, 102, John T. Smith personal papers.
22. Memo, "Summary of Chronology re: Cox Firing, Richardson-Ruckelshaus Resignation."
23. Letter, Elliot L. Richardson to author, February 27, 1997; Elliot L. Richardson, author's interview, November 25, 1992; "The Saturday Night Massacre," program, December 3, 1993.
24. Elliot L. Richardson, author's interview, November 25, 1992.
25. Memo, "Summary of Chronology re: Cox Firing, Richardson-Ruckelshaus Resignation."
26. Richard Nixon to ELR, October 19, 1973, box 229, Watergate SP: Nixon letter re: Cox, October 19, 1973, folder, ELR papers; U.S. Senate Committee on the Judiciary, *Hearings before the Committee on the Judiciary, United States Senate, Ninety-third Congress, First Session, on Special Prosecutor,* 1 (tab F): 284; *New York Times,* October 20, 1973.
27. Elliot L. Richardson, author's interview, November 25, 1992.
28. AC 27:16; Richardson, *The Creative Balance,* p. 42–43.
29. "The Saturday Night Massacre," program, December 3, 1993.
30. News Release and Statement by the President, October 19, 1973, box 229, Watergate SP—Nixon Richard M., Statements folder, ELR papers; *New York Times,* October 20, 1973; *Washington Post,* October 20, 1973.
31. "The Saturday Night Massacre," program, December 3, 1993; Press Release, October 19, 1973, James Doyle papers, temporary folder 140.
32. News Release, October 19, 1973, James Doyle papers, temporary folder 140.
33. Interview with James Doyle by Phil Heymann et al., May 1, 1974, p. 62, James Doyle papers.
34. Statement (not released), October 19, 1973, box 232, Watergate SP—Unreleased Statement re: Stennis proposal folder, ELR papers.

35. AC 27:17.
36. Interview with J. T. Smith by Phil Heymann et al., April 22, 1974, p. 92, John T. Smith personal papers.
37. John T. Smith, author's interview.
38. Ibid.
39. Ibid.
40. Elliot L. Richardson, author's interview, November 25, 1992. The phrase refers to the fact that mahogany is more expensive than pine.
41. Richardson, *The Creative Balance*, p. 43.
42. U.S. Senate Committee on the Judiciary, *Hearings Before the Committee on the Judiciary, United States Senate, Ninety-third Congress, First Session, on Special Prosecutor*, 1 (tab C): 280.
43. *Washington Evening Star*, October 20, 1973.
44. AC 27:17, 18.
45. AC 27:19.
46. Phyllis Ames Cox, author's interview.
47. Cox, *The Court and the Constitution*, p. 23.
48. Memo, Richard Weinberg to AC, August 24, 1973, AC papers, box 23, folder 4.
49. Cox, *The Court and the Constitution*, p. 23.
50. Phyllis Ames Cox, author's interview, and author's follow-up interview, February 7, 1995.
51. AC 27:18.
52. "The Saturday Night Massacre," program, December 3, 1993.
53. AC 28:1.
54. John F. Barker, author's interview.
55. AC 27:18.
56. Philip B. Heymann, author's interview.
57. Ibid.
58. Doyle, *Not Above the Law*, p. 176.
59. John F. Barker, author's interview.
60. See, generally, Drew, *Washington Journal*, p. 53. Ford was confirmed by the Senate on November 27, 1973, and by the House of Representatives on December 6, 1973. For information on the Carl Albert incident, see *Washington Post*, August 1, 1973.
61. "The Saturday Night Massacre," program, December 3, 1993.
62. Ibid. Cox did not remember the name of his father's friend.
63. AC, author's follow-up interview, August 7, 1996.
64. "The Saturday Night Massacre," program, December 3, 1993.
65. Richardson, *The Creative Balance*, pp. 43–44; ELR to Richard Nixon, August 20, 1973, box 229, Watergate SP—Richardson: Resignation letter folder, ELR papers.
66. Videotape of press conference, October 20, 1973, AC personal collection; *New York Times*, October 21, 1973.
67. "The Saturday Night Massacre," program, December 3, 1993.
68. Videotape of press conference, October 20, 1973, AC personal collection.
69. Transcript, Press Conference with Special Prosecutor Archibald Cox and Members of the Press, October 20, 1973, James Doyle papers, temporary folder 142.

70. John F. Barker, author's interview.
71. James Doyle, letter to author, July 29, 1996.
72. John F. Barker, author's interview.
73. *Boston Globe,* October 22, 1973.
74. Drew, *Washington Journal,* p. 49.
75. James Doyle, author's follow-up interview, May 2, 1997. Commentator George Will told a television news audience that this performance would increase Cox's already large fees for arguing private cases before the Supreme Court. Jim Doyle quickly called the television station and corrected Will. Most of Archie's cases were handled pro bono, free of charge. Will apologized for the misstatement on the air. See Doyle, *Not Above the Law,* p. 38.
76. Theodore Chase, author's interview.
77. John Kenneth Galbraith, author's interview.
78. Gerald Gunther, author's interview.
79. Bertha Perkins Frothingham, author's interview.
80. "The Saturday Night Massacre," program, December 3, 1993. See also Transcript, Press Conference with Special Prosecutor Archibald Cox and Members of the Press, October 20, 1973, James Doyle papers, temporary folder 142. Cox's reply to Mollenhoff was: "You know more about it than I do."
81. Miscellaneous letters and correspondence, box 220, Watergate Public Mail to Richardson—Pre-resignation, Support for Archibald Cox folders, ELR papers.
82. AC 28:3.
83. "The Saturday Night Massacre," program, December 3, 1993.
84. Elliot L. Richardson, author's interview, November 25, 1992.
85. In his interview with this author, Richardson initially used the time 3:00. However, his schedule indicates that he went to the White House at approximately 3:30 (where he first met with Haig) and saw the president at approximately 4:00. See Attorney General's Schedule, October 20, 1973, box 227, Watergate SP—Chron. File, 15–20 October 1973, folder, ELR papers.
86. Elliot L. Richardson, author's interview, November 25, 1992.
87. Ibid.
88. Ibid.
89. Ibid.; "The Saturday Night Massacre," program, December 3, 1993.
90. "The Saturday Night Massacre," program, December 3, 1993.
91. Interview with John T. Smith by Phil Heymann et al., April 22, 1974, p. 88, John T. Smith personal papers. See also William D. Ruckleshaus, author's interview.
92. Elliot L. Richardson, author's interview, November 25, 1992.
93. Ibid.; "The Saturday Night Massacre," program, December 3, 1993.
94. Elliot L. Richardson, author's interview, November 25, 1992.
95. Richardson, *The Creative Balance,* p. 39.
96. "The Saturday Night Massacre," program, December 3, 1993.
97. Elliot L. Richardson, author's interview, November 25, 1992.
98. Leonard Garment, author's interview, October 19, 1994.
99. Elliot L. Richardson, author's interview, November 25, 1992.
100. AC 28:4.
101. AC 28:3.
102. AC 28:5.

103. AC 28:6, 37:1.
104. AC 37:1; Bickel, "The Tapes, Cox, Nixon," *New Republic,* September 29, 1973, 13–14. As a legal matter, Bickel's point was that the courts did not have proper jurisdiction because the president in effect was "litigating with himself," and thus any opinion on the matter would be purely "advisory." When it came to the distinct issue of executive privilege, however, Bickel parted company with his friend Robert Bork. Bickel did not believe that such a privilege "covers material believed on probable cause to constitute evidence of crime." See ibid. A memo from Alexander Haig to the president on August 2, 1973, suggested that Bork "reversed his originally skeptical attitude on our position" relating to executive privilege. See Oudes, *From: The President,* p. 597. See also AC 37:2.
105. AC 37:2.
106. Richardson, *The Creative Balance,* p. 45.
107. AC 28:4.
108. AC 37:9.
109. Maxwell E. Cox, author's interview.
110. AC 28:4.
111. Doyle, *Not Above the Law,* p. 198; AC 28:4.
112. *Washington Post,* October 21, 1973. Some newspaper accounts added the words "to decide" at the end of the sentence, because they were more pleasing to the ear. But Cox's original statement ended with the words "American people."

Chapter 20

1. *Washington Post,* October 21, 1973; *New York Times,* October 21, 1973.
2. *Washington Post,* October 21, 1973.
3. Transcript, *Face the Nation,* interview with Robert Bork, November 11, 1973, pp. 10–12, James Doyle papers, temporary folder 148.
4. Ambrose, *Nixon,* 3:249.
5. Drew, *Washington Journal,* p. 52.
6. Kissinger, *Years of Upheaval,* pp. 550–51; Ambrose, *Nixon,* 3:247.
7. *Washington Post,* October 21, 1973.
8. Florence L. Campbell, author's interview.
9. Doyle, *Not Above the Law,* p. 201; *Village Voice,* October 24, 1973; *New York Times,* October 21, 1973; *Washington Evening Star,* October 21, 1973.
10. James Vorenberg, author's interview.
11. Peter M. Kreindler, author's interview.
12. William D. Ruckelshaus, author's interview.
13. Ibid.
14. Sirica, *To Set the Record Straight,* p. 130; D. Todd Christofferson, author's interview.
15. Interview with Robert Bork by James Doyle, circa 1975, pp. 1–53, 54, James Doyle papers. Alexander Haig initially declined to be interviewed for this book because he was working on his own memoirs. Alexander M. Haig, Jr., letter to author, August 12, 1991. He later scheduled an interview for November 10, 1995, but cancelled it.

16. Nixon, *RN*, pp. 929, 933.
17. John T. Smith, author's interview.
18. Notes and clippings re: Western Union, James Doyle papers, temporary folder 166; *Washington Post*, November 14, 1973.
19. *Valdosta (Ga.) Daily Times*, October 22, 1973.
20. In 1973, Veteran's Day (traditionally November 11) was celebrated on Monday, October 22. See *Washington Post*, October 23, 1973. The experiment of celebrating the holiday on the fourth Monday of October quickly fizzled out. The suggestion by George Bush is recorded in the chronology of Len Garment's secretary for October 21, Chronology, September–November 1973 folder, box 9, Leonard Garment papers, Library of Congress.
21. White, *Breach of Faith*, p. 268.
22. Edward J. Domaleski, Jr., to Richard M. Nixon, October 23, 1973, box 34, Criminal Matters October 18–November 4, 1973, folder, Richard M. Nixon Presidential Materials Project, National Archives.
23. Chet Long to Richard M. Nixon, October 22, 1973, box 32, Criminal Matters September 5, 1973, folder, ibid.
24. AC 28:7.
25. *Bangor (Maine) Daily News*, October 27, 1973.
26. *Washington Post*, October 23, 1973.
27. Drew, *Washington Journal*, p. 56; interview with James Doyle by Phil Heymann et al., May 1, 1974, p. 57, James Doyle papers.
28. James Vorenberg, author's interview.
29. Memo, Office of the Watergate Special Prosecutor, undated, James Doyle papers, temporary folder 151.
30. AC 28:8.
31. Ibid.
32. Erwin N. Griswold, author's interview.
33. AC 36:35.
34. William D. Ruckelshaus, author's interview.
35. Ibid.
36. Ibid.
37. Ibid.
38. Bork had met President Nixon just a year earlier in connection with drafting legislation to limit school busing as a means of remedying segregation. See Robert H. Bork, author's interview.
39. Ibid.
40. Elliot L. Richardson, author's interview, November 25, 1992.
41. John T. Smith, author's interview.
42. Elliot L. Richardson, author's interview, November 25, 1992.
43. Interview with Robert H. Bork by James Doyle, circa 1975, pp. 1–22, 23, 35, James Doyle papers.
44. Robert H. Bork, author's interview.
45. Ibid.
46. William D. Ruckelshaus, author's interview; Press Conference of William D. Ruckelshaus, October 23, 1973, James Doyle papers, temporary folder 154. During the confirmation hearings of Robert Bork for appointment to the

Supreme Court in 1987, Senator Edward M. Kennedy questioned Elliot Richardson sharply regarding the logic of this assessment. Kennedy's principal point was that the charter spelling out the circumstances under which the special prosecutor could be fired was ultimately published by Richardson in the Federal Register and thus applied to any subsequent attorney general with as much force as it applied to Richardson. See *Nomination of Robert H. Bork to Be Associate Justice of the Supreme Court of the United States,* September 29, 1987, pp. 3112–24. This was the same strict legal interpretation adopted by Judge Gesell in a federal suit brought by Ralph Nader. However, none of the principal Watergate actors, including Cox, ever considered it a major issue. Even if technically true, Bork could have rehired Cox after the Saturday Night Massacre, revoked or amended the charter, and then fired him. Cox and Richardson both assumed that the president could ultimately "work his will" and fire the special prosecutor, if he made that decision.

47. AC 36:35.

48. Robert H. Bork, author's interview. Not everyone agrees that Bork was receptive to the idea of installing a new *independent* special prosecutor, i.e., one from outside the Justice Department. On the Tuesday after Cox's firing, Bork apparently "waffled" on this issue, and told Special Prosecution Force members that the "Department" would undoubtedly oppose the idea, whether he was acting attorney general or not. Ben-Veniste and Frampton, *Stonewall,* p. 148, 156; Henry Ruth, author's follow-up interview, April 12, 1997.

49. Ibid.

50. AC 37:3.

51. Leonard Garment, author's interview, October 19, 1994.

52. Order No. 546-73, October 23, 1973, James Doyle papers, temporary folder 150.

53. Press Release (Robert H. Bork), October 24, 1973, and Press Conference (Robert H. Bork and Henry Petersen), October 24, 1973, James Doyle papers, temporary folder 156. Bork did state at one point during his press conference that the appointment of a new special prosecutor "had crossed my mind." However, as of October 24, there was no indication that Bork believed that a new special prosecutor, if appointed, would report to anyone but Petersen. One Richardson aide even recalled that the White House asked Elliot Richardson to say something in his final press conference about the "qualifications and integrity" of Henry Petersen, since Petersen was to inherit the Watergate investigation. See interview with Elliot Richardson by James Doyle, June 3, 1975, pp. 4–41, 42, James Doyle papers. Richardson opted to say nothing about Petersen in his press conference on Tuesday, October 23.

54. Robert H. Bork, author's interview.

55. Ibid., author's follow-up interview, December 19, 1996.

56. Although it took President Nixon's own tapes to place dates and times on many of these contacts, Cox and his staff understood the basic facts.

57. Many contacts between President Nixon and Henry Petersen are discussed in the secret memorandum that George Frampton prepared shortly after the release of the first tapes by the White House. See Report (George Frampton), undated, James Doyle papers, temporary folder 187. Other information concerning the unusual links between Henry Petersen and the White House are

generally documented in the following sources: Pincus, "The Silbert-Petersen Puzzle," *New Republic*, July 6 and 13, 1974, pp. 15–16; Memo, Earl J. Silbert to AC, June 5, 1973, James Doyle papers, temporary folder 74; Memo, Harold H. Titus et al. to ELR, April 30, 1973, James Doyle papers, temporary folder 74; Henry Petersen, D.C. Grand Jury No. 2, August 23, 1973, James Doyle papers, temporary folder 74; "Agnew's Nemesis at Justice," *Time*, October 8, 1973, 16–17; Mollenhoff, *Game Plan for Disaster*, p. 295; Meeting Notes (ELR), May 4, 1973, Administrative Files of the Watergate Special Prosecution Force, RG 460, BSD-1, Authority & Establishment, National Archives. Key conversations between the President and Petersen can be found in *The White House Transcripts*, beginning on p. 538 (April 16, 1973), p. 665 (April 17, 1973), and p. 774 (April 27, 1973). Not all entries are damning to Petersen. At one point during the April conversations, Petersen told President Nixon that if he found any evidence incriminating the president, he (Petersen) would "waltz it right over to the House of Representatives." See Ben-Veniste and Frampton, *Stonewall*, pp. 217–18.

58. John W. Dean, III, author's interview. On the night of the Saturday Night Massacre, Dean met with Richard Ben-Veniste of the special prosecution staff in a Washington hotel. He told Ben-Veniste: "Petersen's extremely loyal to Nixon, loyal to Mitchell. I don't think it's going to be independent. It's going to have limits on it. The whole playing field was going to change." See ibid.

59. John T. Smith, author's interview. Petersen had admitted earlier that summer that he had suspected "higher-ups" were involved in the Watergate break-in within days of the burglary. He later confessed that he had not pushed his suspicions far enough because he was "ashamed" to have them. See *New York Times*, June 5, 1973, June 21, 1974.

60. Robert H. Bork, author's follow-up interview, December 19, 1996.

61. Ibid.

62. *Washington Post*, October 24, 1973; press conference (Robert H. Bork and Henry Petersen), October 24, 1973, James Doyle papers, temporary folder 156. Petersen made clear that he disapproved of the idea of a separate special prosecutor from the start: "I would hope that the investigation can proceed with confidence in the criminal justice system, with confidence in Mr. Bork and me, with confidence in the Special Prosecution staff."

63. John T. Smith, author's interview.

64. Henry Ruth, author's interview; and author's follow-up interview, April 12, 1997.

65. Henry Ruth, author's interview. Not everyone interviewed for this book felt that Henry Petersen should be faulted for the unwitting role he played in the Watergate cover-up. John C. Keeney, who worked alongside Petersen in the Justice Department and later headed the Criminal Division himself, pointed out that Petersen was "reporting to Nixon at a time he was not aware of Nixon's involvement." According to Keeney, there was nothing nefarious about such contact in 1973, particularly because Petersen was acting attorney general with respect to the Watergate matter after the recusal of Attorney General Kleindienst, and thus had final authority over the case. Historically, explained Keeney, such contacts between presidents and the Justice Department were not unheard of. Today, such communications are sharply restricted by internal

Department of Justice guidelines. But at the time, Keeney explained, Petersen's conduct was not out of line. Even after the Watergate debacle, said Keeney, few lawyers in the Justice Department felt that Henry Petersen was to blame: "Nobody felt he screwed up. He was idolized by lawyers here." John C. Keeney, author's interview, and author's follow-up interview, March 4, 1997. Henry Ruth, Cox's deputy who dealt with Petersen immediately after Cox's firing (and who had been hired by Petersen in the Justice Department in 1961), concurred. "[Petersen] would agree that he was duped," said Ruth. "But if people can remember back to that time, the President was king and national security was king." Despite Petersen's missteps in Watergate, Ruth still felt that he was a devoted government lawyer. "I would put Henry Petersen well above most lawyers I've ever met." Henry Ruth, author's follow-up interview, April 12, 1997. Robert Bork expressed a similar view concerning Petersen. Concluded Bork: "He was not an evil guy. I don't know what mistakes he may have made. But he was not an evil guy." Robert Bork, author's interview.

66. AC 37:4.
67. Leonard Garment, author's interview, October 19, 1994.
68. *Boston Globe*, November 11, 1973.
69. Comments by Archibald Cox, October 23, 1973, James Doyle papers, temporary folder 151; *New York Times*, October 24, 1973.
70. *Harvard Crimson*, October 30, 1973; *Harvard University Gazette*, November 2, 1973.
71. *Boston Globe*, November 15, 1973.
72. Elliot L. Richardson, author's follow-up interview, November 23, 1993.
73. Ibid.
74. "The Saturday Night Massacre," program, December 3, 1993.
75. Elliot L. Richardson, author's interview, November 25, 1992; "The Saturday Night Massacre," program, December 3, 1993.
76. This material is contained in chronological notes kept by Leonard Garment's secretary for Monday, October 15 through Sunday, October 21. See box 9, Chron. File September–November 1973, Leonard Garment papers, Library of Congress.
77. *Washington Post*, April 28, 1973; *New York Times*, April 28, 1973; Dr. Robert Warren Muir, author's interview. President Nixon recounts his trip with Stennis in his memoirs. See Nixon, *RN:*, 844.
78. *Time*, "Richard Nixon Stumbles to the Brink," October 29, 1973, 14.
79. R. James Woolsey, author's interview. Others concurred that stories of Stennis's hearing "problems" were highly exaggerated, as of 1973. See Dr. Robert Warren Muir, author's interview; Rex G. Buffington, author's interview; William "Eph" Cresswell, author's interview.
80. The robbers had taken Stennis's billfold, twenty-five cents, his watch, and his Phi Beta Kappa key.
81. *New York Times*, January 31, 1973; *Washington Post*, January 31, 1973.
82. Dr. Robert Warren Muir, author's interview.
83. *New York Times*, February 8, 1973.
84. Stennis underwent a total of three operations to repair damage to his abdomen

and thigh. *Washington Post,* June 12, 1973, July 27, 1973, July 31, 1973; *New York Times,* June 13, 1973.

85. *Washington Post,* August 8, 1973; *New York Times,* August 8, 1973.

86. *Congressional Record* 119 (1973): 28471–77; *Washington Post,* September 6, 1973; *New York Times,* September 6, 1973.

87. Dr. Robert Warren Muir, author's interview.

88. The president's personal secretary, Rose Mary Woods, spent more than twenty-five hours transcribing the first one-hour conversation. See Price, *With Nixon,* p. 251.

89. Even a quick listen to several minutes of the "Nixon Tapes" at the National Archives allows the average listener to appreciate the enormous difficulty posed by the task of transcribing them.

90. Robert H. Bork, author's interview.

91. William "Eph" Cresswell, author's interview.

92. Memoranda of Conversations, May–October 1973, October 15, 1973 (no. 3), box 205, Haig folder, ELR papers; John T. Smith, author's interview.

93. Henry Ruth, author's interview.

94. John T. Smith, author's interview.

95. Memoranda of Conversations, May–October 1973, October 16, 1973 (no. 3), box 205, Haig folder, ELR papers; John T. Smith, author's interview.

96. "Stennis Compromise" notes, undated, and Statement by Senator John C. Stennis on Proposed Watergate Tapes Compromise, October 20, 1973, John C. Stennis papers, Special Collection, Mississippi State University; Lukas, *Nightmare,* p. 425.

97. Leonard Garment, author's interview, October 19, 1994.

98. John T. Smith, author's interview.

99. Ibid.

100. *Congressional Record* 118 (1972): 11121.

101. Nixon, *RN,* p. 382.

102. *New York Times,* February 9, 1962, February 11, 1962.

103. Stennis had written the following generous words in ruling in favor of the president, eleven years earlier: "I know of no case where the Court has ever made the Senate or the House surrender records from its files, or where the Executive has made the Legislative Branch surrender records from its files— and I do not think either of them could. So the rule works three ways. Each is supreme within its field, and each is responsible within its field." See Nixon, *Public Papers of the President of the United States,* (1974): 479. President Nixon's letter to the House Judiciary Committee, in which he quoted the Stennis ruling, was dated June 10, 1974.

104. Peter M. Kreindler, author's interview. The third-person "summaries" prepared by President Nixon and his staff no longer exist, or remain buried in the papers of Fred Buzhardt that are off-limits in the National Archives. The author sought to obtain access to the Buzhardt papers through the estate of former President Nixon, but that request was denied. Nonetheless, various portions had been read to staffers over the phone, and it is clear that they provided a favorable slant to the president and omitted damaging passages. See ibid. The House Judiciary Committee later drafted impeachment articles that raised the misleading nature

of the president's more extensive summaries as grounds for removing the president from office. See U.S. House Committee on the Judiciary, *Impeachment of Richard M. Nixon, President of the United States. Report of the Committee on the Judiciary, House of Representatives*, pp. 203–5.

105. Author's informal recollections following "Saturday Night Massacre" program, December 3, 1993, University of Pittsburgh, Pennsylvania, author's notes.

106. The author wrote to President Nixon on several occasions requesting interviews under whatever conditions the former president deemed appropriate. President Nixon did not reply. See letters, author to President Richard M. Nixon, January 30, 1991, and May 7, 1991.

Chapter 21

1. Letter quoted in the *Boston Globe,* December 5, 1973.
2. Jonathan Soroff to AC, April 24, 1974, box 47, folder 11, AC papers; *Harvard Magazine,* June 1974, p. 53.
3. Eliggio Moretti to AC, November 26, 1973, Phyllis Ames Cox personal papers. Loosely translated, this means "Nixon, why does he have to go there?"
4. One of these songs was put to the music of Beethoven, and titled "Watergate Lament." Eamon O'Connor to AC, undated, Phyllis Ames Cox personal papers.
5. Sarah Cohen to Florence Campbell, October 19, 1973, and enclosed report "Get to Know Archibald Cox," Phyllis Ames Cox personal papers.
6. TRB, "Supreme Performances," *New Republic,* November 10, 1973, p. 4.
7. *Newsweek,* October 29, 1973; *Time,* November 29, 1973.
8. *Christian Science Monitor,* August 19, 1980.
9. Miscellaneous clippings, Phyllis Ames Cox personal papers.
10. Richard W. Lyman to AC, October 25, 1974, Phyllis Ames Cox personal papers.
11. Alfred A. Knopf to AC, October 24, 1973, AC papers, box 48, folder 4.
12. "Yesterday's News," *Harvard Magazine,* November-December 1993, p. 97.
13. This unsigned letter is reproduced in the *Boston Globe,* December 5, 1973.
14. Among other things, the White House had learned in the interim that Judge Sirica intended to hold the president in contempt and impose stiff monetary fines for each day he continued to defy the court order. See Sirica, *To Set the Record Straight,* pp. 132–40.
15. *Watergate: Chronology of a Crisis,* 2:76; News Conference, October 23, 1973; Notes, October 23, 1973, Chronology, September–November 1973 folder, box 9, Leonard Garment papers, Library of Congress; *Weekly Compilation of Presidential Documents,* 9 (October 29, 1973): 1275; Doyle, *Not Above the Law,* p. 223. Over the long holiday weekend, the president's lawyers had filed a memo with Judge Sirica, stating that the Stennis "verification" would be submitted in lieu of the tapes. James Doyle's discussion of this little-known memo can be found in his interview with Robert Bork (circa 1975), pp. 1–66, 67, James Doyle papers.
16. *Watergate: Chronology of a Crisis,* 2:69, 76.
17. *New York Daily News,* November 2, 1973; *New York Times,* November 2, 1973.
18. *The Economist,* October 27, 1973, 13.

19. Mankiewicz, *U.S. v. Richard M. Nixon*, p. 51; Lewis J. Paper, *The Promise and the Performance*, p. 357.

20. Ambrose, *Nixon*, 3:255. For a perspective from the White House, lauding the president's efforts, see Price, *With Nixon*, pp. 262–63. Whether President Nixon's fear of nuclear confrontation in the Mideast as a result of Watergate was real or imagined will never be known. There is certainly room to conclude that the Mideast was a real problem for the president, which Nixon believed could be simultaneously used to deliver him from the hell of Watergate. There is also room to suspect that the Mideast war was the trump card that President Nixon planned to play on Senator Stennis, a lifelong believer in deferring to the president on military matters, just as the president had attempted to play it on Elliot Richardson.

21. On October 30, the House Judiciary Committee granted sweeping subpoena power to Chairman Peter Rodino, who pledged to proceed "full steam ahead." See Mollenhoff, *Game Plan for Disaster*, p. 319.

22. *New York Times*, October 27, 1973; Drew, *Washington Journal*, p. 75.

23. The story was particularly hard for observers to swallow, because Nixon himself had reportedly listened to the tapes as early as September 29 at Camp David, in preparing his "summaries" for Senator Stennis, yet he had never mentioned that any of the tapes were missing.

24. Kutler, *The Wars of Watergate*, p. 426; *Watergate: Chronology of a Crisis*, 2:111.

25. This was accomplished through an order of Acting Attorney General Robert Bork, dated November 2, entitled "Establishing the Office of Watergate Special Prosecution Force," WSPF, SP—Admin. Files, BSD-1, RG 460, Robert Bork folder, National Archives. See also Mollenhoff, *Game Plan for Disaster*, p. 323; Ambrose, *Nixon*, 3:260–61; Cook, *The Crimes of Watergate*, pp. 148–49, 152–53; *New York Times*, November 11, 1973; *Washington Post*, November 6, 1973; "The Mystery of the Missing Tapes," *Time*, November 12, 1973, 22.

26. *Wall Street Journal*, October 30, 1973.

27. AC 28:20.

28. "Instant Replay—the ITT Case," *Newsweek*, November 12, 1973, 29.

29. AC 28:20, 21.

30. *Washington Post*, October 31, 1973. The White House termed the conduct "inexcusable," and Cox agreed.

31. "Instant Replay—the ITT case," *Newsweek*, November 12, 1973, 29.

32. Ibid., 29–30; *Chicago Tribune*, November 2, 1973.

33. *Newsweek*, November 12, 1973.

34. Henry Ruth, author's interview.

35. Philip B. Heymann, author's interview.

36. In fact, some evidence surfaced that the story was funneled to the *Times* by the White House or Kleindienst's own lawyer. See AC 28:21; AC to Leon Jaworski, March 16, 1974, AC papers, box 24, folder 2.

37. *Philadelphia Evening Bulletin*, July 18, 1974; AC 28:22.

38. *Washington Post*, November 15, 1973; Transcript of Proceedings, *Ralph Nader et al. v. Robert H. Bork*, November 9, 1973, and Memorandum Opinion, November 14, 1973, AC papers, box 21, folder 14.

39. AC 28:10, 37:10.

40. Mary "Molly" Cox, author's interview, August 15, 1990. Phyllis Cox saw a genuine "admiration" in her husband's eyes for the man who succeeded him as special prosecutor. Years after Jaworski's death, Archie would pay him the supreme New England compliment. He confided to Phyllis one day that when it came time to "meet his Maker," he hoped that he "would go" just like Leon Jaworski— "splitting wood." See Phyllis Ames Cox, author's interview.

41. *Blue Hill (Maine) Weekly Packet*, November 22, 1973.

42. *Ellsworth (Maine) American*, November 15, 1973; *Biddeford-Saco (Maine) Journal*, November 19, 1973.

43. Cook, *The Crimes of Watergate*, pp. 150–52.

44. "The Secretary and the Tapes Tangle," *Time*, December 10, 1973, 15; *New York Times*, December 2, 1973; *Washington Post*, January 20, 1974. General Alexander Haig attributed the infamous 18½-minute gap on the June 20, 1972, tape to a "sinister force" or "some other energy force." Although Haig would later make light of his comment, there was no laughter in December 1973, when he struggled to explain the gap to Judge Sirica. See *Washington Post*, December 7, 1973. H. R. Haldeman's diaries later confirmed that the gap corresponded with a discussion of Watergate, one that went into "considerable detail." See Haldeman, *The Haldeman Diaries*, p. 473.

45. Drew, *Washington Journal*, p. 91. Nixon's loyal secretary of twenty-two years, Rose Mary Woods, testified that she might have caused the erasure by stretching to answer the phone and keeping her foot on the foot pedal of the transcriber at the same time. Few bought that explanation. See *New York Times*, November 27, 1973, December 7, 1973; Pincus, "Who Dunnit: The Rose Mary Woods Mystery," *New Republic*, February 2, 1974, 14; "Rosemary's Boo-Boo," *Newsweek*, December 10, 1973, 26; Ambrose, *Nixon*, 3:261.

46. "New White House Blast," *Time*, November 12, 1973, 78.

47. Richard Ben-Veniste, author's interview.

48. *White House Transcripts*, pp. 146–47; Doyle, *Not Above the Law*, pp. 262–65.

49. Richard Ben-Veniste, author's interview.

50. Report (George Frampton), undated, James Doyle papers, temporary folder 187. On the subject of what evidence Cox's subpoena unearthed, see ibid.; *Subpoena duces tecum*, July 23, 1973, AC papers, box 21, folder 11; *White House Transcripts*, pp. 146–47; Doyle, *Not Above the Law*, pp. 247–86; *Akron Beacon Journal*, July 28, 1973.

51. Alexander Haig later wrote that "Cox subpoenaed the wrong tapes," and that "none of the eight recordings [there were nine] demanded by him on July 23 contained any information that suggested, much less established, criminal conduct on the part of the President." See Haig, *Inner Circles*, p. 383. However, this seems to be a wishful minimization rather than the objective assessment of one schooled in criminal law. Both of the "missing" tapes involved critical dates and thus provided circumstantial evidence of wrongdoing. The first was the June 20, 1972, phone conference between the president and John Mitchell just three days after the Watergate break-in. (White House lawyers said this conversation did not exist on tape because the president had used a hall telephone.) The second was the April 15, 1973, "Dictabelt" of the conversation between John Dean and President Nixon, in which Dean testified that the president sought to cover up his

agreement to make a one-million-dollar payoff. The president had personally told Henry Petersen that there was a recording of this conversation. See "The Mystery of the Missing Tapes," *Time,* November 12, 1973, 22; *New York Times,* December 2, 1973; *Washington Post,* November 24, 1973.

With respect to those tapes handed over, they contained numerous portions damaging to the president. The September 15, 1972, meeting in the Oval Office between the president, Haldeman, and Dean—the same day the grand jury indicted seven men for the Watergate burglary—contained a passage in which the president congratulated Dean for "skillfully putting your fingers in the leaks that have sprung here and sprung there." This portion of the tape thus suggested that the president already knew of, and approved of, the cover-up. See *White House Transcripts,* pp. 57–61; report (George Frampton), undated, James Doyle papers, temporary folder 187, pp. 6–7. The March 21, 1973, meeting between Nixon, Dean, and Haldeman shows the president fully aware of a cover-up in progress and contains Dean's infamous remarks about a "cancer within the Presidency." See *White House Transcripts,* pp. 28–55, 132–80; report (George Frampton), pp. 55–60. The March 13 and March 22 tapes also contain evidence of a continued cover-up. Thus, Alexander Haig's statements notwithstanding, the tapes Cox subpoenaed were both incriminating to the president and instrumental in obtaining the next, larger, batch of tapes after Leon Jaworski became special prosecutor.

52. Richard Ben-Veniste, author's interview.
53. Doyle, *Not Above the Law,* p. 329.
54. "Cox at Cambridge," *New Yorker,* January 20, 1975, 27.
55. *U.S. v. Nixon,* 418 U.S. 683 (1974).
56. "The Court's Middle Man," *Newsweek,* October 15, 1973, 24.
57. Warren E. Burger, author's interview.
58. 8 U.S. (4 Cranch) 469 (1807).
59. Warren E. Burger, author's interview.
60. Doyle, *Not Above the Law,* 336; Schwartz, *The Ascent of Pragmatism,* pp. 81–89.
61. Warren E. Burger, author's interview; James E. Gauch (law clerk to Chief Justice Burger), letter to author, June 7, 1994.
62. Charles Wright to Leonard Garment, July 5, 1974, box 8, Charles Alan Wright 1973–74 folder, Leonard Garment papers, Library of Congress.
63. Woodward and Bernstein, *The Final Days,* p. 231.
64. Leonard Garment, letter to author, April 2, 1997. Garment explained that the "maelstrom of criticism" that followed the publication of the president's edited tape transcripts, even before the "belated challenge" in the Supreme Court, signaled the beginning of the downward slide.
65. For Cox's views about the issue of impeaching the president, see *New York Times,* January 24, 1974; Cox, "Reflections on a Firestorm," *Saturday Review,* March 9, 1974, 12.
66. *Chicago Tribune,* July 28, 1974. Regarding the "smoking gun," see Kutler, *The Wars of Watergate,* p. 470; Doyle, *Not Above the Law,* pp. 340–44.
67. W. Thomas McGough, Jr., author's interview.
68. Donna Chiozzi, author's interview.
69. AC 28:9.

70. Phyllis Ames Cox, author's interview.
71. *Boston Globe,* March 31, 1976.
72. AC 37:15.
73. AC to Archie C. Epps III, August 28, 1974, AC papers, box 44, folder 10.
74. Statement Released to Press on Nixon Pardon, September 8, 1974, box 24, folder 14, AC papers.
75. See also *Yale News,* September 25, 1974. Cox parted company with those who believed that the pardon was unconstitutional and who felt it should be tested in the Supreme Court. But it was still, he believed, a "great mistake." He told reporters that his problem was not with the legality of Ford's move. "My disapproval is of its wisdom." See *New Haven Register,* September 25, 1974; *Hartford Courant,* September 25, 1974.
76. Gerald R. Ford, author's interview.
77. Ford, *A Time to Heal,* pp. 163–64.
78. Ibid., pp. 170–71; Gerald R. Ford, author's interview.
79. It was "a time to heal," the phrase from Ecclesiastes, that Ford would borrow as the title for his own autobiography.
80. AC 37:18.
81. Ibid.
82. *Washington Evening Star,* September 9, 1974; Vladimir Pregelj, author's interview.
83. AC 28:14.
84. Doyle, *Not Above the Law,* pp. 378–89. The jury also convicted Robert Mardian, an assistant to John Mitchell, but his conviction was later overturned because the appellate court found that he should have been tried separately. Only Kenneth W. Parkinson, a lawyer for the Committee to Re-elect the President, was acquitted.
85. Philip B. Heymann, author's interview.
86. *Washington Post,* March 2, 1978.
87. *New York Times,* March 24, 1976.
88. Karen L. Middaugh to AC, July 2, 1974, AC papers, box 45, folder 2. The quotation was "Upon our joint human adventure we do not know the goal . . . but can catch glimpses of a bright potential and perhaps can see that by reason, mutual trust and forbearance, man can learn to walk a little straighter."
89. Susan Ferraro to AC, July 18, 1974, AC papers, box 44, folder 14. Cox replied that her letter "leaves me a bit at a loss for words." Although notable public figures like Henry Commanger and Corliss Lamont had "suggested the possibility" of running for president, Cox stated that he had "too much respect for the office and what can be done [as President]" to even entertain the notion, because "I find it remote indeed." See AC to Susan Ferraro, August 2, 1974, AC papers, box 44, folder 14.
90. Deirdre Henderson to AC, May 27, 1974, AC papers, box 45, folder 6.
91. Alice I. Fisher to AC, February 28, 1974, AC papers, box 44, folder 14.
92. Philip B. Heymann, author's interview.
93. Robert H. Bork, author's interview.
94. Gerald R. Ford, author's interview.
95. Warren E. Burger, author's interview.

96. Elliot L. Richardson, author's interview, November 25, 1992.
97. Karnow, "Elliot Richardson," *New Republic,* May 17, 1975, 14.

Chapter 22

1. AC to Major League Players Association, August 19, 1974, AC papers, box 44, folder 18.
2. The vice chancellor of the university had personally extended the invitation, writing a letter in which he reminded Cox that "the skull of Oliver Cromwell was buried at Sidney Sussex." Cox graciously accepted, but promised: "I shall not commit regicide while at Sidney." AC, author's follow-up interview, December 10, 1996.
3. AC to Dean Albert Sacks, January 25, 1973, AC personnel file, Harvard Law School; "Cox at Cambridge," *New Yorker,* January 20, 1975, 25.
4. Memos, AC to Elliot L. Richardson, March 7, 1975 and March 10, 1975, and Richardson to AC, March 21, 1975, Cox file, box 285, ELR papers.
5. American Chamber of Commerce (United Kingdom) announcement, March 18, 1975, Cox file, box 285, ELR papers; Cox, "More Reasons for Confidence Than Despair," *Anglo American Trade News,* June 1975, 8, 14, contained in Cox file, box 285, ELR papers.
6. "Cox at Cambridge," *New Yorker,* January 20, 1975, 26.
7. The Isle of Skye had figured in legends that Cox had read about since he was a boy, including the story of "Bonnie Prince Charlie" returning the Stuarts back to the throne in the mid-eighteenth century. AC, author's follow-up interview, December 10, 1996; AC, letter to author, October 31, 1996.
8. *Daily Telegraph* (London), October 17, 1975.
9. *Guardian* (London), October 17, 1975.
10. Elliot L. Richardson to AC, October 20, 1975, Cox file, box 285, ELR papers.
11. AC to Richardson, October 31, 1975, ELR papers.
12. Richardson to AC, November 10, 1975, ELR papers.
13. *Harvard Crimson,* June 12, 1975; William G. Anderson to Dean Albert M. Sacks, April 28, 1975, AC personnel file, HLS.
14. *Harvard Gazette,* May 29, 1981; Derek C. Bok to Albert M. Sacks, June 9, 1976, AC personnel file, HLS.
15. Typical of Cox's writing during this time period were the following: "Federalism and Individual Rights under the Burger Court," *Northwestern University Law Review* 73 (1978): 1; "The Lawyer's Independent Calling," *Kentucky Law Journal* 67 (1978–79): 5; "Recent Developments in Federal Labor Law Preemption," *Ohio State Law Journal* 41 (1980): 277; "Constitutional Issues in the Regulation of the Financing of Election Campaigns," *Cleveland State Law Review* 31 (1982): 395; "Freedom of the Press," *University of Illinois Law Review* 1983 (1983): 3.
16. Board of Student Advisor (BSA) evaluations, Constitutional Law, 1978–79, Advanced Constitutional Law: First Amendment, Fall 1983, BSA archives, HLS. The reviews of Cox as a Labor Law professor, after that subject became of secondary interest to him, were much more mixed. See ibid., Labor Law evaluations, Spring 1979.

17. Derek C. Bok, author's interview.
18. Roland S. Homet, Jr., author's interview.
19. Harry H. Wellington, author's interview. Cox was frequently sighted in the Harkness Commons in the morning, having coffee and a doughnut with students. See Maurice Ford letter to *Harvard Law Bulletin,* James Doyle papers. Cox was also known for writing extensive comments on student papers at the end of each semester. One student remembered rushing to Cox's secretary to determine if he had received an A or an A minus, since the grade marked at the bottom of the paper was unclear. The secretary scrutinized the handwriting and said, "Oh, neither. That's an 'AC' for Archibald Cox." The student had in fact received a B. Daniel L. Wessels, author's interview.
20. Helen Sorrentino, author's interview.
21. Regarding the Windsor bicentennial, see F. D. Churchill to AC, undated, and AC to F. D. Churchill, January 11, 1978, AC papers, box 53, folder 1. Regarding the speech at Miss Porter's School, see "Miss Porter's School—Graduation 1976," AC personal papers, and *The Bulletin* (Miss Porter's School), Spring 1977.
22. Alfred A. Knopf, Jr., to AC, October 30, 1973; Simon Michael Bessie to AC, August 15, 1974, AC to Elizabeth Knappman, October 23, 1974; and AC to Richard B. McAdoo, November 28, 1973, AC papers, box 48, folder 5.
23. Sally Cox, author's interview; Clark Byse, author's interview.
24. Sally Cox, author's interview.
25. Clark Byse, author's interview; Phyllis Ames Cox, author's interview; "Talk of the Town," *New Yorker,* December 19, 1977.
26. *Boston Phoenix,* December 14, 1976; *Harvard Law Record,* February 6, 1976; Massachusetts, Governor's Select Committee on Judicial Needs, "Report on the State of the Massachusetts Courts." The reforms implemented by Cox's panel dealt with the organization, management, and financing of the state courts, as well as jurisdictional matters.
27. AC 28:28.
28. Cox had helped convince Stewart Udall to support Senator John F. Kennedy's bid for the presidency during a car trip through Arizona in 1959, as Cox was returning from a summer teaching stint at Stanford, California.
29. *Tucson Star,* January 6, 1974; *Washington Post,* June 5, 1976; *New York Times,* March 21, 1976; remarks of AC at Dinner Honoring Congressman Morris K. Udall, January 5, 1974, AC personal papers; AC 28:23–29.
30. *Boston Evening Globe,* March 3, 1976.
31. AC 28:23–29; text of Udall Nomination Speech by AC, July 14, 1976, AC personal papers.
32. Cox had begun working with Senator Kennedy on the matter while the bill was still pending. AC, author's follow-up interview, December 10, 1996. For general background, see Edward M. Kennedy to AC, July 9, 1975, and AC to Edward M. Kennedy, July 15, 1975, files of Senator Edward M. Kennedy; *Boston Globe,* July 27, 1975; *Harvard Crimson,* July 29, 1975; *Philadelphia Inquirer,* July 27, 1975; News Release, Senators Edward M. Kennedy and Hugh Scott, July 27, 1975, Phyllis Ames Cox personal papers. The principal plaintiffs in the suit were former Senator Eugene McCarthy (a liberal candidate for president) and Senator James Buckley (a conservative senator from New York), who claimed the Federal

Election Reform Act violated their constitutional rights because it limited political contributions and expenditures in ways that favored centrist candidates and penalized political dissenters. The defendants were various federal officials and agencies responsible for enforcing the law, and intervening parties including Common Cause.

33. *Buckley v. Valeo,* 424 U.S. 1, 1–5 (1976); News Release, Senators Edward M. Kennedy and Hugh Scott, Phyllis Ames Cox personal papers; *Boston Globe,* July 27, 1975.

34. In the time allocated to Common Cause, Cox was permitted to argue on the issue of whether ceilings on contributions and expenditures were constitutional. Common Cause's counsel, Lloyd Cutler, disagreed with Common Cause's position on this issue. It was agreed among the lawyers that Cox, who would not otherwise be entitled to argue on behalf of Senators Scott and Kennedy as amicus, would present the argument in the time reserved for Common Cause. See AC, author's follow-up interview, December 10, 1996.

35. *Boston Globe,* November 11, 1975; Kurland and Casper, *Landmark Briefs and Arguments,* 100:623–38.

36. *Buckley v. Valeo,* 424 U.S., pp. 3–5, 19–23, 109–13, 140–44; *New York Times,* January 31, 1976; *Washington Post,* January 31, 1976. To the extent that Cox's oral argument focused primarily on expenditures, it is fair to say that the Court rejected most of his contentions. See 424 U.S. pp. 14–23. However, to the extent that Cox worked to defend the entire statute in *Buckley,* the case represented a significant victory.

37. *Washington Post,* January 31, 1976. At the same time, the Court invalidated other portions of the act. It struck down caps on spending by candidates for House and Senate seats; it allowed individual citizens to spend any amount in an independent effort to elect or defeat a candidate through advertising efforts; it allowed presidential candidates who did not accept federal funds to spend virtually unrestricted amounts of money; and it sharply curtailed the power of the Federal Election Commission. See ibid.; *New York Times,* January 31, 1976. The Court thus drew a sharp line between "expenditures" and "contributions," giving the former greater protection under the First Amendment.

38. The California Supreme Court had ordered Allan Bakke admitted, applying a "strict scrutiny" test under the equal protection clause of the Fourteenth Amendment, and concluding that there was no "compelling state interest" in treating applicants differently based upon race. See AC 28:29, 30; *Regents of the University of California v. Bakke,* 438 U.S. 265 (1978).

39. "What Rights for Whites?" *Time,* October 24, 1977, 97.

40. Ibid., 98.

41. At the time, Cox was swamped with outside commitments. He agreed to take the *Bakke* case only on condition that the California lawyers bear the primary responsibility for writing the brief. Cox was responsible for handling the oral argument.

42. In *DeFunis,* Harvard had supported the policy of the University of Washington Law School that used race as one criterion in selecting members of the entering class in order to achieve a "reasonable representation of minority group members." The Supreme Court ultimately mooted the case, because DeFunis, a white man, had been admitted to the law school by order of the trial court, was in his

third year of law school by the time the litigation reached the Supreme Court and would not be affected by a decision either way. See *Harvard Law Record,* February 8, 1974; *DeFunis v. Odegaard,* 416 U.S. 312 (1974).

43. "What Rights for Whites?" *Time,* October 24, 1977, 95; *Boston Globe,* October 13, 1977.

44. Tom Eagleton to AC, October 12, 1977, AC papers, box 50, folder 6.

45. "What Rights for Whites?" *Time,* October 24, 1977, 95. Other lawyers could, and occasionally did, wear formal attire in the Court. AC, author's follow-up interview, December 10, 1996. However, by the 1970s Cox was one of the few. His status as a former solicitor general was viewed by most observers as an appropriate warrant for this special attire.

46. AC 28:31–33; *Boston Globe,* October 13, 1977. Lincoln Caplan's book tallies that Cox argued a total of eighty-seven times in the Supreme Court, although the author's count indicates eighty-six. In any event, the *Bakke* case was his next to last appearance. See Caplan, *The Tenth Justice,* p. 191.

47. Kurland, *Landmark Briefs and Arguments,* 100:623.

48. AC, author's follow-up interview, October 4, 1996.

49. Kurland, *Landmark Briefs and Arguments,* 199:627; *New York Times,* October 13, 1977; *Pittsfield (Mass.) Berkshire Eagle,* October 13, 1977; *Boston Globe,* October 13, 1977.

50. AC 28:32, 33; Kurland, *Landmark Briefs and Arguments,* 100:627–28.

51. Ibid.

52. Harry A. Blackmun, letter to author, February 3, 1995.

53. *Boston Globe,* October 13, 1977; *Pittsfield (Mass.) Berkshire Eagle,* October 14, 1977; Kurland, *Landmark Briefs and Arguments,* 100:645–63; *New York Times,* October 13, 1977.

54. Potter Stewart to Phyllis Ames Cox, and William Brennan to Phyllis Ames Cox, undated, Phyllis Ames Cox personal papers.

55. Kurland, *Landmark Briefs and Arguments,* 100:665.

56. Drew S. Days III, author's interview. Solicitor General Wade McCree, a black former federal judge, argued for the United States as amicus. Solicitor General McCree departed from Cox's position however, by urging that the case be sent back to the California courts for further consideration because the record was inadequate. See *Boston Globe,* October 13, 1977; "What Rights for Whites?" *Time,* October 24, 1977, 68.

57. *Boston Globe,* October 13, 1977.

58. *Washington Post,* June 29, 1978; *New York Times,* June 29, 1978.

59. *Regents of the University of California v. Bakke,* 438 U.S. 265 (1978).

60. Ibid., 316–17; *New York Times,* June 30, 1978. Justice Powell quoted this passage from the amicus brief submitted by Columbia, Stanford, Penn, and Harvard universities.

61. *Washington Post,* June 29, 1978.

62. *New York Times,* June 29, 1978.

63. AC 28:35, 36.

64. Miscellaneous cards, Phyllis Ames Cox personal papers. The quote about the gerbil comes from granddaughter Melissa Hart to Phyllis Ames Cox, April 10, 1978.

65. Archibald Cox, Jr., author's interview.

66. *New York Times,* August 20, 1977.
67. Charlie Wright, Cox's old Watergate opponent, received an advance copy of the book and wrote a brief note of congratulations: "I was genuinely impressed." See Charles Alan Wright to AC, April 1, 1976, AC papers, box 53, folder 3.
68. Cyril Clemens to AC, September 20, 1978, AC papers, box 85, folder 15.
69. *Bangor (Maine) Daily News,* undated, Phyllis Ames Cox personal papers.
70. Cox's publications and honorary degrees until the year 1979 can be found listed in his "Personal Data Questionnaire" submitted to the First Circuit selection panel in the early months of 1979. This document is contained in AC personal papers held by the author, and will be transferred to the Harvard Law School Library collection.
71. Florence R. Rubin to AC, March 1, 1979, AC personal papers; *Boston Globe,* March 8, 1979.
72. AC, author's follow-up interview, December 10, 1996; AC letter to author, October 31, 1996.
73. Theodore Chase, author's interview; Personal Data Questionnaire, AC personal papers.
74. AC 30:12. The "reasoned elaboration" language was a reference to Herbert Wechsler's famous article, "Toward Neutral Principles of Constitutional Law," 73 *Harvard Law Review* 1 (1959).
75. AC 30:11–15.
76. *New York Times,* June 3, 1979.
77. *Boston Globe,* August 3, 1979. Griffin Bell would remain clear on the subject two decades later. He stated: "We were trying to follow the ABA guidelines. We were flooded with names of people over 70. The Democrats had been out of office for some time; now many Senators were coming forward with names of older candidates. It would have been departing from what we were doing for a lot of other Senators." Griffin B. Bell, author's interview.
78. Charles E. Wyzanski, Jr., to Attorney General, November 30, 1978, AC papers, box 52, folder 19.
79. Griffin B. Bell, author's interview.
80. Edward M. Kennedy, author's interview.
81. Memo, Griffin B. Bell to President Carter, May 8, 1979, Carter Presidential Papers, Staff Offices, Counsel, Lipshutz, Cox, Archibald (and Age Limit for Judges), 7/77–9/79, [CF, O/A 434], box 11, Jimmy Carter Library, Atlanta, Georgia. For a discussion of Chief Justice Hughes's contributions to the Court, see Freund, "Charles Evans Hughes as Chief Justice," *Harvard Law Review* 81 (1967): 4.
82. Memo, Bob Lipshutz to President Carter, May 8, 1979, Carter Presidential Papers, Staff Offices, Counsel, Lipshutz, Cox, Archibald (and Age Limit for Judges), 7/77–9/79, (CF, O/A 434), box 11, Jimmy Carter Library.
83. Notes (author unknown), April 12, 1979, Carter Presidential Papers, Staff Offices, Counsel, Lipshutz, Cox, Archibald (and Age Limit for Judges), 7/77–9/79, (CF, O/A 434), box 11, Jimmy Carter Library. These notes appear to be written while a presidential aide in Lipshutz's office interviewed key individuals about the possibility of the Cox appointment.
84. Notes ("Ken Feinberg") April 12, 1979, author unknown, Carter Presidential Papers, Staff Offices, Counsel, Lipshutz, Cox, Archibald (and Age Limit for Judges), 7/77–9/79, (CF, O/A 434), box 11, Jimmy Carter Library.

85. Kenneth R. Feinberg, author's interview.
86. *Boston Sunday Globe*, April 8, 1979. Cox himself was aware that Learned Hand had worked full time on the U.S. Court of Appeals until his eightieth year and continued to write opinions for another decade. See Gunther, *Learned Hand*, pp. 639–79.
87. Cohen, "Another White House Folly," *National Journal*, September 8, 1979, 1492.
88. Ibid.
89. AC to Louis McClennan, September 24, 1979, AC personal papers.
90. AC to Herome P. Facher, April 29, 1980, AC personal papers.
91. AC, author's follow-up interview, November 24, 1996; Kenneth R. Feinburg, author's interview.
92. Stephen Breyer, author's follow-up interview, December 10, 1996.
93. Kenneth R. Feinberg, author's interview.
94. AC, author's follow-up interview, November 24, 1996; AC 1:36.
95. *Boston Globe*, October 20, 1979. Various memorabilia from the Kennedy Library dedication are contained in Phyllis Ames Cox personal papers.
96. Standard Diary, March 8, 1965, AC personal papers.
97. *Concord (N.H.) Monitor*, February 10, 1982. The rule requiring mandatory retirement at age seventy was rescinded by the university in later years.
98. Derek C. Bok, author's interview.
99. John J. McCloy to AC, April 19, 1984, Phyllis Ames Cox personal papers.
100. This comes from a speech by Cox to the Phi Beta Kappa society at Harvard, "The University and Public Life," that is reprinted in part in the *Wall Street Journal*, June 25, 1974.
101. Derek C. Bok to AC, undated, Phyllis Ames Cox personal papers.
102. AC, author's follow-up interview, November 24, 1996.
103. Clark Byse, author's interview.
104. AC, author's follow-up interview, September 5, 1995.
105. David J. Seipp, letter to author, May 1, 1997. Dean Ronald A. Cass of Boston University School of Law had decided upon his own "retirement" policy for Cox: "He teaches as long as he wants to," said Cass. Cox had been "through so many of the wars the students heard about elsewhere," Cass explained, that students and faculty considered him a walking piece of history. See Ronald A. Cass, author's interview.
106. The HEI may have sounded more like an organization for a scientist than a lawyer. It consisted of leaders from the motor vehicle industry, the scientific community, and the EPA, but it appealed to Cox's intellectual curiosity. He viewed it as a healthy way to tackle shared societal problems, much like the old tripartite boards of his labor days. See AC 31:22–31. Cox made a similar point in a speech to the American Bar Association Section of Labor Relations Law in Chicago on August 10, 1977, p. 13, AC personal papers.
107. AC 31:4–6.
108. AC 31:5.
109. AC to Fred Wertheimer, November 13, 1975, AC papers, box 49, folder 11.
110. AC 31:8. 9.
111. John W. Gardner, author's interview.
112. Gardner retired in 1977 and was succeeded by Nan Waterman. In 1980, Cox was seeking a successor for Waterman.

113. AC 31:3, 4.
114. John W. Gardner, author's interview.
115. Dorothy Cecelski, author's interview.
116. AC 31:16, 17.
117. Dorothy Cecelski, author's interview.
118. Fred Wertheimer, letter to author, April 17, 1997.
119. Cox lost by the vote of an equally divided Court, with justices split three votes to three. See *Common Cause v. Schmitt*, 455 U.S. 129; 512 F. Supp. 489 (D.D.C. 1980). By the end of his career, Cox had argued a total of eighty-six cases in the Supreme Court. He won sixty-one (71 percent), lost eighteen (21 percent), and split seven (8 percent), thus prevailing in a total of 79 percent of the cases he argued. These figures are based upon the author's review of the *U.S. Reports*, as well as upon Supreme Court records. A list of all cases won, lost, and split is contained in author's papers.
120. The 1982 amendment to the Voting Rights Act was designed to undo *City of Mobile v. Bolden*, 446 U.S. 55 (1980), in which the Supreme Court had held that a discriminatory *purpose* had to be proven before a violation of the Voting Rights Act and the Fifteenth Amendment occurred. The 1982 amendment specifically provided that a discriminatory *effect* was sufficient to prove a violation. The final compromise bill that Congress adopted to accomplish this revamping of the Voting Rights Act was introduced by Republican Senator Bob Dole of Kansas, immediately after a session in which Cox lobbied him on this subject. AC, author's follow-up interview, December 10, 1996.
121. Much of the work of Common Cause is summarized in "Twenty Years of Citizen Action: Common Cause 1970–1990," and "Memorandum to the National Governing Board. The 103rd Congress: Opportunities to Advance the Common Cause Core Agenda," January 1993, Common Cause Archives. See also AC 31:1–21; AC, author's follow-up interview, December 10, 1996.
122. Statements of Common Cause President Fred Wertheimer, February 27, 1991 and February 28, 1991, Common Cause archives.
123. Terry Sanford to Fred Wertheimer, February 28, 1991; AC to Senator Sanford, March 5, 1991; and Terry Sanford to AC, March 5, 1991, AC personal papers.
124. Caplan, *The Tenth Justice*, p. 195.
125. "I've got my peas up," Cox told a reporter. "I fed the horse and put it out to pasture before I got on the plane this morning. Made for an early rising, I must say." See *Christian Science Monitor*, August 19, 1980.
126. Phyllis Ames Cox, author's interview.
127. AC 31:12. See also Dorothy Cecelski, author's interview.
128. *Washington Post*, July 2, 1987; *New York Times*, July 26, 1987.
129. *Washington Post*, July 2, 1987.
130. Ibid., September 16, 1987, September 19, 1987.
131. Ibid., August 4, 1987.
132. Kramer, "The Brief on Judge Bork," *U.S. News & World Report*, September 14, 1987, 18.
133. *Washington Post*, August 4, 1987.
134. AC 31:13. Fred Wertheimer later stated: "[Cox] never told anyone where he stood on Bork. No one knew." Fred Wertheimer, author's interview.

135. *Nomination of Robert H. Bork to Be Associate Justice of the Supreme Court of the United States,* September 29, 1987, pp. 3112–24. With respect to the issue of Judge Gesell's ruling, and the publication of the regulation in the Federal Register, Cox himself never put much stock in this theory. Although Bork's decision to fire him may have been "technically illegal," he always assumed that Bork could have changed the sequence of events, revoked the regulation first, and then fired him. Consequently, he tended to agree with Elliot Richardson on this point. He viewed Gesell's ruling as a "distraction" from the larger issue of whether the president was entitled to defy the court order. AC, author's follow-up interview, October 4, 1996.

136. For an interesting review of Cox's book, compared and contrasted with the writing of Judge Robert Bork, see Selig, "Book Reviews," *Land and Water Law Review* 25 (1990): 625. As this review shows, the two men did not always disagree when it came to fundamental legal principles.

137. *Nomination of Robert H. Bork to Be Associate Justice of the Supreme Court of the United States,* September 19, 1987, pp. 844–45.

138. Edward M. Kennedy to AC, August 7, 1987, office files of Senator Edward M. Kennedy, Washington, D.C.

139. AC to Senator Kennedy, undated, office files of Senator Edward M. Kennedy, Washington, D.C.

140. *Washington Post,* October 24, 1987.

Epilogue

1. *The Court and the Constitution* had started out as a project for a thirteen-part television series on the Supreme Court that Cox would narrate. Much of the research was completed, but producer Adrian Malone, who had produced important programs such as *The Ascent of Man,* could not raise enough funds from foundations for production. All that came of the project was Cox's book, which he agreed to write for Houghton Mifflin since they had financed much of the project. See AC 2:10.

2. *New York Times,* August 8, 1988; obituary and related notes, August 16, 1988, AC file, St. Paul's School.

3. Theodore Chase, author's interview.

4. "Austin Wakeman Scott," undated, AC personal papers. This speech in honor of Mr. Scott was apparently delivered at Scott's ninetieth birthday party.

5. AC, author's follow-up interview, April 28, 1994.

6. Melissa Hart to Mr. and Mrs. A. Cox, June 12, 1978, Phyllis Ames Cox personal papers.

7. Remarks by Dean Robert Clark at ceremony in honor of Archibald Cox, September 13, 1991, transcript contained in AC papers, HLSL. The *Doonesbury* character used the phrase "Doing an Archie," which was defined as "pressing your investigation with such integrity that you end up getting fired." The cartoon appeared in 1977, copyright G. B. Trudeau.

8. Ibid.; *Harvard Crimson,* September 16, 1991. At this ceremony Cox was also made an honorary member of the prestigious Order of the Coif. The presenta-

tion was made by the national president and Cox's colleague at Harvard, Professor Bernard Wolfman.

9. Dorothy Cecelski, author's interview.
10. Ibid.
11. AC 32:2, 3.
12. Phyllis's own mother, to whom the house still belonged, was ill and would die at the age of one hundred in a retirement home in nearby Concord, Massachusetts, in 1985. See Phyllis Ames Cox, author's follow-up interview, August 21, 1996.
13. Application for Building Permit, July 23, 1984, Phyllis Ames Cox personal papers.
14. Sally Cox, author's interview.
15. Phyllis Cox, author's interview.
16. Sally Cox, author's interview.
17. This quote came from the period after Watergate. See James Doyle interview with AC, circa 1975, p. 2–16, James Doyle papers. Cox's hearing problem only intensified in later years.
18. Clark Byse, author's interview; Phyllis Amex Cox, author's follow-up interview, August 10, 1994.
19. Phyllis Ames Cox, author's follow-up interviews, August 21, 1996, August 10, 1994.
20. Anna Ela, author's interview.
21. Phyllis Ames Cox, author's interview.
22. The Cox grandchildren consisted of Archie, Jr.'s three children (Archie III, Suzanne, and Christopher—adopted via his second wife, Jean) and young Phyllis's three children (Melissa, Jennifer, and Russell—the son of Phyllis's second husband).
23. Sarah "Sally" Cox earned her executive M.B.A. from Northeastern University in 1981 and held a series of corporate posts in the New England area, the most recent as owner of a tile company in Maine.
24. Archibald Cox, Jr., worked as an investment banker at the firm of Morgan Stanley in New York and London for twenty-four years. See "The New Style at Morgan Stanley," *Business Week,* January 19, 1974, 47. In 1990 he became president and CEO of First Boston Corporation, a position he held until 1993, when the investment bank was restructured. See *Wall Street Journal,* July 14, 1993. Presently, Archibald Cox, Jr., runs his own investment banking firm, Sextant Grouping, in New York. He married Nina Sharpe in 1962; divorced in 1976; and married Jean Leventes in 1977.
25. Phyllis Cox attended University of Denver School of Law, graduating in 1974. She remained in the Denver area, focusing her practice on family law, and traveled extensively around the world. She was married to Robert Hart in 1968; divorced in 1972; married to Sidney Werkman in 1974; and divorced again five years later. Her oldest daughter, Melissa Hart, recently clerked for Justice John Paul Stevens on the U.S. Supreme Court after graduating from Harvard Law School. Phyllis's second daughter, Jennifer, is currently pursuing a graduate degree in health services.
26. AC 6:23.
27. AC, author's follow-up interview, August 23, 1996. Syndicated columnist Mary

McGrory would express disbelief that such a "gentleman" would watch football. Cox insisted that it was not the violence but "the enormous skill and grace of these passings and receivings, that are so brilliant." He added, "Maybe it's an unconscious yen for the violence repressed, you know, in other respects." See *Christian Science Monitor,* August 19, 1980.

28. It was at an early meeting of one such lawyer's club that Cox became acquainted with the famous poet Archibald MacLeish, who was also a lawyer and Librarian of Congress. MacLeisch confided that he had been "vexed for many years by the name Archibald." Cox replied that he had no problem with the name. He found it surprising that a great man like MacLeisch would worry about something as inconsequential as a given name, but upon further reflection concluded, "he doubtless was vexed by it before he became a great man." See AC 36:10, 11.

29. The Saturday Club is discussed at AC 32:14–16. See also John Kenneth Galbraith, author's interview. The club consisted largely of literary figures in its early years, but gradually included distinguished intellectuals in a wide array of fields including science, law, journalism, and other disciplines. Cox served for a time as its chairman.

30. Donald, *Lincoln;* Ambrose, *Undaunted Courage;* Bowen, *Francis Bacon;* Wolfe, *The Bonfire of the Vanities.*

31. Sally Cox, author's interview.

32. *Harvard University Gazette,* June 2, 1989 (Harvard Medal); Phyllis Ames Cox personal papers (Founders Medal).

33. Phyllis Ames Cox, author's follow-up interview, August 21, 1996. Among other things, Phyllis Ames Cox drafted "The Members Manual for Youth Horse Clubs," which was used extensively by 4-H groups across the country.

34. Archie would comment on his wife's speech: "Her 'few words' proved the high point of the evening." AC, letter to author, April 7, 1997.

35. Sally Cox, author's interview.

36. Phyllis Cox, author's interview. One of the Christmas poems the Coxes shared during their last holiday in Windsor summed up Phyllis's contributions to the family. Written by young Phyllis, it went into the yellowing book of Christmas verse kept by the family:

> *You are young, wife Phyllis, her husband said,*
> *And you keep exceedingly limber*
> *Do you do this by tending our gardens green*
> *Or by cutting our winter timber?*
>
> *In my youth I engaged in many a sport*
> *That developed my athletic ability*
> *In fact I've continued the practice to date*
> *Which explains my present agility.*
>
> *You are wise, Grandma Phyllis, her grandchildren said*
> *And you know our psychological conditions*
> *Did you learn this acumen by studying Freud*
> *Or by following your native intuition?*

. . . You are kind, mother dear, her children said,
And you thought once we'd grown that you'd rest
How do you bear with our uncertain life styles
Without becoming excessively stressed?

There are times, she admitted, when I can't but conclude
That your lives are a bit too chaotic
But I'll continue to offer my whole family
A haven from the world neurotic.

Poem, undated, Phyllis Ames Cox personal papers. This verse was based on "You Are Old, Father William," by Lewis Carroll, in *Alice's Adventures in Wonderland.*

37. The independent counsel statute, as finally enacted, provided that the attorney general, after a preliminary investigation of alleged criminal misconduct by the president or one holding high executive office, would determine if there was a basis for further investigation. If so, the matter would be turned over to a three-judge panel, who would select a special prosecutor. The special prosecutor would continue the investigation divorced from the Justice Department. See Ethics in Government Act of 1978, Pub.L.No. 95-521, tit. 6, 92 Stat. 1824, 1867 (codified as amended at 28 U.S.C. Sec. 591-599 [1988]). Some of Cox's views are discussed in Queijo, "Witness to Justice," *Bostonia* magazine, September/October 1987, 49.

38. AC, author's follow-up interview, August 23, 1996. For an excellent discussion of problems encountered by Congress in the Iran-Contra affair, based upon its friction with the executive branch, see Shane, "Presidents, Pardons and Prosecutors: Legal Accountability and the Separation of Powers," *Yale Law and Policy Review* 11:361.

39. AC, author's follow-up interview, August 13, 1996; *Ottowa Citizen*, August 8, 1987.

40. AC, author's follow-up interview, August 13, 1996; *Boston Globe*, November 21, 1996; *New York Times*, December 12, 1996.

41. AC 31:14.

42. AC 31:14, 15.

43. *New York Times*, December 12, 1996; AC, author's follow-up interview, August 23, 1996.

44. AC, author's follow-up interview, August 23, 1996.

45. *New York Times*, December 12, 1996; AC, author's follow-up interview, August 23, 1996. Many of the points discussed by Cox in his conversation with the author on August 23 were later refined and incorporated into the *New York Times* article, which is quoted in places here.

46. *New York Times*, December 12, 1996; AC, author's follow-up interview, August 23, 1996.

47. Ibid.; AC 30:15.

48. When it came to abortion, Cox explained, *Roe v. Wade* had existed as law in the United States for over two decades. "And has been law in the sense that people have acted on it and it's been the predicate of all kinds of action." Whatever one thought of its original wisdom: "States have had no occasion to repeal their antiabortion laws because they're now going to be unconstitutional. Political movement to modify antiabortion laws is abandoned because it has been taken

care of by the Supreme Court. All those things enter into what I mean when I say those decisions are existing law, law in practice, law being counted on, built on." See AC 30:16.

49. AC 30:17, 18. In the same vein, Cox did not believe that Congress would, or should, succeed in overturning these entrenched constitutional principles by legislation. See AC, "Congress v. the Supreme Court," Mercer Law Review 33 (1982): 707. Nor did Cox believe that the increasing politicization of the Supreme Court selection process, such as the battles over the appointment of Judge Robert Bork and Justice Clarence Thomas, would diminish the Court's legitimacy over the long haul. "The politics [of Supreme Court appointment] today is a little cruder and louder," admitted Cox. "But politics was involved in the past, and everyone knew it. I don't think it's a serious danger." See AC, author's follow-up interview, August 23, 1996.

50. Bertha Perkins Frothingham, author's follow-up interview, May 28, 1994.

51. Bertha Perkins Frothingham, author's interview; AC, author's follow-up interview, August 23, 1996; this general point was also made in a book by Michael Sandel of Harvard, *Democracy's Discontent: America in Search of a Public Philosophy*, with which Cox found himself in strong agreement.

52. AC, author's follow-up interview, August 24, 1994, December 17, 1996.

53. AC, author's follow-up interview, August 23, 1996, December 17, 1996.

54. Ibid.

55. AC lecture, "Ethics, Campaign Finance and Democracy," (Chicago, Illinois) November 3, 1995, pp. 18–20, AC personal papers. The quote from Learned Hand came from a speech Hand gave before the Federal Bar Association in 1932, entitled "Democracy: Its Presumptions and Realities." It appears in Hand, *The Spirit of Liberty*, p. 90.

56. AC 30:19, 20.

57. AC 30:20.

58. Louise Brown, author's interview.

59. Phyllis Ames Cox, author's follow-up interview, August 21, 1996.

60. Hay, "Jim Bludso of the *Prairie Belle*," in Stevenson, *Home Book* (7th ed.), pp. 3342–44.

61. Phyllis Ames Cox, author's follow-up interview, December 17, 1996.

Acknowledgments

The work on this biography, beginning on a cold winter day in 1990 when I traveled to Boston on a train to discuss the idea with Archibald Cox in his Harvard office, spanned over seven years and would have undoubtedly fizzled out if it were not for the help of many people. The biography of the dead is difficult enough; the biography of the living is fraught with unique problems, because it requires candor and frank direction from individuals who might prefer to remain anonymous as long as the subject is alive.

Fortunately, I received countless hours of interview time, research leads, and honest appraisals of the man whose life I was to study from a slew of busy people who could have just as easily ignored my letters and phone calls, particularly since this was my first book. Over one hundred people listed in the bibliography agreed to be interviewed, some for multiple sessions. Most of the interviews were taped, unless the interviewee requested otherwise. Tapes and/or transcripts have been donated to the Harvard Law School Library Special Collections, along with original handwritten notes.

Several interviewees require special thanks: Phyllis Ames Cox surmounted her usual discomfort with microphones and electronic contraptions to spend a long snow-covered afternoon in front of the fireplace in Wayland, Massachusetts, talking to me about her husband. After her initial inspection of the putative author, she opened up her house and basement and treasure trove of personal letters and clippings to me, without which this biography would have been terribly incomplete. Molly Cox (now deceased) made the old family homestead in Windsor, Vermont, a welcome stopping point for the author, and supplied hours of recollections of her brother's childhood; as did Betty Bigelow, Louis Cox, and Max Cox (the other siblings), and Bert Frothingham (Cox's cousin who lived next door in Windsor). The Cox children—Sarah, Archibald, Jr., and Phyllis—gave up their time freely, and carefully read over the chapters dealing with family history for factual missteps. Melissa Hart, one of the Cox grandchildren (who followed in her grandfather's footsteps as a lawyer), read an early draft and critiqued it thoroughly, to the author's benefit. Elliot Richardson gave me access to his papers, and spent an enormous amount of time carefully reconstructing Watergate events. His help was invaluable. Richardson's former aide J. T. Smith took the time to painstakingly decipher Richardson's handwritten notes—a complicated scrawl akin to hieroglyphics on an ancient Egyptian tomb—and without his help much of the riddle of President

Nixon's proposed "Stennis Compromise" could not have been unraveled. Jim Doyle, Cox's Watergate press spokesman, allowed me to drive away from his home in Bethesda, Maryland, with eight boxes of critical Watergate files (now donated to Harvard), which formed the mother-lode for my research on Watergate. John Barker took me on a memorable walking tour of Washington one crisp October day, retracing the steps that Cox had walked from his office on K Street to his press conference at the National Press Club, just hours before President Nixon fired him during the infamous Saturday Night Massacre.

Professor Phil Heymann at Harvard Law School was instrumental in pushing the project along from its inception; without him, there would be no book. Dean Robert Clark and Vice Dean David Smith provided assistance from the earliest stages, and opened up documents in the Harvard Law School Special Collections which proved priceless. They also provided support to transcribe the author's lengthy tape-recorded interviews with Cox, which will hopefully serve as an important source of research materials for future scholars. Professor Jim Vorenberg dug out handwritten Watergate notes and painstakingly decoded them. Professor Clark Byse (born in 1912, the same year as Cox) was an active cheerleader and a tireless supporter.

A number of individuals agreed to read select chapters of the draft manuscript, due to their special knowledge or expertise, which turned out to be an enormous help to the author in unearthing factual errors and avoiding considerable embarrassment. These special readers included Chief Justice William H. Rehnquist, who reviewed the prologue dealing with the impeachment of Andrew Johnson; Gerald Gunther, who read the materials on Judge Learned Hand and kept on reading the entire manuscript; Clark Byse, who read Harvard segments with great care; Harold Enarson, who provided valuable insight on the Truman chapter; Ralph Dungan, an aide to then-Senator John F. Kennedy in the 1950s, who helped enormously on the chapter dealing with Cox's work on the Landrum-Griffin Act; Arthur M. Schlesinger, Jr., and John Kenneth Galbraith, who read the Kennedy campaign chapters with zeal and provided useful comments to a first-time biographer; Burke Marshall and Nick Katzenbach, who reviewed the solicitor general materials with great enthusiasm; Sam Williamson, who spent considerable time on the lengthy chapter dealing with student uprisings at Harvard; and Jim Doyle, J. T. Smith, Phil Heymann, Jim Vorenberg, Richard Ben-Veniste, Elliot Richardson, John Dean, and Dr. Robert Muir, all of whom read Watergate chapters with great care.

Other people who read drafts of the manuscript deserve special thanks: Judge Robert J. Cindrich, who forced me to rewrite the first few chapters even though the editing process was rolling forward like a locomotive; David Seipp, a legal historian at Boston University School of Law, who plowed through the entire manuscript with amazing thoroughness in the face of severe time constraints, and provided invaluable comments; and my sister-in-law Leslie Kozler, Esq., who was my most careful reader and most trusted second pair of eyes.

This biography required that a lawyer learn to become an historian; numerous librarians and archivists eased that transformation along the way. Many thanks to the staff at the Harvard Law School Library Special Collections: Erika Chadbourn, who did a magnificent job in organizing the Cox papers and exhibit; David DeLorenzo, my principal source at Harvard and a true professional; library director David Warrington; archivist Judy Mellins; and photo expert Steven Smith. Danielle Green at the central Harvard Archives was unusually resourceful, and helped liberate boxes of documents dealing with the student uprisings at Harvard. I am also extremely grateful to the Truman Library Institute for a grant that took me to Independence, Missouri, and I am indebted to that library's excellent staff who made my stay there both memorable and productive: Ray Geselbracht, Dennis Bilger, Liz Safly, Sam Rushay, and Randy Sowell. Thanks, also, to Mrs. Haroldine Helm, keeper of the cozy bed and breakfast for wayward scholars in Independence.

The John F. Kennedy Library Foundation supplied me with two different research grants, enabling me to spend portions of two consecutive summers at their glistening haven overlooking Boston Harbor at Columbia Point. The Library's director, William Johnson, and the archivists—Maura Porter, June Payne, Megan Desnoyers, Ron Whealan, Allan Goodrich, and Ismael Garcia—made possible an exhaustive review of Cox's work with John and Robert Kennedy that became a critical ingredient in the book. At the Library of Congress in Washington, D.C., James H. Hutson, John Haines, Ernest Emrich, Kathleen McDonough, and Fred Bauman provided invaluable assistance. At the National Archives in College Park, Maryland, David Paynter and Patricia Anderson were particularly helpful in poring through the massive collection of Watergate documents. At the U.S. Department of Justice, Harriet Shapiro, Hon. Drew S. Days III, and Gloria Branker led the author through a bureaucratic maze to retrieve important documents in the archives, while George Duke and S. Craig Crawford helped locate elusive photos. At St. Paul's School, Alan Hall gave me a tour of the beautiful campus where Cox had spent important teenage years; George Grove and Ann Locke made available useful material from St. Paul's library. Joel Marks, a reference librarian at the Weston (Massachusetts) Public Library, looked up minutiae in old *Town Crier* newspapers, often on his own time. And Louise Brown at the Wayland (Massachusetts) Public Library provided help on miscellaneous local facts.

Over the years, numerous research assistants assisted on this project. I am indebted to Dan Cooper, Craig Milsten, John Shaw, Elizabeth Wachsman, Leslie Kozler (again), David Gildernew, Jennifer DiGiovanni, Maria L. Henderson, Lance D. Lewis, Dan Troy, and Anthony Frigo. As well, a legion of secretaries and typists have contributed their talents and patience over the past seven years: LuAnn Driscoll, Karen Knochel, Darlene Mocello, Carolyn Rohan, Barb Salopek, and Libby Jacaszek, all at the University of Pittsburgh School of Law; Marsha Tsouris, Donna Myers, Bea Kierzkowski, and Mary Ann Kaper at the University of Pittsburgh Department of Political Science; Melanie Uziel and Debby Yankello at the law firm of Mansmann, Cindrich & Titus (now Titus & McConomy); Lori Godshall, Kathy Koehler, Phyllis Karczewski, and Marie Zagrocki at Duquesne University School of Law; and Cheri Hinnebusch, who endured years of van shuttling and slim funding to type thousands of pages of interview transcripts.

Finally, a special thanks to Mary Jo "M.J." Korinek (along with Bob and Rebecca), who suffered through visits on every major holiday—including the Christmas of 1996 that never was—to type endless drafts of this manuscript in order to keep the book on schedule. They displayed unswerving loyalty to the project, even when the sanity of the author was open to serious question.

A number of mentors, past and present, have provided support that has been essential in writing this biography while practicing law, teaching, and otherwise engaging in the mundane task of earning a living. These include: Bob Cindrich, Paul

Titus, Jerry Mansmann, and Bert McConomy in law practice; Mark Nordenberg, now chancellor, and Dick Seeburger at the University of Pittsburgh; John E. Murray, Jr., president, and Michael P. Weber, provost, at Duquesne University; Dean Nicholas P. Cafardi at the Duquesne University School of Law, who believed in this project from the start and supported it every step of the way; as well as Associate Dean Raymond F. Sekula and Assistant Dean John T. Rago.

So many other people have contributed to this book through their kindness that it would be impossible to list them all. They include: Donna Chiozzi, Joan Noel, Joan Flammia, and Rocco Forgione, who located abandoned dormrooms, empty couches, and vacant offices for me to occupy during my many trips to Cambridge; Cox's secretaries Carolyn Marshall and Delona Wilkin; Peter Shane, for a useful discussion of separation of powers; Matt and Louetta Kambic, for photos and French translations; Victor Navasky and Bruce Terris, who made papers available; Evelyn Lincoln (already missed); Finlay McQuade, an old English writing teacher; Eleanor Van Middlesworth, for lectures on Republicanism; Enrico Bellisario, Jr., for many haircuts; Garrett Epps, A.C. Epps, Dr. James A. Fallows, and James M. Fallows, who loaned me elusive *Harvard Crimsons*; John B. Fox, Jr., Secretary of the Faculty of Arts and Sciences at Harvard University; Dr. Michael B. Ballard from the John C. Stennis Library at Mississippi State; William J. Keefe and Holbert N. Carroll, two special professors of government; Judge Donald E. Zeigler, Bill Lapiana, Jim McElroy, Nancy Bigelow Krause, Jeff Blattner, Manning J. O'Connor II, Bernita Brooks, Mac Schweibinz, Mick Livingston, Peg Mulvihill (and both Meads), Darlene and Tom Mocello, Pat and Lisa Sorek, and Harry and Dee Paras, all of whom provided support and encouragement; the Bucknell contingency; the residents of the elite Atwood Complex; Rex Van Middlesworth, Mark Warner, Joel Pelz, Steve Nock, Rick Cromartie, Tom Lucero, and other members of the Somerville Bar Review; my distinguished faculty colleagues at Duquesne University School of Law, who have been gracious in allowing me to monopolize support staff; and the excellent library staff at the Law School, headed by Frank Liu.

My family was a constant source of love, support, and good humor during the seemingly endless period of labor that turned into a book: My parents, Elena and Bill Gormley, who loaned me my old room and Aunt Gertrude's desk to find a quiet retreat overlooking West Swissvale Avenue, still the happiest of homes; my parents-in-law, Noreen and Joe Kozler, who read the entire book with inordinate rapture; my great-grandmother-in-law, Winnie Brennan Gallagher, who—at the spry age of 92—consumed the book in between televised Yankee games; my uncle, John Furia, Jr., who provided much-valued writing assistance; my brother, Professor Bill Gormley, who helped at many stages; B.J. and Cindy Gormley, plus Jessie and Matt; Nancy and Frank Pfenning, plus Andreas, Marina, and Nils—an inspiration to all of us; Suzie and Mark Hogan, plus Natalie and Greta; Beth and Mark Scarpato, plus Daniel, Meredith, and Brandon; Amy and Tom Maxey, plus Samuel James (who arrived during revisions); Leslie Wesley and Bryant Wesley, who supplied much-needed weekend escapes; the Galdis, Hackerts, Furias, Estills, Gilkisons, Gormleys, Tilghmans, Morgans, Delaches, and the various issue of John and Jessica Furia (from New York) and Will and Katherine Gormley (from Kentucky), all of whom helped the author appreciate the raw materials of life that go into storytelling.

My agent, Julian Bach, visualized this completed project before I knew what I had begun, and I am forever grateful for all that I learned from him. Although 83 years of age, Mr Bach's contract thankfully mandates that he be present for the arrival of the millennium, and work another forty years beyond that, all to the benefit of the literary world. His assistant, Carolyn Krupp, gave much assistance. Patty Boyd is a friend and a skilled copyeditor, whom I was able to trust absolutely in the humbling process of readying an imperfect manuscript for the world. Jess Brallier at Addison-Wesley helped the book land at that publishing house, much to my good fortune. My thanks also to Suzanne Heiser, a talented designer, for her excellent work on the jacket; Ruth Kolbert, for outstanding text design; Lynn Hutchinski, for excellent indexing; and Michele Hanson, who helped with advance publicity. Beth Burleigh Fuller did an exceptional job leading the book through production, always with great care and a sense of fresh enthusiasm. And my editor, John Bell, although younger than I expected when I first met him, turned out to be one of the most seasoned, advanced professionals with whom I have ever dealt. Without his careful attention to detail, and vision of perfection in the grand tradition of Max Perkins, this book would have revealed far more of the author's flaws, and far less of the sounds of something approaching literature.

Finally, my wife, Laura, stuck with the project for seven years—at times without paychecks and absent a husband in body and mind—always exhibiting great love, support, and good spirit as she endured her spouse's aberrant career notions. My three children, Carolyn, Luke, and Rebecca spent many hours in the attic coloring and stapling while tramping over chapters of the book, giving it their own magical imprint. For all of them, I would write three biographies, and then start all over.

Ken Gormley
Pittsburgh, Pennsylvania
March 1997

Index